Beginning PHP5, Apache, and MySQL® Web Development

Beginning PHP5, Apache, and MySQL® Web Development

Elizabeth Naramore, Jason Gerner, Yann Le Scouarnec,
Jeremy Stolz, Michael K. Glass

Wiley Publishing, Inc.

Beginning PHP5, Apache, and MySQL® Web Development

Published by
Wiley Publishing, Inc.
10475 Crosspoint Boulevard
Indianapolis, IN 46256
www.wiley.com

Copyright © 2005 by Wiley Publishing, Inc., Indianapolis, Indiana

Published simultaneously in Canada

ISBN: 0-7645-7966-5

Manufactured in the United States of America

10 9 8 7 6 5 4 3

1B/SQ/QR/QV/IN

For general information on our other products and services or to obtain technical support, please contact our Customer Care Department within the U.S. at (800) 762-2974, outside the U.S. at (317) 572-3993 or fax (317) 572-4002.

Wiley also publishes its books in a variety of electronic formats. Some content that appears in print may not be available in electronic books.

Library of Congress Cataloging-in-Publication Data available from the publisher.

Trademarks: Wiley, the Wiley Publishing logo, Wrox, the Wrox logo, Programmer to Programmer, and related trade dress are trademarks or registered trademarks of John Wiley & Sons, Inc. and/or its affil-iates, in the United States and other countries, and may not be used without written permission. MySQL is a registered trademark of MySQL AB Limited Company. All other trademarks are the prop-erty of their respective owners. Wiley Publishing, Inc., is not associated with any product or vendor mentioned in this book.

About the Authors

Elizabeth Naramore

Elizabeth graduated from Miami University (Ohio) with a degree in Organizational Behavior and has been a Web developer since 1997. Her main focus is in e-commerce, but she develops sites across numerous industries. She is currently a moderator at PHPBuilder.com, an online help center for PHP. She lives in Cincinnati, Ohio with her husband and two children, and looks forward to someday returning to Miami to get her Masters in Computer Science.

Thanks to my husband and soul mate who continues to be supportive of everything I do, and who inspires me to always do a little better. Thanks to my children who make me understand the importance of looking outside the box and keeping my sense of humor, and for making me proud to be a mom. Also, thank you to Debra for always keeping us on track, and for having faith in us.

Jason "goldbug" Gerner

Jason currently spends his days working as a Web developer in Cincinnati and burns free time complaining about lack of support for Web standards and abusing XML. He can often be found lurking in the PHPBuilder.com discussion forums, waiting to chime in with nagging comments about CSS or code efficiency.

Yann "Bunkermaster" Le Scouarnec

Yann is the senior developer for Jolt Online Gaming, a British gaming company. He is a moderator at PHPBuilder.com and a developer of open source PHP software for the gaming community. He has also worked for major software corporations as a software quality expert.

I thank all the innocent bystanders who got pushed around because of this project: Debra and Nancy, who were patient enough not to have homicidal thoughts; and my wife and kids, who barely saw me for six months.

Jeremy "stolzyboy" Stolz

Jeremy is a Web Developer at J&M Companies, Inc. (www.jmcompanies.com), a print company in Fargo, North Dakota. Jeremy is primarily a PHP/MySQL developer, but he has also worked with many other languages. When not working, he frequents the Internet and tries to keep his programming skills sharp and up to date. He is a contributor to and moderator at PHPBuilder.com.

I'd like to thank my wife, my baby daughter, and the rest of my family for being patient with me while working on this project.

Michael "BuzzLY" Glass

Michael Glass has been a gladiator in the software/Web site development arena for more than eight years. He has more than ten years of commercial programming experience with a wide variety of technologies, including PHP, Java, Lotus Domino, and Vignette StoryServer. He divides his time between computer programming, playing pool in the APA, and running his Web site at www.ultimatespin.com. You can usually find him slinking around on the PHPBuilder.com forums, where he is a moderator with the nickname BuzzLY.

Thanks, Staci, for putting up with long and late hours at the computer. Elizabeth and Jason, it wouldn't have been the same project without you two. And thanks to my code testers at www.ultimatespin.com: Spidon, Kaine, Garmy, Spidermanalf, Ping, Webhead, and FancyDan. You guys rock!

To Donna and Gerry, who have influenced my life more than they can ever know, and who taught me the importance of finishing what you've started.

Credits

Acquisitions Editor
Debra Williams Cauley

Development Editor
Brian MacDonald

Senior Production Editor
Angela Smith

Technical Editor
Jason Gerner

Copy Editor
Kim Cofer

Editorial Manager
Mary Beth Wakefield

Vice President & Executive Group Publisher
Richard Swadley

Vice President and Publisher
Joseph B. Wikert

Project Coordinator
Erin Smith

Graphics and Production Specialists
Carrie A. Foster
Denny Hager
Jennifer Heleine

Quality Control Technician
Brian H. Walls

Proofreading and Indexing
TECHBOOKS Production Services

Contents

Contents

Contents

Contents

Contents

Contents

Part I: Getting Started

Chapter 1: Configuring Your Installation

Configuring Your Installation

You've spent your hard-earned money and purchased this book, so you undoubtedly know the enormous benefits of using PHP, Apache, and MySQL together to create your Web site. But in case you found this book on your desk one Monday morning with a sticky note reading "Learn this!," this chapter looks at the basics of PHP, MySQL, and Apache to show you what makes the "AMP" combination so popular. This chapter also walks you through the procedure for installing all three components of the AMP module and advises you on how to best configure the software to meet your specific needs.

Projects in This Book

Over the course of this book, you will develop two complete Web sites:

❑ **Movie Review Web site.** Developing this site introduces you to writing a PHP program, making your pages look professional, working with variables and includes, and integrating PHP with MySQL to make your site truly dynamic as pages are created on the fly for your Web site visitor. You will also get experience in error handling and data validation while working on this site.

❑ **Comic Book Fan Web site.** The creation of this Web site takes you through the steps of building databases from scratch, manipulating images and sending out e-mails using PHP, authenticating users, managing content through CMS, creating a mailing list, setting up an e-commerce section, and developing and customizing a discussion forum.

Finally, this book covers how to learn about your visitors through the use of log files and how to troubleshoot common mistakes or problems. The appendixes in this book provide you with the necessary reference materials you'll need to assist you in your Web site development journey and offer tools to make you more efficient.

After reading this book, you will be able to create a well-designed, dynamic Web site using tools available for free. Although this book is not intended to be a detailed analysis of Apache, PHP, and MySQL, it points you in the right direction to explore further issues you may wish to delve into.

Brief Intro to PHP, Apache, MySQL, and Open Source

PHP, Apache, and MySQL are all part of the *open source* group of software programs. The open source movement is a collaboration of some of the finest minds in computer programming. By allowing the open exchange of information, programmers from all over the world contribute to make a truly powerful and efficient piece of software available to everyone. Through the contributions of many people to the publicly available source code, bugs get fixed, improvements are made, and a good software program becomes a great one over time.

A Brief History of Open Source Initiatives

The term *open source* was coined in 1998 after Netscape decided to publish the source code for its popular Navigator browser. This announcement prompted a small group of software developers who had been long-time supporters of the soon-to-be open source ideology to formally develop the Open Source Initiatives (OSI) and the Open Source Definition.

Although the OSI ideology was initially promoted in the hacker community, upon Netscape's release of Navigator's source code, programmers from all walks of life began to offer suggestions and fixes to improve the browser's performance. The OSI mission was off and running, as the mainstream computing world began to embrace the idea.

Linux became the first operating system that could be considered open source (although BSD was a close runner-up, distributed from Berkeley in 1989), and many programs followed soon thereafter. Large software corporations, such as Corel, began to offer versions of their programs that worked on Linux machines.

Although there are now numerous classifications of OSI open source licenses, any software that bears the OSI Certification seal can be considered open source because it has passed the Open Source Definition test. These programs are available from a multitude of Web sites; the most popular is www.sourceforge.net, which houses more than 83,000 open source projects.

Why Open Source Rocks

Open source programs are very cool because:

❑ **They are free.** The greatest thing about open source software is that it is free and available to the general public. Software developers and programmers volunteer their time to improve existing software and create new programs. Open source software cannot, by definition, require any sort of licensing or sales fees.

- **They are cross-platform and "technology-neutral."** By requiring open source software to be non–platform specific, the open source community has ensured that the programs are usable by virtually everyone. According to the Open Source Definition provided by the Open Source Initiative at http://opensource.org/docs/definition.php, open source programs must not be dependent on any "individual technology or style of interface" and must be "technology-neutral." As long as the software can run on more than one operating system, it meets the criterion.

- **They must not restrict other software.** This basically means that if an open source program is distributed along with other programs, those other programs may be open source or commercial in nature. This gives software developers maximum control and flexibility.

- **They embrace diversity.** Diversity of minds and cultures simply produces a better result. For this reason, open source programs cannot, by definition, discriminate against any person or group of persons, nor against any "field of endeavor." For example, a program designed for use in the medical profession cannot be limited to that field if someone in another field wants to take the program and modify it to fit his or her needs.

For a complete list of the criteria a piece of software must meet before it can be considered "open source," or for more information about the OSI or the open source community, visit the OSI Web site at www.opensource.org.

How the Pieces of the AMP Module Work Together

Now that you've learned some of the history of open source, it's important to understand the role each of these programs (Apache, MySQL, and PHP) plays in creating your Web site.

Imagine that your dynamic Web site is a fancy restaurant. Diners come to your place, and each one wants something different and specific. They don't worry so much about how the food is prepared, as long as it looks and tastes delicious. Unlike a buffet-type spread, where everything is laid out and your patrons simply choose from what's available, a nice restaurant encourages patron/waiter interaction and complete customization for any specific dietary needs. Similarly, a Web site shouldn't be a static page with little interaction from visitors; it should be a dynamic site where the visitor can choose what he or she wants to see.

In this scenario, you can characterize the three components of the AMP module as follows:

- **Apache:** This is your highly trained master of culinary arts, the chef. Whatever people ask for, she prepares it without complaint. She is quick, flexible, and able to prepare a multitude of different types of foods. Apache acts in much the same way as your HTTP server, parsing files and passing on the results.

- **PHP:** This is the waiter. He gets requests from the patron and carries them back to the kitchen with specific instructions about how the meal should be prepared.

- **MySQL:** This is your stockroom of ingredients (or in this case, information).

When a patron (or Web site visitor) comes to your restaurant, he or she sits down and orders a meal with specific requirements, such as a steak, well done. The waiter (PHP) takes those specific requirements back to the kitchen and passes them off to the chef (Apache). The chef then goes to the stockroom (MySQL) to retrieve the ingredients (or data) to prepare the meal and presents the final dish to the patron, exactly the way he or she ordered it.

You can choose to install one, two, or all three components of the AMP package based on your specific needs. For example, if you are responsible for providing a company-wide intranet, or hosting your own Web site, you should probably install all three. If your site is hosted by a third-party Web hosting company, however, you do not necessarily need to install all three components (or, for that matter, any of them).

Installing the three components, even if you don't have to, enables you to develop and test your site in the comfort of your own workspace without having to upload to the file server just to test at every little step. Even if you do a lot of off-line testing, however, we highly recommend that you still perform a complete test once your site is live and running, because your settings may differ from those on your Web-hosting company's server. Even a small difference can cause you big headaches.

Apache

Apache acts as your Web server. Its main job is to parse any file requested by a browser and display the correct results according to the code within that file. Apache is quite powerful and can accomplish virtually any task that you, as a Webmaster, require.

The version of Apache covered in this book is the most recent and stable at the time of this writing: version 2.0.50. The features and server capabilities available in this version include the following:

- ❑ Password-protected pages for a multitude of users
- ❑ Customized error pages
- ❑ Display of code in numerous levels of HTML, and the capability to determine at what level the browser can accept the content
- ❑ Usage and error logs in multiple and customizable formats
- ❑ Virtual hosting for different IP addresses mapped to the same server
- ❑ DirectoryIndex directives to multiple files
- ❑ URL aliasing or rewriting with no fixed limit

According to the Netcraft Web site (www.netcraft.com), at the time of this writing Apache is running over 34 million Internet servers, more than Microsoft, Sun ONE, and Zeus combined. Its flexibility, power, and, of course, price make it a popular choice. It can be used to host a Web site for the general public, or a company-wide intranet, or for simply testing your pages before they are uploaded to a secure server on another machine. Later in this chapter, you learn to configure your Apache setup to accommodate all of these options.

PHP

PHP is a server-side scripting language that allows your Web site to be truly dynamic. PHP stands for *PHP: Hypertext Preprocessor* (and, yes, we're aware PHP is a "recursive acronym" — probably meant to confuse the masses). Its flexibility and relatively small learning curve (especially for programmers who have a background in C, Java, or Perl) make it one of the most popular scripting languages around. PHP's popularity continues to increase as businesses, and individuals everywhere embrace it as an alternative to Microsoft's ASP language and realize that PHP's benefits most certainly outweigh the costs (three cheers for open source!). According to Netcraft, PHP code can now be found in approximately 16 million Web sites.

The version of PHP referenced in this book is the most recent stable release at the time of publication: version 5.0.0. Although we discuss several of the most common uses and functions of PHP, you can find a complete list of PHP functions in Appendix B of this book. As you continue to program in PHP and your comfort level increases (or the demands of your boss grow), we encourage you to expand your use of built-in PHP functions to take advantage of its tremendous power. You can download the PHP software from PHP's Web site at www.php.net.

MySQL

Another open source favorite, MySQL is the database construct that enables PHP and Apache to work together to access and display data in a readable format to a browser. It is a Structured Query Language server designed for heavy loads and processing of complex queries. As a relational database system, MySQL allows many different tables to be joined together for maximum efficiency and speed.

This book references version 4.0.20, the most stable release of MySQL at the time of writing. You can find a complete list of features at the MySQL Web site (www.mysql.com), but some of the more popular features of this program are as follows:

❑ Multiple CPUs usable through kernel threads

❑ Multi-platform operation

❑ Numerous column types cover virtually every type of data

❑ Group functions for mathematical calculations and sorting

❑ Commands that allow information about the databases to be easily and succinctly shown to the administrator

❑ Function names that do not affect table or column names

❑ A password and user verification system for added security

❑ Up to 32 indexes per table permitted; this feature has been successfully implemented at levels of 60,000 tables and 5,000,000,000 rows (version 4.1.2, currently in development, will allow 64 indexes)

❑ International error reporting usable in many different countries

MySQL is the perfect choice for providing data via the Internet because of its ability to handle heavy loads and its advanced security measures.

For more information on how MySQL was developed, or other specific information not covered in this book, visit the resource Web site at www.mysql.com.

AMP Installers

If you'd like to take your entire Saturday afternoon to install each of these components separately, feel free to refer to Appendix I at the back of this book. However, we can also tell you about some third-party software programs that will complete the installation for you. You can find an extended list of these types of installers at www.hotscripts.com.

Foxserv

Foxserv is an Apache/MySQL/PHP installer that is available at www.foxserv.net. It is offered as an open source program and is free to the general public. Foxserv allows you to customize your configuration files during installation and also allows for PEAR modules to be downloaded. (You can read more about the use of PEAR in Appendix H.) This installer is compatible with both Windows and Linux systems.

PHPTriad

PHPTriad is another open source installer that is available at no charge. It is available for download at http://sourceforge.net/projects/phptriad/ but is currently applicable to Windows systems only. Along with Apache, PHP, and MySQL, the package includes Perl and phpMyAdmin (another powerful database administration system we discuss in Chapter 3).

XAMPP

XAMPP, available at http://sourceforge.net/projects/xampp, is an open source installer that will install Apache, MySQL, PHP, Perl, phpMyAdmin, and an FTP server. It is suitable for Linux, Solaris, and Windows systems.

Configuring Your Apache Installation

For the purposes of working through this book, we assume that you have installed Apache on your computer. If you haven't done so but would like to, you can find detailed installation instructions in Appendix I.

Before you begin configuring and customizing your installation, take a minute to make sure you have installed everything correctly.

You can access the Apache executable file in three ways:

❑ During installation, the default option is to add Apache to your Start menu, so unless you disabled this, you can locate the Apache HTTP Server listing directly from your Start button. This gives you shortcuts to starting the server and to testing and configuring features, as well.

❑ Open Windows Explorer and go to the directory where you have installed Apache, the default being c:\program files\Apache Group\Apache2\bin\; click Apache.exe to start your Apache HTTP server.

❑ At the DOS prompt, change directories to the location where the Apache file has been loaded, and type **apache**. This starts the server.

Testing Your Installation

To test installation of your Apache server, open your Web browser and type the following:

```
http://localhost/
```

If your installation was successful, you will see an Apache "success" page in your browser. If not, check your error log by opening the `error. log` file, which you can find in `c:\program files\Apache Group\Apache2\logs\`. This gives you an indication of where your installation went wrong. For a more in-depth discussion of logs, please refer to Chapter 17.

If you had installation problems, note that you might experience errors, such as the "no services installed" error if Apache is trying to share port 80 with another Web server or application, such as a firewall. To fix this, open your `httpd.conf` file in the `c:\program files\Apache group\Apache2\conf` directory and locate the following lines:

```
# Listen: Allows you to bind Apache to specific IP addresses and/or
# ports, instead of the default. See also the <VirtualHost>
# directive.
#
# Change this to Listen on specific IP addresses as shown below to
# prevent Apache from glomming onto all bound IP addresses (0.0.0.0)
#
#Listen 12.34.56.78:80
Listen 80
```

Change the last line of this block to read

```
Listen 8080
```

Then locate the following lines:

```
#
# ServerName gives the name and port that the server uses to identify itself.
# This can often be determined automatically, but we recommend you specify
# it explicitly to prevent problems during startup.
#
# If this is not set to valid DNS name for your host, server-generated
# redirections will not work.  See also the UseCanonicalName directive.
#
# If your host doesn't have a registered DNS name, enter its IP address here.
# You will have to access it by its address anyway, and this will make
# redirections work in a sensible way.
#
ServerName www.yourdomainnamehere.com:80
```

Change the last line of this code to the following:

```
ServerName www.yourdomainnamehere.com:8080
```

Finally, if you are still experiencing problems and you are running a Windows system, The Apache Foundation has provided a nifty document about some other issues that may arise during installation. You can view the document by going to http://httpd.apache.org/docs-2.0/platform/ windows.html.

Customizing Your Installation

Now that you know that everything works okay, you can adjust the configuration file to better suit your needs. The main configuration file you use to make changes is httpd.conf; this is found in the c:\ program files\Apache group\Apache2\conf directory by default or wherever you have installed Apache. You can open this file with any common text editor, such as Notepad.

Adding PHP to the Equation

In order for Apache to recognize a PHP file as one that needs to be parsed with the PHP engine, you need to first locate the following lines in your httpd.conf file:

```
#
# AddType allows you to add to or override the MIME configuration
# file mime.types for specific file types.
#
AddType application/x-tar .tgz
AddType image/x-icon .ico
```

Then add the following lines:

```
AddType application/x-httpd-php .php
AddType application/x-httpd-php-source .phps
```

Now add the PHP module into your httpd.conf program so that Apache can properly parse PHP. In your script, locate the following lines:

```
#
# Dynamic Shared Object (DSO) Support
#
# To be able to use the functionality of a module which was built as a DSO you
# have to place corresponding `LoadModule' lines at this location so the
# directives contained in it are actually available _before_ they are used.
# Statically compiled modules (those listed by `httpd -l') do not need
# to be loaded here.
#
# Example:
# LoadModule foo_module modules/mod_foo.so
#
LoadModule access_module modules/mod_access.so
LoadModule actions_module modules/mod_actions.so
LoadModule alias_module modules/mod_alias.so
LoadModule asis_module modules/mod_asis.so
LoadModule auth_module modules/mod_auth.so
```

```
#LoadModule auth_anon_module modules/mod_auth_anon.so
#LoadModule auth_dbm_module modules/mod_auth_dbm.so
#LoadModule auth_digest_module modules/mod_auth_digest.so
LoadModule autoindex_module modules/mod_autoindex.so
#LoadModule cern_meta_module modules/mod_cern_meta.so
LoadModule cgi_module modules/mod_cgi.so
#LoadModule dav_module modules/mod_dav.so
#LoadModule dav_fs_module modules/mod_dav_fs.so
LoadModule dir_module modules/mod_dir.so
LoadModule env_module modules/mod_env.so
#LoadModule expires_module modules/mod_expires.so
#LoadModule file_cache_module modules/mod_file_cache.so
#LoadModule headers_module modules/mod_headers.so
LoadModule imap_module modules/mod_imap.so
LoadModule include_module modules/mod_include.so
#LoadModule info_module modules/mod_info.so
LoadModule isapi_module modules/mod_isapi.so
LoadModule log_config_module modules/mod_log_config.so
LoadModule mime_module modules/mod_mime.so
#LoadModule mime_magic_module modules/mod_mime_magic.so
#LoadModule proxy_module modules/mod_proxy.so
#LoadModule proxy_connect_module modules/mod_proxy_connect.so
#LoadModule proxy_http_module modules/mod_proxy_http.so
#LoadModule proxy_ftp_module modules/mod_proxy_ftp.so
LoadModule negotiation_module modules/mod_negotiation.so
#LoadModule rewrite_module modules/mod_rewrite.so
LoadModule setenvif_module modules/mod_setenvif.so
#LoadModule speling_module modules/mod_speling.so
#LoadModule status_module modules/mod_status.so
#LoadModule unique_id_module modules/mod_unique_id.so
LoadModule userdir_module modules/mod_userdir.so
#LoadModule usertrack_module modules/mod_usertrack.so
#LoadModule vhost_alias_module modules/mod_vhost_alias.so
#LoadModule ssl_module modules/mod_ssl.so
```

Add the following line:

```
LoadModule php5_module "c:/php/sapi/php5apache2.dll"
```

Make sure your path matches the location of this file, as determined during your installation.

Document Root

By default, the directory under which Apache looks for files is c:\program files\Apache Group\ Apache2\htdocs\. You can change this to whatever is applicable for your directory structure, but for the purposes of this discussion, create a directory named c:\program files\Apache Group\ Apache2\test\ where you can put files to test them. After you have created the directory, you must point Apache to the new directory.

To point Apache to the new directory, you must change the document root in your httpd.conf file by following these steps:

1. Locate the section of the file that resembles this text:

```
#
# DocumentRoot: The directory out of which you will serve your
# documents. By default, all requests are taken from this directory, but
# symbolic links and aliases may be used to point to other locations.
#
DocumentRoot "C:/Program Files/Apache Group/Apache2/htdocs"
```

2. Change the last line of this section to

```
DocumentRoot "C:/Program Files/Apache Group/Apache2/test"
```

Notice that this uses forward slashes instead of backslashes.

3. Locate the section of the file that resembles this text:

```
#
# Note that from this point forward you must specifically allow
# particular features to be enabled - so if something's not working as
# you might expect, make sure that you have specifically enabled it
# below.
#


#
# This should be changed to whatever you set DocumentRoot to.
#
<Directory "C:/Program Files/Apache Group/Apache2/htdocs">
```

4. Change the last line of this section to

```
<Directory "C:/Program Files/Apache Group/Apache2/test">
```

5. Save your file and restart Apache so it can recognize the changes you made to the config file. (Make sure you have created this directory before restarting Apache or you will get an "Operation Failed!" error.)

Now create a small "test" program to make sure Apache can find your directory.

Open Notepad and type the following:

```
<HTML>
<HEAD>
<TITLE>Apache testing</TITLE>
</HEAD>
<BODY>
If this works, we did it!
</BODY>
</HTML>
```

Save this as index.html in the "test" directory you created. Now open your browser, and type **http://localhost**. You should see the screen shown in Figure 1-1.

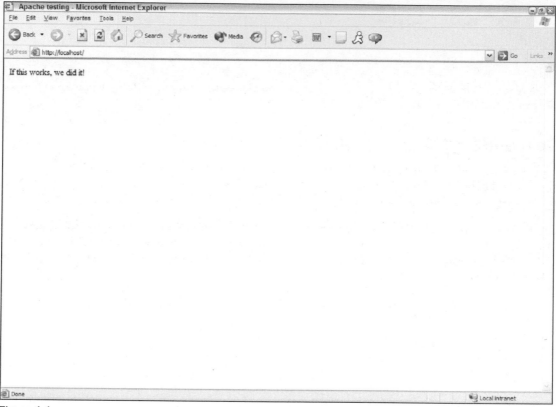

Figure 1-1

Configuring Your PHP Installation

Once PHP has been installed on your computer, you can customize it to fit your needs. Although some of the configuration settings deal with how the information is shown through the browser, a great many of the settings relate to how the server handles errors and how those errors are displayed to you and your users. You will also be able to have some control over how PHP interacts with MySQL.

Testing Your Installation

To ensure that both PHP and Apache have been installed together, write another test program. Open Notepad and type the following program:

```
<HTML>
<HEAD>
<TITLE>PHP Testing</TITLE>
</HEAD>
<BODY>
```

```
<?php
echo "If this works, we <i>really</i> did it!";
?>
</BODY>
</HTML>
```

Save this file as phptest.php. Open your browser and type **http://localhost/phptest.php** and you should see the screen shown in Figure 1-2.

Customizing Your Installation

The configuration file that holds the key to how PHP runs on your computer is named php.ini; it can be found in the root directory where you extracted your installation files. In Windows, this file was saved to c:\windows so Apache could find it.

The php.ini file includes a brief explanation of each of the configuration settings, which are beyond the scope of this discussion. However, you are encouraged to read through the entire introduction of the php.ini file before you begin making changes. In the table that follows, we touch on some of the more commonly changed settings.

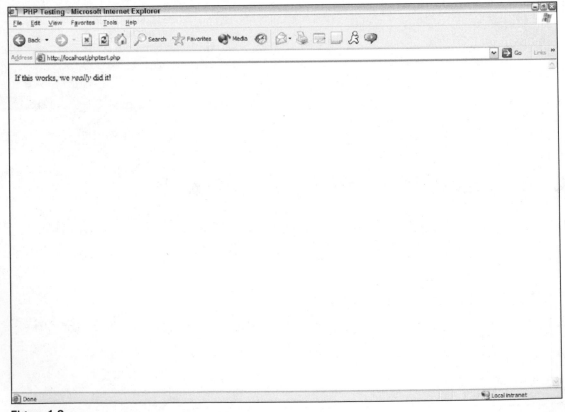

Figure 1-2

Setting	What It Does
short_open_tag	Allows short tags to be parsed (`<?` and `?>` as opposed to `<?php` and `?>`).
asp_tags	Allows ASP-style tags to be parsed (`<%` and `%>`).
precision	Determines the number of digits to be displayed in floating-point numbers. The default is 12, and this should suffice for most applications.
output_buffering	Allows header lines to be sent after HTML has already been sent to the server. The default is "Off," and most third-party hosts maintain this default. It is not advisable to change this setting, especially if you depend on a third-party host.
max_execution_time	Sets the limit for how long a script can take to run; expressed in seconds.
max_input_time	Sets the limit for how long a script can take to parse the data; expressed in seconds.
memory_limit	Sets the limit for how much memory a script can use to run; expressed in MB.
error_reporting	There are many levels you can use to set what errors will be shown to you, but for the purposes of this book, we assume that error_reporting is set to E_ALL. When set to E_ALL, all errors and warnings are shown.
display_errors	Determines whether or not errors will be printed. Leave this feature on while you develop your site and you learn PHP, but once the site is ready to go live, we recommend that this setting be switched to "off" for security purposes.
log_errors	Allows errors to be written into a log file for future reference. We recommend that you switch this setting to "on."
error_log	Points to the name of your PHP error log file.
variables_order	Determines the order in which variables are registered. The default is EGPCS, which translates into Environment, GET, POST, COOKIE, and Built-in variables. We recommend that you leave this as the default setting until you are more familiar with PHP and the way variables work. In addition, your third-party host will most likely keep the default setting. This setting applies to all variables on all PHP pages, which we discuss in greater detail in Chapter 2.
register_globals	Determines whether variables sent through forms are available globally. This was a recent change from "on" to "off" as the default, and we recommend you leave this set to "off." You can read more about register_globals in Chapter 2.

Table continued on following page

Setting	What It Does
`file_uploads`	Enables Web site visitors to upload files to your server.
`upload_max_filesize`	Sets the limit for how large an uploaded file may be, in MB.
`mysql.allow_persistent`	Determines whether or not a persistent connection can be established with the MySQL server.
`mysql.max_persistent`	Sets the limit of how many persistent connections are allowed. For no limit, set this to -1.
`mysql.max_links`	Sets the limit of how many total links are allowed (persistent and non-persistent together). For no limit, set this to -1.
`session.save_path`	Determines where session information will be stored on your computer. You must specify a valid path, such as `c:\php\sess\tmp` or `c:\tmp` if you are using Windows. You must also create this directory beforehand, because PHP will not set this up for you.

Numerous other variables in your file can be altered, but we encourage you to work with the defaults until you feel more comfortable with PHP and your Web site setup. Changing these defaults can raise functionality, security, and performance issues, adversely affecting your site.

Configuring PHP5 to Use MySQL

Pre-PHP5, MySQL support was included in PHP installation by default. With the release of PHP5, you now have to specifically enable this.

If you are using Unix, you most likely built PHP with MySQL during installation. If you are using Windows, however, in order for your PHP and MySQL to play nice with each other, you will need to make two changes to your `php.ini` file. Open the file using your text editor (such as Notepad). Locate the following lines:

```
; Directory in which the loadable extensions (modules) reside.
extension_dir = "./"
```

Change the last line to

```
extension_dir = "c:\php\ext"
```

The next change involves locating and "uncommenting" the following line:

```
;extension=php_mysql.dll
```

Simply remove the semicolon at the beginning of the line to uncomment it.

You will also need to copy the file `libmysql.dll` from your `c:\php` directory into your `c:\windows\system32` or `c:\winnt\system32` directory.

Configuring Your MySQL Installation

MySQL needs TCP/IP protocols to run properly, regardless of the Windows environment. You must install TCP/IP before you can continue if it is not already on your computer. (Most computers have this set up already by default.) In Windows, this will be under your Control Panel ⇨ Network Settings, and in Linux, this is under your /proc filesystem.

Testing Your Installation

As with the other applications, it's a good idea to test your installation. You can do this from a DOS prompt so that you can view any error messages your MySQL server encounters.

Follow these steps to test your installation:

1. For Windows 95/98/Me, at the DOS prompt, change directories until you are in the MySQL server main directory (the default is c:\mysql\bin\). Then type

   ```
   c:\mysql\bin>mysqld
   ```

   For Windows 2000/XP/NT, at the DOS prompt, change directories until you are in the MySQL server main directory and type

   ```
   C:\>C:\mysql\bin\mysqld --install
   ```

   You should see a screen that looks similar to the one shown in Figure 1-3.

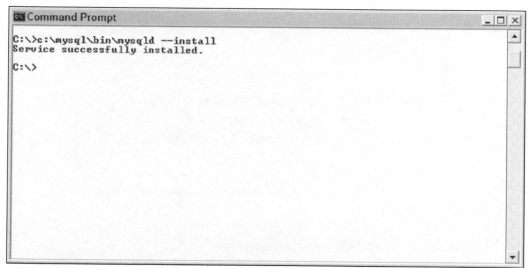

Figure 1-3

2. To start the MySQL server, type the following:

   ```
   c:\>NET START MySQL
   ```

   Your screen will look like the one shown in Figure 1-4.

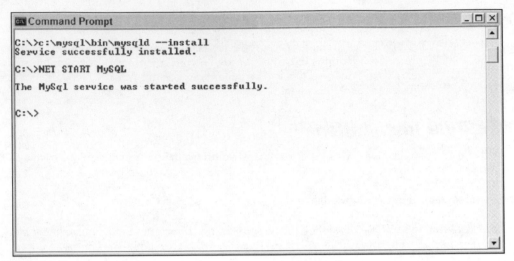

Figure 1-4

3. Now you should test to make sure your MySQL server is running. Although there are many possible commands to test the server, to keep things simple use the following:

```
C:\>c:\mysql\bin\mysql test
```

Your screen should look something like the one shown in Figure 1-5.

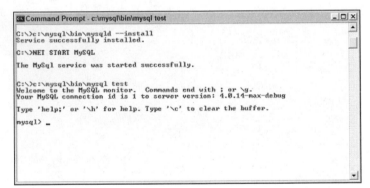

Figure 1-5

4. To return to the DOS prompt, enter the following:

```
mysql>exit
```

or

```
mysql>quit
```

5. To stop the server from running, type the following:

```
c:\>NET STOP MySQL
```

6. To shut down the MySQL service, type

```
C:\>c:\mysql\bin\mysqladmin -u root shutdown
```

It's time to configure your system to improve security, set up some user permissions, and alter your settings according to your preferences.

Configuring Your Installation

Before you configure any of your settings, start the MySQL service again.

1. Enter the following:

```
c:\>c:\mysql\bin\mysql mysql -u root
```

Now your screen should look like Figure 1-6.

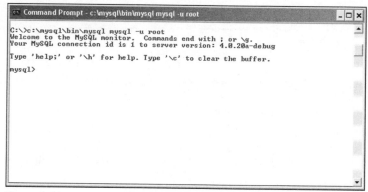

Figure 1-6

2. Next, see what database tables have been set up by default. Type the following:

```
mysql> show databases;
```

You should see the two existing databases, mysql and test, as shown in Figure 1-7.

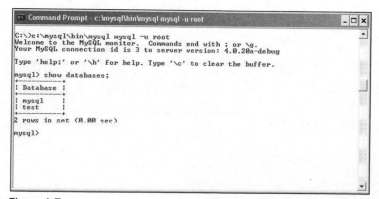

Figure 1-7

3. Now see what tables are there. Type the following:

```
mysql> show tables;
```

You should see what is depicted in Figure 1-8.

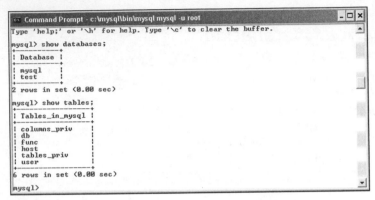

Figure 1-8

4. By default, MySQL on Windows sets up all users with all privileges. For this reason, you want to focus on the user table for a moment. If you would like to see all the privileges that can be assigned, you can type the following:

```
mysql> SHOW COLUMNS FROM user FROM mysql;
```

You only want to look at what users are already there, so type the following:

```
mysql> SELECT user, host FROM user;
```

You should see what is depicted in Figure 1-9.

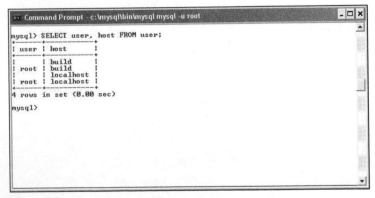

Figure 1-9

5. Because you want to set up a secure service, you want to change the blank user for the `localhost` host. Type the following:

```
mysql> DELETE FROM user WHERE Host='localhost' AND User='';
```

You will get a response from MySQL that states:

```
Query OK, 1 row affected (0.07 sec)
```

The time it takes to process the query may differ based on the speed of your computer, but the important thing here is that you get the "OK" from the MySQL gods.

6. Then get out of MySQL again and reset the users by entering the following:

```
mysql> quit
c:\>c:\mysql\bin\mysqladmin -u root reload
c:\>c:\mysql\bin\mysqladmin -u root password mysqlpass
```

7. Insert whatever password you would like for your root access; in this example, we chose the word "mysqlpass."

8. To reconnect to the server, try your new password:

```
C:\>c:\mysql\bin\mysql -h localhost -u root -p
```

You will be prompted for your password; in this case, enter "mysqlpass" or whatever you chose for your root password. You should then see the prompt shown in Figure 1-10.

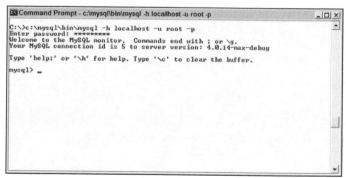

Figure 1-10

The my.cnf File

The `my.cnf` file, which you can open with any text editor, such as Notepad, is the main file that MySQL uses to read configuration options you have set up in your installation. You can alter this file at any time to tweak your configuration down the road.

By default, the installation of MySQL provides four sample `my.cnf` configuration files to use as examples: `my-small.cnf`, `my-medium.cnf`, `my-large.cnf`, and `my-huge.cnf`. If you used the default directory during installation, these were all saved under the `c:\mysql\` directory. If for some reason your copy of the installation zip file did not include these sample files, you can use the one provided here (you will just need to type it in from scratch using Notepad).

The difference in these files is presumably the amount of space you have on your computer dedicated to processing query requests and so on. For the purposes of the Web sites used in this book, the my-medium.cnf file will suffice, so save it to your root c:\ directory so it can be accessed by the MySQL server. Be sure to rename this file my.cnf so the server can find it.

Your my.cnf file looks like this:

```
# Example mysql config file.
# Copy this file to c:\my.cnf to set global options
#
# One can use all long options that the program supports.
# Run the program with --help to get a list of available options

# This will be passed to all mysql clients
[client]
#password=my_password
port=3306
#socket=MySQL

# Here is entries for some specific programs
# The following values assume you have at least 32M ram
# The MySQL server
[mysqld]
port=3306
#socket=MySQL
skip-locking
set-variable       = key_buffer=16M
set-variable       = max_allowed_packet=1M
set-variable       = table_cache=64
set-variable       = sort_buffer=512K
set-variable       = net_buffer_length=8K
set-variable       = myisam_sort_buffer_size=8M
server-id          = 1

# Uncomment the following if you want to log updates
#log-bin

# Uncomment the following rows if you move the MySQL
# distribution to another location
#basedir = d:/mysql/
#datadir = d:/mysql/data/


# Uncomment the following if you are NOT using BDB tables
#skip-bdb

# Uncomment the following if you are using BDB tables
#set-variable       = bdb_cache_size=4M
#set-variable       = bdb_max_lock=10000

# Uncomment the following if you are using Innobase tables
#innodb_data_file_path = ibdata1:400M
#innodb_data_home_dir = c:\ibdata
#innodb_log_group_home_dir = c:\iblogs
```

```
#innodb_log_arch_dir = c:\iblogs
#set-variable = innodb_mirrored_log_groups=1
#set-variable = innodb_log_files_in_group=3
#set-variable = innodb_log_file_size=5M
#set-variable = innodb_log_buffer_size=8M
#innodb_flush_log_at_trx_commit=1
#innodb_log_archive=0
#set-variable = innodb_buffer_pool_size=16M
#set-variable = innodb_additional_mem_pool_size=2M
#set-variable = innodb_file_io_threads=4
#set-variable = innodb_lock_wait_timeout=50

[mysqldump]
quick
set-variable        = max_allowed_packet=16M

[mysql]
no-auto-rehash
# Remove the next comment character if you are not familiar with SQL
#safe-updates

[isamchk]
set-variable        = key_buffer=20M
set-variable        = sort_buffer=20M
set-variable        = read_buffer=2M
set-variable        = write_buffer=2M

[myisamchk]
set-variable        = key_buffer=20M
set-variable        = sort_buffer=20M
set-variable        = read_buffer=2M
set-variable        = write_buffer=2M

[mysqlhotcopy]
interactive-timeout
```

Although you can find a complete reference of configuration at the source (www.mysql.com), the options a beginner will be most concerned with follow. To set any of these options, simply type the appropriate line directly in your my.cnf file under the appropriate section.

First, we'll discuss the local-infile option, which can be found in the my.cnf file as follows:

```
[mysqld]

local-infile     =1
```

This allows you to load large amounts of data from a tab-delimited file or .csv file directly into your MySQL database. While this option can be very helpful if you are running your own Web site, or if you are the only one accessing the MySQL configurations, many third-party hosts have this set to 0 to block their MySQL hosts from accessing this command, primarily for security reasons. If you are contemplating having your Web site hosted by a third party and you will need this feature, you may want to verify that they have this setting enabled to save yourself some major headaches later on, such as having to manually input large amounts of data a bit at a time, or having to write a subroutine that inputs the data for you. If you haven't yet chosen your third-party host, this will be an important selling point.

Second, we'll discuss altering the `log-bin` configuration option that can be found in the following section of the `my.cnf` file:

```
# Uncomment the following if you want to log updates
#log-bin
```

This is very important if you care at all about monitoring which updates are made to your MySQL tables (and you should). This logs all activity to the tables, and this topic is covered in greater detail in Chapter 17. We recommend that you uncomment the `log-bin` line to at least make the data available. Whether or not you do anything with it is another story.

Setting Up Users and Privileges

Hackers (or the malicious breed known as "crackers") can be quite crafty in the ways in which they break into your system, especially if you are directly connected to the Internet. MySQL allows you to pick and choose what user is allowed to perform what function based on the "privileges" that you establish. All user privilege information is stored in a database called mysql, which is located, by default, in your `c:\mysql\data` directory.

If you're the only one accessing the MySQL database, you may not have to worry about adding users. However, what if you have, say, an Aunt Edna who is going to help you out by inputting some back-logged information? You want her to be able to go into the tables and look at things, and even insert some information. But you probably don't want her to be able to delete your entire database. By restricting her privileges as a user, you help to protect your data.

Try It Out   Setting Up Privileges

To set up the initial privileges parameters, you need to make sure you're logged on as "root." Then you're going to GRANT Aunt Edna some privileges as a new user, so type the following:

```
mysql> GRANT SELECT,INSERT,UPDATE
    -> ON *.*
    -> TO edna@localhost
    -> IDENTIFIED BY 'ednapass';
```

How It Works

You have now established that "edna" is a valid user who will be allowed access to your MySQL system, provided two things:

❑   She attempts her connection from the "localhost" host—not a different connection from somewhere else.

❑   She supplies the correct password: "ednapass."

Your Aunt Edna will now be allowed to select information from the database, insert new information in the database, and update old information in the database. By giving her access to all the tables in the database (via the use of ON *.*), you have allowed her to modify any table in existence.

As you become more familiar with working with tables and MySQL commands, modifying privileges or user information will become easier for you because the information is all stored in a table (just like everything else in MySQL).

A complete list of privileges that you can grant is available at the MySQL Web site, www.mysql.com.

Where to Go for Help and Other Valuable Resources

Although we've certainly tried to make this as easy as possible for you, there are so many different variables in computers and their setups that it is virtually impossible to cover every possible situation. Anyone who works with computers on a regular basis is surely aware that, while in theory everything seems relatively simple, things don't always go as planned (or as you think they should). To your advantage, there are several avenues for help should you find yourself in a difficult situation.

Help within the Programs

Before getting online and searching for help, you can try looking for answers to your problems within the programs themselves.

In Apache, the manual was installed with the standard installation and can be accessed in c:\program files\apache group\apache2\manual. A check of your error log will be most helpful as well.

In MySQL, you can enter this realm by typing the following at your DOS prompt:

```
c:\>c:\mysql\bin\mysql --help
```

This provides a multitude of commands that will help you find what you need, or at the very least, a valuable "cheat sheet" for administering your MySQL server. In addition, this will allow you to see the current settings for your server at a glance so you can potentially troubleshoot any problem spots.

The MySQL manual is also installed to your computer and can be found under c:\mysql\docs\manual.htm.

Source Web Sites

You undoubtedly know where to find these by now, but just in case, the Web sites associated with each of our three components have incredibly detailed information to help you work out any issues, or report any bugs you may find in the programs:

- ❏ For Apache questions and information: www.apache.org
- ❏ For PHP questions and information: www.php.net
- ❏ For MySQL questions and information: www.mysql.com

Summary

By now, you should have an idea of what AMP is and how it fits into the open source initiative. You know that the abbreviation AMP refers to Apache, MySQL, and PHP, all of which work together to help you develop dynamic Web sites.

So now you've installed, configured, and tested the installation for Apache, MySQL, and PHP, and you should be ready to start making some Web sites! You'll get your hands dirty in the next chapter, starting with PHP code and your movie review Web site.

Part II: Movie Review Web Site

Creating PHP Pages Using PHP5

This chapter discusses the basics of PHP and starts you on your way to creating your first complete Web site, one featuring movie reviews. After you complete your Web site, your visitors will be able to locate information about a particular movie, and you will be able to program in PHP.

Even if you are familiar with PHP4, we encourage you to read through this chapter and to pay particular attention to the section on Object Oriented Programming (OOP), which is a new feature of PHP5.

This chapter covers the following basic PHP commands and structures:

- ❑ Using `echo` to display text
- ❑ Formatting text with both HTML and PHP
- ❑ Constants and variables
- ❑ Using a URL to pass variable values
- ❑ Sessions and cookies
- ❑ HTML forms
- ❑ `if/else` statements
- ❑ Includes
- ❑ Functions
- ❑ Arrays and `foreach`
- ❑ `while` and `do/while`
- ❑ Using classes and methods with OOP

By the end of this chapter, if you actually try all the "Try It Out" exercises, you will be able to create a simple login form, give your users an option to either see a review of your favorite movie or see a list of your top favorite movies, and offer them a numbered list of your movies based on how many they decide they want to see. You can even alphabetize the list for them, if so desired.

Overview of PHP Structure and Syntax

PHP programs are written using a text editor, such as Notepad or WordPad, just like HTML pages. Unlike HTML, though, PHP pages, for the most part, end in a .php extension. This extension signifies to the server that it needs to parse the PHP code before sending the resulting HTML code to the viewer's Web browser.

In a five-star restaurant, patrons see just a plate full of beautiful food served up just for them. They don't see where the food comes from, nor how it was prepared. In a similar fashion, PHP fits right into your HTML code and is invisible to the people visiting your site.

How PHP Fits with HTML

We assume that you know some HTML before you embark on your PHP/Apache/MySQL journey, and you've undoubtedly seen how JavaScript code and other languages can be interspersed within the HTML code in an HTML page. What makes PHP so different is that it not only allows HTML pages to be created on the fly, but it is invisible to your Web site visitors. The only thing they see when they view the source of your code is the resulting HTML output. This gives you more security for your PHP code and more flexibility in writing it.

HTML can also be written inside the PHP section of your page; this allows you to format text while keeping blocks of code together. This will also help you write organized, efficient code, and the browser (and, more importantly, the viewer) won't know the difference.

PHP can also be written as a standalone program, with no HTML at all. This is helpful for storing your connection variables, redirecting your visitors to another page of your site, or performing other functions discussed in this book.

The Rules of PHP Syntax

One of the benefits of using PHP is that it is relatively simple and straightforward. As with any computer language, there is usually more than one way to perform the same function. Once you feel comfortable writing some PHP programs, you can research shortcuts to make your code more efficient. For the sake of simplicity, we cover only the most common uses, rules, and functions of PHP.

You should always keep in mind these two basic rules of PHP:

❑   PHP is denoted in the page with opening and closing tags, as follows:

```
<?php
?>
```

❑   PHP lines end with a semicolon, generally speaking:

```
<?php
// First line of code goes here;
// Second line of code goes here;
// Third line of code goes here;
?>
```

You can add comments in your program, as in the preceding code, through double slashes (//) for one-liners or /* and */ for opening and closing comment tags that may extend over several lines of code. Indents don't matter, and, generally speaking, neither do line returns. This gives you freedom as a programmer, but a little freedom can be a dangerous thing, as we discuss in the next section.

And there you have it! Now you're an expert. Okay—there might be a few more things you need to learn, but this gets you started.

The Importance of Coding Practices

Before you jump in, you should realize how the structure of your code can affect your script. As far as the Web server parsing the PHP code is concerned, the structure of your code really doesn't matter. To the server, your code will show up as one continuous line, regardless of tabs, indents, and line returns. But to the human eye, how well your code is organized can really make a difference.

Take a look at the following examples.

Example 1:

```php
<?php
if ($_POST["fname"] == "Joe") {
  echo "<p>Hi $_POST['fname']</p>";
}
else {
  echo "<h2>Your name's not Joe, so you can't enter the Web site.</h2>"
}
?>
```

Example 2:

```php
<?php
//check to make sure the first name is equal to Joe before granting access
    if ($_POST["fname"] == "Joe")
        {
        echo "<p>";
        echo "Hi ";
        echo $_POST['fname'];
        echo "</p>";
        }
    else
        {
        echo "<h2>";
        echo "Your name's not Joe, so you can't enter the Web site!";
        echo "</h2>";
        }
?>
```

You can see that although Example 2 involves more typing, it will be much easier to spot any missing syntax or locate a specific portion of the code for troubleshooting purposes. This is especially important when you are just starting out. When you become more experienced as a coder, you can condense the code as in Example 1.

What Makes a Great Program?

Truly professional code follows three general guidelines:

❑ **Consistency:** Blocks of well-written code always look the same and have the same indents and ways of coding, such as syntax shortcuts that use bracket placement and formatting styles consistently throughout the program. The great thing about PHP is that it really doesn't care about tabs or indents, so you are free to create a style all your own, one that works best for you.

In addition, although there may be more than one syntax for accomplishing the same goal, good coders will be consistent throughout their code with whichever method they choose. For example, as far as PHP is concerned, the following two snippets of code mean the same thing:

```
<?php
// php code goes here;
?>


<?
// php code goes here;
?>
```

You should simply pick one and stick with it throughout your program.

❑ **Frequent comments:** The more you use comments throughout your code, the better off you will be. Although it's not so important in smaller, simpler programs, as your programs become more and more complex, it will be hard for you to remember what you did, where you did it, and why you did it the way you did. Detailed comments can help you find your way. Also, if you are working on a collaborative project, using comments will help your fellow code monkeys follow your logic.

❑ **The use of line numbers:** Some text editors insert line numbers for you, but others do not. Text editors are discussed later in this chapter, but you should know that it is important to denote line numbers somehow in your code, if they are not provided for you, because PHP lets you know when your program generates errors, and it notifies you of the line number in which the error occurs. If you have to count the lines manually every time you encounter an error, you can imagine how time consuming and inefficient your debugging will be.

Why Should You Care about What Your Code Looks Like?

It's important to follow good coding practices for three reasons:

❑ **For efficiency:** The easier your code is to read and follow, the easier it will be to keep track of where you are with your code, and the quicker it will be to pick up where you left off after a break.

❑ **For debugging:** Knowing where your problem lies is a major debugging tool. If you used comments, you can easily follow your own logic, and if you have line numbers and consistent formatting, you can easily scan your document to pinpoint a trouble area.

❑ **For future expansions and modifications:** Using comments in your code is especially important for future changes, because it's difficult to remember the logic behind code that was written years or even just months ago. Also, if you are working on code that involves a team, if everyone is using the same coding styles, it will be much easier to make changes or additions to someone else's work down the road.

Okay, enough preaching about good code—let's get to it.

Creating Your First Program

You can't get much simpler than this first program, but try it out to get a feel for what the results look like. The PHP function echo, seen in the material that follows, is one of the most commonly used PHP functions and one that, undoubtedly, you will become intimate with. It is used to send text (or variable values or a variety of other things) to the browser.

Try It Out   Using echo

Try using echo to see what results you achieve.

1. Enter the following program in your favorite text editor (Notepad, WordPad, or whatever), and save it as firstprog.php.

    Make sure you save it in a "plain text" format to avoid parsing problems, and if you're using Notepad, double-check to ensure that the file is not saved as firstprog.php.txt by default.

    ```
    <html>
    <head>
    <title>My First PHP Program</title>
    </head>
    <body>
    <?php
    echo "I'm a lumberjack.";
    ?>
    </body>
    </html>
    ```

2. Open this program using your browser. Your resulting screen should look like the one in Figure 2-1.

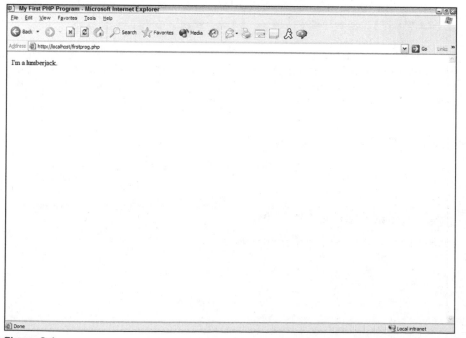

Figure 2-1

3. Now view the source of the HTML code so you can see what happened with the PHP portions of the code. As you can see, the PHP portion of the code has vanished, leaving only the resulting HTML code.

4. Now add the following highlighted line to your script so you can get a better feel for how your PHP code will be parsed:

```
<html>
<head>
<title>My First PHP Program</title>
</head>
<body>
<?php
echo "I'm a lumberjack.";
echo "And I'm okay.";
?>
</body>
</html>
```

5. Save the revised file and open it in your browser. As you can see, the line runs together without a line break, even though you had your PHP code on two different lines.

How It Works

When a browser calls a PHP program, it first searches through the entire code line by line to locate all PHP sections (those encased in the appropriate tags) and it then processes them one at a time. To the server, all PHP code is treated as one line, which is why your two lines of code were shown as one continuous line on the screen. After the PHP code has been parsed accordingly, the server goes back and gobbles up the remaining HTML and spits it out to the browser, PHP sections included.

Using HTML to Spice Up Your Pages

As you can see in the previous example, using only PHP code results in rather bland pages. You can make them look more professional and less utilitarian by adding some HTML to your PHP. HTML can be inserted within your PHP block of code using the echo function. Anything you can code in HTML, from frames, to tables, to font characteristics, can be inserted within a PHP section of code.

Integrating HTML with PHP

You will be better able to see how easily you can use HTML in the PHP program with the following practical example.

Try It Out   **Using PHP within HTML**

In this example, you'll use some PHP and HTML together.

1. Modify the highlighted lines of firstprog.php:

```
<html>
<head>
<title>My First PHP Program</title>
</head>
```

```
<body>
<?php
echo "<h1>I'm a lumberjack.</h1>";
echo "<h2>And I'm okay.</h2>";
?>
</body>
</html>
```

2. Save your file and reload the page. Your screen should now look something like the one in Figure 2-2.

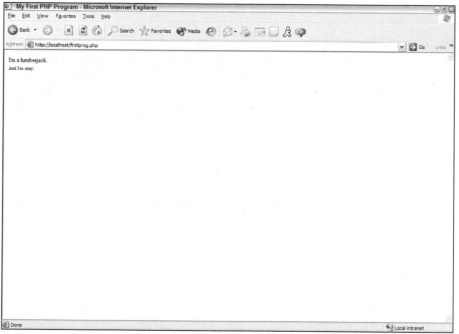

Figure 2-2

How It Works

The echo function basically outputs whatever it's told to the browser, whether it be HTML code, variable values, plain text — whatever. We wanted to prove a point, so we simply chose to echo HTML code in this example, as shown in the following lines:

```
echo "<h1>I'm a lumberjack.</h1>";
echo "<h2>And I'm okay.</h2>";
```

You can see that by inserting some HTML code within the PHP section of the program, you accomplish two things:

❑   You can improve the look of your site.

❑   You can keep PHP lines of code together without having to jump back and forth between HTML and PHP.

If you view the source of your HTML code you will see the HTML code you inserted using the `echo` function displayed just as you intended.

Considerations with HTML Inside PHP

The following list discusses some pitfalls commonly seen with the practice of inserting HTML inside PHP:

❑ **You have to check for double quotes.** As you may have noted when you worked through the previous example, using the `echo` function may involve the use of double quotation marks. Because HTML also uses double quotes, you can do one of two things to avoid problems:

  ❑ Use single quotes inside your HTML.

  ❑ Escape your HTML double quotes with a backslash, as in the following:

```
echo "<font size=\"2\">";
```

This is especially useful if you want to display double quotes in your text, such as:

```
echo "He was about 6'5\" tall.";
```

❑ **Remember that you still have to follow PHP rules, even though you're coding in HTML.** Sometimes when you begin to code in HTML within your PHP section, you can temporarily forget that you need to follow PHP guidelines and end your sentences with a semicolon, as well as close all quotes at the end of your `echo` statements.

❑ **Don't try to cram too much HTML into your PHP sections.** If you find yourself in the middle of a PHP portion of your program, and your HTML is becoming increasingly complex or lengthy, consider ending the PHP section and coding strictly in HTML. Consider the following examples:

Example 1:

```
<?php
    echo "<table width='100%' border='2' bgcolor='#FFFFFF'>";
    echo "<tr>";
    echo "<td width='50%'>";
    echo "<font face='Verdana, Arial' size='2'>";
    echo "First Name:";
    echo "</font></td">";
    echo "<td width='50%'>";
    echo "<font face='Verdana, Arial' size='2'>";
    echo $_POST["fname"]
    echo "</font></td>";
    echo "</tr>";
    echo "</table>";?>
```

Example 2:

```
<table width="100%" border="2" bgcolor="#FFFFFF">;
  <tr>
    <td width="50%">
      <font face="Verdana, Arial" size="2">
        First Name:
      </font>
    </td>
```

```
    <td width="50%">
      <font face="Verdana, Arial" size="2">
        <?php
          echo $_POST["fname"];
        ?>
      </font>
    </td>
  </tr>
</table>
```

Although we have not yet discussed variables, you can see in the first example that the only thing PHP was really needed for was to provide the value held in the variable fname and display it on the screen. The rest of the related code was in HTML. In this instance, you're better off just staying in HTML and pulling out the PHP line when you need it, instead of coding the HTML inside the PHP. Although it really doesn't matter to the server, it makes for easier formatting, easier debugging, and less typing (which is always a good thing). In essence, it is up to you to balance your HTML with PHP and discover what works best for your coding style.

Using Constants and Variables to Add Functionality

We've covered the basics of using the echo function to display text the way you want it. Really, this works no differently from coding an HTML page. However, using constants and variables allows you to take advantage of the power of PHP.

Overview of Constants

A constant is a placeholder for a value that you reference within your code. Constants are typically named with capital letters (so you can easily find them within your code), and the values are usually formally defined before using them. Constant names must begin with a letter or an underscore and cannot begin with a number. Names are also case-sensitive.

You define a value assigned to a constant with the PHP function define(). Once you've defined a constant, it can't be changed or undefined.

Try It Out   **Using Constants**

In this exercise, you'll see how you can use constants in your program.

1.   Open your text editor and type the following program:

```
<html>
<head>
<title>My Movie Site</title>
</head>
<body>
<?php
  define ("FAVMOVIE", "The Life of Brian");
  echo "My favorite movie is ";
```

```
      echo FAVMOVIE;
   ?>
   </body>
   </html>
```

2. Save this file as `moviesite.php` and open it in your browser. You should see the text shown in Figure 2-3.

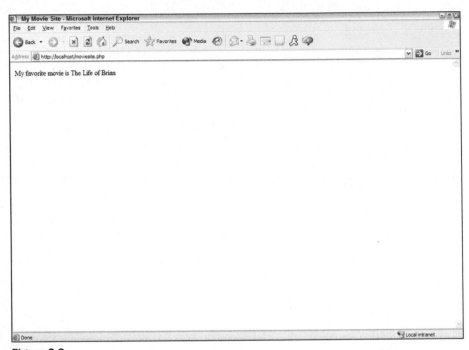

Figure 2-3

How It Works

By defining the constant known as FAVMOVIE, you have set the value as "The Life of Brian," which can be recalled and displayed later on. Although this constant can't be changed or reset throughout your script, it is available for use by any part of your script.

Overview of Variables

Unlike constants, variables are obviously meant to be variable — they are meant to change or be changed at some point in your program. Variables also do not need to be defined or declared and can simply be assigned when needed. Variables can hold either numeric or text values.

Variables are denoted with a dollar sign ($) and are case-sensitive, as are constants (in other words, $dateEntered and $DateEntered are not the same thing). The first letter of the variable name must be an underscore or letter and cannot be a number.

Previously, in PHP4, by default, variables were not passed by reference unless you prefaced them with an ampersand to force use of that practice. Beginning with PHP5, all variables will be passed by reference with no additional syntax required. This significantly increases the speed and power of your PHP programs. Don't worry if you don't understand what that means; it becomes more important in more advanced applications.

Using Variables

In this exercise, you'll add variables to your existing script.

1. Open your text editor and make the following changes to your `moviesite.php` file (noted in highlighted lines):

```
<html>
<head>
<title>My Movie Site</title>
</head>
<body>
<?php
  define("FAVMOVIE", "The Life of Brian");
  echo "My favorite movie is ";
  echo FAVMOVIE;
  echo "<br>";
  $movierate = 5;
  echo "My movie rating for this movie is: ";
  echo $movierate;
?>
</body>
</html>
```

2. Save the changes and access the file in your browser. Your screen should now look like the one in Figure 2-4.

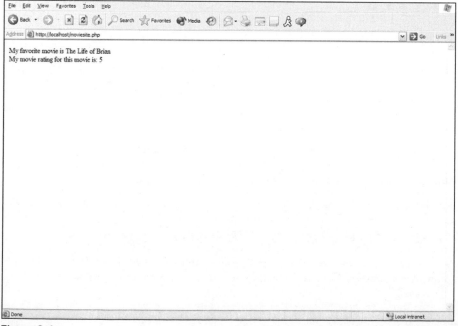

File   Edit   View   Favorites   Tools   Help

Back ·   ·   Search   Favorites   Media

Address   http://localhost/moviesite.php

My favorite movie is The Life of Brian
My movie rating for this movie is: 5

Done   Local intranet

Figure 2-4

How It Works

The value "5" is assigned to the variable `movierate`, and it is assigned as an integer value (number) instead of a string (text). The following line of code would cause the value of "5" to be seen as a string:

```
$movierate = "5";
```

By keeping this value as an integer, you can then perform mathematical calculations on this number later on (such as giving the viewer the average movie rate), as in this example:

```php
<?php
  $bobsmovierate = 5;
  $joesmovierate = 7;
  $grahamsmovierate = 2;
  $zabbysmovierate = 1;
  $avgmovierate = (($bobsmovierate + $joesmovierate + $grahamsmovierate
                  + $zabbysmovierate) / 4);
  echo "The average movie rating for this movie is: ";
  echo $avgmovierate;
?>
```

PHP also has numerous built-in mathematical functions that you can use on variables that contain numbers, such as the following:

❑   `rand([min],[max])`: Generates a random integer.

❑   `ceil(number)`: Rounds a decimal up to the next highest integer.

❑   `floor(number)`: Rounds a decimal down to the next lowest integer.

❑   `number_format(number [,dec places] [,dec point] [,thousands])`: Formats the number based on the chosen number of decimal places, and uses the designated decimal point and thousands separator, if applicable. By default, PHP uses a period for the decimal point and a comma for the thousands separator, so if that's acceptable for you, then you can leave off the optional parameters, as noted in brackets above. If you would like to take out the comma, for example, you would type the following code:

```php
$price = 12345.67;
number_format($price); //returns 12,345.67
number_format($price, 2, ".", ""); //returns 12345.67
```

❑   `max(argument1, argument2, ...)`: Returns the maximum value of the supplied arguments.

❑   `min(argument1, argument2, ...)`: Returns the minimum value of the supplied arguments.

For a complete listing of PHP's mathematical functions, please refer to Appendix C.

Passing Variables between Pages

Suppose your site allows viewers to enter their name on the front page. You'd like to be able to greet the user by name on each page in your site, but to do so, you need some way to pass the value of the name variable from page to page. There are basically four ways to accomplish this task: pass the variables in the URL, through a session, via a cookie, or with an HTML form. The method you choose is based on the situation and what best fits your needs at the time.

A Word about register_globals

Before we begin discussing the four methods of parsing variables between pages, you need to understand a little concept called `register_globals`. This is a configuration setting in your `php.ini` file that, when turned off, prevents the variable value from being falsely inserted by an outside source. While previous versions of PHP set the default setting in `php.ini` to "on," ever since version 4.2, the default has been switched to "off." This was the cause of many a programmer's sleepless night, because you must refer to your variables differently if `register_globals` is turned off, or else find all your variables' values coming up empty.

Although many third-party Web hosts have turned on `register_globals`, for security reasons not everyone does; we decided to assume that `register_globals` is off for the purposes of the exercises in this book. Coding with the assumption that `register_globals` has been turned off is the safest way to code because your program will work regardless of the server's setting.

Instead of calling variable values by the standard `$varname` syntax, when `register_globals` is "off" and you need to pass variables across pages, you need to refer to them in a different way, but only in the receiving page. You will see this in action in the next "Try It Out" section, but the various ways to refer to variables depend on how they are being sent.

Syntax	When to Use It
`$_GET['varname']`	When the method of passing the variable is the `"GET"` method in HTML forms
`$_POST['varname']`	When the method of passing the variable is the `"POST"` method in HTML forms
`$_SESSION['varname']`	When the variable has been assigned the value from a particular session
`$_COOKIE['varname']`	When the variable has been assigned a value from a cookie
`$_REQUEST['varname']`	When it doesn't matter (`$_REQUEST` includes variables passed from any of the above methods)
`$_SERVER['varname']`	When the variable has been assigned a value from the server
`$_FILES['varname']`	When the variable has been assigned a value from a file upload
`$_ENV['varname']`	When the variable has been assigned a value from the operating environment

If you do not retrieve the variables using this syntax, the variable value will appear to be empty in your program and can cause you much grief in debugging!

Passing Variables through a URL

The first method of passing variables between pages is through the page's URL. You've undoubtedly seen URLs such as this:

```
http://www.mydomain.com/news/articles/showart.php?id=12345
```

This is an example of passing variable values through the URL. It requests that the article with the ID number of "12345" be chosen for the `showart.php` program. The text after the URL is called the *query string*.

You can also combine variables in a URL by using an ampersand (`&`), as in this example:

```
http://www.mydomain.com/news/articles/showart.php?id=12345&lang=en
```

This asks to retrieve the file with an ID of "12345" and the language presumably equal to "en," for English.

There are a few disadvantages to passing variables through a URL:

❑   Everyone can see the values of the variables, so passing sensitive information isn't really very secure using this method.

❑   The user can change the variable value in the URL, leaving your site potentially open to showing something you'd rather not show.

❑   A user might also pull up inaccurate or old information using a saved URL with older variables embedded in it.

Try It Out   Using URL Variables

In this exercise, you'll modify your program to show the URL variables in action.

1.   Modify your `moviesite.php` file as follows (changes are highlighted):

```
<html>
<head>
<title>My Movie Site - <?php echo $favmovie; ?></title>
</head>
<body>
<?php
    //delete this line: define("FAVMOVIE", "The Life of Brian");
    echo "My favorite movie is ";
    echo $favmovie;
    echo "<br>";
    $movierate = 5;
    echo "My movie rating for this movie is: ";
    echo $movierate;
?>
</body>
</html>
```

2. Save your `moviesite.php` file and start a new document in your text editor.

3. Type the following code:

```
<html>
<head>
<title>Find my Favorite Movie!</title>
</head>
<body>
<?php
  echo "<a href='moviesite.php?favmovie=Stripes'>";
  echo "Click here to see information about my favorite movie!";
  echo "</a>";
?>
</body>
</html>
```

4. Save this file as `movie1.php` and open it in your browser. Your screen should look like the one in Figure 2-5.

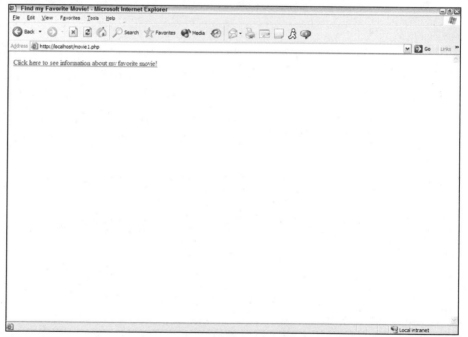

Figure 2-5

5. Now click the link and see what you get (see Figure 2-6).

You see the value for `$favmovie` as "Stripes" in the URL, as shown in Figure 2-6, but notice there is nothing shown for the value in the body of your page, nor in the title as it's supposed to be. If you have `E_ALL` turned on in your `php.ini` file, you will see the "undefined variable" error message.

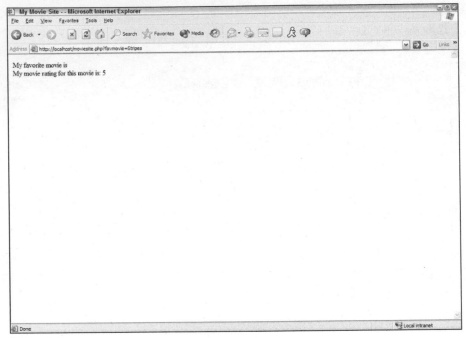

Figure 2-6

What went wrong? You guessed correctly if you said `register_globals`! This is a prime example of how not retrieving the variables in the correct way can leave your pages not working and leave you perplexed. Now modify the `moviesite.php` file to fix the mistake.

1. Edit the following lines in your script (changes are highlighted):

```
<html>
<head>
<title>My Movie Site - <?php echo $_REQUEST['favmovie']; ?></title>
</head>
<body>
<?php
  echo "My favorite movie is ";
  echo $_REQUEST['favmovie'];
  echo "<br>";
  $movierate = 5;
  echo "My movie rating for this movie is: ";
  echo $movierate;
?>
</body>
</html>
```

2. Now save your file and reopen `movie1.php`. The link should now work fine, and your screen should look like the one in Figure 2-7.

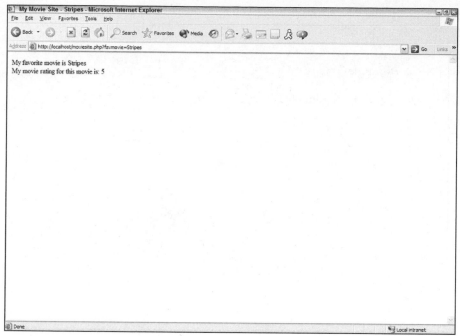

Figure 2-7

How It Works

Here are a few points to note about your program:

❑ As you can see from the "Title" section of your program, PHP code can be inserted in a straight line in the midst of your HTML code. This is helpful when you just need to insert one tidbit of information grabbed from PHP.

❑ You can also insert PHP information anywhere in your HTML program, including the title.

❑ You saw first-hand the effects of not taking into account register_globals when accessing a variable from another page, but did you notice that when you referred to $movierate, you did not have to include the register_globals syntax? This is because the value of $movierate is kept within moviesite.php; you did not get the information from another page or source.

❑ $_REQUEST was chosen for your variable syntax because it really didn't matter in this example where the value for $favmovie came from. You were not trying to validate anything or prevent an unauthorized user from entering this page of the site: You simply wanted to pass the value across.

Special Characters in URLs

Passing variables through a URL poses an interesting problem if there are spaces, ampersands, or other special characters in the value of your variable. Luckily, substitutes exist for special characters that maintain the integrity of the variables' values. There is a special function called urlencode() to use when passing these values through a URL. If you wanted to change your favorite movie from "Stripes" to "Life of Brian," you would use `urlencode()` to encode the value and insert the proper HTML special characters.

To try this out, perform these steps:

1. Make the following highlighted changes to your `movie1.php` file:

```
<html>
<head>
<title>Find my Favorite Movie!</title>
</head>
<body>
<?php
    //add this line:
    $myfavmovie = urlencode("Life of Brian");

    //change this line:
    echo "<a href='moviesite.php?favmovie=$myfavmovie'>";
    echo "Click here to see information about my favorite movie!";
    echo "</a>";
?>
</body>
</html>
```

2. Save the file and open it again in your browser. Clicking the link now displays the page shown in Figure 2-8.

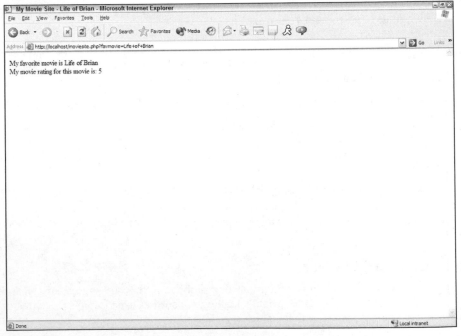

Figure 2-8

Passing Variables with Sessions

As we mentioned before, passing a value through a URL is fine if the information is not of a particularly sensitive nature or if it is relatively static and there is no danger of a user pulling up old information from a previously saved page. If you are transmitting information such as usernames or passwords, however, or personal information such as addresses and phone numbers, better methods exist for passing the information while keeping it private.

A *session* is basically a temporary set of variables that exists only until the browser has shut down (unless you set this up differently in your php.ini file, which is another story altogether). Examples of session information include a session ID and whether or not an authorized person has "logged in" to the site. This information is stored temporarily for your PHP programs to refer back to whenever needed.

Every session is assigned a unique session ID, which keeps all the current information together. Your session ID can either be passed through the URL or through the use of cookies. Although it is preferable for security reasons to pass the session ID through a cookie so that it is hidden from the human eye, if cookies are not enabled, the backup method is through the URL.

This setting is determined in your php.ini file. If you would like to force the user to pass variables through cookies (instead of allowing a backup plan), you would set the following line in your file:

```
session.use_only_cookies = 1
```

To begin a session, use the function session_start(). Because we assume you have register_globals set to "off," you should not use the session_register() function you may have seen in other PHP scripts. Make sure before using sessions that your php.ini file has been modified to show a valid path in the session.save_path variable, as described in Chapter 1.

First, you need to decide what information will be stored in your session. Anything that has been stored in a database can be retrieved and stored temporarily along with your session information. Usually, it is information such as username and login information, but it can also be preferences that have been set at some point by the user. An SID (session ID) will also be stored in the session array of variables.

Try It Out   Passing the Visitor's Username

Suppose you want to pass your visitor's username, and whether or not he or she has authentically logged into the site between the first page and the second page. Because we won't discuss the use of forms until later in this chapter, we'll fake it for now.

Follow these steps:

1.   Change your movie1.php file to include the following highlighted lines.

```
<?php
session_start();
$_SESSION['username'] = "Joe12345";
$_SESSION['authuser'] = 1;
?>
<html>
<head>
<TITLE>Find my Favorite Movie!</TITLE>
```

```
</head>
<body>
<?php
  $myfavmovie = urlencode("Life of Brian");
  echo "<a href='moviesite.php?favmovie=$myfavmovie'>";
  echo "Click here to see information about my favorite movie!";
  echo "</a>";
?>
</body>
</html>
```

2. Now save your `movie1.php` file.

3. Open `moviesite.php` to make the following highlighted changes:

```
<?php
session_start();

//check to see if user has logged in with a valid password
if ($_SESSION['authuser'] != 1) {
  echo "Sorry, but you don't have permission to view this page, you loser!";
  exit();
}
?>
<html>
<head>
<title>My Movie Site - <?php echo $_REQUEST['favmovie']; ?></title>
</head>
<body>
<?php
  echo "Welcome to our site, ";
  echo $_SESSION['username'];
  echo "! <br>";
  echo "My favorite movie is ";
  echo $_REQUEST['favmovie'];
  echo "<br>";
  $movierate = 5;
  echo "My movie rating for this movie is: ";
  echo $movierate;
?>
</body>
</html>
```

4. Click the link in `movie1.php`, and you should see the text for `moviesite.php` shown in Figure 2-9.

How It Works

Here are a few important things to note about this procedure:

❏   All the session information is at the top of the page, before any HTML code. This is very important! If there is even a leading space before the PHP code at the top of the page, you will get
this error:

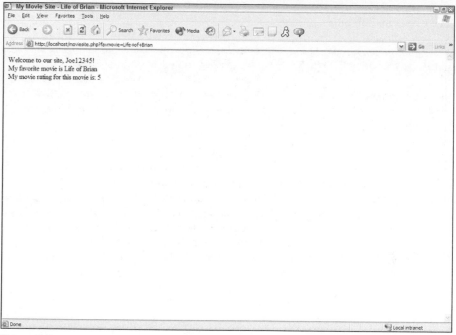

Figure 2-9

Warning: `session_start(): Cannot send session cache limiter - headers already sent (output started at c:\program files\Apache Group\Apache2\test\moviesite.php:1) in` **c:\program files\Apache Group\Apache2\test\moviesite.php** `on line` **2**

Some other situations also will give you the "headers already sent" error, which we discuss in Chapter 18.

❑   Refer to the session variables using the `register_globals` syntax, `$_SESSION['varname']`; if you don't, the variables will contain empty values.

❑   You must use the function `session_start()` at the beginning of every page that references the session variables.

❑   You used an `if` statement, which we delve into later in this chapter. It's a good idea to take a quick glance at this syntax, just to familiarize yourself with it.

Passing Variables with Cookies

Cookies are tiny bits of information stored on your Web site visitor's computer. There appears to be some sort of paranoia about using cookies, so many people choose to disable this feature in their Web browsers. In theory, cookies can be intercepted to gain information such as a person's IP address and operating system, but cookies are primarily used for storing information only. A few ad campaigns have developed technology to use cookies to track your browsing habits, and many people see this as an invasion of privacy. Also, because cookies are stored in a commonly named directory, anyone with access to someone else's computer (either via a hack or physical location) can potentially open cookie files and glean information about the owner. Because of these possibilities it's not a good idea to store any poten-tially private information on a computer.

For more information on cookies and the potential security risks (however minute), you are encouraged to visit the W3 Security FAQ Web site at `www.w3.org/Security/faq/wwwsf2.html`.

Therefore, because your visitors may either have cookies turned off or may physically delete cookies from their computers, relying on cookie information probably isn't the brightest idea from a Web devel-opment standpoint.

So why do developers use cookies, anyway? The advantage to storing information in a cookie versus a session is longevity. Sessions alone can't store information for more than the length of time the browser window is open. Like the elusive and mean-spirited video game that loses all high scores once it's unplugged, once a browser closes, all session information is lost. Cookies, on the other hand, can live on a person's computer until the developer has decided it's been long enough and they automatically "die." It is because of this longevity that cookies are fabulous for storing information such as a visitor's user-name or language preferences. These are the pieces of information that users won't have to retype every time they visit your site, but if for some reason someone did get wind of the information, it wouldn't be the end of the world.

We mentioned earlier that sessions alone can't store information for very long. However, you can alter this limitation if you use sessions in conjunction with cookies. If your sessions are passing variables using cookies, you *can* set the life of these cookies to longer than the life of the browser using the `session.cookie_lifetime` configuration in your `php.ini` file. Keep in mind, however, that not only will the session information be stored on the person's computer, but the session ID also will be stored, and that can cause you problems later on.

To set a cookie, you use the appropriately named `setcookie()` function. When setting a cookie, you can determine that the following information be set along with it:

❑ Cookie name (this is mandatory).

❑ Value of the cookie (such as the person's username).

❑ Time in seconds when the cookie will expire. (This time is based on a Unix timestamp, but you can set it using the syntax `time()+60*60*24*365`, which keeps the cookie alive for a year. This is optional, but if it is not set, the cookie will expire when the browser is closed.)

❑ Path (the directory where the cookie will be saved — the default is usually sufficient; this is optional).

❑ Domain (domains that may access this cookie — this is optional).

❑ Whether a cookie must have a secure connection to be set (defaults to 0; to enable this feature set this to 1).

You make each of these settings as follows:

```
setcookie('cookiename', 'value', 'expiration time', 'path', 'domain',
    'secure connection');
```

As you can probably guess by now, those values will be referenced in the script as `$_COOKIE['cookiename']`.

Try It Out   **Setting a Cookie**

In this exercise, you'll have the Web site set a cookie on Joe's machine so that he (theoretically) doesn't have to type his username (Joe12345) every time he comes back to visit. To do this, follow these steps:

1.   Modify your `movie1.php` file as shown:

```php
<?php
setcookie('username', 'Joe', time()+60);
session_start();
//delete this line: $_SESSION['username']="Joe12345";
$_SESSION['authuser'] = 1;
?>
<html>
<head>
<title>Find my Favorite Movie!</title>
</head>
<body>
<?php
  $myfavmovie = urlencode("Life of Brian");
  echo "<a href='moviesite.php?favmovie=$myfavmovie'>";
  echo "Click here to see information about my favorite movie!";
  echo "</a>";
?>
</body>
</html>
```

2.   Save the file.

3.   Make the following changes to your `moviesite.php` file:

```php
<?php
session_start();

//check to see if user has logged in with a valid password
if ($_SESSION['authuser'] != 1) {
  echo "Sorry, but you don't have permission to view this
          page, you loser!";
  exit();
}
?>
<html>
<head>
<title>My Movie Site - <?php echo $_REQUEST['favmovie']; ?></title>
</head>
<body>
<?php
  echo "Welcome to our site, ";
  echo $_COOKIE['username'];
  echo "! <br>";
  echo "My favorite movie is ";
  echo $_REQUEST['favmovie'];
  echo "<br>";
  $movierate=5;
```

```
    echo "My movie rating for this movie is: ";
    echo $movierate;
?>
</body>
</html>
```

4. Save the file.

5. Open a new browser window (in case you have any session information from the previous example lingering about) and open the movie1.php file. Click the link and your screen should look like the one in Figure 2-10.

Figure 2-10

How It Works

When using cookies, remember the following:

❑ Like sessions, cookies must be placed at the very top of the page, before your first <html> line. Otherwise, you get the "headers already sent" error.

❑ If you didn't notice, you changed the username from Joe12345 when you were using sessions, to Joe when you were using cookies. This was to double-check that the information was coming from the cookie and not the session.

❑ The expire time for the cookie was set to 60 seconds so you could play with and test your cookies without having to wait around for them to kick off. For a normal application storing usernames, it would be logical to set this higher.

❑ Unlike sessions, cookie information can't be accessed in the current page where the cookies have been set. You have to move on to the next page for the cookie to be set and accessible to your program.

Passing Information with Forms

Up until now, you've passed information among pages successfully, but you've been the one to supply all the information, not the visitor. Although it would be a great world if you really knew that much about your Web site visitors, it might get a little labor-intensive on your part. What do you say to letting them supply you with information for a change?

If you've never filled out a form online, then you have probably been living in a cave somewhere with no Internet access. Forms are the great Venus Fly Traps, just lying in wait to gobble up useful information from Web site visitors. Forms allow your Web site to be truly interactive; they take data from the user and send it off somewhere where it gets massaged, manipulated, perhaps stored, and then some result is sent back to the user. We discuss forms in greater detail in Chapter 5, but we will briefly touch on them here so you get a basic understanding of how they work.

Fast Primer on Forms

In case you are a bit rusty on the syntax of forms, or if you just need a quick reference, here is a quick, down-and-dirty discussion of forms. Forms are coded in HTML and stay in HTML. A form is made up of four parts:

❑ **Opening tag line, indicated by the** `<form>` **tag.** This tag line must include an *action* and a *method*. An action gives the form a URL or path to another program that will take the data included in the form and carry it from there. A method (`GET` or `POST`) tells the form how the data is to be carried. (`POST` is, generally speaking, the preferred method because it's more secure.)

❑ **Content of the form, including input fields.** Input fields are the areas where the user types in the information (or selects it in the case of a checkbox or radio button). An input field must include a *type* and a *name*, and can include other parameters, such as `maxlength`.

The type of input field can be one of many different selections, the most common being:

    ❑ **Text.** Used for collecting from 2 characters up to 2,000 characters. The parameter used to limit the number of accepted characters for a particular input field is `maxlength`. For large input fields (such as comments) the input field `textarea` is recommended over `text`.

    ❑ **Checkbox.** Used to allow users to make a selection from a list of choices; also permits users to make more than one choice. Individual choices must be indicated with a value parameter.

    ❑ **Radio.** Also known as radio buttons. Used for allowing users to choose from a list, but they permit only one choice. Individual choices must be indicated with a `value` parameter.

    ❑ **Select.** Also known as drop-down boxes. Used for allowing users to choose from a list. Individual choices can be indicated with a `value` parameter.

    ❑ **Password.** Hides what the user is typing behind asterisks, but does not compromise the value of the variable.

The name of the input field will be known as your variable name in your PHP program. To avoid issues with PHP parsing, you should name your input fields according to the PHP variable naming guidelines covered earlier in this chapter.

❑ **Action button(s) or images, typically submit/clear or a user-defined button, technically considered input types as well.** These are indicated with the input types submit, reset, and image for user-created buttons.

❑ **Closing tag line, indicated with a** </form> **tag.**

Got it?

Try It Out   **Using Forms to Get Information**

Because your program is slowly increasing in size, for this exercise, we suggest you switch to a text editor that will add line numbers to your document. If you are using a text editor that inserts these line numbers already, you do not need to worry about adding these in. Otherwise, you may want to add periodic line numbers as comments to help you keep track. In addition to adding line numbers to your program, you are also going to insert comments to help you keep track of what is going on.

Here's how to use forms to get information from visitors:

1.   Open your movie1.php file and make the following changes:

```php
<?php
//delete this line: setcookie('username', 'Joe', time()+60);
session_start();
$_SESSION['username'] = $_POST['user'];
$_SESSION['userpass'] = $_POST['pass'];
$_SESSION['authuser'] = 0;

//Check username and password information
if (($_SESSION['username'] == 'Joe') and
    ($_SESSION['userpass'] == '12345')) {
  $_SESSION['authuser'] = 1;
} else {
  echo "Sorry, but you don't have permission to view this
        page, you loser!";
  exit();
}
?>
<html>
<head>
<title>Find my Favorite Movie!</title>
</head>
<body>
<?php
  $myfavmovie = urlencode("Life of Brian");
  echo "<a href='moviesite.php?favmovie=$myfavmovie'>";
  echo "Click here to see information about my favorite movie!";
  echo "</a>";
?>
</body>
</html>
```

2. Now make these changes to your `moviesite.php` file:

```php
<?php
session_start();

//check to see if user has logged in with a valid password
if ($_SESSION['authuser'] !=1 ) {
  echo "Sorry, but you don't have permission to view this
        page, you loser!";
  exit();
}
?>
<html>
<head>
<title>My Movie Site - <?php echo $_REQUEST['favmovie']; ?></title>
</head>
<body>
<?php
  echo "Welcome to our site, ";
  //delete this line: echo $_COOKIE['username'];
  echo $_SESSION['username'];
  echo "! <br>";
  echo "My favorite movie is ";
  echo $_REQUEST['favmovie'];
  echo "<br>";
  $movierate = 5;
  echo "My movie rating for this movie is: ";
  echo $movierate;
?>
</body>
</html>
```

3. Start a new file:

```php
<?php
session_unset();

?>
<html>
<head>
<title>Please Log In</title>
</head>

<body>
<form method="post" action="movie1.php">
  <p>Enter your username:
    <input type="text" name="user">
  </p>
  <p>Enter your password:
    <input type="password" name="pass">
  </p>
  <p>
    <input type="submit" name="Submit" value="Submit">
  </p>
```

```
    </form>
    </body>
    </html>
```

4. Save this file as `login.php`.

5. Load the `login.php` file into your browser and log in with the username Joe12345 and the password 12345.

Let's see what happens. If the authorization script works, your screen should look like the one shown in Figure 2-11.

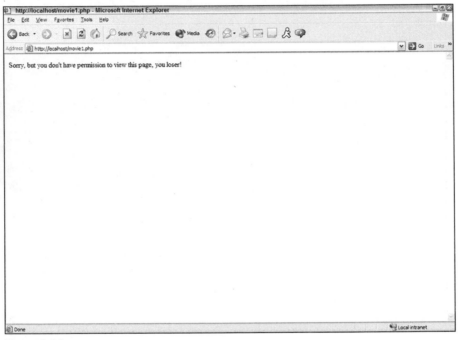

Figure 2-11

Now try logging in with the correct username (Joe) and password (12345). Your `movie1.php` site should load as it did before, and the link should take you to the `moviesite.php` page.

How It Works

In `login.php`, you first release any variables from sessions that may be lingering around with the command `session_unset()`. Then you ask for two variables from the user: username and password (variable names `user` and `pass`, respectively). These are submitted to `movie1.php` (the "action" in the form) via the POST method (the "method" in the form). This is why you have to refer to them using the `$_POST` syntax at the beginning of `movie1.php`.

The file `movie1.php` actually accomplishes several things:

❑ It starts the session and, by default, registers the variables. Values are set based on the information sent from the form in login.php.

❑ It checks to see if the username and password are acceptable. In real life, you would match this information to a database for authentication and verification.

❑ It sets the authuser to 1 if the acceptable username/password combination has been supplied, which grants the user permission to then proceed to other pages in the site, such as moviesite.php.

❑ If the username/password combination is not acceptable, a tactful error message is displayed to the user.

Because the information is passed on to moviesite.php as before, the only thing moviesite.php has to check for is that the user is authorized through the authuser variable.

Using if/else Arguments

You've seen now that you can assign many different values to variables. At some point in the course of your script, you're going to want to take specific actions based on the value of a variable. For example, consider a $password variable. If the user supplies the correct password, you'll want to grant him access to the site. If the password is incorrect, you might want to ask the user to try again, or maybe lock him out. You can use the if statement to dictate the action your script takes based on the value of a variable. If you add the else statement to an if, you open up a whole range of possible actions.

Using if Statements

Unlike some other programming languages, in PHP, the if statement can be used alone. The syntax is as follows:

```
if (condition1 operator condition2) action to be taken if true;
```

As in this example:

```
if ($stockmarket >= 10000) echo "Hooray! Time to Party!";
```

If the action to take is longer than a simple statement that will easily fit on one line, you must use brackets ({}) to enclose your action section:

```
if ($stockmarket >= 10000) {
  echo "Hooray! Time to Party!";
  $mood = "happy";
  $retirement = "potentially obtainable";
}
```

Operators

The operators used to compare the two conditions are similar to those comparison operators you likely encountered in elementary-school math. A list of these operators follows. Please note that these are only for use within the if statement itself and are not to be used when assigning values to variables.

Operator	Appropriate Syntax
equal to	==
not equal to	!= or <>
greater than	>
less than	<
greater than or equal to	>=
less than or equal to	<=
equal to, AND data types match (both are integers, or both are strings)	===
not equal to, OR the data types are not the same	!==

Special Syntax Considerations

You should pay special attention to the use of semicolons in `if` statements. Semicolons are required in individual lines within the `if` statement, but not at the end of the `if` statement itself. Also, take special note of the use of the double equals sign when comparing condition1 and condition2. This takes some getting used to for the newbie and can slip you up if you're not careful.

The way you indent your lines does not matter to PHP, but it matters to the human eye, so if possible, try to keep your indents consistent and easy to read.

Try It Out   Using if

This exercise will start you off with a brief script to illustrate `if` by itself.

1. Open your text editor and type the following program:

```
<html>
<head>
<title>How many days in this month?</title>
</head>
<body>
<?php
$month = date("n");
if ($month==1) echo "31";
if ($month==2) echo "28 (unless it's a leap year)";
if ($month==3) echo "31";
if ($month==4) echo "30";
if ($month==5) echo "31";
if ($month==6) echo "30";
if ($month==7) echo "31";
if ($month==8) echo "31";
if ($month==9) echo "30";
if ($month==10) echo "31";
if ($month==11) echo "30";
if ($month==12) echo "31";
?>
</body>
</html>
```

2.   Save this as `date.php` and open it in your browser.

The result should display the number of days in the current month.

How It Works

The script gets the value for variable `$month` by tapping into one of PHP's numerous built-in date functions; `date("n")` returns a value equal to the numerical equivalent of the month as set in your server, such as 1 for January, 2 for February, and so on. (We talk more about `date()` in Appendix C.)

Then the script tests the `if` statements for each potential value for `$month` until it gets the right answer. If the first `if` statement is false, the program immediately goes to the next line and executes it. When it gets to the right month, it carries out the rest of the statement in the line and then goes to the next line and executes it as well. It does not stop once it comes across a true statement but continues on as if nothing happened.

Using if and else Together

Using `if` by itself is fine and dandy in some cases, but there are other times when the `if/else` combination is more appropriate. For example, suppose you want to show a certain message on your site, but you have a holiday message you'd like shown for the month of December. Or suppose that on your movie review site, you want to show an abbreviated version of a movie review for those who haven't yet seen the movie. It's these "either/or" cases where you need to whip out the all-powerful `if/else` combination.

Try It Out   Using if and else

Keep with the date theme to let the user know whether or not the current year is a leap year. Follow these steps to accomplish this:

1.   Open your text editor and enter the following code:

```
<html>
<head>
<title>Is it a leap year?</title>
</head>
<body>
<?php
$leapyear = date("L");
if ($leapyear == 1) echo "Hooray! It's a leap year!";
else echo "Aww, sorry, mate. No leap year this year.";
?>
</body>
</html>
```

2.   Save this file as `leapyear.php` and open it in your browser.

You should now see a statement based on whether or not the current year is a leap year.

How It Works

Suppose the year is 2003. That's not a leap year, so the value of `$leapyear` would be 0. When the script reads the `if` statement, the condition is false, so the script skips down to the next line, the `else` statement, and executes the code it finds there. This is basically the same as when `if` is used alone. Now, however, suppose the year is 2004. That is a leap year, so the code in the `if` statement is executed. When that's done, the script skips the `else` statement, and continues on with the script.

In this example, if you were to take out the word `else` and leave the rest of the statement, the "Aww, sorry, mate" message would appear every time, which is something you don't want to happen.

The `if` and `else` statements can be very helpful in controlling the flow and resulting output of your scripts. With them, you can tailor your site accordingly with basically unlimited possibilities. You can display different messages based on a person's age (if users are over 18, they see one message; if they are under 18, they see another one). You can display a message if it's Tuesday versus if it's Wednesday. You can display a "good morning," "good afternoon," or "good evening" message based on the time of day. You can also `nest` your `if` statements so that your script checks for the day of the week, and if it's a certain day, it checks for the time and displays a message, such as "it's Friday afternoon—the weekend's almost here!"

Using Includes for Efficient Code

Are you getting sick of typing the same things over and over again? The makers of PHP have blessed us frustrated developers with a little time-saving device called "includes" that save you from reentering frequently used text over and over.

Suppose that you want to type the same message on every page of your site. Perhaps it is your company's name and address, or maybe today's date. If you are coding each page of your site from scratch, this is not very efficient for a couple of reasons:

❏ You are typing the same information over and over again, which is never good.

❏ In the case of an update or a change, you have to make the change in every single page of your site. Again, this is redundant and time consuming, and it elevates the potential for human error.

A solution to this problem is to use an include. *Includes* are PHP files tucked into other PHP files. You take commonly used information and put it in a separate file. For example, if you have a set of defined variables that need to be referenced in every page on your site, you could define them once, in a single PHP script. Then, on each of your pages where you want the variables to appear, you use an `include` statement that specifies the file that defines the variables. When your script is parsed, the parser inserts the code from the include file into your page, just as if you'd typed it there yourself. The final output is then sent to the browser.

Includes can use any extension, but are sometimes referenced as `.inc` files. If you are adding potentially sensitive information, for example, server variables such as passwords, then it is advisable to save these in `.php` files so they are never accessible to anyone because the information is parsed before it is sent to the browser. You can add an include in any other file, and if you place the `include` statement in an `if` statement, you can control when the include is inserted.

Try It Out   Adding a Welcome Message

Suppose you want every page in the movie review site to show a welcome message and perhaps today's date. You want to create a file that includes this information, so follow these steps:

1. Open your text editor and type the following:

```
<div align="center"><font size="4">Welcome to my movie review site!</font>
<br>
<?php
echo "Today is ";
echo date("F d");
echo ", ";
echo date("Y");
?>
</div>
```

2. Save this file as header.php.

3. To include this file in the three existing movie Web site files, add the following line immediately after the <body> tag to login.php, movie1.php, and moviesite.php:

```
<?php include "header.php"; ?>
```

4. Save your files.

5. Take a look at the files again. If you open login.php, you should see the screen shown in Figure 2-12.

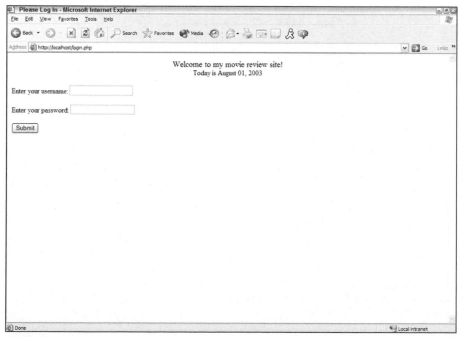

Figure 2-12

You will see the same two lines on every page where you have included the header.php file.

How It Works

When PHP comes across an `include` line in a script, it stops working on the current program and immediately shoots on over to whatever file it's told to include. The server parses that second file and carries the results back to the original file, where the parsing continues from where it left off.

Suppose you decided you didn't really want the date to be shown with the leading zeros. Luckily, PHP has a solution for that when formatting the date function. Make the following change to your `header.php` file and see what happens:

```
<div align="center"><font size="4">Welcome to my movie review site!</font>
<br>
<?php
echo "Today is ";
echo date("F j");
echo ", ";
echo date("Y");
?>
</div>
```

Your problem is fixed, and it's fixed in all the pages in your site, in one fell swoop.

Using Functions for Efficient Code

As with includes, functions make your code (and your typing) more efficient and easier to debug. *Functions* are blocks of code that can be called from anywhere in your program. They enable you to execute lines of code without having to retype them every time you want to use them. Functions can help set or update variables, and can be nested. You can also set a function to execute only if a certain criterion has been fulfilled.

Functions are mini-programs within themselves. They don't know about any other variables around them unless you let the other variables outside the function in through a door called "global." You use the `global $varname` command to make an outside variable's value accessible to the function. This does *not* apply to any values assigned to any variables that are global by default, such as `$_POST`, `$_GET`, and so on.

Your function can be located anywhere within your script and can be called from anywhere within your script. Therefore, you can list all your commonly used functions at the top of your program, and they can all be kept together for easier debugging. Better yet, you can put all your functions in a file and *include* them in your programs. Now you're rolling!

> *PHP provides you with a comprehensive set of built-in functions (which you can find in Appendix C), but sometimes you need to create your own customized functions.*

Try It Out   Working with Functions

This exercise demonstrates functions in action by adding a list of favorite movies to your movie reviews site.

1. Open your `movie1.php` page and modify it as shown in the highlighted text:

```php
<?php
session_start();
$_SESSION['username'] = $_POST['user'];
$_SESSION['userpass'] = $_POST['pass'];
$_SESSION['authuser'] = 0;

//Check username and password information
if (($_SESSION['username'] == 'Joe') and
    ($_SESSION['userpass'] == '12345')) {
  $_SESSION['authuser'] = 1;
} else {
  echo "Sorry, but you don't have permission to view this
        page, you loser!";
  exit();
}
?>
<html>
<head>
<title>Find my Favorite Movie!</title>
</head>
<body>
<?php include "header.php"; ?>
<?php
  $myfavmovie = urlencode("Life of Brian");
  echo "<a href='moviesite.php?favmovie=$myfavmovie'>";
  echo "Click here to see information about my favorite movie!";
  echo "</a>";
  echo "<br>";
  echo "<a href='moviesite.php?movienum=5'>";
  echo "Click here to see my top 5 movies.";
  echo "</a>";
  echo "<br>";
  echo "<a href='moviesite.php?movienum=10'>";
  echo "Click here to see my top 10 movies.";
  echo "</a>";
?>
</body>
</html>
```

2. Now modify `moviesite.php` as shown:

```php
<?php
session_start();

//check to see if user has logged in with a valid password
if ($_SESSION['authuser'] != 1) {
  echo "Sorry, but you don't have permission to view this
        page, you loser!";
```

63

```php
    exit();
  }
?>
<html>
<head>
<title>My Movie Site</title>
</head>
<body>
<?php include "header.php"; ?>
<?php
function listmovies_1() {
  echo "1. Life of Brian<br>";
  echo "2. Stripes<br>";
  echo "3. Office Space<br>";
  echo "4. The Holy Grail<br>";
  echo "5. Matrix<br>";
}

function listmovies_2() {
  echo "6. Terminator 2<br>";
  echo "7. Star Wars<br>";
  echo "8. Close Encounters of the Third Kind<br>";
  echo "9. Sixteen Candles<br>";
  echo "10. Caddyshack<br>";
}

if (isset($_REQUEST['favmovie'])) {
  echo "Welcome to our site, ";
  echo $_SESSION['username'];
  echo "! <br>";
  echo "My favorite movie is ";
  echo $_REQUEST['favmovie'];
  echo "<br>";
  $movierate = 5;
  echo "My movie rating for this movie is: ";
  echo $movierate;
} else {
  echo "My top ";
  echo $_REQUEST['movienum'];
  echo " movies are:";
  echo "<br>";

  listmovies_1();
  if ($_REQUEST['movienum'] == 10) listmovies_2();
}
?>
</body>
</html>
```

3. Now you must go through the login.php file before you can see your changes. Log in as Joe and use the password 12345. Your movie1.php page should look like the one in Figure 2-13.

4. Click the "5 Movies" link. Your screen should look like Figure 2-14.

5. Go back and click the "Top 10" link; your screen will look like the one in Figure 2-15.

Figure 2-13

Figure 2-14

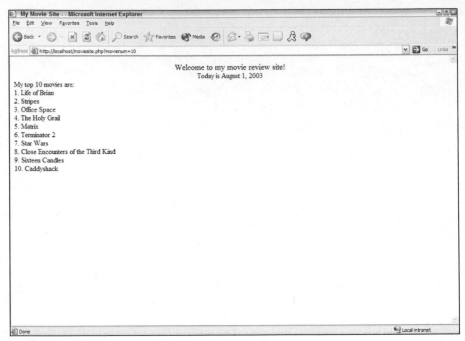

Figure 2-15

How It Works

This has been a rudimentary look at how to use functions, but you can see how they work. The moviel.php page gave users the option of looking at 5 or 10 of your favorite movies. Whichever link they choose sets the value for $movienum.

In addition, moviesite.php accomplishes several other tasks:

- ❑ It sets up the functions listmovies_1() and listmovies_2(), which prints a portion of the total top 10 list.

- ❑ You also added this line:

```
if (isset($_REQUEST['favmovie'])) {
```

  The isset function checks to see if a variable has been set yet (this doesn't check the value, just whether or not it has been used). You didn't want to show users the information about your favorite movie if they didn't click on the link to see it, so you used if/else to take it right outta there. If the variable favmovie has not yet been sent, the program jumps on down to the else portion.

- ❑ The script performs another if statement to check the value of movienum to run the correct corresponding functions.

- ❑ It also references the movienum variable for the title of the list, so the program displays the correct number of movies in the list.

As you get more advanced in your PHP programming skills, you might store a list of all your favorite movies in a database and reference them that way, changing your `listmovies()` function to list only one movie at a time and running the function `listmovies()` a number of times. You could also give your users the option of choosing how many movies they want displayed, perhaps through a drop-down box or radio buttons. That would be your new `movienum` variable.

All About Arrays

You've learned about variables and how they are used, but what if you need to have more than one value assigned to that variable? That, my friend, is a good old-fashioned array. *Arrays* are nothing more than lists of information mapped with keys and stored under one variable name. For example, you can store a person's name and address or a list of states in one variable.

Arrays can be a hard thing to wrap your brain around, so let's take a visual approach. Say you see a man sitting at a table at a local restaurant. He has several characteristics that are unique to him, such as first name, last name, and age. You could easily store his pertinent information in three variables, `$firstname`, `$lastname`, and `$age`.

Now, suppose his wife sits down to join him. How can you store her information? If you use the same variable names, how will you know which is her information and which is her husband's? This is where arrays come in. You can store all of his information under one variable, and all of her information under another.

If you put all the information in a chart, it would look like this:

	First Name	Last Name	Age
Husband	Albert	Einstein	124
Wife	Mileva	Einstein	123

An array is just a row of information, and the "keys" are the column headers. Keys are identifiers to help keep the information organized and easy to use. In this instance, if you didn't have column headers, you wouldn't know what each of those variables represented. Now let's see how you can use arrays in PHP syntax.

Array Syntax

With an array, you can store a person's name and age under one variable name, like this:

```php
<?php
$husband = array("firstname"=>"Albert",
                 "lastname"=>"Einstein",
                 "age"=>"124");

echo $husband["firstname"];

?>
```

Notice how you use => instead of = when assigning values to keys of arrays. This gives you an output of "Albert" and all the values are still stored in the variable name husband. You can also see how you keep track of the information inside the variable with the use of keys such as "firstname" and "lastname."

You can also set an array value in the following way:

```php
<?php
$husband["firstname"] = "Albert";
$husband["lastname"] = "Einstein";
$husband["age"] = 124;
?>
```

This is the equivalent of the previous example.

You can also have arrays within arrays (also known as *multi-dimensional arrays*). In the earlier example, you had two people sitting at one table. What if you pulled up another table and added a few more people to the mix? How in the heck would you store everyone's information and keep it all separate and organized? Like this!

```php
<?php
$table1 = array("husband" => array("firstname"=>"Albert",
                                   "lastname"=>"Einstein",
                                   "age"=>124),
                "wife" => array("firstname"=>"Mileva",
                                "lastname"=>"Einstein",
                                "age"=>123));
//do the same for each table in your restaurant
?>
```

Then if someone asks you, "Hey, what are the first names of the couple sitting at table one?," you can easily print the information with a few simple echo statements:

```php
<?php
echo $table1["husband"]["firstname"];
echo " & ";
echo $table1["wife"]["firstname"];
?>
```

This script would produce the output "Albert & Mileva."

If you want to simply store a list and not worry about the particular order, or what each value should be mapped to (such as a list of states or flavors of shaved ice), you don't need to explicitly name the keys; PHP will assign invisible internal keys for processing; numeric integers starting with 0. This would be set up as follows:

```php
<?php
$flavor[] = "blue raspberry";
$flavor[] = "root beer";
$flavor[] = "pineapple";
?>
```

These would then be referenced like this:

```
echo $flavor[0]; //outputs "blue raspberry"
echo $flavor[1]; //outputs "root beer"
echo $flavor[2]; //outputs "pineapple"
```

Sorting Arrays

PHP provides many easy ways to sort array values. The table that follows lists some of the more common array-sorting functions, although you can find a more extensive list in Appendix C.

Function	Description
arsort(array)	Sorts the array in descending value order and maintains the key/value relationship
asort(array)	Sorts the array in ascending value order and maintains the key/value relationship
rsort(array)	Sorts the array in descending value order
sort(array)	Sorts the array in ascending value order

Try It Out   Sorting Arrays

Before we go further, let's do a quick test on sorting arrays so you can see how the array acts when it is sorted. Type the following program in your text editor and call it sorting.php.

```php
<?php
$flavor[] = "blue raspberry";
$flavor[] = "root beer";
$flavor[] = "pineapple";

sort($flavor);
print_r($flavor);
?>
```

How It Works

Notice anything weird in the preceding code? Yes, we've introduced a new function: print_r. This simply prints out information about a variable so that people can read it. It is frequently used to check array values, specifically. The output would look like that in Figure 2-16.

You can see that the sort() function has done what it's supposed to and sorted the values in ascending alphabetical order. You can also see the invisible keys that have been assigned to each value (and reassigned in this case).

foreach Constructs

PHP also provides a foreach command that applies a set of statements for each value in an array. What an appropriate name, eh? It works only on arrays, however, and will give you an error if you try to use it with another type of variable.

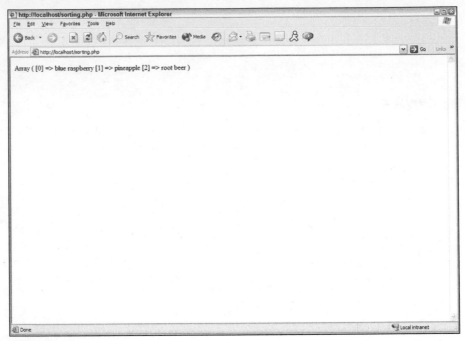

Figure 2-16

Your syntax for the `foreach` command looks like this:

```php
<?php
$flavor[] = "blue raspberry";
$flavor[] = "root beer";
$flavor[] = "pineapple";
echo "My favorite flavors are:<br>";
foreach ($flavor as $currentvalue) {
    //these lines will execute as long as there is a value in $flavor
    echo $currentvalue . "<br>\n";
}
?>
```

This produces a list of each of the flavors in whatever order they appear in your array.

When PHP is processing your array, it keeps track of what key it's on with the use of an internal array *pointer*. When your `foreach` function is called, the pointer is at the ready, waiting patiently at the first key/value in the array. At the end of the function, the pointer has moved down through the list and remains at the end, or the last key/value in the array. The position of the pointer can be a helpful tool, one which we'll touch on later in this chapter.

Try It Out   Adding Arrays

In this exercise, you'll see what happens when you add arrays to the `moviesite.php` file. You'll also sort them and use the `foreach` construct.

1. Make the following highlighted changes to the `moviesite.php` file:

```php
<?php
session_start();

//check to see if user has logged in with a valid password
if ($_SESSION['authuser'] != 1) {
  echo "Sorry, but you don't have permission to view this
        page, you loser!";
  exit();
}
?>
<html>
<head>
<title>My Movie Site</title>
</head>
<body>
<?php include "header.php"; ?>
<?php
$favmovies = array("Life of Brian",
                   "Stripes",
                   "Office Space",
                   "The Holy Grail",
                   "Matrix",
                   "Terminator 2",
                   "Star Wars",
                   "Close Encounters of the Third Kind",
                   "Sixteen Candles",
                   "Caddyshack");

//delete these lines:
function listmovies_1() {
  echo "1. Life of Brian<br>";
  echo "2. Stripes<br>";
  echo "3. Office Space<br>";
  echo "4. The Holy Grail<br>";
  echo "5. Matrix<br>";
}

function listmovies_2() {
  echo "6. Terminator 2<br>";
  echo "7. Star Wars<br>";
  echo "8. Close Encounters of the Third Kind<br>";
  echo "9. Sixteen Candles<br>";
  echo "10. Caddyshack<br>";
}
//end of deleted lines

if (isset($_REQUEST['favmovie'])) {
  echo "Welcome to our site, ";
  echo $_SESSION['username'];
  echo "! <br>";
  echo "My favorite movie is ";
```

```
        echo $_REQUEST['favmovie'];
        echo "<br>";
        $movierate = 5;
        echo "My movie rating for this movie is: ";
        echo $movierate;
    } else {
        echo "My top 10 movies are:<br>";

        if (isset($_REQUEST['sorted'])) {
            sort($favmovies);
        }

        //delete these lines
        echo $_REQUEST['movienum'];
        echo " movies are:";
        echo "<br>";

        listmovies_1();
        if ($_REQUEST['movienum'] == 10) listmovies_2();
        //end of deleted lines

        foreach ($favmovies as $currentvalue) {
            echo $currentvalue;
            echo "<br>\n";
        }
    }
    ?>
    </body>
    </html>
```

2.   Then change `movie1.php` as shown here:

```
<?php
session_start();
$_SESSION['username'] = $_POST['user'];
$_SESSION['userpass'] = $_POST['pass'];
$_SESSION['authuser'] = 0;

//Check username and password information
if (($_SESSION['username'] == 'Joe') and
    ($_SESSION['userpass'] == '12345')) {
    $_SESSION['authuser'] = 1;
} else {
    echo "Sorry, but you don't have permission to view this
        page, you loser!";
    exit();
}
?>
<html>
<head>
<title>Find my Favorite Movie!</title>
</head>
<body>
<?php include "header.php"; ?>
<?php
```

```
$myfavmovie = urlencode("Life of Brian");
echo "<a href='moviesite.php?favmovie=$myfavmovie'>";
echo "Click here to see information about my favorite movie!";
echo "</a>";
echo "<br>";
//delete these lines
echo "<a href='moviesite.php?movienum=5'>";
echo "Click here to see my top 5 movies.";
echo "</a>";
echo "<br>";
//end of deleted lines

//change the following line:
echo "<a href='moviesite.php'>";

echo "Click here to see my top 10 movies.";
echo "</a>";
echo "<br>";
echo "<a href='moviesite.php?sorted=true'>";
echo "Click here to see my top 10 movies, sorted alphabetically.";
echo "</a>";
```

```
?>
</body>
</html>
```

3. Now log in with the `login.php` file (log in as Joe, with password 12345), and when you get the choice, click the link that lists the top 10 movies. You should see something like Figure 2-17.

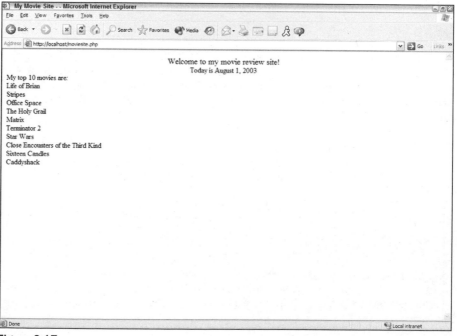

Figure 2-17

4. Go back to `movie1.php`, and this time click the link that lists the movies sorted in alphabetical order. This time, you should see something like Figure 2-18.

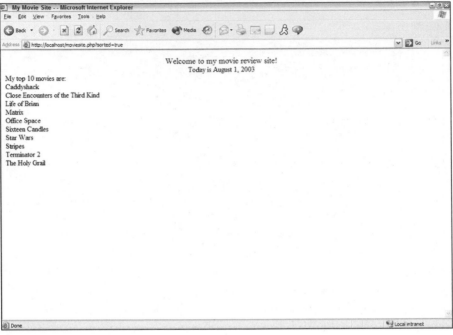

Figure 2-18

How It Works

You first put the movie list in one variable, `$favmovies`, with the array function. Then you were able to list the movies individually using the `foreach` construct in `moviesite.php`. You also added a link that would allow users to show the list sorted alphabetically, by adding a variable named `$_REQUEST[sorted]`. When this variable was set to "true," the `sort()` function executed, and you passed that "true" variable through the URL in the link.

You may have noticed a shortcoming in the program . . . okay, you may have noticed many shortcomings, but one in particular stands out. You can no longer control how many movies are shown in your list. You are stuck with showing the total number of movies in the array. There's a way to fix that, which we talk about next.

While You're Here . . .

You've seen that `foreach` will take an action on each element of an array until it reaches the end, but you can also take an action on just some of the elements in an array with the `while` statement. A `while` statement tells the server to execute a command or block of commands repeatedly, as long as a given condition is true.

Here's an example of how you would use the `while` command. This code simply counts from 1 to 5, printing each number on a separate line. Each time through the loop, the variable $num is increased by 1. At the top of the loop, the `while` checks to see that the value of $num is less than or equal to 5. After five times through the loop, the value of $num is 6, so the loop ends.

```
$num = 1;
while ($num <= 5) {
   echo $num;
   echo "<br>";
   $num = $num + 1;
}
```

The following code does the same thing, but it uses a `do/while` loop instead. This code works exactly the same way, except that the condition is checked at the end of the loop. This guarantees that the commands inside the loop will always be executed at least once.

```
$num = 1;
do {
   echo $num;
   echo "<br>";
   $num = $num + 1
} while ($num <= 5);
```

Try It Out   Using the while Function

This exercise allows users to tell you how many movies they want to see, and enables you to number the list as you did before, using the `while` function.

1. Make the following changes to your `movie1.php` program:

```
<?php
session_start();
$_SESSION['username'] = $_POST['user'];
$_SESSION['userpass'] = $_POST['pass'];
$_SESSION['authuser'] = 0;

//Check username and password information
if (($_SESSION['username'] == 'Joe') and
    ($_SESSION['userpass'] == '12345')) {
   $_SESSION['authuser'] = 1;
} else {
   echo "Sorry, but you don't have permission to view this
       page, you loser!";
   exit();
}
?>
<html>
<head>
<title>Find my Favorite Movie!</title>
</head>
<body>
<?php include "header.php" ?>
<?php
```

```php
$myfavmovie=urlencode("Life of Brian");
echo "<a href='moviesite.php?favmovie=$myfavmovie'>";
echo "Click here to see information about my favorite movie!";
echo "</a>";
echo "<br>";

//delete these lines
echo "<a href='moviesite.php'>";
echo "Click here to see my top 10 movies.";
echo "</a>";
echo "<br>";
echo "<a href='moviesite.php?sorted=true'>";
echo "Click here to see my top 10 movies, sorted alphabetically.";
echo "</a>";
//end of deleted lines

echo "Or choose how many movies you would like to see:";
echo "</a>";
echo "<br>";
?>
<form method="post" action="moviesite.php">
  <p>Enter number of movies (up to 10):
    <input type="text" name="num">
    <br>
    Check here if you want the list sorted alphabetically:
    <input type="checkbox" name="sorted">
  </p>
  <input type="submit" name="Submit" value="Submit">
</form>
</body>
</html>
```

2.   Make the following changes to `moviesite.php`:

```php
<?php
session_start();

//check to see if user has logged in with a valid password
if ($_SESSION['authuser'] != 1) {
  echo "Sorry, but you don't have permission to view this
        page, you loser!";
  exit();
}
?>
<html>
<head>
<title>My Movie Site</title>
</head>
<body>
<?php include "header.php"; ?>
<?php
$favmovies = array("Life of Brian",
                   "Stripes",
```

```
                       "Office Space",
                       "The Holy Grail",
                       "Matrix",
                       "Terminator 2",
                       "Star Wars",
                       "Close Encounters of the Third Kind",
                       "Sixteen Candles",
                       "Caddyshack");

    if (isset($_REQUEST['favmovie'])) {
      echo "Welcome to our site, ";
      echo $_SESSION['username'];
      echo "! <br>";
      echo "My favorite movie is ";
      echo $_REQUEST['favmovie'];
      echo "<br>";
      $movierate = 5;
      echo "My movie rating for this movie is: ";
      echo $movierate;
    } else {
      echo "My top ". $_POST["num"] . " movies are:<br>";

      if (isset($_REQUEST['sorted'])) {
        sort($favmovies);
      }

      //list the movies
      $numlist = 1;
      while ($numlist <= $_POST["num"]) {
        echo $numlist;
        echo ". ";
        echo pos($favmovies);
        next($favmovies);
        echo "<br>\n";
        $numlist = $numlist + 1;
      }

      //delete these lines
      foreach ($favmovies as $currentvalue) {
        echo $currentvalue;
        echo "<br>\n";
      }
      //end of deleted lines
    }
    ?>
  </body>
</html>
```

3. Now play around with your new `movie1.php` and `moviesite.php` files.

How It Works

Your code should show a list of the top movies based on how many you as the user chose to see and whether or not you wanted them listed alphabetically.

You'll notice several things in the code:

❑ We added a little trick to the normal echo statement — the use of periods to concatenate the statement like this:

```
echo "My top ". $_POST["num"] . " movies are:<br>";
```

This way you can slip in and out of quotes virtually undetected.

❑ You set $numlist to 1, and this will keep track of what number you're on.

❑ You are using the variable $_POST["num"] to place a limit on the number of movies to be listed; this is the number the user input from the form in movie1.php.

❑ The function pos($favmovies) is also a new one for you. This function returns the current value where the array "pointer" is (starts at the beginning). You echoed this function because you wanted to see the current value.

❑ The function next($favmovies) is another new array function that moves the array pointer to the next value in line. This gets the array ready for the next iteration of while statements.

Now see, that wasn't so hard, was it? You're really cooking now!

Alternate Syntax for PHP

As a programmer, it's always great when you can find a quicker and easier way to make something happen. We have included some useful shortcuts or alternate syntax for tasks you are already familiar with.

Alternates to the <?php and ?> Tags

You can denote PHP code in your HTML documents in other ways:

❑ <? and ?>. This must be turned on in your php.ini file with the short open tags configuration.

❑ <% and %>. This must be turned on in your php.ini file with the ASP tags configuration.

❑ <script language="PHP"> and </script>. These are available without changing your php.ini file.

Alternates to the echo Command

You already got a taste of print_r(), but you can also use the print() command to display text or variable values in your page. The difference between echo() and print() is that when you use print(), a value of 1 or 0 will also be returned upon the success or failure of the print command. In other words, you would be able to tell if something didn't print using the print() command, whereas echo() just does what it's told without letting you know whether or not it worked properly. For all other intents and purposes, the two are equal.

Alternates to Logical Operators

You may remember that and and or are obvious logical operators you use when comparing two expressions, but there are other ways to express these operators:

❑   && can be used in place of and, the only difference being the order in which the operator is evaluated during a mathematical function.

❑ || can be used in place of or, the only difference being the order in which the operator is evaluated during a mathematical function.

Alternates to Double Quotes: Using heredoc

Besides using double quotes to block off a value, you can also use the heredoc syntax:

```
$value = <<<ABC
This is the text that will be included in the value variable.
ABC;
```

This is especially helpful if you have double quotes and single quotes within a block of text, such as:

```
$value = <<<ABC
Last time I checked, I was 6'-5" tall.
ABC;
```

This keeps you from having to escape those characters out, and keeps things much simpler. Your "ABC" syntax can consist of any characters, just as long as they match.

Alternates to Incrementing/Decrementing Values

You can have variable values incremented or decremented automatically, like this:

Syntax Shortcut	What It Does to the Value
++$value	Increases by one, and returns the incremented value
$value++	Returns the value, then increases by one
--$value	Decreases by one, and returns the decremented value
$value--	Returns the value, then decreases by one
$value=$value+1	Increases the value by one
$value+=1	Increases the value by one

OOP Dreams

You may or may not have heard some hoopla about PHP5 and the use of OOP. OOP stands for Object Oriented Programming, and while it's not always the best logical way to code, it can provide for some pretty darn efficient scripts. The big deal about OOP in PHP5 is that, although the OOP methodology was acceptable in PHP4, with the release of PHP5 it became a whole lot easier to use and implement. As a beginner, you won't really need to delve in to the world of OOP (we do that in later chapters of this book) but it's important for you to understand the concepts behind OOP.

In a nutshell, OOP takes commonly accessed functions, and instead of putting them in an include as you did before, it puts them in a *class*. A class is a collection of variables (called *members* in OOP-speak) and functions (called *methods* in OOP-speak) that are processed when called upon to do so. The *object* is what results from the class being *instantiated*, or started.

A Brief OOP Example

Using OOP is like ordering at a pizza parlor. No, it will not make you gain weight and give you greasy fingers, but it will put a few things in motion (such as instantiating an object and calling a class). It would probably go something like this:

First, your waiter will take your order and go to the kitchen. He will request that a certain pizza made to your requirements be cooked. The cooks will open their recipe books and see that they need someone to make the dough. Then they will need to place the toppings on the pizza and cook it for a specified amount of time. Lastly, they will present your ready-made pizza to your waiter, who will deliver it all hot and bubbly to your table.

In this example, the methods would be the making of the dough, the application of the toppings, the cooking of the pizza, and the removal from the oven. The members are the specifications you gave to the waiter to begin with, and your object is your pizza.

If we were to write your pizza experience in PHP/OOP terminology, it might look something like this:

```php
<?php
//this will be our "class" file.

class Pizza {
  public $dough;
  public $toppings;

  public function MakeDough($dough) {
    $this->dough = $dough;
    //roll out $this->dough
  }

  public function addToppings($toppings) {
    $this->toppings = $toppings;
    //chop $this->toppings;
    //place $this->toppings on dough;
  }

  public function bake() {
    //bake the pizza
    return true;
  }

  public function make_pizza($dough, $toppings) {
```

```
      //Make the pizza
      $step1 = $this->MakeDough($dough);
      if ($step1) {
        $step2 = $this->addToppings($toppings);
      }
      if ($step2) {
        $step3 = $this->bake();
      }
  }

}
?>
```

Then you can create your object (pizza) whenever you feel like it and you can make sure that the right pizza gets to the right table.

```
<?php
//this is our php script
$table1 = new Pizza();
$table1->make_pizza('hand-tossed', 'pepperoni');
if ($table1->bake()) {
//deliver $pizza to table 1;
}
else echo "uh-oh, looks like you should have gone to eat fast food.";
?>
```

Obviously, if you run this script as-is it won't work; this was simply for show. Now you can see how you can create your object (your "pizza" in this case) any time you want without having to have numerous variables such as $dough1, $toppings1, $pizza1, $dough2, $toppings2, $pizza2, table1, table2, and so on in your pizza parlor. Anytime someone wants to order a pizza you simply call the class Pizza and voila! A new pizza is born. Also, when this table of patrons gets up and leaves and you have a new customer back at table 1, you can create a new pizza for them without getting your variables confused with any prior pizzas that have been created for table 1.

Here are a few things to note about your class script:

❑   You named your class and methods (functions) using a mix of upper- and lowercase letters. This is called "studlyCaps" or "camel case," and it was adopted as the standard for OOP in PHP5.

❑   If you wanted a function to begin immediately every time the class was instantiated, you would name that function __construct(), list it immediately as the first function in the class, and it would be called a *constructor*. For example:

```
function __construct() {
  //for every order of a pizza, no matter what goes on it, set that
  //it will be delivered on a round tray.
  $this->tray = $round;
}
```

❑   Make special note of the $this->variable command. This is similar to your array syntax and has similar meaning. $this can be thought of as "this particular object you're creating." Therefore, when used in the pizza scenario, $this->dough=$dough means "make this particular pizza's dough the same as whatever is in the $dough variable ('hand-tossed' in this case)."

❏ Did you notice that your class began with some initial variable lines? The only time you need to declare a variable in PHP is within a class. You declare the variables as "public," "private," or "protected." Public variables are visible to any class, private variables are visible only within that class, and protected variables are visible to that class and any other class that extends the first (this is a whole other can of worms). It is probably okay to keep most of your variables as public, except perhaps any that might contain personal information.

❏ In order to begin your object creation, you used the keyword new in the line

```
$table1 = new Pizza();
```

This keeps all the pizza information together in the $table1 variable.

For simplicity's sake, you created a function in your class that called all the other functions in the order you wanted (makePizza). What if you were being carb-conscious and wanted to avoid the dough altogether, and then decided you didn't need to bake the pizza after all? Can you still use your class Pizza? Of course you can. You would simply call only the addToppings method instead of the makePizza method.

Why Use OOP?

Using OOP has a few benefits over simply including a file with functions in it. First, with OOP, you can easily keep bits of related information together and perform complex tasks with that data. Second, you can process the data an unlimited number of times without worrying about variables being overwritten. Third, you can have multiple instances of the class running at the same time without variables being corrupted or overwritten.

OOP is a relatively advanced concept to understand, which is why we won't use it until later on in this book. For now, we'll keep it simple and let you digest the basics.

Summary

Although we've covered many different topics in this chapter, our goal was to give you enough ammunition to get started on your own Web site. Our hope is that you are beginning to realize the power of PHP and how easy it is to jump in and get started. As we talk about database connectivity in Chapter 3, you will start to see how PHP can work with a database to give you a very impressive site.

PHP is straightforward, powerful, and flexible. There are numerous built-in functions that can save you hours of work (date() for example, which takes one line to show the current date). You can find an extensive list of PHP functions in Appendix C; browse that list to find bits and pieces you can use in your own site development.

Exercises

To build your skills even further, here is an exercise you can use to test yourself. The answers are provided in Appendix A, but keep in mind that there is always more than one way to accomplish a given task, so if you choose to do things a different way, and the results display the way you want, more power to you.

Try modifying your PHP files in the following ways:

1.   Go back to your date.php file and instead of displaying only the number of days in the current month, add a few lines that say:

      The month is _____.

      There are ____ days in this month.

      There are _____ months left in the current year.

2.   On your movie Web site, write a file that displays the following line at the bottom center of every page of your site, with a link to your e-mail address. Set your font size to 1.

      This site developed by: <u>ENTER YOUR NAME HERE</u>.

3.   Write a program that displays a different message based on the time of day. For example, if it is in the morning, have the site display "Good Morning!"

4.   Write a program that formats a block of text (to be input by the user) based on preferences chosen by the user. Give your user options for color of text, font choice, and size. Display the output on a new page.

5.   In the program you created in step 4, allow your users the option of saving the information for the next time they visit, and if they choose "yes," save the information in a cookie.

6.   Using functions, write a program that keeps track of how many times a visitor has loaded the page.

Using PHP5 with MySQL

So now that you've done some really cool stuff with PHP in Chapter 2, such as using includes and functions, it's time to make your site truly dynamic and show users some real data. You may or may not have had experience with databases, so we'll take a look at what MySQL is and how PHP can tap into the data. We will also show you what a MySQL database looks like in terms of the different tables and fields and give you some quickie shortcuts to make your life much easier (you can thank us later for those).

By the end of this chapter, you will be able to:

- ❑ Understand a MySQL database
- ❑ View data contained in the MySQL database
- ❑ Connect to the database from your Web site
- ❑ Pull specific information out of the database, right from your Web site
- ❑ Use third-party software to easily manage tables
- ❑ Use the source Web site to troubleshoot problems you may encounter

Although some of this information is expanded upon in later chapters, this chapter lays the groundwork for more complex issues.

Overview of MySQL Structure and Syntax

MySQL is a relational database system, which basically means that it can store bits of information in separate areas and link those areas together. You can store virtually anything in a database: the contents of an address book, a product catalog, or even a wish list of things you want for your birthday.

In the sites you create as you work through this book, you are storing information pertinent to a movie review site (such as movie titles and years of release) and comic book fan information (such as a list of authentic users/comic book fans and their passwords).

MySQL commands can be issued through the command prompt, as you did in Chapter 1 when you were installing it and granting permissions to users, or through PHP. We primarily use PHP to issue commands in this book, and we will discuss more about this shortly.

MySQL Structure

Because MySQL is a relational database management system, it allows you to separate information into *tables* or areas of pertinent information. In nonrelational database systems, all the information is stored in one big area, which makes it much more difficult and cumbersome to sort and extract only the data you want. In MySQL, each table consists of separate *fields*, which represent each bit of information. For example, one field could contain a customer's first name, and another field could contain his last name. Fields can hold different types of data, such as text, numbers, dates, and so on.

You create database tables based on what type of information you want to store in them. The separate tables of MySQL are then linked together with some common denominator, where the values of the common field are the same.

For an example of this structure, imagine a table that includes a customer's name, address, and ID number, and another table that includes the customer's ID number and past orders he has placed. The common field is the customer's ID number, and the information stored in the two separate tables would be linked together via fields where the ID number is equal. This enables you to see all the information related to this customer at one time.

Let's take a look at the ways in which you can tailor database tables to fit your needs.

Field Types

When you create a table initially, you need to tell MySQL server what types of information will be stored in each field. The different types of fields and some examples are listed in the table that follows.

MySQL Field Type	Description	Example
char(length)	Any character can be in this field, but the field will have a fixed length.	Customer's State field always has two characters.
varchar(length)	Any character can be in this field, and the data can vary in length from 0 to 255 characters. Maximum length of field is denoted in parentheses.	Customer's Address field has letters and numbers and varies in length.
int(length)	Numeric field that stores integers that can range from -2147483648 to +2147483647, but can be limited with the length parameter. The length parameter limits the number of digits that can be shown, not the value. Mathematical functions can be performed on data in this field.	Quantity of a product on hand.

MySQL Field Type	Description	Example
int(length) unsigned	Numeric field that stores positive integers (and zero) up to 4294967295. The length parameter limits the number of digits that can be displayed. Mathematical functions can be performed on data in this field.	Customer ID (if entirely numerical).
text	Any character can be in this field, and the maximum size of the data is 65536 characters.	Comments field that allows longer text to be stored, without limiting field to 255 characters.
decimal(length,dec)	Numeric field that can store decimals. The length parameter limits the number of digits that can be displayed, and the dec parameter limits the number of decimal places that can be stored. For example, a price field that would store prices up to 999.99 would be defined as decimal(5,2).	Prices.
enum("option1", "option2", ...)	Allows only certain values to be stored in this field, such as "true" and "false," or a list of states. 65535 different options are allowed.	Gender field for your users will have a value either "male" or "female."
date	Stores a date as yyyy-mm-dd.	Date of order, a birthday, or the date a user joined as a registered user.
time	Stores time as hh:mm:ss.	Time a news article was added to the Web site.
datetime	Multipurpose field that stores date and time as yyyy-mm-dd hh:mm:ss.	Last date and time a user visited your Web page.

Although the preceding field types should suffice for most needs, the table that follows lists some perhaps less-often-used types.

MySQL Field Type	Description
tinyint(length)	Numeric field that stores integers from -128 to 127. (Adding the unsigned parameter allows storage of 0 to 255.)
smallint(length)	Numeric field that stores integers from -32768 to 32767. (Adding the unsigned parameter allows storage of 0 to 65535.)

Table continued on following page

MySQL Field Type	Description
mediumint(length)	Numeric field that stores integers from -8388608 to 8388607. (Adding the unsigned parameter allows storage of 0 to 16777215.)
bigint(length)	Numeric field that stores integers from -9223372036854775808 to 9223372036854775807. (Adding the unsigned parameter allows storage of 0 to 18446744073709551615.)
tinytext	Allows storage of up to 255 characters.
mediumtext	Allows storage of up to 1677215 characters.
longtext	Allows storage of up to 4294967295 characters.
blob	Equal to a text field, except it is case-sensitive when sorting and comparing. Stores up to 65535 characters.
tinyblob	Equal to the tinytext field, except it is case-sensitive when sorting and comparing.
mediumblob	Equal to the mediumtext field except it is case-sensitive when sorting and comparing.
longblob	Equal to the longtext field except it is case-sensitive when sorting and comparing.
year(length)	Stores a year in four-character format (by default). It is possible to specify a two-year format by signifying that with the length parameter.

Believe it or not, even more data types are supported by MySQL; you can find a comprehensive list of them in Appendix D.

Choosing the Right Field Type

Although you won't actually be creating a database from scratch just yet, you should know how to figure out what field type will best serve your needs. We've put together a list of questions about fields that you can ask yourself before your database tables have been created. As you answer each of these questions, keep in mind the potential values that could exist for the particular field you're setting up.

First, ask yourself, will the field contain both letters and numbers?

❑ If the answer is "yes," consider char, varchar, text, tinytext, mediumtext, longtext, blob, tinyblob, mediumblob, longblob. Then ask yourself how many characters will need to be stored? Will it vary from entry to entry?

   ❑ How many characters will need to be stored? Will it vary from entry to entry?

   ❑ **0–255 characters, variable length:** Use varchar if you want to delete any trailing spaces, or if you want to set a default value. Use tinytext if you don't care about trailing spaces or a default value or if your text does not need to be case-sensitive. Use tinyblob if you don't care about trailing spaces or a default value, but your text does need to be case-sensitive.

- ❑ **256–65536 characters:** Use text if your text does not need to be case-sensitive in searches, sorts, or comparisons. Use blob if your text is case-sensitive.

- ❑ **65537–1677215 characters:** Use mediumtext if your text does not need to be case-sensitive; use mediumblob if your text is case-sensitive.

- ❑ **1677216–4294967295 characters:** Use longtext if your text does not need to be case-sensitive, use longblob if your text is case-sensitive.

❑ If the answer is "Yes, it may contain letters or numbers, but it must be one of a finite number of values," use enum.

❑ If the answer is "No, it will consist of dates and/or times only," use timestamp if you need to store the time and date the information was entered or updated. If you need to store only the date, use date. If you need to store both the date and time, use datetime. If you need only the year, use year.

❑ If the answer is "No, it will consist only of numbers, and mathematical functions will be performed on this field," use one of the following, depending on the size of the number:

- ❑ Integers from -127 to 127, use tinyint.
- ❑ Integers from -32768 to 32767, use smallint.
- ❑ Integers from -8388608 to 8388607, use mediumint.
- ❑ Integers from -2147483648 to 2147483647, use int.
- ❑ Integers from -9223372036854775808 to 9223372036854775807, use bigint.
- ❑ Integers from 0 to 255, use tinyint unsigned.
- ❑ Integers from 0 to 65535, use smallint unsigned.
- ❑ Integers from 0 to 16777215, use mediumint unsigned.
- ❑ Integers from 0 to 4294967295, use int unsigned.
- ❑ Integers from 0 to 18446744073709551615, use bigint unsigned.
- ❑ Decimals with fixed decimal places, use dec.

❑ If the answer is "No, it will consist of only numbers, but mathematical functions will not be performed on this field," use the preceding guidelines for text/number mix in the field.

If your field requirements do not fall into any of these categories, check Appendix D for a complete list of all available field types. If you are still unsure about what type of field you need, you can also check the documentation at the MySQL source Web site, www.mysql.com.

null/not null

Your MySQL server also wants to know whether or not the field can be empty. You do this with the null or not null option. null tells MySQL that it is okay if nothing is stored in the field, and not null tells MySQL to require something, *anything*, to be stored there. Don't forget that a number zero is different from a null entry.

If a field has been defined as not null and nothing is entered by the user, MySQL will enter a "0" in the field instead of producing an error. It is for this reason that you should not rely on MySQL to check data for accuracy and instead put checks into place using PHP. We talk more about data validation in Chapter 8.

Indexes

MySQL uses *indexes* to expedite the process of searching for a particular row of information. Here's how indexes work: Imagine you have a room full of stacks and stacks of receipts from everything you have ever bought in your life. Then you find you have to return some zippered parachute pants you bought in 1984, but unfortunately you need the receipt. So you start sifting through the massive stacks of papers. Lo and behold, five days later you find the receipt in the last pile in the room. After cursing to yourself that perhaps you should get a little more organized, you realize you could at least group them by year of purchase. And then you start getting *really* organized and group them further into categories, such as apparel, 8-track tapes, and so on. So the next time you need to return something you purchased many years ago, you can at least jump to the correct pile and even know what category to look in. Makes sense, right?

Now imagine that your data is stored willy-nilly in your table so that every time you wanted to search for something, it would start at the first record and make its way down through all the rows until it found what it was looking for. What if you had 10,000 rows and the one you happened to be looking for was at the very end? Pull up your chair and take your shoes off, because it could be a while.

By using an internal filing system, MySQL can jump to the approximate location of your data much more quickly. It does this through the use of indexes, also known as *keys*. In the receipt example, you decided to group your receipts by year, so if your receipts were stored in a database, an index entry would be "year." You also decided to further group your receipts, so another index would be "category."

MySQL requires at least one index on every table, so that it has something to go by. Normally, you would use a *primary key*, or unique identifier that helps keep the data separate. This field must be "not null" and "unique"; an example would be a customer ID number to keep your customers separate. (You could easily have two "John Smith" entries, so you need a way to tell the difference.) In the receipts table example, you would create a primary key and assign each receipt its own identifying number so you can tell each receipt apart.

MySQL also provides a feature that allows a value in a field to be automatically incremented by one. This `auto_increment` parameter is useful for making sure your primary key is being populated with unique numbers.

Unique

We all like to think we're unique, but when this parameter is turned on, MySQL makes sure that absolutely no duplicates exist for a particular field. Typically, this is used for only the primary key in your table, but it can be used with any field.

For example, what if you ran a contest in which only the first person from every state who visited would be allowed to join your Web site? You could use the `unique` parameter; then anyone who tries to insert data into your database from a state where someone has already filled the slot will get an error message.

Auto Increment

Say you have a field that you want to automatically increase by one whenever a new record is added. This can be a quite useful function when assigning ID numbers. You don't have to worry about what the last ID number was; the field automatically keeps track for you.

You can designate a field to be auto incremented by simply adding the `auto_increment` command when setting up your table. You can also determine what the first number in the count will be, if you don't want it to be 1. You will see this in action later in the chapter.

Other Parameters

You can make other specifications when creating your database, but those are for more advanced MySQL users. For a complete list of these parameters, we encourage you to visit the source: www.mysql.com.

Types of MySQL Tables and Storage Engines

Now that you understand some of the general features of tables, you should know that there are two different types of tables: transaction-safe tables (TSTs) and non-transaction-safe tables (NTSTs). Transaction-safe tables allow lost data to be recovered, or a rollback of data to revert changes recently made. Non-transaction-safe tables are much faster and require much less memory to process updates, but changes are permanent.

The current version of MySQL uses five main types of storage engines to store and update data in those tables:

- ❏ MyISAM
- ❏ MERGE
- ❏ MEMORY (formerly known as HEAP)
- ❏ InnoDB
- ❏ BDB

A brief summary of each of these types follows, but if you would like to find out more about them, we encourage you to visit the source at www.mysql.com.

MyISAM

This is the default storage engine and will usually be sufficient for the average user's needs. It supports all the field types, parameters, and functions we've talked about. It supports NTSTs and replaces the ISAM storage engine from long ago.

MERGE

This storage engine can manipulate several identical MyISAM tables as one entity. It supports NTSTs.

MEMORY

These are mostly used for temporary tables because of their incredible speed, but they don't support a lot of the common features of the MyISAM table, such as auto_increment and blob/text columns. This type should be used in unique circumstances only. You might use it, for example, if you were working with user logs and you wanted to store the information in a temporary table to massage the data, but you didn't necessarily need to keep the data long-term. This storage engine supports NTSTs.

InnoDB

This type, along with the BDB type, supports TSTs. It is meant for extremely large and frequently accessed applications. It features a "row-locking" mechanism to prevent different users from attempting to change or add the same row to the table. According to the source Web site, one instance of this type of table has been shown to support 800 inserts and updates per second—not too shabby! You can also read more about this type at its own Web site: www.innodb.com.

BDB

BDB, or BerkeleyDB, is the other type of table that supports TSTs. It is actually its own entity that works closely with the MySQL server and can be downloaded from www.sleepycat.com. Like InnoDB tables, it is meant to support very large applications with literally thousands of users attempting to insert and update the same data at the same time. There is a complete reference manual available at its source Web site, which we invite you to read.

MySQL Syntax and Commands

Although it is quite possible to access MySQL directly through a shell command prompt, for the purposes of this book, we are going to access it through PHP. Regardless of the mode by which the MySQL server gets its information and requests, the syntax is basically the same.

Typically, you keep the MySQL commands in all caps, although this is not necessary. The purpose of this is to help keep the MySQL syntax separate from the variables and table or database names.

Common commands you will be using in this book include:

- ❏ CREATE: Creates (duh) new databases and tables
- ❏ ALTER: Modifies existing tables
- ❏ SELECT: Chooses the data you want
- ❏ DELETE: Erases the data from your table
- ❏ DESCRIBE: Lets you know the structure and specifics of the table
- ❏ INSERT INTO *tablename* VALUES: Puts values into the table
- ❏ UPDATE: Lets you modify data already in a table
- ❏ DROP: Deletes an entire table or database

How PHP Fits with MySQL

With the onset of PHP5, you need to take a few extra steps to convince PHP and MySQL to play well with each other. Before your MySQL functions will be recognizable by PHP, make sure to enable MySQL in your php.ini file, which we covered in Chapter 1.

You can use MySQL commands within PHP code almost as seamlessly as you do with HTML. Numerous PHP functions work specifically with MySQL to make your life easier; you can find a comprehensive list in Appendix C.

Some of the more commonly used functions are:

- ❏ mysql_connect ("*hostname*", "*user*", "*pass*"): Connects to the MySQL server.
- ❏ mysql_select_db("*database name*"): Equivalent to the MySQL command USE; makes the selected database the active one.
- ❏ mysql_query("*query*"): Used to send any type of MySQL command to the server.

- ❏ `mysql_fetch_rows("results variable from query")`: Used to return a row of the entire results of a database query.

- ❏ `mysql_fetch_array("results variable from query")`: Used to return several rows of the entire results of a database query.

- ❏ `mysql_error()`: Shows the error message that has been returned directly from the MySQL server.

You will most likely become very familiar with these commands, and many more.

You can also send any MySQL command to the server through PHP and the `mysql_query` command, as in the preceding example. You do this by sending the straight text through PHP either through a variable or through the `mysql_query` command directly, like this:

```
$query = "SELECT * from TABLE";
$results = mysql_query($query);
```

You can also do it like this:

```
$results = mysql_query("SELECT * from TABLE");
```

The results of your query are then put into a temporary array known as `$results`, which you'll learn more about later.

Connecting to the MySQL Server

Before you can do anything with MySQL, you must first connect to the MySQL server using your specific connection variables. Connection variables consist of the following parameters:

- ❏ **Host name:** In your case, it's the local host because you've installed everything locally. You will need to change this to whatever host is acting as your MySQL server.

- ❏ **Username and password:** We're going to use a new username that we created for use with the examples throughout the rest of the book. Refer to the instructions in Chapter 1 on how to create a new user, and create a user named "bp5am" with the password "bp5ampass."

You issue this connection command with the PHP function called `mysql_connect`. As with all of your PHP/MySQL statements, you can either put the information into variables, or leave them as text in your MySQL query.

Here's how you would do it with variables:

```
$host = "localhost";
$user = "bp5am";
$pass = "bp5ampass";
$connect = mysql_connect($host, $user, $pass);
```

The following statement has the same effect:

```
$connect = mysql_connect("localhost", "bp5am", "bp5ampass");
```

For the most part, your specific needs and the way you are designing your table dictate what piece of code you use. Most people use the first method for security's sake, and they may even put those variables in a different file and include them wherever they need to make a connection to the database.

So now that you're hooked up with the server, whaddya say we actually do something with a database?

Looking at a Ready-Made Database

Create the database that you will be using for your movie site. It consists of three tables:

❑ A movie table, which stores the names of the movies and information about them

❑ A movietype table, which stores the different categories of movies

❑ A people table, which stores the names of the actors and directors in the movies

Try It Out   Creating a Database

In this exercise, you'll create the database and tables that you'll use in the next several chapters of the book.

1. Open your browser and type the following code. This creates your database and the tables you need to hold the data.

```php
<?php
//connect to MySQL; note we've used our own parameters- you should use
//your own for hostname, user, and password
$connect = mysql_connect("localhost", "bp5am", "bp5ampass") or
     die ("Hey loser, check your server connection.");

//create the main database if it doesn't already exist
$create = mysql_query("CREATE DATABASE IF NOT EXISTS moviesite")
  or die(mysql_error());

//make sure our recently created database is the active one
mysql_select_db("moviesite");

//create "movie" table
$movie = "CREATE TABLE movie (
  movie_id int(11) NOT NULL auto_increment,
  movie_name varchar(255) NOT NULL,
  movie_type tinyint(2) NOT NULL default 0,
  movie_year int(4) NOT NULL default 0,
  movie_leadactor int(11) NOT NULL default 0,
  movie_director int(11) NOT NULL default 0,
  PRIMARY KEY  (movie_id),
  KEY movie_type (movie_type,movie_year)
)";

$results = mysql_query($movie)
  or die (mysql_error());
```

```php
//create "movietype" table
$movietype = "CREATE TABLE movietype (
  movietype_id int(11) NOT NULL auto_increment,
  movietype_label varchar(100) NOT NULL,
  PRIMARY KEY  (movietype_id)
)";

$results = mysql_query($movietype)
  or die(mysql_error());

//create "people" table
$people = "CREATE TABLE people (
  people_id int(11) NOT NULL auto_increment,
  people_fullname varchar(255) NOT NULL,
  people_isactor tinyint(1) NOT NULL default 0,
  people_isdirector tinyint(1) NOT NULL default 0,
  PRIMARY KEY  (people_id)
)";

$results = mysql_query($people)
  or die(mysql_error());

echo "Movie Database successfully created!";

?>
```

2. Save this file as `createmovie.php`.

3. Create a new file, and name it `moviedata.php`. This is the file that will populate the database:

```php
<?php
//connect to MySQL
$connect = mysql_connect("localhost", "bp5am", "bp5ampass")
  or die ("Hey loser, check your server connection.");

//make sure we're using the right database
mysql_select_db("moviesite");

//insert data into "movie" table
$insert = "INSERT INTO movie (movie_id, movie_name, movie_type, " .
          "movie_year, movie_leadactor, movie_director) " .
          "VALUES (1, 'Bruce Almighty', 5, 2003, 1, 2), " .
          "(2, 'Office Space', 5, 1999, 5, 6), " .
          "(3, 'Grand Canyon', 2, 1991, 4, 3)";
$results = mysql_query($insert)
  or die(mysql_error());

//insert data into "movietype" table
$type = "INSERT INTO movietype (movietype_id, movietype_label) " .
        "VALUES (1,'Sci Fi'), " .
        "(2, 'Drama'), " .
        "(3, 'Adventure'), " .
        "(4, 'War'), " .
        "(5, 'Comedy'), " .
        "(6, 'Horror'), " .
        "(7, 'Action'), " .
```

```
                "(8, 'Kids')" ;
$results = mysql_query($type)
  or die(mysql_error());

//insert data into "people" table
$people = "INSERT INTO people (people_id, people_fullname, " .
          "people_isactor, people_isdirector) " .
          "VALUES (1, 'Jim Carrey', 1, 0), " .
          "(2, 'Tom Shadyac', 0, 1), " .
          "(3, 'Lawrence Kasdan', 0, 1), " .
          "(4, 'Kevin Kline', 1, 0), " .
          "(5, 'Ron Livingston', 1, 0), " .
          "(6, 'Mike Judge', 0, 1)";
$results = mysql_query($people)
  or die(mysql_error());

echo "Data inserted successfully!";
?>
```

4.   First, run `createmovie.php` from your browser; then run `moviedata.php`.

How It Works

We hope you didn't have too many errors when running the previous files and you saw the two "success" statements. Although we tried to insert useful comments throughout the code, let's dissect this thing one step at a time.

First, you connected to the MySQL server so that you could begin sending MySQL commands and working with the database and tables. You also wanted to be told if there was an error, and you wanted your program to immediately stop running. You did this in the first few lines of code:

```
<?php
//connect to MySQL; note we've used our own parameters- you should use
//your own for hostname, user, and password
$connect = mysql_connect("localhost", "bp5am", "bp5ampass") or
  die ("Hey loser, check your server connection.");
```

Then you actually created the database itself, and if for some reason the database could not be created, you told the server to stop running and show you what the problem was:

```
//create the main database if it doesn't already exist
$create = mysql_query("CREATE DATABASE IF NOT EXISTS moviesite")
  or die(mysql_error());
```

You also made sure to select your database so the server would know which database you would be working with next:

```
//make sure our recently created database is the active one
mysql_select_db("moviesite");
```

Then you began making your individual tables, starting with the movie table. You defined the individual field names and set up their parameters:

```
//create "movie" table
$movie = "CREATE TABLE movie (
  movie_id int(11) NOT NULL auto_increment,
  movie_name varchar(255) NOT NULL,
  movie_type tinyint(2) NOT NULL default 0,
  movie_year int(4) NOT NULL default 0,
  movie_leadactor int(11) NOT NULL default 0,
  movie_director int(11) NOT NULL default 0,
  PRIMARY KEY  (movie_id),
  KEY movie_type (movie_type,movie_year)
)";
```

Once you had your MySQL statement ready to go, you just had to send it to the server with the `mysql_query` command. Again, you told the server to stop executing the program and let you know what the error was, if there was one:

```
$results = mysql_query($movie)
  or die (mysql_error());
```

You also created a movie type and people tables in much the same way:

```
//create "movietype" table
$movietype = "CREATE TABLE movietype (
  movietype_id int(11) NOT NULL auto_increment,
  movietype_label varchar(100) NOT NULL,
  PRIMARY KEY  (movietype_id)
)";

$results = mysql_query($movietype)
  or die(mysql_error());

//create "people" table
$people = "CREATE TABLE people (
  people_id int(11) NOT NULL auto_increment,
  people_fullname varchar(255) NOT NULL,
  people_isactor tinyint(1) NOT NULL default 0,
  people_isdirector tinyint(1) NOT NULL default 0,
  PRIMARY KEY  (people_id)
)";

$results = mysql_query($people)
  or die(mysql_error());
```

You assume that everything was successful if your program runs all the way to the end, so you echoed yourself a success statement, just so you know:

```
echo "Movie Database successfully created!";

?>
```

With your `moviedata.php` file, you populated the tables with information. As always, you have to connect to the MySQL server and select the database. (Hint: This would be great as an included file.)

```
<?php
//connect to MySQL
$connect = mysql_connect("localhost", "bp5am", "bp5ampass")
  or die ("Hey loser, check your server connection.");

//make sure we're using the right database
mysql_select_db("moviesite");
```

Then you began by inserting data into the `movie` table. You first listed the columns you would be accessing. You then listed the values for each record, as follows:

```
//insert data into "movie" table
$insert = "INSERT INTO movie (movie_id, movie_name, movie_type, " .
          "movie_year, movie_leadactor, movie_director) " .
          "VALUES (1, 'Bruce Almighty', 5, 2003, 1, 2), " .
          "(2, 'Office Space', 5, 1999, 5, 6), " .
          "(3, 'Grand Canyon', 2, 1991, 4, 3)";
$results = mysql_query($insert)
  or die(mysql_error());
```

You did the same with the other tables, `movietype` and `people`.

```
//insert data into "movietype" table
$type = "INSERT INTO movietype (movietype_id, movietype_label) " .
        "VALUES (1,'Sci Fi'), " .
        "(2, 'Drama'), " .
        "(3, 'Adventure'), " .
        "(4, 'War'), " .
        "(5, 'Comedy'), " .
        "(6, 'Horror'), " .
        "(7, 'Action'), " .
        "(8, 'Kids')";
$results = mysql_query($type)
  or die(mysql_error());

//insert data into "people" table
$people = "INSERT INTO people (people_id, people_fullname, " .
          "people_isactor, people_isdirector) " .
          "VALUES (1, 'Jim Carrey', 1, 0), " .
          "(2, 'Tom Shadyac', 0, 1), " .
          "(3, 'Lawrence Kasdan', 0, 1), " .
          "(4, 'Kevin Kline', 1, 0), " .
          "(5, 'Ron Livingston', 1, 0), " .
          "(6, 'Mike Judge', 0, 1)";
$results = mysql_query($people)
  or die(mysql_error());
```

Then, because you instructed your program to die if there is any error, you echoed a success statement to yourself to let you know that the entire program executed and you received no errors:

```
echo "Data inserted successfully!";
?>
```

Querying the Database

Now that you have some data in the database, you probably want to retrieve it. You use the SELECT statement to choose data that fits your criteria.

Typical syntax for this command is as follows:

```
SELECT [fieldnames]
    AS [alias]
    FROM [tablename]
    WHERE [criteria]
    ORDER BY [fieldname to sort on] [DESC]
    LIMIT [offset, maxrows]
```

You can set numerous other parameters, but these are the most commonly used:

❑ SELECT [fieldnames]: First decide what specific fieldnames you want to retrieve; if you want to see them all, you simply insert *.

❑ AS: You use the alias to group two or more fieldnames together so that you can reference them later as one giant variable. An example would be:

```
SELECT first_name, last_name AS full_name. . . ORDER BY full_name . . .
```

You cannot use the AS parameter with the WHERE parameter, because this is a limitation of MySQL. When the WHERE clause is executed, the column value may not be known.

❑ FROM: This is pretty self-explanatory: You just need to name the table or tables you are pulling the data from.

❑ WHERE: List your criteria for filtering out the data, as described in the following section.

❑ ORDER BY: Use this parameter if you want the data sorted on a particular field; if you want the results returned in descending order, add DESC.

❑ LIMIT: This enables you to limit the number of results returned and offset the first record returned to whatever number you choose. An example would be:

```
LIMIT 9, 10
```

This would show records 10 through 19. This is a useful feature for showing only a certain number of records on a page, and then allowing the user to click a "next page" link to see more.

For a complete reference, you are advised to — yet again — visit the source at www.mysql.com.

WHERE, oh WHERE

The beast clause called WHERE deserves its own little section because it's really the meat of the query. (No offense to the other guys, but they are pretty much "no brainers.") WHERE is like a cool big brother that can really do some interesting stuff. While SELECT tells MySQL which fields you want to see, WHERE tells it which records you want to see. It is used as follows:

```
SELECT * FROM customers
//retrieves all information about all customers

SELECT * FROM customers WHERE gender = "Male"
//retrieves all information about male customers
```

Let's look at the WHERE clause a little more in-depth:

❑ **Comparison operators** are the heart of the WHERE clause, and they include the following:

  ❑ =, <, >, <=, >=, !=

  ❑ **LIKE** and **%:** Oh how we like LIKE. LIKE lets you compare a piece of text or number and gives you the % as a wildcard. The wildcard allows you to search even if you only know a piece of what's in the field, but you don't want an exact match.

  Example:

```
SELECT * FROM products WHERE description LIKE "%shirt%"
```

  This gives you any records that have the word or text pattern of "shirt" in the description, such as "t-shirt," "blue shirts," or "no shirts here." Without the %s you would get only those products that have a description of "shirt" and nothing else.

❑ **Logical operators** are also accepted in the WHERE clause:

```
SELECT * FROM products WHERE description LIKE "%shirt%" AND price < 25
```

  This gives you all the products that have the word or text pattern of "shirt" in the description and that have a price of less than $25.

Now that you have the SELECT query down to a science, let's look at this baby in action, shall we?

Try It Out   Using the SELECT Query

In this exercise, you'll create a short script that demonstrates how the SELECT query works.

1.   Open your text editor and type this code:

```php
<?php
//connect to MySQL
$connect = mysql_connect("localhost", "bp5am", "bp5ampass")
  or die("Hey loser, check your server connection.");

//make sure we're using the right database
mysql_select_db("moviesite");

$query = "SELECT movie_name, movie_type " .
         "FROM movie " .
         "WHERE movie_year>1990 " .
         "ORDER BY movie_type";
$results = mysql_query($query)
  or die(mysql_error());
```

```
while ($row = mysql_fetch_array($results)) {
  extract($row);
  echo $movie_name;
  echo " - ";
  echo $movie_type;
  echo "<br>";
}

?>
```

2.   Save this file as `select.php`, and then run it from your browser.

How It Works

You should see the screen shown in Figure 3-1 after running `select.php`.

First, as always, you had to connect to the MySQL server and the specific database. Next you plan out your query and assign it to the `$query` variable.

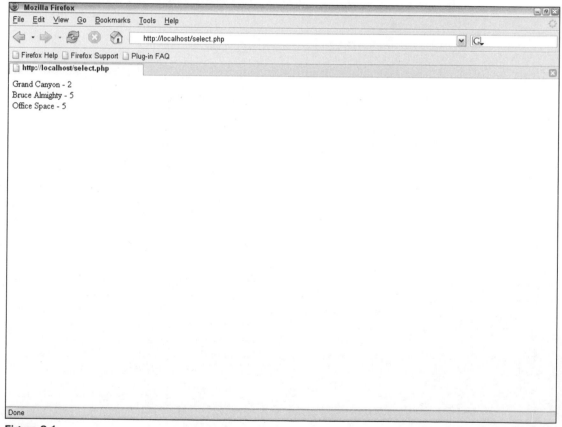

Figure 3-1

You wanted to choose only the fieldnames movie_name and movie_type because you decided you didn't care about seeing the rest of the information contained in the table at this time. If you wanted to retrieve everything, you simply would have written:

```
SELECT * FROM ...
```

but instead you wrote:

```
$query = "SELECT movie_name, movie_type " .
```

Next, you told the server from what table you want to retrieve the information.

```
"FROM movie " .
```

Then you gave it the conditions of your query. In this case, you wanted to see only movies made since 1990, so you wrote:

```
"WHERE movie_year>1990 " .
```

And you asked the server to sort the results by movie type and ended your query and the PHP line:

```
"ORDER BY movie_type";
```

Next, you collect all the rows that match your criteria with these lines:

```
$results = mysql_query($query)
  or die(mysql_error());
```

Then, you loop through the results with these lines:

```
while ($row = mysql_fetch_array($results)) {
   extract($row);
   echo $movie_name;
   echo " - ";
   echo $movie_type;
   echo "<br>";
}
```

For each row you find (based on the above query), you store those results in an array named $row using the mysql_fetch_array() function. You then extract all the variables in $row using the extract function, echo out what you need, and then go on to the next row of results from your query. When there are no more rows that match your criteria, the while loop ends.

Pretty easy, eh? Let's try using the foreach function instead of the while function and see how it works.

Working with PHP and Arrays of Data: foreach

The foreach function is similar to the while function if you're using while to loop through a list of results from your query. Its purpose is to apply a block of commands to every row in your results set. It is used in this way:

```
foreach ($row as $value) {
  echo $value;
  echo "<br>";
}
```

The preceding code would take all the variables in the $row array and list each value with a line break in between them. You can see this in action in Chapters 4 and 5 and get a better idea of how it can be used.

Try It Out   Using foreach

This exercise contrasts foreach with the while you used in the previous exercise.

1. In your select.php file, make the following highlighted changes:

```
<?php
//connect to MySQL
$connect = mysql_connect("localhost", "bp5am", "bp5ampass")
  or die("Hey loser, check your server connection.");

//make sure we're using the right database
mysql_select_db("moviesite");

$query = "SELECT movie_name, movie_type " .
         "FROM movie " .
         "WHERE movie_year>1990 " .
         "ORDER BY movie_type";
$results = mysql_query($query)
  or die(mysql_error());

while ($row = mysql_fetch_assoc($results)) {
  foreach ($row as $val1) {
    echo $val1;
    echo " ";
  }
  echo "<br>";
}
?>
```

How It Works

You should see the same results as before, except that there is now no dash between the elements. Pretty sneaky, huh? Because using mysql_fetch_array actually returns two sets of arrays (one with associative indices, one with number indices), you see duplicate values if you use the foreach function without clarifying. You can therefore either use mysql_fetch_array($results,MYSQL_ASSOC) or mysql_fetch_assoc to perform the same thing and return only one array at a time. You still need to use the while function to proceed through the selected rows one at a time, but you can see that using foreach applies the same sets of commands to each value in the array regardless of their contents.

Sometimes you will need to have more control over a specific value, and you can't apply the same formatting rules to each value in the array, but the foreach function can also come in handy when using formatting functions such as creating tables. In the following exercise, you'll create another version of the select.php program that illustrates this.

Using foreach to Create a Table

In this exercise, you'll use `foreach` to apply some formatting rules to the results of your query.

1. Open your text editor and enter the following script:

```php
<?php
//connect to MySQL
$connect = mysql_connect("localhost", "bp5am", "bp5ampass")
or die("Hey loser, check your server connection.");

//make sure we're using the right database
mysql_select_db("moviesite");

$query = "SELECT * " .
        "FROM movie " .
        "WHERE movie_year>1990 " .
        "ORDER BY movie_type";
$results = mysql_query($query)
  or die(mysql_error());

echo "<table border=\"1\">\n";
while ($row = mysql_fetch_assoc($results)) {
  echo "<tr>\n";
  foreach($row as $value) {
    echo "<td>\n";
    echo $value;
    echo "</td>\n";
  }
  echo "</tr>\n";
}
echo "</table>\n";
?>
```

2. Save this script as `select2.php`, then run it in your browser. You should see something like Figure 3-2.

How It Works

You use the `mysql_query` and `while` statements to retrieve your desired records and fields. Then for each value you retrieve, you place it in a separate cell in your table using your `foreach` function and a combination of HTML code and `echo`.

You can see that this script would easily show a long string of array variables with a few lines of code, whereas if you had to echo out each separate variable with the accompanying HTML code, this script would be quite lengthy.

A Tale of Two Tables

The preceding code is all nice and neat and pretty, but it doesn't do you a whole lot of good if you don't have a secret decoder ring to tell you what those cryptic "movie type" numbers correspond to in plain English. That information is all stored in a separate table, the `movietype` table. So how do you get this information?

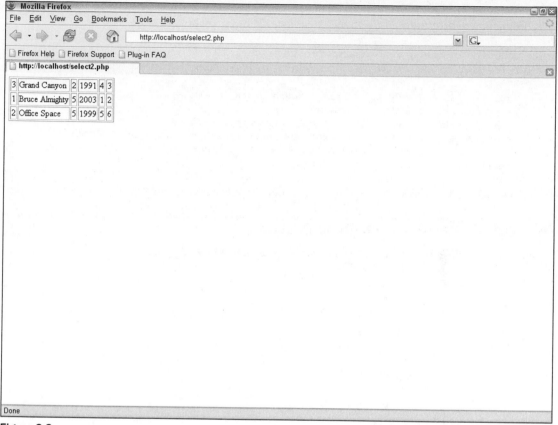

Figure 3-2

You can get information from more than one table in two ways:

❑ Reference the individual tables in your query and link them temporarily through a common field

❑ Formally JOIN the individual tables in your query

Let's try out these methods and then talk about each of them in more detail.

Referencing Two Tables

You can distinguish between two tables in your database by referencing them in the SELECT statement as follows:

```
$query = "SELECT customers.name, orders.order_total
          FROM customers, orders
          WHERE customers.cust_ID = orders.cust_ID";
//retrieves customers' names from customers table and order_total from
//orders table where the cust_ID field in the customers table equals the
//cust_ID field in the orders table.
```

If a customer's ID is 123, you will see all the `order_totals` for all the orders for that specific customer, enabling you to determine all the money customer 123 has spent at your store.

Although you are linking the two tables through the `cust_ID` field, the names do not have to be the same. You can compare any two field names from any two tables. An example would be:

```
$query = "SELECT customers.name, orders.order_total
        FROM customers, orders
        WHERE customers.email = orders.shiptoemail";
//retrieves customers' names from customers table and order_total from
//orders table where the email field in the customers table equals the
//shiptoemail field in the orders table.
```

This would link your tables through the `email` and `shiptoemail` fields from different tables.

Try It Out   Referencing Individual Tables

This exercise will show you how to reference multiple tables in your query.

1. Change your `select2.php` program as shown here (changes are highlighted):

```php
<?php
//connect to MySQL
$connect = mysql_connect("localhost", "bp5am", "bp5ampass")
or die ("Hey loser, check your server connection.");

//make sure we're using the right database
mysql_select_db("moviesite");

$query = "SELECT movie.movie_name, movietype.movietype_label " .
        "FROM movie, movietype " .
        "WHERE movie.movie_type = movietype.movietype_id " .
        "AND movie.movie_year>1990 " .
        "ORDER BY movie_type";
$results = mysql_query($query)
  or die(mysql_error());

echo "<table border=\"1\">\n";
while ($row = mysql_fetch_assoc($results)) {
  echo "<tr>\n";
  foreach($row as $value) {
    echo "<td>\n";
    echo $value;
    echo "</td>\n";
  }
  echo "</tr>\n";
}
echo "</table>\n";
?>
```

2. Save your script and run it. Your screen should look something like Figure 3-3.

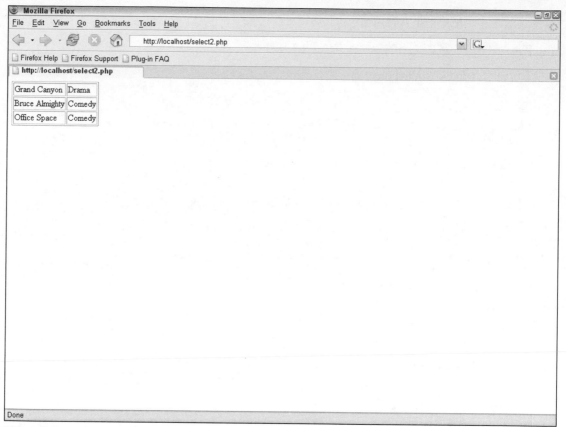

Figure 3-3

How It Works

Now you can see a table with the movie names and actual words for the type of movie instead of your cryptic code, as was the case in Figure 3-2. The common fields were linked in the WHERE portion of the statement. ID numbers from the two different tables (fieldname movie_type in the movie table and fieldname movietype_id in the movietype table) represented the same thing, so that's where you linked them together.

Joining Two Tables

In life as in code, regardless of the circumstances under which two things join together, it is rarely a simple thing, and more often than not, it comes with conditions and consequences.

In the world of MySQL, joins are also complex things that we discuss in greater detail in Chapter 10; meanwhile, we walk you through a very simple and commonly used join so you can get a taste of what joining is all about. The JOIN function gives you greater control over how your database tables relate to and connect with each other, but it also requires a greater understanding of relational databases (another topic covered in Chapter 10).

Try It Out   **Joining Two Tables**

In this exercise, you'll link the two tables with a JOIN.

1.   Make the following highlighted changes to `select2.php`:

```php
<?php
//connect to MySQL
$connect = mysql_connect("localhost", "bp5am", "bp5ampass")
  or die("Hey loser, check your server connection.");

//make sure we're using the right database
mysql_select_db("moviesite");

$query = "SELECT movie_name, movietype_label " .
         "FROM movie " .
         "LEFT JOIN movietype " .
         "ON movie_type = movietype_id " .
         "WHERE movie.movie_year>1990 " .
         "ORDER BY movie_type";
$results = mysql_query($query)
  or die(mysql_error());

echo "<table border=\"1\">\n";
while ($row = mysql_fetch_assoc($results)) {
  echo "<tr>\n";
  foreach($row as $value) {
    echo "<td>\n";
    echo $value;
    echo "</td>\n";
  }
  echo "</tr>\n";
}
echo "</table>\n";
?>
```

2.   Save the script and run it.

How It Works

You should see the same result as in the previous example. As you can see, you simply listed all the fields you wanted to see, regardless of the table they were in. (MySQL will find them as long as the table name is referenced there somewhere.) You did this in the first line of the SELECT statement:

```
SELECT movie_name, movietype_label
```

Then you told MySQL what tables you wanted to access and what type of join should be used to bring them together in these statements:

```
FROM movie
LEFT JOIN movietype
```

You used the LEFT join statement in this case. Although there are other things that go along with this, the LEFT join in layman's terms simply means that the second table (movietype in the example) is dependent on the first table (movie). You are getting the main information from movie, and "looking up" a bit of information from movietype.

You then told the server which field to use to join them together in this line:

```
ON movie_type = movietype_id
```

Again, you don't need to clarify which table is being used, but if you have overlapping fieldnames across tables, you can add this if you like, to avoid confusion.

You kept your condition about only showing the movies that were made after 1990, and sorted them by numerical movie type with these lines:

```
WHERE movie.movie_year>1990
ORDER BY movie_type";
```

And the rest of the code is the same. See, joining wasn't that bad, was it?

Helpful Tips and Suggestions

Now and then, we all get into a little trouble. Instead of sitting in the corner and sucking your thumb, or banging your fist against your keyboard, relax! We are here to help.

Documentation

The guys at MySQL have provided wonderfully thorough documentation covering more than you ever wanted to know about its capabilities, quirks, and plans for the future. We have stated this time and time again, but the source Web site really can provide you with the most up-to-date and accurate information.

You can search the documentation, or even add your own comments if you've discovered something especially helpful that might help out other folks just like you. Because this is all open source, you really do get a community feeling when you read through the documentation.

Once again, you can find the manual at www.mysql.com.

Using PHPMyAdmin

Okay, now that you've been given the task of learning MySQL and PHP on your own from scratch, we're going to let you in on a dirty little secret: It's called PHPMyAdmin, and it will probably be your new best friend.

PHPMyAdmin is another wonderful open source project that enables you to access your MySQL databases through a GUI. It's easy to set up and manage, and it makes administering your databases, tables, and data a breeze. It does have some limitations, but for the most part, it will make you a lot more efficient.

## Chapter 3

With this software, you can easily do the following:

- ❑ Drop and create databases
- ❑ Create, edit, and delete tables
- ❑ Create, edit, and delete fields
- ❑ Enter any MySQL statements
- ❑ View and print table structure
- ❑ Generate PHP code
- ❑ View data in table format

You can download the software by visiting the source Web site at www.phpmyadmin.net. This software works whether your MySQL server is on your local machine or hosted by a third party.

Summary

We've covered some pretty fundamental programming concepts here, and we'll delve more into those in future chapters. But for now you should have a pretty good handle on the basics.

You should have a good understanding of databases and tables and how to insert and retrieve information stored within those tables. You should also have a good understanding of how MySQL works with PHP to make dynamic pages in your Web site. In the next few chapters, you build on this knowledge to create more complex applications.

Exercises

We have started you on the MySQL/PHP journey, and in the next few chapters we take you places you've never dreamed of. To fine-tune your skills, here are a few exercises to really make sure you know your stuff.

1. Create a PHP program that prints the lead actor and director for each movie in the database.

2. Pick only comedies from the movie table, and show the movie name and year it was produced. Sort the list alphabetically.

3. Show each movie in the database on its own page, and give the user links in a "page 1, page 2 ..." type navigation system. Hint: Use OFFSET to control which movie is on which page.

Using Tables to Display Data

So now that you can successfully marry PHP and MySQL to produce dynamic pages, what happens when you have rows and rows of data that you need to display? You need to have some mechanism for your viewers to easily read the data, and it needs to be in a nice, neat, organized fashion. The easiest way to do this is to use tables.

This chapter covers the following:

❑   Creating a table to hold the data from the database

❑   Creating column headings automatically

❑   Populating the table with the results of a basic MySQL query

❑   Populating the table with the results of more complex MySQL queries

❑   Making the output user-friendly

Creating a Table

Before you can list your data, you need to set up the structure, column headings, and format of your table.

Try It Out   **Defining the Table Headings**

In this exercise, you'll define the table headings for your table.

1.   Open your favorite text/HTML editor and enter the following code:

```php
<?php
$movie=<<<EOD
<h2><center>Movie Review Database</center></h2>
<table width="70%" border="1" cellpadding="2"
        cellspacing="2" align="center">
  <tr>
    <th>Movie Title</th>
```

```
      <th>Year of Release</th>
      <th>Movie Director</th>
      <th>Movie Lead Actor</th>
      <th>Movie Type</th>
    </tr>
</table>
EOD;

echo $movie;
?>
```

2. Save this file as `table1.php` and upload it to your Web server.

3. Load your favorite browser and view the page that you have just uploaded.

Your table should look like the one shown in Figure 4-1.

How It Works

All the code between `<<<EOD` and `EOD;` is held in the variable `$table`, so instead of printing each element of the HTML table, you are adding that element to the variable `$table`. Incidentally, the border has been left on just to show that it is actually working.

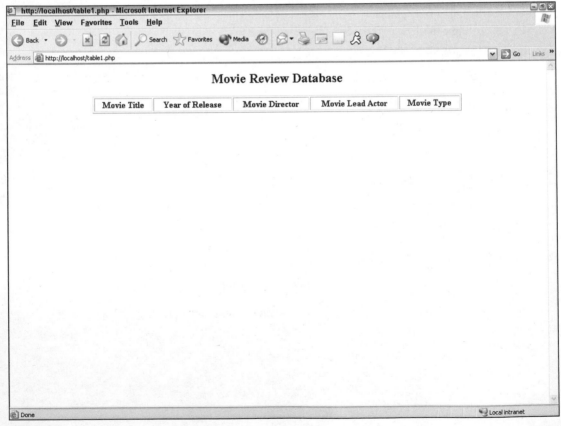

Figure 4-1

Then you simply echo the contents of $table. And finally, you close the PHP script using the ?> tag.

By using these two tags, you can use raw HTML code (that is, HTML code that does not need any modification at all).

As you may recall from Chapter 2 in the discussion regarding using heredoc, you can change the text "EOD" to whatever you'd like, but the beginning and ending tags must match. For example, this will work fine:

```
$table =<<<HAHAHA
        code here
HAHAHA;
```

But this will not work:

```
$table =<<<HAHAHA
        code here
BOOHOO;
```

You will receive an error such as the one shown in Figure 4-2.

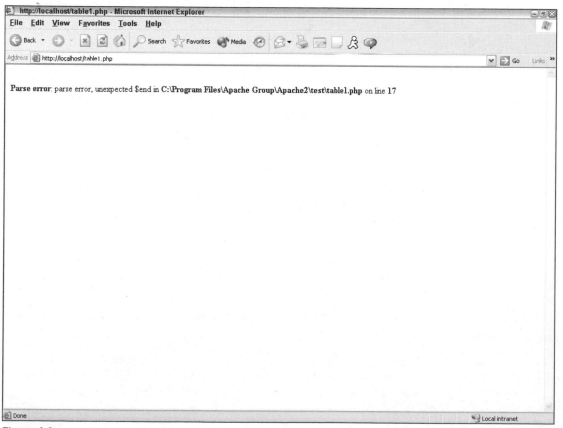

Figure 4-2

Note that there must be *no* spaces after the =<<<EOD and the EOD; tags. In addition, there can be no leading space, indents, or any other characters on the heredoc closing tag line (semicolons are permissible). If there is even one space, you'll receive an error. (You can potentially spend *hours* trying to fix an error as a result of having a single space after these tags!) Always remember to delete all spaces after these tags.

Now that you can create a table, you should fill it with some data from your movie review database. After all, that's what you're here for!

Populating the Table

Looking at your empty skeleton of a table gives you the blueprint for how your data will be laid out once it is retrieved from the database.

Try It Out   **Filling the Table with Data**

Because this is quite a large piece of code, we'll explain what's going on as you go through it. All changes are highlighted. A few things are taken out from the original script (we'll soon see who has been paying attention).

1. Open the file `table1.php`, and with your favorite text/HTML editor make the following changes to the existing code. We use the databases created in Chapter 3 for the purposes of the example here.

Remember to replace the server name, username, password, and database name with your own values.

```php
<?php
$link = mysql_connect("localhost","bp5am","bp5ampass")
  or die(mysql_error());
mysql_select_db("moviesite")
  or die (mysql_error());
```

2. Start by making a connection to the database. (You have remembered to change the settings to reflect your own, haven't you? Good.)

```php
$query = "SELECT movie_name, movie_director, movie_leadactor " .
       "FROM movie";

$result = mysql_query($query, $link)
  or die(mysql_error());
$num_movies = mysql_num_rows($result);
```

3. Run a SQL query against the database and get the results. And while you are at it, count how many records were returned from the query.

As we discussed in Chapter 3, we've put the SQL words in capital letters. This is good practice, because it allows you to easily identify which words are field names and which ones are SQL keywords. It is also good practice to make your SQL query as easy to read as possible. That is also why we have written the SQL query over several lines.

```
$movie_header =<<<EOD
<h2><center>Movie Review Database</center></h2>
<table width="70%" border="1" cellpadding="2"
       cellspacing="2" align="center">
  <tr>
    <th>Movie Title</th>
    <th>Movie Director</th>
    <th>Movie Lead Actor</th>
  </tr>
EOD;
```

4. Then enter the block of code that was originally there (minus the echo statement).

Pay attention to the fact that it's called $movie_header, *not* $movie (as it was in the first example).

```
$movie_details = '';
while ($row = mysql_fetch_array($result)) {
  $movie_name = $row['movie_name'];
  $movie_director = $row['movie_director'];
  $movie_leadactor = $row['movie_leadactor'];

  $movie_details .=<<<EOD
  <tr>
    <td>$movie_name</td>
    <td>$movie_director</td>
    <td>$movie_leadactor</td>
  </tr>
EOD;
}

$movie_details .=<<<EOD
  <tr>
   <td> </td>
  </tr>
  <tr>
    <td>Total :$num_movies Movies</td>
  </tr>
EOD;
```

How It Works

The preceding code does quite a lot of work for you, so let's look at it in more detail.

As you know, the while { } statement loops through the records that have been returned. For each record, it executes the block of code that is between the brackets. Don't worry; PHP is smart enough to know how many records there are and what record number it is currently on in this case. There is no danger of having the wrong values assigned to the wrong record.

The first line within the while loop tells the script to pull out the value of the field movie_name in the current record and put it into a variable called $movie_name. The next four lines do pretty much the same thing—they simply assign different field values to differently named variables.

Then you come across the familiar tag that you saw at the beginning of this chapter. It's not quite the same as the one before because this one has .=<<<EOD instead of just =<<<EOD. So instead of just having one record's values, $movie_details contains all of the record values that have been returned. Then at the end you have included the total number of movies in your database.

> *By adding a period (.) in front of* =<<<EOD, *you are appending the existing value of* $movie_details *with the current value of* $movie_details. *If you forget to add the period (.), then you will replace the existing value with the current value. That's because in PHP* $var = "1" *means "make* $var *become equal to the value of 1" and* $var .= "1" *means "take the current value of* $var *and add* "1" *to it."*

In the preceding example, notice that you've assigned the name of the movie to the variable $movie_name and then used $movie_name instead of doing the following:

```
while ($row = mysql_fetch_row($result)) {
  $movie_details .=<<<EOD
  <tr>
    <td>$row['movie_name']</td>
  </tr>
EOD;
}
```

The preceding snippet does exactly the same thing, but it would then limit you if you wanted to do any formatting on the variable's values (you'll see what we mean a bit later on).

Try It Out   Putting It All Together

The data has now been retrieved, but you need to send it all to the browser so it will display in the table.

1. You assign the $movie_footer variable by entering the following:

```
$movie_footer ="</table>";

$movie =<<<MOVIE
              $movie_header
              $movie_details
              $movie_footer
MOVIE;

  echo "There are $num_movies movies in our database";
  echo $movie;
?>
```

2. Append this to your previous code, save this file as table2.php, and upload it to your Web server.

3. Load that page into your Web browser. You should see something similar to the screen shown in Figure 4-3.

How It Works

First, your code took the information stored in $movie_header, $movie_details, and $movie_footer, and rolled all that up, tied it with a bow, and put it in $movie, with the use of heredoc. Then there are the following lines:

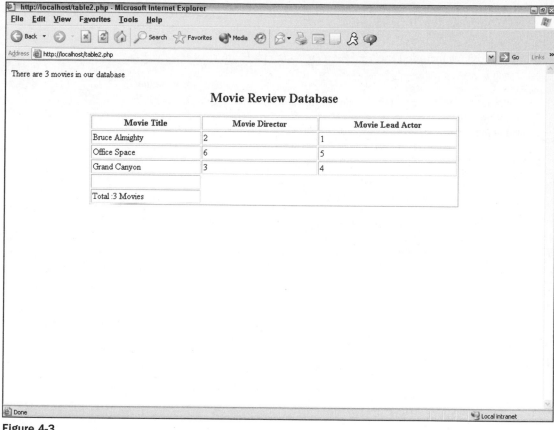

Figure 4-3

```
echo "There are $num_movies movies in our database";
echo $movie;
```

You printed the statement about how many movies there are in your database, and then you sent the whole ball of wax ($movie_header, $movie_details, and $movie_footer) with the next line.

The table may look pretty, but as in Chapter 3, it doesn't do the user much good if they don't have their secret decoder ring to decipher what actors and directors were associated with your movies. You need to link your tables to pull this information.

Try It Out   Improving Your Table

In this exercise, you'll link the tables together, as you saw in Chapter 3, so you can output meaningful data.

1.   Modify your table2.php file as shown in the highlighted text:

```
<?php
$link = mysql_connect("localhost","bp5am","bp5ampass")
```

```
  or die(mysql_error());
mysql_select_db("moviesite")
  or die (mysql_error());

$query = "SELECT movie_name, movie_director, movie_leadactor " .
         "FROM movie";

$result = mysql_query($query, $link)
  or die(mysql_error());
$num_movies = mysql_num_rows($result);

$movie_header=<<<EOD
  <h2><center>Movie Review Database</center></h2>
  <table width="70%" border="1" cellpadding="2"
        cellspacing="2" align="center">
    <tr>
      <th>Movie Title</th>
      <th>Movie Director</th>
      <th>Movie Lead Actor</th>
    </tr>

EOD;

function get_director() {
  global $movie_director;
  global $director;

  $query_d = "SELECT people_fullname " .
             "FROM people " .
             "WHERE people_id='$movie_director'";
  $results_d = mysql_query($query_d)
    or die(mysql_error());
  $row_d = mysql_fetch_array($results_d);
  extract($row_d);
  $director = $people_fullname;
}

function get_leadactor() {
  global $movie_leadactor;
  global $leadactor;

  $query_a = "SELECT people_fullname " .
             "FROM people " .
             "WHERE people_id='$movie_leadactor'";
  $results_a = mysql_query($query_a)
    or die(mysql_error());
  $row_a = mysql_fetch_array($results_a);
  extract($row_a);
  $leadactor = $people_fullname;
}

while ($row = mysql_fetch_array($result)) {
  $movie_name = $row['movie_name'];
```

```
    $movie_director = $row['movie_director'];
    $movie_leadactor = $row['movie_leadactor'];

    //get director's name from people table
    get_director();

    //get lead actor's name from people table
    get_leadactor();

    $movie_details .=<<<EOD
    <tr>
      <td>$movie_name</td>
      <td>$director</td>
      <td>$leadactor</td>
    </tr>
EOD;
}

$movie_details .=<<<EOD
  <tr>
    <td>Total :$num_movies Movies</td>
  </tr>
EOD;

$movie_footer ="</table>";

$movie =<<<MOVIE
                $movie_header
                $movie_details
                $movie_footer
MOVIE;

  echo "There are $num_movies movies in our database";
  echo $movie;
?>
```

2. Save your file and reload it in your browser.

Your screen should now look like that in Figure 4-4.

How It Works

With the functions get_director and get_leadactor added, the script requests that specific information be requested from the server for each separate row in the table. This enables you to pull the information you want without muddling up your original query. You also cleaned up the formatting for the last two rows with the change in code near the end of the script.

Congratulations! You have successfully developed a powerful script that will query a database and put its contents into an HTML table. Give yourself a pat on the back. But like all good explorers, onward we must go.

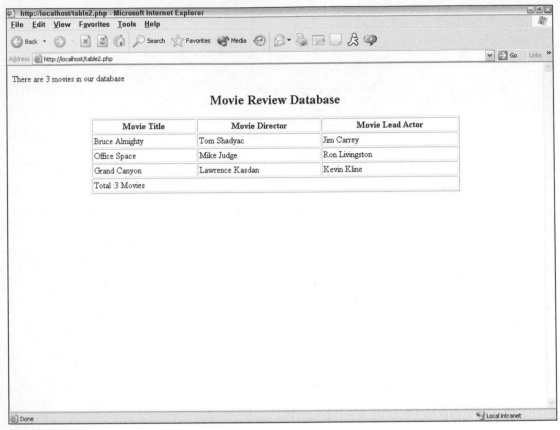

Figure 4-4

Who's the Master?

Now let's build on the good work that you've done so far and add more information and functionality to your table. Implementing master and child relationships in your site can allow your users to click on a movie title in your table for more information about the movie. Of course these would all be dynamically generated, so let's find out how to do such a cool thing, and what master/child relationships mean.

Try It Out   Adding Links to the Table

The steps in this section will enable you to load extra information depending on the movie that you click. This requires you to do the following:

1. Open `table2.php` in your favorite text/HTML editor and add the lines of code that appear highlighted. We haven't displayed the whole page of code, as we're sure you know it by heart already.

```
    $query = "SELECT movie_id, movie_name, " .
             "movie_director, movie_leadactor " .
             "FROM movie";

$result = mysql_query($query, $link)
   or die(mysql_error());
$num_movies = mysql_num_rows($result);

$movie_details = '';
while ($row = mysql_fetch_array($result)) {
   $movie_id = $row['movie_id'];
   $movie_name = $row['movie_name'];
   $movie_director = $row['movie_director'];
   $movie_leadactor = $row['movie_leadactor'];

   //get director's name from people table
   get_director();

   //get lead actor's name from people table
   get_leadactor();

   $movie_details .=<<<EOD
   <tr>
     <td><a href="movie_details.php?movie_id=$movie_id"
          title="Find out more about $movie_name">$movie_name</td>
     <td>$director</td>
     <td>$leadactor</td>
   </tr>
EOD;
}
```

2. Save the file as `table3.php`, upload the file to your Web server, and open the page with your browser.

Your screen should look like that in Figure 4-5.

How It Works

You should notice a change between Figure 4-4 (`table2.php`) and Figure 4-5 (`table3.php`). You now have links to more detailed information about each movie for your visitor to click.

The first change made in the previous section altered the MySQL query to include the `$movie_id` field.

Then you added the new field to the results set returned from the query. (Otherwise, you'd just be selecting a field and not actually doing anything with it, and what's the point of that?)

The final change created the HTML code that produces a hyperlink on the movie name. You've also added a nice little touch with the inclusion of "tooltips" for each of the movies in the list. Unfortunately, some Web browsers don't support this (apologies to those of you who have such browsers).

So now that the changes have been made, what does it actually do? Place your mouse over some hyperlinks, and if you view your status bar, you'll see that each link is unique and is created dynamically. This page is known as the "master page," and the page that we are going to link to is known as the "child page."

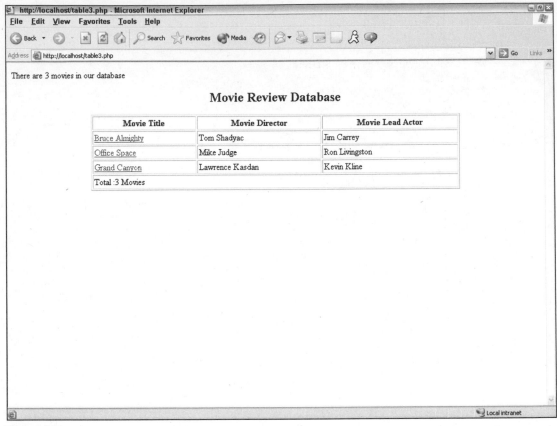

Figure 4-5

Good, eh? No more having to type lots of different hyperlinks (what a bore that used to be).

Before you can go any further, you need to add some data to your existing database that you can use for your movie details. If you recall from Chapter 3, for each movie, you currently have the movie name, director, lead actor, type, and year of release. Let's also add the running time, how much the movie made, and how much it cost to produce. For all you sticklers out there, a word of warning: the dollar amounts we are using are *for instructional purposes only*. In fact, we have no idea how much money these movies actually made, nor how much they cost to produce. Work with us on this one, okay?

Try It Out   Adding Data to the Table

In this exercise, you'll add some additional data about each movie to the database.

1. Open your text editor and type the following code:

```php
<?php
$link = mysql_connect("localhost","bp5am","bp5ampass")
   or die(mysql_error());
```

```
mysql_select_db("moviesite")
  or die (mysql_error());

//alter "movie" table to include running time/cost/takings fields
$add = "ALTER TABLE movie ADD COLUMN ( " .
       "movie_running_time int NULL, " .
       "movie_cost int NULL, " .
       "movie_takings int NULL)";
$results = mysql_query($add)
  or die(mysql_error());

//insert new data into "movie" table for each movie
$update = "UPDATE movie SET " .
          "movie_running_time=102, " .
          "movie_cost=10, " .
          "movie_takings=15 " .
          "WHERE movie_id = 1";
$results = mysql_query($update)
  or die(mysql_error());

$update = "UPDATE movie SET " .
          "movie_running_time=90, " .
          "movie_cost=3, " .
          "movie_takings=90 " .
          "WHERE movie_id = 2";
$results = mysql_query($update)
  or die(mysql_error());

$update = "UPDATE movie SET " .
          "movie_running_time=134, " .
          "movie_cost=15, " .
          "movie_takings=10 " .
          "WHERE movie_id = 3";
$results = mysql_query($update)
  or die(mysql_error());

?>
```

2.   Save this file as `alter_movie.php`, then open this file in your browser. Don't worry — you will see a blank screen, but your table has been altered and the information has been entered automatically.

How It Works

First, the script used the `ALTER TABLE` command to add the appropriate fields into the existing movie table, and then it used the `UPDATE` command to insert the new data into those fields. If you aren't familiar with these commands, you might try rereading Chapter 3.

Now that you have the data in place, you need to create a new page that you'll use to display the extra movie information (`movie_details.php`).

Try It Out   **Calculating Movie Takings**

In this exercise, you'll create a new page to display the data you added in the previous exercise.

1.   Open your text editor and type the following program:

```php
<?php
$link = mysql_connect("localhost","bp5am","bp5ampass")
  or die(mysql_error());
mysql_select_db("moviesite")
  or die (mysql_error());

/* Function to calculate if a movie made a profit,
loss or broke even */
function calculate_differences($takings, $cost) {
  $difference = $takings - $cost;

  if ($difference < 0) {
    $difference = substr($difference, 1);
    $font_color = 'red';
    $profit_or_loss = "$" . $difference . "m";
  } elseif ($difference > 0) {
    $font_color ='green';
    $profit_or_loss = "$" . $difference . "m";
  } else {
    $font_color = 'blue';
    $profit_or_loss = "Broke even";
  }
  return "<font color=\"$font_color\">" . $profit_or_loss . "</font>";
}
?>
```

This function will make life easier for you. This will become clearer as we proceed through the rest of this example.

2.   Save this file as `movie_details.php`.

How It Works

The line that contains the code `substr` is placed before the `$profit_or_loss` line because a loss will return a negative number, and no one actually says, "The movie made a loss of minus 10 million dollars." Instead we say, "The movie lost 10 million dollars." However, what happens when the movie takings are the same as the movie production costs? That's where the last "else" comes into play. You've covered all eventualities.

The important thing to remember is that in PHP you can very easily create new variables by performing actions on existing ones. Just because you don't hold the information in the database doesn't mean you can't create it.

Try It Out   **Displaying the New Information**

In this exercise you are going to alter the original master table to include the new data, and this will serve as your new "child" table.

1.   Add the following code to `movie_details.php`:

```php
/* Function to get the director's name from the people table */
function get_director() {
  global $movie_director;
  global $director;

  $query_d = "SELECT people_fullname " .
             "FROM people " .
             "WHERE people_id='$movie_director'";
  $results_d = mysql_query($query_d)
    or die(mysql_error());
  $row_d = mysql_fetch_array($results_d);
  extract($row_d);
  $director = $people_fullname;
}


/* Function to get the lead actor's name from the people table */
function get_leadactor() {
  global $movie_leadactor;
  global $leadactor;

  $query_a = "SELECT people_fullname " .
             "FROM people " .
             "WHERE people_id='$movie_leadactor'";
  $results_a = mysql_query($query_a)
    or die(mysql_error());
  $row_a = mysql_fetch_array($results_a);
  extract($row_a);
  $leadactor = $people_fullname;
}

$query = "SELECT * FROM movie " .
         "WHERE movie_id ='" . $_GET['movie_id'] . "'";

$result = mysql_query($query, $link)
  or die(mysql_error());

$movie_table_headings=<<<EOD
  <tr>
    <th>Movie Title</th>
    <th>Year of Release</th>
    <th>Movie Director</th>
    <th>Movie Lead Actor</th>
    <th>Movie Running Time</th>
    <th>Movie Health</th>
  </tr>
EOD;


while ($row = mysql_fetch_array($result)) {
  $movie_name = $row['movie_name'];
  $movie_director = $row['movie_director'];
  $movie_leadactor = $row['movie_leadactor'];
  $movie_year = $row['movie_year'];
  $movie_running_time = $row['movie_running_time']." mins";
  $movie_takings = $row['movie_takings'];
```

```
    $movie_cost = $row['movie_cost'];

    //get director's name from people table
    get_director();

    //get lead actor's name from people table
    get_leadactor();

}
```

How It Works

Because you've already written the functions to get the director's and lead actor's names, you "borrowed" this code from the `table2.php` file. Then you've changed the query to return everything in each record, as opposed to only a few fields. It does mean that you are returning one field that you are not actually using. The query now contains a WHERE clause. This determines which record you are going to retrieve the data from.

Take a look at the WHERE clause (it's not as daunting as it first seems):

❑   You have used `$_GET['movie_id']` in the WHERE clause. This is the ID of the movie that was passed from the hyperlink in `table3.php`.

❑   You've also created the variable `$movie_table_headings` to contain the headings for the fields that you'll be using.

❑   The rest of the code is very similar to the code in `table3.php`. You've added four extra fields to the `while` control loop.

Didn't we say previously that returning fields that you don't need is not good practice? Yes, we did. However, in this case you are returning only one more field than you need, as opposed to returning many redundant fields. So are we going against our own advice? To be 100 percent truthful, yes. However, because you are using the vast majority of fields in each record, PHP will not suffer from this tradeoff, and it is worth it. You would *not* want to do this when, for example, you want the values of (say) 5 fields and the record structure contains 50 fields. If you did this in that instance, PHP would be wasting resources to return the other 45 fields.

So now that you've arranged to return information from records, what next? Now you put this extra information to work.

Try It Out   **Displaying Movie Details**

In this exercise, you'll enhance the `movie_details` page with your new data.

1.   Add the following lines of code to the end of `movie_details.php`:

```
$movie_health = calculate_differences($movie_takings, $movie_cost);
$page_start =<<<EOD
<html>
<head>
<title>Details and Reviews for: $movie_name</title>
```

```
</head>
<body>
EOD;

$movie_details =<<<EOD
<table width="70%" border="0" cellspacing="2"
        cellpadding="2" align="center">
  <tr>
    <th colspan="6"><u><h2>$movie_name: Details</h2></u></th>
  </tr>
  $movie_table_headings
  <tr>
    <td width="33%" align="center">$movie_name</td>
    <td align="center">$movie_year</td>
    <td align="center">$director</td>
    <td align="center">$leadactor</td>
    <td align="center">$movie_running_time</td>
    <td align="center">$movie_health</td>
  </tr>
</table>
<br>
<br>
EOD;
$page_end =<<<EOD
</body>
</html>
EOD;
$detailed_movie_info =<<<EOD
    $page_start
    $movie_details
    $page_end
EOD;

echo $detailed_movie_info;
mysql_close();
```

2.   Save the file as `movie_details.php`, upload the file to your Web server, and browse to `table3.php`.

3.   Click a movie name.

You should now see a page similar to Figure 4-6.

How It Works

Remember the function you created at the top? When you add the line in step 1 of the previous "Try It Out" section, you call the function and ask it to execute. Whatever value is returned from the `calculate_difference` function will be placed in the variable `$movie_health` (after all, if a movie is healthy then it has made a profit). Passing the `$movie_takings` and the `$movie_costs` to the function will produce the correct result.

When you define the `$page_start` variable, you start sorting out the actual page structure. By adding the variable `$movie_name`, you can get it displayed in the browser's title bar. You can see now how handy the `=<<<EOD` syntax is becoming.

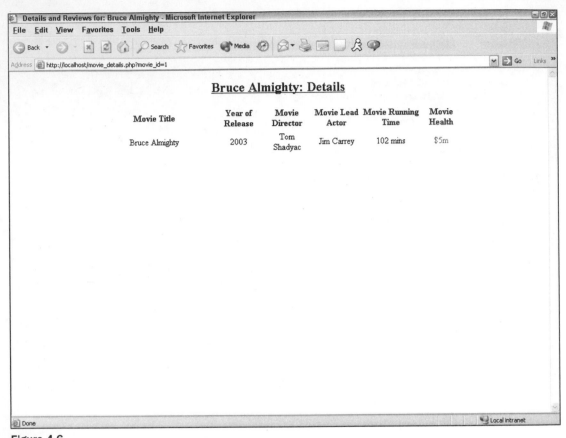

Figure 4-6

Next, you define the $movie_details variable. This should be fairly self-explanatory. Remember the $movie_table_headings variable you created previously? All you've done is slot it into place within the $movie_details variable and, hey presto, it appears.

Finally, you define the $page_end variable and bring it all together in the closing lines.

Phew! That was a lot of code there! Now is a good time to take a break and reward yourself (mine's coffee with milk and two sugars, thanks).

A Lasting Relationship

What if you wanted to find all the reviews for a particular movie? As it stands, you'd need to create a new SQL query in the movies_details.php page and execute it when the page loads, which would make a total of two SQL queries in one page. It would work, but it would not be very efficient. (We're all efficient coders, aren't we?) This also results in unnecessary code.

It's time to answer the question, what's a relationship?

A *relationship* is a way of joining tables so that you can access the data in all those tables. The benefit of MySQL is that it is a relational database and, as such, supports the creation of relationships between tables. When used correctly (this can take a bit of time to get your head around) relationships can be very, very powerful and can be used to retrieve data from many, many tables in one SQL query.

The best way to demonstrate this is to build upon what you have done so far, so let's do it.

Try It Out   Creating and Filling a Movie Review Table

Before you can access movie reviews in your movie review table, you need to create the table and then fill it with data.

1.   Open your text editor and type the following code:

```php
<?php
//connect to MySQL
$connect = mysql_connect("localhost", "bp5am", "bp5ampass")
  or die ("Hey loser, check your server connection.");
mysql_select_db("moviesite");

//create "reviews" table
$reviews = "CREATE TABLE reviews (
  review_movie_id int(11) NOT NULL,
  review_date date NOT NULL,
  review_name varchar(255) NOT NULL,
  review_reviewer_name varchar(255) NOT NULL,
  review_comment varchar(255) NOT NULL,
  review_rating int(11) NOT NULL default 0,
  KEY (review_movie_id)
)";

$results = mysql_query($reviews)
  or die (mysql_error());

//populate the "reviews" table
$insert = "INSERT INTO reviews
    (review_movie_id, review_date, review_name,
    review_reviewer_name, review_comment, review_rating)
  VALUES
    ('1', '2003-08-02', 'This movie rocks!',
    'John Doe','I thought this was a great movie even though
    my girlfriend made me see it against my will.' ,'4'),
    ('1','2003-08-01','An okay movie',
    'Billy Bob','This was an okay movie. I liked Eraserhead
    better.','2'),
    ('1','2003-08-10','Woo hoo!',
    'Peppermint Patty','Wish I\'d have seen it sooner!','5'),
    ('2','2003-08-01','My favorite movie',
    'Marvin Marian','I didn\'t wear my flair to the movie but
    I loved it anyway.','5'),
```

```
    ('3','2003-08-01','An awesome time',
     'George B.','I liked this movie, even though I thought it
     was an informational video from our travel agent.','3')";

$insert_results = mysql_query($insert)
  or die(mysql_error());

?>
```

2. Save this file as `createreviews.php`, upload it to your server, and open it in your browser. Your reviews table has now been created and filled!

How It Works

By now you should be familiar with creating tables using MySQL and PHP, and this should be pretty self-explanatory. If you're having trouble, you might try going back to Chapter 3.

Try It Out   **Querying for the Reviews**

In this example, you're going to link two tables (movies and reviews) to show the reviews for a particular movie. This requires a lot of changes to the `movie_details.php` page, so you'd best make a copy of the file (can't ever be too careful). Then follow these steps:

1. Open `movie_details.php` in your favorite text/HTML editor.

2. Make the following changes to the code (changes are highlighted):

```
$movie_query = "SELECT * FROM movie " .
               "WHERE movie_id ='" . $_GET['movie_id'] . "'";

$movie_result = mysql_query($movie_query, $link)
  or die(mysql_error());
```

And later in the code, change the following:

```
while ($row = mysql_fetch_array($movie_result)) {
    $movie_name = $row['movie_name'];
    $movie_director = $row['movie_director'];
```

3. Add the following lines after the closing bracket of your `while` statement:

```
$review_query = "SELECT * FROM reviews " .
                "WHERE review_movie_id ='" . $_GET['movie_id'] . "' " .
                "ORDER BY review_date DESC";

$review_result = mysql_query($review_query, $link)
  or die(mysql_error());
```

How It Works

You've changed the name of `$query` to `$movie_query`, and also changed `$result` to `$movie_result`. This was done to ensure that you do not confuse yourself when accessing the relevant results set returned from a SQL query. There is also an "order by" clause, which ensures that the most recent reviews are at the top of the page.

A fundamental mistake that a lot of beginners make is to simply use the same variable names when creating SQL queries (for example, $sql = "SELECT ...). Assume that you simply copied and pasted, and then modified the movie query and movie result when it was called query. You'd have two SQL queries called query and two results sets called $result. When the first result ran it would produce the expected results, as would the second one. However, if you ever wanted to refer to the results set that was returned from the first SQL, you'd have a big problem.

Why? The first results set would have been overwritten by the results of the second SQL query. For this reason, always ensure that you use different names for additional SQL queries and results sets returned from the query.

Try It Out   **Displaying the Reviews**

The next chunk of code is the function that allows you to display a cool little graphic for the rating that each film received from the reviewer. We've used one of our images (thumbsup.gif) but you can use anything on your local machine. Just make sure to use your own filename.

1.   Add this code to movie_details.php:

```
function generate_ratings($review_rating) {
  $movie_rating = '';
  for($i=0; $i<$review_rating; $i++) {
    $movie_rating .= "<img src=\"thumbsup.gif\"> ";
  }
  return $movie_rating;
}
```

2.   Now add the code in the following lines immediately below the $movie_table_headings variable:

```
$review_table_headings=<<<EOD
  <tr>
    <th>Date of Review</th>
    <th>Review Title</th>
    <th>Reviewer Name</th>
    <th>Movie Review Comments</th>
    <th>Rating</th>
  </tr>
EOD;
```

3.   You need to add the next few lines after the review table headings section:

```
while($review_row = mysql_fetch_array($review_result)) {
  $review_flag =1;
  $review_title[] = $review_row['review_name'];
  $reviewer_name[] = ucwords($review_row['review_reviewer_name']);
  $review[] = $review_row['review_comment'];
  $review_date[] = $review_row['review_date'];
  $review_rating[] = generate_ratings($review_row['review_rating']);
}
```

4.   Next, you need to add the following lines to the page:

```
$i = 0;
$review_details = '';
while ($i<sizeof($review)) {
  $review_details .=<<<EOD
  <tr>
    <td width="15%" valign="top" align="center">$review_date[$i]</td>
    <td width="15%" valign="top">$review_title[$i]</td>
    <td width="10%" valign="top">$reviewer_name[$i]</td>
    <td width="50%" valign="top">$review[$i]</td>
    <td width="10%" valign="top" align="center">$review_rating[$i]</td>
  </tr>
EOD;
  $i++;
}
```

5. Make the changes as shown here. Go slowly, and ensure that you make all the changes correctly.

```
      <td>$movie_health</td>
    </tr>
  </table>
  <br>
  <br>
EOD;
```

```
if ($review_flag) {
  $movie_details .=<<<EOD
<table width="95%" border="0" cellspacing="2"
      cellpadding="20" align="center">
  $review_table_headings
  $review_details
</table>
EOD;
}
```

6. Save the file as movie_details.php (overwriting the existing one — we hope you have made a backup copy as suggested).

7. Upload to your Web server, load table3.php, and click a movie.

You'll see something similar to Figure 4-7.

How It Works

The generate_ratings function is fairly straightforward. You send it the value that is in the ratings field for a movie and it creates a "rating" image for that movie and returns it. Notice that you are using .= (which is similar to .=<<<). This ensures that movies with a rating of more than 1 will get additional images added to the single rating image.

The $review_table_headings variable contains the table headings for the reviews that you have just pulled out via the previous SQL query. This uses exactly the same concept as the movie table headings in the previous example. So now you have all the review table headings in a nice, neat variable.

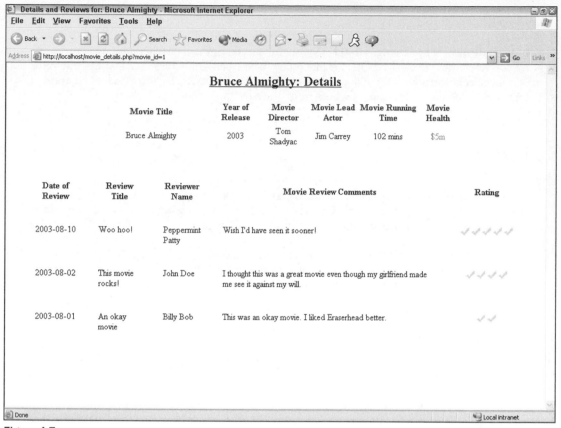

Figure 4-7

While the script is collecting rows of reviews, if there are any reviews for the movie, you set a flag indicating this using the $review_flag variable. The code creates arrays to hold the values that will be returned. Why are you putting them into arrays and not just ordinary variables? This allows the variables to hold data for more than one review for the movie. After all, you expect that there'll be many, many reviews for each film. If you didn't create the review variables as arrays, then you'd return only the last review for the movie. In the previous discussion, we looked at why we preferred to put the field values into a variable rather than echo out the field values. Take a look at the line reviewer_name. You'll notice that we have placed the line $review_row['review_name'] inside the PHP function ucwords. This allows you to automatically perform the ucwords function (which capitalizes the first letter of each word) on the value returned from that field.

The code then loops through the array and assigns values to each of the fields that you are going to display to the user for the review. You use the PHP sizeof function to calculate how many records have been returned.

Finally, you've broken the $movie_details variable up into several smaller chunks and added them through the use of .=<<<. Just as you have done before, you used an already-defined variable (in this case, $review_table_headings and $review_details) and just slotted it into the correct place. If the review flag has been set, then you'll see the items that make up the reviews (review table headings and the reviews).

You've made quite a few changes in this section. But as you can see, the changes have been well worth it. Now you know how to use MySQL to create relationships between tables. You successfully retrieved all the reviews from the review table depending on the `movie_id` variable. You also looked at using the `$_GET` super global variable to pass values from one page to another.

Summary

You've learned how to work with HTML tables to display your data, how to pull data from more than one database table and have it displayed seamlessly with data from another table, and how to create dynamic pages that display detailed information about the rows in your database. You should also be able to include those nifty little images to graphically display data to your Web site visitors.

So far, you've hard-coded all the additions to the database yourself, which isn't very dynamic. We'll teach you how to let the user add items to the database and edit them later in Chapter 6, but first, you need to know how to use forms with PHP, which is the subject of Chapter 5.

Exercises

1. Add a column in the top table of your `movie_details.php` file that shows the average rating given by reviewers.

2. Change each column heading of the review table in your `movie_details.php` file to a link that allows the user to sort by that column (i.e., the user would click on "Date of Review" to sort all the reviews by date).

3. Alternate the background colors of each row in the review table of your `movie_details.php` file to make them easier to read. *Hint:* Odd-numbered rows would have a background of one color, even-numbered rows would have a background of another color; check each row number to see if it is divisible by 2 to determine if it is even or odd.

Form Elements: Letting the User Work with Data

An interactive Web site requires user input, which is generally gathered through forms. As in the paper-based world, the user fills in a form and submits its content for processing. In a Web application, the processing is performed by a PHP script, not a sentient being. Hence, the script requires coded intelligence.

When you fill in a paper form, you generally use a means to deliver its content (for example, the postal service) to a known address (such as a mail-order bookstore). The same logic applies to online forms. An HTML form is sent to a specific location and processed.

In HTML, the form element is rather simple; it states where and how it will send the contents of the elements it contains once submitted. At this point, PHP comes into play. Your PHP script receives the data from the form and uses it to perform an action, such as updating the contents of a database, sending an e-mail, testing the data format, and so on.

PHP uses a set of simple yet powerful expressions that, once combined, provide you with the means to do virtually anything you want.

In this chapter, you begin to build a simple application that allows you to add, edit, or delete members of a data set (in this instance, movies, actors, and directors). This chapter welcomes you into a world of PHP/MySQL interaction by covering the following:

- ❑ Creating forms using buttons, text boxes, and other form elements
- ❑ Creating PHP scripts to process HTML forms
- ❑ Mastering $_POST and $_GET to retrieve data
- ❑ Passing hidden information to the form processing script via hidden form controls and a URL query string

Your First Form

As a wise man once said, every journey starts with a single step. To start this particular journey, you will focus on a very simple form. It will include only a text field and a submit button in a table layout. The processing script will display only the value entered in the text field.

Try It Out   Say My Name

In this exercise, you are going to get PHP to respond to a name entered in a form. This is a simple variation of the typical "hello world" program, allowing you to take your first step into interactivity.

1.   Create a text file named `form1.html` and open it in your favorite text editor.

2.   Enter the following code:

```html
<html>
<head>
<title>Say My Name</title>
<style type="text/css">
TD{color:#353535;font-family:verdana}
TH{color:#FFFFFF;font-family:verdana;background-color:#336699}
</style>
</head>
<body>
<form action="formprocess1.php" method="post">
<table border="0" cellspacing="1" cellpadding="3"
        bgcolor="#353535" align="center">
  <tr>
    <td bgcolor="#FFFFFF" width="50%">Name</td>
    <td bgcolor="#FFFFFF" width="50%">
      <input type="text" name="Name"><br>
    </td>
  </tr>
  <tr>
    <td bgcolor="#FFFFFF" colspan="2" align="center">
      <input type="submit" name="SUBMIT" value="Submit">
    </td>
  </tr>
</table>
</form>
</body>
</html>
```

3.   Create another empty file named `formprocess1.php` and enter the following code:

```php
<html>
<head>
<title>Say My Name</title>
</head>
<body>
<?php
  echo "Hello " . $_POST['Name'];
```

```
?>
<pre>
  DEBUG :
<?php
  print_r($_POST);
?>
</pre>
</body>
</html>
```

4. Upload the files to your Apache work directory.

5. Open form1.html in your browser.

6. Type **test** in the name text box (as shown in Figure 5-1) and click the Submit button.

You can see two distinct parts on the resulting page: the "Hello Test" portion and the DEBUG part shown in Figure 5-2.

You just coded your first form processing script.

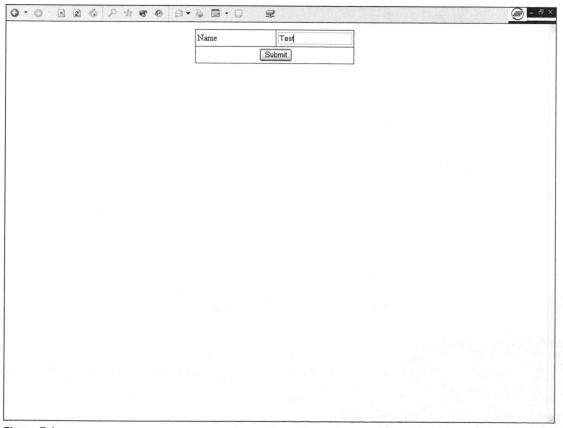

Figure 5-1

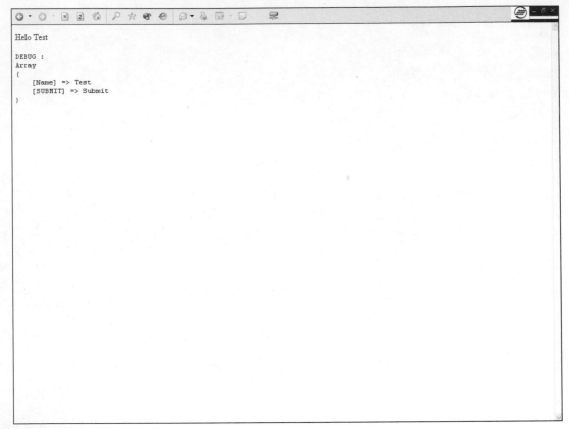

Figure 5-2

How It Works

As with any recipe, it's a good idea to start working on forms by understanding the ingredients. To familiarize yourself with forms, you'll need some background information about HTML form elements and a few new PHP functions.

Let's start with the HTML form itself.

You can find HTML references at the World Wide Web Consortium Web site at www.w3.org/MarkUp.

FORM Element

First, we'll introduce the first HTML element you'll need: FORM. It delimits the form area in the page and holds the fields you want your Web site users to fill in.

```
<form action="formprocess1.php" method="post">
<!--form controls here-->
</form>
```

Notice that the FORM element has an ending tag and two attributes. The first attribute (action) is the recipient page address (the form processing script). The second attribute (method) is the way in which you will send the data to the recipient. There are two separate ways of sending a form to its processing script: the POST and the GET methods.

The POST method (see Figure 5-3) takes the data from the form fields and sends it through an HTTP header. In this case, the data cannot be seen in the URL.

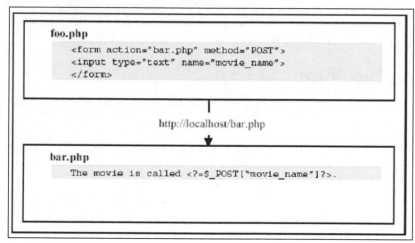

Figure 5-3

The GET method gets the data from the form fields, encodes it, and adds it to the destination URL, as shown here:

```
http://localhost/formprocess1.php?field1=valuea&field2=value%20b
```

As you can see, the field names and their values are easy to read inside the script URL. Having the script parameters in the URL allows the user to change them manually. This can lead to errors in the script processing or access to data not originally meant to be accessed.

INPUT Element

The second new HTML element included here is INPUT. This is the basis of most forms and can be used in many different ways to gather many different types of information. In this case, you use two different types of INPUT: the text and submit types.

Here's the INPUT TEXT type:

```
<input type="text" name="Name">
```

The INPUT text type is a standard, single-line text box. As with all form controls, it needs a name so that the processing script can access its content using the following syntax:

```
<?php
  echo $_POST['Name']; // will display the value typed in
?>
```

And here's the INPUT submit type:

```
<input type="submit" name="SUBMIT" value="Submit">
```

As its name cleverly hints, the submit element displays a button that, when pressed, submits the form. The button text is set through the value attribute. As mentioned for the text INPUT, this form control needs a name for a processing reference.

Processing the Form

In this little script, you may have noticed a few new functions and syntaxes, and you are probably curious about them.

The first form processing script is an interactive variation of the famous "hello world," but in this case it displays "hello" and the name you type in the text box. To make this happen, you need to print the value of the text field you filled in on the form. You know the echo command, so let's move on to the other piece, $_POST['Name'].

The $_POST global array contains all form data submitted with the POST method. The array index of the field is its name. In a moment you'll see how to check the content of your $_POST array using the print_r() function.

```
<?php
  echo "Hello " . $_POST['Name'];
?>
```

In this example, $_POST['name'] displays what you entered in the "Name" box.

```
Hello test
```

You might wonder what print_r($_POST) does. It simply dumps the whole contents of the super global $_POST array to the output. This is a great way to debug your forms.

The $_POST array, as with all arrays, has case-sensitive indexes. Use this tip to check for case and display the state of your objects when building a script.

Your formprocess1.php script outputs something similar to the following:

```
Hello test
DEBUG :
Array
(
    [Name] => test
    [SUBMIT] => Submit
)
```

When receiving the submitted form, PHP sets the POST array with the data that the form sends. As with any array, you can directly access any of the indexes by name. In this instance, you can clearly see that the Name index contains the value test. This trick works for all forms, even the most complicated ones.

Let's move on to see how you can use more HTML elements during form input to interact with the user.

Driving the User Input

The form in this example allows you to lead the user to choose values from a set of values you provide. Defining a value set is done through the use of specific HTML elements, such as list boxes, radio buttons, and checkboxes.

Two kinds of predefined user input are in HTML forms. The first kind allows you to choose one item from the available options; the second allows the user to choose multiple items. Drop-down list boxes and radio buttons allow for one selection only. Checkboxes and multiline list boxes provide for multiple choices.

Try It Out   Limiting the Input Choice

Let's start with the simple type of input. Follow these steps to create a single selection list:

1. Create a text file named form2.html and open it in your favorite text editor.

2. Enter the following code:

```
<html>
<head>
<title>Greetings Earthling</title>
<style type="text/css">
TD{color:#353535;font-family:verdana}
TH{color:#FFFFFF;font-family:verdana;background-color:#336699}
</style>
</head>
<body>
<form action="formprocess2.php" method="post">
<table border="0" cellspacing="1" cellpadding="3"
      bgcolor="#353535" align="center">
  <tr>
    <td bgcolor="#FFFFFF" width="50%">Name</td>
    <td bgcolor="#FFFFFF" width="50%">
      <input type="text" name="Name">
    </td>
  </tr>
  <tr>
    <td bgcolor="#FFFFFF">Greetings</td>
    <td bgcolor="#FFFFFF">
      <select name="Greeting">
        <option value="Hello">Hello</option>
        <option value="Hola">Hola</option>
        <option value="Bonjour">Bonjour</option>
      </select>
```

```
        </td>
      </tr>
      <tr>
        <td bgcolor="#FFFFFF" width="50%">Display Debug info</td>
        <td bgcolor="#FFFFFF" width="50%">
          <input type="checkbox" name="Debug" checked>
        </td>
      </tr>
      <tr>
        <td bgcolor="#FFFFFF" colspan=2 align="center">
          <input type="submit" name="SUBMIT" value="Submit">
        </td>
      </tr>
    </table>
  </form>
</body>
</html>
```

3. Create another empty file named `formprocess2.php` and enter the following code:

```
<html>
<head>
<title>Greetings Earthling</title>
<style type="text/css">
TD{color:#353535;font-family:verdana}
TH{color:#FFFFFF;font-family:verdana;background-color:#336699}
</style>
</head>
<body>
<?php
  if (isset($_POST['Debug']) and $_POST['Debug'] == "on") {
?>
<pre>
<?php
    print_r($_POST);
?>
</pre>
<?php
  }
?>

<p align="center"><?php echo $_POST['Greeting']; ?>
<?php echo $_POST['Name']; ?></p>
</body>
</html>
```

4. Save `formprocess2.php` and upload it to your work folder.

5. Call the page from your browser. As you can see from the resulting page, displayed in Figure 5-4, the form got a bit more complicated.

6. Enter your name and click the Submit button. The display page that appears, shown in Figure 5-5, is rather simple; it holds only debug information and a greeting.

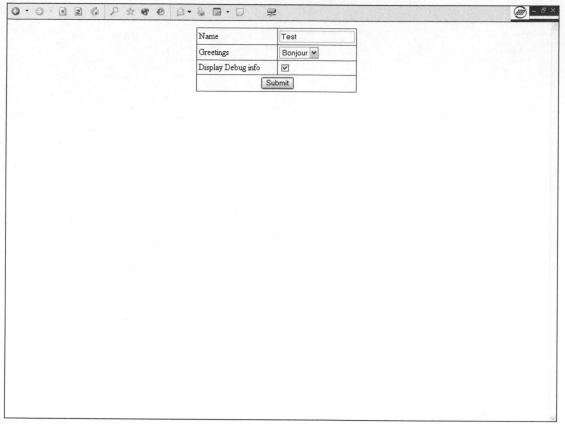

Figure 5-4

How It Works

As you see, this code uses logic similar to that in formprocess1.php. Two fields have been added (a drop-down list box and a checkbox).

formprocess2.php does the same thing as formprocess1.php but with an added twist. It displays the debugging information only if the Debug checkbox is selected and greets you using any of the drop-down list choices in the subsections that follow.

INPUT Checkbox Type

The checkbox can represent only two possibilities: When checked, it passes the value on to the $_POST array, but otherwise it just doesn't send anything. This is a great way to represent Boolean typed data.

```
    *    SELECT element
<select name="Greeting">
  <option value="Hello">Hello</option>
  <option value="Hola">Hola</option>
  <option value="Bonjour">Bonjour</option>
</select>
```

Figure 5-5

The SELECT element (also known as list) allows you to display a fixed list of choices from which the user has to choose an element. The item selected won't be sent as displayed but will be sent as its value. In this example, the value and its display are identical, but in a database-driven system you would probably see record IDs as the values and their text label as list choices. A good example is a product number and its name.

When using lists, be sure to set the value part of the OPTION items. If these are not set, the list looks the same but is totally useless because all choices will send the same null value.

One Form, Multiple Processing

Forms always react in a predefined way based on how you code your processing script to handle the data that the user sends to the system. A single form can have more than one defined action by using different submit buttons.

Radio Button, Multiline List Boxes

In the following example, you create a form that prepares a search and creates a movie/actor/director interface.

1. Create a text file named `form3.php` and open it in your text editor. Then type the following code:

```html
<html>
<head>
<title>Add/Search Entry</title>
<style type="text/css">
TD{color:#353535;font-family:verdana}
TH{color:#FFFFFF;font-family:verdana;background-color:#336699}
</style>
</head>
<body>
<form action="formprocess3.php" method="post">
<table border="0" cellspacing="1" cellpadding="3"
      bgcolor="#353535" align="center">
  <tr>
    <td bgcolor="#FFFFFF" width="50%">Name</td>
    <td bgcolor="#FFFFFF" width="50%">
      <input type="text" name="Name">
    </td>
  </tr>
  <tr>
    <td bgcolor="#FFFFFF">What you are looking for</td>
    <td bgcolor="#FFFFFF">
      <select name="MovieType">
        <option value="" selected>Select a movie type...</option>
        <option value="Action">Action</option>
        <option value="Drama">Drama</option>
        <option value="Comedy">Comedy</option>
        <option value="Sci-Fi">Sci-Fi</option>
        <option value="War">War</option>
        <option value="Other">Other...</option>
      </select>
    </td>
  </tr>
  <tr>
    <td bgcolor="#FFFFFF">Add what?</td>
    <td bgcolor="#FFFFFF">
      <input type="radio" name="type" value="Movie" checked>
      Movie<br>
      <input type="radio" name="type" value="Actor">
      Actor<br>
      <input type="radio" name="type" value="Director">
      Director<br>
    </td>
  </tr>
  <tr>
    <td bgcolor="#FFFFFF" width="50%">Display Debug info</td>
    <td bgcolor="#FFFFFF" width="50%">
```

```
        <input type="checkbox" name="Debug" checked>
      </td>
    </tr>
    <tr>
      <td bgcolor="#FFFFFF" colspan=2 align="center">
        <input type="submit" name="Submit" value="Search">
        <input type="submit" name="Submit" value="Add">
      </td>
    </tr>
  </table>
  </form>
  </body>
  </html>
```

2.   Create another file named `formprocess3.php` and edit it to add the following code:

```php
<?php
if ($_POST['type'] == "Movie" && $_POST['MovieType'] == "") {
  header("Location:form3.php");
}
$title = $_POST['Submit'] . " " .
         $_POST['type'] . " : " .
         $_POST['Name'];
?>
<html>
<head>
<title><?php echo $title; ?></title>
</head>
<body>
<?php
  if ($_POST['Debug'] == "on") {
?>
<pre>
<?php
    print_r($_POST);
?>
</pre>
<?php
  }
  $name = $_POST['Name'];
  $name[0] = strtoupper($name[0]);
  if ($_POST['type'] == "Movie") {
    $foo = $_POST['MovieType'] . " " . $_POST['type'];
  } else {
    $foo = $_POST['type'];
  }
?>

<p align="center">
  You are <?php echo $_POST['Submit']; ?>ing
  <?php echo $_POST['Submit'] == "Search" ? "for " : ""; ?>
  a <?php echo $foo ?>
  named "<?php echo $name; ?>"
</p>
</body>
</html>
```

3. Start your browser and open `http://localhost/form3.php`. The form shown in Figure 5-6 appears. Notice that the form has two submit buttons. One is labeled Search, the other Add.

4. Type **Kevin Kline** in the Name field.

5. Leave `Movie Type` as is; then move on to the `Item Type` field, in which you'll select Actor.

6. Clear the Display Debug Dump checkbox if you like; then click the Search button. The results appear, as shown in Figure 5-7.

7. Now play around a bit with the form. Look at the output and how it changes when you modify the data.

How It Works

You just coded a simple form with two possible actions. Depending on the button you click and the data you choose to enter, this code outputs different information.

What's new in the form page itself? A group of radio buttons and a new submit button have been added. Let's have a closer look at these.

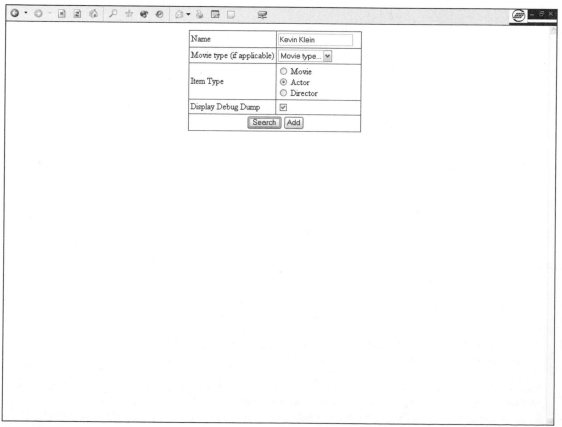

Figure 5-6

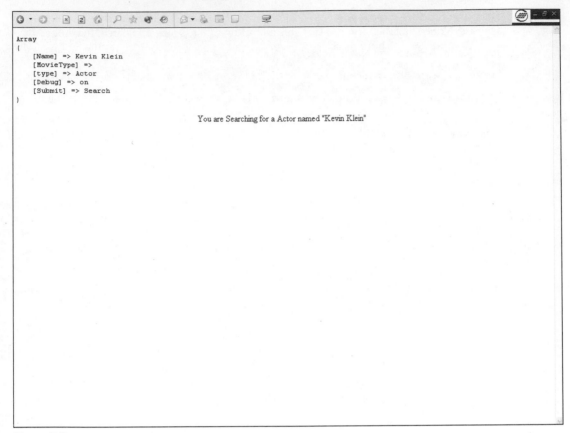

```
Array
(
    [Name] => Kevin Klein
    [MovieType] =>
    [type] => Actor
    [Debug] => on
    [Submit] => Search
)
```

You are Searching for a Actor named "Kevin Klein"

Figure 5-7

Radio INPUT Element

The radio button is a very simple element. By default, if no radio button is specified as CHECKED, no default choice is made. Always remember that choosing the default value is a very important part of building a form. Users often leave defaults in forms. (It is a form of laziness, so to speak.)

```
<input type="radio" name="type" value="Movie" checked>
Movie<br>
<input type="radio" name="type" value="Actor">
Actor<br>
<input type="radio" name="type" value="Director">
Director<br>
```

For multiple radio buttons to be linked together to form a group and be processed as a single form element, they need to share the same name and different values (quite obviously). In the preceding code, the name is always type. This tells the browser that selecting one of the radio buttons clears the others.

Multiple Submit Buttons

As with radio buttons, submit buttons share the same name with a different value. Clicking one of these buttons simply submits the form.

```
<input type="submit" name="Submit" value="Search">
<input type="submit" name="Submit" value="Add">
```

As you can see in the DEBUG block, the submit button sends its own information to the script. You can access the submit button value through the $_POST['Submit'] array.

Basic Input Testing

What about the processing script? What's new in there?

The following code checks that the item type is Movie, and, if it is, it checks that the user has selected a valid movie type from the list. If he or she has not, he or she is redirected to the form page.

The test is a simple if with an and operator. (In simple Monopoly parlance, if the item type is movie and the movie type is not specified, you go back to square one and you do not collect $200.)

```
if ($_POST['type'] == "Movie" && $_POST['MovieType'] == "") {
  header("Location:form3.php");
}
```

The header function allows you to send a raw HTTP header. It is useful for handling security problems and access restrictions. In this instance it redirects the user to the specified page.

A very common error with beginning PHP users is that they fail to understand a very simple fact: Once sent, the headers cannot be sent again. This means that any echo, any space, any tabulation left before the call to the header function will trigger a warning in the script execution. Here are a few typical errors:

```
<?php
header("Location:form3.php");
?>
```

This code will fail. The empty line starting the script will send the headers with a carriage return and a line feed (depending on the operating system).

```
<?php
echo "foobar";
header("Location:form3.php");
?>
```

This code will fail. The echo function will send the headers with the text "foobar".

Dynamic Page Title

This code is rather simple to understand: You don't start outputting as soon as you start executing the PHP script. What often happens is that at the start of the scripts there will be a check for intrusion and context verification. In this instance, you don't have that sort of complex verification code, but you do dynamically set the page title using the action type and item type you will use to handle the page.

149

```
$title = $_POST['Submit'] . " " .
         $_POST['type'] . " : " .
         $_POST['Name'];
?>
<html>
<head>
<title><?php echo $title; ?></title>
```

Manipulating a String as an Array to Change the Case of the First Character

Single string characters can be accessed through a very simple syntax that is similar to array index access. Specify the index of the character you want to access and voilà! To change the case of a character or an entire string, use the strtoupper() function:

```
$name = $_POST['Name'];
$name[0] = strtoupper( $name[0]);
```

You could have used the ucfirst() *function (which essentially does what this code did), but a bit of creativity can't hurt.*

Ternary Operator

This line holds a ternary comparison operation. Ternary operators are not PHP-specific; many other languages, such as C, use them.

```
<?php echo $_POST['Submit'] == "Search" ? "for " : ""; ?>
```

These work in a very simple way and can be compared to an if-else structure:

```
[expression]?[execute if TRUE]: [execute if FALSE];
```

The ternary operator is a known maintainability hazard. Using this operator will make your code less readable and will probably cause errors during maintenance stages.

Using Form Elements Together

Now that you know most of the form elements, let's create a skeleton for the movie application. The system will add new items or search for existing ones. Database interaction is covered in Chapter 6, however, so for now you'll just build the forms and echo the results to the screen.

Try It Out Bonding It All Together

In this exercise, you'll create several new scripts that work together to simulate allowing the user to add information to the database.

1.   Create a file named form4.php and open it in your text editor.

2.   Enter the following code:

```php
<?php
// Debug info Display
function debugDisplay() {
?>
<pre>
$_POST
<?php
  print_r($_POST);
?>
$_GET
<?php
  print_r($_GET);
?>
</pre>
<?php
}

if (!isset($_GET['step'])) {
  require('startform.php');
} else {

// Switch on search/add wizard step
switch ($_GET['step']) {
// ################
//  Search/Add form
// ################
  case "1":
    $type = explode(":", $_POST['type']);
    if ($_POST['Submit'] == "Add") {
      require($_POST['Submit'] . $type[0] . '.php');
    } else {
      if ($_POST['type'] == "Movie:Movie" &&
          $_POST['MovieType'] == ""){
        header("Location:form4.php");
      }
?>
<h1>Search Results</h1>
<p>You are looking for a "<?php echo $type[1]; ?>" named
"<?php echo $_POST['Name']; ?>"</p>
<?php
    }
    if ($_POST['Debug'] == "on") {
      debugDisplay();
    }
    break;
// ################
//  Add Summary
// ################
  case "2":
    $type = explode(":", $_POST['type']);
?>
<h1>New <?php echo $type[1]; ?> : <?php echo $_POST['Name']; ?></h1>
<?php
    switch ($type[0]) {
      case "Movie":
```

```
?>
<p>Released in <?php echo $_POST['MovieYear']; ?></p>
<p><?php echo nl2br(stripslashes($_POST['Desc'])); ?></p>
<?php
        break;
      default:
?>
<h2>Quick Bio</h2>
<p><?php echo nl2br(stripslashes($_POST['Bio'])); ?></p>
<?php
        break;
    }
    break;
// ##############
//  Starting form
// ##############
  default:
    require('startform.php');
    break;
}

}
?>
```

3. Create a new file called `startform.php` and enter the following code:

```
<html>
<head>
<title>Multipurpose Form</title>
<style type="text/css">
TD{color:#353535;font-family:verdana}
TH{color:#FFFFFF;font-family:verdana;background-color:#336699}
</style>
</head>
<body>
<form action="form4.php?step=1" method="post">
<table border="0" width="750" cellspacing="1" cellpadding="3"
       bgcolor="#353535" align="center">
  <tr>
    <td bgcolor="#FFFFFF" width="30%">Name</td>
    <td bgcolor="#FFFFFF" width="70%">
      <input type="TEXT" name="Name">
    </td>
  </tr>
  <tr>
    <td bgcolor="#FFFFFF">Item Type</td>
    <td bgcolor="#FFFFFF">
      <input type="radio" name="type" value="Movie:Movie" checked>
      Movie<br>
      <input type="radio" name="type" value="Person:Actor">
      Actor<br>
      <input type="radio" name="type" value="Person:Director">
      Director<br>
    </td>
```

```
      </tr>
      <tr>
        <td bgcolor="#FFFFFF">Movie type (if applicable)</td>
        <td bgcolor="#FFFFFF">
          <select name="MovieType">
            <option value="" selected>Movie type...</option>
            <option value="Action">Action</option>
            <option value="Drama">Drama</option>
            <option value="Comedy">Comedy</option>
            <option value="Sci-Fi">Sci-Fi</option>
            <option value="War">War</option>
            <option value="Other">Other...</option>
          </select>
        </td>
      </tr>
      <tr>
        <td bgcolor="#FFFFFF" width="50%">Display Debug Dump</td>
        <td bgcolor="#FFFFFF" width="50%">
          <input type="checkbox" name="Debug" checked>
        </td>
      </tr>
      <tr>
        <td bgcolor="#FFFFFF" colspan=2 align="center">
          <input type="submit" name="Submit" value="Search">
          <input type="submit" name="Submit" value="Add">
        </td>
      </tr>
    </table>
  </form>
</body>
</html>
```

4. Create another new, empty file named AddMovie.php, in which you will add this code:

```php
<?php
if ($_POST['type'] == "Movie:Movie" &&
    $_POST['MovieType'] == "") {
  header("Location:form4.php");
}
$title = $_POST['Submit'] . " " .
         $_POST['type'] . " : " .
         $_POST['Name'];
$name = $_POST['Name'];
$name[0] = strtoupper($name[0]);
?>
<html>
<head>
<title><?php echo $title; ?></title>
<style type="text/css">
TD{color:#353535;font-family:verdana}
TH{color:#FFFFFF;font-family:verdana;background-color:#336699}
</style>
</head>
<body>
```

```php
<form action="form4.php?step=2" method="post">
<input type="hidden" name="type" value="<?php echo $type[1]; ?>">
<input type="hidden" name="action"
  value="<?php echo $_POST['Submit']; ?>">
<table border="0" width="750" cellspacing="1" cellpadding="3"
       bgcolor="#353535" align="center">
  <tr>
    <td bgcolor="#FFFFFF" width="30%">Movie Name</td>
    <td bgcolor="#FFFFFF" width="70%">
      <?php echo $name; ?>
      <input type="hidden" name="Name" value="<?php echo $name; ?>">
    </td>
  </tr>
  <tr>
    <td bgcolor="#FFFFFF">Movie Type</td>
    <td bgcolor="#FFFFFF">
      <?php echo $_POST['MovieType']?><br>
      <input type="hidden" name="type"
        value="Movie: <?php echo $_POST['MovieType']; ?>">
    </td>
  </tr>
  <tr>
    <td bgcolor="#FFFFFF">Movie Year</td>
    <td bgcolor="#FFFFFF">
      <select name="MovieYear">
        <option value="" selected>Select a year...</option>
<?php
for ($year=date("Y"); $year >= 1970 ;$year--) {
?>
        <option value="<?php echo $year; ?>"><?php
        echo $year; ?></option>
<?php
}
?>
      </select>
    </td>
  </tr>
  <tr>
    <td bgcolor="#FFFFFF">Movie Description</td>
    <td bgcolor="#FFFFFF">
      <textarea name="Desc" rows="5" cols="60"></textarea>
    </td>
  </tr>
  <tr>
    <td bgcolor="#FFFFFF" colspan="2" align="center">
      <input type="submit" name="SUBMIT" value="Add">
    </td>
  </tr>
</table>
</form>
</body>
</html>
```

5.   Create a file named `AddPerson.php` and enter the following code:

```php
<?php
$title = $_POST['Submit'] . " " .
         $_POST['type'] . " : " .
         $_POST['Name'];
$name = $_POST['Name'];
$name[0] = strtoupper($name[0]);
?>
<html>
<head>
<title><?php echo $title; ?></title>
<style type="text/css">
TD{color:#353535;font-family:verdana}
TH{color:#FFFFFF;font-family:verdana;background-color:#336699}
</style>
</head>
<body>
<form action="form4.php?step=2" method="post">
<input type="hidden" name="type"
  value="Person: <?php echo $type[1]; ?>">
<input type="hidden" name="action"
  value="<?php echo $_POST['Submit']; ?>">
<table border="0" width="750" cellspacing="1" cellpadding="3"
       bgcolor="#353535" align="center">
  <tr>
    <td bgcolor="#FFFFFF" width="30%">
      <?php echo $type[1]; ?> Name
    </td>
    <td bgcolor="#FFFFFF" width="70%">
      <?php echo $name?>
      <input type="hidden" name="Name" value="<?php echo $name; ?>">
    </td>
  </tr>
  <tr>
    <td bgcolor="#FFFFFF">Quick Bio</td>
    <td bgcolor="#FFFFFF">
      <textarea name="Bio" rows="5" cols="60"></textarea>
    </td>
  </tr>
  <tr>
    <td bgcolor="#FFFFFF" colspan="2" align="center">
      <input type="submit" name="SUBMIT" value="Add">
    </td>
  </tr>
</table>
</form>
</body>
</html>
```

6.   Upload the files to your Apache server and launch a browser, entering the address `http://localhost/chapter5/form4.php` (adapt this URL to your setup). A new form, shown in Figure 5-8, pops up, asking for more details.

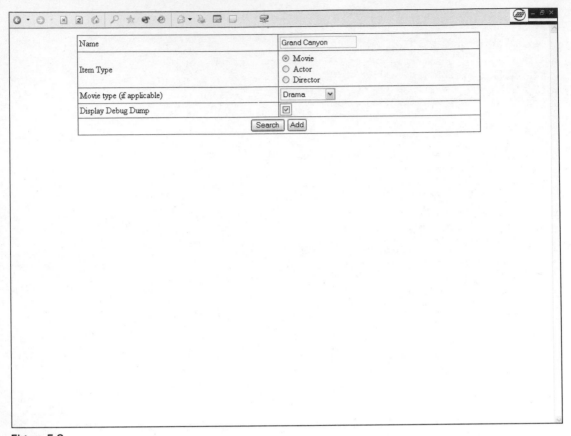

Figure 5-8

7. Enter the name of the movie you want to add: "Grand Canyon."

8. Click the Add button; this takes you to the add form shown in Figure 5-9.

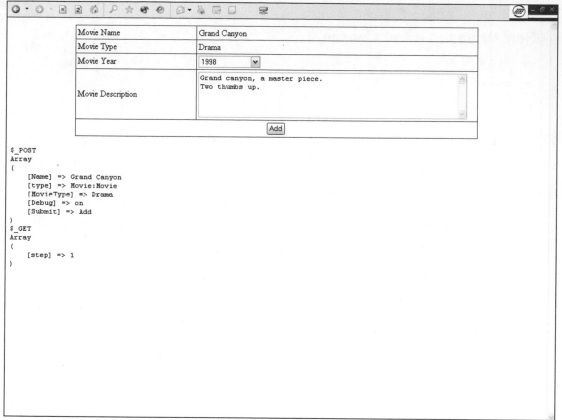

Figure 5-9

9. Select a date for the year the movie was made (1991, if memory serves).

10. Select Drama in the Movie type list.

11. Type a quick movie description, making sure you enter multiple lines, and press the Enter key between them.

12. Click the Add button and see how the information is displayed (see Figure 5-10).

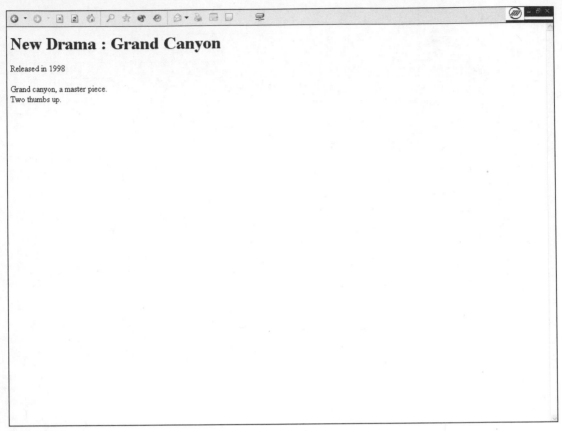

Figure 5-10

How It Works

This script is designed around a simple idea: one skeleton script (`form4.php`) and multiple flesh-and-muscle scripts doing the job under one URL with query strings.

This raises a question, however: Why use one skeleton script and multiple flesh-and-muscle scripts? One word: maintainability. One of the things most beginners never think about when they start a new language is maintainability. It is a very common error that most people regret.

Suppose that you have a site you made in the month after reading this book and you made a darn good job of it for a first site. Six months later you've learned a lot and want to improve this site.

At this very moment, the full force of chaos theory hits you square in the face: You can't read your code anymore. How unfortunate. The goal now is to help you to separate things out in such a way that, when you come back to your code in six months, you won't have to start from scratch (which, trust me, happens to most of us).

So, let's get back to work. How does this thing work, anyway? We discuss the elements you must decipher in the sections that follow.

The Skeleton Script

The skeleton here is the `form4.php` script. It all revolves around a use of the switch case structure. It starts with a function definition for the debug display (which now holds the display of the $_GET super global array).

The trick resides in the fact that the forms will use the POST methods and thus transmit their information through the $_POST array; the actual page content switching will be made through query strings passed through the $_GET array.

Each step in the building of the data is guided by the $_GET['step'] index value. It holds the information passed on by the ?step=1 part of the URL.

Each value of the step GET parameter has a specific script attached to it. This parameter tells the main script (index.php) where to branch to process the data received.

Default Response

What happens when you call the page the first time and the step URL parameter is not set? Logically enough, the script evaluates the switch condition and finds that it doesn't match any of the specified cases, so it executes the default behavior:

```
switch ($_GET['step']) {
...
  default:
    require('startform.php');
    break;
}
```

The `require()` function gets the content of the file that is specified and includes it in the script at interpretation time. The `require()` function differs from the `include()` in that it triggers a fatal error instead of a warning if the file is not found. In this instance, not having the `startform.php` script would slightly reduce your script's functionality, so you want to know if it doesn't find the file.

Adding Items

You need two different forms to add an item, depending on whether the user adds a person or a movie (at least if you consider that you store the same data in the database for the actors and directors). So you need a second branching (the first branching being the step switch) to determine which form will be displayed.

Now we hit a part of the script in which there is a little trick. The list item value is used to store two values instead of one. The trick is to use a separator and then to explode the value into an array and access the piece you need (the `explode()` function takes each bit of text delimited by the separator and inserts it as new array elements). Let's take a closer look.

In this case you have three types of items (Actors, Directors, and Movies), each of which requires a form to create. But you have decided that, so far, an Actor item and a Director item hold the same information. So you don't need two different forms, just one. You handle this by adding a tree structure level above the item level, Person or Movie. Under Person you include the Actor and Director level. The whole point is to be able to use the new hierarchy level name to name the file so that the including is automatic and you can add new levels later without too much effort.

In startform.php you have:

```
<input type="radio" name="type" value="Person:Actor">
Actor<br>
```

Note that the value part of the type element is composed of two different values, separated by a semicolon.

In form4.php you have:

```
...
$type = explode(":", $_POST['type']);
if ($_POST['Submit'] == "Add") {
  require($_POST['Submit'] . $type[0] . '.php');
}
...
```

In this script, you retrieve the type element value using the $_POST['type'] array index and then use the explode() function on its content. The explode() function is fairly easy to use; it just needs a string that specifies the delimiter and a string that holds the text to be exploded.

For example, you have "Person:Actor" as the value to explode and a colon (:) as the delimiter. The resulting $type variable will be an array holding the pieces of the string cut at each instance of the semicolon. If you represent it in the print_r format, you have:

```
Array
(
    [0] => Person
    [1] => Actor
)
```

The goal of having simple filenames inclusion is achieved. You have two Add scripts, and one name: AddPerson.php and AddMovie.php.

```
require($_POST['Submit'] . $type[0] . '.php');
```

This line recomposes your filenames automatically.

Summary

You've learned a lot of about forms in this chapter. Forms are composed of fields. Each field type has a specific purpose and allows a certain data type to be entered. Text fields can be used to enter text or numeric data. Lists can be used to enter any type of data and have a limited set of possible values. Lists are a good way to drive user input when multiple choices are available.

Forms are processed by the PHP script using the super global array $_GET and $_POST, which is a sub-array of $_QUERY. Each super global array has its use, as you saw, and contributes to making your script access the form data.

Exercises

See how you might accomplish the following:

1. Create a form and a processing page that let you choose a rating (stars, thumbs up, # out of 5, whatever), and provide comments for a movie.

2. Create a form with several text input boxes that allow you to populate the options of a select field on a subsequent page.

3. Create a calculator form that takes two numbers and calculates their sum.

Letting the User Edit the Database

Retrieving data from a database is all well and good when you've fed the database some data. But databases don't generate their own contents, and only a few get fed data by other systems, such as integrated systems. That means you have to feed your system with data that comes from PHP.

All database interaction is based on SQL (you will one day encounter XML and other sources, but let's not go there now). You know the basic SQL syntax to get data from a table; now let's look at the other side of the equation.

Most people use SQL to insert data that PHP modifies or generates. You will try a slightly different approach and let SQL do its thing, data processing.

This chapter covers database editing, including:

- ❑ Adding entries, which is quite simple, but you will find that adding entries in a relational database is yet another exercise
- ❑ Deleting entries without corrupting the database structure and referential integrity
- ❑ Modifying entries to replace some existing fields with new content in an existing record

Preparing the Battlefield

This may sound a bit Vulcan, but if you want to manage a database, the first logical thing to do is to create one. To save time, let's use an existing database to avoid any problems in the coming exercises. Create a new empty database in phpMyAdmin named moviesite. In the newborn database, execute the chapter6.mysql script (available at www.wrox.com), which holds the database definition and its start data.

Try It Out   Setting Up the Environment

First, you need a start page. Follow these steps to create one:

1. Create a new directory called `chap6` under your `htdocs` (or create an alias, if you wish).

2. Create an `index.php` script and enter the following code:

```php
<?php
  $link = mysql_connect("localhost", "bp5am", "bp5ampass")
    or die("Could not connect: " . mysql_error());
  mysql_select_db('moviesite', $link)
    or die(mysql_error());
?>
<html>
<head>
<title>Movie database</title>
<style type="text/css">
TD{color:#353535;font-family:verdana}
TH{color:#FFFFFF;font-family:verdana;background-color:#336699}
</style>
</head>
<body>
<table border="0" width="600" cellspacing="1" cellpadding="3"
       bgcolor="#353535" align="center">
  <tr>
    <td bgcolor="#FFFFFF" colspan="2" align="center">
      Movies <a href="movie.php?action=add&id=">[ADD]</a>
    </td>
  </tr>
<?php
  $moviesql = "SELECT * FROM movie";
  $result = mysql_query($moviesql)
    or die("Invalid query: " . mysql_error());
  while ($row = mysql_fetch_array($result)) {
?>
  <tr>
    <td bgcolor="#FFFFFF" width="50%">
      <?php echo $row['movie_name']; ?>
    </td>
    <td bgcolor="#FFFFFF" width="50%" align="right">
      <a href="movie.php?action=edit&id=<?php
        echo $row['movie_id']; ?>">[EDIT]</a>
      <a href="delete.php?type=movie&id=<?php
        echo $row['movie_id']?>">[DELETE]</a>
    </td>
```

```
      </tr>
<?php
    }
?>
  <tr>
    <td bgcolor="#FFFFFF" colspan="2" align="center">
      People <a href="people.php?action=add&id=">[ADD]</a>
    </td>
  </tr>
<?php
  $moviesql = "SELECT * FROM people";
  $result = mysql_query($moviesql)
    or die("Invalid query: " . mysql_error());
  while ($row = mysql_fetch_array($result)) {
?>
  <tr>
    <td bgcolor="#FFFFFF" width="50%">
      <?php echo $row['people_fullname']; ?>
    </td>
    <td bgcolor="#FFFFFF" width="50%" align="right">
      <a href="people.php?action=edit&id=<?php
        echo $row['people_id']; ?>">[EDIT]</a>
      <a href="delete.php?type=people&id=<?php
        echo $row['people_id']; ?>">[DELETE]</a>
    </td>
  </tr>
<?php
    }
?>
</table>
</body>
</html>
```

3. Now open your browser and go to `http://localhost/chapter6/index.php` as shown in Figure 6-1.

All links are broken at the moment, but do not worry; that's perfectly normal because you haven't yet created the pages.

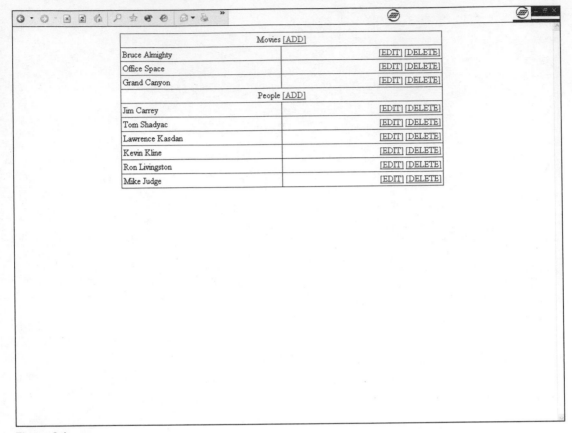

Figure 6-1

How It Works

You must always have a central administration interface that allows you to perform actions on the data and easily see the content. This script is the admin interface. It shows you everything and allows you to manage everything in sight.

What does it do and how does it do what it does? As in Chapter 4, where you connected to the database and displayed its contents, you will do the same thing here. The table holds the name of each known movie and person, and generates EDIT and DELETE links.

Inserting a Simple Record from phpMyAdmin

Note that the following scripts follow a simple rule concerning SQL: Always try the query in MySQL before trying to insert it in your code. The simple reason is that you are probably better off debugging one language at a time.

Try It Out   Inserting Simple Data

In this exercise, you'll insert some data into your table.

1.   Open your database in phpMyAdmin or your favorite MySQL client, and enter the following SQL code (yes, there is an error) as in Figure 6-2.

```
INSERT INTO movie (movie_name, movie_type, movie_year)
VALUES ('Bruce Almighty', '1', '2003)
```

2.   The following message appears (see Figure 6-3 for details):

```
You have an error in your SQL syntax.  Check the manual that corresponds to your
MySQL server version for the right syntax to use near ''2003)' at line 2
```

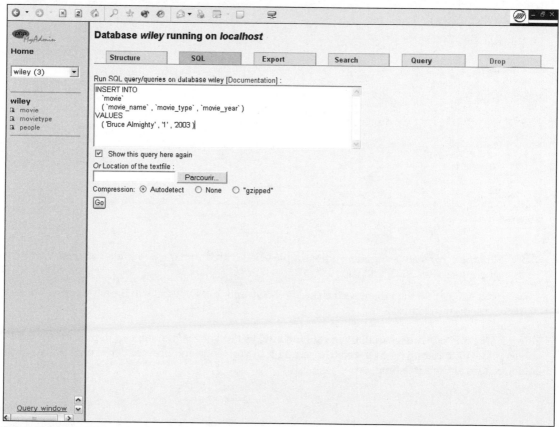

Figure 6-2

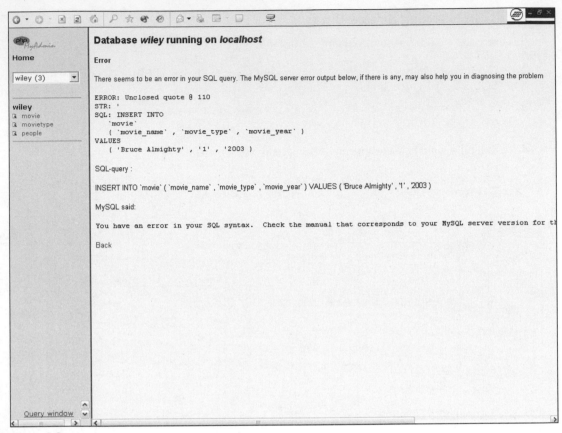

Figure 6-3

3. Fix the error as this suggests (quite simple to do with the character number reference, just close the quote after 2003) and run.

   phpMyAdmin then displays the executed SQL and takes you back to the table content display as shown in Figure 6-4.

Before doing any SQL query in PHP, you should always test your SQL statement in phpMyAdmin. It will enable you to debug the SQL before inserting it in your code and prevent debugging in two different languages at the same time.

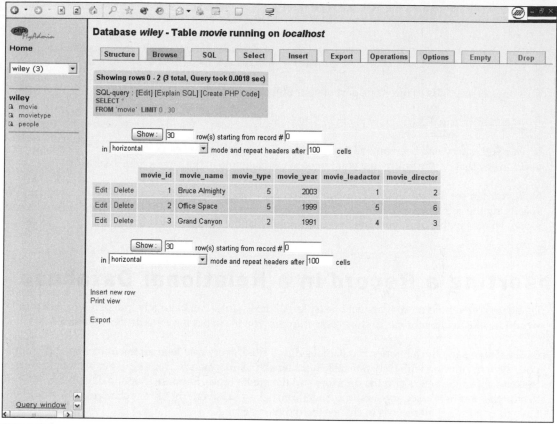

Figure 6-4

How It Works

When inserting a record in a table, you don't need to insert the ID if you set the primary key field to auto increment. SQL will gladly handle that for you. This enables you to be sure you don't have duplicate keys in the table.

To get the just-inserted record's auto increment id, just use the PHP `mysql_insert_id()` function right after the `mysql_query()` function call. This function returns the primary key field when inserting a new record.

You can find the `mysql_insert_id` *function syntax on the PHP site at* www.php.net/mysql_insert_id.

Because you have created the SQL query on more than one line, you can use the line number returned in the following error message:

```
You have an error in your SQL syntax.  Check the manual that corresponds to your
MySQL server version for the right syntax to use near ''2003)' at line 2
```

This line corresponds to the value part of your SQL statement, as shown here:

```
VALUES ('Bruce Almighty', '1', '2003)
```

If your SQL query had been on one line, you'd have had only a useless "error in line 1" message. Here you can see that on the guilty line you forgot to close a quote in the `movie_year` value.

Now you can see that we omitted the `movie.movie_id` field. We did this on purpose (yes, we did). Not specifying the primary key value forces the MySQL engine to automatically determine the auto increment value. Thanks to this trick, you don't need to know what the next key will be.

Inserting a Record in a Relational Database

Databases often hold more than just one table. All those tables can be totally independent, but that would be like using your car to store some things in the trunk but never to drive you around.

In old systems in which relational databases didn't exist, every row held all the information. Imagine your system running with only one table holding all the information. Your `movie` table would store all the data about the actors and the directors and the movie types. Suppose that one day you were to decide that a movie category should change from action to adventure (things change). You would then have to go through all records to change the movie type label.

In modern RDBMS (relational database management systems), this is not the case anymore; you will create a `movietype` table storing a reference of all the possible movie types, and you will link movies to the relevant movie type.

To link those tables, you will use a primary key/foreign key team. The primary key of the `movietype` table is a numeric identification of each type of movie. For example, in your database the id 1 references comedy. The foreign key is the reference in the `movie` table to the `movietype` primary key.

In the following exercise, you use PHP and SQL to insert a movie in your database. This movie is of a known movie type from the `movietype` reference table.

Try It Out   Inserting a Movie with Known Movie Type and People

This time, let's do something a bit more complicated. You'll be able to add a movie to the system while specifying an existing movie type and existing actor and director.

1. Create a new empty file named `movie.php` and enter the following code:

```php
<?php
 $link = mysql_connect("localhost", "bp5am", "bp5ampass")
    or die("Could not connect: " . mysql_error());
```

```php
    mysql_select_db('moviesite', $link)
      or die ( mysql_error());
    $peoplesql = "SELECT * FROM people";

    $result = mysql_query($peoplesql)
      or die("Invalid query: " . mysql_error());
    while ($row = mysql_fetch_array($result)) {
      $people[$row['people_id']] = $row['people_fullname'];
    }
?>
<html>
<head>
<title>Add movie</title>
<style type="text/css">
TD{color:#353535;font-family:verdana}
TH{color:#FFFFFF;font-family:verdana;background-color:#336699}
</style>
</head>
<body>
<form action="commit.php?action=add&type=movie" method="post">
<table border="0" width="750" cellspacing="1" cellpadding="3"
       bgcolor="#353535" align="center">
  <tr>
    <td bgcolor="#FFFFFF" width="30%">Movie Name</td>
    <td bgcolor="#FFFFFF" width="70%">
      <input type="text" name="movie_name">
    </td>
  </tr>
  <tr>
    <td bgcolor="#FFFFFF">Movie Type</td>
    <td bgcolor="#FFFFFF">
      <select id="game" name="movie_type" style="width:150px">
<?php
  $sql = "SELECT movietype_id, movietype_label " .
         "FROM movietype ORDER BY movietype_label";
  $result = mysql_query($sql)
    or die("<font color=\"#FF0000\">Query Error</font>" .
           mysql_error());
  while ($row = mysql_fetch_array($result)) {
    echo '<option value="' . $row['movietype_id'] . '">' .
         $row['movietype_label'] . '</option>' . "\r\n";
  }
?>
      </select>

    </td>
  </tr>
  <tr>
    <td bgcolor="#FFFFFF">Movie Year</td>
    <td bgcolor="#FFFFFF">
      <select name="movie_year">
        <option value="" selected>Select a year...</option>
<?php
  for ($year = date("Y"); $year >= 1970; $year--) {
```

171

```
?>
        <option value="<?php echo $year; ?>"><?php
        echo $year; ?></option>
<?php
  }
?>
      </select>
    </td>
  </tr>
  <tr>
    <td bgcolor="#FFFFFF">Lead Actor</td>
    <td bgcolor="#FFFFFF">
      <select name="movie_leadactor">
        <option value="" selected>Select an actor...</option>
<?php
  foreach ($people as $people_id => $people_fullname) {
?>
        <option value="<?php echo $people_id; ?>" ><?php
        echo $people_fullname; ?></option>
<?php
  }
?>
      </select>
    </td>
  </tr>
  <tr>
    <td bgcolor="#FFFFFF">Director</td>
    <td bgcolor="#FFFFFF">
      <select name="movie_director">
        <option value="" selected>Select a director...</option>
<?php
  foreach ($people as $people_id => $people_fullname) {
?>
        <option value="<?php echo $people_id; ?>" ><?php
        echo $people_fullname; ?></option>
<?php
  }
?>
      </select>
    </td>
  </tr>
  <tr>
    <td bgcolor="#FFFFFF" colspan="2" align="center">
      <input type="submit" name="SUBMIT" value="Add">
    </td>
  </tr>
</table>
</form>
</body>
</html>
```

2. Save your file and upload it to the `chapter6` directory on your server.

3. Create a new empty file named `commit.php` and enter the following code:

```php
<?php
// COMMIT ADD
  $link = mysql_connect("localhost", "bp5am", "bp5ampass")
    or die("Could not connect: " . mysql_error());
  mysql_select_db('moviesite', $link)
    or die ( mysql_error());
  switch ($_GET['action']) {
    case "add":
      switch ($_GET['type']) {
        case "movie":
          $sql = "INSERT INTO movie
                    (movie_name,
                     movie_year,
                     movie_type,
                     movie_leadactor,
                     movie_director)
                  VALUES
                    ('" . $_POST['movie_name'] . "',
                    '" . $_POST['movie_year'] . "',
                    '" . $_POST['movie_type'] . "',
                    '" . $_POST['movie_leadactor'] . "',
                    '" . $_POST['movie_director'] . "')";
          break;
      }
      break;
  }

  if (isset($sql) && !empty($sql)) {
    echo "<!--" . $sql . "-->";
    $result = mysql_query($sql)
      or die("Invalid query: " . mysql_error());
?>
  <p align="center" style="color:#FF0000">
    Done. <a href="index.php">Index</a>
  </p>
<?php
  }
?>
```

4. Save your file and upload it to the `chapter6` directory on your server.

5. Open your browser on the `index.php` page and click ADD next to the `movie` table header. You should see the screen shown in Figure 6-5.

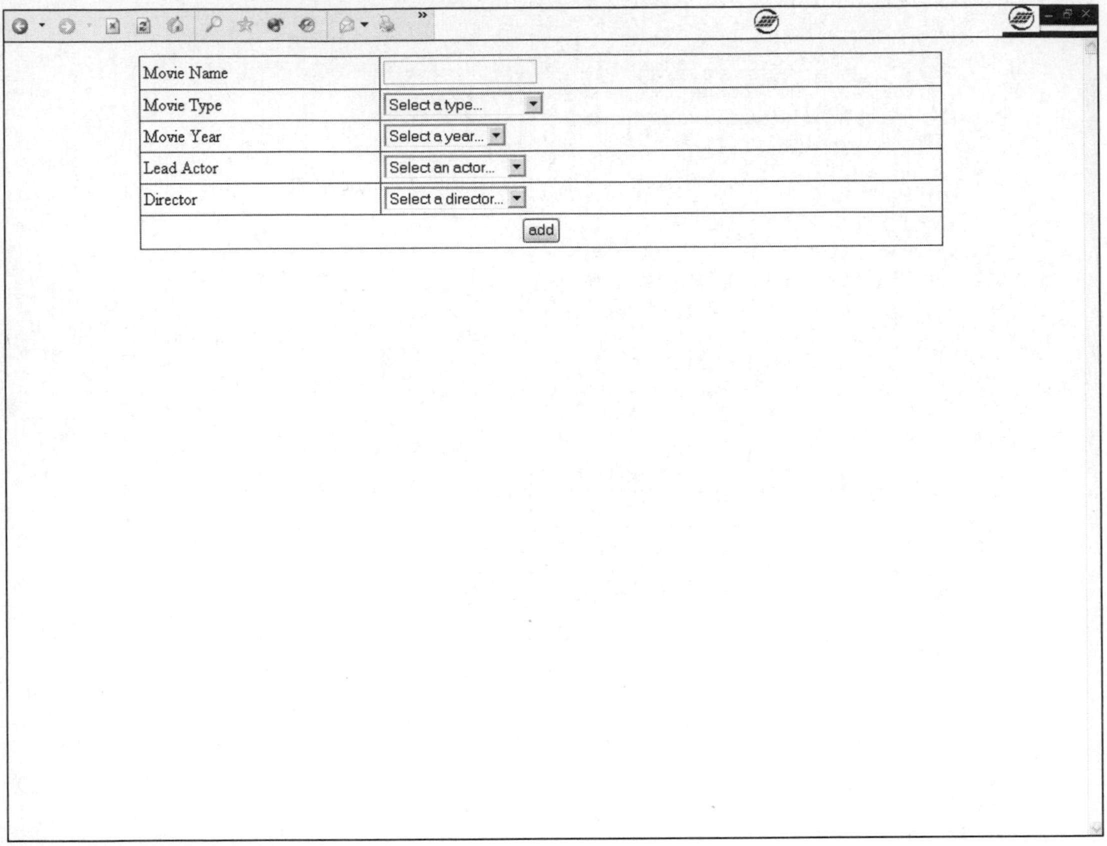

Figure 6-5

6. Add a movie named "Test" with random type, actor, and director as shown in Figure 6-6.

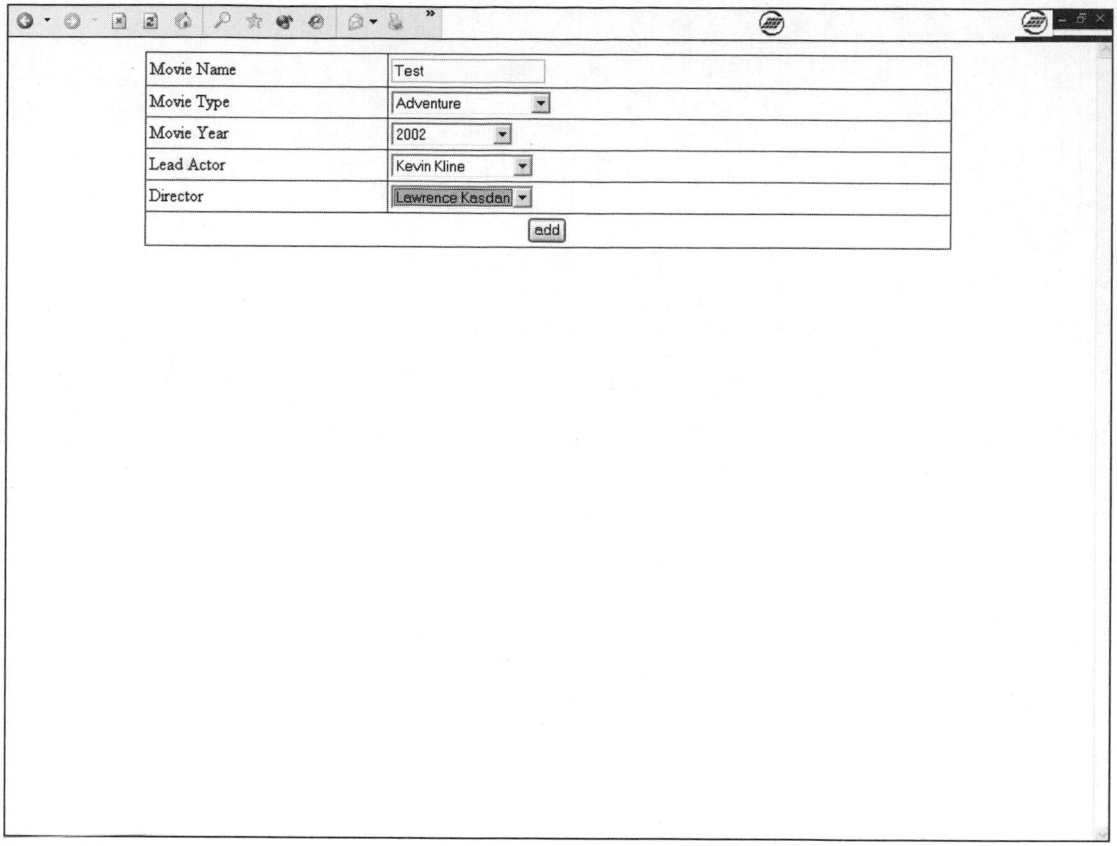

Figure 6-6

7. Click the "add" button and you will see the confirmation message as in Figure 6-7.

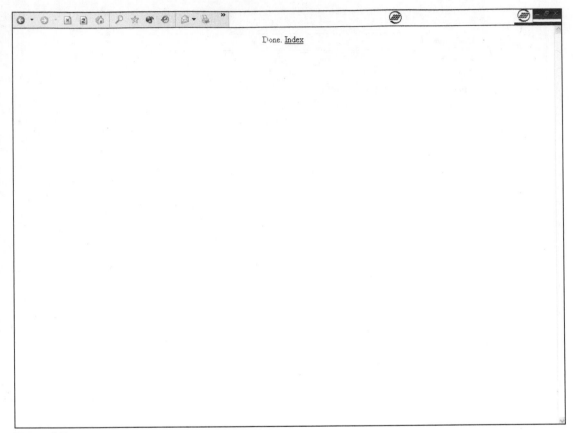

Done. Index

Figure 6-7

How It Works

HTML forms allow you to drive the way the user enters the data. Once submitted, the form sends the server information that PHP can use to generate and run the SQL INSERT statement.

As you see in the movie insertion form in movie.php, you have four combo boxes and a text field. The text field content is left to your discretion, but the combos are quite directive. Let's review the content of the combos generated from the database contents.

First, let's concentrate on the people combos. Each combo lists all persons present in a people table.

```php
<?php
  $link = mysql_connect("localhost", "bp5am", "bp5ampass")
    or die("Could not connect: " . mysql_error());
  mysql_select_db('moviesite', $link)
    or die ( mysql_error());
  $peoplesql = "SELECT * FROM people";
```

```
    $result = mysql_query($peoplesql)
      or die("Invalid query: " . mysql_error());
    while ($row = mysql_fetch_array($result)) {
      $people[$row['people_id']] = $row['people_fullname'];
    }
  ?>
```

At the beginning of the form script, you query the `people` table and put its content in an array. The data regarding people known to the system is stored in the `people` table.

To generate the list of people, you simply query the database, retrieve all the known people in the system, and display the names in the combo and reference their primary key as the item value. Each known person will have an item in the combo box:

```
<select name="movie_director">
  <option value="" selected>Select a director...</option>
<?php
  foreach ($people as $people_id => $people_fullname) {
?>
  <option value="<?php echo $people_id; ?>" ><?php
  echo $people_fullname; ?></option>
<?php
  }
?>
</select>
```

Here you've used the `foreach` syntax to walk the array to generate all the options.

Now generate the movie type combo box. This is a more conventional use of SQL to generate contents. You'll reuse this code soon to create a generic form to edit and add, so you need to understand the details of how this works.

```
      <select id="game" name="movie_type" style="width:150px">
<?php
  $sql = "SELECT movietype_id, movietype_label " .
       "FROM movietype ORDER BY movietype_label";
  $result = mysql_query($sql)
    or die("<font color=\"#FF0000\">Query Error</font>" .
        mysql_error());
  while ($row = mysql_fetch_array($result)) {
    echo '<option value="' . $row['movietype_id'] . '">' .
        $row['movietype_label'] . '</option>' . "\r\n";
  }
?>
      </select>
```

This code generates the options in combo box by querying the `movietype` table to extract all available movie types. Each option will have the movie type id as a value and the movie type itself as a label.

Now that your form is ready, you need to have a script that uses this data to create records. As you can see, the `switch case` on `$_GET['action']` is totally useless for now. In the next exercises, you add a lot of code to the `movie.php` script so you can use it to edit the movies.

Deleting a Record

Deleting records is easy (a bit too easy at times—you will know what we mean soon). As mentioned earlier, always be sure to test your queries on a test database. Deleting records in a test database never threatens your system, and testing your query helps you find any SQL error before deleting all the records in your production database because you forgot a little thing such as a WHERE clause. MySQL deletes everything that matches the SQL statement. If you omit a WHERE clause in your query, all the records will match the SQL statement, and thus will be deleted.

Deleting always means losing data. To delete a record you need to point the record to the database engine through a set of conditions in a WHERE statement. Once this statement is executed, there is no turning back. The record(s) will be deleted without hope of return; that's why we advise caution when using the DELETE statement.

Try It Out   Deleting a Single Record

Before asking PHP to delete anything, you should try deleting a record from phpMyAdmin to familiarize yourself with the DELETE statement.

1. Open phpMyAdmin and enter the following code:

```
DELETE FROM movie
WHERE movie_id = 12
LIMIT 1
```

2. phpMyAdmin returns a nice message saying you deleted a record from the movie table.

How It Works

The DELETE SQL statement is very simple to use. As you see, you used the LIMIT 1 statement to limit the deletion to only one record (in the event of the WHERE statement returning more than one record).

As you know, a database often holds related records in different tables. Deleting some records without considering their relations introduces you to chaos and heavy database manual tweaking. MySQL unfortunately doesn't manage relations for you and thus will not automatically preserve referential integrity.

To avoid that problem, you can use a more elaborate form of the DELETE statement, the *Cascade Delete*, as discussed in the following section.

Try It Out   Cascade Delete

Now that you know how to use DELETE, you will add it to your system to delete a known person from the system. As you store references to known people in the movie table, you will need to update the movie table content so you don't reference deleted people. (The update-specific exercises come next in this chapter.) Deleting the person only would be like throwing away your car keys and expecting your parking spot to be empty. You need to make sure no reference is left to a deleted record in the remaining data.

Follow these steps to implement the Cascade Delete:

1. Create a new text file named delete.php and enter the following code:

```php
<?php
  $link = mysql_connect("localhost", "bp5am", "bp5ampass")
    or die("Could not connect: " . mysql_error());
  mysql_select_db('moviesite', $link)
    or die ( mysql_error());
// DELETE SCRIPT
  if (!isset($_GET['do']) || $_GET['do'] != 1) {
?>
  <p align="center" style="color:#FF0000">
    Are you sure you want to delete this <?php
    echo $_GET['type']; ?>?<br>
    <a href="<?php echo $_SERVER['REQUEST_URI']; ?>&do=1">yes</a>
    or <a href="index.php">Index</a>
  </p>
<?php
  } else {
    if ($_GET['type'] == "people") {
      // delete references to people from the movie table
      // delete reference to lead actor
      $actor = "UPDATE movie
               SET movie_leadactor = '0'
               WHERE movie_leadactor = '" . $_GET['id'] . "'";
      $result = mysql_query($actor)
        or die("Invalid query: " . mysql_error());

      // delete reference to director
      $director = "UPDATE movie
                  SET movie_director = '0'
                  WHERE movie_director = '" . $_GET['id'] . "'";
      $result = mysql_query($director)
        or die("Invalid query: " . mysql_error());
    }
    // generate SQL
    $sql = "DELETE FROM " . $_GET['type'] . "
           WHERE " . $_GET['type'] . "_id = '" . $_GET['id'] . "'
           LIMIT 1";
    // echo SQL for debug purpose
    echo "<!--" . $sql . "-->";
    $result = mysql_query($sql)
      or die("Invalid query: " . mysql_error());
?>
  <p align="center" style="color:#FF0000">
    Your <?php echo $_GET['type']; ?> has been deleted.
    <a href="index.php">Index</a>
  </p>
<?php
  }
?>
```

2. Save `delete.php` and upload it to your chap6 directory.

3. Open `index.php` in your browser. You will see the DELETE links next to each movie or person as in Figure 6-8.

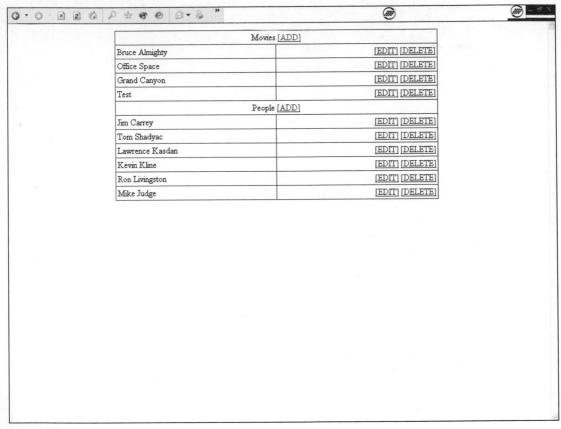

Figure 6-8

4. Try deleting the test movie you added in the previous exercise by clicking the DELETE link next to the "Test" movie name. You will be asked for confirmation as in Figure 6-9.

Are you sure you want to delete this movie?
yes or Index

Figure 6-9

5. Click the "yes" link to confirm the deletion and wait for the confirmation message as in Figure 6-10.

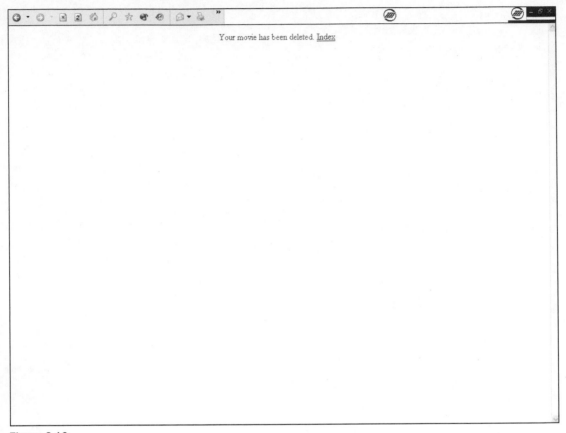

Your movie has been deleted. Index

Figure 6-10

How It Works

Here you are, planning the annihilation of an innocent set of data. Putting any moral issues aside, let's see how this script works.

First, you need to understand that in a relational database you cannot delete records and just forget about them. Deleting has to be considered carefully. For example, if you delete a person from the `people` table, this prevents you from finding a potential reference to that person in the `movie` table. If you delete Jim Carrey from the `people` table, who will *Bruce Almighty*'s lead actor be? If you don't do anything, Jim Carrey's id will remain in the record and you will have a corrupted database. You don't want that, do you? (The answer is no.)

The solution to this problem is to make sure that you always have the round peg (a foreign key) in the round hole (a record). In the code that follows, you update the movie table with a 0 value (the default value telling the script you have not set the people part) before deleting the people record. This also allows you to check the behavior of the UPDATE SQL statement. (Isn't life great?)

```
// delete reference to lead actor
$actor = "UPDATE movie
          SET movie_leadactor = '0'
          WHERE movie_leadactor = '" . $_GET['id'] . "'";
$result = mysql_query($actor)
  or die("Invalid query: " . mysql_error());

// delete reference to director
$director = "UPDATE movie
          SET movie_director = '0'
          WHERE movie_director = '" . $_GET['id'] . "'";
$result = mysql_query($director)
  or die("Invalid query: " . mysql_error());
```

In the preceding code, you set any field in the movie table that might hold a reference to your unfortunate, soon-to-be-deleted person. The UPDATE statement works in a very simple way. It sets the fields specified to the new value specified in all records, meeting the requirements of the WHERE statement.

You might wonder what would happen if someone were to forget the WHERE part. Well, curiosity is a fine quality: This would update all records in the table, which is probably not something you want to do in real life.

Once your tidying up is done, you do the deleting:

```
// generate SQL
$sql = "DELETE FROM " . $_GET['type'] . "
        WHERE " . $_GET['type'] . "_id = '" . $_GET['id'] . "'
        LIMIT 1";
// echo SQL for debug purpose
echo "<!--" . $sql . "-->";
$result = mysql_query($sql)
  or die("Invalid query: " . mysql_error());
```

This DELETE query is a bit dynamic, but it's fairly understandable. You don't want to code a SQL statement for each type. (Well, you did for the movies update, but it doesn't count, does it?) So you use the information passed through the URL to generate your SQL statement. The table and primary key field are generated dynamically from the item type to delete.

Editing Data in a Record

Having data in the database is all well and good, but data has a mind of its own and tends to want to be updated. To update data, you need to identify the data to update and present the system user with a nice interface to do so. Using the same interface as was used to create the data is often a good practice.

Try It Out   **Editing a Movie**

In this exercise, you create a script that enables you to edit a movie. You will build on the existing `movie.php` script you created earlier.

1. Open `movie.php` in your favorite text editor and enter this code:

```php
<?php
  $link = mysql_connect("localhost", "bp5am", "bp5ampass")
    or die("Could not connect: " . mysql_error());
  mysql_select_db('moviesite', $link)
    or die ( mysql_error());
  $peoplesql = "SELECT * FROM people";

  $result = mysql_query($peoplesql)
    or die("Invalid query: " . mysql_error());
  while ($row = mysql_fetch_array($result)) {
    $people[$row['people_id']] = $row['people_fullname'];
  }

    switch ($_GET['action']) {
      case "edit":
        $moviesql = "SELECT * FROM movie
                     WHERE movie_id = '" . $_GET['id'] . "'";
        $result = mysql_query($moviesql)
          or die("Invalid query: " . mysql_error());
        $row = mysql_fetch_array($result);
        $movie_name = $row['movie_name'];
        $movie_type = $row['movie_type'];
        $movie_year = $row['movie_year'];
        $movie_leadactor = $row['movie_leadactor'];
        $movie_director = $row['movie_director'];
        break;

      default:
        $movie_name = "";
        $movie_type = "";
        $movie_year = "";
        $movie_leadactor = "";
        $movie_director = "";
        break;
    }
  ?>
  <html>
  <head>
  <title><?php echo $_GET['action']; ?> movie</title>
  <style type="text/css">
  TD{color:#353535;font-family:verdana}
  TH{color:#FFFFFF;font-family:verdana;background-color:#336699}
  </style>
  </head>
  <body>
```

```php
<form action="commit.php?action=<?php
  echo $_GET['action']; ?>&type=movie&id=<?php
  echo $_GET['id']; ?>" method="post">
<table border="0" width="750" cellspacing="1" cellpadding="3"
       bgcolor="#353535" align="center">
  <tr>
    <td bgcolor="#FFFFFF" width="30%">Movie Name</td>
    <td bgcolor="#FFFFFF" width="70%">
      <input type="text" name="movie_name"
        value="<?php echo $movie_name; ?>">
    </td>
  </tr>
  <tr>
    <td bgcolor="#FFFFFF">Movie Type</td>
    <td bgcolor="#FFFFFF">
      <select id="game" name="movie_type" style="width:150px">
<?php
  $sql = "SELECT movietype_id, movietype_label " .
         "FROM movietype ORDER BY movietype_label";
  $result = mysql_query($sql)
    or die("<font color=\"#FF0000\">Query Error</font>" .
           mysql_error());
  while ($row = mysql_fetch_array($result)) {
    if ($row['movietype_id'] == $movie_type) {
      $selected = " selected";
    } else {
      $selected = "";
    }
    echo '<option value="' . $row['movietype_id'] . '"' .
         $selected.'>' . $row['movietype_label'] . '</option>' .
         "\r\n";
  }
?>
      </select>
    </td>
  </tr>
  <tr>
    <td bgcolor="#FFFFFF">Movie Year</td>
    <td bgcolor="#FFFFFF">
      <select name="movie_year">
        <option value="" selected>Select a year...</option>
<?php
  for ($year = date("Y"); $year >= 1970; $year--) {
    if ($year == $movie_year) {
      $selected = " selected";
    } else {
      $selected = "";
    }
?>
        <option value="<?php echo $year; ?>"<?php
        echo $selected; ?>><?php echo $year; ?></option>
<?php
  }
?>
```

```
        </select>
      </td>
   </tr>
   <tr>
     <td bgcolor="#FFFFFF">Lead Actor</td>
     <td bgcolor="#FFFFFF">
       <select name="movie_leadactor">
         <option value="" selected>Select an actor...</option>
<?php
   foreach ($people as $people_id => $people_fullname) {
     if ($people_id == $movie_leadactor) {
       $selected = " selected";
     } else {
       $selected = "";
     }
?>
         <option value="<?php echo $people_id; ?>"<?php
         echo $selected; ?>><?php echo $people_fullname; ?></option>
<?php
   }
?>
       </select>
     </td>
   </tr>
   <tr>
     <td bgcolor="#FFFFFF">Director</td>
     <td bgcolor="#FFFFFF">
       <select name="movie_director">
         <option value="" selected>Select a director...</option>
<?php
   foreach ($people as $people_id => $people_fullname) {
     if ($people_id == $movie_director) {
       $selected = " selected";
     } else {
       $selected = "";
     }
?>
         <option value="<?php echo $people_id; ?>"<?php
         echo $selected; ?>><?php echo $people_fullname; ?></option>
<?php
   }
?>
       </select>
     </td>
   </tr>
   <tr>
     <td bgcolor="#FFFFFF" colspan="2" align="center">
       <input type="submit" name="SUBMIT" value="<?php
         echo $_GET['action']; ?>">
     </td>
   </tr>
</table>
</form>
</body>
</html>
```

2. Open the `commit.php` script and edit its content to match this new code:

```php
<?php
// COMMIT ADD AND EDITS
  $link = mysql_connect("localhost", "bp5am", "bp5ampass")
    or die("Could not connect: " . mysql_error());
  mysql_select_db('moviesite', $link)
    or die ( mysql_error());
  switch ($_GET['action']) {
    case "edit":
      switch ($_GET['type']) {
        case "movie":
          $sql = "UPDATE movie SET
                  movie_name = '" . $_POST['movie_name'] . "',
                  movie_year = '" . $_POST['movie_year'] . "',
                  movie_type = '" . $_POST['movie_type'] . "',
                  movie_leadactor = '" .$_POST['movie_leadactor']."',
                  movie_director = '" . $_POST['movie_director'] . "'
                WHERE movie_id = '" . $_GET['id'] . "'";
        break;
      }
      break;
    case "add":
      switch ($_GET['type']) {
        case "movie":
          $sql = "INSERT INTO movie
                    (movie_name,
                    movie_year,
                    movie_type,
                    movie_leadactor,
                    movie_director)
                  VALUES
                    ('" . $_POST['movie_name'] . "',
                    '" . $_POST['movie_year'] . "',
                    '" . $_POST['movie_type'] . "',
                    '" . $_POST['movie_leadactor'] . "',
                    '" . $_POST['movie_director'] . "')";
        break;
      }
      break;
  }
  if (isset($sql) && !empty($sql)) {
    echo "<!--" . $sql . "-->";
    $result = mysql_query($sql)
      or die("Invalid query: " . mysql_error());
?>
  <p align="center" style="color:#FF0000">
    Done. <a href="index.php">Index</a>
  </p>
<?php
  }
?>
```

3. Now open your browser and go to `http://localhost/chapter6/index.php` as shown in Figure 6-11.

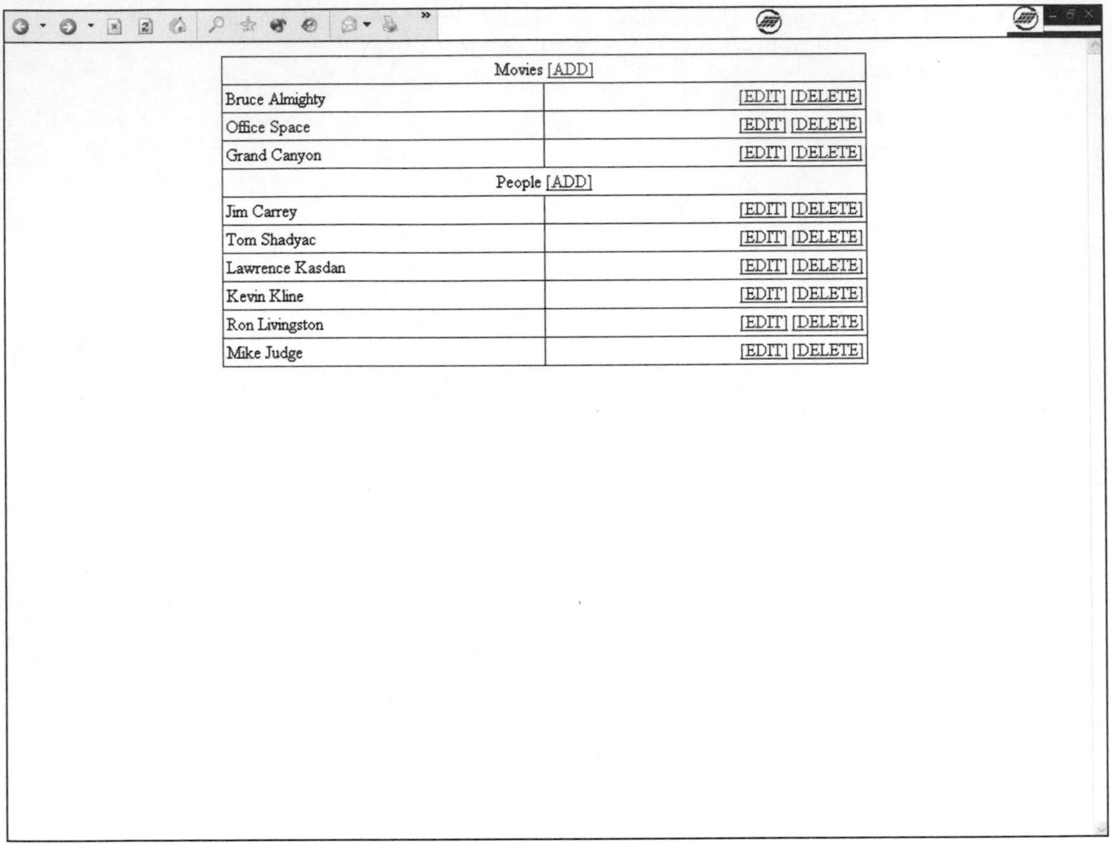

Movies [ADD]		
Bruce Almighty		[EDIT] [DELETE]
Office Space		[EDIT] [DELETE]
Grand Canyon		[EDIT] [DELETE]
People [ADD]		
Jim Carrey		[EDIT] [DELETE]
Tom Shadyac		[EDIT] [DELETE]
Lawrence Kasdan		[EDIT] [DELETE]
Kevin Kline		[EDIT] [DELETE]
Ron Livingston		[EDIT] [DELETE]
Mike Judge		[EDIT] [DELETE]

Figure 6-11

4. Try clicking the EDIT link next to the "Bruce Almighty" movie, change a few boxes and the movie name, and press the "edit" button in the form shown in Figure 6-12.

5. Edit the "Bruce Almighty" entry again with the procedure in step 4, and fix it so it's back to its own old self.

   Now the EDIT links for movies will actually do something!

You see that the script loads the stored values and allows you to edit the data easily. Play around a bit, and get a feel for the way it all works.

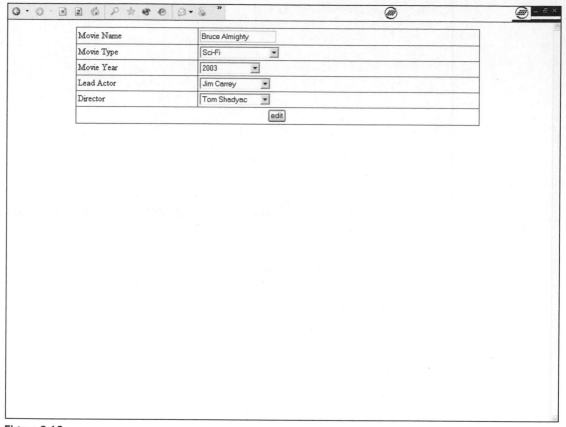

Figure 6-12

How It Works

The commit.php code is very much the same as what you saw already, but there is an interesting twist in movie.php. Let's look at it in some detail.

First, look at the switch at the start of the script. You defined a switch on a query string parameter named action. If the action is edit, you query the database for a record corresponding to the id specified in the id query string parameter and set some variables. These variables are set to void if action is not edit.

```
switch ($_GET['action']) {
  case "edit":
    $moviesql = "SELECT * FROM movie
                 WHERE movie_id = '" . $_GET['id'] . "'";
    $result = mysql_query($moviesql)
      or die("Invalid query: " . mysql_error());
    $row = mysql_fetch_array($result);
    $movie_name = $row['movie_name'];
    $movie_type = $row['movie_type'];
```

```
            $movie_year = $row['movie_year'];
            $movie_leadactor = $row['movie_leadactor'];
            $movie_director = $row['movie_director'];
            break;

        default:
            $movie_name = "";
            $movie_type = "";
            $movie_year = "";
            $movie_leadactor = "";
            $movie_director = "";
            break;
    }
?>
```

The variables set in the preceding code are used to set the default value of the form fields. Each field has a known value if you are editing a record and has a void value if you are creating a record.

```
<tr>
  <td bgcolor="#FFFFFF" width="30%">Movie Name</td>
  <td bgcolor="#FFFFFF" width="70%">
    <input type="text" name="movie_name"
      value="<?php echo $movie_name; ?>">
  </td>
</tr>
```

In this example, the movie_name field takes the $movie_name variable content as a default value. This allows you to reload the form with data from the record to edit it.

Editing a text field is pretty straightforward. Editing a value in a list is another story. You can't just display the list and hope the user will reset the value to the original when he or she edits the record. You need to reload the whole list and make the previously set value appear as the default in the list so the user can just skip it if he or she doesn't want to edit it.

How do you do this? The script holds the solution:

```
<tr>
  <td bgcolor="#FFFFFF">Movie Type</td>
    <td bgcolor="#FFFFFF">
      <select id="game" name="movie_type" style="width:150px">
<?php
$sql = "SELECT movietype_id, movietype_label " .
        "FROM movietype ORDER BY movietype_label";
$result = mysql_query($sql)
  or die("<font color=\"#FF0000\">Query Error</FONT>" .
          mysql_error());
while ($row = mysql_fetch_array($result)) {
  if ($row['movietype_id'] == $movie_type) {
    $selected = " selected";
  } else {
    $selected = "";
  }
  echo '<option value="' . $row['movietype_id'] . '"' .
```

```
        $selected . '>' . $row['movietype_label'] . '</option>' .
        "\r\n";
  }
  ?>
      </select>
    </td>
  </tr>
```

You load the list as you would have done if adding a record, but you compare the current value to the default value. If they are identical, add a simple SELECTED flag to the option value. This sets the default list value to the current value in the table.

```
if ($row['movietype_id'] == $movie_type) {
  $selected = " selected";
} else {
  $selected = "";
}
```

Summary

As you've learned in this chapter, there are three basic actions in modifying the content of a database:

❑   Insert

❑   Delete

❑   Update

These actions are performed by the database itself through SQL queries PHP executes on MySQL. Read up on the SQL statements used in this chapter to get a good feel for how far they can take you and at what level you feel confident using these commands.

Often, using MySQL revolves around the same few PHP functions. The SQL executed through those commands on the database changes the way the system reacts. Don't hesitate to learn more about SQL to enhance your PHP systems.

And finally, always remember that testing your query alone in phpMyAdmin saves you a lot of time debugging it when working in a PHP script.

Exercise

It may seem like we're about to take it easy on you, with only one exercise, but don't be fooled. This single exercise covers a lot of what we mentioned in this chapter.

1.   Create the edit/delete code for the people table. Use the movie code as an example.

Manipulating and Creating Images with PHP

Now that you've been rocking and rolling with manipulating and displaying data using PHP, why stop there? Did you know that PHP can also manipulate and create images on the fly? Well it can, admittedly with a little help from the GD library. "GD" loosely stands for "Graphics Draw" according to the folks at Boutell.com, the makers of this software, but the industry generally refers to it as the GD library.

This chapter covers the following:

- ❑ Enabling your PHP setup to include the GD library
- ❑ Allowing your users to upload their own images
- ❑ Retrieving information about an image, such as size or file type
- ❑ Creating a new image
- ❑ Copying an image or a portion of an image
- ❑ Creating thumbnails (smaller versions of images)
- ❑ Creating black-and-white versions of images
- ❑ Adding watermarks and captions to images

Working with the GD Library

GD is written in C++ and allows for the manipulation of certain image types. Because PHP can't automatically process images with built-in functions, you need to make sure you have the GD library enabled. Fortunately, a bundled version comes with all recent versions of PHP. If you don't have the bundled version, though, you can find it externally at http://www.boutell.com/gd/. However, we recommend that you use the bundled version as opposed to the external version available for downloading, if possible.

What File Types Can I Use with GD and PHP?

GD itself can work with a multitude of images, but when you use it with PHP you can get information about any GIF, JPG, PNG, SWF, SWC, PSD, TIFF, BMP, IFF, JP2, JPX, JB2, JPC, XBM, or WBMP image format. You can also manipulate and create images in GIF, JPG, PNG, WBMP, and XBM image formats. GD can also allow PHP to create shapes such as squares, polygons, and ellipses, as well as text boxes using True Type Fonts.

> *Depending on your version of GD, GIF support may or may not be enabled. You can tell if GIF support is enabled with the use of the* gd_info *function described in the "Try It Out - Testing Your GD" section that follows.*

Compiling PHP with GD

If you are using a Web host, chances are that they have already enabled GD on their installation of PHP. If you are running your own server, enabling the GD functions in PHP is really not so hard. In Windows, simply find the following line in your php.ini file:

```
;extension=php_gd2.dll
```

Uncomment that line like this:

```
extension=php_gd2.dll
```

You need to restart Apache for your changes to take effect.

In Linux, you need to enable GD with the --with-gd configure option. Again, because the bundled version of GD is recommended for use with PHP, you do not need to identify GD's installation directory — it will find the bundled version by default.

Easy enough? Thought so. Let's test the thing.

Try It Out   Testing Your GD

Make sure everything is working properly before you go any further:

1. Open your favorite text/HTML editor and enter the following code:

```
<?php
print_r(gd_info());
?>
```

2. Save this file as gdtest.php (and upload it to your Web server if needed).

3. Load your favorite browser and view the page that you have just uploaded.

   Your screen should look like the one shown in Figure 7-1.

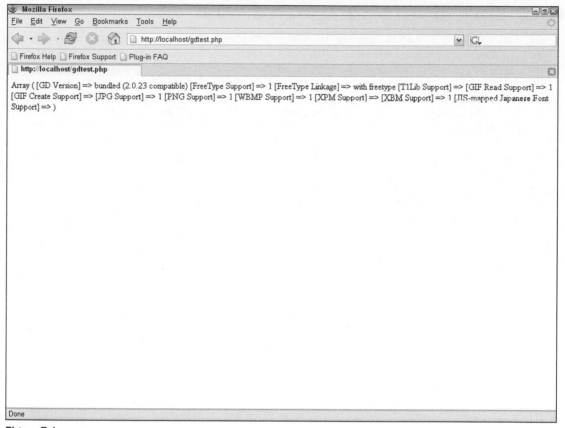

Figure 7-1

How It Works

The gd_info function is quite useful, because it tells you what capabilities you have with the current version of GD that was bundled with your version of PHP. Its purpose is to put all the information about the GD version into an array that you can then view. This not only serves as a test to make sure that GD and PHP are playing nice with each other, but it lets you see what your limitations are for using the GD functions in PHP. For the purposes of the examples in this chapter, you will need to have JPG, GIF, and PNG support. If your version of GD doesn't support any of these image types, you will need to upgrade. You can find full upgrade instructions and source files at http://www.boutell.com/gd.

The print_r() function takes all the information stored in a variable (including arrays) and outputs it to the browser so you can see it.

Now that you know that your GD library is working well, and what image types are supported in your version, let's move along.

Allowing Users to Upload Images

Suppose you wanted to add a little spice to your movie review site and thought it would be a good idea to let users upload pictures of themselves dressed as their favorite movie actors in their favorite roles. In the rest of this chapter, you will create this "look-alike" photo gallery.

No man is an island, and the same can be said for PHP. To let other people submit their own pictures to your little old site, you will need to enlist the help of HTML. You will also need some MySQL to keep track of all these images.

There is some debate about whether or not actual images can be efficiently stored in a database using the `blob` MySQL column type. My personal preference is not to store the actual image, but to store only information about the image, and if needed, a link to the image. The images themselves are then stored in a regular old directory of your choosing. That being said, create a table in your movie review database that will store the links to the images your users upload.

Try It Out   Creating the Image Table

First, you need to create a table that will hold information about your images. You are going to store basic information about each image, such as the user's name and the title of the image. Then, give your users a form where they can submit an image for display on your site. You will ask some basic information about the image, then you will let users upload the file directly from the comfort of their own browser, without the aid of any FTP software.

1. If you do not have a directory to house your images, you will need to create one. In this exercise, the images will be stored in /images/.

2. Open your text editor and type the following:

```php
<?php

//connect to the database
$link = mysql_connect("localhost", "bp5am", "bp5ampass")
  or die("Could not connect: " . mysql_error());
mysql_select_db("moviesite", $link)
  or die (mysql_error());

//create images table
$sql = "CREATE TABLE IF NOT EXISTS images (
        image_id INT(11) NOT NULL AUTO_INCREMENT,
        image_caption VARCHAR(255) NOT NULL,
        image_username VARCHAR(255) NOT NULL,
        image_date DATE NOT NULL,
        PRIMARY KEY (image_id)
        )";
$results = mysql_query($sql)
  or die(mysql_error());

echo "Image table successfully created.";

?>
```

3. Save this file as `create_images_table.php`. Open this file in your browser and you should see the message "Image table successfully created."

4. Open your editor and type the following code:

```html
<html>
<head>
<title>Upload your pic to our site!</title>
</head>
<body>

<form name="form1" method="post" action="check_image.php"
    enctype="multipart/form-data">

<table border="0" cellpadding="5">
  <tr>
    <td>Image Title or Caption<br>
      <em>Example: You talkin' to me?</em></td>
    <td><input name="image_caption" type="text" id="item_caption" size="55"
        maxlength="255"></td>
  </tr>
  <tr>
    <td>Your Username</td>
    <td><input name="image_username" type="text" id="image_username" size="15"
        maxlength="255"></td>
  </tr>
    <td>Upload Image:</td>
    <td><input name="image_filename" type="file" id="image_filename"></td>
  </tr>
</table>
<br>
<em>Acceptable image formats include: GIF, JPG/JPEG, and PNG.</em>
<p align="center"><input type="submit" name="Submit" value="Submit">
   
  <input type="reset" name="Submit2" value="Clear Form">
</p>
</form>
</body>
</html>
```

5. Save this file as `upload_image.htm`. In this simple example, you haven't included any PHP code in this form, so you don't need to use the `.php` extension.

6. Create a new file in your editor by typing the following code:

```php
<?php
//connect to the database
$link = mysql_connect("localhost", "bp5am", "bp5ampass")
  or die("Could not connect: " . mysql_error());
mysql_select_db("moviesite", $link)
  or die (mysql_error());

//make variables available
$image_caption = $_POST['image_caption'];
```

```php
$image_username = $_POST['image_username'];
$image_tempname = $_FILES['image_filename']['name'];
$today = date("Y-m-d");

//upload image and check for image type
//make sure to change your path to match your images directory
$ImageDir ="c:/Program Files/Apache Group/Apache2/test/images/";
$ImageName = $ImageDir . $image_tempname;

if (move_uploaded_file($_FILES['image_filename']['tmp_name'],
                       $ImageName)) {

  //get info about the image being uploaded
  list($width, $height, $type, $attr) = getimagesize($ImageName);

  switch ($type) {
    case 1:
      $ext = ".gif";
      break;
    case 2:
      $ext = ".jpg";
      break;
    case 3:
      $ext = ".png";
      break;
    default:
      echo "Sorry, but the file you uploaded was not a GIF, JPG, or " .
           "PNG file.<br>";
      echo "Please hit your browser's 'back' button and try again.";
  }

   //insert info into image table

  $insert = "INSERT INTO images
             (image_caption, image_username, image_date)
             VALUES
             ('$image_caption', '$image_username', '$today')";
  $insertresults = mysql_query($insert)
    or die(mysql_error());

  $lastpicid = mysql_insert_id();

  $newfilename = $ImageDir . $lastpicid . $ext;

  rename($ImageName, $newfilename);

}

?>

<html>
<head>
```

```
<title>Here is your pic!</title>
</head>
<body>
<h1>So how does it feel to be famous?</h1><br><br>
<p>Here is the picture you just uploaded to our servers:</p>
<img src="images/<?php echo $lastpicid . $ext; ?>" align="left">
<strong><?php echo $image_name; ?></strong><br>
This image is a <?php echo $ext; ?> image.<br>
It is <?php echo $width; ?> pixels wide
and <?php echo $height; ?> pixels high.<br>
It was uploaded on <?php echo $today; ?>.
</body>
</html>
```

7. Save this file as check_image.php. Now open upload_image.htm in your browser. Your screen should look like Figure 7-2.

8. Upload your image. Your screen should look something like Figure 7-3.

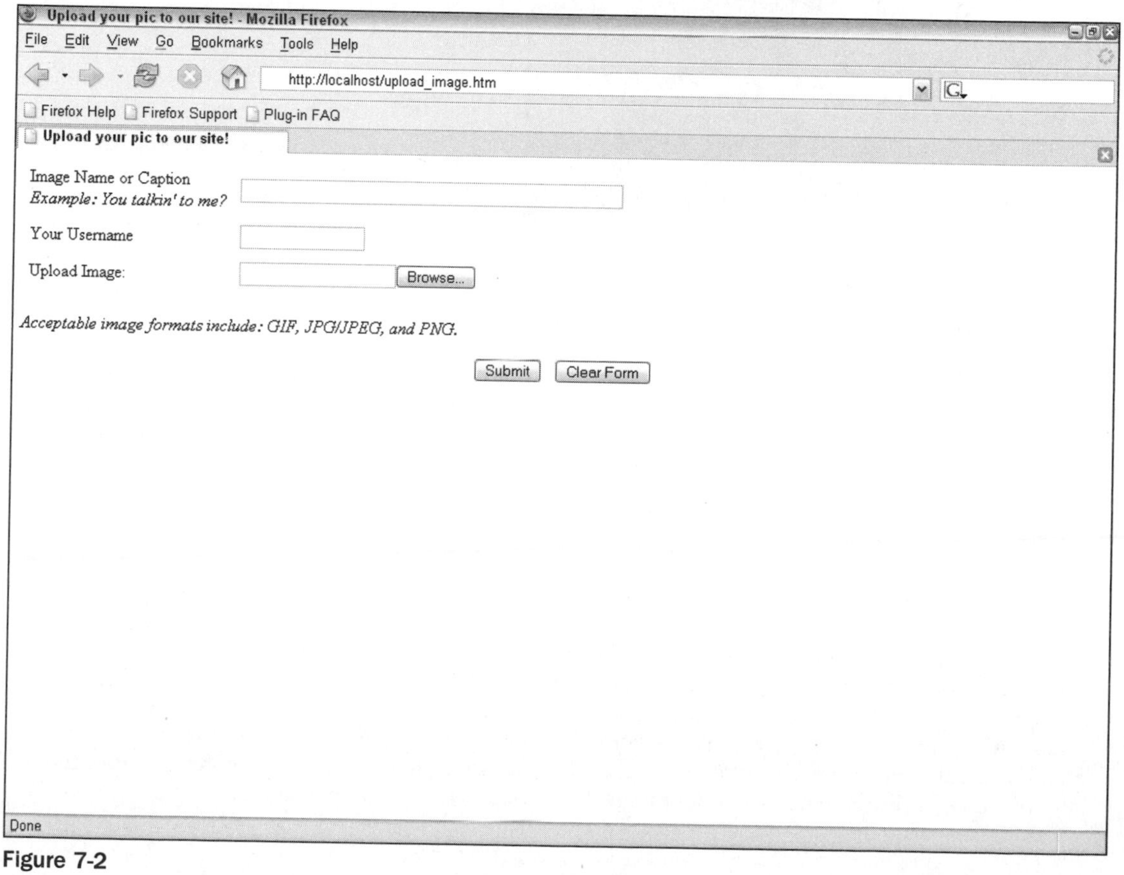

Figure 7-2

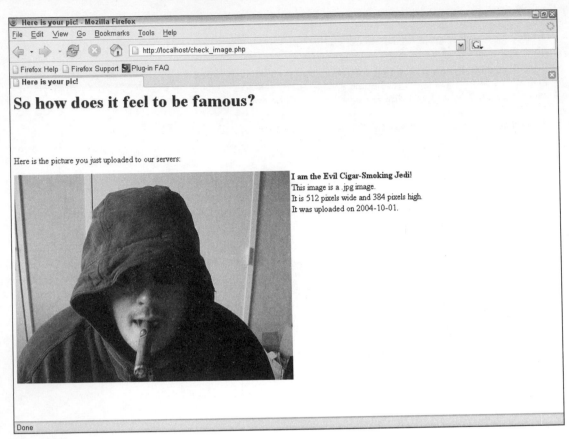

Figure 7-3

How It Works

In `upload_image.htm`, you have given HTML the power to search the user's local disk with the "Browse" button, simply by adding the `enctype` to the form attributes:

```
<form name="form1" method="post" action="check_image.php"
    enctype="multipart/form-data">
```

Then you have a few input fields, including the input type, `"file"`, which takes the file and passes it to the server, in a temporary place.

Then, in `check_image.php`, you have several different things going on. First, you connect to the database and make the variables easy to access in your script. Next, you define your directory that holds all your images, and the name of your image. Let's look at this line in particular:

```
$image_tempname = $_FILES['image_filename']['name'];
```

You can use several different methodologies when dealing with images. If you think you will have numerous files for each user, you can create a directory for each user, then reference the images in each one. In this instance, you are keeping all the image files in one big directory, just for simplicity's sake. Regardless of the directory structure you choose, you should apply some check for duplicate filenames. In this case, you renamed each incoming file the same name as the unique ID assigned to it. This ensures that each file will have its own unique name, and you won't have any problems if two users upload a file named photo1.jpg. So you will temporarily hang on to the name of the file that was uploaded using the variable $image_tempname, and rename it once it has uploaded successfully and been inserted into your table, using the variable $newfilename, which you see later on in the script.

Next you check to make sure the file was uploaded successfully with this line:

```
if (move_uploaded_file($_FILES['image_filename']['tmp_name'],
                $ImageName))
```

The move_uploaded_file function does just that—it moves an uploaded file from the original image filename that was provided by the user to the 'tmp_name' assigned by the server to the ultimate destination, $ImageName (the filename that was provided by the user concatenated to the images directory). It is important to include the 'tmp_name' step in your scripts, and to note that you really don't have anything to do with this value held in this variable—it is assigned by the server. The value is hidden from you, but it's important that you don't rename or alter the way that variable is referenced.

The next step is to get information about the file that was just uploaded. In the example, you are only allowing those more common file types that play well with the current version of the PHP/GD combo. This includes GIF, JPG, and PNG files. Other file types are easily manipulated in PHP, such as WBMP, but for now we will skip over those.

> WBMP is not the same type of file as a Windows Bitmap (BMP). WBMP files are Wireless Bitmap files, used in Palm Pilots and the like. At the time of this writing, the PHP/GD combo does not provide for direct manipulation of BMP files. You will need another application such as ImageMagick to convert BMP files into GIF, JPG, or PNG files if you want to work with them using PHP/GD.

The getimagesize function is very valuable for gleaning information about an image file. It can give you the width, height, and type of the image, and for JPG files, it can give you the number of channels and bits. It spits out the information in an array, which you access using the list function in this line:

```
list($width, $height, $type, $attr) = getimagesize($ImageName);
```

Width and height of the image are returned as integers in pixels. The type of the file is portrayed as an integer with the following key:

1	GIF	9	JPC
2	JPG	10	JP2
3	PNG	11	JPX
4	SWF	12	JB2
5	PSD	13	SWC
6	BMP	14	IFF
7	TIFF (Intel byte order)	15	WBMP
8	TIFF (Motorola byte order)	16	XBM

The $attr variable contains a string with the width and height included, which you would use in an HTML image tag. An example of the contents of this variable is

```
width="640" height="480
```

But alas, we digress. Going back to the script at hand, you use the switch function to filter out the unusable image types like this:

```
switch ($type) {
    case 1:
      $ext = ".gif";
      break;
    case 2:
      $ext = ".jpg";
      break;
    case 3:
      $ext = ".png";
      break;
    default:
      echo "Sorry, but the file you uploaded was not a GIF, JPG, or " .
           "PNG file.<br>";
      echo "Please hit your browser's 'back' button and try again.";
}
```

You assign the file extension based on the file type, and you will need to have that information available when you rename your file. If the uploaded file doesn't match any of your cases, the default is applied, and that is that the reader will see the "Sorry, but the file you uploaded was not a GIF, JPG or PNG file" statements. This way you can filter out unacceptable file types, non-image files, or corrupted files that may have been uploaded.

Assuming everything is going smoothly, you then insert the information in the table, in the following lines:

```
//insert info into image table

$insert = "INSERT INTO images
           (image_caption, image_username, image_date)
           VALUES
           ('$image_caption', '$image_username', '$today')";
$insertresults = mysql_query($insert)
  or die(mysql_error());

$lastpicid = mysql_insert_id();
```

You then rename the file to avoid any future filename conflicts, using the image's auto-incremented ID:

```
$newfilename =  $ImageDir . $lastpicid . $ext;

rename($ImageName, $newfilename);
```

Then in the HTML portion of the script, you simply spit the picture back out to the user, so he or she knows the image was successfully uploaded.

Converting Image File Types

You may have noticed something interesting about the way you referenced your image when showing it back to the user. Look at this line:

```
<img src="images/<?php echo $lastpicid . $ext; ?>" align="left">
```

You used the two variables `$lastpicid` and `$ext` to return your image's filename. (You could have also used the variable `$newfilename` and left off the image path, but bear with us, we're going to make a point here.) Did you notice that this information isn't stored anywhere in your image table? How will you access this picture again when the information in the variables has expired? You can access the first portion of the filename, because it's the same as the `image_id`. How do you know the file extension, though, if it's different for each image? You can do one of three things to remedy this:

1. Add a field to your image table to allow you to store the full image filename.

2. Add a field to your image table to allow you to store the extension.

3. Convert all your incoming images to the same file type so the extension will always be the same.

We're going for door number 3, Monty. You'll see why in the next few sections, but for now, alter your `check_image.php` file accordingly. You won't be "converting" the images per se, but you will be creating duplicates in the `.jpg` file type, and saving those. You can choose GIF, JPG, or PNG; this example uses JPG files because we are dealing mostly with photos and won't need to worry about things like transparency.

To convert your file to another type, you have to do four (optionally five) steps:

1. Create a new GD-friendly image from your original image to act as your temporary source image.

2. Create a new GD-friendly blank image to act as your temporary destination image.

3. Copy your new source image to your new destination image.

4. Save or output your altered destination image.

5. (Optional, but recommended) Destroy your temporary source and destination images.

PHP has file type–specific functions for steps 1 and 4 (for example, `imagecreatefromgif`, `image createfromjpg`, and so on), so it's important to know the file type you're working with. By keeping the file types consistent on your site, you can manipulate all the images using the same set of functions. Of course it is possible to maintain and work with multiple image types, but remember you're going for simplicity here.

Try It Out   Streamlining the Process

To fix your file, you will need to alter `check_image.php`.

1. Open your file and make the following changes (changes are highlighted):

```php
<?php

//connect to the database
$link = mysql_connect("localhost", "bp5am", "bp5ampass")
  or die("Could not connect: " . mysql_error());
mysql_select_db("moviesite", $link)
  or die (mysql_error());

//make variables available
$image_caption = $_POST['image_caption'];
$image_username = $_POST['image_username'];
$image_tempname = $_FILES['image_filename']['name'];
$today = date("Y-m-d");

//upload image and check for image type
$ImageDir ="c:/Program Files/Apache Group/Apache2/test/images/";
$ImageName = $ImageDir . $image_tempname;

if (move_uploaded_file($_FILES['image_filename']['tmp_name'],
                       $ImageName)) {

  //get info about the image being uploaded
  list($width, $height, $type, $attr) = getimagesize($ImageName);

  //**delete these lines
  switch ($type) {
    case 1:
      $ext = ".gif";
      break;
    case 2:
      $ext = ".jpg";
      break;
    case 3:
      $ext = ".png";
      break;
    default:
      echo "Sorry, but the file you uploaded was not a GIF, JPG, or " .
          "PNG file.<br>";
      echo "Please hit your browser's 'back' button and try again.";
  }
  //**end of deleted lines

  //**insert these new lines
  if ($type > 3) {
    echo "Sorry, but the file you uploaded was not a GIF, JPG, or " .
        "PNG file.<br>";
    echo "Please hit your browser's 'back' button and try again.";
  } else {

    //image is acceptable; ok to proceed

  //**end of inserted lines

  //insert info into image table
```

```php
$insert = "INSERT INTO images
          (image_caption, image_username, image_date)
          VALUES
          ('$image_caption', '$image_username', '$today')";
$insertresults = mysql_query($insert)
  or die(mysql_error());

$lastpicid = mysql_insert_id();
```

```php
//change the following line:
$newfilename = $ImageDir . $lastpicid . ".jpg";

//**insert these lines
if ($type == 2) {
  rename($ImageName, $newfilename);
} else {
  if ($type == 1) {
    $image_old = imagecreatefromgif($ImageName);
  } elseif ($type == 3) {
    $image_old = imagecreatefrompng($ImageName);
  }

  //"convert" the image to jpg
  $image_jpg = imagecreatetruecolor($width, $height);
  imagecopyresampled($image_jpg, $image_old, 0, 0, 0, 0,
                     $width, $height, $width, $height);
  imagejpeg($image_jpg, $newfilename);
  imagedestroy($image_old);
  imagedestroy($image_jpg);
}

$url = "location: showimage.php?id=" . $lastpicid;
header($url);
//**end of inserted lines
}
```

```php
?>
```

```html
<!-- DELETE THESE LINES
<html>
<head>
<title>Here is your pic!</title>
</head>
<body>
<h1>So how does it feel to be famous?</h1><br><br>
<p>Here is the picture you just uploaded to our servers:</p>
<img src="images/<?php echo $lastpicid . $ext;  ?>" align="left">
<strong><?php echo $image_caption; ?></strong><br>
This image is a <?php echo $ext; ?> image.<br>
It is <?php echo $width; ?> pixels wide
and <?php echo $height; ?> pixels high.<br>
It was uploaded on <?php echo $today; ?>.
</body>
</html>
END OF DELETED LINES-->
```

2. Open your text editor and type the new `showimage.php` file as shown:

```php
<?php

//connect to the database
$link = mysql_connect("localhost", "bp5am", "bp5ampass")
  or die("Could not connect: " . mysql_error());
mysql_select_db("moviesite", $link)
  or die (mysql_error());


//make variables available
$id = $_REQUEST['id'];

//get info on the pic we want
$getpic = mysql_query("SELECT * FROM images WHERE image_id = '$id'")
  or die(mysql_error());
$rows = mysql_fetch_array($getpic);
extract($rows);

$image_filename = "images/" . $image_id . ".jpg";

list($width, $height, $type, $attr) = getimagesize($image_filename);

?>

<html>
<head>
<title>Here is your pic!</title>
</head>
<body>
<h1>So how does it feel to be famous?</h1><br><br>
<p>Here is the picture you just uploaded to our servers:</p>
<img src="<?php echo $image_filename; ?>" align="left"
  <?php echo $attr; ?> >
<strong><?php echo $image_caption; ?></strong><br>
It is <?php echo $width; ?> pixels wide a
nd <?php echo $height; ?> pixels high.<br>
It was uploaded on <?php echo $image_date; ?>
by <?php echo $image_username; ?>.
</body>
</html>
```

3. If you save the file, load it in your browser, and upload your picture, you will notice that you basically get the same screen as before (with a few minor tweaks).

How It Works

Let's look at the main section that you added to your program, and let's take it line by line. First, we will deal with the JPG files because they are already in the format you want.

```php
if ($type == 2) {
  rename($ImageName, $newfilename);
```

Here you are saying if the file is a JPG file, you just want to rename it to match your image ID, plus the ".jpg" extension. Piece of cake, right?

Otherwise, if the file is a GIF or a PNG, you want to use the appropriate function to deal with them. You first check to see if the file is a GIF file:

```
} else {
  if ($type == 1) {
    $image_old = imagecreatefromgif($ImageName);
```

imagecreatefromgif() is the appropriate function because your source image is in a GIF format. Likewise if the image was a PNG image, you would use the imagecreatefrompng function:

```
} elseif ($type == 3) {
    $image_old = imagecreatefrompng($ImageName);
}
```

Now that you have your GD-friendly source image, you need to go step 2 of the conversion list presented earlier and create a GD-friendly temporary destination image. You do this in the next line:

```
$image_jpg = imagecreatetruecolor($width, $height);
```

You use the imagecreatetruecolor() function to maintain color quality in your image, and because you want your destination image to be identical in size to the source image, you use the $width and $height variables that were obtained from the getimagesize function earlier in the script.

Now you can proceed to step 3 of the conversion list — copy the temporary source image into the temporary destination image. You do this in the next line:

```
imagecopyresampled($image_jpg, $image_old, 0, 0, 0, 0,
                    $width, $height, $width, $height);
```

You use imagecopyresampled to maintain the quality of your image. As you can see, you denote the destination image, the source image, starting coordinates (x, y) of both images, and the width and height of each image. If you only wanted to copy a portion of the source image into your destination image, you could do this through the coordinates and the width/height variables.

Next, you have to save your image somewhere to make it permanent, as you can see in the next line:

```
imagejpeg($image_jpg, $newfilename);
```

This is where the actual conversion takes place. Before this line, your temporary images were "generic." You decide to make the destination file a JPG with the imagejpeg function. You could also have used imagepng or imagegif, but again, you want to work with JPGs because the majority of your uploaded files will be photos. In this function, you name the new temporary source file (your previous destination file) and the new permanent destination file. It's important to note that you needed to include the path name in the variable $newfilename, which you did above.

You also then can destroy your temporary images, as in the lines that follow:

```
imagedestroy($image_old);
imagedestroy($image_jpg);
```

In summary, you have either renamed your JPG files to be *image_id*.jpg, or you have created duplicate images and saved them as JPG files with the name *image_id*.jpg. Now you can reference the images the same way every time.

The script also relocates you to a new file, showimage.php, which basically pulls the information you just entered into the database, looks it up again, then spits it back to the browser. The difference is that you can access the showimage.php page any time, and for any image ID. This file is also going to be where you allow your users to modify their image to include captions, watermarks, and all kinds of other fun things.

Black and White

Now that you've got a directory full of images, what comes next? To play with them of course! What if you wanted to allow your users to make their images black and white? Let's add that option to your showimage page, so your users can choose whether or not they want to see their image in grayscale. You will be using the imagefilter() function, which can do many things, only one of which is to convert the image to grayscale. This function can also make a negative of your image, alter the brightness or contrast of your image, emboss, blur, smooth, detect edges within and colorize your image. Whew! It's a pretty powerful function, and one you want to remember. (You can find complete syntax for using this function and the filter types at http://us2.php.net/manual/en/function.imagefilter.php.) You can use this function to clean up or create funky versions of uploaded photos, or better yet, transfer that power over to your users!

Try It Out   Adding Grayscale

In this exercise, you'll add just one of the imagefilter() features to your site. You'll give users the option to show their image in grayscale.

1. Open showimage.php and make the following highlighted changes:

```
<?php

//connect to the database
$link = mysql_connect("localhost", "bp5am", "bp5ampass")
   or die("Could not connect: " . mysql_error());
mysql_select_db("moviesite", $link)
   or die (mysql_error());


//make variables available
$id = $_REQUEST['id'];

//**INSERT THE FOLLOWING LINE:
if (isset($_REQUEST['mode'])) {
  $mode = $_REQUEST['mode'];
```

```
} else {
  $mode = '';
}
//**END OF INSERT

//get info on the pic we want
$getpic = mysql_query("SELECT * FROM images WHERE image_id = '$id'")
  or die(mysql_error());
$rows = mysql_fetch_array($getpic);
extract($rows);

$image_filename = "images/" . $image_id . ".jpg";

list($width, $height, $type, $attr) = getimagesize($image_filename);

?>

<html>
<head>
<title>Here is your pic!</title>
</head>
<body>
<h1>So how does it feel to be famous?</h1><br><br>
```

```
<!--INSERT THE FOLLOWING LINES: -->
<?php
if ($mode == 'change') {
  echo "<font color=\"CC0000\"><em><strong>Your image has been
      modified.</strong></em></font>";
  echo "<img src=\"" . $image_filename . "\" align=\"left\" " .
      $attr . ">";

} else {
?>
<!--END OF INSERTED LINES-->
```

```
<p>Here is the picture you just uploaded to our servers:</p>
<img src="<?php echo $image_filename; ?>" align="left"
  <?php echo $attr; ?> >
<strong><?php echo $image_caption; ?></strong><br>
It is <?php echo $width; ?> pixels wide
and <?php echo $height; ?> pixels high.<br>
It was uploaded on <?php echo $image_date; ?>
by <?php echo $image_username; ?>.
```

```
<!--INSERT THE FOLLOWING LINES:-->
<?php
//end the else
}
?>
```

```
<hr>
<p><em><strong>Modifying Your Image</strong></em></p>
<form action="modifyimage.php" method="post">
<p>
```

```
   Please choose if you would like to modify your image with any of
   the following options. If you would like to preview the image
   before saving, you will need to hit your browser's 'back' button
   to return to this page. Saving an image with any of the
   modifications listed below <em>cannot be undone.</em>
</p>
<input name="id" type="hidden" value="<?php echo $image_id; ?>">
<input name="bw" type="checkbox">black &amp; white<br>

<p align="center">
  <input type="submit" name="action" value="preview">
  <input type="submit" name="action" value="save">
</p>
</form>

<!--END OF INSERTED LINES-->

</body>
</html>
```

2.   Next, you want to create a new file that will modify your image accordingly. Open your
      browser and type the following, saving it as modifyimage.php:

```php
<?php

//connect to the database
$link = mysql_connect("localhost", "bp5am", "bp5ampass")
  or die("Could not connect: " . mysql_error());
mysql_select_db("moviesite", $link)
  or die (mysql_error());


//make variables available
$id = $_POST['id'];
if (isset($_POST['bw'])) {
  $bw = $_POST['bw'];
} else {
  $bw = '';
}
$action = $_POST['action'];

//get info on the pic we want
$getpic = mysql_query("SELECT * FROM images WHERE image_id = '$id'")
  or die(mysql_error());
$rows = mysql_fetch_array($getpic);
extract($rows);

$image_filename = "images/" . $image_id . ".jpg";

list($width, $height, $type, $attr) = getimagesize($image_filename);

$image = imagecreatefromjpeg("$image_filename");

if ($bw == 'on') {
```

```
      imagefilter($image, IMG_FILTER_GRAYSCALE);
   }


   if ($action == "preview") {
     header("Content-type:image/jpeg");
     imagejpeg($image);
   }

   if ($action == "save") {
     imagejpeg($image, $image_filename);

     $url = "location:showimage.php?id=". $id . "&mode=change";
     header($url);
   }

?>
```

3. Now, try this out. You don't need to upload another image, because you haven't changed anything in that step of the process. Go to `http://localhost/showimage.php?id=1` (or whatever your specific URL is). You should see something similar to that in Figure 7-4.

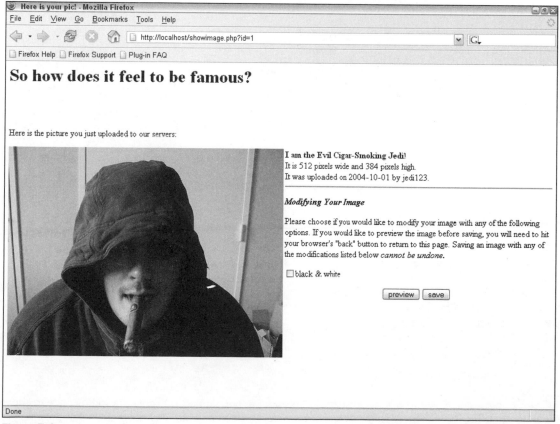

Figure 7-4

If you preview your image in black and white, you will get a screen with nothing but the image. Try hitting your browser's "back" button and try saving the file in black and white this time. You should see something like that shown in Figure 7-5 (of course in this book the images *always* show up in black and white, but bear with us, okay?).

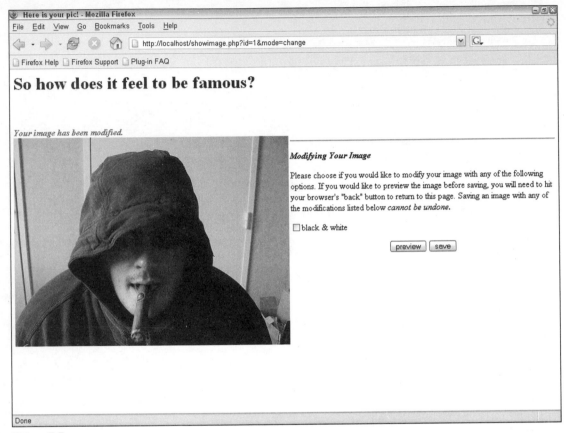

Figure 7-5

How It Works

If you look at the lines you added in showimage.php, you see the following lines first:

```
//**INSERT THE FOLLOWING LINE:
if (isset($_REQUEST['mode'])) {
  $mode = $_REQUEST['mode'];
} else {
  $mode = '';
}
//**END OF INSERT
```

You have added this variable because in modifyimage.php you send users back to this page to show them their newly modified image. You want to send them some kind of confirmation that the change(s) they submitted were saved successfully, so this mode lets you do just that. You see the prime example of that later in the script when you add the lines

```
<!--INSERT THE FOLLOWING LINES: -->
<?php
if ($mode == change) {
  echo "<font color=\"CC0000\"><em><strong>Your image has been
       modified.</strong></em></font>";
  echo "<img src=\"" . $image_filename . "\" align=\"left\" " .
       $attr . ">";

} else {
```

You show the "Your image has been modified" line just to let users know what's going on. You also show the image again, so they can see their changes in action. You left out the size and when the image was uploaded, because users already saw that info when they first uploaded the thing.

In the following lines, you added a form to give users the black and white option:

```
<hr>
<p><em><strong>Modifying Your Image</strong></em></p>
<form action="modifyimage.php" method="post">
<p>
  Please choose if you would like to modify your image with any of
  the following options. If you would like to preview the image
  before saving, you will need to hit your browser's 'back' button
  to return to this page. Saving an image with any of the
  modifications listed below <em>cannot be undone.</em>
</p>
<input name="id" type="hidden" value="<?php echo $image_id; ?>">
<input name="bw" type="checkbox">black &amp; white<br>

<p align="center">
  <input type="submit" name="action" value="preview">
  <input type="submit" name="action" value="save">
</p>
</form>

<!--END OF INSERTED LINES-->
```

Since we're on the subject of the new form, look at your newly created modifyimage.php file. Everything should look pretty standard, until you get to this line:

```
$image = imagecreatefromjpeg("$image_filename");
```

Remember the five-step conversion process? There is a similar process when simply altering images. First, you create a GD-friendly duplicate of your source image, which you did in the line above. Next you do whatever it is you want to do to your GD-friendly image, as seen in the following lines:

```
if ($bw == 'on') {
  imagefilter($image, IMG_FILTER_GRAYSCALE);
}
```

Next you decide whether or not you want to keep the changes you are making, and you do so in the following lines:

```
if ($action == "preview") {
  header("Content-type:image/jpeg");
  imagejpeg($image);
}
```

If you are only previewing the image, you will spit it directly out to the browser (which is done using the `imagejpeg()` function and without a specific filename for the destination). But why did you send a header to the browser, and why is there no HTML? Again, because you are spitting out the image directly, you don't need (and actually can't send) any text along with the image. You are only sending the image itself. If you don't specify what content type is in your page, the browser will assume it is text and you will get a page full of garbage. Don't believe us? Go ahead and comment out the header line and reload the page. See what we mean? You send the header so the browser will interpret the image stream correctly.

Because the browser is expecting an image, if you try to send any text along with the image, after the header has been sent, you will see a big ol' error.

If your users want to save the changes to the image, and they click "save" when submitting, you process the following lines of code:

```
if ($action == "save") {
  imagejpeg($image, $image_filename);
  $url = "location:showimage.php?id=". $id . "&mode=change";
  header($url);
}
```

Notice the use of the mode variable (so your users will see the confirmation text when the page loads) and the filename specified in the `imagejpeg()` function. Specifying a destination filename saves the temporary image to a permanent place, and in this case, it overwrites the file that was already there, making your change permanent.

Think you got it? Great! Let's let your users play with their images some more, shall we?

Adding Captions

A special group of functions allow you to add captions (or a copyright notice or other text) to your images. PHP/GD is relatively advanced in allowing you to control the size and type of font that is used, even allowing you to load your own font on demand. While you're absolutely encouraged to experiment with all the cool font functions available to you, we will try and keep it simple here to get you started. That being said, let's get to it!

Embedding Text in Images

You will be modifying your `showimage.php` and `modifyimage.php` files to show captions along with the images, but they will be minor changes.

1. Locate the following section in your `showimage.php` file, and add the highlighted lines:

```
<hr>
<p><em><strong>Modifying Your Image</strong></em></p>
<form action="modifyimage.php" method="post">
<p>
  Please choose if you would like to modify your image with any of
  the following options. If you would like to preview the image
  before saving, you will need to hit your browser's 'back' button
  to return to this page. Saving an image with any of the
  modifications listed below <em>cannot be undone.</em>
</p>
<input name="id" type="hidden" value="<?php echo $image_id; ?>">
<input name="bw" type="checkbox">black & white<br>

<!--INSERT THE FOLLOWING LINE-->
<input name="text" type="checkbox">embedded caption<br>
<!--END OF INSERTED LINES-->

<p align="center">
  <input type="submit" name="action" value="preview">
  <input type="submit" name="action" value="save">
</p>
</form>
```

2. The "arial.ttf" font is used in this exercise, but you should use a font that is installed on your server. If you attempt to run the following script with a font that is not installed on the server, you will get an error. Now that that's cleared up, add the following highlighted lines to your `modifyimage.php` file:

```
<?php

//connect to the database
$link = mysql_connect("localhost", "bp5am", "bp5ampass")
  or die("Could not connect: " . mysql_error());
mysql_select_db("moviesite", $link)
  or die (mysql_error());


//make variables available
$id = $_POST['id'];
if (isset($_POST['bw'])) {
  $bw = $_POST['bw'];
} else {
  $bw = '';
```

```
}
$action = $_POST['action'];
//**INSERT THE FOLLOWING LINES:
if (isset($_POST['text'])) {
  $text = $_POST['text'];
} else {
  $text = '';
}
//**END OF INSERT

//get info on the pic we want
$getpic = mysql_query("SELECT * FROM images WHERE image_id = '$id'")
  or die(mysql_error());
$rows = mysql_fetch_array($getpic);
extract($rows);

$image_filename = "images/" . $image_id . ".jpg";

list($width, $height, $type, $attr) = getimagesize($image_filename);

$image = imagecreatefromjpeg("$image_filename");

if ($bw == 'on') {
  imagefilter($image, IMG_FILTER_GRAYSCALE);
}

//**INSERT THE FOLLOWING LINES:
if ($text == 'on') {
  imagettftext($image, 12, 0, 20, 20, 0, "arial.ttf", $image_caption);
}
//**END OF INSERT

if ($action == "preview") {
  header("Content-type:image/jpeg");
  imagejpeg($image);
}

if ($action == "save") {
  imagejpeg($image, $image_filename);
  $url = "location:showimage.php?id=". $id . "&mode=change";
  header($url);
}

?>
```

3. Now go back to http://localhost/showimage.php?id=1 and try previewing your image with the "embed caption" feature checked. You should see something similar to Figure 7-6.

You can see how easy it is to automatically add copyright notices or any text at all to your images. Let's break it down.

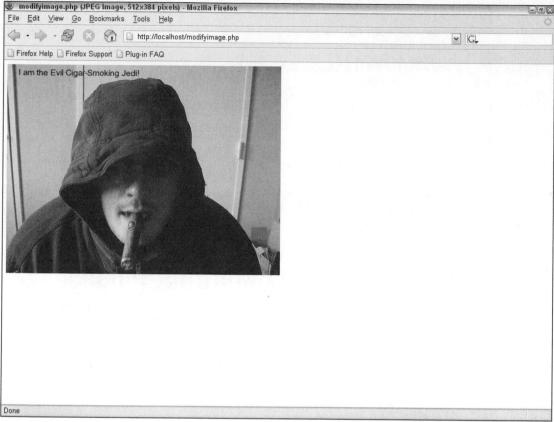

Figure 7-6

How It Works

First, you add the "embed caption" option to your form in showimage.php. This is a no-brainer, right? Good.

Then you add the imagettftext() function to your modifyimage.php file like this:

```
//**INSERT THE FOLLOWING LINES:
if ($text == 'on') {
  imagettftext($image, 12, 0, 20, 20, 0, "arial.ttf", $image_caption);
}
//**END OF INSERT
```

The imagettftext() function is only one of the many text/string functions available in PHP/GD. The function is made up of eight values, in this order:

1. The image where the text is to go ($image in this example)

2. The font size of the text (12 in this example)

3. The rotation of the text (0 in this example)

4. The x coordinate for the starting position of the text, with 0 being the leftmost boundary of the image (20 in this example)

5. The y coordinate for the starting position of the text, with 0 being the upper boundary of the image (20 in this example)

6. The color of the text using the color index (0, or black, in this example)

7. The name of the font file you want to reference, to be located automatically in the default font directory (`arial.ttf` in this example)

8. The string of text to be shown (contents of the `$image_caption` variable in this example)

Again, feel free to experiment with different fonts, colors, and locations for your text—this is only one small example. In the course of your experimentation, be sure you fill in values for each one of the eight parameters, or you will get an error message.

Adding Watermarks and Merging Images

Because you are showing these images on the Movie Review Site, make your logo show up lightly behind each image that is hosted by you, as a sort of watermark. You can do this with your own logo to protect any copyrighted images, as we did easily enough with the text.

In this section, you will actually be merging two images (your source image and your logo image) to create the desired effect. Let's make the changes.

Try it Out **Merging Two Images**

To merge the two images, you will again need to change your `showimage.php` file and your `modify image.php` file.

1. Add the following line to your `showimage.php` file, in the same section as before:

```
<input name="watermark" type="checkbox">include Movie Review Site watermark<br>
```

2. Add the following line to your `modifyimage.php` file, as before:

```
//**INSERT NEAR THE TOP OF THE FILE
if (isset($_POST['watermark'])) {
  $watermark = $_POST['watermark'];
} else {
  $watermark = '';
}
```

Then add the following lines later on in the script:

```
if ($watermark == 'on') {
  $image2 = imagecreatefromgif("images/logo.gif");
  imagecopymerge($image, $image2, 0,0,0, 0, $width, $height, 15);
}
```

3. Okay, now do as you're told. Try it out, already! Although you don't have the `logo.gif` file, use any file you like—just make sure your script can find it. Your screen should look something remotely resembling that in Figure 7-7.

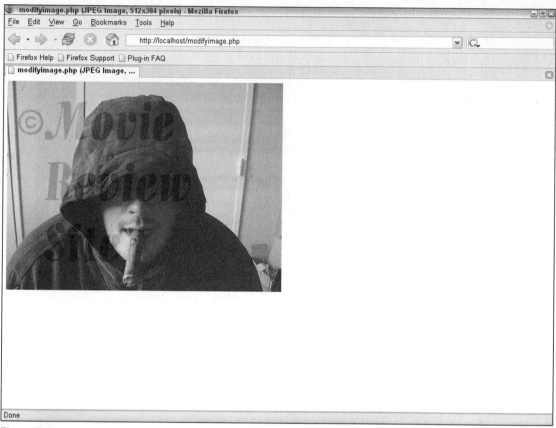

Figure 7-7

How It Works

You have simply added another option for your users; and you did it using the `imagecopymerge()` function in `modifyimage.php`. Note that before you could merge the two images, you had to make the second image "GD friendly" by creating a duplicate copy. Because your image was a GIF image, you used the `imagecreatefromgif` function.

Look at this line from that script:

```
imagecopymerge($image, $image2, 0,0,0, 0, $width, $height, 15);
```

The parameters for the `imagecopymerge` function are as follows, in this order:

1. The name of the destination image (`$image` in this example, since the `$image` file is the one you are making all the changes to, and the one that will be shown at the end of your script)

2. The name of the second, or "source" image ($image2 in this example)

3. The x coordinate of the destination image (0 in this example, representing the leftmost boundary)

4. The y coordinate of the destination image (0 in this example, representing the upper boundary)

5. The x coordinate of the second image (0 in this example)

6. The y coordinate of the second image (0 in this example)

7. The width of the portion of the second image to be merged ($width in this example, representing as much of the second image that will fit on the destination image)

8. The height of the portion of the second image to be merged ($height in this example, representing as much of the second image that will fit on the destination image)

9. The percent of transparency of the two images to be merged, with 100 being equal to the second image completely overwriting the first (15 in this example)

Let's talk briefly about numbers seven and eight. Because imagecopymerge() can merge only a portion of one image with another, you have to specify how much of the image you want merged. The CBA logo is huge, and bigger than the user's photo. You only wanted to merge the portion as big as your user's photo, which is why you used $width and $height. If your logo is tiny, you would specify its width and height, assuming you want to merge the whole thing with your first image.

We hope you're still with us because there is one more thing we would like to do.

Creating Thumbnails

Of course, showing your users' images at full size is fine if they want to see them up close. However, it's not too conducive for showing a photo gallery or list of many photos on a page. This section discusses discuss how you can automatically create a thumbnail of each of your uploaded files that will be used for just that purpose — a photo gallery of all your photos.

Try It Out   **Creating Thumbnails**

You want to automatically create a thumbnail version of all the images that are uploaded by the users, so you will be modifying check_image.php and including this function.

1. Create a subdirectory of your images folder to house the thumbnails. For this example, we created c:\Program Files\Apache Group\Apache2\images\thumbs. Make sure your directory has "write" permissions.

2. Modify your check_image.php file as follows (changes are highlighted):

```php
<?php

//connect to the database
$link = mysql_connect("localhost", "bp5am", "bp5ampass")
   or die("Could not connect: " . mysql_error());
mysql_select_db("moviesite", $link)
   or die (mysql_error());
```

```
//make variables available
$image_caption = $_POST['image_caption'];
$image_username = $_POST['image_username'];
$image_tempname = $_FILES['image_filename']['name'];
$today = date("Y-m-d");

//upload image and check for image type
$ImageDir = "c:/Program Files/Apache Group/Apache2/test/images/";

//**INSERT THIS LINE:
$ImageThumb = $ImageDir . "thumbs/";
//**END OF INSERT

$ImageName = $ImageDir . $image_tempname;

if (move_uploaded_file($_FILES['image_filename']['tmp_name'],
                       $ImageName)) {

  //get info about the image being uploaded
  list($width, $height, $type, $attr) = getimagesize($ImageName);

  if ($type > 3) {
    echo "Sorry, but the file you uploaded was not a GIF, JPG, or " .
        "PNG file.<br>";
    echo "Please hit your browser's 'back' button and try again.";
  } else {

  //image is acceptable; ok to proceed


  //insert info into image table

  $insert = "INSERT INTO images
            (image_caption, image_username, image_date)
            VALUES
            ('$image_caption', '$image_username', '$today')";
  $insertresults = mysql_query($insert)
    or die(mysql_error());

  $lastpicid = mysql_insert_id();

  $newfilename =  $ImageDir . $lastpicid . ".jpg";

  if ($type == 2) {
    rename($ImageName, $newfilename);
  } else {
    if ($type == 1) {
      $image_old = imagecreatefromgif($ImageName);
    } elseif ($type == 3) {
      $image_old = imagecreatefrompng($ImageName);

    //"convert" the image to jpg
    $image_jpg = imagecreatetruecolor($width, $height);
```

```
        imagecopyresampled($image_jpg, $image_old, 0, 0, 0, 0,
                          $width, $height, $width, $height);
      imagejpeg($image_jpg, $newfilename);
      imagedestroy($image_old);
      imagedestroy($image_jpg);

  }
```

```
//**INSERT THESE LINES

  $newthumbname = $ImageThumb . $lastpicid . ".jpg";

  //get the dimensions for the thumbnail
  $thumb_width = $width * 0.10;
  $thumb_height = $height * 0.10;

  //create the thumbnail
  $largeimage = imagecreatefromjpeg($newfilename);
  $thumb = imagecreatetruecolor($thumb_width, $thumb_height);
  imagecopyresampled($thumb, $largeimage, 0, 0, 0, 0,
                    $thumb_width, $thumb_height, $width, $height);
  imagejpeg($thumb, $newthumbname);
  imagedestroy($largeimage);
  imagedestroy($thumb);
//**END OF INSERT
```

```
  $url = "location: showimage.php?id=" . $lastpicid;
  header ($url);
  }
}

?>
```

3.   Now you're going to create gallery.php, which will act as your photo gallery. Type the following in your editor:

```
<?php

//connect to the database
$link = mysql_connect("localhost", "bp5am", "bp5ampass")
  or die("Could not connect: " . msql_error());
mysql_select_db("moviesite", $link)
  or die (mysql_error());

$ImageDir = "images";
$ImageThumb = $ImageDir . "/thumbs/";
?>
```

```
<html>
<head>
<title>Welcome to our Photo Gallery</title>
</head>
<body>
<p align="center">Click on any image to see it full sized.</p>
<table align="center">
  <tr>
    <td align="center">Image</td>
    <td align="center">Caption</td>
    <td align="center">Uploaded By</td>
    <td align="center">Date Uploaded</td>
  </tr>

<?php
//get the thumbs
$getpic = mysql_query("SELECT * FROM images")
  or die(mysql_error());
while ($rows = mysql_fetch_array($getpic)) {
  extract($rows);
  echo "<tr>\n";
  echo "<td><a href=\"".$ImageDir . $image_id . ".jpg\">";
  echo "<img src=\"" . $ImageThumb . $image_id . ".jpg\" border=\"0\">";
  echo "</a></td>\n";
  echo "<td>" . $image_caption . "</td>\n";
  echo "<td>" . $image_username . "</td>\n";
  echo "<td>" . $image_date . "</td>\n";
  echo "</tr>\n";
}

?>

</table>
</body>
</html>
```

4. Now upload some images using your `upload_image.htm` page. When you have a few, go to `gallery.php` in your browser and see what you have. Your screen should look something like Figure 7-8.

Ok, so it's not pretty, and mostly utilitarian in appearance. The important thing is that it works! You can add the bells and whistles later; we just want to make sure you can make a thumbnail.

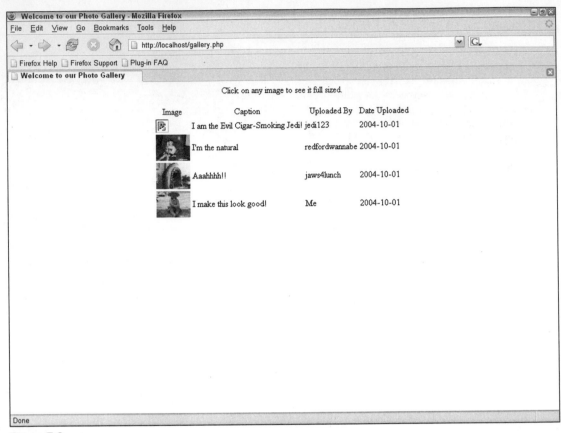

Figure 7-8

How It Works

The actual thumbnail itself is created in your `check_image.php` file, so let's take a look at that first. You added the following lines that complete that task for you:

```
//**INSERT THESE LINES

$newthumbname = $ImageThumb . $lastpicid . ".jpg";

//get the dimensions for the thumbnail
$thumb_width = $width * 0.10;
$thumb_height = $height * 0.10;

//create the thumbnail
$largeimage = imagecreatefromjpeg($newfilename);
$thumb = imagecreatetruecolor($thumb_width, $thumb_height);
imagecopyresampled($thumb, $largeimage, 0, 0, 0, 0,
                    $thumb_width, $thumb_height, $width, $height);
```

```
imagejpeg($thumb, $newthumbname);
imagedestroy($largeimage);
imagedestroy($thumb);
//**END OF INSERT
```

You first give your thumbnail its own directory, and you're using the same naming scheme for simplicity's sake. You then decide to make your thumbnails equal to 10% of the size of the original pictures. By using percentages instead of hard integers, you ensure that the proportions are kept equal and no skewing of your image occurs. Of course, you can make this smaller or larger depending on your users' preferences and typical file uploads.

You then create the thumbnail using the 5-step process as before:

1. Create a GD-friendly image from your source.

2. Create a blank GD-friendly image, with your smaller dimensions.

3. Copy the source image into the smaller blank image.

4. Save the newly created small image in its proper directory with its proper name.

5. Destroy the temporary images.

Just like before, easy as pie, right?

You may notice a broken image in the screenshot above; do you know why it is broken? If you said "because we uploaded that photo before we implemented the thumbnail process," then you get 100 points and you get to take a break. Not a long one, mind you, but a break nonetheless.

Summary

This chapter covered a lot, and has only scratched the surface on image manipulation using the PHP/GD combination. Hopefully by now, you can upload images, resize them, change their coloring, create an automatic thumbnail, create new images, and merge two images together.

In this chapter, you used a form to get the image from the user. What if the user tried to upload a file that wasn't an image at all, either by mistake or out of malicious intent? In this chapter, such a file would have been caught by the code that checked for the image type. Not all forms are so straightforward to check, though. In the next chapter, you'll learn about how to check that users enter information in your form in the proper format, and how to give them appropriate feedback when they don't.

Exercises

1. Create a site called a "virtual vacation." Offer different backgrounds for people to superimpose photos of themselves in, and let them send virtual postcards to their friends and family.

## Chapter 7

2. Have a page on your site with funny photographs or cartoons and allow your users to write the caption for them. Place the text in a speech bubble that is appropriately sized based on the length of the caption they submit.

3. Create a page for kids where they can choose different heads, bodies, and tails from animals, and put them together to make a new creation and a new image. Or create a virtual paper doll site where kids can place different outfits on a model, then save the images they create.

Validating User Input

If you plan to accept user input on your site, you have to be prepared for mistakes. This could be simple human error, or a deliberate attempt to circumvent your Web forms. The most common human errors include basic typographical errors and format errors — failing to give a year in a date, for example. Deliberate errors could be a user who doesn't want to provide his e-mail address, or it could be an attacker deliberately trying to corrupt your database with unexpected characters. No matter what the source, your script needs to be able to handle incorrect input, usually by identifying the bad data and returning the user to the form page with an appropriate error message. This chapter covers user input validation, including:

❑ Validating simple string values

❑ Validating integer values

❑ Validating formatted text input

Users Are Users Are Users . . .

Consider an example: You work in a bank. You are developing a new system to allow the employees to manage a customer account updating process on the company intranet. You use your well-known MM-DD-YYYY format for the date. It all works quite well when testing, but when put in production, your users say it doesn't work. Why? Because all your company systems use the ISO 8601 YYYY-MM-DD date format (a standard used in many systems because the date can be sorted alphabetically). Your users are confused between the two different formats and input wrong information in the system. If the data is in the wrong format, you can end up with a corrupted database or trigger errors in your application.

You can avoid this by using well-known formats and *validating* the user input. When you expect an integer value, for example, you can check that it is an integer before you try to use it. It's a simple enough rule, and you'll learn how to do it later in this chapter.

Incorporating Validation into the Movie Site

To really understand the role of user input and validation, you need to see it in action. So, first you need to add a few fields to your beloved movie database. The modifications are all in the `movie` table.

The movie application provides a lot of opportunities to check for user input. You will need to add a few features to the application, however, to provide more case studies. It will also help you to review what you learned in the previous chapters.

Add a `movie_release` field `INT(11)` with default value 0 after the existing `movie_year` field, as shown in Figure 8-1. This allows you to store a timestamp for the movie release date. Then add a field named `movie_rating` at the end of the table type `TINYINT (2)`. That information holds the movie rating you gave the movie when viewing it (see Figure 8-2). This rating goes from 0 to 10.

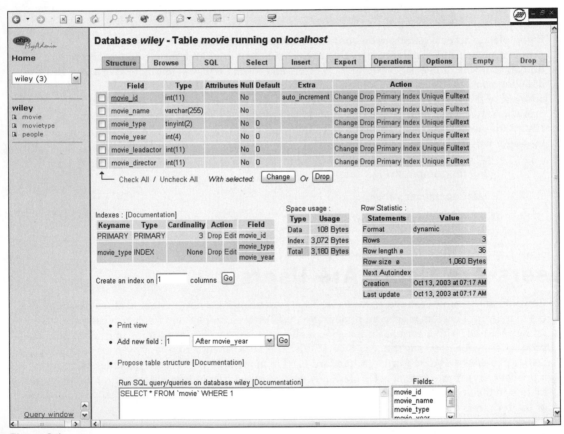

Figure 8-1

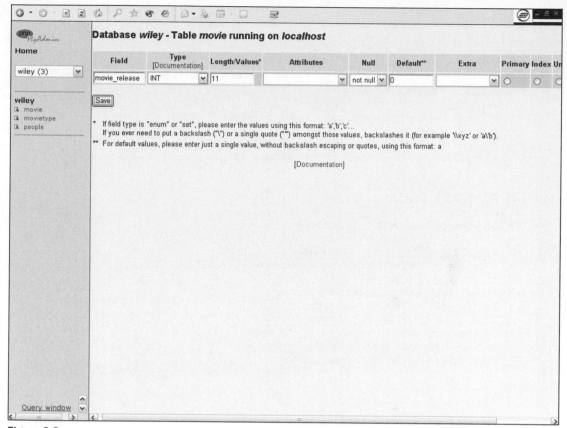

Figure 8-2

Forgot Something?

Sometimes, when a user enters data in a form, he or she forgets to fill in a field. When this happens, the system has to react so that the insertion of the invalid or incomplete data will not corrupt the database. In some cases, these errors are made on purpose. In some cases, blank fields will appear first during searches and make the searching process harder than necessary; in other cases you will have erroneous statistics on your data (in your billing system, for example). In fact, these attempts to find cracks in the walls around your system are quite frequent. You need to design your system so it can react to such errors or malicious attempts to corrupt the database.

Try It Out   Adapting Your Script to the User Input

In this exercise, you'll be making sure that the script can adapt when the user fails to enter all the fields.

1.   Copy the code you made in Chapter 6 into a new directory, open the movie.php script, and modify it as shown in the highlighted lines:

```php
<?php
$link = mysql_connect("localhost", "bp5am", "bp5ampass")
  or die("Could not connect: " . mysql_error());
mysql_select_db('moviesite', $link)
  or die ( mysql_error());

$peoplesql = "SELECT * FROM people";
$result = mysql_query($peoplesql)
   or die("Invalid query: " . mysql_error());

while ($row = mysql_fetch_array($result)) {
  $people[$row['people_id']] = $row['people_fullname'];
}

switch ($_GET['action']) {
  case "edit":
    $moviesql = "SELECT * FROM movie " .
                "WHERE movie_id = '" . $_GET['id'] . "'";
    $result = mysql_query($moviesql)
      or die("Invalid query: " . mysql_error());

    $row = mysql_fetch_array($result);
    $movie_name = $row['movie_name'];
    $movie_type = $row['movie_type'];
    $movie_year = $row['movie_year'];
    $movie_leadactor = $row['movie_leadactor'];
    $movie_director = $row['movie_director'];
    break;

  default:
    $movie_name = "";
    $movie_type = "";
    $movie_year = "";
    $movie_leadactor = "";
    $movie_director = "";
    break;
}
?>
<html>
<head>
<title><?php echo $_GET['action']; ?> movie</title>
<style type="text/css">
  TD{color:#353535;font-family:verdana}
  TH{color:#FFFFFF;font-family:verdana;background-color:#336699}
</style>
</head>
<body>
<form action="commit.php?action=<?php
  echo $_GET['action']; ?>&type=movie&id=<?php
  if (isset($_GET['id'])) { echo $_GET['id']; } ?>" method="post">
<?php
if (!empty($_GET['error'])) {
  echo "<div align=\"center\" " .
       "style=\"color:#FFFFFF;background-color:#FF0000;" .
```

```
            "font-weight:bold\">" . nl2br(urldecode($_GET['error'])) .
            "</div><br />";
    }
    ?>
<table border="0" width="750" cellspacing="1"
    cellpadding="3" bgcolor="#353535" align="center">
  <tr>
    <td bgcolor="#FFFFFF" width="30%">Movie Name</td>
    <td bgcolor="#FFFFFF" width="70%">
      <input type="text" name="movie_name"
        value="<?php echo $movie_name?>">
    </td>
  </tr>
  <tr>
    <td bgcolor="#FFFFFF">Movie Type</td>
    <td bgcolor="#FFFFFF">
      <select id="game" name="movie_type" style="width:150px">
        <option value="" selected>Select a type...</option>
<?php
$sql = "SELECT movietype_id, movietype_label " .
       "FROM movietype ORDER BY movietype_label";
$result = mysql_query($sql)
  or die("<font color=\"#FF0000\">Query Error</font>" . mysql_error());
while ($row = mysql_fetch_array($result)) {
  if ($row['movietype_id'] == $movie_type) {
    $selected = " selected";
  } else {
    $selected = "";
  }
  echo '<option value="' . $row['movietype_id'] . '"' . $selected .
       '>' . $row['movietype_label'] . "</option>\r\n";
}
?>
      </select>
    </td>
  </tr>
  <tr>
    <td bgcolor="#FFFFFF">Movie Year</td>
    <td bgcolor="#FFFFFF">
      <select name="movie_year">
        <option value="" selected>Select a year...</option>
<?php
for ($year=date("Y"); $year >= 1970 ; $year--) {
  if ($year == $movie_year) {
    $selected = " selected";
  } else {
    $selected = "";
  }
?>
        <option value="<?php echo $year; ?>"
          <?php echo $selected; ?>><?php echo $year; ?></option>
<?php
}
?>
```

```
        </select>
      </td>
    </tr>
    <tr>
      <td bgcolor="#FFFFFF">Lead Actor</td>
      <td bgcolor="#FFFFFF">
        <select name="movie_leadactor">
          <option value="" selected>Select an actor...</option>
<?php
foreach ($people as $people_id => $people_fullname) {
  if ($people_id == $movie_leadactor) {
    $selected = " selected";
  } else {
    $selected = "";
  }
?>
          <option value="<?php echo $people_id; ?>"
            <?php echo $selected; ?>><?php echo $people_fullname;
            ?></option>
<?php
}
?>
        </select>
      </td>
    </tr>
    <tr>
      <td bgcolor="#FFFFFF">Director</td>
      <td bgcolor="#FFFFFF">
        <select name="movie_director">
          <option value="" selected>Select a director...</option>
<?php
foreach ($people as $people_id => $people_fullname) {
  if ($people_id == $movie_director) {
    $selected = " selected";
  } else {
    $selected = "";
  }
?>
          <option value="<?php echo $people_id; ?>"
            <?php echo $selected; ?>><?php echo $people_fullname;
            ?></option>
<?php
}
?>
        </select>
      </td>
    </tr>
    <tr>
      <td bgcolor="#FFFFFF" colspan="2" align="center">
        <input type="submit" name="submit"
          value="<?php echo $_GET['action']; ?>">
      </td>
    </tr>
</table>
```

```
  </form>
  </body>
  </html>
```

2.   Save the file as movie.php and upload the new code to your work directory.

3.   Open the commit.php script and modify it as shown in the highlighted lines:

```php
<?php
// COMMIT ADD AND EDITS
$error = '';
$link = mysql_connect("localhost", "bp5am", "bp5ampass")
  or die("Could not connect: " . mysql_error());
mysql_select_db('moviesite', $link)
  or die ( mysql_error());

switch ($_GET['action']) {
  case "edit":
    switch ($_GET['type']) {
      case "people":
        $sql = "UPDATE people SET " .
               "people_fullname = '" . $_POST['people_fullname'] .
               "' WHERE people_id = '" . $_GET['id'] . "'";
        break;
      case "movie":
        $movie_name = trim($_POST['movie_name']);
        if (empty($movie_name)) {
          $error .= "Please+enter+a+movie+name%21%0D%0A";
        }
        if (empty($_POST['movie_type'])) {
          $error .= "Please+select+a+movie+type%21%0D%0A";
        }
        if (empty($_POST['movie_year'])) {
          $error .= "Please+select+a+movie+year%21%0D%0A";
        }
        if (empty($error)) {
          $sql = "UPDATE movie SET " .
            "movie_name = '" . $_POST['movie_name'] . "'," .
            "movie_year = '" . $_POST['movie_year'] . "'," .
            "movie_type = '" . $_POST['movie_type'] . "'," .
            "movie_leadactor = '" . $_POST['movie_leadactor'] . "'," .
            "movie_director = '" . $_POST['movie_director'] . "' " .
            "WHERE movie_id = '".$_GET['id']."'";
        } else {
          header("location:movie.php?action=edit&error=" .
                 $error . "&id=" . $_GET['id'] );
        }
        break;
    }
    break;
  case "add":
    switch ($_GET['type']) {
      case "people":
        $sql = "INSERT INTO people (people_fullname) " .
               "VALUES ('" . $_POST['people_fullname'] . "')";
```

```
          break;
       case "movie":
          $movie_name = trim($_POST['movie_name']);
          if (empty($movie_name)) {
            $error .= "Please+enter+a+movie+name%21%0D%0A";
          }
          if (empty($_POST['movie_type'])) {
            $error .= "Please+select+a+movie+type%21%0D%0A";
          }
          if (empty($_POST['movie_year'])) {
            $error .= "Please+select+a+movie+year%21%0D%0A";
          }
          if (empty($error)) {
            $sql = "INSERT INTO movie (movie_name,movie_year," .
                   "movie_type,movie_leadactor,movie_director) " .
                   "VALUES ('" . $_POST['movie_name'] . "'," .
                   "'" . $_POST['movie_year'] . "'," .
                   "'" . $_POST['movie_type'] . "'," .
                   "'" . $_POST['movie_leadactor'] . "'," .
                   "'" . $_POST['movie_director'] . "')";
          } else {
            header("location:movie.php?action=add&error=" . $error);
          }
          break;

    }
    break;
}
if (isset($sql) && !empty($sql)) {
  echo "<!--".$sql."-->";
  $result = mysql_query($sql)
    or die("Invalid query: " . mysql_error());
?>
<p align="center" style="color:#FF0000">
  Done. <a href="index.php">Index</a>
</p>
<?php
}
?>
```

4. Save the file as `commit.php` and upload it to your server.

5. Now open your browser and go to http://localhost/chapter8/index.php (adapt this URL to fit your setup) and try adding a movie with no name, as shown in Figure 8-3.

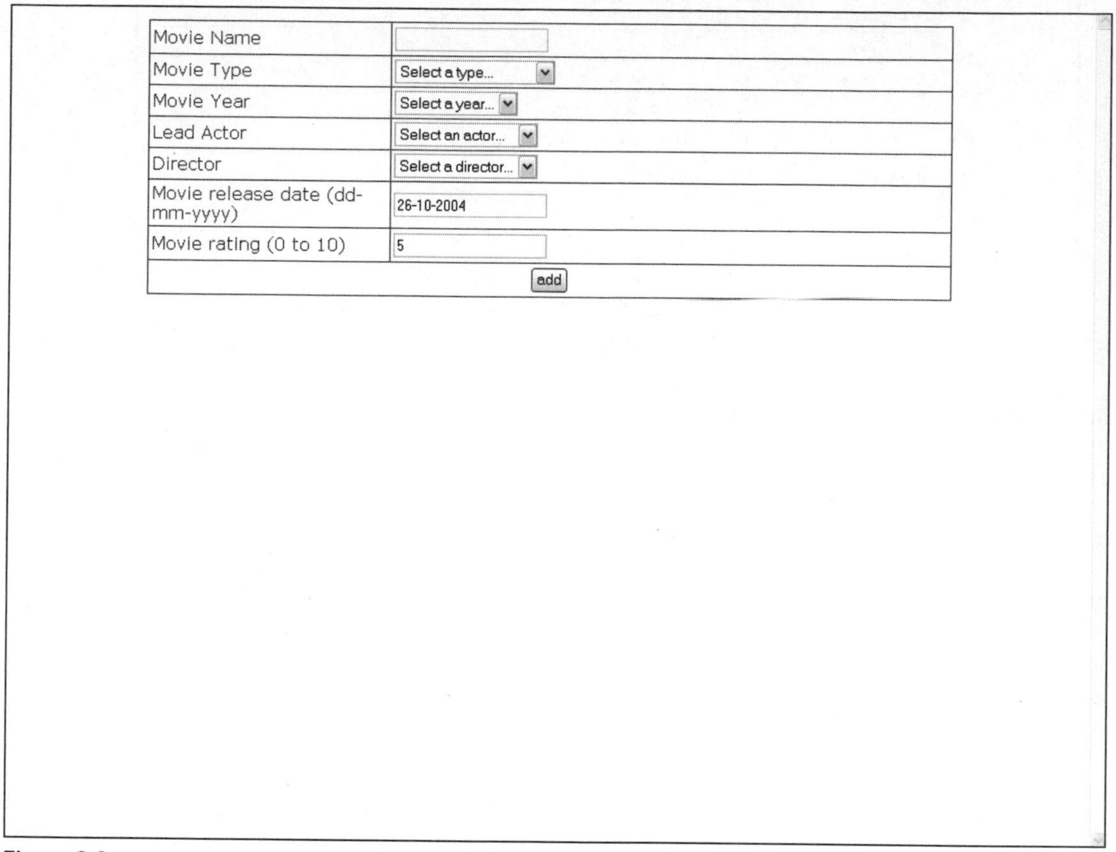

Movie Name	
Movie Type	Select a type...
Movie Year	Select a year...
Lead Actor	Select an actor...
Director	Select a director...
Movie release date (dd-mm-yyyy)	26-10-2004
Movie rating (0 to 10)	5
	add

Figure 8-3

6. Now try to enter a new movie without setting the year and the movie type (see Figure 8-4).

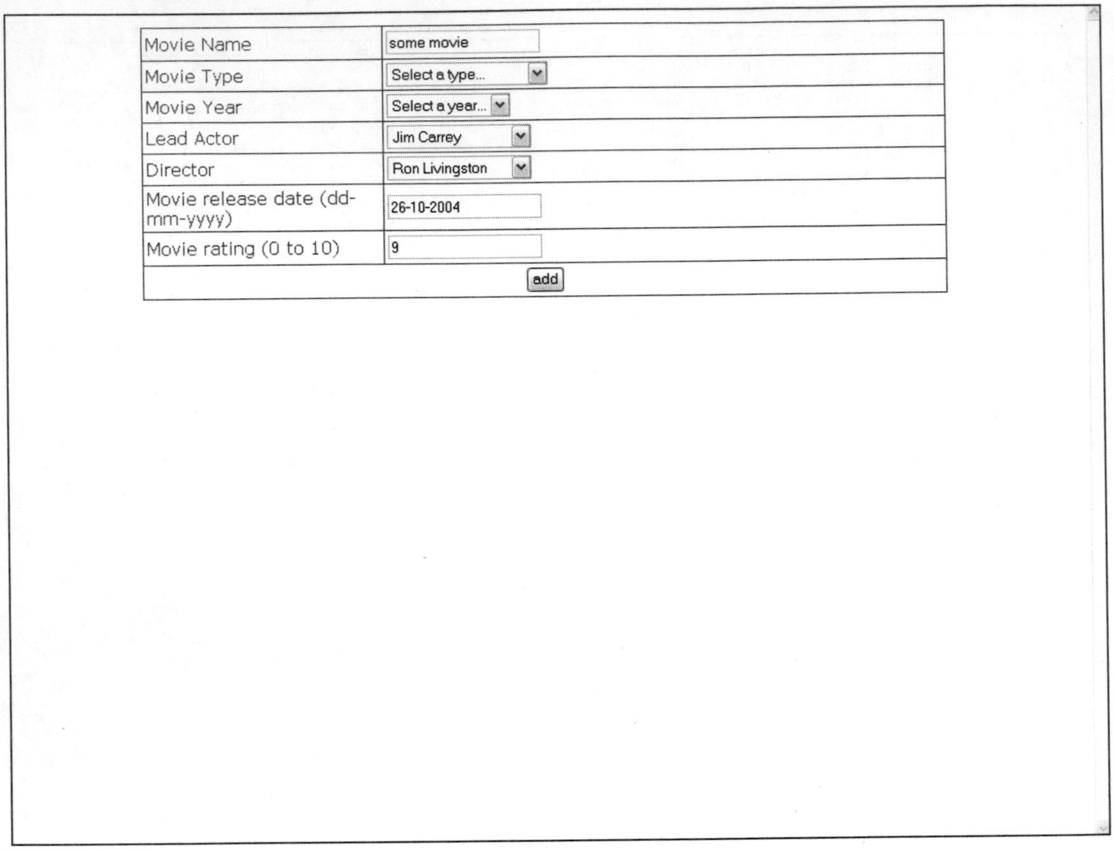

Movie Name	some movie
Movie Type	Select a type...
Movie Year	Select a year...
Lead Actor	Jim Carrey
Director	Ron Livingston
Movie release date (dd-mm-yyyy)	26-10-2004
Movie rating (0 to 10)	9
	add

Figure 8-4

7. Edit a movie from the index and try deleting the name and submitting the form (see Figure 8-5).

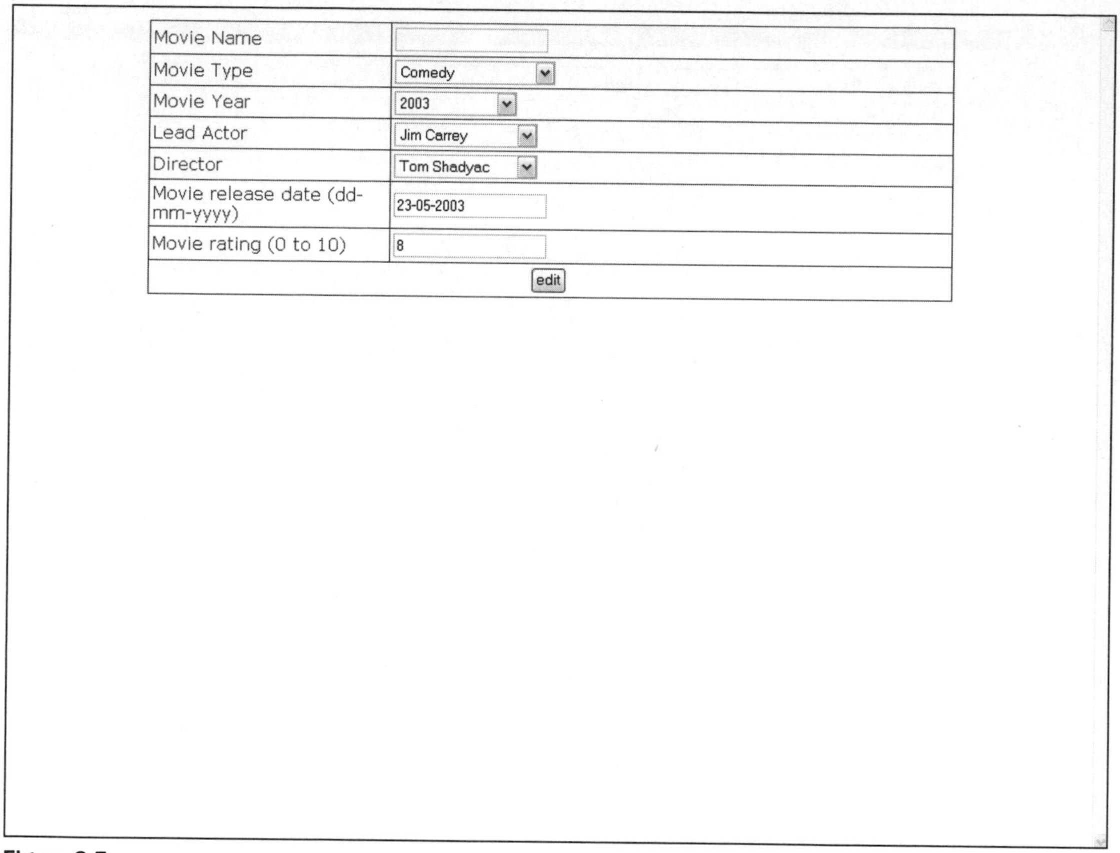

Movie Name	
Movie Type	Comedy ▾
Movie Year	2003 ▾
Lead Actor	Jim Carrey ▾
Director	Tom Shadyac ▾
Movie release date (dd-mm-yyyy)	23-05-2003
Movie rating (0 to 10)	8
	edit

Figure 8-5

8. Notice the error message stating the mistake made in filling in the form (see Figure 8-6).

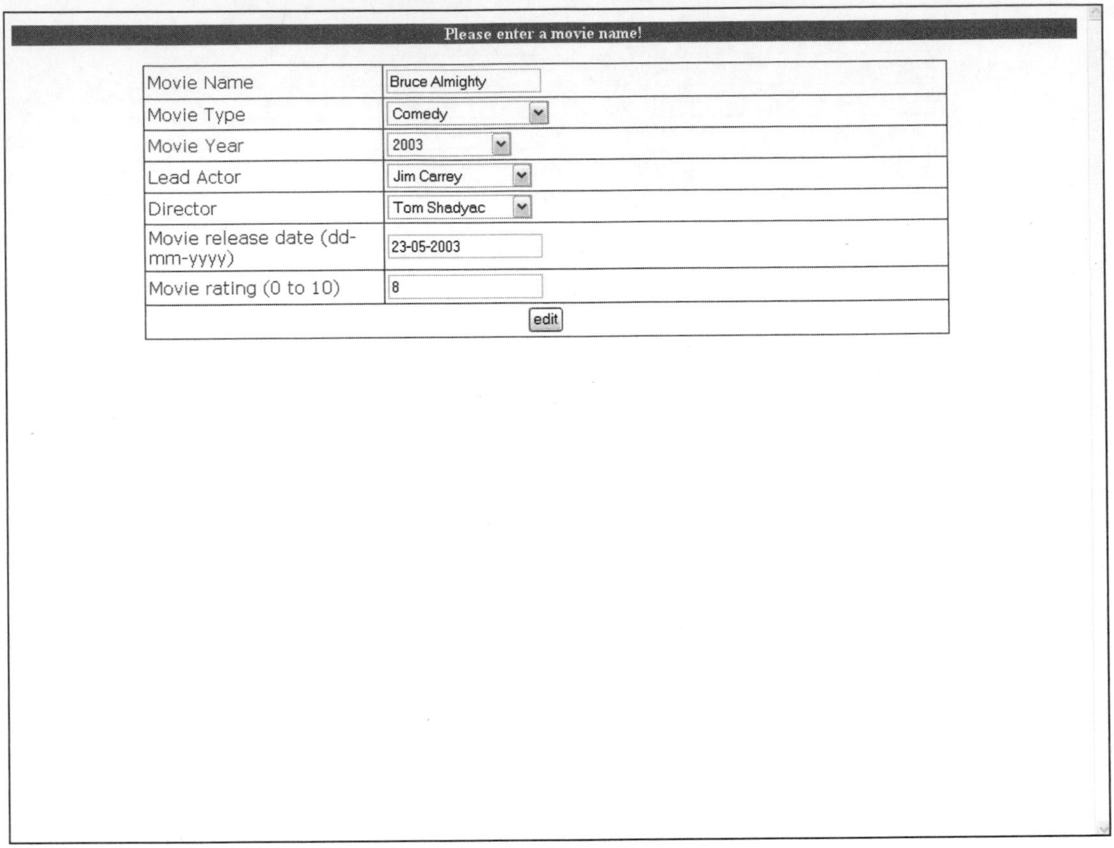

Movie Name	Bruce Almighty
Movie Type	Comedy
Movie Year	2003
Lead Actor	Jim Carrey
Director	Tom Shadyac
Movie release date (dd-mm-yyyy)	23-05-2003
Movie rating (0 to 10)	8
	edit

Please enter a movie name!

Figure 8-6

How It Works

When the form passes information to the commit script, the data has to be verified. In this case, you use a simple verification method: The empty() function returns true if the string is empty and false if not. To ensure that the user did not submit the form with a simple space in the movie name field, you use trim() on the field's content to eliminate any space leading or trailing the string. (Some people like to trigger errors in Web sites by entering erroneous input; don't make their job easy.)

At the same time, if an error is detected, you add a message to the $error variable that collects all the error messages. The error messages are URL encoded before being added to the code. (See urlencode and urldecode functions in the manual; for more information, check the PHP Web site at www.php.net/url.)

```
if (empty($movie_name)) {
    $error .= "Please+enter+a+movie+name%21%0D%0A";
}
```

Once you are sure that an error has occurred, you redirect the user to the form with an error message stating the problem. The error message is URL encoded to ensure that it will be passed to the movie.php script without being corrupted.

```
if (empty($error)) {
  ...
} else {
  header("location:movie.php?action=add&error=" . $error);
}
```

Once redirected to the form, the system needs to display the decoded error message.

```
<?
if (!empty($_GET['error'])) {
  echo "<div align=\"center\" " .
       "style=\"color:#FFFFFF;background-color:#FF0000;" .
       "font-weight:bold\">" . nl2br(urldecode($_GET['error'])) .
       "</div><br />";
}
?>
```

This displays a rather colorful message that your user will not miss.

The update itself is performed at the end of the code, along with all the controls and debug messages you need.

```
if (isset($sql) && !empty($sql)) {
  echo "<!--".$sql."-->";
  $result = mysql_query($sql)
    or die("Invalid query: " . mysql_error());
?>
<p align="center" style="color:#FF0000">
  Done. <a href="index.php">Index</a>
</p>
<?php
}
```

If the $sql variable is not previously set (which could happen if the page is called out of context), the code will not try to execute and will do nothing. (Note that it would be a good exercise for you to code a response to this occurrence, such as a message or a logging of the error in the database.)

Checking for Format Errors

Checking for errors in dates or other formatted data is a requirement in most systems because users can't always be guided in their input. You should always check the data that the user enters if you require a specific format or set of values.

At this point, you need the feared and powerful *regular expressions*. The regular expressions allow you to define a pattern and check to see if it can be applied to your data. It's very useful to check for dates, Social Security numbers, and any data that has to respect a predefined set of format requirements. (It helps to be sure to always indicate the format in the source field.)

Try It Out   Checking Dates and Numbers

In this exercise, you'll change a few pages so that you can check the format of the dates the user enters.

1.   Open the well-known `movie.php` file and modify it as follows (modifications are highlighted):

```php
<?php
$link = mysql_connect("localhost", "bp5am", "bp5ampass")
  or die("Could not connect: " . mysql_error());
mysql_select_db('moviesite', $link)
  or die(mysql_error());

$peoplesql = "SELECT * FROM people";
$result = mysql_query($peoplesql)
  or die("Invalid query: " . mysql_error());

while ($row = mysql_fetch_array($result)) {
  $people[$row['people_id']] = $row['people_fullname'];
}

switch ($_GET['action']) {
  case "edit":
    $moviesql = "SELECT * FROM movie " .
                "WHERE movie_id = '" . $_GET['id'] . "'";
    $result = mysql_query($moviesql)
      or die("Invalid query: " . mysql_error());
    $row = mysql_fetch_array($result);
    $movie_name = $row['movie_name'];
    $movie_type = $row['movie_type'];
    $movie_year = $row['movie_year'];
    $movie_release = $row['movie_release'];
    $movie_leadactor = $row['movie_leadactor'];
    $movie_director = $row['movie_director'];
    $movie_rating = $row['movie_rating'];
    break;

  default:
    $movie_name = "";
    $movie_type = "";
    $movie_year = "";
    $movie_release = time();
    $movie_leadactor = "";
    $movie_director = "";
    $movie_rating = "5";
    break;
}
?>
<html>
<head>
```

```
<title><?php echo $_GET['action']; ?> movie</title>
<style type="text/css">
  TD{color:#353535;font-family:verdana}
  TH{color:#FFFFFF;font-family:verdana;background-color:#336699}
</style>
</head>
<body>
<form action="commit.php?action=<?php
  echo $_GET['action']; ?>&type=movie&id=<?php
  if (isset($_GET['id'])) { echo $_GET['id']; } ?>" method="post">
<?php
if (!empty($_GET['error'])) {
  echo "<div align=\"center\" " .
      "style=\"color:#FFFFFF;background-color:#FF0000;" .
      "font-weight:bold\">" . nl2br(urldecode($_GET['error'])) .
      "</div><br />";
}
?>
<table border="0" width="750" cellspacing="1"
    cellpadding="3" bgcolor="#353535" align="center">
  <tr>
    <td bgcolor="#FFFFFF" width="30%">Movie Name</td>
    <td bgcolor="#FFFFFF" width="70%">
      <input type="text" name="movie_name"
        value="<?php echo $movie_name?>">
    </td>
  </tr>
  <tr>
    <td bgcolor="#FFFFFF">Movie Type</td>
    <td bgcolor="#FFFFFF">
      <select id="game" name="movie_type" style="width:150px">
        <option value="" selected>Select a type...</option>
<?php
$sql = "SELECT movietype_id, movietype_label " .
      "FROM movietype ORDER BY movietype_label";
$result = mysql_query($sql)
  or die("<font color=\"#FF0000\">Query Error</font>" . mysql_error());
while ($row = mysql_fetch_array($result)) {
  if ($row['movietype_id'] == $movie_type) {
    $selected = " selected";
  } else {
    $selected = "";
  }
  echo '<option value="' . $row['movietype_id'] . '"' . $selected .
      '>' . $row['movietype_label'] . "</option>\r\n";
}
?>
      </select>
    </td>
  </tr>
  <tr>
    <td bgcolor="#FFFFFF">Movie Year</td>
    <td bgcolor="#FFFFFF">
      <select name="movie_year">
```

```
        <option value="" selected>Select a year...</option>
<?php
for ($year=date("Y"); $year >= 1970 ;$year--) {
  if ($year == $movie_year) {
    $selected = " selected";
  } else {
    $selected = "";
  }
?>
        <option value="<?php echo $year; ?>"
          <?php echo $selected; ?>><?php echo $year; ?></option>
<?php
}
?>
      </select>
    </td>
  </tr>
  <tr>
    <td bgcolor="#FFFFFF">Lead Actor</td>
    <td bgcolor="#FFFFFF">
      <select name="movie_leadactor">
        <option value="" selected>Select an actor...</option>
<?php
foreach ($people as $people_id => $people_fullname) {
  if ($people_id == $movie_leadactor) {
    $selected = " selected";
  } else {
    $selected = "";
  }
?>
        <option value="<?php echo $people_id; ?>"
          <?php echo $selected; ?>><?php echo $people_fullname;
          ?></option>
<?php
}
?>
      </selected>
    </td>
  </tr>
  <tr>
    <td bgcolor="#FFFFFF">Director</td>
    <td bgcolor="#FFFFFF">
      <select name="movie_director">
        <option value="" selected>Select a director...</option>
<?php
foreach ($people as $people_id => $people_fullname) {
  if ($people_id == $movie_director) {
    $selected = " selected";
  } else {
    $selected = "";
  }
?>
        <option value="<?php echo $people_id; ?>"
          <?php echo $selected; ?>><?php echo $people_fullname;
```

```
                  ?></option>
<?php
}
?>
      </select>
    </td>
  </tr>
  <tr>
    <td bgcolor="#FFFFFF" width="30%">
      Movie release date (dd-mm-yyyy)
    </td>
    <td bgcolor="#FFFFFF" width="70%">
      <input type="text" name="movie_release"
        value="<?php echo date("d-m-Y", $movie_release); ?>">
    </td>
  </tr>
  <tr>
    <td bgcolor="#FFFFFF" width="30%">
      Movie rating (0 to 10)
    </td>
    <td bgcolor="#FFFFFF" width="70%">
      <input type="text" name="movie_rating"
        value="<?php echo $movie_rating; ?>">
    </td>
  </tr>
  <tr>
    <td bgcolor="#FFFFFF" colspan="" align="center">
      <input type="submit" name="submit"
        value="<?php echo $_GET['action']; ?>">
    </td>
  </tr>
</table>
</form>
</body>
</html>
```

2.   Now open `commit.php` and modify it as follows (modifications are highlighted):

```php
<?php
// COMMIT ADD AND EDITS
$error = '';
$link = mysql_connect("localhost", "bp5am", "bp5ampass")
  or die("Could not connect: " . mysql_error());
mysql_select_db('moviesite', $link)
  or die ( mysql_error());

switch ($_GET['action']) {
  case "edit":
    switch ($_GET['type']) {
      case "people":
        $sql = "UPDATE people SET " .
                "people_fullname = '" . $_POST['people_fullname'] .
                "' WHERE people_id = '" . $_GET['id'] . "'";
        break;
```

```php
    case "movie":
      $movie_rating = trim($_POST['movie_rating']);
      if (!is_numeric($movie_rating)) {
            $error .= "Please+enter+a+numeric+rating+%21%0D%0A";
      } else {
        if ($movie_rating < 0 || $movie_rating > 10) {
          $error .= "Please+enter+a+rating+" .
                    "between+0+and+10%21%0D%0A";
        }
      }
      if (!ereg("([0-9]{2})-([0-9]{2})-([0-9]{4})",
                $_POST['movie_release'] ,
                $reldatepart)) {
        $error .= "Please+enter+a+date+" .
                  "with+the+dd-mm-yyyy+format%21%0D%0A";
      } else {
        $movie_release = @mktime(0, 0, 0, $reldatepart['2'],
                                 $reldatepart['1'],
                                 $reldatepart['3']);
        if ($movie_release == '-1') {
          $error .= "Please+enter+a+real+date+" .
                    "with+the+dd-mm-yyyy+format%21%0D%0A";
        }
      }
      $movie_name = trim($_POST['movie_name']);
      if (empty($movie_name)) {
        $error .= "Please+enter+a+movie+name%21%0D%0A";
      }
      if (empty($_POST['movie_type'])) {
        $error .= "Please+select+a+movie+type%21%0D%0A";
      }
      if (empty($_POST['movie_year'])) {
        $error .= "Please+select+a+movie+year%21%0D%0A";
      }
      if (empty($error) ){
        $sql = "UPDATE movie SET " .
           "movie_name = '" . $_POST['movie_name'] . "'," .
           "movie_year = '" . $_POST['movie_year'] . "'," .
           "movie_release = '$movie_release'," .
           "movie_type = '" . $_POST['movie_type'] . "'," .
           "movie_leadactor = '" . $_POST['movie_leadactor'] . "'," .
           "movie_director = '" . $_POST['movie_director'] . "'," .
           "movie_rating = '$movie_rating'" .
           "WHERE movie_id = '" . $_GET['id'] . "'";
      } else {
         header("location:movie.php?action=edit&error=" .
                $error . "&id=" . $_GET['id']);
      }
      break;
    }
    break;
  case "add":
    switch ($_GET['type']) {
      case "people":
```

```
      $sql = "INSERT INTO people (people_fullname) " .
            "VALUES ('" . $_POST['people_fullname'] . "')";
      break;
    case "movie":
      $movie_rating = trim($_POST['movie_rating']);
      if (!is_numeric($movie_rating)) {
        $error .= "Please+enter+a+numeric+rating+%21%0D%0A";
      } else {
        if ($movie_rating < 0 || $movie_rating > 10) {
          $error .= "Please+enter+a+rating+" .
                    "between+0+and+10%21%0D%0A";
        }
      }
      $movie_release = trim($_POST['movie_release']);
      if (!ereg("([0-9]{2})-([0-9]{2})-([0-9]{4})",
                $movie_release,
                $reldatepart) || empty($movie_release)) {
        $error .= "Please+enter+a+date+" .
                  "with+the+dd-mm-yyyy+format%21%0D%0A";
      } else {
        $movie_release = @mktime(0, 0, 0, $reldatepart['2'],
                                 $reldatepart['1'],
                                 $reldatepart['3']);
        if ($movie_release == '-1') {
          $error .= "Please+enter+a+real+date+" .
                    "with+the+dd-mm-yyyy+format%21%0D%0A";
        }
      }
      $movie_name = trim($row['movie_name']);
      if (empty($movie_name)) {
        $error .= "Please+enter+a+movie+name%21%0D%0A";
      }
      if (empty($_POST['movie_type'])) {
        $error .= "Please+select+a+movie+type%21%0D%0A";
      }
      if (empty($_POST['movie_year'])) {
        $error .= "Please+select+a+movie+year%21%0D%0A";
      }
      if (empty($error)) {
        $sql = "INSERT INTO movie (movie_name,movie_year," .
               "movie_release,movie_type,movie_leadactor," .
               "movie_director,movie_rating) " .
               "VALUES ('" . $_POST['movie_name'] . "'," .
               "'" . $_POST['movie_year'] . "'," .
               "'$movie_release'," .
               "'" . $_POST['movie_type'] . "'," .
               "'" . $_POST['movie_leadactor'] . "'," .
               "'" . $_POST['movie_director'] . "'," .
               "'$movie_rating')";
      } else {
        header("location:movie.php?action=add&error=" . $error);
      }
      break;
```

```
      }
    break;
}
if (isset($sql) && !empty($sql)) {
  echo "<!--".$sql."-->";
  $result = mysql_query($sql)
    or die("Invalid query: " . mysql_error());
?>
<p align="center" style="color:#FF0000">
  Done. <a href="index.php">Index</a>
</p>
<?php
}
?>
```

3. Now save the files, upload them, and open your browser to the site index.

4. Click any movie and try entering **2003-10-10** in the release date field. You will be brought back to the form with a nice, yet very explicit, message telling you what format to use, as shown in Figure 8-7.

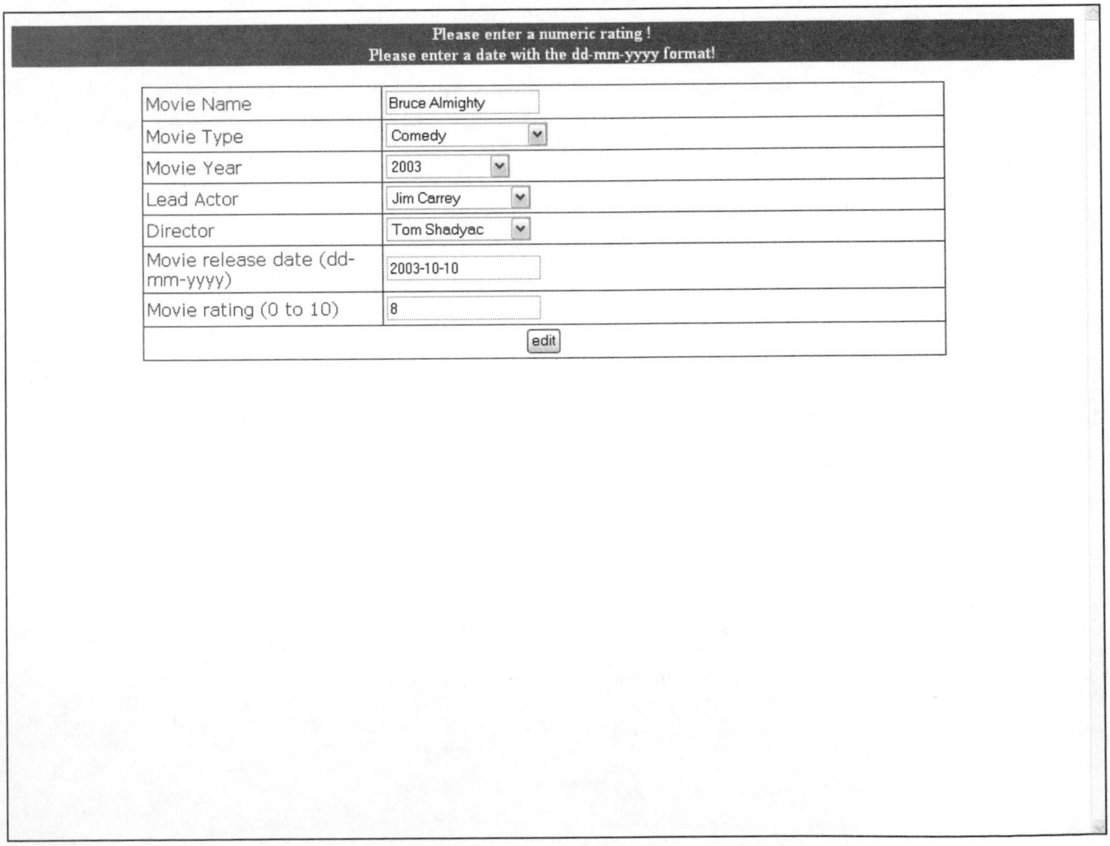

Please enter a numeric rating !	
Please enter a date with the dd-mm-yyyy format!	
Movie Name	Bruce Almighty
Movie Type	Comedy
Movie Year	2003
Lead Actor	Jim Carrey
Director	Tom Shadyac
Movie release date (dd-mm-yyyy)	2003-10-10
Movie rating (0 to 10)	8
edit	

Figure 8-7

5. Try entering alphanumeric values in the rating field, as in Figure 8-8 (which could easily have been a drop-down but is a text field for the purpose of the exercise).

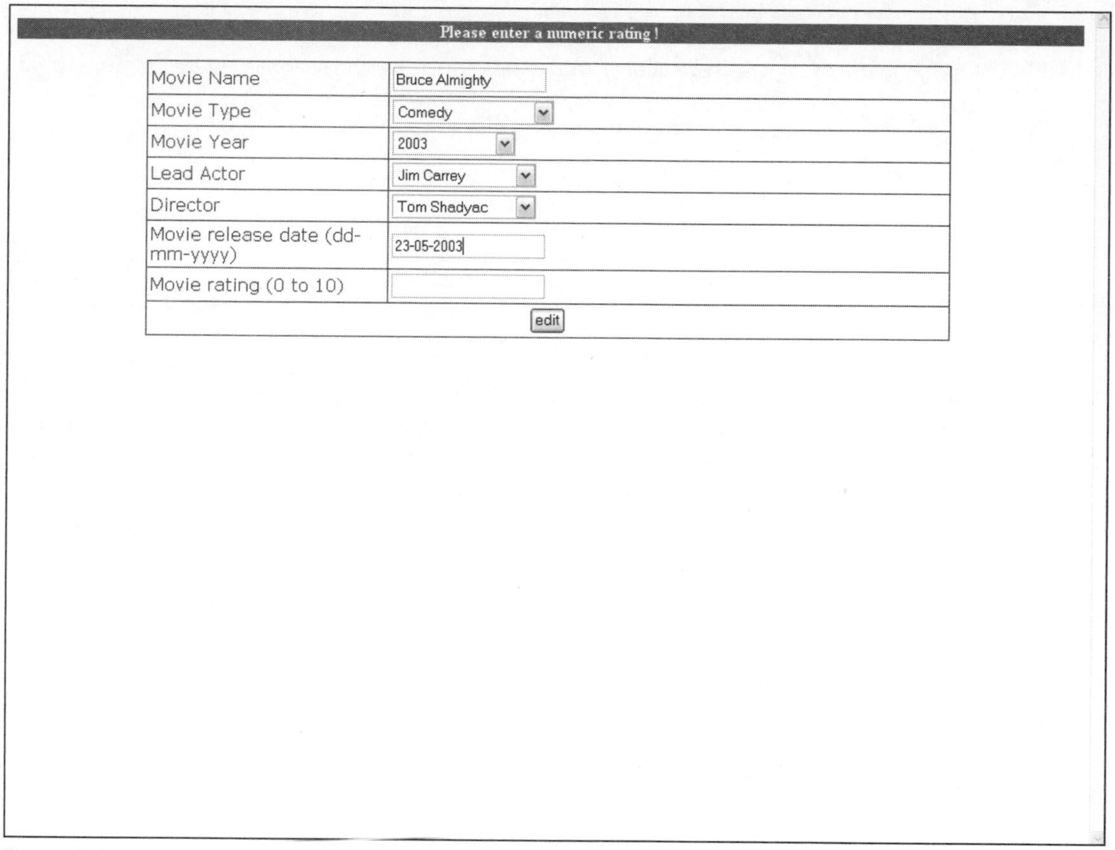

Figure 8-8

If the entered value is not in the 0 to 10 range, it will be refused. (Note that the decimals are not managed in this code and will be lost.)

How It Works

First, let's look into the type validating functions. In the commit.php code, you use the is_numeric() function. This function returns a Boolean TRUE if the value is indeed numeric and FALSE if not. More of these validating functions are available, including:

❑ is_string, which checks to see if the value is of the string format

❑ is_bool, which checks for Boolean type (TRUE, FALSE, 0, or 1)

❑ is_array, which tells you if the variable holds an array

❏ `is_object`, which determines if the variable stores an object (remember this one when you try object-oriented coding using PHP; it is very useful)

These functions are all documented in the PHP manual at www.php.net/variables.

In this instance, the use of `is_numeric` allows you to make sure that the user has entered a numeric value.

```php
$movie_rating = trim($_POST['movie_rating']);
if (!is_numeric($movie_rating)) {
  $error .= "Please+enter+a+numeric+rating+%21%0D%0A";
} else {
  if ($movie_rating < 0 || $movie_rating > 10) {
      $error .= "Please+enter+a+rating+" .
              "between+0+and+10%21%0D%0A";
  }
}
```

The code first cleans up the value of leading and trailing spaces with the `trim()` function (always try to be prepared for typos and mishaps) and then tests to see if the value is numeric. If it's not, the error message queue is fed; if it is, the code tests the value to see if it is between 0 and 10. If the value is not between 0 and 10, it adds an error message to the error message queue.

The date validation is almost as simple to understand, if you know about regular expressions. Here's a closer look at it:

```php
$movie_release = trim($_POST['movie_release']);
if (!ereg("([0-9]{2})-([0-9]{2})-([0-9]{4})",
          $movie_release,
          $reldatepart) || empty($movie_release)) {
  $error .= "Please+enter+a+date+" .
            "with+the+dd-mm-yyyy+format%21%0D%0A";
} else {
  $movie_release = @mktime(0, 0, 0, $reldatepart['2'],
                          $reldatepart['1'],
                          $reldatepart['3']);
  if ($movie_release == '-1') {
    $error .= "Please+enter+a+real+date+" .
            "with+the+dd-mm-yyyy+format%21%0D%0A";
  }
}
```

As you saw in this chapter's first exercise, you use the `trim()` function to clear all leading and trailing spaces in the received string to make sure your user entered something other than just a space.

You can find the string manipulation functions at the PHP Web site at www.php.net/strings. *You can find* trim() *and some other very useful functions there.*

The next statement contains two conditions. The first condition tests for a regular expression match. The regular expression is "`([0-9]{2})-([0-9]{2})-([0-9]{4})`". What does this do? `[0-9]{2}` specifies that you want to check for numbers between 0 and 9 with two occurrences. For example, 02 will match, but not 2. The same logic applies to the `[0-9]{4}` statement: The only difference is that you are expecting four digits in the number, which indicate the year part of the date.

So, in English, it means "I want my string to start with a number with two digits, followed by a hyphen, and then another group of two digits, and then a hyphen, and finish with a four-digit number."

```
if (!ereg("([0-9]{2})-([0-9]{2})-([0-9]{4})",
        $movie_release,
        $reldatepart) || empty( $movie_release )) {
    ...
}
```

This is exactly what your regular expression says. If the string matches your condition, you will split it in three different chunks, each chunk delimited with the parentheses.

This cutting is performed by the `ereg()` function. If the `$movie_release` string matches the pattern, `ereg` will cut the string into parts and then store each part as an element of the `$reldatepart` array.

Be sure to read the PHP manual about regular expressions at `www.php.net/regex` *and consult a few tutorials to understand the real power of using regular expressions. (You can find a good starting tutorial at* `www.phpbuilder.com/columns/dario19990616.php3.)*

If the user entered the date 02-03-2004, the array would be as follows:

```
Array
(
    [0] => 02-03-2004
    [1] => 02
    [2] => 03
    [3] => 2004
)
```

As you can see here, the first index holds the whole string, and each remaining index holds a cut-off part of the string, delimited by the parentheses.

Now that you have the date in an understandable format, you can change it into a timestamp using the `mktime()` function, which allows you to create a timestamp from chunks of dates. It is also a very useful function to manipulate dates.

```
$movie_release = mktime(0, 0, 0, $reldatepart['2'],
                        $reldatepart['1'],
                        $reldatepart['3']);
```

This code stores a timestamp from the day, month, and year information fed to the system in the `$movie_release` variable. The format is int mktime (int hour, int minute, int second, int month, int day, int year). The returned value is the number of seconds between January 1, 1970, and the specified date.

See documentation at `www.php.net/mktime` *for additional information regarding optional parameters such as daylight saving flag.*

If `mktime` fails to create a timestamp from the date you passed to it, it will return -1. This happens when the input is invalid, although it matches the regular expression. For example, 99-99-9999 will pass the regular expression test but is obviously not a valid date. To be sure that the date is indeed a date, you test for the return value from `mktime` and respond accordingly.

```
if ($movie_release == '-1') {
  $error .= "Please+enter+a+real+date+" .
            "with+the+dd-mm-yyyy+format%21%0D%0A";
}
```

In this case, a false date entry triggers an error message asking for a valid date.

Here's an alternative technique: You could have performed the same timestamp generation using SQL. Many things that PHP does on the string manipulation side can be done straight from SQL, as shown here:

```
if (!ereg("([0-9]{2})-([0-9]{2})-([0-9]{4})",
          $movie_release,
          $reldatepart) || empty($movie_release)) {
  ...
}
$reldate = $reldatepart['3'] . "-" .
           $reldatepart['2'] . "-" .
           $reldatepart['1'] . " 00:00:00";

$sql = "INSERT INTO movie (movie_release) " .
       "VALUES (UNIX_TIMESTAMP('$reldate'))";
```

In this code, the SQL does the timestamp generation. The `UNIX_TIMESTAMP()` SQL function expects a YYYY-MM-DD HH:MM:SS (2004-12-05 02:05:00) format and creates a timestamp from it. In the code, you force the creation of the timestamp at 00:00 on the date of the movie release. You can save yourself some lengthy coding by using SQL features wherever possible.

See documentation on MySQL date *and* time *functions at* www.mysql.com/doc/en/ Date_and_time_functions.html.

Summary

Validating user data is all about being prepared for the worst. Users make mistakes — that's the nature of users. Most errors are unintentional, but some are made intentionally to deny the service. It happens every day. The developer has to help the system deal with user input errors.

Regular expressions help you meet many user input validation challenges. Learning how to use them is often the key to success in an interactive system.

Exercise

1. Add validation to make the lead actor and director selections required.

Handling and Avoiding Errors

You will probably be spending a fair amount of time contemplating errors in your code, as do most Web developers when they start programming. No matter how good you are, how well you code, how long you have been coding, or how hard you try, you will encounter times when you have errors in your code.

It is of the utmost importance that you know how to handle your errors and debug your own code. Being able to efficiently and properly debug your code is an invaluable time-saver; and in Web development, $time == $money!

Luckily, PHP comes with a full-featured Applications Programming Interface (API) that provides you with many ways to trap and resolve those unwanted errors. PHP also allows you to use the API to capture the errors and create your own custom error functions or pages. These features are useful when debugging your code and when notifying your Webmaster about errors that seem to be happening to your applications as users are running them. Not only can you use PHP code to trap errors and customize them; you can use the Apache Web Server to help do this.

How the Apache Web Server Deals with Errors

Apache has a directive, the ErrorDocument, that you can configure in the httpd.conf file to create custom error pages with PHP so visitors to your site don't see the old, boring, server-created error pages. You have limitless possibilities when creating these custom messages. As with the PHP error-catching pages, you can have the ErrorDocument call PHP pages to do whatever you would like them to do — from simply displaying a friendly error message to the user to e-mailing a system administrator to notify him or her of the failure.

Unlike PHP error pages, the Apache ErrorDocument pages are used more for instances of missing pages (that is, a "Page Not Found" error or "Forbidden access" error pages and other requests of that sort). So, if someone visits your site, and he or she runs into the "Page Not Found" error page, the script will e-mail the administrator and he or she can in turn check to see whether this was a valid request and there is something wrong with the page or server, or whether someone was just looking for pages or trying to sniff around where they weren't supposed to be.

Apache's ErrorDocument Directive

Error handling is an invaluable resource and a "must have" for Web developers to keep their sites up and running with the fewest end-user problems or complaints. If you rely on people contacting you to tell you about errors on your site, you will never get any decent input. Allowing the server to do this for you will greatly increase your success at running a smooth server. This section first looks at Apache's ErrorDocument method of error handling.

Try It Out	Using Apache's ErrorDocument Method

First of all, you need to make some changes to the httpd.conf file to allow you to create a custom error page. Apache is usually set up by default to go to its own internal error pages, but you don't want that. You want Apache to go to your custom error page, no matter what error has occurred.

To do this, you change the default settings to your own specific settings by following these steps:

1. Open up your httpd.conf file, and around line 750 or so, you will find some lines that look like this (if you do not have access to httpd.conf, the following can usually be added to a .htaccess file in the base directory of your Web site):

```
# Customizable error responses come in three flavors:
# 1) plain text 2) local redirects 3) external redirects
#
# Some examples:
#ErrorDocument 500 "The server made a boo boo."
#ErrorDocument 404 /missing.html
#ErrorDocument 404 "/cgi-bin/missing_handler.pl"
#ErrorDocument 402 http://www.example.com/subscription_info.html
```

2. Change that information to the following, then restart Apache:

```
# Customizable error responses come in three flavors:
# 1) plain text 2) local redirects 3) external redirects
#
# Some examples:
ErrorDocument 400 /error.php?400
ErrorDocument 401 /error.php?401
ErrorDocument 403 /error.php?403
ErrorDocument 404 /error.php?404
ErrorDocument 500 /error.php?500
```

How It Works

You have just edited Apache's configuration file to help you with error handling. By using the ErrorDocument directive, you are able to send users to specific error pages depending on what error the server has encountered. For example, if you receive a 404 error, the typical "Page Cannot Be Found" page, you can redirect it to a page you have created to look like your Web site but still get the message through to the user that there has been a problem. You can do that with any and all error messages that the server can encounter.

Many `ErrorDocument` codes exist, but we will focus on the error messages you see typically in everyday Web browsing:

- ❑ **400:** Bad Request
- ❑ **401:** Authorization Required
- ❑ **403:** Forbidden
- ❑ **404:** Not Found
- ❑ **500:** Internal Server Error

Numerous other error codes exist, of course. You can find a complete list at www.apache.org.

> *Although you are seeing just a few error codes in this exercise, you can catch others as well by simply adding another ErrorDocument to the* httpd.conf *file. For example, if you want to implement the 501 error code, you would simply add **ErrorDocument 501 /error.php?501** to your code and add the error handling in the* error.php *page, which you'll see shortly.*

Next, you'll see a simple way to show the user error messages, and then get into some more complex ways to notify the Webmaster of errors occurring on the Web site by using the `mail()` command that you learned previously.

Try It Out   Displaying Custom Error Messages

To show the user error messages, follow these steps:

1. Open your text editor and save a page called `error.php`.

2. Enter the following code:

```php
<?php
$error_no = $_SERVER['QUERY_STRING'];

switch ($error_no) {
  case 400:
    $error_output = "<h1>&quot;Bad Request&quot; Error Page - " .
                    "(Error Code 400)</h1>";
    $error_output .= "The browser has made a Bad Request<br>";
    $error_output .= "<a href=\"mailto:sysadmin@localhost.com\">" .
                    "Contact</a> the system administrator";
    $error_output .= " if you feel this to be in error";
    break;

  case 401:
    $error_output = "<h1>&quot;Authorization Required&quot; " .
                    "Error Page - (Error Code 401)</h1>";
    $error_output .= "You have supplied the wrong information to " .
                    "access a secure area<br>";
    $error_output .= "<a href=\"mailto:sysadmin@localhost.com\">" .
```

```
                         "Contact</a> the system administrator";
      $error_output .= " if you feel this to be in error";
      break;

   case 403:
      $error_output = "<h1>&quot;Forbidden Access&quot; Error Page - " .
                     "(Error Code 403)</h1>";
      $error_output .= "You are denied access to this area<br>";
      $error_output .= "<a href=\"mailto:sysadmin@localhost.com\">" .
                     "Contact</a> the system administrator";
      $error_output .= " if you feel this to be in error";
      break;

   case 404:
      $error_output = "<h1>&quot;Page Not Found&quot; Error Page - " .
                     "(Error Code 404)</h1>";
      $error_output .= "The page you are looking for cannot " .
                     "be found<br>";
      $error_output .= "<a href=\"mailto:sysadmin@localhost.com\">" .
                     "Contact</a> the system administrator";
      $error_output .= " if you feel this to be in error";
      break;

   case 500:
      $error_output = "<h1>&quot;Internal Server Error&quot; " .
                     "Error Page - (Error Code 500)</h1>";
      $error_output .= "The server has encountered an internal " .
                     "error<br>";
      $error_output .= "<a href=\"mailto:sysadmin@localhost.com\">" .
                     "Contact</a> the system administrator";
      $error_output .= " if you feel this to be in error";
      break;

   default:
      $error_output = "<h1>Error Page</h1>";
      $error_output .= "This is the custom error Page<br>";
      $error_output .= "You should be <a href=\"index.php\">here</a>";
}
?>
<html>
<head>
<title>Beginning PHP5, Apache, MySQL Web Development</title>
</head>
<body>
<?php
echo $error_output;
?>
</body>
</html>
```

3. Open your browser and type **http://localhost/asdf/qwerty/page.html**, or any other page you know for certain doesn't reside on your server, into the address bar. You should see the "Page Not Found" message on the screen, similar to the message shown in Figure 9-1.

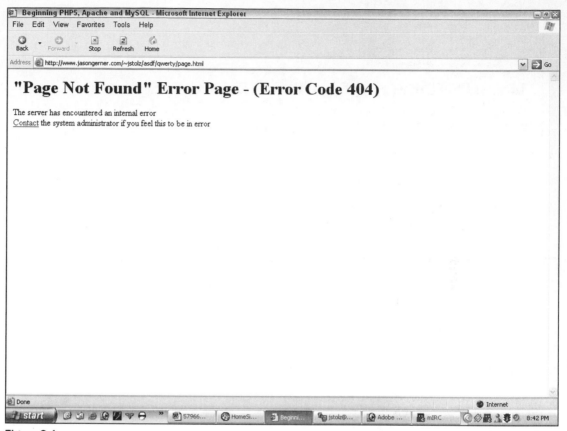

Figure 9-1

4. Another way to test or simulate the error messages so that you can ensure you coded the page correctly is to supply the page with the query string information via the browser. For example, to simulate an "Internal Server Error" error message, type **http://localhost/error.php?500** into your address bar. The page will use the query string information and run the code just as if there were an Internal Server Error on one of your pages. The result will look pretty similar to the previous example but will contain a different message. The "Internal Server Error" page will look like the one shown in Figure 9-2, displaying the "Internal Server Error" message on the screen.

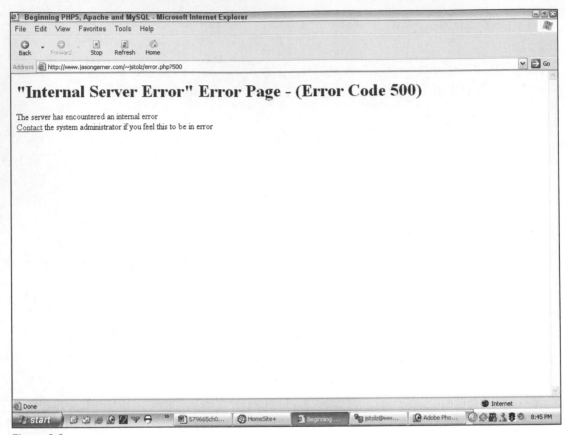

Figure 9-2

How It Works

You have just created a simple error handling PHP page. You created a PHP page that will handle the most common errors that servers encounter. By using the query string information along with the `switch()` statement, you are able to display custom error message pertinent to the error itself. This is useful if you don't want Apache to display its somewhat cryptic-looking error message to your users.

Apache's ErrorDocument: Advanced Custom Error Page

Up until this point, you've been showing the user a custom error message only. You can do countless other things, such as e-mailing the administrator or Webmaster of the site so he or she can look into the issue further should there be a problem with certain pages. This is a great way for you to keep track of your pages without having to check up on the server periodically. More than likely, if you haven't received any error e-mails, there haven't been problems with your server.

Try It Out   **Creating an Error E-Mail**

In this exercise, you will create a script that generates an automatic e-mail that tells the administrator what time the error occurred, on what day, what the error was, what page generated the error, and what error message was displayed to the user who navigated to the page.

1. Open your `error.php` file. You're going to change the code substantially, so if you want to keep the original file, save a copy under the original name.

2. Enter the following code. (This is almost completely new code, so we won't show you the changed lines with highlighting this time.)

```php
<?php
function email_admin($error_no,
                     $error_output,
                     $full_date,
                     $full_time,
                     $request_page) {

  $to = "Administrator <admin@yourdomain.com>";

  $subject = "Apache Error Generation";

  $body = "<html>";
  $body .= "<head>";
  $body .= "<title>Apache Error</title>";
  $body .= "</head>";
  $body .= "<body>";
  $body .= "Error occurred on <b>" . $full_date . "</b> " .
          "at <b>" . $full_time . "</b><br>";
  $body .= "Error received was a <b>" . $error_no . "</b> error.<br>";
  $body .= "The page that generated the error was: <b>" .
          $request_page . "</b><br>";
  $body .= "The generated error message was:" . $error_output;
  $body .= "</body>";
  $body .= "</html>";

  $headers = "MIME-Version: 1.0\r\n";
  $headers .= "Content-type: text/html; charset=iso-8859-1\r\n";

  $headers .= "From: Apache Error <host@yourdomain.com>\r\n";
  $headers .= "Cc: webmaster@yourdomain.com\r\n";

  mail($to, $subject, $body, $headers);
}

$date = getdate();
$full_date = $date['weekday'] . ", " .
             $date['month'] . " " .
             $date['mday'] . ", " .
             $date['year'];
```

```
$full_time = $date['hours'] . ":" .
             $date['minutes'] . ":" .
             $date['seconds'] . ":" .
             $date['year'];

$error_no = $_SERVER['QUERY_STRING'];
$request_page = $_SERVER['REQUEST_URI'];

switch ($error_no) {
  case 400:
    $error_output = "<h1>\"Bad Request\" Error Page - " .
                    "(Error Code 400)</h1>";
    $error_output .= "The browser has made a Bad Request<br>";
    $error_output .= "<a href=\"mailto:sysadmin@localhost.com\">" .
                    "Contact</a> the system administrator";
    $error_output .= " if you feel this to be in error";

    email_admin($error_no,
               $error_output,
               $full_date,
               $full_time,
               $request_page);
    break;

  case 401:
    $error_output = "<h1>\"Authorization Required\" Error Page - " .
                    "(Error Code 401)</h1>";
    $error_output .= "You have supplied the wrong information to " .
                    "access a secure area<br>";
    $error_output .= "<a href=\"mailto:sysadmin@localhost.com\">" .
                    "Contact</a> the system administrator";
    $error_output .= " if you feel this to be in error";

    email_admin($error_no,
               $error_output,
               $full_date,
               $full_time,
               $request_page);
    break;

  case 403:
    $error_output = "<h1>\"Forbidden Access\" Error Page - " .
                    "(Error Code 403)</h1>";
    $error_output .= "You are denied access to this area<br>";
    $error_output .= "<a href=\"mailto:sysadmin@localhost.com\">" .
                    "Contact</a> the system administrator";
    $error_output .= " if you feel this to be in error";

    email_admin($error_no,
               $error_output,
               $full_date,
               $full_time,
```

```
                                $request_page);
        break;

    case 404:
        $error_output = "<h1>\"Page Not Found\" Error Page - " .
                        "(Error Code 404)</h1>";
        $error_output .= "The page you are looking for " .
                        "cannot be found<br>";
        $error_output .= "<a href=\"mailto:sysadmin@localhost.com\">" .
                        "Contact</a> the system administrator";
        $error_output .= " if you feel this to be in error";

        email_admin($error_no,
                    $error_output,
                    $full_date,
                    $full_time,
                    $request_page);
        break;

    case 500:
        $error_output = "<h1>\"Internal Server Error\" Error Page - " .
                        "(Error Code 500)</h1>";
        $error_output .= "The server has encountered " .
                        "an internal error<br>";
        $error_output .= "<a href=\"mailto:sysadmin@localhost.com\">" .
                        "Contact</a> the system administrator";
        $error_output .= " if you feel this to be in error";

        email_admin($error_no,
                    $error_output,
                    $full_date,
                    $full_time,
                    $request_page);
        break;

    default:
        $error_output = "<h1>Error Page</h1>";
        $error_output .= "This is the custom error Page<br>";
        $error_output .= "You should be <a href=\"index.php\">here</a>";
}
?>
<html>
<head>
<title>Beginning PHP5, Apache, MySQL Web Development</title>
</head>
<body>
<?php
echo $error_output;
?>
</body>
</html>
```

How It Works

The output that you see in the browser will be the same as you saw before, but behind the scenes, the mail() function is used to send an e-mail to the administrator. Some other PHP functions, such as getdate(), are used to note the time and day the error occurred. The mail() function allows you to e-mail anyone you desire when an error occurs. You will learn about the mail() function in more detail in Chapter 11. Also, by using getdate(), you are able to retrieve when exactly the error occurred so you can make note of the error's time of occurrence. You can get the date in many ways, including the date() function, but the getdate() function is a little easier to decipher. We threw in some function practice for you to get the hang of sending variables as parameters to and from functions. Now the administrator or Webmaster will be getting an HTML-formatted e-mail concerning the error message that the user received when he or she happened to go to that page.

That's it! You just used Apache's ErrorDocument directive to help you maintain your server.

Error Handling and Creating Error Handling Pages with PHP

This section looks at how you can troubleshoot your PHP scripts using simple logical steps. First, however, you need to understand what PHP does when it encounters an error and what it does with certain errors.

When a PHP script gets executed and encounters an error, it displays a message in the browser showing you what the error was. Depending on what type of error occurred, the script may not finish executing. You are likely to run into these sorts of errors when writing your own scripts. Don't feel ashamed if you receive errors; everybody makes errors when writing code, no matter what your level of expertise. Even though it is normal to receive errors during the development of your script, you don't want errors (which are normally complicated for the layperson to understand) popping up to end users when your site has gone live. For this reason, it's important to know how to catch those unwanted errors and generate more user-friendly errors that let the user know that there will be a solution forthcoming.

Error Types in PHP

There are 12 types of errors in PHP, which are listed in the following table, along with the Report All Errors option. Each of these can be called by either an integer value or a named constant. Slight changes have been made as of PHP5: the addition of E_STRICT, and that E_ALL does not include E_STRICT.

Error	Integer Value	NAMED CONSTANT
E_ERROR	1	Fatal runtime error.
E_WARNING	2	Non-fatal runtime error.
E_PARSE	4	Compile-time parse error.
E_NOTICE	8	Non-fatal runtime notice.
E_CORE_ERROR	16	Fatal error occurring at startup.

Error	Integer Value	NAMED CONSTANT
E_CORE_WARNINGS	32	Non-fatal runtime error caused by initial startup.
E_COMPILE_WARNING	128	Non-fatal compile-time error.
E_USER_ERROR	256	User-generated error by PHP function `trigger_error()`.
E_USER_WARNING	512	User-generated warning by PHP function `trigger_error()`.
E_USER_NOTICE	1024	User-generated notice by PHP function `trigger_error()`.
E_ALL	2047	All errors and warnings reported.
E_STRICT	2048	Run-time notices. When enabled, will suggest changes to your code to ensure forward compatibility.

Typically, you don't have to worry about all of the error types; your main concern is with runtime errors such as notices, warnings, and errors, along with the user-generated equivalents. The simple, more trivial errors, such as warnings, aren't useful to users or yourself, since they simply notify you that you forgot to initialize a variable or something similar. Because initializing variables is purely for your benefit while you are coding to track down errors before your Web site launch, it is of no use to display these errors to users once your Web site goes live. Your error-handling code helps resolve these cryptic errors to offer helpful, user-friendly messages.

The three main types of errors discussed in full here are:

❑ **Fatal errors:** Fatal runtime errors. These indicate errors that the program can't recover from. Script execution is halted.

❑ **Warnings:** Runtime warnings (non-fatal errors). Script execution is not halted.

❑ **Notices:** Runtime notices. These indicate that the script has encountered something that could indicate an error, but could also happen in the normal course of running the script.

Generating PHP Errors

Now let's generate some errors so that you can check out what you need to do to resolve them. Consider this code snippet, for example:

```php
<?php
//set string with "Wrox" spelled wrong
$string_variable = "Worx books are great!";

//try to use str_replace to replace Worx with Wrox
//this will generate an E_WARNING
//because of wrong parameter count
str_replace("Worx", "Wrox");
?>
```

If you run this snippet, you should see the following error:

```
Warning: Wrong parameter count for str_replace() in·
c:\FoxServ\www\errorhandling\error1.php on line 8
```

The error occurred because `str_replace` requires a third parameter for the function. The third parameter is the variable, `$string_variable`, or a string of text in which you want to search for the first parameter, "Worx," and replace it with "Wrox." Because this is a non-fatal error that does not halt script execution, you can still run code after the point where the error occurred. If you change the snippet to this:

```php
<?php
//set string with "Wrox" spelled wrong
$string_variable = "Worx books are great!";

//try to use str_replace to replace Worx with Wrox
//this will generate an E_WARNING
//because of wrong parameter count
str_replace("Worx", "Wrox");

//this is a non-fatal error, so the original
//variable should still show up after the warning
echo $string_variable;
?>
```

The string will continue to execute after the error, and will produce the following output:

```
Warning: Wrong parameter count for str_replace() in
c:\FoxServ\www\errorhandling\error1.php on line 8
Worx books are great!
```

Next, we throw out a fatal error to show you how it produces different results when the error occurs. Let's create a fatal error by using the following code:

```php
<?php
//beginning of page
echo "Beginning";

//we are going to make a call to
//a function that doesn't exist
//this will generate an E_ERROR
//and will halt script execution
//after the call of the function
fatalerror();

//end of page
echo "End";
//won't be output due to the fatal error
?>
```

This produces the following output:

```
Beginning
Fatal error: Call to undefined function: fatalerror() in
c:\FoxServ\www\errorhandling\error2.php on line 10.
```

Notice that "Beginning" was output because it was before the function call, but "End" was not because the fatal error halted the script execution. You can suppress the fatal error calls by putting an ampersand in front of the function call, like so: @fatalerror(). This suppresses the error, but the script still halts its execution.

As of PHP4 the default error reporting does not show E_NOTICE errors. However, you may want to show them during development. Enabling E_NOTICE errors for debugging can warn you about possible bugs or bad programming practices. For example, you might use something such as $row[variable], but actually it is better to write this as $row['variable'] because PHP will try and treat "variable" as a constant. If, however, it isn't a constant, PHP assumes it to be a string for the array. You can set error reporting by simply putting error_reporting(number), where number is the constant value in the table shown earlier in the chapter, in your PHP page.

If you don't know at what level your error reporting is set, you can simply run the error_reporting() function without any arguments, like this:

```php
<?php
echo error_reporting();
?>
```

By default, all error handling is handled by PHP's built-in error handler, which tells you the error and displays the message associated with that error. The message displays the error type, the error message, the filename, and the line number where the error occurred.

You may have noticed an error similar to this one in a previous code snippet:

Warning: Wrong parameter count for str_replace() in
c:\FoxServ\www\errorhandling\error1.php on line 8

Usually, letting PHP generate its own errors is fine, but with complicated applications you may want to *catch* the errors so you can do something specific with the error, such as notifying an administrator so he or she can look into the problem further.

Try It Out   Creating a Custom Error Handler

You will now create a custom error handler to catch the errors and display a more friendly error message.

1.   Edit the script used in the previous examples like this:

```php
<?php
//create your error handler function
function handler($error_type,
                 $error_message,
                 $error_file,
                 $error_line) {

  echo "<h1>Page Error</h1>";
  echo "Errors have occurred while executing this page. Contact the ";
  echo "<a href=\"mailto:admin@yourdomain.com\">administrator</a> " .
      "to report errors<br><br>";
  echo "<b>Information Generated</b><br><br>";
  echo "<b>Error Type:</b> $error_type<br>";
```

```
    echo "<b>Error Message:</b> $error_message<br>";
    echo "<b>Error Filename:</b> $error_file<br>";
    echo "<b>Error Line:</b> $error_line";
}

//set the error handler to be used
set_error_handler("handler");
```

```
//set string with "Wrox" spelled wrong
$string_variable = "Worx books are great!";

//try to use str_replace to replace Worx with Wrox
//this will generate an E_WARNING
//because of wrong parameter count
str_replace("Worx", "Wrox");
?>
```

2. Save the file as `custom_error.php` and open it in your browser. The output should look similar to that in Figure 9-3.

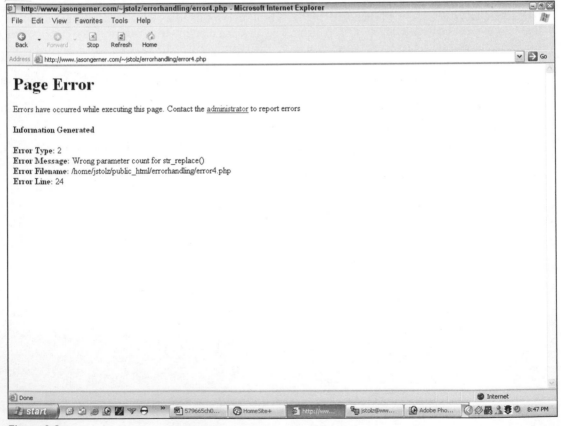

Figure 9-3

3. Because your error handler is user-defined, you can catch the errors, and you can re-create the error messages based on the error type. Create a snippet for this sort of error handler by editing your custom_error.php file like this:

```php
<?php
//create your error handler function
function handler($error_type,
                 $error_message,
                 $error_file,
                 $error_line) {

    switch ($error_type) {

        //fatal error
        case E_ERROR:
          echo "<h1>Fatal Error</h1>";
          die("A fatal error has occured at line $error_line of file " .
              "$error_file.<br>" .
              "Error message created was &quot;$error_message&quot;");
          break;

        //warnings
        case E_WARNING:
          echo "<h1>Warning</h1>";
          echo "A warning has occured at line $error_line of file " .
              "$error_file.<br>";
          echo " Error message created was &quot;$error_message&quot;";

        //notices
        case E_NOTICE:
          //don't show notice errors
          break;
    }
}

//set the error handler to be used
set_error_handler("handler");

//set string with "Wrox" spelled wrong
$string_variable = "Worx books are great!";

//try to use str_replace to replace Worx with Wrox
//this will generate an E_WARNING
//because of wrong parameter count
str_replace("Worx", "Wrox");
?>
```

4. Save the file and load it in your browser. The results should look like Figure 9-4. One of the earlier code snippets you created produced a fatal error, which is why the E_ERROR case was called in the switch statement. This sort of handler is nice to use to trap any sort of error and perform different actions based on the error.

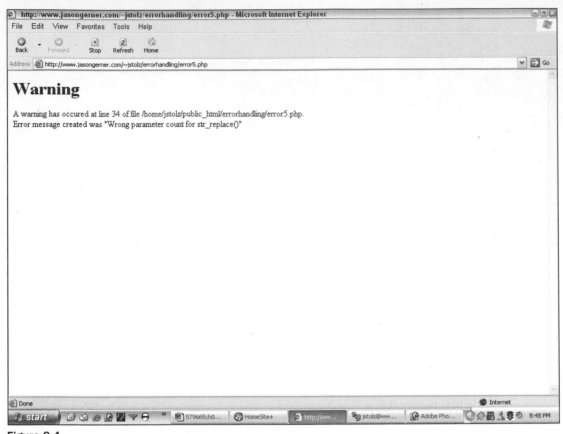

Figure 9-4

How It Works

Creating custom error message gives you near full control over your pages, regardless of success or failure when they are loading. What you have done is create a function called handler, which will catch the type of error, the error message, the file in which the error occurred, and the line in which the error occurred. By knowing those details, you can take whatever steps necessary to ensure the success of your Web site. The heart of the script you created was the switch(), where you are able to display a certain error message or send specific error message e-mails, depending on what error was served up by Apache. For example, if you were to encounter an E_ERROR, the code would run the case E_ERROR: section of the switch(). Depending on what section of the switch() was used, you will see a different error message, or an administrator will be e-mailed a different message.

Now, when trapping errors, you can display whatever you want to display, but you may not want the user to see the error message you created previously. You can create an error message that simply says there was an error on the page. Then you can apologize for the inconvenience and allow the user to go to another page. Finally, you can write the error message to a log file, write it to a database, or send it to the Webmaster or administrator via e-mail so that person can further review the error.

We personally prefer the e-mail method because it requires that the person be notified of the problem right away, and it doesn't require him or her to check the database or log files periodically. The only problem with this method is if there are a lot of requests to the page where the error is occurring; in that case the admin will be bombarded with e-mails.

Try It Out   **Creating a Full-Featured Error Page**

For this exercise, you'll set up your full-featured error handler to do just what you want it to. You can then include this page in all your pages so you can trap all the errors without using PHP's built-in handler.

1.   Edit the `feature_error.php` script as follows:

```php
<?php
//create your error handler function
function handler($error_type,
                 $error_message,
                 $error_file,
                 $error_line) {

  switch($error_type) {

    //fatal error
    case E_ERROR:
      $to = "Administrator <admin@yourdomain.com>";

      $subject = "Custom Error Handling";

      $body = "<html>";
      $body .= "<head>";
      $body .= "<title>Website error</title>";
      $body .= "</head>";
      $body .= "<body>";
      $body .= "<h1>Fatal Error</h1>";
      $body .= "Error received was a <b>" . $error_type .
               "</b> error.<br>";
      $body .= "The page that generated the error was: <b>" .
               $error_file . "</b>";
      $body .= " and was generated on line: <b>" . $error_line .
               "</b><br>";
      $body .= "The generated error message was:" . $error_message;
      $body .= "</body>";
      $body .= "</html>";

      $headers = "MIME-Version: 1.0\r\n";
      $headers .= "Content-type: text/html; charset=iso-8859-1\r\n";

      $headers .= "From: Apache Error <host@yourdomain.com>\r\n";
      $headers .= "Cc: webmaster@yourdomain.com\r\n";

      mail($to, $subject, $body, $headers);
      die(); //kill the script
      break;

    //warnings
    case E_WARNING:
```

```
        $to = "Administrator <admin@yourdomain.com>";

        $subject = "Custom Error Handling";

        $body = "<html>";
        $body .= "<head>";
        $body .= "<title></title>";
        $body .= "</head>";
        $body .= "<body>";
        $body .= "<h1>Warning</h1>";
        $body .= "Error received was a <b>" . $error_type .
            "</b> error.<br>";
        $body .= "The page that generated the error was: <b>" .
            $error_file . "</b>";
        $body .= " and was generated on line: <b>" . $error_line .
            "</b><br>";
        $body .= "The generated error message was:" . $error_message;
        $body .= "</body>";
        $body .= "</html>";

        $headers = "MIME-Version: 1.0\r\n";
        $headers .= "Content-type: text/html; charset=iso-8859-1\r\n";

        $headers .= "From: Apache Error <host@yourdomain.com>\r\n";
        $headers .= "Cc: webmaster@yourdomain.com\r\n";

        mail($to, $subject, $body, $headers);
        break;
        //script will continue

    //notices
    case E_NOTICE:
      //don't show notice errors
      break;
  }
}
/*
set error handling to 0
we will handle all error reporting
only notifying admin on warnings and fatal errors
don't bother with notices as they are trivial errors
really only meant for debugging
*/
error_reporting(0);

//set the error handler to be used
set_error_handler("handler");

/*
Create the rest of your page here.
We will not be displaying any errors
We will be e-mailing the admin an error message
Keep in mind that fatal errors will still halt the
execution, but they will still notify the admin
*/
?>
```

How It Works

Once you run this page, the code is almost exactly the same for what the logic is doing, as far as the `switch()`. The only real difference is that it will be e-mailing the administrator, instead of merely displaying an error message to the user. It can still do that, but this example showed you the e-mail function instead of simply displaying a message to the users.

So, in short, once you run this page and you receive an error, the script e-mails the admin with the error and some useful information about the user who visited the page that generated the error.

Other Methods of Error Handling

You've just seen some of what you can do with custom error messages, but there are other ways to deal with errors. Exceptions are a new feature that enables your scripts to take specific behaviors based on the type of errors that you define. Other methods of error handling are more manual: inserting `echo` statements to check the value of your variables and watching out to make sure your condition statements are being met properly. The PHP parser also provides some error messages for simple parse errors.

Exceptions

PHP5 introduced a new feature called *exceptions*. These are very similar to other languages, such as Java. Exceptions handle unforeseen conditions in your Web applications and allow you an efficient way to handle those errors that are encountered. PHP5 uses the `try/catch` method to handle the Exceptions.

Try It Out   Experimenting with Exceptions

In this exercise, you'll create a script that deliberately throws some exceptions so you can see how they work.

1. Create a PHP page with the following code:

```php
<?php
//$x = "";        //Throws null Exception
//$x = "500";     //Throws less than Exception
$x = "1000";      //Throws NO Exception

try {
  if ($x == "") {
    throw new Exception("Variable cannot be null");
  }
  if ($x < 1000) {
    throw new Exception("Variable cannot be less than 1000");
  }
  echo "Validation Accepted!";
}
catch (Exception $exception) {
  echo $exception->getMessage();
  echo " - Validation Denied!";
}
?>
```

2. Save this code as `exceptions.php` and then run it in your browser. You shouldn't see any errors.

3. Comment out the `$x = "1000"` line, and remove the comment marks from the `$x = ""` line.

4. Save the file and run it again. Now you should see the "null" message.

5. Comment out the `$x = ""` line, and remove the comment marks from the `$x = "500"` line.

6. Save the file and run it again. Now you should see the "less than 1000" message.

How It Works

The usefulness of the `try` block is that all conditions in the `try` must be met or the `catch` will be triggered. This is useful when you need to check many instances of different variables and situations and don't want to hop through so many `if`/`else` statements for your desired results. All you need is your `if` statement, and a thrown Exception with a little error message specific to that `if` statement to be thrown when needed. If any `if` statement in the `try` block is true, the exception will be thrown and passed to the `catch` block. The `catch` block will then trigger the appropriate error message, depending on which exception was caught.

In the `catch` area, you can handle the error in any way you prefer. You may just want to tell the user about something, you may want to set some default variables, a combination of both, or whatever you feel is needed at that point.

Another advantage to using Exceptions is the way they propagate through nested functions and code. For example, if you have a function A that calls function B which in turn calls function C, and an Exception is thrown in function C without using `try{}`, the exception will stop processing the script immediately and bubble up through the call chain until a `catch` block is found.

If no `try{}...catch{}` block is found when traversing up the code, an error will be shown on the screen indicating that an Unhandled Exception has occurred.

Exceptions can also be rethrown as follows:

```php
<?php
try {
  throw new Exception("This will be rethrown");
}
catch (Exception $e) {
  throw $e;
}
?>
```

You can rethrow your Exceptions in this way to deal with Exceptions at different points in the code, or in one single place of your choosing.

All in all, Exceptions act like `return`/`break` statements but allow you a far easier way to handle your errors when they do occur.

Not Meeting Conditions

Error trapping cannot catch all problems in your code. It will catch only problems related to PHP itself. Any problems you are having with conditions in your code will not be caught by simple error trapping. You'll have to do this manually by using several different methods of troubleshooting in your code.

For example, say you are submitting a form and you are wondering why the condition isn't true when you are checking for submission. Suppose you have an input such as this:

```
<input type="submit" name="submit" value="Submit">
```

You are checking to see whether the submit button has been pressed to then see whether or not you should process the form information. You are probably doing a check similar to this:

```
if ($_POST['submit'] == "submit") {
  //form has been submitted
} else {
  //form has not been submitted
}
```

See if you can figure out what is wrong with the code causing you not to get the `if` statement. Here's a hint: The value of the submit button is `"Submit"`, not `"submit"`. To troubleshoot to see if your condition is working or not, you can simply put a line in your `if` statement such as this:

```
echo "In the if statement";
```

If you get into the `if` statement, the echoed line is output to the browser. If you don't change the lower-case "submit" to an uppercase "Submit," you don't see that echo in the browser, so you can then further investigate why you aren't getting into the `if` statement. Once you realize the error, you can change the case and test it again, and voilà, the line has been echoed.

You will find that you need to use this technique to establish where in your code actions are happening. Not only do you want to do this with `if` statements, but you will probably be using it to test `for` loops, `while` loops, `foreach` loops, `do while` loops, and many others at other times when you are running conditions, or are expecting results and you can't figure out why something isn't working.

Another common problem is when variables aren't being output. Most of the time, the variables are just fine, but the programmer can't figure out why they aren't being output. Again, the conditions aren't being met, and if a condition isn't met and the expected variables are in the condition, they obviously aren't going to be output. Many programmers run into this problem and have a hard time figuring it out. They tend to lay blame on the variables before checking to see whether or not their conditions have been met.

Sometimes the variables are the reason for the condition not being met, as shown in the previous paragraph. The programmer uses the wrong value to check the `if` statement and the condition fails. The best thing for you to do in this situation is to troubleshoot. Throw an `echo` here and an `echo` there to see where your problems are. Don't give up at the first sign of defeat: You should exhaust all of your own programming resources before you go looking for help elsewhere.

Parse Errors

A parse error is another main error type. Parse errors occur when you forget a semicolon, when curly braces are mismatched, when square brackets aren't used properly, and so on. These parse errors usually don't have to do with a condition statement; they are mainly syntax errors that will cause the script to halt execution. Parse errors are worse than fatal errors because they won't even let the script run at all; they merely give you the error information.

Summary

You have read through a lot of useful information in this chapter. Learning from your own mistakes and errors will help you to be quicker at noticing small, trivial mistakes that are causing problems in your code. The single best action a programmer can learn is how to troubleshoot. Once you have that figured out, nothing can hold you back from creating seamless applications that will impress you and your clients.

Exercises

Here are three short snippets of code to sift through. Try to spot the errors and figure out how to fix them. The answers are provided in Appendix A. Once you are finished, based on what you have learned, create a little error-catching script to catch the errors.

1.

```php
<?php
$query = "SELECT * FROM table_name " .
         "WHERE name = '" . $_POST['name'] . "';"
$result = mysql_query($result)
  or die(mysql_error());
?>
```

2.

```php
<?php
if ($_POST['first_name'] = "Jethro") {
  echo "Your name is " . $_POST['first_name'];
}
?>
```

3.

```php
<?php
$full_name = $_POST['mrmiss'] ". " $_POST['first_name'] " " $_POST['last_name'];
?>
```

Part III: Comic Book Fan Site

Building Databases

In previous chapters, you created a very nice movie review Web site, but now the hand-holding is over, my friend. It's time for us to push you out of the nest. In this chapter, you will have the opportunity to create your own databases and your own Web site.

We show you how to put together a comic book appreciation Web site, but you can take the concepts we teach you and branch off to create that online auction or antique car site you have always dreamed about. We think the comic book appreciation Web site is cooler, but *whatever*. You do your thing.

This chapter covers the basics of creating your own database. Topics discussed include:

- ❏ Planning the design of your database
- ❏ Database normalization
- ❏ Creating your database
- ❏ Creating and modifying tables in your database
- ❏ Building Web pages to access your data with PHP

Getting Started

You have a great idea for a site, right? Excellent. Open up your PHP editor and start coding! Believe it or not, many people approach the creation of a Web site in just this way. You may be tempted to do this yourself. It is not impossible to create a good site in this manner, but you are seriously handicapping your chances for greatness. Before you begin, you need a plan.

We're not going to tell you how to plan out an entire Web site, complete with charts and maps and business models. That's not what this book is about. We are going to assume that you or somebody in your company has already done that by reading other great books on business models, attending seminars, reading great articles on the Web, and perhaps even hiring a business consultant who will help you with everything but building the site (because that's what we're going to teach you how to do).

So you have a great idea for a Web site *and* a plan. What do you suppose is the first step in creating a successful Web application using PHP, Apache, and MySQL? We'll give you a clue: Look at the title of this chapter.

You need to build the database this site will be based on. Don't worry — one of the great things about relational database design is that you don't have to create *every* table your site will use. You can start with a few, and build on it. As long as you follow the basic principles of good database design, your database should be quite scalable (that is, expandable to any size).

Sound like a daunting task? Don't worry. You see, we know a secret that has been kept hidden like the magician's code: *Efficient database design is easy.* No, really, we promise! You see, most of us computer geeks like to seem invaluable and very intelligent, and it sounds quite impressive to most interviewers to see on a resume "Designed a comprehensive Web site utilizing an RDBMS backend." When you are done with this chapter, you will be able to put that on your resume as well!

What Is a Relational Database?

Let's first cover a few basics of database design. The relational database is a concept first conceived by E. F. Codd of IBM, in 1970. It is a collection of data organized in tables that can be used to create, retrieve, delete, and update that data in many different ways. This can be done without having to reorganize the tables themselves, especially if the data is organized efficiently.

Take a look at the first table that follows. You can see that it contains a very simple collection of data consisting of superheroes' aliases and real names, and their superhero ID. Nothing too amazing, of course, but notice how it relates to the league table that follows it. Each superhero user has a League_ID that corresponds to an ID in the league table. Through this link, or *relationship*, you can see that Average Man is a member of the Dynamic Dudes League because the ID in the league table matches his League_ID in the superhero table.

ID	League_ID	Alias	Real Name
1	2	Average Man	Bill Smith
2	2	The Flea	Tom Jacobs
3	1	Albino Dude	George White
4	3	Amazing Woman	Mary Jones

ID	League
1	Extraordinary People
2	Dynamic Dudes
3	Stupendous Seven
4	Justice Network

At first glance, it may seem silly to create a table with one data column and an ID. Why not just put the league name in the superhero table? Imagine that you had a database of 10,000 superheroes, and 250 of them were in the Dynamic Dudes league. Now imagine that the Superhero Consortium decided to do a reorganization and "Dynamic Dudes" was changed to the "Incredible Team." If the league name were in the superhero table, you would have to edit 250 records to change the value. With the leagues in a separate, *related* table, you have to change the name in only one place.

That relationship is the key to a relational database. And speaking of keys . . .

Keys

A *key* is a column where each item of data appears only once in that column. Therefore, the key uniquely identifies each row within the table, because no two rows can have the same key. Each table is allowed to have one special key that serves as a primary unique identifier for the table, called a *primary key*.

Most of the time, the primary key is a single column, but it is not uncommon to use more than one column to make up a primary key. The important distinction is that for each row, the primary key must be unique. Because of that characteristic, you can use the key to identify a specific row of data.

The primary key must contain the following characteristics:

- ❑   It cannot be empty (null).

- ❑   It will never change in value. Therefore, a primary key cannot contain information that might change, such as part of a last name (for example, smith807).

- ❑   It must be unique. In other words, no two rows can contain the same primary key.

The League_ID column in the superhero table is also a key. It matches the primary key of the league table, but it is in a different, or *foreign*, table. For this reason, it is called a foreign key. Although it is not a requirement, many programmers will give the foreign key a name that identifies what table it refers to ("League") and some identifier that marks it as a key ("_ID"). This, along with the fact that keys are usually numeric, makes it fairly clear which column is the foreign key, if one exists in the table at all.

> *Keys do not have to be purely numeric. Other common values used as primary keys include Social Security numbers (which contain dashes) and e-mail addresses. Any value is valid as a primary key as long as it is guaranteed to be unique for each individual record in the table and will not change over time.*

Relationships

In order to be related, the two tables need a column they can use to tie them together. The superhero and league tables are related to each other by the League_ID column in the superhero table and the ID field in the league table. There is no explicit link created in the database; rather, you create the relationship by linking them with a SQL statement:

```
SELECT * FROM superhero s, league l WHERE s.League_ID = l.ID
```

In plain English, this statement tells the MySQL server to "select all records from the superhero table (call it 's') and the league table (call it 'l'), and link the two tables by the superhero League_ID column and the league ID column."

There are three types of relationships: one-to-one (1:1), one-to-many (1:M), and many-to-many (M:N). The previous example is a one-to-many relationship. To figure out what type of relationship the tables have, ask yourself how many superheroes you can have in a league. The answer is more than one, or "many." How many leagues can a superhero belong to? The answer is "one." That is a one-to-many relationship. (Of course, in some universes, a superhero might belong to more than one league. But for this example, our superheroes exhibit league loyalty.)

One-to-many is the most common database relationship. 1:1 relationships don't happen often, and a many-to-many relationship is actually two one-to-many relationships joined together with a linking table. We explore that further later in the chapter.

Although they are more rare, here's an example of a one-to-one (1:1) relationship just so you know. Say you have a link between a company and its main office address. Only one company can have that exact address. In many applications, however, the main office address is included in the company table, so no relationship is needed. That's one of the great things about relational database design. If it works for your needs, then there is no "wrong" way to do it.

Referential Integrity

The concept of referential integrity may be a little lofty for a beginner book like this, but we think it is important to touch on this briefly. If your application has referential integrity, then when a record in a table refers to a record in another table (as the previous example did), the latter table will contain the corresponding record. If the record it references is deleted, you have lost referential integrity.

In many cases, this is not disastrous. You might have an article written by an author whose name no longer exists in the author table. You still want to keep the article, so losing the referential integrity between authors and articles is okay. However, if you have an order in your database that can't be related to a customer because the customer was deleted, then you might be hard-pressed to figure out where to send the product and who to charge for it.

Ways exist to enforce referential integrity in a MySQL database, but these concepts and procedures are beyond the scope of this book. If you are interested in obtaining more information about referential integrity and foreign keys, visit `www.mysql.com/doc/en/InnoDB_foreign_key_constraints.html`.

Normalization

"Database normalization" is one of those big fancy terms that database administrators like to throw around, along with "Boyce-Codd Normal Form," "trivial functional dependency," and "Heisenberg compensator." They aren't really important terms to know to be able to design a good database, but we'll touch on normalization here.

For our purposes, we will simply define normalization as the process of modifying your database table structure so that dependencies make sense, and there is no redundant data. In a moment, you are going to go through this process. The best way to learn is to do!

Designing Your Database

It's time to design your application. This will be a relatively simple application, but it will help you learn important concepts such as normalization and expose you to various SQL commands. Typically, this is where you would go through a "Try It Out" section and learn "How It Works." When first designing a database, however, you do not need your computer. All you need is a pad of paper and a pencil. So, go get a pad of paper and a pencil. We'll wait.

OK, let's draw some tables. The application you are going to design is a comic book character database. You will store a little bit of information about various characters, such as their alter ego, their real names, the powers they possess, and the location of their lair. (Yes, that's right. We said "lair.")

Creating the First Table

Before you open MySQL and start mucking around with tables, you need to figure out how you are going to store all of the data. For simplicity, create one big table with all of the relevant data. You can draw it out on your piece of paper, or if you just can't stay away from your computer, use your favorite spreadsheet program. Copy the information you see in the table that follows.

name	real name	power 1	power 2	power 3	lair address	city	st	zip
Clean Freak	John Smith	Strength	X-ray vision	Flight	123 Poplar Avenue	Townsburg	OH	45293
Soap Stud	Efram Jones	Speed			123 Poplar Avenue	Townsburg	OH	45293
The Dustmite	Dustin Huff	Strength	Dirtiness vision	Laser	452 Elm Street #3D	Burgtown	OH	45201

Call this table "zero," because you're not even at the first step yet, and that data is just *ugly* (from a relational database standpoint).

The first thing you should notice is that there are multiple power columns. What would you do if you had to add a character with more than three powers? You would have to create a new column, and that's not good. Instead, you should combine all the powers into one column, and then separate each power into its own separate row. The other columns are duplicated in these additional rows (so, Clean Freak would have three rows instead of one, each row including a different power in the power column, but the name, address, and so on would remain identical among the three listings). This concept is called *atomicity*. Each value (cell) is *atomic*, or has only one item of data.

You also should create a unique primary key for each character. Yes, you could use the character's name, but remember that a primary key should never be something that could change, and it must be unique. To handle this requirement you'll create an ID column.

Because in this pass you have multiple rows with the same character and the multiple rows are a result of the existence of multiple powers, you'll combine the ID column with the power column to create the primary key. When more than one column makes up the primary key, it is called a *composite primary key*. We'll mark the primary key columns with an asterisk (*) to highlight them for you.

Your table should look like the one that follows. Call this table "one" because it's your first pass at normalizing. (Yes, you are in the middle of a normalization process. We told you it wasn't difficult.)

id*	name	real name	power*	lair address	city	st	zip
1	Clean Freak	John Smith	Strength	123 Poplar Avenue	Townsburg	OH	45293
1	Clean Freak	John Smith	X-ray vision	123 Poplar Avenue	Townsburg	OH	45293
1	Clean Freak	John Smith	Flight	123 Poplar Avenue	Townsburg	OH	45293
2	Soap Stud	Efram Jones	Speed	123 Poplar Avenue	Townsburg	OH	45293
3	The Dustmite	Dustin Hare	Strength	452 Elm Street #3D	Burgtown	OH	45201
3	The Dustmite	Dustin Hare	Dirtiness	452 Elm Street #3D	Burgtown	OH	45201
3	The Dustmite	Dustin Hare	Laser vision	452 Elm Street #3D	Burgtown	OH	45201

Looking better, but there is still repeated data in there. In fact, the power column is what is causing the duplicate data. Separate out the power column and use a foreign key to relate it to the original table. You will also further normalize the power table so that you get rid of duplicate data. This is pass number "two." See the three tables that follow.

id*	name	real name	lair address	city	st	zip
1	Clean Freak	John Smith	123 Poplar Avenue	Townsburg	OH	45293
2	Soap Stud	Efram Jones	123 Poplar Avenue	Townsburg	OH	45293
3	The Dustmite	Dustin Hare	452 Elm Street #3D	Burgtown	OH	45201

id*	power
1	Strength
2	X-ray vision
3	Flight
4	Speed
5	Dirtiness
6	Laser vision

char_id*	power_id*
1	1
1	2
1	3
2	4
3	1
3	5
3	6

As you can see, you have much less repeated data than you did before. The powers have been separated out, and a link table has been created to link each power to each appropriate character.

It may seem a bit nitpicky, but you still have some duplicate data that you can take care of in the character table. It is quite possible for more than one character to be in the same lair, as is the case with Clean Freak and Soap Stud. Create a lair table, and link it to the character table with keys. Also add a new column to the character table for alignment. See the two tables that follow.

id*	lair_id	name	real name	align
1	1	Clean Freak	John Smith	Good
2	1	Soap Stud	Efram Jones	Good
3	2	The Dustmite	Dustin Hare	Evil

id*	lair address	city	st	zip
1	123 Poplar Avenue	Townsburg	OH	45293
2	452 Elm Street #3D	Burgtown	OH	45201

We waited to add the alignment column to illustrate a point. If you are in the middle of the normalization process, and discover that there is some other data you need to add, it isn't difficult to do so. You could even add a completely new table if you needed to. That is one of the great things about relational database design.

The city and state fields are not only duplicates, but they are redundant data with the ZIP code (which is in itself a representation of the city/state). City and state are also not directly related to the lairs (because other lairs could exist in the same city). For these reasons, you will put city and state in a separate table. Because the ZIP code is numeric, and a direct representation of city/state, you will make the zip column a primary key. This is pass "three," shown in the three tables that follow.

id*	lair_id	name	real name	align
1	1	Clean Freak	John Smith	Good
2	1	Soap Stud	Efram Jones	Good
3	2	The Dustmite	Dustin Hare	Evil

id*	zip_id	lair address
1	45293	123 Poplar Avenue
2	45201	452 Elm Street #3D

id*	city	st
45293	Townsburg	OH
45201	Burgtown	OH

You may have noticed that you have created a many-to-many (M:N) relationship between the characters and their powers (a character can have multiple powers, and many characters may have the same power). There are two tables with primary keys, and a linking table between them has two foreign keys, one for each of the tables. The combination of the foreign keys is a primary key for the char_power table. This enables the M:N relationship.

Just for fun, add a small table that links the superheroes to villains, and vice versa. This is another M:N relationship because any superhero can have multiple villain enemies, and any villain can have multiple superhero enemies. Of course, you have the character table as one of the "many" sides of the equation— can you figure out what table to use for the other "many" side? If you said the character table, you are correct! This is just like the character-power relationship, but this time you reference the table to itself via a good_bad linking table. The goodguy_id and badguy_id columns *each* link to the id column in the character table. Each column in the good_bad table is a foreign key, and both columns make up a composite primary key.

goodguy_id*	badguy_id*
1	3
2	3

And just like that, you have created your database design. Congratulations! You now have a "map" that will help you create your database tables on the server. Not only that, but you just normalized your database design as well by modifying your database table structure so that dependencies make sense, and there is no redundant data. In fact, you have actually gone through the proper normalization steps of First, Second, and Third Normal Form.

What's So Normal About These Forms?

Remember we told you to call the first table "zero"? That's called Zero Form. It is basically the raw data, and is usually a very flat structure, with lots of repeated data. You see data like this sometimes when a small company keeps records of its customers in a spreadsheet.

The first pass through the table, which you called pass "one," was the first step of normalization, called "First Normal Form," or 1NF. This step requires that you eliminate all repeating data in columns (which you did with the power column), create separate rows for each group of related data, and identify each record with a primary key. The first step satisfies the requirements of 1NF.

You can see where we're going with this, can't you? The Second Normal Form (2NF) requirements state that you must place subsets of data in multiple rows in separate tables. You did that by separating the power data into its own table. Second Normal Form also requires that you create a relationship with the original table by creating a foreign key. You did that in pass "two," when you satisfied the requirements for 2NF.

On your third pass, you removed all the columns not directly related to the primary key (city and state), and used the ZIP code as the foreign key to the new `city_state` table. Third Normal Form (3NF) is then satisfied. Congratulations! You normalized a database just like the pros do.

There are further requirements for database normalization, but Third Normal Form is generally accepted as being good enough for most business applications. The next step is Boyce-Codd Normal Form, followed by Fourth Normal Form and Fifth Normal Form. In this case, the other Forms don't apply — the database is as normalized as it needs to get. All tables are easily modifiable and updateable, without affecting data in the other tables.

> We know there are some database gurus out there who would tell you that in order to completely satisfy the Forms of normalization, that the align column should be put into its own table and linked with a foreign key. While that may be true in the strictest sense of the rules, we usually think of normalization as a guideline. In this case, we have only two values, good and evil. Those values will never change, and they will be the only values available to the user. Because of this, we can actually create a column with the ENUM datatype. Because the values good and evil will be hardcoded into the table definition, and we don't ever see a need to change the values in the future, there is no problem with keeping those values in the `char_main` table.

Standardization

When you are designing a new application, it is a very good idea to come up with *standards*, or design rules, that you adhere to in all cases. These can be extensive, such as the standards published by the W3C for HTML, XML, and other languages. They can be very short, but very strict, such as the list of 10 standards brought down from a mountain by an old bearded man. For now you'll just standardize your table structure. For this application, we came up with the following table standards:

❑ **Table names:** Table names should be descriptive, but relatively short. Table names will be in lowercase. They should describe what main function they serve, and what application they belong to. All six tables should start with "char_" to show that they belong to the character application.

❑ **Column names:** Table columns are similar to table names. All column names will be in lower-case. They will be kept short, but multiple words (such as lair and address) will be separated by an underscore "_" (`lair_addr`).

❑ **Primary keys:** Single primary keys will always be called "id". Except in special cases, primary keys will be an integer datatype that is automatically incremented. If they consist of a single column, they will always be the first column of the table.

❑ **Foreign keys:** Foreign keys will end with "_id". They will start with the table descriptor. For example, in the `char_lair` table, the foreign key for the `char_zipcode` table will be called `zip_id`.

Finalizing the Database Design

One other thing we like to do during the database design process is put the datatypes into the empty cells of each table. You can print these tables and easily refer to them when you are writing the SQL code. You may want to do this yourself (or just use the tables provided).

If you don't understand datatypes, you can learn about them in Chapter 3, and datatypes are discussed in more detail a little later in this chapter as well. For now, just understand that datatypes are the type of data stored in each table column, such as INT (integer), VARCHAR (variable-length character string), or ENUM (enumerated list). When appropriate, they are followed by the length in parentheses; for example, `varchar(100)` is a character column that can contain up to 100 characters.

If you have been working in a spreadsheet, simply erase all of the actual data in those tables. If you used a pad and pencil, just follow along. Reduce the tables to two rows, one with column names, the other row blank. If you want, you can make a copy before erasing the data.

In keeping with the previously listed table standards, we arrive at the following tables. Yours should look very similar.

id*	lair_id	name	real_name	align
int(11)	int(11)	varchar(40)	varchar(80)	enum('good','evil')

id*	power
int(11)	varchar(40)

char_id*	power_id*
int(11)	int(11)

id*	zip_id	lair_addr
int(11)	varchar(10)	varchar(40)

id*	city	state
varchar(10)	varchar(40)	char(2)

good_id*	bad_id*
int(11)	int(11)

We think it is about time you actually created these tables on the server. Ready? Not so fast: You have to create the database first.

Creating a Database in MySQL

You can create a database in a number of ways. All require the execution of a SQL statement in one way or another, so let's look at that first:

```
CREATE DATABASE yourdatabase;
```

What, were you expecting something more complicated? Well, an optional parameter is missing: IF NOT EXISTS. We're pretty sure you know whether or not it exists, but if it makes you feel better, you can certainly add that:

```
CREATE DATABASE IF NOT EXISTS yourdatabase;
```

That's all there is to it. Think of the database as an empty shell. There is nothing special about it, really. The interesting stuff comes later, when you create the tables and manipulate the data.

That said, you still have to figure out how you are going to execute that SQL statement. Here are a few suggestions:

❑ From the MySQL command prompt. Do it this way only if you have access to the server on which MySQL is installed. If you are running your own server, or you have telnet access to the server, this may be an option for you.

❑ If you are being hosted by an ISP, you may need to request that the ISP create a database for you. For example, on one author's site the ISP has CPanel installed, and he simply clicks the module called MySQL Databases. From the next page, he simply types in the database he wants to create and clicks a button, and it's created for him.

ISPs will usually give you this option because you have a limit in your contract on how many databases you are allowed to create. On one of our sites, for example, the limit is 10 databases.

❑ If you have PHPMyAdmin installed (either on your own server or through your ISP), you can then run the SQL command from there. PHPMyAdmin is a valuable tool, and we recommend you use it if that is an option for you. It allows you to see your table structures and even browse data. It is a dangerous tool, however, because you can easily drop tables or entire databases with the click of a button, so use it carefully.

❑ Another option is to run your SQL statement from a PHP file. Most likely, if you are hosted by an ISP, it won't allow the creation of databases in this manner. However, almost any other SQL statement will work using this method. This is the way we will be running SQL commands through the rest of this chapter.

Once you have determined how you are going to run that SQL command, go ahead and do it. Make sure you substitute your own database name for yourdatabase. Because you are going to develop a comic book appreciation Web site, you could call it comicsite:

```
CREATE DATABASE IF NOT EXISTS comicsite;
```

Now that you have a design mapped out and a database created in MySQL, it is time to create some tables.

Try It Out   Creating the Tables

In this exercise, you'll create the file that will hold the hostname, username, password, and database values.

1. Open your favorite text editor, and enter the following code (making sure you use the proper values for your server):

```php
<?php

define('SQL_HOST','localhost');
define('SQL_USER','bp5am');
define('SQL_PASS','bp5ampass');
define('SQL_DB','comicsite');

?>
```

2. Save the file as config.php. This file will be included in each subsequent PHP file that needs to access the database.

3. Type the following code in your favorite PHP editor, and save it as make_table.php:

```php
<?php
require('config.php');

$conn = mysql_connect(SQL_HOST, SQL_USER, SQL_PASS)
  or die('Could not connect to MySQL database. ' . mysql_error());

mysql_select_db(SQL_DB,$conn);

$sql1 =
  "CREATE TABLE IF NOT EXISTS char_main (
    id int(11) NOT NULL auto_increment,
    alias varchar(40) NOT NULL default '',
    real_name varchar(80) NOT NULL default '',
    lair_id int(11) NOT NULL default 0,
    align enum('good','evil') NOT NULL default 'good',
```

```
        PRIMARY KEY (id)
        )";

$sql2 =
  "CREATE TABLE IF NOT EXISTS char_power (
     id int(11) NOT NULL auto_increment,
     power varchar(40) NOT NULL default '',
     PRIMARY KEY (id)
     )";

$sql3 =
  "CREATE TABLE IF NOT EXISTS char_power_link (
     char_id int(11) NOT NULL default 0,
     power_id int(11) NOT NULL default 0,
     PRIMARY KEY (char_id, power_id)
     )";

$sql4 =
  "CREATE TABLE IF NOT EXISTS char_lair (
     id int(11) NOT NULL auto_increment,
     zip_id varchar(10) NOT NULL default '00000',
     lair_addr varchar(40) NOT NULL default '',
     PRIMARY KEY (id)
     )";

$sql5 =
  "CREATE TABLE IF NOT EXISTS char_zipcode (
     id varchar(10) NOT NULL default '',
     city varchar(40) NOT NULL default '',
     state char(2) NOT NULL default '',
     PRIMARY KEY (id)
     )";
$sql6 =
  "CREATE TABLE IF NOT EXISTS char_good_bad_link (
     good_id int(11) NOT NULL default 0,
     bad_id int(11) NOT NULL default 0,
     PRIMARY KEY (good_id,bad_id)
     )";

mysql_query($sql1) or die(mysql_error());
mysql_query($sql2) or die(mysql_error());
mysql_query($sql3) or die(mysql_error());
mysql_query($sql4) or die(mysql_error());
mysql_query($sql5) or die(mysql_error());
mysql_query($sql6) or die(mysql_error());

echo "Done.";
?>
```

4. Run `make_table.php` by loading it in your browser. Assuming all goes well, you should see the message "Done" in your browser. The database now should contain all six tables.

How It Works

Every PHP script that needs to access your database on the MySQL server will include `config.php`. These constants will be used in your scripts to gain access to your database. By putting them here, in one file, you can change the values any time you move servers, change the name of the database, or change your username or password. Any time you have information or code that will be used in more than one PHP script, you should include it in a separate file. That way, you'll only need to make your changes in one location.

```
define('SQL_HOST','localhost');
define('SQL_USER','bp5am');
define('SQL_PASS','bp5ampass');
define('SQL_DB','comicsite');
```

The `make_tables.php` file is a one-time script: You should never have to run it again, unless you needed to drop all of your tables and re-create them. So, rather than explain all of the code in the page, we'll just look at one of the SQL statements:

```
CREATE TABLE IF NOT EXISTS char_main (
   id int(11) NOT NULL auto_increment,
   alias varchar(40) NOT NULL default '',
   real_name varchar(80) NOT NULL default '',
   lair_id int(11) NOT NULL default 0,
   align enum('good','evil') NOT NULL default 'good',
   PRIMARY KEY (id)
   )
```

The syntax for creating a table in MySQL is the following:

```
CREATE [TEMPORARY] TABLE [IF NOT EXISTS] tbl_name
    [(create_definition,...)] [table_options] [select_statement]
```

Obviously, you are not using the `TEMPORARY` keyword, because you want this table to be permanent and exist after your connection with the database. You are using the `IF NOT EXISTS` keyword, but only if this page is loaded twice. If you attempt to load the page again, MySQL will not attempt to re-create the tables and will not generate an error.

The table name in this case is `char_main`. The columns the script creates are `id`, `alias`, `real_name`, `lair_id`, and `alias`, which are the names we came up with earlier.

Let's look at each column:

❑   `id int(11) NOT NULL auto_increment`: The `id` column is set as an integer, with 11 maximum places. An integer datatype can contain the values -2147483648 to 2147483648. A sharp observer would note that the max value is only 10 digits. The eleventh digit is for negative values.

     `NOT NULL` will force a value into the column. With some exceptions, numeric columns will default to 0, and string columns will default to an empty string (`' '`). Very rarely will you allow a column to carry a `NULL` value.

The code `auto_increment` causes the column to increase the highest value in the table by 1 and store it in this column. A column set to `auto_increment` does not have a default value.

❏ `alias varchar(40) NOT NULL default ''`: the `alias` column is set as a `varchar` datatype, a string of 0 to 255 characters. You are allotting 40 characters, which should be enough for any character name. A `varchar` differs from a `char` datatype by the way space is allotted for the column.

A `varchar` datatype occupies only the space it needs, whereas `char` datatypes will always take up the space allotted to them by adding spaces at the end. The only time you really need to use the `char` datatype is for strings of known fixed length (such as the `State` column in the `char_zipcode` table).

❏ `real_name varchar(80) NOT NULL default ''`: Similar to `alias`. You are allotting 80 characters, which should be enough for your needs.

Note that you did not separate the `real_name` column into `first_name` and `last_name` columns. If you wanted to do that, you certainly could, but in this small application it really isn't necessary. On the other hand, in a human resources application for your company, having separate columns for first and last name is almost a requirement, so that you can do things such as greet employees by their first names in a company memo.

❏ `lair_id int(11) NOT NULL default 0`: The foreign key to the `char_lair` table is also an integer of length 11, with a default value of 0.

❏ `align enum('good', 'evil') NOT NULL default 'good'`: The `align` column can be one of two values: "good" or "evil." Because of this, you use an `enum` datatype, and default it to "good." (Everyone has some good in them, right?)

You now have a database. You have tables. If you just had a way to enter some data into your tables in your database, you'd have an application you could give to your users, where they could store information about their favorite superheroes and villains.

You could enter the data with some query statements in PHPMyAdmin, but that probably wouldn't be too efficient, not to mention that your users wouldn't have any access to it. You need some sort of interface for them that they can use to create and edit data, which means you need to design some Web pages for them.

Creating the Comic Character Application

It's back to the drawing board. Literally. Get away from your computer. You're going to put together some ideas for a Web application.

First of all, you need a page to display a list of comic book characters along with some information about them. It doesn't need to include every detail about them (such as the location of their secret lair), but it should have enough data so that users can distinguish who they are and read a little bit of information about them.

You will list the following information:

❏ Character name (alias)

❏ Real name

❑   Alignment (good or evil)

❑   Powers

❑   Enemies

You also need a character input form. This form will serve two purposes. It will allow you to create a new character, in which case the form will load with blank fields and a create button, or it will allow you to edit an existing character, in which case it will load with the fields filled in, and an update button. The form will also have a reset button that either clears the new form, or restores the edited form fields. A delete button should also be available when editing an existing character.

The fields on your form will be as follows:

❑   Character name (alias)

❑   Real name

❑   Powers (multiple select field)

❑   Lair address, city, state, and ZIP

❑   Alignment (radio button: good/evil, default good)

❑   Enemies (multiple select field)

You also need a form for adding and deleting powers. This form will be relatively simple and will contain the following elements:

❑   A checkbox list of every power currently available

❑   A Delete Selected button

❑   A text field to enter a new power

❑   An Add Power button

You also need a PHP script that can handle all database inserts, deletes, and so on. This is called a *transaction page*, and it simply does a required job and redirects the user on to another page. This page handles *all* transactions for the character application (with redirect), including the following:

❑   Inserting a new character (character listing page)

❑   Editing an existing character (character listing page)

❑   Deleting a character (character listing page)

❑   Adding a new power (power editor page)

❑   Deleting a power (power editor page)

That's basically all there is to the application. Four pages (five if you count the config.php file you created earlier — it will be used again) shouldn't be too difficult. You'll write them first, and then we'll talk about how they work.

Some of these files are a bit long. Don't let that scare you. Most of the code consists of SQL statements, and they are explained clearly for you in the "How It Works" section that follows. Remember that this code can also be downloaded from the Web site (www.wrox.com).

1. Let's start with a transaction script. This code is the longest, but that's because it contains a lot of SQL statements. It's not as bad as it looks. But if you want to download this code from the Web site, go ahead, and be guilt-free. Consider it our gift to you. If you are typing it, you know the drill. After entering it, save this one as char_transact.php:

```php
<?php
require('config.php');

foreach ($_POST as $key => $value) {
  $$key = $value;
}

$conn = mysql_connect(SQL_HOST, SQL_USER, SQL_PASS)
  or die('Could not connect to MySQL database. ' . mysql_error());
mysql_select_db(SQL_DB, $conn);

switch ($action) {
  case "Create Character":
    $sql = "INSERT IGNORE INTO char_zipcode (id, city, state) " .
           "VALUES ('$zip', '$city', '$state')";
    $result = mysql_query($sql)
      or die(mysql_error());

    $sql = "INSERT INTO char_lair (id, zip_id, lair_addr) " .
           "VALUES (NULL, '$zip', '$address')";
    $result = mysql_query($sql)
      or die(mysql_error());
    if ($result) {
      $lairid = mysql_insert_id($conn);
    }
    $sql = "INSERT INTO char_main (id,lair_id,alias,real_name,align) " .
           "VALUES (NULL, '$lairid', '$alias', '$name', '$align')";
    $result = mysql_query($sql)
      or die(mysql_error());
    if ($result) {
      $charid = mysql_insert_id($conn);
    }

    if ($powers != "") {
      $val = "";
      foreach ($powers as $key => $id) {
        $val[] = "('$charid', '$id')";
      }
      $values = implode(',', $val);
      $sql = "INSERT IGNORE INTO char_power_link (char_id, power_id) " .
```

```
            "VALUES $values";
  $result = mysql_query($sql)
    or die(mysql_error());
}

if ($enemies != '') {
  $val = "";
  foreach ($enemies as $key => $id) {
    $val[] = "('$charid', '$id')";
  }
  $values = implode(',', $val);
  if ($align = 'good') {
    $cols = '(good_id, bad_id)';
  } else {
    $cols = '(bad_id, good_id)';
  }
  $sql = "INSERT IGNORE INTO char_good_bad_link $cols " .
         "VALUES $values";
  $result = mysql_query($sql)
    or die(mysql_error());
}

$redirect = 'charlist.php';
break;

case "Delete Character":
  $sql = "DELETE FROM char_main, char_lair " .
         "USING char_main m, char_lair l " .
         "WHERE m.lair_id = l.id AND m.id = $cid";
  $result = mysql_query($sql)
    or die(mysql_error());

  $sql = "DELETE FROM char_power_link WHERE char_id = $cid";
  $result = mysql_query($sql)
    or die(mysql_error());

  $sql = "DELETE FROM char_good_bad_link " .
         "WHERE good_id = $cid OR bad_id = $cid";
  $result = mysql_query($sql)
    or die(mysql_error());
  $redirect = 'charlist.php';
  break;

case "Update Character":
  $sql = "INSERT IGNORE INTO char_zipcode (id, city, state) " .
         "VALUES ('$zip', '$city', '$state')";
  $result = mysql_query($sql)
    or die(mysql_error());

  $sql = "UPDATE char_lair l, char_main m " .
         "SET l.zip_id='$zip', l.lair_addr='$address', " .
         "alias='$alias', real_name='$name', align='$align' " .
```

```
              "WHERE m.id = $cid AND m.lair_id = l.id";
    $result = mysql_query($sql)
      or die(mysql_error());

    $sql = "DELETE FROM char_power_link WHERE char_id = $cid";
    $result = mysql_query($sql)
      or die(mysql_error());

    if ($powers != "") {
      $val = "";
      foreach ($powers as $key => $id) {
        $val[] = "('$cid', '$id')";
      }
      $values = implode(',', $val);
      $sql = "INSERT IGNORE INTO char_power_link (char_id, power_id) " .
            "VALUES $values";
      $result = mysql_query($sql)
        or die(mysql_error());
    }

    $sql = "DELETE FROM char_good_bad_link " .
          "WHERE good_id = $cid OR bad_id = $cid";
    $result = mysql_query($sql)
      or die(mysql_error());

    if ($enemies != '') {
      $val = "";
      foreach ($enemies as $key => $id) {
        $val[] = "('$cid', '$id')";
      }
      $values = implode(',', $val);
      if ($align == 'good') {
        $cols = '(good_id, bad_id)';
      } else {
        $cols = '(bad_id, good_id)';
      }
      $sql = "INSERT IGNORE INTO char_good_bad_link $cols " .
            "VALUES $values";
      $result = mysql_query($sql)
        or die(mysql_error());
    }
    $redirect = 'charlist.php';
    break;

case "Delete Powers":
  if ($powers != "") {
    $powerlist = implode(',', $powers);

    $sql = "DELETE FROM char_power WHERE id IN ($powerlist)";
    $result = mysql_query($sql)
      or die(mysql_error());
```

```
       $sql = "DELETE FROM char_power_link " .
              "WHERE power_id IN ($powerlist)";
       $result = mysql_query($sql)
          or die(mysql_error());
     }

     $redirect = 'poweredit.php';
     break;

   case "Add Power":
     if ($newpower != '') {
       $sql = "INSERT IGNORE INTO char_power (id, power) " .
              "VALUES (NULL, '$newpower')";
       $result = mysql_query($sql)
          or die(mysql_error());
     }

     $redirect = 'poweredit.php';
     break;

   default:

     $redirect = 'charlist.php';
 }
 header("Location: $redirect");
 ?>
```

How It Works

You may have noticed, unlike some of the previous exercises in the book, you're not loading a page in your browser to test the script. In this situation, the script you just wrote has nothing to display — it only processes transactions and redirects the user. One tremendous advantage to using a transaction page in this manner is that, because no data was sent to the client browser, once the browser gets to the destination page, the history will have no memory of this page. Further, if the user refreshes his or her browser, it won't re-execute the transaction. This makes for a very clean application.

For example, say a user starts on the Character List page. He or she clicks the Edit Powers link. From the Edit Powers page, the user enters a new power and clicks Add Power. The user might do this five times, adding five new powers. Each time, the PHP server submits the form to the transaction page and redirects the user back to the power page. However, if the user then clicks Back on his or her browser, the user is taken back to the Character List page, as if he or she just came from there. This is almost intuitive to the average user and is the way applications should work.

It looks like there is a lot happening on this page, but it's not that complicated. There are simply many different tasks that are performed by this page, depending on how the data got here. Let's open it up and see what makes it tick.

On many PHP servers, the php.ini option register_globals is set to ON. That registers all $_REQUEST variables (POST, GET, and COOKIE) as global variables. In other words, if your form posted a field called username using the post method, then this page could access it as $username in addition to $_POST ['username']. We're not going to go into the security problems you might have by setting register_ globals = ON. However, we do recommend that you set it to OFF, if you have control over that. In fact, it is set to OFF by default in PHP versions after 4.2.0. (If you would like more information about this, visit www.php.net/register_globals.)

You should always assume that register_globals is turned OFF to make your application more portable, and for this reason, we assume that you have access to the posted variables through the $_POST array only. What you are doing here is looping through $_POST and setting each variable yourself. If username was passed as $_POST['username'], then it will now be accessible as $username, regardless of the register_globals setting.

```
foreach($_POST as $key => $value) {
  $$key = $value;

}
```

Remember that each button is named action and that each one has a different value. In the code that follows, you determine which button was clicked, and run the appropriate code. For example, if the Delete Character button was clicked, you want to run the SQL commands only for removing character data.

```
switch ($action) {
```

The switch command is a fancy way of providing a multiple choice. It is easier to read than a complex if...else statement. The only "gotcha" you need to be aware of is to use break; at the end of each case to prevent the rest of the code in the other case blocks from executing.

The INSERT query that follows is relatively simple. In plain English: "Insert the values $zip, $city, and $state into the columns id, city, and state in the char_zipcode table." The IGNORE keyword is a very cool option that allows you do an insert without first using a SELECT query to see if the data is already in the table. In this case, you know there might already be a record for this ZIP code. So, IGNORE tells the query "If you see this ZIP code in the database already, don't do the INSERT."

```
case "Create Character":
  $sql = "INSERT IGNORE INTO char_zipcode (id, city, state) " .
         "VALUES ('$zip', '$city', '$state')";
  $result = mysql_query($sql)
    or die(mysql_error());
```

Note that the IGNORE statement compares primary keys only. Therefore, even if another ZIP code is in the database with the same state, the INSERT still takes place. Using IGNORE when inserting into a table where the primary key is automatically incremented has no effect at all; the INSERT will *always* happen in that case. This might seem obvious to you, but just keep this fact in mind; with some complex tables it won't be so intuitive.

In the INSERT that follows, you see the use of NULL as the first value. When you insert NULL into a column, MySQL does the following: If the column allows NULL values, it inserts the NULL; if it does not allow NULL (the column is set to NOT NULL), it will set the column to the default value. If a default value has not been determined, then the standard default for the datatype is inserted (empty string for varchar/char, 0 for integer, and so on). If, as is the case here, the column is set to auto_increment, then the next highest available integer for that column is inserted. In this case, id is the primary key, so this is what you want to happen.

```
$sql = "INSERT INTO char_lair (id, zip_id, lair_addr) " .
       "VALUES (NULL, '$zip', '$address')";
$result = mysql_query($sql)
   or die(mysql_error());
```

You also could have left out the id field from the insert, and inserted values into the zip_id and lair_addr columns only. MySQL treats ignored columns as if you had attempted to insert NULL into them. We like to specify every column when doing an insert, though. If you needed to modify your SQL statement later, having all the columns in the INSERT query gives you a nice placeholder so all you have to do is modify the inserted value.

The following is a neat little function. Assuming the insert worked properly ($result returned TRUE), the mysql_insert_id() function will return the value of the last auto_increment from the last run query. This works only after running a query on a table with an auto_incremented column. In this case it returns the primary key value of the row you just inserted into the char_lair table. You will need that value to insert into the char_main table.

```
if ($result) {
   $lairid = mysql_insert_id($conn)
}
```

The connection variable is optional, but we think it's a good habit to always include it. If you omit it, it will use the most recently opened connection. In a simple application like this one, that's not a problem; in a more complex application where you might have more than one connection, it could get confusing.

Again, note the use of NULL for the primary key id, and the use of mysql_insert_id() to return the primary key in the following:

```
$sql = "INSERT INTO char_main (id, lair_id, alias, real_name, align) " .
       "VALUES (NULL, '$lairid', '$alias', '$name', '$align')";
$result = mysql_query($sql)
   or die(mysql_error());
if ($result) {
   $charid = mysql_insert_id($conn)
}
```

You are always interested in minimizing the number of times you run a query on the database. Each hit takes precious time, which can be noticeable in a more complex application. At this point, you need to figure out how to insert all the powers with only one SQL command:

```
if ($powers != "") {
   $val = "";
   foreach ($powers as $key => $id) {
      $val[] = "('$charid', '$id')";
   }
   $values = implode(',', $val);
   $sql = "INSERT IGNORE INTO char_power_link (char_id, power_id) " .
          "VALUES $values";
   $result = mysql_query($sql)
      or die(mysql_error());
}
```

There are a couple of concerns here. First, if there is already a power for this user (there shouldn't be; it's a new character, but always be prepared), you need to not insert the row. You already know how to take care of this by using the IGNORE keyword.

Second, you must insert multiple rows of data with only one query. Easy enough; all you have to do is supply a comma-separated list of value groupings that matches up to the column grouping in the query. For example:

```
INSERT INTO table (col1, col2) VALUES (val1, val2), (val3, val4)
```

You accomplish this by looping through the $powers array and putting the values for character ID and power ID into a new array. You then concatenate that array with a comma separator, and *voilà!* There are your multiple rows of data to insert.

You then do the same thing with the $enemies array that you did with $powers. This time, however, you insert into the columns based on whether the character is good or evil. It doesn't really matter too much which column gets which ID, but for the most part you want evil character IDs in the bad_id column.

```
if ($enemies != '') {
  $val = "";
  foreach ($enemies as $key => $id) {
    $val[] = "('$charid', '$id')";
  }
  $values = implode(',', $val);
  if ($align = 'good') {
    $cols = '(good_id, bad_id)';
  } else {
    $cols = '(bad_id, good_id)';
  }
  $sql = "INSERT IGNORE INTO char_good_bad_link $cols " .
         "VALUES $values";
  $result = mysql_query($sql)
    or die(mysql_error());
}
```

When it comes to the char_good_bad_link table, you have a little bit of referential integrity that you have to handle (beyond what MySQL does for you). Namely, you don't want to have a good_id/bad_id combination to match up to a bad_id/good_id combination. For the purposes of a relational database, that isn't bad, but for your purposes, that is considered a duplication. You will handle this contingency when updating a character, but because this is a new character (with a brand new id), you don't have to worry about that just yet.

You're done inserting new character data, so you now set the page you are going to load next, and break out of the switch statement.

```
$redirect = 'charlist.php';
break;
```

When deleting a character, you simply remove all instances of it from all relevant tables. To remove the relevant data from the char_lair table, you have to JOIN it to the char_main table by matching up the lair ids first. Then you delete all matching rows where the character ID matches.

```
case "Delete Character":
  $sql = "DELETE FROM char_main, char_lair " .
         "USING char_main m, char_lair l " .
         "WHERE m.lair_id = l.id AND m.id = $cid";
  $result = mysql_query($sql)
    or die(mysql_error());

  $sql = "DELETE FROM char_power_link WHERE char_id = $cid";
  $result = mysql_query($sql)
    or die(mysql_error());
```

You don't really need to put the results of the `mysql_query` command in a variable. We like to do this as a matter of habit because if you ever need the return value later, it will be available. In the case of a DELETE, you don't get a result set, you get a return value of either TRUE or FALSE.

Remembering that the `char_good_bad_link` needs to maintain what we call "reverse" referential integrity (1, 3 matches 3, 1), you remove all rows that contain the character's ID in either column:

```
$sql = "DELETE FROM char_good_bad_link " .
       "WHERE good_id = $cid OR bad_id = $cid";
$result = mysql_query($sql)
  or die(mysql_error());
```

Updating a character is where things get interesting. First of all, you can simply do an INSERT IGNORE on the ZIP code table. If the address and ZIP code change, you don't really need to delete the old data because it might be used for other characters — it's perfectly fine to leave the old data alone. So, you just do an INSERT IGNORE as you did for a new character, and leave it at that.

```
case "Update Character":
  $sql = "INSERT IGNORE INTO char_zipcode (id, city, state) " .
         "VALUES ('$zip', '$city', '$state')";
  $result = mysql_query($sql)
    or die(mysql_error());
```

Here is the first UPDATE query, and incidentally, the only one in the entire application. It is very similar to INSERT and SELECT queries, with the exception of the SET keyword. The SET keyword tells MySQL what columns to set, and what values to set them to. The old values in the row are overwritten. This is a JOIN query because there is more than one table. The WHERE keyword specifies both the linking column (`lair_id`) and the condition that only rows for this character will be updated.

```
$sql = "UPDATE char_lair l, char_main m " .
       "SET l.zip_id='$zip', l.lair_addr='$address', " .
       "alias='$alias', real_name='$name', align='$align' " .
       "WHERE m.id = $cid AND m.lair_id = l.id";
$result = mysql_query($sql)
  or die(mysql_error());
```

Because the `char_power_link` table does not have an automatically incremented column as the primary key, you don't have to do an update to the table. An update is possible, but it is much easier to simply delete all the old links of character to power, and insert new link rows. In some cases, you may be deleting and inserting the same data (for instance, you might be adding `flight` as a power, but `invisibility` did not change; `invisibility` will still be deleted and reinserted). When updating data in an M:N relationship, you will usually simply delete the old data, and insert the updated/new data.

```
$sql = "DELETE FROM char_power_link WHERE char_id = $cid";
$result = mysql_query($sql)
  or die(mysql_error());

if ($powers != "") {
  $val = "";
  foreach ($powers as $key => $id) {
    $val[] = "('$cid', '$id')";
  }
  $values = implode(',', $val);
  $sql = "INSERT IGNORE INTO char_power_link (char_id, power_id) " .
       "VALUES $values";
  $result = mysql_query($sql)
    or die(mysql_error());
}
```

This brings you to the Enemies data, where not only do you have to maintain referential integrity, but you have to worry about updating rows where the ID can be present in either of the two linking columns. You must maintain the "reverse" referential integrity.

```
$sql = "DELETE FROM char_good_bad_link " .
     "WHERE good_id = $cid OR bad_id = $cid";
$result = mysql_query($sql)
  or die(mysql_error());

if ($enemies != '') {
  $val = "";
  foreach ($enemies as $key => $id) {
    $val[] = "('$cid', '$id')";
  }
  $values = implode(',', $val);
  if ($align == 'good') {
    $cols = '(good_id, bad_id)';
  } else {
    $cols = '(bad_id, good_id)';
  }
  $sql = "INSERT IGNORE INTO char_good_bad_link $cols " .
       "VALUES $values";
  $result = mysql_query($sql)
    or die(mysql_error());
}
```

How did you deal with referential integrity? It turns out that it takes care of itself when you follow the same method you employed when updating the `char_power_link` table. By simply running the same DELETE query you ran when deleting a character, and then immediately running the same INSERT query you ran when creating a new character, you ensure that only one set of rows exists to match up each character to his/her enemy. It's simple, elegant, and it works!

By this time, queries should seem quite familiar to you. The DELETE query is one of the simplest of the SQL statements. In these DELETE queries, you need to delete each power that was selected on the Add/Delete Power page. You must do this not only in the char_power table, but in the char_power_link table as well. (In this application, if a power is removed, you remove that power from the characters as well.) To perform a DELETE on multiple rows, you use the IN keyword, with which each ID in the supplied comma-separated list of power IDs is matched against the id, and each matching row is deleted.

```
case "Delete Powers":
  if ($powers != "") {
    $powerlist = implode(',', $powers);

    $sql = "DELETE FROM char_power WHERE id IN ($powerlist)";
    $result = mysql_query($sql)
      or die(mysql_error());

    $sql = "DELETE FROM char_power_link " .
           "WHERE power_id IN ($powerlist)";
    $result = mysql_query($sql)
      or die(mysql_error());
  }
```

When adding a power, you first check to make sure a value was passed (no need to run a query if there is nothing to add), and then attempt to insert the value into the power table. Once again, you use the IGNORE keyword in what follows to avoid duplication of powers. We have mentioned that you really use IGNORE only on tables that have a primary key that is not autogenerated. There is an exception. IGNORE will not allow any duplicate data in any column that is designated as UNIQUE. In the char_power table, the power column is a UNIQUE column, so attempting to insert a duplicate value would result in an error. The IGNORE keyword prevents the insertion, so you don't get an error returned. If the power already exists, the script simply returns to the poweredit.php page and awaits further instructions.

```
case "Add Power":
  if ($newpower != '') {
    $sql = "INSERT IGNORE INTO char_power (id, power) " .
           "VALUES (NULL, '$newpower')";
    $result = mysql_query($sql)
      or die(mysql_error());
  }
```

You should always have a default: option in your case statements. You don't need to do anything there, but it is good programming practice to include it. In this case, you are simply going to redirect the user back to the charlist.php page.

```
default:
  $redirect = 'charlist.php';
```

Finally, you reach the last command of char_transact.php. To use the header() function, no data can have been previously sent to the client. If it has, you will get an error. In this case, char_transact.php has no data sent to the client, so the header() function will work as advertised.

```
header("Location: $redirect");
```

Each case sets a destination page after running its queries. This command will now send the user to that destination.

Editing Superhero Powers

The next page you're going to create is a script to allow you to create and modify superhero powers.

1. Enter the following code in your favorite PHP editor, and save it as `poweredit.php`:

```php
<?php
require('config.php');

$conn = mysql_connect(SQL_HOST, SQL_USER, SQL_PASS)
  or die('Could not connect to MySQL database. ' . mysql_error());
mysql_select_db(SQL_DB, $conn);

$sql = "SELECT id, power FROM char_power ORDER BY power";
$result = mysql_query($sql)
  or die(mysql_error());
if (mysql_num_rows($result) > 0) {
  while ($row = mysql_fetch_array($result)) {
    $pwrlist[$row['id']] = $row['power'];
  }
  $numpwr = count($pwrlist);
  $thresh = 5;
  $maxcols = 3;
  $cols = min($maxcols, (ceil(count($pwrlist)/$thresh)));
  $percol = ceil(count($pwrlist)/$cols);
  $powerchk = '';
  $i = 0;
  foreach ($pwrlist as $id => $pwr) {
    if (($i>0) && ($i%$percol == 0)) {
      $powerchk .= "</td>\n<td valign=\"top\">";
    }
    $powerchk .= "<input type=\"checkbox\" name=\"powers[]\" " .
                 "value=\"$id\"> $pwr<br>\n";
    $i++;
  }
  $delbutton = " <tr>
    <td colspan=\"$cols\" bgcolor=\"#CCCFF\" align=\"center\">
      <input type=\"submit\" name=\"action\" value=\"Delete Powers\">
      <font size=\"2\" color=\"#990000\"><br><br>
      deleting will remove all associated powers<br>
      from characters as well -- select wisely</font>
    </td>
    </tr>";
} else {
  $powerchk = "<div style=\"text-align:center;width:300;
    font-family:Tahoma,Verdana,Arial\">No Powers entered...</div>";
  $delbutton = '';
  $cols = 1;
}
```

```
?>
<html>
<head>
<title>Add/Delete Powers</title>
</head>
<body>
<img src="CBA_Tiny.gif" align="left" hspace="10">
<h1>Comic Book<br>Appreciation</h1><br>
<h3>Editing Character Powers</h3>
<form action="char_transact.php" method="post" name="theform">
<table border="0" cellpadding="5">
  <tr bgcolor="#FFCCCC">
    <td valign="top"><?php echo $powerchk; ?></td>
  </tr>
  <?php echo $delbutton; ?>
  <tr>
    <td colspan="<?php echo $cols; ?>" bgcolor="#CCCCFF" align="center">
      <input type="text" name="newpower" value="" size=20>
      <input type="submit" name="action" value="Add Power">
    </td>
  </tr>
</table>
</form>
<a href="charlist.php">Return to Home Page</a>
</body>
</html>
```

2. Load `poweredit.php` in your browser. When the page appears (see Figure 10-1), it initially will be empty.

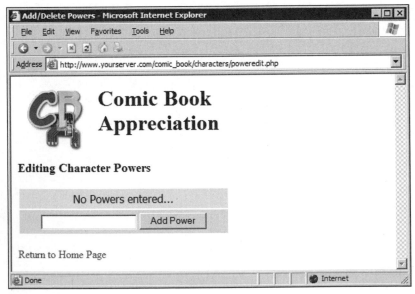

Figure 10-1

3. Enter an ultra-cool superpower such as invisibility or X-ray vision in the text box, and click Add Power. If you need help with power ideas, here are a few: super strength, invisibility, X-ray vision, speed, soccer mom, stretchable, flight, breathes underwater. Add a total of six powers. Moving on, you should now see a new button and a list of powers with checkboxes next to them.

4. Check one or two powers and click Delete Powers. They should go away.

How It Works

You will see this on every page, but we will mention it this one time only. You include the `config.php` file that contains the constants used in the next couple of lines. By putting these constants in an included file, you can make any required changes in one place. You use the `require` command instead of `include` because of the way PHP works: An included file will not stop the processing of the rest of the page, whereas a required file, if not found, would immediately stop processing.

```
require('config.php');
```

Next, a connection to the server is made, and the appropriate database is selected. Notice the use of the constants you defined in `config.php`:

```
$conn = mysql_connect(SQL_HOST, SQL_USER, SQL_PASS)
    or die('Could not connect to MySQL database. ' . mysql_error());
mysql_select_db(SQL_DB, $conn);
```

What follows is a somewhat simple SQL `select` statement. It grabs the `id` and `power` columns from the `char_power` table and sorts them by power. This way, when you iterate through them later and put the data on the Web page, they will be in alphabetical order.

```
$sql = "SELECT id, power FROM char_power ORDER BY power";
```

The following code executes the SQL statement and throws an error if there are any problems:

```
$result = mysql_query($sql)
    or die(mysql_error());
```

Now the script checks to make sure at least one row was returned. If so, it iterates through each row, building up an array of powers, using the power ID as the array key. Note the use of `mysql_fetch_array`. Other options are `mysql_fetch_row` and `mysql_fetch_assoc`. Using `mysql_fetch_array` gives you the flexibility to reference the results by numerical index or named index.

```
if (mysql_num_rows($result) > 0) {
  while ($row = mysql_fetch_array($result)) {
    $pwrlist[$row['id']] = $row['power'];
  }
}
```

When the script retrieves data from the database, it will usually need to retrieve appropriate ids so that you can later insert or update the correct record. In this case, the ID serves as the key to the array, making it easy to retrieve the values. You could have certainly used a multi-value array, but that gets a little more confusing, and it's just not necessary here. Just be sure you understand that many times in this application (and many applications using relational databases) you will use the table ID as an array key.

Now we're going to get a little tricky. Because the list of powers could get quite large, you want to try to distribute them across multiple columns. However, you would probably like to distribute them fairly evenly. The following 13 lines of code do this for you (if math is not interesting to you at all, or you simply don't want to know how this part of the code works, skip this section).

First, you get a count of the number of powers in the array. Next, you set the threshold to 5 lines (after which a second column will be created), and a maximum number of columns (in this case, 3).

```
$numpwr = count($pwrlist);
$thresh = 5;
$maxcols = 3;
```

Next, you determine how many columns to create. Assume there are 7 powers to display. First, you divide the count by the threshold (7/5), which gives you 1.4. Next, you use `ceil()` to round up to the nearest integer (`ceil(1.4) = 2`). Then you take the smaller of the two values (3 and 2), and store it in the `$cols` variable. In this example, `$cols` would equal 2.

To figure out how many powers go into each column, you divide the count by the number of columns, and round up to the nearest integer. In this case, `ceil(7/2) = 4`. So, you'll have two columns, with four values in each column (the last column will contain the remainder of powers if there are fewer than four). `$powerchk` is a string that will contain each power, with a checkbox attached to it. For now, you initialize it to an empty string `' '`.

```
$cols = min($maxcols, (ceil(count($pwrlist)/$thresh)));
$percol = ceil(count($pwrlist)/$cols);
$powerchk = '';
```

Now you loop through each element of the `$pwrlist` array, which contains the ID as the key (`$id`), and power as the value (`$pwr`). The counter `$i` will start at 0 and increment each time through the loop. In each loop, you add the `<input>` tag to create the checkbox, using the ID as the value, and the name of the power as the label. When the counter reaches a value that is divisible by `$percol`, you add a close table definition and start a new one.

```
$i = 0;
foreach ($pwrlist as $id => $pwr) {
   if (($i>0) && ($i%$percol == 0)) {
      $powerchk .= "</td>\n<td valign='top'>";
   }
   $powerchk .= "<input type=\"checkbox\" name=\"powers[]\" " .
               "value=\"$id\"> $pwr<br>\n";
   $i++;
}
```

In this example, increments 0, 1, 2, and 3 end up in the first column. When `$i` reaches 4 (the value of `$percol`), the script starts a new column. If this is confusing, don't worry. You can play around with it by changing your `$thresh` and `$maxcols` values and adding a bunch of random power values to see how the table is built. For now, let's check out the rest of the code.

This is the rest of the if statement. If there is even one power, a row is created that contains a delete button. If not, the script creates a row that simply states that no powers have yet been entered.

```
$delbutton = " <tr>
  <td colspan=\"$cols\" bgcolor=\"#CCCCFF\" align=\"center\">
    <input type=\"submit\" name=\"action\" value=\"Delete Powers\">
    <font size=\"2\" color=\"#990000\"><br><br>
    deleting will remove all associated powers<br>
    from characters as well -- select wisely</font>
  </td>
  </tr>";
} else {
  $powerchk = "<div style=\"text-align:center;width:300;
   font-family:Tahoma,Verdana,Arial\">No Powers entered...</div>";
  $delbutton = '';
  $cols = 1;
}
?>
```

We have left off some of the HTML. We assume you know HTML well enough that we don't need to explain it. As you can see in the <form> tag, when the user clicks the Add Power or Delete Powers button, you'll be sending values to char_transact.php:

```
<form action="char_transact.php" method="post" name="theform">
```

At this point, $powerchk either contains the No Powers display, or the built-up table columns. Either way, the script inserts $powerchk into the table. Note the open and close table definitions (<td valign="top"> and </td>). You didn't add them to $powerchk earlier, but you *did* add the internal close/open definitions to create the columns as necessary.

```
<table border="0" cellpadding="5">
  <tr bgcolor="#FFCCCC">
    <td valign="top"><?php echo $powerchk; ?></td>
```

In the following, $delbutton either contains the row with the delete button (if powers were found), or it's blank. That is how you control when it shows up, and this is where it's inserted into the table.

```
<?php echo $delbutton; ?>
```

The following code deals with the add button. Notice that it is called 'action' and that it has a value of Add Power. When submitting a form, PHP passes these values on to the next page. Because you are using the post method on the form, you will have a $_POST variable called 'action' that contains the value of the button. Because of this, and because all of your forms load char_transact.php, all of your buttons are named 'action' and have different values so that you can determine what to do with the data that is sent. We go into more detail about this when we look at char_transact.php.

```
<input type="submit" name="action" value="Add Power">
```

Try It Out   Managing the Characters

The next file you're going to create will display a list of the characters in your database.

1.   Enter the following code, and save it as `charlist.php`:

```php
<?php
require('config.php');

if (isset($_GET['o']) && is_numeric($_GET['o'])) {
  $ord = round(min(max($_GET['o'], 1), 3));
} else {
  $ord = 1;
}
$order = array(1 => 'alias ASC',
               2 => 'name ASC',
               3 => 'align ASC, alias ASC'
);

$conn = mysql_connect(SQL_HOST, SQL_USER, SQL_PASS)
  or die('Could not connect to MySQL database. ' . mysql_error());
mysql_select_db(SQL_DB, $conn);

$sql = "SELECT c.id, p.power " .
       "FROM char_main c " .
       "JOIN char_power p " .
       "JOIN char_power_link pk " .
       "ON c.id = pk.char_id AND p.id = pk.power_id";

$result = mysql_query($sql)
  or die(mysql_error());
if (mysql_num_rows($result) > 0) {
  while ($row = mysql_fetch_array($result)) {
    $p[$row['id']][] = $row['power'];
  }
  foreach ($p as $key => $value) {
    $powers[$key] = implode(", ", $value);
  }
}

$sql = "SELECT c.id, n.alias " .
       "FROM char_main c " .
       "JOIN char_good_bad_link gb " .
       "JOIN char_main n " .
       "ON (c.id = gb.good_id AND n.id = gb.bad_id) " .
       "OR (n.id = gb.good_id AND c.id = gb.bad_id)";

$result = mysql_query($sql)
  or die(mysql_error());
if (mysql_num_rows($result) > 0) {
  while ($row = mysql_fetch_array($result)) {
    $e[$row['id']][] = $row['alias'];
  }
  foreach ($e as $key => $value) {
```

```
      $enemies[$key] = implode(", ", $value);
   }
}
$table = "<table><tr><td align=\"center\">No characters " .
          "currently exist.</td></tr></table>";
?>
<html>
<head>
<title>Comic Book Appreciation</title>
</head>
<body>
<img src="CBA_Tiny.gif" align="left" hspace="10">
<h1>Comic Book<br>Appreciation</h1><br>
<h3>Character Database</h3>

<?php
$sql = "SELECT id, alias, real_name AS name, align " .
       "FROM char_main ORDER BY ". $order[$ord];

$result = mysql_query($sql)
  or die(mysql_error());
if (mysql_num_rows($result) > 0) {
  $table = "<table border=\"0\" cellpadding=\"5\">";
  $table .= "<tr bgcolor=\"#FFCCCC\"><th>";
  $table .= "<a href=\"" . $_SERVER['PHP_SELF'] . "?o=1\">Alias</a>";
  $table .= "</th><th><a href=\"" . $_SERVER['PHP_SELF'] . "?o=2\">";
  $table .= "Name</a></th><th><a href=\"" . $_SERVER['PHP_SELF'];
  $table .= "?o=3\">Alignment</a></th><th>Powers</th>";
  $table .= "<th>Enemies</th></tr>";

  // build each table row
  $bg = '';
  while ($row = mysql_fetch_array($result)) {
    $bg = ($bg=='F2F2FF'?'E2E2F2':'F2F2FF');
    $pow = ($powers[$row['id']]==''?'none':$powers[$row['id']]);
    if (!isset($enemies) || ($enemies[$row['id']]=='')) {
      $ene = 'none';
    } else {
      $ene = $enemies[$row['id']];
    }
    $table .= "<tr bgcolor=\"#" . $bg . "\">" .
              "<td><a href=\"charedit.php?c=" . $row['id'] . "\">" .
              $row['alias']. "</a></td><td>" .
              $row['name'] . "</td><td align=\"center\">" .
              $row['align'] . "</td><td>" . $pow . "</td>" .
              "<td align=\"center\">" . $ene . "</td></tr>";
  }

  $table .= "</table>";
  $table = str_replace('evil',
                    '<font color="red">evil</font>',
                    $table);
  $table = str_replace('good',
                    '<font color="darkgreen">good</font>',
```

```
                              $table);

}
echo $table;
?>
<br /><a href="charedit.php">New Character</a> &bull;
<a href="poweredit.php">Edit Powers</a>
</body>
</html>
```

2. In the last file for this chapter, you'll create the ability to add and modify characters. Enter the next block of code and save it as `charedit.php`:

```php
<?php
require('config.php');

if (!isset($_GET['c']) || $_GET['c'] == '' || !is_numeric($_GET['c'])) {
  $char='0';
} else {
  $char = $_GET['c'];
}
$subtype = "Create";
$subhead = "Please enter character data and click " .
           "'$subtype Character.'";
$tablebg = '#EEEEFF';

$conn = mysql_connect(SQL_HOST, SQL_USER, SQL_PASS)
  or die('Could not connect to MySQL database. ' . mysql_error());
mysql_select_db(SQL_DB, $conn);

$sql = "SELECT id, power FROM char_power";
$result = mysql_query($sql)
  or die(mysql_error());
if (mysql_num_rows($result) > 0) {
  while ($row = mysql_fetch_array($result)) {
    $pwrlist[$row['id']] = $row['power'];
  }
}

$sql = "SELECT id, alias FROM char_main WHERE id != $char";
$result = mysql_query($sql)
  or die(mysql_error());
if (mysql_num_rows($result) > 0) {
  $row = mysql_fetch_array($result);
  $charlist[$row['id']] = $row['alias'];
}

if ($char != '0') {
  $sql = "SELECT c.alias, c.real_name AS name, c.align, " .
         "l.lair_addr AS address, z.city, z.state, z.id AS zip " .
         "FROM char_main c, char_lair l, char_zipcode z " .
         "WHERE z.id = l.zip_id " .
         "AND c.lair_id = l.id " .
```

```php
              "AND c.id = $char";
    $result = mysql_query($sql)
      or die(mysql_error());
    $ch = mysql_fetch_array($result);

    if (is_array($ch)) {
      $subtype = "Update";
      $tablebg = '#EEFFEE';
      $subhead = "Edit data for <i>" . $ch['alias'] .
                  "</i> and click '$subtype Character.'";

      $sql = "SELECT p.id " .
            "FROM char_main c " .
            "JOIN char_power p " .
            "JOIN char_power_link pk " .
            "ON c.id = pk.char_id " .
            "AND p.id = pk.power_id " .
            "WHERE c.id = $char";
      $result = mysql_query($sql)
        or die(mysql_error());
      if (mysql_num_rows($result) > 0) {
        while ($row = mysql_fetch_array($result)) {
          $powers[$row['id']] = 'selected';
        }
      }

      // get list of character's enemies
      $sql = "SELECT n.id " .
            "FROM char_main c " .
            "JOIN char_good_bad_link gb " .
            "JOIN char_main n " .
            "ON (c.id = gb.good_id AND n.id = gb.bad_id) " .
            "OR (n.id = gb.good_id AND c.id = gb.bad_id) " .
            "WHERE c.id = $char";
      $result = mysql_query($sql)
        or die(mysql_error());
      if (mysql_num_rows($result) > 0) {
        while ($row = mysql_fetch_array($result)) {
          $enemies[$row['id']] = 'selected';
        }
      }
    }
  }
}
?>

<html>
<head>
<title>Character Editor</title>
</head>
<body>
<img src="CBA_Tiny.gif" align="left" hspace="10">
<h1>Comic Book<br />Appreciation</h1><br />
<h3><?php echo $subhead; ?></h3>
```

```
<form action="char_transact.php" name="theform" method="post">
<table border="0" cellpadding="15" bgcolor="<?php echo $tablebg; ?>">
  <tr>
    <td>Character Name:</td>
    <td><input type="text" name="alias" size="41"
        value="<?php if (isset($ch)) { echo $ch['alias']; } ?>">
    </td>
  </tr>
  <tr>
    <td>Real Name:</td>
    <td><input type="text" name="name" size="41"
        value="<?php if (isset($ch)) { echo $ch['name']; } ?>">
    </td>
  </tr>
  <tr>
    <td>Powers:<br><font size="2" color="#990000">
      (Ctrl-click to<br>select multiple<br>powers)</font>
    </td>
    <td>
      <select multiple name="powers[]" size="4">
<?php
foreach ($pwrlist as $key => $value) {
  echo "<option value=\"$key\" ";
  if (isset($powers) && array_key_exists($key,$powers)) {
    echo $powers[$key];
  }
  echo ">$value</option>\n";
}
?>
      </select>
    </td>
  </tr>

  <tr>
    <td>Lair Location:<br><font size="2" color="#990000">
      (address,<br>city, state, zip)</font>
    </td>
    <td><input type="text" name="address" size="41"
        value="<?php if (isset($ch)) { echo $ch['address']; } ?>"><br>
      <input type="text" name="city"
        value="<?php if (isset($ch)) { echo $ch['city']; } ?>">
      <input type="text" name="state" size="2"
        value="<?php if (isset($ch)) { echo $ch['state']; } ?>">
      <input type="text" name="zip" size="10"
        value="<?php if (isset($ch)) { echo $ch['zip']; } ?>">
    </td>
  </tr>

  <tr>
    <td>Alignment:</td>
```

```
    <td>
      <input type="radio" name="align" value="good"
      <?php if (isset($ch)) {
        echo($ch['align']=='good' ? ' checked' : '');
      } ?>>
      good<br>
      <input type="radio" name="align" value="evil"
      <?php if (isset($ch)) {
        echo($ch['align']=='evil' ? ' checked' : '');
      } ?>>
      evil
    </td>
  </tr>

<?php if (isset($charlist) && is_array($charlist)) { ?>
  <tr>
    <td>Enemies:<br><font size="2" color="#990000">
      (Ctrl-click to<br>select multiple<br>enemies)</font>
    </td>
    <td>
      <select multiple name="enemies[]" size="4">
<?php
foreach ($charlist as $key => $value) {
  echo "<option value=\"$key\" ";
  if (isset($enemies)) {
    echo $enemies[$key];
  }
  echo ">$value</option>\n";
}
?>
      </select>
    </td>
  </tr>
<?php } ?>
  <tr>
    <td colspan="2">
      <input type="submit" name="action"
        value="<?php echo $subtype; ?> Character">
      <input type="reset">
<?php if ($subtype == "Update") { ?>
          
      <input type="submit" name="action" value="Delete Character">
<?php } ?>
    </td>
  </tr>
</table>
<input type="hidden" name="cid" value="<?php echo $char; ?>">
</form>
<a href="charlist.php">Return to Home Page</a>
</body>
</html>
```

3. Open your browser, and point it to the location of `charlist.php`. This is your Character Database home page. It should look something like Figure 10-2. If the logo is missing, you can download it from the Web site, edit the four pages to eliminate the image, or change it to anything you want. Because you don't currently have any characters to look at, let's move on.

Figure 10-2

4. Click the New Character link. A shiny new page appears, ready for your data input (see Figure 10-3). You will notice that the powers you entered are choices in the Powers field. (Relational databases rule!)

5. Enter the appropriate data, and click Create Character. You should be taken to the home page, where you'll now see the character you entered (as in Figure 10-4).

Character Editor - Microsoft Internet Explorer
File Edit View Favorites Tools Help
Address http://www.yourserver.com/comic_book/characters/charedit.php
Comic Book Appreciation
Please enter character data and click 'Create Character.'
Character Name:
Real Name:
Powers:
(Ctrl-click to select multiple powers)
invisibility
dirtiness
cleanliness
x-ray vision
Lair Location:
(address, city, state, zip)
Alignment:
good
evil
Create Character
Reset
Return to Home Page
Done
Internet

Figure 10-3

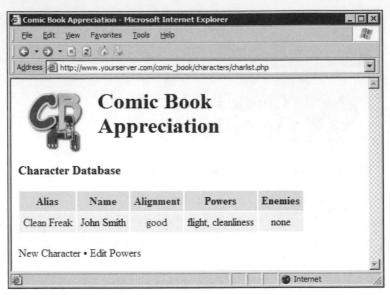

Figure 10-4

6. If you click New Character again, you should now see an extra field for Enemies. You can select any previously created character in the database as the current character's enemy.

7. From the home page, click one of your characters' names. The Character Editor page loads again, but now the background is green, and the character's data will be automatically entered into the fields (see Figure 10-5). If you look at the URL for this page, you see ?c=x at the end, where x is the character's number.

8. Change some of the data, and click Update Character. You are taken back to the home page, and you should immediately see the results of your changes. In fact, if you selected an enemy for this character, you should see the results change in the enemy's row as well.

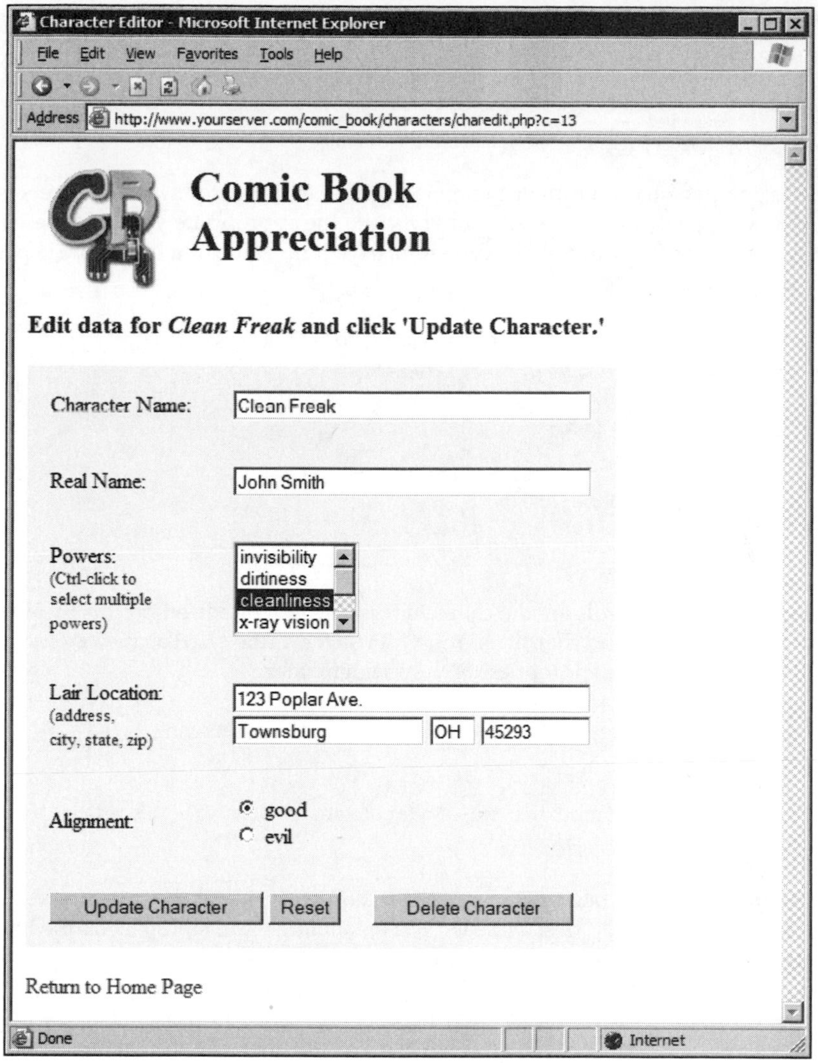

Figure 10-5

How It Works

You created two different files in this exercise, so we're going to take them apart and look at them individually here.

charlist.php

The `charlist.php` page has an optional parameter that can be passed: `?o=x`, where x is 1, 2, or 3. This code retrieves that variable if it exists, and converts it to the appropriate value if necessary. If some smart-aleck types o=4 in the browser, the code returns 3. If no value or a bad value is passed, it will default to 1. The value is stored in `$ord`.

```
if (isset($_GET['o']) && is_numeric($_GET['o'])) {
  $ord = round(min(max($_GET['o'], 1), 3));
} else {
  $ord = 1;
}
$order = array(1 => 'alias ASC',
               2 => 'name ASC',
               3 => 'align ASC, alias ASC'
);
```

This value determines which column the character display will be sorted on: 1 is by alias, 2 is by real name, and 3 is by alignment and then alias. You will use the value `$ord` as the key to your order array, which will be appended to the appropriate SQL statement later.

Make a connection, and choose a database. You know the drill by now.

```
$conn = mysql_connect(SQL_HOST, SQL_USER, SQL_PASS)
  or die('Could not connect to MySQL database. ' . mysql_error());
mysql_select_db(SQL_DB, $conn);
```

Ah . . . your first JOIN. This SELECT statement might look confusing to the uninitiated, but it is not that complicated. First, look at the JOIN statements. You are joining three tables, using the `char_power_link` table to link the `char_power` table and the `char_main` table. This is a many-to-many (M:N) relationship. You define how they are joined with the ON statement. As you can see, you are linking up the character table to the link table using the character id, and you're linking the power table to the link table using the power id. With that link established, you can see that you are grabbing the character's ID and the powers assigned to each character.

```
$sql = "SELECT c.id, p.power " .
       "FROM char_main c " .
       "JOIN char_power p " .
       "JOIN char_power_link pk " .
       "ON c.id = pk.char_id AND p.id = pk.power_id";
$result = mysql_query($sql)
  or die(mysql_error());
```

Notice the use of aliases for the tables. The character table is c, the power link table is pk, and the power table is p. This allows you to refer to the appropriate columns with a shorter syntax (for example pk.char_id instead of char_power_link.char_id). It is not necessary to use table.column syntax if the column name is unique across all tables. However, it is a good practice to keep so that you are always aware of which data you are accessing. It is required, of course, for column names that are duplicated across multiple tables (such as id). Some might recommend that you *always* use unique names for all of your fields, but we prefer the practice of naming all primary keys "id" and using proper table.column syntax in SQL queries.

Next, you create a multidimensional array. That's fancy talk for an array with more than one index. This one is two-dimensional. Think of a two-dimensional array as being like a spreadsheet, and it isn't difficult to understand.

```
if (mysql_num_rows($result) > 0) {
  while ($row = mysql_fetch_array($result)) {
    $p[$row['id']][] = $row['power'];
  }
```

The trick here is that you have multiple powers for the same id. By adding [] to the $p array, a new array item is created for each row that has the same id. The end result is that you have a $p array of *x* characters, each element of which contains a $p[x] array of *y* powers. That is a multidimensional array.

Now you go back through the temporary array $p, and pull out each array that it holds. The $key variable contains the character id, and $value contains the array of that character's powers. You then implode the powers into a comma-separated list of powers, and store that in the $powers array, using the character ID ($key) as the array index. You end up with an array that contains a list of powers for each character.

```
foreach ($p as $key => $value) {
  $powers[$key] = implode(", ", $value);
}
```

Oh boy, another JOIN. This one is similar to the previous M:N query, with a couple of exceptions. First of all, you are linking the character table twice. You can see that you are creating two instances of that table, one called c for "character" and one called n for "nemesis." This distinction is very important.

```
$sql = "SELECT c.id, n.alias " .
       "FROM char_main c " .
       "JOIN char_good_bad_link gb " .
       "JOIN char_main n " .
       "ON (c.id = gb.good_id AND n.id = gb.bad_id) " .
       "OR (n.id = gb.good_id AND c.id = gb.bad_id)";
```

The other exception is the ON statement. You have characters that you are attempting to link to other characters as "enemies." Call them opponents, or nemeses, or whatever. Typically, you expect good versus evil and vice versa. However, you are allowing *any* character to be the enemy of *any other* character. That makes linking more interesting because you are using a table with a bad_id and a good_id. If you have two evil characters that are enemies, which one gets stored in the good_id column?

The answer is that it doesn't matter. What you want to do is to make sure that you not only don't have any duplicates in the char_good_bad_link table, but also that you don't have what we call *reverse duplication.* In other words, if you have a row with good_id=3 and bad_id=7, then good_id=7 and bad_id=3 must be considered a duplicate. There is no way to prevent that in MySQL using primary keys, so you must take care of that contingency in your code. You do that in a couple of places.

In this instance, you are combining two queries in one. The first one grabs all instances of each character where the character's ID is in the good_id field and his enemies' IDs are in the bad_id field. The second part of the ON statement reverses that, and pulls all instances of each character where the character's ID is in the bad_id field and his enemies' IDs are in the good_id field. This does not prevent reverse duplication (that is handled elsewhere), but it does make sure you have grabbed every possible link to a character's enemy.

This code is virtually identical to the multidimensional powers array. This time, you are creating a multidimensional array of each character and that character's enemies. You then implode the enemies list and store it in the $enemies array, using the character's ID as the array index.

```
$result = mysql_query($sql)
  or die(mysql_error());
if (mysql_num_rows($result) > 0) {
  while ($row = mysql_fetch_array($result)) {
    $e[$row['id']][] = $row['alias'];
  }
  foreach ($e as $key => $value) {
    $enemies[$key] = implode(", ", $value);
  }
}
```

You are going to build a table of characters in a moment. In case there are no characters to display (as when you first tested your charlist.php page), you want to display a "No characters" message. This code builds the $table variable (even though it doesn't contain an actual table) using a <div> tag. If any characters do exist, this variable will be overwritten with an actual table of data.

```
$table = "<table><tr><td align=\"center\">No characters " .
        "currently exist.</td></tr></table>"
?>
```

Next is another simple SQL SELECT, pulling the appropriate data: character's id, alias, real name, alignment, and address info. Note the $order array. You set that value at the beginning of this page, using the $_GET value "o" in the URL. This is where it's used to sort the characters.

```
$sql = "SELECT id, alias, real_name AS name, align " .
       "FROM char_main ORDER BY ". $order[$ord];
$result = mysql_query($sql)
  or die(mysql_error());
```

You are now building up the table of characters, as long as you returned at least one record from the database. Note the first three columns' links. They refer back to this same page, adding the ?o=x parameter. This will re-sort the data and display it sorted on the column the user clicked.

```
if (mysql_num_rows($result) > 0) {
  $table = "<table border=\"0\" cellpadding=\"5'>";
```

```
$table .= "<tr bgcolor=\"#FFCCCC\"><th>";
$table .= "<a href=\"" . $_SERVER['PHP_SELF'] . "?o=1\">Alias</a>";
$table .= "</th><th><a href=\"" . $_SERVER['PHP_SELF'] . "?o=2\">";
$table .= "Name</a></th><th><a href=\"" . $_SERVER['PHP_SELF'];
$table .= "?o=3\">Alignment</a></th><th>Powers</th>";
$table .= "<th>Enemies</th></tr>";
```

Next, you alternate the background colors of the table, to make it a little easier to read.

```
// build each table row
$bg = '';
while ($row = mysql_fetch_array($result)) {
  $bg = ($bg=='F2F2FF'?'E2E2F2':'F2F2FF');
```

Remember the power and enemy arrays you built earlier? You use the character's ID to grab the list of values and put them into a variable to be inserted shortly into the appropriate table cell.

```
$pow = ($powers[$row['id']]==''?'none':$powers[$row['id']]);
if (!isset($enemies) || ($enemies[$row['id']]=='')) {
  $ene = 'none';
} else {
  $ene = $enemies[$row['id']];
}
```

The table is built, row by row, inserting the appropriate data in each cell; then it's closed:

```
    $table .= "<tr bgcolor=\"#" . $bg . "\">" .
              "<td><a href='charedit.php?c=" . $row['id'] . "\">" .
              $row['alias']. "</a></td><td>" .
              $row['name'] . "</td><td align=\"center\">" .
              $row['align'] . "</td><td>" . $pow . "</td>" .
              "<td align=\"center\">" . $ene . "</td></tr>";
}
$table .= "</table>";
```

Just for kicks, and to make them more visible, the script changes the color of the "good" and "evil" values in the table. This isn't necessary, but it makes the values pop out more.

```
$table = str_replace('evil',
                     '<font color="red">evil</font>',
                     $table);
$table = str_replace('good',
                     '<font color="darkgreen">good</font>',
                     $table);
```

This variable contains either the <div> tag you created earlier or the table of character data. It's inserted in the page here.

```
echo $table;
```

charedit.php

This file does double-duty, so it's a little longer. But a lot of it is HTML, and much of what it does you have already done before, so this shouldn't be too difficult.

The default functionality of this page is New Character mode. If there is a value in $char other than 0, the script will pull the data and change the default values.

```
if (!isset($_GET['c']) || $_GET['c'] == '' || !is_numeric($_GET['c'])) {
  $char='0';
} else {
  $char = $_GET['c'];
}
$subtype = "Create";
$subhead = "Please enter character data and click " .
          "'$subtype Character.'";
$tablebg = '#EEEEFF';
```

Next, the script gets all the powers, and puts them into an array to be accessed later (when building the power select field on the form).

```
$sql = "SELECT id, power FROM char_power";
$result = mysql_query($sql)
  or die(mysql_error());
if (mysql_num_rows($result) > 0) {
  while ($row = mysql_fetch_array($result)) {
    $pwrlist[$row['id']] = $row['power'];
  }
}
```

All characters except the chosen character will be pulled from the database to be used for the Enemies field. If the character ID is not valid, then *all* characters will be pulled for the Enemies field.

```
$sql = "SELECT id, alias FROM char_main WHERE id != $char";
$result = mysql_query($sql)
  or die(mysql_error());
if (mysql_num_rows($result) > 0) {
  $row = mysql_fetch_array($result);
  $charlist[$row['id']] = $row['alias'];
}
```

If there is a character id, the script attempts to pull the data from the database. This SQL statement is also a JOIN, although the JOIN keyword is not used. You can identify such a JOIN because there are two or more tables, and the WHERE keyword is matching columns from each of the tables. The JOIN in this case is implied. Once all the tables are joined, all the appropriate fields are pulled as long as the character ID in the character table matches $char. If there is no match, no records will be returned. If there is a match, one record is returned and the row is stored in $ch.

```
if ($char != '0') {
  $sql = "SELECT c.alias, c.real_name AS name, c.align, " .
         "l.lair_addr AS address, z.city, z.state, z.id AS zip " .
         "FROM char_main c, char_lair l, char_zipcode z " .
         "WHERE z.id = l.zip_id " .
```

```
          "AND c.lair_id = l.id " .
          "AND c.id = $char";
   $result = mysql_query($sql)
     or die(mysql_error());
   $ch = mysql_fetch_array($result);
```

Once the script determines there was a record retrieved, it alters the default variables to reflect the edited document. The background is green, and you are "Updating" rather than "Creating."

```
if (is_array($ch)) {
  $subtype = "Update";
  $tablebg = '#EEFFEE';
  $subhead = "Edit data for <i>" . $ch['alias'] .
             "</i> and click '$subtype Character.'";
```

The next SQL statement retrieves all powers associated with this character. All you really need is the ID so that you can create a $powers array with each element containing the word "selected." This will be used in the Powers field on the form, so that each power assigned to the character will be automatically selected.

```
$sql = "SELECT p.id " .
       "FROM char_main c " .
       "JOIN char_power p " .
       "JOIN char_power_link pk " .
       "ON c.id = pk.char_id " .
       "AND p.id = pk.power_id " .
       "WHERE c.id = $char";
$result = mysql_query($sql)
  or die(mysql_error());
if (mysql_num_rows($result) > 0) {
  while ($row = mysql_fetch_array($result)) {
    $powers[$row['id']] = 'selected';
  }
}
```

Now you do exactly the same thing with the character's enemies. Note the similarity in this SQL statement to the one in charlist.php. The only difference is that you want only the enemies that match your character.

```
// get list of character's enemies
$sql = "SELECT n.id " .
       "FROM char_main c " .
       "JOIN char_good_bad_link gb " .
       "JOIN char_main n " .
       "ON (c.id = gb.good_id AND n.id = gb.bad_id) " .
       "OR (n.id = gb.good_id AND c.id = gb.bad_id) " .
       "WHERE c.id = $char";
$result = mysql_query($sql)
  or die(mysql_error());
if (mysql_num_rows($result) > 0) {
  while ($row = mysql_fetch_array($result)) {
    $enemies[$row['id']] = 'selected';
  }
}
```

You next build the table in HTML, and insert values into the appropriate places as defaults. This is how you fill in the fields with character data. Note how the script checks to see if the variable is set before echoing it to the page. If it didn't, and the error reporting for PHP was set to E_ALL, there might be a warning printed to the screen if $ch didn't contain a value. Checking is usually a good idea if you aren't certain a variable will be set.

```
<td>Character Name:</td>
<td><input type="text" name="alias" size="41"
     value="<?php if (isset($ch)) { echo $ch['alias']; "?>">
</td>
```

Now you build the Powers select field. As the script loops through each power in the $pwrlist array (which contains *all* powers), it concatenates the $powers array value for that power ("selected"). If that power's key (from $pwrlist) doesn't exist in the $powers array, $powers[$key] will simply be blank instead of "selected." In this way, the script builds a field of *all* powers where the character's chosen powers are selected in the list. Neato, huh?

```
<td>Powers:<br><font size="2" color="#990000">
  (Ctrl-click to<br>select multiple<br>powers)</font>
</td>
<td>
  <select multiple name="powers[]" size="4">
<?php
foreach ($pwrlist as $key => $value) {
  echo "    <option value=\"$key\" ";
  if (isset($powers) && array_key_exists($key,powers)) {
    echo $powers[$key];
  }
  echo ">$value</option>\n";
}
?>
  </select>
</td>
```

Note the [] in the select name attribute. That is necessary for PHP to recognize the variable as an array when it gets POSTed to the next page. This is a requirement for any field that might post with multiple values.

The following code creates a set of radio buttons for "good" and "evil." The character's alignment is selected with the checked attribute.

```
<td>
  <input type="radio" name="align" value="good"
  <?php if (isset($ch)) {
    echo($ch['align']=='good' ? ' checked="checked"' : '');
  } ?>>
  good<br>
  <input type="radio" name="align" value="evil"
  <?php if (isset($ch)) {
    echo($ch['align']=='evil' ? ' checked="checked"' : '');
  } ?>>
  evil
</td>
```

Remember what you did with the Powers field? Ditto all of that for the Enemies field. The only difference here is that if there are no values in the $charlist variable (list of all characters except the chosen character), the Enemies field will not show up on the form.

```php
<?php if (isset($charlist) && is_array($charlist)) { ?>
  <tr>
    <td>Enemies:<br><font size="2" color="#990000">
      (Ctrl-click to<br>select multiple<br>enemies)</font>
    </td>
    <td>
      <select multiple name="enemies[]" size="4">";
<?php
foreach ($charlist as $key => $value) {
  echo "<option value=\"$key\" ";
  if (isset($enemies)) {
    echo $enemies[$key];
  }
  echo ">$value</option>\n";
}
```

If the character entry form is not in Update mode, then the script will hide the Delete Character button (you can't delete a character you haven't created yet):

```php
<?php if ($subtype == "Update") { ?>
        
    <input type="submit" name="action" value="Delete Character">
<?php } ?>
```

Finally, the character ID is not passed through any form fields, so you create a hidden field to hold that information. You need that ID if you are going to update an existing character. Of course, if you are creating a new character, then the ID will be created for you when you insert all the appropriate data.

```php
<input type="hidden" name="cid" value="<?php echo $char; ?>">
```

Summary

Whew! This chapter covered a lot of ground. You learned about how to plan the design of your application, including database design. You learned how to normalize your data, so that it can easily be linked and manipulated. You created a brand new database for your Web site and started building your Web site by creating tables and creating the Web application needed to access and update those tables.

Congratulations! You just created your first, fully functioning Web application with a relational database backend. (That's going to look *so* good on your resume.)

This chapter is only the beginning, however. With the knowledge you gained here, you can create almost any application you desire. Here are some examples of what you could do:

❑ **Content Management (CMS):** Create a data entry systems that will allow users and administrators to alter the content of the Web site and your database without knowing any HTML.

❏ **Maintain a database of users visiting your site:** You can enable user authentication, e-mail your users to give them exciting news, sign them up for newsletters, and so on.

❏ **Create an online e-commerce site:** Create shopping carts where users can store the merchandise they will purchase. (This can be daunting—many choose to use a third-party shopping cart application.)

❏ **Create an online discussion forum where your users can go to discuss how wonderful your site looks!**

These are just a few ideas. In fact, you are going to see how to do each of these things over the course of upcoming chapters. With a little imagination, you can come up with solutions to almost any problem you might face in building your site.

If any of the ideas presented in this chapter are difficult for you to grasp, that's okay. It is a lot of material, especially if you are a beginning programmer. The great thing about a book is that you can keep coming back! You will also be revisiting many of these concepts in later chapters. For example, in Chapter 16 where you learn to build your own forum, you will go through database normalization again on a new set of databases. You will also have many more opportunities to create SQL queries, some familiar and some new.

For now, take some time to play with your new toy, the Character Database. You have the basic knowledge for creating even the most complex sites. You have the first incarnation installed on your server.

Now all you need to do is let all of your friends and family know about your cool new site. If only you knew how to send e-mails using PHP. Well, we'll handle that in Chapter 11.

Exercises

See how you might accomplish the following tasks:

1. Add a "costume description" field to the character record, and provide a way to modify the costume description.

2. Modify the character listing to display the characters' locations alongside their powers.

Sending E-mail

So far, the chapters in this book have walked you through the creation of a comprehensive Web site. You have designed your site so that users can add and modify data, which is being stored in databases. You have built pages dynamically for your users, ensuring they have a rich and unique experience when they visit your Web site. You are even displaying helpful error messages in case something goes wrong. Now it's time to get a little more interactive with your users with e-mail. But we are not talking about standard e-mail, in which you write to your mother to tell her about the cool site you've been building. (You did tell her, didn't you? She would be so proud.) We're talking about sending out e-mails using PHP.

Why would you want a server-side scripting language to send e-mails? Perhaps you want to create a simple feedback form to be submitted to an administrator, as introduced in Chapter 9. Or maybe you want certain errors to be automatically e-mailed to the Webmaster. Or perhaps you would like to create an application that allows users to send their friends and family electronic postcards. (Nod your head in vigorous agreement here because that is exactly what you are going to do!)

Specifically, this chapter covers:

- ❑ Sending a basic e-mail
- ❑ Sending an e-mail formatted with HTML
- ❑ Multipart messages
- ❑ Sending images
- ❑ Getting confirmation

Setting Up PHP to Use E-mail

To be able to send e-mail with PHP, you need an e-mail server. This chapter doesn't delve too deeply into the setup of a mail server for PHP, but here are the basics.

If you are in a UNIX or Linux environment, you will most likely have sendmail installed on your server. If you are using a hosting service, check with your service provider to make sure sendmail or some equivalent is being used.

If you are not using sendmail, or you have Apache installed on a Windows server, you have a couple of choices. You can use your existing SMTP (Simple Mail Transport Protocol) service, or you can install a mail server such as Mailtraq on your computer. If you have questions or concerns about setting up or using a mail server, many online resources are available to help you. We suggest using a search engine.

Once you have your mail server squared away, you'll need to modify your php.ini file. There are a couple of parameters you need to set. Of course, if you are using a hosting service, the host should already have these parameters set up.

❑ SMTP: Set this to the IP address or DNS name of your SMTP server. For example, if you have a mail server installed on the same server as your PHP server, you should be able to set SMTP to localhost. This applies to Windows installations only.

❑ smtp_port: Set this to the port PHP uses to connect to the SMTP server. This applies to Windows installations only and is valid for PHP version 4.3 and above.

❑ sendmail_from: The From address used by default by the PHP mail() command.

❑ sendmail_path: The path to the sendmail program (UNIX/Linux servers only). For most servers, this is usr/sbin/sendmail.

That's just about all there is to setting up PHP for e-mail. You will test to make sure it works correctly in the next section, "Sending an E-mail." You can find more information about setting up PHP for mail at http://us3.php.net/manual/en/ref.mail.php.

Sending an E-mail

The actual method of sending an e-mail is quite simple. Of course, it can be made much more complex with the addition of headers, and sending HTML and images. However, you are going to start off with something simple.

Try It Out   Sending a Simple E-mail

This example is just about the simplest code you can write to send an e-mail. Of course, it's not very flexible, but it does demonstrate the mail() function quite well.

1. Start your favorite text/PHP/HTML editor.

2. Enter the following code. Make sure you put your own e-mail address in as the first parameter:

```php
<?php
mail("your@e-mailaddress.com", "Hello World", "Hi, world. Prepare for our arrival.
We're starving!");
?>
```

3. Save the text file as firstmail.php and load it in your browser. You should see a blank page and should receive an e-mail shortly at the address entered as the first parameter.

How It Works

Pretty cool, huh? That's all there is to it!

The mail() function automatically sends an e-mail, using the following format:

```
Mail(to, subject, message, headers, other_parameters)
```

The parameters headers and other_parameters are optional. If you want to send a message to multiple recipients, their addresses must be separated with a comma in the to parameter:

```
Mail("first@e-mail.com, second@e-mail.com", "Hi", "Whazzup??")
```

We will cover the headers parameter soon. The other_parameters are beyond the scope of this book, but if you want more information about the mail() function, point your browser to www.php.net/manual/en/function.mail.php.

You may have noticed when receiving this e-mail that there was no From address (or, your service provider may have automatically put in a bogus address). Ours says "Nobody." In the next example, you'll see how to add a "From:" parameter to your e-mail, and you'll collect information from the user before sending the e-mail. Let's dig in!

Try It Out   Collecting Data and Sending an E-mail

In this exercise, you are going to create two Web pages, postcard.php and sendmail.php. The file postcard.php will collect the data you are going to send. The file sendmail.php will actually send the message, using the data you enter.

1. Start up your favorite text/PHP/HTML editor, and enter the following code:

```
<html>
<head>
<title>Enter E-mail Data</title>
</head>
<body>
<form name="theform" method="post" action="sendmail.php">
<table>
  <tr>
    <td>To:</td>
    <td><input type="text" name="to" size="50"></td>
  </tr>
  <tr>
    <td>From:</td>
    <td><input type="text" name="from" size="50"></td>
  </tr>
  <tr>
    <td>Subject:</td>
    <td><input type="text" name="subject" size="50"></td>
  </tr>
  <tr>
    <td valign="top">Message:</td>
    <td>
```

```
          <textarea cols="60" rows="10" name="message"
          >Enter your message here</textarea>
      </td>
    </tr>
    <tr>
      <td></td>
      <td>
        <input type="submit" value="Send">
        <input type="reset" value="Reset the form">
      </td>
    </tr>
  </table>
  </form>
  </body>
  </html>
```

2. Save the page as `postcard.php`. Note that `postcard.php` doesn't actually have any PHP code in it. It simply collects the required data in an HTML form. You're giving it a `.php` extension in case you decide to add PHP code to it later (and you will).

3. Start a new text document and enter the following code:

```
<html>
<head>
<title>Mail Sent!</title>
</head>
<body>
<?php
$to = $_POST["to"];
$from = $_POST["from"];
$subject = $_POST["subject"];
$message = $_POST["message"];
$headers = "From: " . $from . "\r\n";
$mailsent = mail($to, $subject, $message, $headers);
if ($mailsent) {
  echo "Congrats! The following message has been sent: <br><br>";
  echo "<b>To:</b> $to<br>";
  echo "<b>From:</b> $from<br>";
  echo "<b>Subject:</b> $subject<br>";
  echo "<b>Message:</b><br>";
  echo $message;
} else {
  echo "There was an error...";
}
?>
</body>
</html>
```

4. Save this page as `sendmail.php`. This second page will take the values entered into the first page and send them in an e-mail.

5.   Load up the first page, `postcard.php`, in your browser, and enter some data. Make sure you use a valid e-mail address so that you can verify their receipt. It should look something like Figure 11-1.

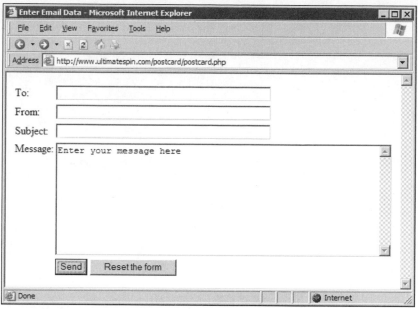

Figure 11-1

6.   Click the Send button. A second page appears, similar to the one shown in Figure 11-2.

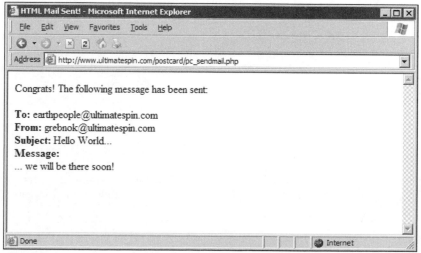

Figure 11-2

7. Open your e-mail client and check your e-mail (which should look like the one shown in Figure 11-3).

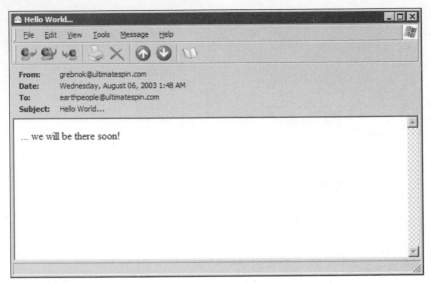

Figure 11-3

How It Works

We assume that you know HTML well enough that we don't have to explain postcard.php in great detail. Just remember that if your sendmail.php page is not in the same folder as postcard.php, you have to provide the correct path:

```
<form name="theform" method="post" action="yourdir/sendmail.php">
```

Once the user presses the Send button, sendmail.php is loaded. The first step in your PHP code assigns all the fields from postcard.php to variables. This step is not necessary if register_globals is set to On in your php.ini file, but we strongly recommend you use this code anyway, in case register_globals is ever turned Off:

```
$to = $_POST["to"];
$from = $_POST["from"];
$subject = $_POST["subject"];
$message = $_POST["message"];
```

To specify from whom the e-mail is coming, use the optional fourth parameter for the mail() function, headers. Headers are explained in more detail in the section "Sending HTML by Using Headers," later in this chapter.

```
$headers = "From: " . $from . "\r\n";
```

The `mail()` function returns a value of `True` if it is successful and `False` if it fails. You can use this function to make your application a little more robust:

```php
$mailsent = mail($to, $subject, $message, $headers);
if ($mailsent) {
  echo "Congrats! The following message has been sent: <br><br>";
  echo "<b>To:</b> $to<br>";
  echo "<b>From:</b> $from<br>";
  echo "<b>Subject:</b> $subject<br><br>";
  echo "<b>Message:</b><br>";
  echo $message;
} else {
  echo "There was an error...";
}
?>
```

Of course, you can modify this to handle errors more elegantly. Use the knowledge you acquired in Chapter 9 to do so.

You have now created your first PHP e-mail application. Congratulations! (Call your mother! She'll be so proud.) But you'll probably soon get tired of ugly, plain-text e-mails. I'm sure you're champing at the bit to create colorful, formatted e-mails, right? How else are you going to enable users to send some pretty postcards? Okay, let's do something about that!

Dressing Up Your E-mails with HTML

Because you are creating a postcard application, sending plain-text e-mails just won't do. You want to dress them up a bit, and make them look professional, yet attractive. So, add a bit of HTML to your e-mail code to dress it up.

Try It Out   Sending HTML Code in an E-mail

First, let's try a little experiment. This step isn't vital, but it will help illustrate a later point about headers.

1.   Go to step 5 of the previous "Try It Out" section and send another e-mail. This time, put some HTML in the message. An example would be:

```
<h3>Hello World!</h3><br>Prepare for our arrival.<br><br><b>We are starving!!!</b>
```

2.   When you have entered all relevant data in the form, click the Send button, and check your e-mail. It should look something like the e-mail shown in Figure 11-4.

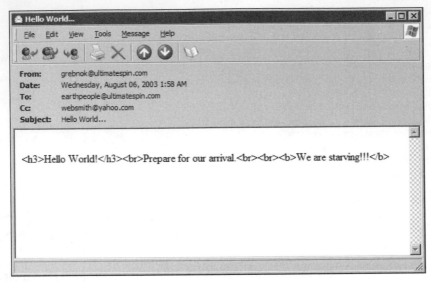

Figure 11-4

How It Works

Perhaps this heading should be "How It *Doesn't* Work." That's because your e-mail client does not know that it has received HTML. Why? Because you didn't tell it! In order for any HTML-capable client to display HTML, the client needs to be told that the incoming e-mail is going to have some HTML tags on it. Only then will it know how to properly display your message.

Try It Out   **Sending HTML by Using Headers**

You need a way for your e-mail to tell the client it contains HTML. This is accomplished by using headers. You already saw how to use headers to include a "From:" parameter. Now you are going to use a similar header to tell the client that the e-mail message contains HTML.

1. Edit your copy of `sendmail.php` in your favorite text editor. Back up `sendmail.php` before making changes if you want to keep the old version.

2. Make the following highlighted modifications to this file:

```
<html>
<head>
<title>HTML Mail Sent!</title>
</head>
<body>
<?php
$to = $_POST["to"];
$from = $_POST["from"];
$subject = $_POST["subject"];
$message = $_POST["message"];
```

```
$headers = "MIME-Version: 1.0\r\n";
$headers .= "Content-type: text/html; charset=iso-8859-1\r\n";
$headers .= "Content-Transfer-Encoding: 7bit\r\n";
$headers .= "From: " . $from . "\r\n";
$mailsent = mail($to, $subject, $message, $headers);
if ($mailsent) {
  echo "Congrats! The following message has been sent: <br><br>";
  echo "<b>To:</b> $to<br>";
  echo "<b>From:</b> $from<br>";
  echo "<b>Subject:</b> $subject<br>";
  echo "<b>Message:</b><br>";
  echo $message;
} else {
  echo "There was an error...";
}
?>
</body>
</html>
```

3. Save the file.

4. Load `postcard.php` into your browser and fill in the fields with appropriate information. Be sure to include some HTML in the message field, such as

```
<h3>Hello World!</h3><br>Prepare for our arrival.<br><br><b>We are starving!!!</b>
```

5. Click the Send button, and open your e-mail client to see the new message, which will look something like Figure 11-5.

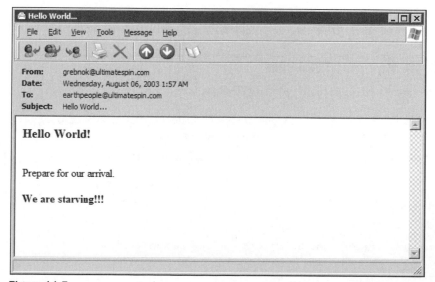

Figure 11-5

How It Works

You added a couple of new lines to the variable $headers. This allows you to do many additional things with your e-mail, including adding HTML. This line is required in order to use extended MIME capabilities (such as HTML).

```
$headers = "MIME-Version: 1.0\r\n";
```

Note the \r\n. This is a carriage return and new line, which must be entered between each header. UNIX sometimes allows just \n, but to be on the safe side, you should always use \r\n.

The following indicates that you will be using HTML in your message:

```
$headers .= "Content-type: text/html; charset=iso-8859-1\r\n";
$headers .= "Content-Transfer-Encoding: 7bit\r\n";
```

It is concatenated to the $headers variable.

That's all there is to adding HTML to your messages. All you have to do is tell the e-mail client to expect HTML, and it will work. You can really get fancy now — with tables, style sheets, images, and so on.

However, there is still a concern — what about e-mail programs that don't accept or recognize HTML? What happens to them? You certainly want this application to be as user-friendly as possible, right? Not to worry — you'll take care of them with multipart (or mixed) messages.

Multipart Messages

You want to be able to send your postcards to anyone. However, some people don't have HTML capabilities in their e-mail client. Therefore, you will send your postcards using both plain text and HTML.

Try It Out   Multipart Messages

To send messages with both plain text and HTML, you will use Multipart Messages. Here's how to do it:

1. Edit your copy of postcard.php in your favorite text editor. Back up postcard.php before making changes if you want to keep the old version.

2. Make the following modifications (shown highlighted) to postcard.php:

```
<html>
<head>
<title>Enter Data</title>
</head>
<body>
<form name="theform" method="post" action="sendmail.php">
<table>
  <tr>
    <td>To:</td>
    <td><input type="text" name="to" size="50"></td>
  </tr>
  <tr>
    <td>From:</td>
```

```
        <td>
          <input type="text" name="from" size="50">
        </td>
      </tr>
      <tr>
        <td>Cc:</td>
        <td>
          <input type="text" name="cc" size="50">
        </td>
      </tr>
      <tr>
        <td>Bcc:</td>
        <td><input type="text" name="bcc" size="50"></td>
      </tr>
      <tr>
        <td>Subject:</td>
        <td><input type="text" name="subject" size="50"></td>
      </tr>
      <tr>
        <td valign="top">Message:</td>
        <td>
          <textarea cols="60" rows="10" name="message"
          >Enter your message here</textarea>
        </td>
      </tr>
      <tr>
        <td></td>
        <td>
          <input type="submit" value="Send">
          <input type="reset" value="Reset the form">
        </td>
      </tr>
    </table>
  </form>
  </body>
  </html>
```

3. Edit your copy of `sendmail.php` in your favorite text editor. Back up `sendmail.php` before making changes if you want to keep the old version.

4. Make the following highlighted changes to `sendmail.php`:

```
<html>
<head>
<title>Multipart Mail Sent!</title>
</head>
<body>
<?php
$to = $_POST["to"];
$cc = $_POST["cc"];
$bcc = $_POST["bcc"];
$from = $_POST["from"];
$subject = $_POST["subject"];
```

```
$messagebody = $_POST["message"];
$boundary = "==MP_Bound_xyccr948x==";
$headers = "MIME-Version: 1.0\r\n";
$headers .= "Content-type: multipart/alternative; boundary=\"$boundary\"\r\n";
$headers .= "CC: " . $cc . "\r\n";
$headers .= "BCC: " . $bcc . "\r\n";
$headers .= "From: " . $from . "\r\n";
$message = "This is a Multipart Message in MIME format\n";
$message .= "--$boundary\n";
$message .= "Content-type: text/html; charset=iso-8859-1\n";
$message .= "Content-Transfer-Encoding: 7bit\n\n";
$message .= $messagebody . "\n";
$message .= "--$boundary\n";
$message .= "Content-Type: text/plain; charset=\"iso-8859-1\"\n";
$message .= "Content-Transfer-Encoding: 7bit\n\n";
$message .= $messagebody . "\n";
$message .= "--$boundary--";
$mailsent = mail($to, $subject, $message, $headers);
if ($mailsent) {
   echo "Congrats! The following message has been sent: <br><br>";
   echo "<b>To:</b> $to<br>";
   echo "<b>From:</b> $from<br>";
   echo "<b>Subject:</b> $subject<br>";
   echo "<b>Message:</b><br>";
   echo $message;
} else {
   echo "There was an error...";
}
?>
</body>
</html>
```

How It Works

Multipart messages are not really that complicated. You must tell the e-mail client that data is coming in multiple parts—in this instance, plain text and HTML. This is done in the header:

```
$headers .= "Content-type: multipart/alternative;
   boundary=\"$boundary\"\r\n";
```

This tells the e-mail client to look for additional "Content-type" information in the message, which includes boundary information. The boundary is what separates the multiple parts of the message. It begins with two dashes (--) and goes at the beginning of the message, between each part, and at the end. There is *no* significance to the content of this boundary. The key here is to make it as unique as possible so that it most likely is not a value that would be repeated anywhere within the message. You can use symbols, numbers, and letters in any combination. Many people choose to use a random number generator or an md5() hash. The method you use is entirely up to you.

The following line simply tells older e-mail programs why they may not see the information they expected in their browser. It's not necessary, but it's user-friendly:

```
$message = "This is a Multipart Message in MIME format\n";
```

The HTML portion of your e-mail follows. Note the double dashes (--) in front of the boundary. Also note the use of two new lines (\n\n) on the Content-Transfer-Encoding line. Do not neglect those — the code will not work correctly without them.

```
$message .= "--$boundary\n";
$message .= "Content-type: text/html; charset=iso-8859-1\n";
$message .= "Content-Transfer-Encoding: 7bit\n\n";
$message .= $messagebody . "\n";
```

Next is the text portion of your e-mail. Note the similarity to the HTML portion. You do not need to include the same $messagebody here. In fact, you would usually include an alternate message in text format.

```
$message .= "--$boundary\n";
$message .= "Content-Type: text/plain; charset=\"iso-8859-1\"\n";
$message .= "Content-Transfer-Encoding: 7bit\n\n";
$message .= $messagebody . "\n";
```

This is the final boundary. Note the double dashes (--) at the end. This signifies that it's the end of the e-mail.

```
$message .= "--$boundary--";
```

Your boundary in this case was set by the following line:

```
$boundary = "==MP_Bound_xyccr948x==";
```

Storing Images

To create a postcard application, you need to have digital postcards available for the user to choose from. For the purposes of this example, you'll have four postcards. If you are ambitious, you can add more, and we hope that you will!

Try It Out   Storing Images

Let's add some nice postcards to the application, shall we? You can create your own, or you can download the images from the Web site (www.wrox.com).

1. First, store your postcard images in a folder on your Apache server. We have ours in the folder postcards/. Place them anywhere you like, but remember where they are.

2. Start up your favorite PHP editor, and type the following code. Make sure you enter your own server, username, password, and database name:

```
<?php
$conn = mysql_connect("localhost", "bp5am", "bp5ampass");
mysql_select_db("postcard", $conn);
?>
```

3. Save this file as `conn_comic.php` in the `includes/` folder. You can call it whatever you like, but you are going to be including it in a few files using the `require()` function, so you'll have to remember to use the filename you came up with. Or, you could go with the name we came up with, because we took the time to come up with such a clever name, and have used it in subsequent PHP pages.

4. Enter the following code, and save it as `db_insertpics.php`. If you used the four pictures we provided for you and put them in the `postcards/` folder, you need not change this file. If you are using a different number of postcards, or have created your own, make sure you modify this code to reflect those changes. And, if you have named the `conn_comic.php` file something you think is more clever than our name, make sure you reflect that change here.

```php
<?php
require("./includes/conn_comic.php");

$sql = "CREATE DATABASE postcard";
$success = mysql_query($sql, $conn) or die(mysql_error());
echo "Database Created. . .";


mysql_select_db("postcard", $conn);

$sql = "CREATE TABLE images (id int NOT NULL primary key
   auto_increment, img_url VARCHAR(255) NOT NULL,
   img_desc text)";
$success = mysql_query($sql, $conn) or die(mysql_error());
echo "'images' table created. . .";

$path = "http://" . $_SERVER['SERVER_NAME'] .
   strrev(strstr(strrev($_SERVER['PHP_SELF']),"/"));

$imagepath = $path . "postcards/";

$imgURL = array('punyearth.gif', 'grebnok.gif', 'sympathy.gif',
   'congrats.gif');
$imgDESC = array('Wish you were here!', 'See you soon!',
   'Our Sympathies', 'Congratulations!');

for ($i=0; $i<4; $i++) {
   $sql = "INSERT INTO images ( images.img_url , images.img_desc )
         VALUES ( '$imagepath$imgURL[$i]', '$imgDESC[$i]')";
   $success = mysql_query($sql, $conn) or die(mysql_error());
}
echo "Data entered. . ."
?>
```

How It Works

First, the script connected to the server using the correct username and password.

```
$conn = mysql_connect("localhost", "bp5am", "bp5ampass");
```

The next step is to create the database, called "postcard." If the creation is successful, the script prints "Database created" to the screen and moves on.

```
$sql = "CREATE DATABASE postcard";
$success = mysql_query($sql, $conn) or die(mysql_error());
echo "Database created. . .";
```

Now that the database is created, the script then selects that database.

```
mysql_select_db("postcard", $conn);
```

Next, you create the images table in the database, containing three columns. As before, if the creation is successful, the script prints "images table created" to the screen and moves on.

```
$sql = "CREATE TABLE images (id int NOT NULL primary key
   auto_increment, img_url VARCHAR(255) NOT NULL,
   img_desc text )";
$success = mysql_query($sql, $conn) or die(mysql_error());
echo "'images' table created. . .";
```

Next, you need to create two arrays of values to place in the images table. You need to know the location of the postcards entered previously in step 1 and their descriptions. Each URL corresponds to a description in the other array.

```
$imgURL = array('punyearth.gif', 'grebnok.gif', 'sympathy.gif',
   'congrats.gif');
$imgDESC = array('Wish you were here!', 'See you soon!',
   'Our Sympathies', 'Congratulations!');
```

Next, the script loops through the arrays, pulling the location and description text and inserting them into the images table. If there are no errors, the script prints "Data entered" to the screen.

```
for ($i=0; $i<4; $i++) {
  $sql = "INSERT INTO images ( images.img_url , images.img_desc )
         VALUES ( '$imagepath$imgURL[$i]', '$imgDESC[$i]')";
  $success = mysql_query($sql, $conn) or die(mysql_error());
}
Echo "Data entered. . .";
```

When you run this PHP script, if anything goes wrong, make sure you delete the postcard database before running it again. Otherwise, you will get an error (database exists) and the script will stop executing.

You'll include the code to view and use the images in the next section.

Getting Confirmation

So far, you have a pretty cool postcard application. Any user can send a postcard to whomever he or she wants, and PHP takes care of mailing it. Unfortunately, there is still a small problem with the application.

As the application stands right now, it is quite easy for the user to use any e-mail address in the "From" field. This is a bad thing because nasty e-mails can be sent on someone else's behalf, and you don't want that, do you? To prevent such maliciousness, you must first send a confirmation e-mail to the "From" address. Once you get the confirmation, you know the user entered a good e-mail address, and you can go ahead and send the e-mail.

This act of achieving confirmation is the first step toward creating a workflow application. Workflow applications are covered in more detail in Chapter 13, but for now just understand that a workflow application is one that requires input from various parties before it reaches its final destination.

To accommodate this workflow, your application must undergo a metamorphosis from what it was in the past. The `sendmail.php` script must be split into two separate processes such that, in between the two processes, you wait for confirmation.

Much of the code you have used so far in `sendmail.php` will be recycled. If you are an experienced developer, we are sure you know very well how to cannibalize your old code! If you are not familiar with cannibalization, now is the time to learn. Sometimes you need to write a function that you have written before in another application. With a couple of modifications, it would work in your new app. So, you copy and paste it into your new application and make the necessary changes. Voila, your first cannibalization!

To confirm an e-mail address, the postcard information needs to be temporarily stored in a table, to be retrieved later on, once confirmation has been established:

Try It Out   Getting Confirmation

In this exercise, you'll implement the confirmation e-mail into your application. (You may want to save your old `postcard.php` and `sendmail.php` files and start new files from scratch before making this change.)

1. Open your favorite PHP editor and create a new PHP file called `db_makeconfirm.php`. Make sure you use the correct server, username, and password.

```php
<?php
$conn = mysql_connect("localhost", "bp5am", "bp5ampass");
mysql_select_db("postcard", $conn);
$sql = <<<EOD
CREATE TABLE confirm (
  id int NOT NULL PRIMARY KEY AUTO_INCREMENT,
  validator VARCHAR(32) NOT NULL,
  to_email VARCHAR(100) NOT NULL,
  toname VARCHAR(50) NOT NULL,
  from_email VARCHAR(100) NOT NULL,
  fromname VARCHAR(50) NOT NULL,
  bcc_email VARCHAR(100),
  cc_email VARCHAR(100),
  subject VARCHAR(255),
  postcard VARCHAR(255) NOT NULL,
  message text
)
EOD;
$query = mysql_query($sql, $conn) or die(mysql_error());
echo "Table <i>confirm</i> created."
?>
```

2. Run db_makeconfirm.php, and then check your MySQL server to make sure the confirm table was indeed created in the database.

3. Enter this as postcard.php in your favorite PHP editor and save it:

```
<html>
<head>
<title>Enter E-mail Data</title>
</head>
<body>
<form name="theform" method="post" action="sendconf.php">
<center>
<table width="640" border="0" cellpadding="4" cellspacing="0">
  <tr>
    <td colspan="4"><h2>Postcard Sender</h2></td>
  </tr>
  <tr bgcolor="#CCCCCC">
    <td>To:</td>
    <td><input type="text" name="toname" size="30"></td>
    <td>e-mail:</td>
    <td><input type="text" name="to" size="40"></td>
  </tr>
  <tr>
    <td>From:</td>
    <td><input type="text" name="fromname" size="30"></td>
    <td>e-mail:</td>
    <td><input type="text" name="from" size="40"></td>
  </tr>
  <tr bgcolor="#CCCCCC">
    <td>Cc:</td>
    <td><input type="text" name="cc" size="40"></td>
    <td>Bcc:</td>
    <td><input type="text" name="bcc" size="40"></td>
  </tr>
  <tr>
    <td colspan="2">Choose a Postcard:
      <select name="postcard[]" onchange="changepostcard(this.value)">
      <?php
        include("./includes/conn_comic.php");
        $sql = "SELECT * FROM images ORDER BY img_desc";
        $images = mysql_query($sql, $conn) or die(mysql_error());
        $iloop = 0;
        while ($imagearray = mysql_fetch_array($images)) {
          $iloop++;
          $iurl = $imagearray['img_url'];
          $idesc = $imagearray['img_desc'];
          if ($iloop == 1) {
            echo "<option selected value=\"$iurl\">$idesc</option>\n";
            $image_url = $imagearray['img_url'];
          } else {
            echo "<option value=\"$iurl\">$idesc</option>\n";
          }
        }
      ?>
      </select><br>
```

```
        </td>
        <td>Subject:</td>
        <td><input type="text" name="subject" size="40"></td>
      </tr>
      <tr>
        <td colspan="2"><img src="<?php echo($image_url)?>" width=320
          height=240 border=0 id="postcard"></td>
        <td valign="top"> </td>
        <td align="right">
          <textarea cols="30" rows="12" name="message"
            >Enter your message here</textarea>
          <input type="submit" value="Send">
          <input type="reset" value="Reset the form">
        </td>
      </tr>
</table>
</center>
</form>
<script language="Javascript">
function changepostcard(imgurl) {
  window.document.theform.postcard.src = imgurl;
}
</script>
</body>
</html>
```

4. Next write `sendconf.php`, the page that sends out the confirmation e-mail to the user. Remember that much of this code can be pulled (cannibalized) from `sendmail.php`.

```
<html>
<head>
<title>HTML Mail Sent!</title>
</head>
<body>
<?php
$to = $_POST["to"];
$toname = $_POST["toname"];
$cc = $_POST["cc"];
$bcc = $_POST["bcc"];
$from = $_POST["from"];
$fromname = $_POST["fromname"];
$subject = $_POST["subject"];
if (!empty($_POST["postcard"])) {
  foreach($_POST["postcard"] as $value) {
    $postcard = $value;
  }
}
$messagebody = $_POST["message"];
$boundary = "==MP_Bound_xyccr948x==";
$headers = "MIME-Version: 1.0\r\n";
$headers .= "Content-type: multipart/alternative; boundary=\"$boundary\"\r\n";
$headers .= "From: no-reply@postcardorama.com\r\n";
$html_msg = "<center>";
$html_msg .= "<table width=\"500\" border=0 cellpadding=\"4\">";
```

```php
$html_msg .= "<tr><td>Greetings, $toname!";
$html_msg .= "</td></tr><tr><td>";
$html_msg .= "$fromname has sent you a postcard today.<br>Enjoy!";
$html_msg .= "</td></tr><tr><td align=\"center\">";
$html_msg .= "<img src=\"$postcard\" border=\"0\">";
$html_msg .= "</td></tr><tr><td align=center>";
$html_msg .= $messagebody . "\n";
$html_msg .= "</td></tr></table></center>";
$temp = gettimeofday();
$msec = (int) $temp["usec"];
$msgid = md5(time() . $msec);
require('./includes/conn_comic.php');
$sql = "INSERT INTO confirm (validator, to_email, toname, from_email, " .
   "fromname, bcc_email, cc_email, subject, postcard, message) " .
   "VALUES ('$msgid', '$to', '$toname', '$from', " .
   "'$fromname', '$bcc', '$cc', '$subject', '$postcard', '$messagebody')";
$query = mysql_query($sql, $conn) or die(mysql_error());
$confirmsubject = "Please Confirm your postcard";
$confirmmessage = "Hello " . $fromname . ",\n\n";
$confirmmessage .= "Please click on the link below to confirm that " .
   "you would like to send this postcard:\n\n";
$confirmmessage .= $html_msg . "\n\n";
$confirmmessage .= "<a href=\"http://localhost/bp5am/ch11/confirm.php" .
   "?id=$msgid\">Click here to confirm</a>";
$textconfirm = "Hello " . $fromname . ",\n\n";
$textconfirm .= "Please visit the following URL to confirm your " .
   "postcard:\n\n";
$textconfirm .= "http://localhost/bp5am/ch11/confirm.php" .
   "?id=$msgid";
$message = "This is a Multipart Message in MIME format\n";
$message .= "--$boundary\n";
$message .= "Content-type: text/html; charset=iso-8859-1\n";
$message .= "Content-Transfer-Encoding: 7bit\n\n";
$message .= $confirmmessage . "\n";
$message .= "--$boundary\n";
$message .= "Content-Type: text/plain; charset=\"iso-8859-1\"\n";
$message .= "Content-Transfer-Encoding: 7bit\n\n";
$message .= $textconfirm . "\n";
$message .= "--$boundary--";
$mailsent = mail($from, $confirmsubject, $message, $headers);
if ($mailsent) {
  echo "Here is the postcard you wish to send.<br>";
  echo "A confirmation e-mail has been sent to $from.<br>";
  echo "Open your e-mail and click on the link to confirm that you would
        like to send this postcard to $toname.<br><br>";
  echo "<b>Subject:</b> $subject<br>";
  echo "<b>Message:</b><br>";
  echo $html_msg;
} else {
  echo "There was an error sending the email.";
}
?>
</body>
</html>
```

5. Next is `confirm.php`. This file is loaded in the browser with an ID in the URL to designate which saved postcard is awaiting confirmation, and it then sends the postcard to the intended recipient. Again, parts can be pulled from the old `sendmail.php` file.

```php
<?php
$id = $_GET['id'];
require('./includes/conn_comic.php');
$sql = "SELECT * FROM confirm WHERE validator = '$id'";
$query = mysql_query($sql, $conn) or die(mysql_error());
$pcarray = mysql_fetch_array($query);
if (!is_array($pcarray)) {
  echo "Oops! Nothing to confirm. Please contact your administrator";
  exit;
}
$to = $pcarray["to_email"];
$toname = $pcarray["toname"];
$from = $pcarray["from_email"];
$fromname = $pcarray["fromname"];
$bcc = $pcarray["bcc_email"];
$cc = $pcarray["cc_email"];
$subject = $pcarray["subject"];
$postcard = $pcarray["postcard"];
$messagebody = $pcarray["message"];

$boundary = "==MP_Bound_xyccr948x==";
$headers = "MIME-Version: 1.0\r\n";
$headers .= "Content-type: multipart/alternative; boundary=\"$boundary\"\r\n";
if (!$cc == "") {
  $headers .= "CC: " . $cc . "\r\n";
}
if (!$bcc == "") {
  $headers .= "BCC: " . $bcc . "\r\n";
}
$headers .= "From: " . $from . "\r\n";

$html_msg .= "<center>";
$html_msg .= "<table width=\"500\" border=0 cellpadding=\"4\">";
$html_msg .= "<tr><td>Greetings, $toname!";
$html_msg .= "</td></tr><tr><td>";
$html_msg .= "$fromname has sent you a postcard today.<br>Enjoy!";
$html_msg .= "</td></tr><tr><td align=\"center\">";
$html_msg .= "<img src=\"$postcard\" border=\"0\">";
$html_msg .= "</td></tr><tr><td align=center>";
$html_msg .= $messagebody . "\n";
$html_msg .= "</td></tr></table></center>";

$message = "This is a Multipart Message in MIME format\n";
$message .= "--$boundary\n";
$message .= "Content-type: text/html; charset=iso-8859-1\n";
$message .= "Content-Transfer-Encoding: 7bit\n\n";
$message .= $html_msg . "\n";
$message .= "--$boundary\n";
```

```php
$message .= "Content-Type: text/plain; charset=\"iso-8859-1\"\n";
$message .= "Content-Transfer-Encoding: 7bit\n\n";
$message .= $messagebody . "\n";
$message .= "--$boundary--";
$mailsent = mail($to, $subject, $message, $headers);
?>
<html>
<head>
<title>Postcard Sent!</title>
</head>
<body>
<?php
if ($mailsent) {
  echo "Congrats! The following message has been sent: <br><br>";
  echo "<b>To:</b> $to<br>";
  echo "<b>From:</b> $from<br>";
  echo "<b>Subject:</b> $subject<br>";
  echo "<b>Message:</b><br>";
  echo $html_msg;
} else {
  echo "There was an error...";
}
?>
</body>
</html>
```

6. Next you'll create a form that allows a user to view the postcard. Call this one `viewpostcard.php`. (Funny how the name matches the functionality, isn't it?) The great thing about `viewpostcard.php` is that most of it is very similar to `confirm.php`. Yes, now you get to cannibalize some of your own code!

```php
<?php
$id = $_GET['id'];
require('./includes/conn_comic.php');
$sql = "SELECT * FROM confirm WHERE validator = '$id'";
$query = mysql_query($sql, $conn) or die(mysql_error());
$pcarray = mysql_fetch_array($query);
$path = "http://" . $_SERVER['SERVER_NAME'] .
  strrev(strstr(strrev($_SERVER['PHP_SELF']),"/"));
if (!is_array($pcarray)) {
  echo "Oops! Can't find a postcard. Please contact your administrator.";
  exit;
}
$to = $pcarray["to_email"];
$toname = $pcarray["toname"];
$from = $pcarray["from_email"];
$fromname = $pcarray["fromname"];
$bcc = $pcarray["bcc_email"];
$cc = $pcarray["cc_email"];
$subject = $pcarray["subject"];
$postcard = $pcarray["postcard"];
$messagebody = $pcarray["message"];
```

```
$html_msg .= "<table width=\"500\" border=0 cellpadding=\"4\">";
$html_msg .= "<tr><td>Greetings, $toname!";
$html_msg .= "</td></tr><tr><td>";
$html_msg .= "$fromname has sent you a postcard today.<br>Enjoy!";
$html_msg .= "</td></tr><tr><td align=\"center\">";
$html_msg .= "<img src=\"$postcard\" border=\"0\">";
$html_msg .= "</td></tr><tr><td align=center>";
$html_msg .= $messagebody . "\n";
$html_msg .= "</td></tr></table>";


echo <<<EOD
  <html>
  <head>
  <title>Viewing postcard for $toname</title>
  </head>
  <body>
  $html_msg
  </body>
  </html>
EOD;
?>
```

7. Load postcard.php in your browser to verify that it works. The results should look similar to what's shown in Figure 11-6.

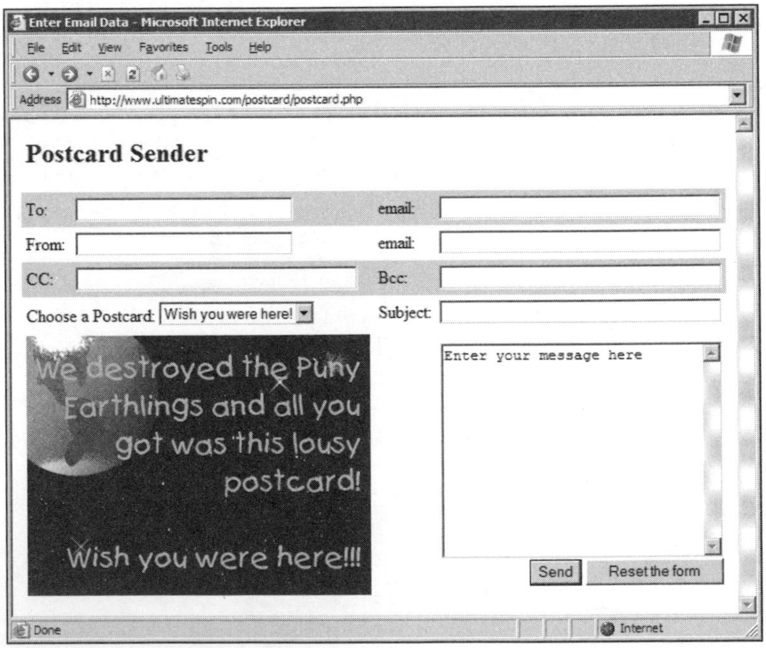

Figure 11-6

8. Enter the appropriate data; remember to put in your valid e-mail address in the From: email field.

9. In the Choose a Postcard field, select a postcard from the drop-down list, enter a message, and click the Send button. A screen similar to the one shown in Figure 11-7 loads.

Figure 11-7

10. Check your e-mail. You should receive an e-mail that looks something like Figure 11-8.

Note the text attachment; this is the part of the e-mail that users would see if their e-mail client did not support HTML. They would see something similar to this:

```
Hello Grebnok,
Please visit the following URL to confirm your postcard:
http://localhost/bp5am/ch11/confirm.php?id=8d3ba748a0aea409fd6b6005be67f262
```

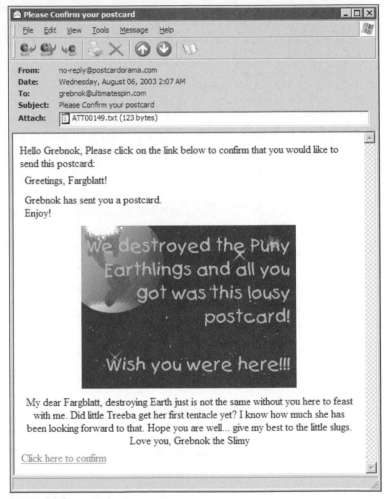

Figure 11-8

11. Click the link at the bottom of the e-mail to confirm that you want to send the postcard.

12. Open the e-mail account this postcard was sent to (see Figure 11-9).

You did send it to an e-mail address you have access to, right? If you sent this to your little sister, we sure hope you didn't scare her!

Figure 11-9

How It Works

Your application is getting more complex. However, it is still fairly basic in its functionality. Here's what it does:

❑ The user loads `postcard.php` and fills out all the fields. He or she also selects a postcard to be sent. In the From field, the user enters his or her e-mail address.

❑ After clicking Send, the user receives an e-mail showing him or her what the postcard and message look like. A link is provided at the bottom of the e-mail asking the user to click to confirm the postcard.

❑ Once the user clicks the confirmation link, the postcard is sent to the intended recipient.

By now, you should be fairly familiar with using PHP to access MySQL. The file db_makeconfirm.php is pretty standard:

```
$sql = <<<EOD
CREATE TABLE confirm (
   id int NOT NULL PRIMARY KEY AUTO_INCREMENT,
   validator VARCHAR(32) NOT NULL,
   to_email VARCHAR(100) NOT NULL,
   toname VARCHAR(50) NOT NULL,
   from_email VARCHAR(100) NOT NULL,
   fromname VARCHAR(50) NOT NULL,
   bcc_email VARCHAR(100),
   cc_email VARCHAR(100),
   subject VARCHAR(255),
   postcard VARCHAR(255) NOT NULL,
   message text
)
EOD;
```

Note the use of the heredoc syntax. This makes the SQL statement a little easier to read. It also allows you to get a more accurate indication of where errors occur because errors usually tell you the line number on which they occurred.

Now let's take a look at the postcard.php file. This is your standard HTML form tag. Make sure sendconf.php is in the same directory as postcard.php. If not, then you will need to provide the proper path for sendconf.php:

```
<form name="theform" method="post" action="sendconf.php">
```

Next is a simple select statement. It will be followed by PHP code that builds the list of postcards the user will be able to select from. Note the square brackets after postcard[]. These are required so that PHP is able to access the $postcard variable as a proper array:

```
<select name="postcard[]" onchange="changepostcard(this.value)">
```

You then connect to the MySQL server and open a connection to the postcard database:

```
include("./includes/conn_comic.php");
```

This gets all image data and puts it into the $images array:

```
$sql = "SELECT * FROM images ORDER BY img_desc";
$images = mysql_query($sql, $conn) or die(mysql_error());
```

You are tracking $iloop; if $iloop is set to 1, the first option tag will be selected by default on the form. This assures you that when the page first loads, you'll see a postcard.

```
$iloop = 0;
```

Next you loop through the $images array, constructing the rest of your HTML select tag (options). The $image_url variable is set to the default image's URL:

```
while ($imagearray = mysql_fetch_array($images)) {
  $iloop++;
  $iurl = $imagearray['img_url'];
  $idesc = $imagearray['img_desc'];
  if ($iloop == 1) {
    echo "<option selected value=\"$iurl\">$idesc</option>\n";
    $image_url = $imagearray['img_url'];
  } else {
    echo "<option value=\"$iurl\">$idesc</option>\n";
  }
}
?>
```

Then you place the default image on the page, just below the select box. You are going to use JavaScript to change this image whenever the user selects a different postcard from the select box. You could use PHP to do this instead, but it would reload the page every time you changed the image. Using JavaScript in this situation helps you reduce loading time and round-trips to the server.

```
<img src="<?php echo($image_url)?>" width=320 height=240 border=0
    id="postcard">
```

What follows, of course, is the JavaScript function that changes the image. It should be pretty self-explanatory if you know JavaScript. If you don't know JavaScript, this is the JavaScript function that changes the image. If you want to know more about JavaScript, you can buy *JavaScript For Dummies, Third Edition*, by Emily A. Vander Veer (Wiley, 2000).

```
<script language="Javascript">
function changepostcard(imgurl) {
  window.document.theform.postcard.src = imgurl;
}
</script>
```

Now you move on to sendconf.php. Much of it is similar to sendmail.php, so we'll just touch on some of the more important points:

```
if (!empty($_POST["postcard"])) {
  foreach($_POST["postcard"] as $value) {
    $postcard = $value;
  }
}
```

Remember, $postcard is an array. A simpler method of getting the value of the postcard would have been to use the 0 key of the $postcard array:

```
$postcard = $_POST["postcard"][0];
```

However, to ensure that you get the first value in the $postcard array regardless of the key, you use the foreach() loop. You must use the if statement because if there is no $postcard array, foreach() returns an "invalid argument" warning. Yes, we know that currently a postcard value is always posted to the sendconf.php page, but if you make a change to postcard.php (for instance, to make the postcard image optional), you don't want sendconf.php to break, right? Let's move on.

Your sendconf.php script performs an extra step you did not take care of in sendmail.php. You must temporarily store the postcard data while you await confirmation.

```
$temp = gettimeofday();
$msec = (int) $temp["usec"];
$msgid = md5(time() . $msec);
```

Note the use of a new PHP function, md5(). This returns a 128-bit "fingerprint," or "hash," of the message passed to it. For example, the md5 hash of "Hello World" is b10a8db164e0754105b7a99be72e3fe5. It is designed as a one-way encryption of the data passed in to it, so you cannot reverse it to discover the original value. Using a one-way hash in this manner allows you to safely have the user click on a link in their e-mail to view their postcard. If you had used a simple number or keyword, a malicious user could more easily guess the URL, and ruin all your fun—guessing an md5 hash would take too long to make it worthwhile for the hacker.

By passing in a time value, you can be fairly certain that the md5 hash returned will be a unique value, which you use as a unique ID for the data. It is not 100 percent guaranteed to be unique, but because it is generated based on the current time in seconds and contains 32 alphanumeric characters, you can be reasonably sure it will be unique.

If you are interested in finding out more information about the md5 hash, visit RFC 1321: The MD5 Message-Digest Algorithm at www.faqs.org/rfcs/rfc1321.

```
require('./includes/conn_comic.php');
$sql = "INSERT INTO confirm (validator, to_email, toname, from_email, " .
  "fromname, bcc_email, cc_email, subject, postcard, message) " .
  "VALUES ('$msgid', '$to', '$toname', '$from', " .
  "'$fromname', '$bcc', '$cc', '$subject', '$postcard', '$messagebody')";
$query = mysql_query($sql, $conn) or die(mysql_error());
```

Next, you store the postcard data temporarily until it is validated. When the user clicks the confirmation link in the e-mail to send it, the postcard is sent on to its intended recipient.

```
$confirmsubject = "Please Confirm your postcard";
$confirmmessage = "Hello " . $fromname . ",\n\n";
$confirmmessage .= "Please click on the link below to confirm that " .
  "you would like to send this postcard:\n\n";
$confirmmessage .= $html_msg . "\n\n";
$confirmmessage .= "<a href=\"http://localhost/bp5am/ch11/confirm.php" .
  "?id=$msgid\">Click here to confirm</a>";
$textconfirm = "Hello " . $fromname . ",\n\n";
$textconfirm .= "Please visit the following URL to confirm your " .
  "postcard:\n\n";
$textconfirm .= "http://localhost/bp5am/ch11/confirm.php" .
  "?id=\"$msgid\"";
```

```
$message = "This is a Multipart Message in MIME format\n";
$message .= "--$boundary\n";
$message .= "Content-type: text/html; charset=iso-8859-1\n";
$message .= "Content-Transfer-Encoding: 7bit\n\n";
$message .= $confirmmessage . "\n";
$message .= "--$boundary\n";
$message .= "Content-Type: text/plain; charset=\"iso-8859-1\"\n";
$message .= "Content-Transfer-Encoding: 7bit\n\n";
$message .= $textconfirm . "\n";
$message .= "--$boundary--";
```

The variable `$confirmmessage` is the HTML version of the confirmation e-mail. The variable `$text confirm` is the plain-text version. The variable `$message` is the entire message, coded to send both plain and HTML e-mails. Note where you insert the `$confirmmessage` and `$textconfirm` variables in the multipart message.

Finally, the following sends the e-mail. Don't be confused by the variable `$from`. That actually controls who this e-mail is being sent *to*. That's the whole idea behind sending out this confirmation e-mail.

```
$mailsent = mail($from, $confirmsubject, $message, $headers);
```

When the user receives the confirmation e-mail, there is a link at the bottom:

```
$confirmmessage .= "<a href=\"http://localhost/bp5am/ch11/confirm.php" .
  "?id=$msgid\">Click here to confirm</a>";
```

When the user clicks the link, `confirmmail.php` is loaded in his or her browser, appended with `?id=` plus the unique validation ID. This is used within `confirmmail.php` to access the proper postcard in the database, compose the e-mail, and send it on its way. A quick reminder: If you always set your variables like this, you never have to worry about the `register_globals` setting in your `php.ini` file.

```
$id = $_GET['id'];
```

The following gets all postcards that match your ID. Of course, there should always be just one match, because `$id` is unique.

```
$sql = "SELECT * FROM confirm WHERE validator = '$id'";
```

The array `$pcarray` contains all of the postcard data you need to send the postcard to its intended recipient:

```
$query = mysql_query($sql, $conn) or die(mysql_error());
$pcarray = mysql_fetch_array($query);
```

Here's a little insurance to make sure you don't try to send out a postcard if no postcard data exists. (Of course, you will think of a much more elegant error message, won't you?) This might be a good place for the PHP `header()` function to redirect the user to a "more information" error page.

```
if (!is_array($pcarray)) {
  echo "Oops! Nothing to confirm. Please contact your administrator";
  exit;
}
```

The following lines are not entirely necessary. They do make life easier, however, if you have to refer to the values multiple times. It's also good to have your variables in a centralized location; if something goes wrong, you have one place to look.

```
$to = $pcarray["to_email"];
$toname = $pcarray["toname"];
$from = $pcarray["from_email"];
$fromname = $pcarray["fromname"];
$bcc = $pcarray["bcc_email"];
$cc = $pcarray["cc_email"];
$subject = $pcarray["subject"];
$postcard = $pcarray["postcard"];
$messagebody = $pcarray["message"];
```

What follows is pretty standard stuff; you did this before in `sendmail.php`. Here's a quick review: To create a multipart message, use the Content-type of multipart/alternative and a boundary that contains unique alphanumeric text to designate the HTML and text portions of the e-mail.

```
$boundary = "==MP_Bound_xyccr948x==";
$headers = "MIME-Version: 1.0\r\n";
$headers .= "Content-type: multipart/alternative; boundary=\"$boundary\"\r\n";
if (!$cc == "") {
  $headers .= "CC: " . $cc . "\r\n";
}
if (!$bcc == "") {
  $headers .= "BCC: " . $bcc . "\r\n";
}
$headers .= "From: " . $from . "\r\n";

$html_msg = "<center>";
$html_msg .= "<table width=\"500\" border=0 cellpadding=\"4\">";
$html_msg .= "<tr><td>Greetings, $toname!";
$html_msg .= "</td></tr><tr><td>";
$html_msg .= "$fromname has sent you a postcard today.<br>Enjoy!";
$html_msg .= "</td></tr><tr><td align=\"center\">";
$html_msg .= "<img src=\"$postcard\" border=\"0\">";
$html_msg .= "</td></tr><tr><td align=center>";
$html_msg .= $messagebody . "\n";
$html_msg .= "</td></tr></table></center>";

$message = "This is a Multipart Message in MIME format\n";
$message .= "--$boundary\n";
$message .= "Content-type: text/html; charset=iso-8859-1\n";
$message .= "Content-Transfer-Encoding: 7bit\n\n";
$message .= $html_msg . "\n";
$message .= "--$boundary\n";
$message .= "Content-Type: text/plain; charset=\"iso-8859-1\"\n";
$message .= "Content-Transfer-Encoding: 7bit\n\n";
$message .= $messagebody . "\n";
$message .= "--$boundary--";
$mailsent = mail($to, $subject, $message, $headers);
?>
```

Until now, nothing has been sent to the browser. That is a good thing. For example, if you had received any errors, and wished to use the `header()` function to redirect the user to a different page, it only works if no text has already been sent to the browser. The lesson here is: Don't put your `<html>` (and other) tags in the code until you are ready to send text to the user's browser.

```html
<html>
<head>
<title>Postcard Sent!</title>
</head>
<body>
<?php
if ($mailsent) {
  echo "Congrats! The following message has been sent: <br><br>";
  echo "<b>To:</b> $to<br>";
  echo "<b>From:</b> $from<br>";
  echo "<b>Subject:</b> $subject<br>";
  echo "<b>Message:</b><br>";
  echo $html_msg;
} else {
  echo "There was an error...";
}
?>
</body>
</html>
```

Creating a Reusable Mail Class

Now that you've seen how to perform basic mail functions using PHP, it's time to take what you've learned and make a nice block of easily reusable code, right? Hopefully you were paying attention previously in the book when PHP objects and classes were discussed. If not, it might be a good idea to go back and brush up on the basics before you continue.

Try It Out   Creating a Reusable Mail Class

You are going to be creating a very handy file, `class.SimpleMail.php`. This file is going to contain a PHP class that will help you reuse the simple mail functionality and help keep your source code clean where you use it.

1.   Open your favorite PHP editor and create a new PHP file called `class.SimpleMail.php`:

```php
<?php

class SimpleMail {
  public $to = NULL;
  public $cc = NULL;
  public $bcc = NULL;
  public $from = NULL;
  public $subject = '';
  public $body = '';
  public $htmlbody = '';
  public $send_text = TRUE;
```

```php
public $send_html = FALSE;
private $message = '';
private $headers = '';

public function send($to = NULL,
                     $subject = NULL,
                     $message = NULL,
                     $headers = NULL) {
  if (func_num_args() >= 3) {
    $this->to = $to;
    $this->subject = $subject;
    $this->message = $message;
    if ($headers) {
      $this->headers = $headers;
    }

  } else {

    if ($this->from) {
      $this->headers .= "From: " . $this->from . "\r\n";
    }
    if ($this->cc) {
      $this->headers .= "Cc: " . $this->cc . "\r\n";
    }
    if ($this->bcc) {
      $this->headers .= "Bcc: " . $this->bcc . "\r\n";
    }

    if ($this->send_text and !$this->send_html) {
      $this->message = $this->body;
    } elseif ($this->send_html and !$this->send_text) {
      $this->message = $this->htmlbody;
      $this->headers .= "MIME-Version: 1.0\r\n";
      $this->headers .= "Content-type: text/html; " .
                        "charset=iso-8859-1\r\n";
    } else {
      $_boundary = "==MP_Bound_xyccr948x==";

      $this->headers = "MIME-Version: 1.0\r\n";
      $this->headers .= "Content-type: multipart/alternative; " .
                        "boundary=\"$_boundary\"\r\n";

      $this->message = "This is a Multipart Message in " .
                       "MIME format\n";
      $this->message .= "--$_boundary\n";
      $this->message .= "Content-Type: text/plain; " .
                        "charset=\"iso-8859-1\"\n";
      $this->message .= "Content-Transfer-Encoding: 7bit\n\n";
      $this->message .= $this->body . "\n";
      $this->message .= "--$_boundary\n";
      $this->message .= "Content-type: text/html; " .
                        "charset=\"iso-8859-1\"\n";
      $this->message .= "Content-Transfer-Encoding: 7bit\n\n";
```

```
          $this->message .= $this->htmlbody . "\n";
          $this->message .= "--$_boundary--";
        }
      }

      if (!mail($this->to,$this->subject,$this->message,$this->headers)) {
        throw new Exception('Sending mail failed.');
        return FALSE;
      } else {
        return TRUE;
      }
    }

  }

?>
```

2. Next, create the file that will be used to demonstrate plain-text functionality, `mail_text.php`. Make sure you change the e-mail address to reflect the account to which you want to send the mail.

```php
<?php
require 'class.SimpleMail.php';

$postcard = new SimpleMail();

$postcard->to = "youremail@yourhost.com";
$postcard->subject = "Testing text email";
$postcard->body = "This is a test using plain text email!";

if ($postcard->send()) {
  echo "Text email sent successfully!";
}
?>
```

3. Now, create a file to send HTML-format e-mails. Remember to change the e-mail account as you desire, like you did in the previous step. Save this file as `mail_html.php`.

```php
<?php
require 'class.SimpleMail.php';

$postcard = new SimpleMail();

$postcard->to = "youremail@yourhost.com";
$postcard->subject = "Testing HTML email";
$postcard->htmlbody = "This is a test using HTML email!";
$postcard->send_html = TRUE;
$postcard->send_text = FALSE;

if ($postcard->send()) {
  echo "HTML email sent successfully!";
}
?>
```

4. Next, create a file that will demonstrate Multipart e-mails, and the rest of the bells-and-whistles that make up the headers. Again, change the e-mail addresses accordingly, and save this file as `mail_multipart.php`.

```php
<?php
require 'class.SimpleMail.php';

$postcard = new SimpleMail();

$postcard->to = "youremail@yourhost.com";
$postcard->from = "fromaddress@yourhost.com";
$postcard->cc = "ccaddress@yourhost.com";
$postcard->bcc = "bccaddress@yourhost.com";
$postcard->subject = "Testing Multipart email";
$postcard->body = "This is the text part of the email!";
$postcard->htmlbody = "This is the HTML part of the email!";
$postcard->send_html = TRUE;

if ($postcard->send()) {
  echo "Multipart email sent successfully!";
}
?>
```

5. Last, create a file to demonstrate the quick-message functionality in the `SimpleMail` class. Save this file as `mail_quick.php`.

```php
<?php

require 'class.SimpleMail.php';

$postcard = new SimpleMail();

if ($postcard->send("youremail@yourhost.com",
                    "Quick message test",
                    "This is a test using SimpleMail::send!")) {
  echo "Quick message sent successfully!";
}
?>
```

6. Load up `mail_text.php`, `mail_html.php`, `mail_multipart.php`, and `mail_quick.php` in your browser. Assuming everything was typed carefully, all four "success" messages will appear.

How It Works

As you might have already discovered, using a PHP class for encapsulating functionality can be a great way to save coding time later on. Looking at `class.SimpleMail.php`, you start out by defining the class and its properties:

```php
<?php

class SimpleMail {
  public $to = NULL;
  public $cc = NULL;
```

```
public $bcc = NULL;
public $from = NULL;
public $subject = '';
public $body = '';
public $htmlbody = '';
public $send_text = TRUE;
public $send_html = FALSE;
private $message = '';
private $headers = '';
```

Pretty straightforward so far. You'll notice the basic e-mail elements to, from, subject, and so on are exposed as public members, while the actual message body and header properties are kept private. Since the class does all the construction work on the message body in the case of multipart mails, and some header construction when sending HTML mails, there's little reason to have them exposed. Also take note of the initial values set for the $send_text and $send_html Booleans. They are currently set to send text-only e-mails by default, but that could obviously be easily changed.

Next, you start the send() function of the class. You've given it four optional parameters that can be used when calling the method:

```
public function send($to = NULL,
                     $subject = NULL,
                     $message = NULL,
                     $headers = NULL) {
```

If the number of arguments passed to send() is three or greater, the send function will behave almost identically to the PHP built-in mail() function:

```
if (func_num_args() >= 3) {
  $this->to = $to;
  $this->subject = $subject;
  $this->message = $message;
  if ($headers) {
    $this->headers = $headers;
  }
}
```

You might be thinking, "Why bother with this, when I can use the normal mail() function instead?" Truthfully, you could in this example. However, the advantage here is that the PHP class can enhance the normal mail-sending process with custom errors or fallback processes, and it will still be only one line in the calling scripts' code.

If fewer than three parameters are passed to the method, the normal send functionality begins, starting by setting the headers:

```
} else {

  if ($this->from) {
    $this->headers .= "From: " . $this->from . "\r\n";
  }
  if ($this->cc) {
    $this->headers .= "Cc: " . $this->cc . "\r\n";
  }
```

```
    if ($this->bcc) {
      $this->headers .= "Bcc: " . $this->bcc . "\r\n";
    }
```

Next, the `send_text` and `send_html` Booleans are checked to determine what format e-mail should be sent in, starting with plain text:

```
if ($this->send_text and !$this->send_html) {
  $this->message = $this->body;
```

If the e-mail is specified as HTML-only, the headers and message body are set accordingly:

```
} elseif ($this->send_html and !$this->send_text) {
  $this->message = $this->htmlbody;
  $this->headers .= "MIME-Version: 1.0\r\n";
  $this->headers .= "Content-type: text/html; " .
                    "charset=iso-8859-1\r\n";
```

In the case of Multipart e-mails, the boundary tokens are set, and the e-mail message body is constructed with both `body` and `html_body` properties.

```
} else {
  $_boundary = "==MP_Bound_xyccr948x==";

  $this->headers = "MIME-Version: 1.0\r\n";
  $this->headers .= "Content-type: multipart/alternative; " .
                    "boundary=\"$_boundary\"\r\n";

  $this->message = "This is a Multipart Message in " .
                   "MIME format\n";
  $this->message .= "--$_boundary\n";
  $this->message .= "Content-Type: text/plain; " .
                    "charset=\"iso-8859-1\"\n";
  $this->message .= "Content-Transfer-Encoding: 7bit\n\n";
  $this->message .= $this->body . "\n";
  $this->message .= "--$_boundary\n";
  $this->message .= "Content-type: text/html; " .
                    "charset=\"iso-8859-1\"\n";
  $this->message .= "Content-Transfer-Encoding: 7bit\n\n";
  $this->message .= $this->htmlbody . "\n";
  $this->message .= "--$_boundary--";
}
}
```

Finally, the `send()` method proceeds to send the e-mail after all the message and header construction is complete. If the mail fails to send, the class will throw an error in the form of PHP5's new `Exception` object:

```
    if (!mail($this->to,$this->subject,$this->message,$this->headers)) {
      throw new Exception('Sending mail failed.');
      return FALSE;
    } else {
      return TRUE;
```

```
        }
      }

   }

   ?>
```

The other scripts should be pretty straightforward. Starting in `mail_text.php`, you include your `SimpleMail` class, and create a new instance of it:

```php
<?php
require 'class.SimpleMail.php';

$postcard = new SimpleMail();
```

Next, the required properties are set:

```php
$postcard->to = "youremail@yourhost.com";
$postcard->subject = "Testing text email";
$postcard->body = "This is a test using plain text email!";
```

And finally, the e-mail is sent, giving a message on success:

```php
if ($postcard->send()) {
   echo "Text email sent successfully!";
}
?>
```

When sending HTML mail, as in `mail_html.php`, you begin roughly the same way, including the `class.SimpleMail.php` file, and creating a new instance of a `SimpleMail` object. Where it differs is when you start setting the properties of the mail:

```php
$postcard->to = "youremail@yourhost.com";
$postcard->subject = "Testing HTML email";
$postcard->htmlbody = "This is a test using HTML email!";
$postcard->send_html = TRUE;
$postcard->send_text = FALSE;
```

There are two things to take note of here. First, you're using the `htmlbody` property instead of the `body` property to store your message. If you used the `body` property instead of `htmlbody`, your e-mail would be empty. Second, you're explicitly turning on HTML e-mail sending, and explicitly turning off plain-text sending. If you didn't turn off plain-text sending, the mail would be sent as Multipart, because the default value for `send_text` is TRUE.

In the multipart example script, `mail_multipart.php`, you add extra header fields, such as `From`, `Cc`, and `Bcc`:

```php
$postcard->to = "youremail@yourhost.com";
$postcard->from = "fromaddress@yourhost.com";
$postcard->cc = "ccaddress@yourhost.com";
$postcard->bcc = "bccaddress@yourhost.com";
$postcard->subject = "Testhing Multipart email";
```

```
$postcard->body = "This is the text part of the email!";
$postcard->htmlbody = "This is the HTML part of the email!";
$postcard->send_html = TRUE;
```

No extra effort is needed to send a Multipart message, other than turning on HTML sending. How simple is that!

In the final example, you use the basic emulation of PHP's `mail()` function the class provides. Witness the short and sweet `mail_quick.php`:

```php
<?php
require 'class.SimpleMail.php';

$postcard = new SimpleMail();

if ($postcard->send("youremail@yourhost.com",
                    "Quick message test",
                    "This is a test using SimpleMail::send!")) {
  echo "Quick message sent successfully!";
}
?>
```

All you had to do was include the class file, and call the send method using the three required parameters!

Summary

In this chapter, you've looked at PHP's `mail()` function and learned how to use it by creating a postcard application. You may have seen similar applications at Hallmark's or Yahoo!'s Web sites. Your application is not as complex as theirs, but with a little bit more work, it shouldn't be too difficult to offer users some terrific features.

You've also created a simple mail-sending PHP class that can be reused in applications that need basic mail functionality, and you won't have to recode those messy Multipart e-mail messages each time! Keep your eyes peeled in future chapters, because it will be popping up from time to time to lend a hand.

The `mail()` function gives PHP the capability to communicate with the outside world, whether it be with users of the Web site, Web site or server administrators, or even another server. There are many opportunities to use `mail()`: A simple form on the Web page that a user fills out to describe a technical problem can be immediately mailed to a tech support person, for example. Or, the PHP server can send the Web site administrator an e-mail any time a Web page displays a fatal error. Complicated workflow applications can be created, such as content management applications.

You've experienced user interaction in this chapter by requiring that the user click a link in a confirmation e-mail before sending the postcard. In the next chapter, you'll take the interaction a step further as you learn how to let the user create an account on your site. With this feature, you can keep track of your users, and present custom information based on each user's preferences.

Exercises

See how you might accomplish the following tasks:

1. Create code to send a message to an e-mail account, and blind carbon-copy (Bcc) yourself or another account.

2. Create a simple Web form that e-mails comments or suggestions to an account of your choosing.

User Logins, Profiles, and Personalization

In this chapter, you'll learn to manipulate Web pages with user logins, profiles, and personalization using PHP's session and cookie functions. You'll create a useful login and personalization application that you can use in conjunction with the applications you have created thus far.

Session and cookie functions are two of the most fundamental, important, and useful functions you will encounter in the PHP programming language. Not convinced about the value of these yet? Think about it this way: You wouldn't want just anyone guessing where you have your important files and messing with information to change your Web site in any way he or she wanted, would you? Well, with htaccess, and better yet, PHP sessions, you can combat hackers or the general public from "stumbling" onto your sensitive files and directories.

Specifically, you learn how to do the following:

- ❑ Restrict access to files and directories via htaccess
- ❑ Use PHP to accomplish the same function as htaccess, but with more control and functionality
- ❑ Store user and admin information in a database to utilize database-driven logins
- ❑ Create a registration system with required and optional fields for users to sign up
- ❑ Use cookies to keep login information between sessions
- ❑ Create a navigation system dependent on whether or not a user has logged in

The Easiest Way to Protect Your Files

Using htaccess is a simple and quick solution to restricting access to files or directory structures. Some Web sites contain sensitive information that you don't want the public to access. Or perhaps you have an administration section where administrators can change the content of the public site, such as in a news or upcoming events section; you don't want just anybody to change that content.

Try It Out — Creating htaccess and htpasswd Files

In this exercise, you'll protect a folder so that when a user visits a page in that directory, a dialog box pops up requiring that a username and password be entered. Take a look at your Apache configuration file, `httpd.conf`. The Linux example is located in something similar to `/usr/local/apache2/conf`, and the Windows example is located in something similar to `C:\Program Files\Apache group\ Apache2\conf`.

Follow these steps:

1. Open the `httpd.conf` file and look for the following lines around line 270 or so. By default the lines are likely to look like this and will reside in the `<Directory />` section that contains your Web root:

```
#
# AllowOverride controls what directives may be placed in .htaccess files.
# It can be "All", "None", or any combination of the keywords:
# Options FileInfo AuthConfig Limit
#
AllowOverride None
#
```

2. For htaccess capabilities, change the lines to look like this:

```
#
# AllowOverride controls what directives may be placed in .htaccess files.
# It can be "All", "None", or any combination of the keywords:
# Options FileInfo AuthConfig Limit
#
AllowOverride AuthConfig
#
```

3. Create a text file named `.htaccess` in the directory that you want to restrict access to. This file will require only the following lines to function correctly:

```
AuthType Basic
AuthUserFile /usr/local/apache2/htdocs/userauth #or your windows path
AuthName "Restricted"
<LIMIT GET POST>
require valid-user
</LIMIT>
```

4. Now, when creating the password file and adding your first user, you need to separate the installation based on your operating system selection. Create your password file in your main login directory by completing these steps:

For Linux htaccess installation:

a. Go to your command prompt and type the following:

```
/usr/local/apache2/bin/htpasswd -c /usr/local/apache/htdocs2/userauth john
```

Use the location of your apache installation's `htpasswd` command, if not located in `/usr/local/apache2/bin`.

b.   You will be prompted to enter john's password; enter it as **doe**. You will then be required to re-enter the password for confirmation. That's it; your Linux htaccess installation is complete.

For Windows htaccess installation:

a.   To run htpasswd, go to Start ⇨ Run and type **cmd** to run commands from the command prompt. The command prompt should look like Figure 12-1.

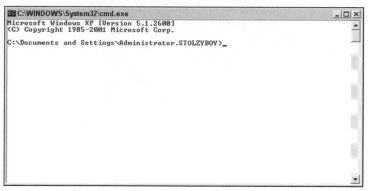

Figure 12-1

b.   Navigate to the `C:\Program Files\Apache group\Apache2\bin` directory (or wherever your `htpasswd.exe` program resides) using the `cd` command and run `htpasswd` with the following syntax at the prompt:

```
C:\>cd "C:\Program Files\Apache group\Apache2\bin"
C:\Program Files\Apache group\Apache2\bin>htpasswd -c userauth john
```

c.   At the prompt to enter john's password, enter it as **doe**; you will then be required to re-enter the password for confirmation. That's it; your Windows htaccess installation is complete.

5.   Navigate to a file in your protected directory, and you should see a screen similar to Figure 12-2.

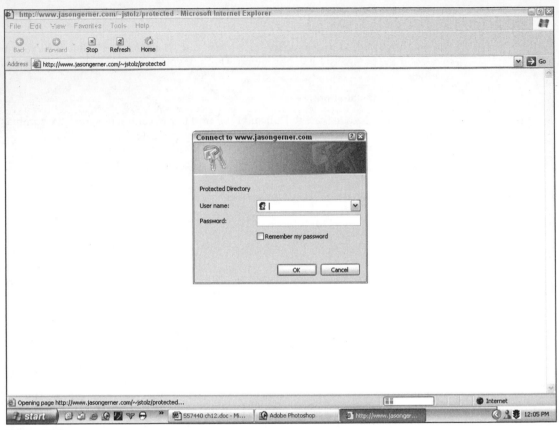

Figure 12-2

6. If you enter the appropriate username and password, you will be allowed to view the page you are requesting, along with any file or folder that resides there. However, if you fail to enter the appropriate username and password three consecutive times, or press Cancel, you will see a screen similar to that shown in Figure 12-3.

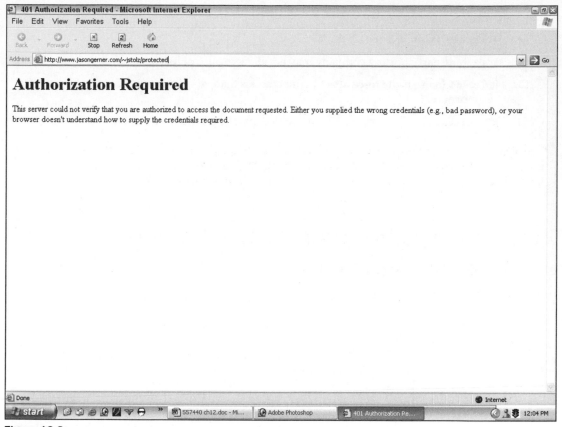

Figure 12-3

How It Works

When you request the page, Apache checks for `.htaccess` files in every folder from the Web site's document root all the way down to the file that you are requesting. Apache then opens the file and interprets it. It does this by reading which directory to protect, according to your file path, and then by reading to whom to allow access. You gave access to valid users only, as in the example of john, so no anonymous users will be allowed access. Anonymous users will see the screen shown in Figure 12-3.

Because no usernames or passwords are submitted with your initial request, Apache sends a message back to the browser, requesting you to enter a username and password to access this section of the site. A dialog box is displayed, and you can submit the username and password by entering them there. Once these are accepted, you will be allowed to view the site. Also, your Web browser will remember to automatically submit this username and password when accessing the particular folder and throughout the directory tree for the rest of the browser session.

There are some problems and drawbacks to using htaccess:

❑ The dialog box that pops up is often ugly.

❑ Your third-party hosting company may not allow the use of htaccess.

❑ It's easier to use brute force attacks with htaccess than when you use program-driven login authorization.

❑ It's not easy to customize "on the fly" for a dynamic, user-driven Web site.

Those are just some of the drawbacks to htaccess. Luckily for you, you can use PHP to solve the access problem to your Web-based files. You are likely to still have to use htaccess to protect files such as down-loadable images, PDFs, Zip files, and other files that can't contain PHP code.

Friendlier Logins Using PHP's Session and Cookie Functions

Sessions and cookies are used to distinguish users apart from one another and to allow or not allow certain users to access pages you want only certain users to see. A *session* is a variable that is kept alive on the server side when someone navigates to a site or page. You can then use this information when tracking a user throughout the site for logins, user preferences, privileges for pages, and much more. *Cookies* work in a similar fashion, although they are stored on a user's computer and allow the user to look at that file if he or she chooses to do so. Cookies are somewhat less secure in that they allow users to tamper with the file where the cookies are stored, but are by no means insecure.

The purpose of this chapter is not just to help you restrict access to certain PHP files; PHP's session and cookie functions are used to require that users of your Web site be authorized before they are allowed to use the Web pages to their full functionality. Keep in mind that this is really useful only when you're protecting sections of Web pages, not for protecting all files and directories. (This will make more sense when you jump into the code.)

You could use this form of authorization in an administration area of a Web site where the administrator can change content that is viewable by the public. Note that this can be used in conjunction with htaccess for higher security, if needed.

Try It Out   Using PHP for Logins

In this exercise, you'll use some code within PHP itself to authorize the user's username and password:

1. Open your favorite text editor.

2. Create a new PHP file and save it as `template.php`. This file will be the template you'll use to illustrate how you protect a page.

3. Start off each Web page you want to protect with this code:

```php
<?php
include "auth.inc.php";
?>
<html>
```

```
<head>
<title>Beginning PHP5, Apache and MySQL</title>
</head>
<body>
<h1>This is the Template Page</h1>
</body>
</html>
```

This preceding template file is just an example of what you would do to protect a PHP page. In a real working situation, you can replace everything between the opening and closing <body> tags to protect any PHP page that you feel necessary.

4. This takes us to the authorization file, which checks to see if the user has successfully started a session by logging in. If not, the user is redirected to the login page. Use the following code to create a page and save it as auth.inc.php:

```
<?php
session_start();
if (isset($_SESSION['logged']) && $_SESSION['logged'] == 1) {
  //Do Nothing
} else {
  $redirect = $_SERVER['PHP_SELF'];
  header("Refresh: 5; URL=login.php?redirect=$redirect");
  echo "You are being redirected to the login page!<br>";
  echo "(If your browser doesn't support this, " .
       "<a href=\"login.php?redirect=$redirect\">click here</a>)";
  die();
}
?>
```

5. Now that you have the template page and the authorization page done, you can create the login page, login.php, that you use to create the sessions that allow you to gain access to your protected pages. Enter the following code, which actually does the login authorization and the creation of the session for the user once he or she has successfully provided the correct username and password:

```
<?php
session_start();
$_SESSION['logged'] = 0;

if (isset($_POST['submit'])) {
  if ($_POST['username'] == "wroxbooks" &&
      $_POST['password'] == "aregreat") {
    $_SESSION['logged'] = 1;
    header ("Refresh: 5; URL=" . $_POST['redirect'] . "");
    echo "You are being redirected to your original page request!<br>";
    echo "(If your browser doesn't support this, " .
         "<a href=\"" . $_POST['redirect']. "\">click here</a>)";
  } else {
?>
<html>
<head>
<title>Beginning PHP5, Apache and MySQL</title>
</head>
<body>
```

```
<p>
  Invalid Username and/or Password<br><br>
  <form action="login.php" method="post">
    <input type="hidden" name="redirect"
      value="<?php echo $_POST['redirect']; ?>">
    Username: <input type="text" name="username"><br>
    Password: <input type="password" name="password"><br><br>
    <input type="submit" name="submit" value="Login">
  </form>
</p>
<?php
  }
} else {
?>
<html>
<head>
<title>Beginning PHP5, Apache and MySQL</title>
</head>
<body>
<p>
  You must be logged in to view this page<br><br>
<?
if (isset($_GET['redirect'])) {
  $redirect = $_GET['redirect'];
} else {
  $redirect = "index.php";
}
?>
  <form action="login.php" method="post">
    <input type="hidden" name="redirect"
      value="<?php echo $_GET['redirect']; ?>">
    Username: <input type="text" name="username"><br>
    Password: <input type="password" name="password"><br><br>
    <input type="submit" name="submit" value="Login">
  </form>
</p>
<?php
}
?>
</body>
</html>
```

6. Navigate to the `template.php` page you created. Because you haven't logged in, the `auth.inc.php` file you included redirects you to the `login.php` page that requires you to log in to view the initial page you requested.

Try inputting the incorrect information so you can see how the login page works. You will see a screen similar to the one shown in Figure 12-4.

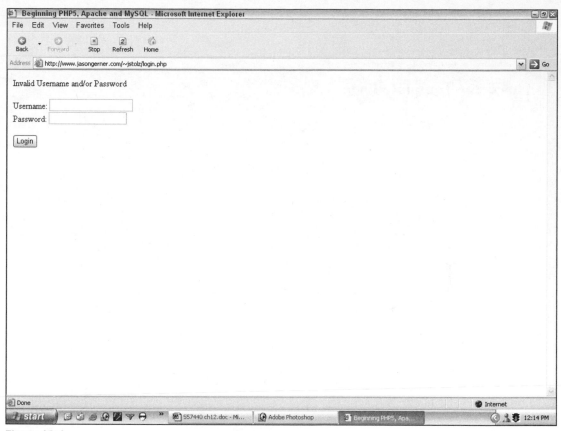

Figure 12-4

7. Input the correct information: `wroxbooks` for the username and `aregreat` for the password. At this point, you are redirected to the page you originally requested because you supplied the correct information. You will see a screen similar to Figure 12-5.

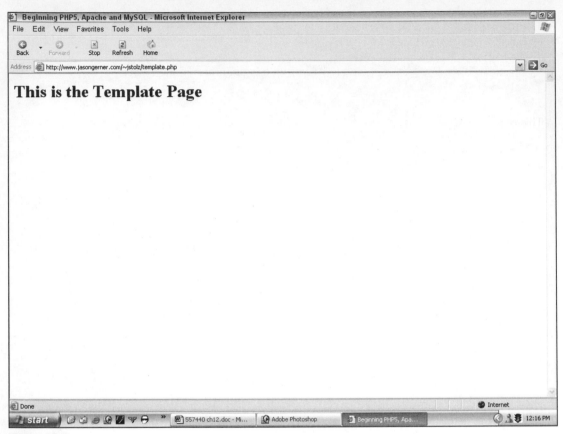

Figure 12-5

How It Works

The PHP pages you just created are used to authorize a user who is trying to view a certain section of your site. When you navigate to a page, the `auth.inc.php` page checks to see if you are or aren't already an authorized user, and then the page either sends you to the login page or displays the page you were requesting. Here is the part of the code that is actually doing the checking:

```
if (isset($_SESSION['logged']) && $_SESSION['logged'] == 1
```

The `$_SESSION['logged']` is the variable you are checking for, and the 1 is another way of checking for true.

Right now, you only have a username and password hard-coded into your page. If you want numerous users, you would have to edit your page accordingly and add those values for those users. Sessions will look more useful when you are using database-driven information rather than the hard-coded values.

This is a very useful way to protect your PHP files to limit use to logged-in users and administrators. However, there are a couple of minor drawbacks that you will solve later when you integrate the database-driven system:

❑   This is manageable only for a few users with login information.

❑   It's somewhat labor intensive when the need to move to a user-driven database system arises.

This may seem to be a less-than-useful example, but it shows that you can protect pages so not just any Joe Shmoe can gain access to them. In fact, this example would work just fine if you needed to have just one or two users or administrators. You can have more, but that isn't easily managed, especially if you get numerous users.

In the next section, you learn how you can use PHP in conjunction with MySQL to create user-driven login systems. You also learn how to allow multiple administrators, multiple usernames and passwords, and privilege levels that can be managed with the MySQL database.

Using Database-Driven Information

This section shows you what you can do with a database-driven Web site. Obviously, you will be using a MySQL database as your preferred database, but keep in mind that PHP can be used with many other databases as well.

You will first set up a couple of tables in your database. For this, you will need a table schema (structured framework or plan). The next few steps are merely setup information so you have some usable data in the database that you can use with your PHP/MySQL pages. Call your database registration and your tables admin and user_info. You can go ahead and create the tables as necessary using one of the methods you learned in previous chapters.

1.   First, create an administration table schema called admin. You won't be using this table information until the last section of the chapter, but because you are creating table schemas, you may as well do it now. This is where you can keep track of the administrators managing your system.

```
CREATE TABLE admin (
  username varchar(50) NOT NULL,
  password varchar(255) NOT NULL,
  first_name varchar(50) NOT NULL,
  last_name varchar(50) NOT NULL,
  email varchar(50) NOT NULL,
  admin_level int(2) NOT NULL,
  id int(10) NOT NULL auto_increment,
  PRIMARY KEY (id)
);
```

2. Create another table to store users and their information. Call this table `user_info` and create it with the following schema:

```
CREATE TABLE user_info (
  email varchar(50) NOT NULL,
  username varchar(50) NOT NULL,
  password varchar(255) NOT NULL,
  first_name varchar(50) NOT NULL,
  last_name varchar(50) NOT NULL,
  city varchar(50) default NULL,
  state varchar(50) default NULL,
  hobbies varchar(255) default NULL,
  id int(10) NOT NULL default '0'
);
```

3. Add a couple of administrators to your database, using your preferred method. (Two will be added here as an example, but you can add as many as you want.) This example uses John Doe and Jane Doe. Keep in mind that you will be using these in all the examples we create here:

```
INSERT INTO admin (username, password, first_name, last_name, email,
  admin_level, id)
VALUES ('johndoe', PASSWORD('jane'), 'John', 'Doe', 'john@johndoe.com',
  '1', '');
```

and

```
INSERT INTO admin (username, password, first_name, last_name, email,
  admin_level, id)
VALUES ('janedoe', PASSWORD('john'), 'Jane', 'Doe', 'jane@janedoe.com',
  '2', '');
```

You now have a couple of administrators set up in your admin table, so you can begin to create the registration portion of your PHP code to allow users to register and log in, and update their information or delete their accounts if needed. You will again be using sessions to track your users, and you will also be using some cookie information to keep persistent logins between sessions should the user want that option.

Try It Out   **Session Tracking with PHP and MySQL**

In this exercise, you create a user login system. You will create it so that the user is required to input a username, password, first name, last name, and e-mail address. The other fields will be optional.

1. First, create an index page that looks for login information similar to the previous example, but don't include an authorization page so that you can show different content based on whether or not the user is logged in. This allows the user the chance to log in if he or she wishes to. Call this page `index.php`, and use the following code to create it:

```
<?php
session_start();
if ((isset($_SESSION['user_logged']) &&
     $_SESSION['user_logged'] != "") ||
    (isset($_SESSION['user_password']) &&
```

```
        $_SESSION['user_password'] != "")) {
   include "logged_user.php";
} else {
   include "unlogged_user.php";
}
?>
```

2. Create `unlogged_user.php` and `logged_user.php` so you can have different content show up depending on whether or not a user is logged in. This first page will be `unlogged_user.php` and will simply contain some information about the benefits that registering provides and how to go about registering:

```
<html>
<head>
<title>Beginning PHP5, Apache and MySQL</title>
</head>
<body>
<h1>Welcome to the home page!</h1>
<p>
  You are currently not logged into our system.<br>
  Once logged in, you will have access to your personal area,
  along with other user information.<br>
  If you have already registered,
  <a href="user_login.php">click here</a> to login,
  or if would like to create an account,
  <a href="register.php">click here</a> to register.
</p>
</body>
</html>
```

3. Next, create the page that tells users they are logged in; then you can show links to the users' own personal area (which you create later) to allow them to update personal information, or delete their account entirely. Call this one `logged_user.php` and use the following code:

```
<html>
<head>
<title>Beginning PHP5, Apache and MySQL</title>
</head>
<body>
<h1>Welcome to the home page!</h1>
<p>
  Thank you for logging into our system
  <b><?php echo $_SESSION['user_logged']; ?></b>.<br>
  You may now <a href="user_personal.php">click here</a>
  to go into your own personal information area, and
  update or remove your information should you wish to do so.
</p>
</body>
</html>
```

4. Create a page called `conn.inc.php` to include in your pages for your MySQL connection information:

```php
<?php
$conn = mysql_connect("localhost", "bp5am", "bp5ampass")
  or die(mysql_error());
$db = mysql_select_db("registration")
  or die(mysql_error());
?>
```

5. Create the registration page, making sure you include the optional fields and that the username chosen by the user registering isn't the same as an existing username. Call it `register.php` (it's a lot of code all at once, but we explain it all later when we get this system together).

If users don't fill out some required fields, or use an already registered username, you will notify them, and keep what had previously been entered in the appropriate fields so they don't have to re-enter everything.

```php
<?php
session_start();
ob_start();
include "conn.inc.php";
?>
<html>
<head>
<title>Beginning PHP5, Apache and MySQL</title>
</head>
<body>
<?php
if (isset($_POST['submit']) && $_POST['submit'] == "Register") {
  if ($_POST['username'] != "" &&
      $_POST['password'] != "" &&
      $_POST['first_name'] != "" &&
      $_POST['last_name'] != "" &&
      $_POST['email'] != "") {

    $query = "SELECT username FROM user_info " .
             "WHERE username = '" . $_POST['username'] . "';";
    $result = mysql_query($query)
      or die(mysql_error());

    if (mysql_num_rows($result) != 0) {
?>
<p>
  <font color="#FF0000"><b>The Username,
  <?php echo $_POST['username']; ?>, is already in use, please choose
  another!</b></font>
  <form action="register.php" method="post">
    Username: <input type="text" name="username"><br>
    Password: <input type="password" name="password"
                value="<?php echo $_POST['password']; ?>"><br>
    Email: <input type="text" name="email"
             alue="<?php echo $_POST['email']; ?>"><br>
    First Name: <input type="text" name="first_name"
                  value="<?php echo $_POST['first_name']; ?>"><br>
```

```
            Last Name: <input type="text" name="last_name"
                       value="<?php echo $_POST['last_name']; ?>"><br>
            City: <input type="text" name="city"
                  value="<?php echo $_POST['city']; ?>"><br>
            State: <input type="text" name="state"
                   value="<?php echo $_POST['state']; ?>"><br>
            Hobbies/Interests: (choose at least one)<br>
            <select name="hobbies[]" size="10" multiple>
              <option value="Golfing"<?php
                if (in_array("Golfing", $_POST['hobbies'])) {
                  echo " selected";
                } ?>>Golfing</option>
              <option value="Hunting"<?php
                if (in_array("Hunting", $_POST['hobbies'])) {
                  echo " selected";
                } ?>>Hunting</option>
              <option value="Reading"<?php
                if (in_array("Reading", $_POST['hobbies'])) {
                  echo " selected";
                } ?>>Reading</option>
              <option value="Dancing"<?php
                if (in_array("Dancing", $_POST['hobbies'])) {
                  echo " selected";
                } ?>>Dancing</option>
              <option value="Internet"<?php
                if (in_array("Internet", $_POST['hobbies'])) {
                  echo " selected";
                } ?>>Internet</option>
              <option value="Flying"<?php
                if (in_array("Flying", $_POST['hobbies'])) {
                  echo " selected";
                } ?>>Flying</option>
              <option value="Traveling"<?php
                if (in_array("Traveling", $_POST['hobbies'])) {
                  echo " selected";
                } ?>>Traveling</option>
              <option value="Exercising"<?php
                if (in_array("Exercising", $_POST['hobbies'])) {
                  echo " selected";
                } ?>>Exercising</option>
              <option value="Computers"<?php
                if (in_array("Computers", $_POST['hobbies'])) {
                  echo " selected";
                } ?>>Computers</option>
              <option value="Other Than Listed"<?php
                if (in_array("Other Than Listed", $_POST['hobbies'])) {
                  echo " selected";
                } ?>>Other Than Listed</option>
            </select><br><br>
            <input type="submit" name="submit" value="Register">  
            <input type="reset" value="Clear">
          </form>
        </p>
<?php
```

```php
      } else {
        $query = "INSERT INTO user_info (username, password, email, " .
                 "first_name, last_name, city, state, hobbies) " .
                 "VALUES ('" . $_POST['username'] . "', " .
                 "(PASSWORD('" . $_POST['password'] . "')), '" .
                 $_POST['email'] . "', '" . $_POST['first_name'] .
                 "', '" . $_POST['last_name'] . "', '" . $_POST['city'] .
                 "', '" . $_POST['state'] . "', '" .
                 implode(", ", $_POST['hobbies']) . "');";
        $result = mysql_query($query)
          or die(mysql_error());
        $_SESSION['user_logged'] = $_POST['username'];
        $_SESSION['user_password'] = $_POST['password'];
?>
<p>
  Thank you, <?php echo $_POST['first_name'] . " " .
  $_POST['last_name']; ?> for registering!<br>
<?php
        header("Refresh: 5; URL=index.php");
        echo "Your registration is complete! " .
             "You are being sent to the page you requested!<br>";
        echo "(If your browser doesn't support this, " .
             "<a href=\"index.php\">click here</a>)";
        die();
      }
    } else {
?>
<p>
  <font color="#FF0000"><b>The Username, Password, Email, First Name,
  and Last Name fields are required!</b></font>
  <form action="register.php" method="post">
    Username: <input type="text" name="username"
               value="<?php echo $_POST['username']; ?>"><br>
    Password: <input type="password" name="password"
               value="<?php echo $_POST['password']; ?>"><br>
    Email: <input type="text" name="email"
             value="<?php echo $_POST['email']; ?>"><br>
    First Name: <input type="text" name="first_name"
             value="<?php echo $_POST['first_name']; ?>"><br>
    Last Name: <input type="text" name="last_name"
               value="<?php echo $_POST['last_name']; ?>"><br>
    City: <input type="text" name="city"
           value="<?php echo $_POST['city']; ?>"><br>
    State: <input type="text" name="state"
            value="<?php echo $_POST['state']; ?>"><br>
    Hobbies/Interests: (choose at least one)<br>
    <select name="hobbies[]" size="10" multiple>
      <option value="Golfing"<?php
        if (in_array("Golfing", $_POST['hobbies'])) {
          echo " selected";
        } ?>>Golfing</option>
      <option value="Hunting"<?php
        if (in_array("Hunting", $_POST['hobbies'])) {
          echo " selected";
```

```
            } ?>>Hunting</option>
        <option value="Reading"<?php
          if (in_array("Reading", $_POST['hobbies'])) {
            echo " selected";
          } ?>>Reading</option>
        <option value="Dancing"<?php
          if (in_array("Dancing", $_POST['hobbies'])) {
            echo " selected";
          } ?>>Dancing</option>
        <option value="Internet"<?php
          if (in_array("Internet", $_POST['hobbies'])) {
            echo " selected";
          } ?>>Internet</option>
        <option value="Flying"<?php
          if (in_array("Flying", $_POST['hobbies'])) {
            echo " selected";
          } ?>>Flying</option>
        <option value="Traveling"<?php
          if (in_array("Traveling", $_POST['hobbies'])) {
            echo " selected";
          } ?>>Traveling</option>
        <option value="Exercising"<?php
          if (in_array("Exercising", $_POST['hobbies'])) {
            echo " selected";
          } ?>>Exercising</option>
        <option value="Computers"<?php
          if (in_array("Computers", $_POST['hobbies'])) {
            echo " selected";
          } ?>>Computers</option>
        <option value="Other Than Listed"<?php
          if (in_array("Other Than Listed", $_POST['hobbies'])) {
            echo " selected";
          } ?>>Other Than Listed</option>
      </select><br><br>
      <input type="submit" name="submit" value="Register">  
      <input type="reset" value="Clear">
    </form>
</p>
<?php
  }
} else {
?>
<p>
  Welcome to the registration page!<br>
  The Username, Password, Email, First Name, and Last Name fields
  are required!
  <form action="register.php" method="post">
    Username: <input type="text" name="username"><br>
    Password: <input type="password" name="password"><br>
    Email: <input type="text" name="email"><br>
    First Name: <input type="text" name="first_name"><br>
    Last Name: <input type="text" name="last_name"><br>
    City: <input type="text" name="city"><br>
    State: <input type="text" name="state"><br>
```

```
       Hobbies/Interests: (choose at least one)<br>
       <select name="hobbies[]" size="10" multiple>
         <option value="Golfing">Golfing</option>
         <option value="Hunting">Hunting</option>
         <option value="Reading">Reading</option>
         <option value="Dancing">Dancing</option>
         <option value="Internet">Internet</option>
         <option value="Flying">Flying</option>
         <option value="Traveling">Traveling</option>
         <option value="Exercising">Exercising</option>
         <option value="Computers">Computers</option>
         <option value="Other Than Listed">Other Than Listed</option>
       </select><br><br>
       <input type="submit" name="submit" value="Register">  
       <input type="reset" value="Clear">
     </form>
  </p>
  <?php
  }
  ?>
  </body>
  </html>
```

How It Works

That whole page is the registration page. It is used to allow users to register for your login system. The page allows users to choose different options for their accounts and restricts users from using someone else's username for registration. Once users are registered, they are allowed to log in to the system and modify their account information as they see fit.

The index.php page checks whether or not a user is logged in. Again, the $_SESSION[''] variable is the one being checked to see if users have already been logged in and they are just revisiting some pages. If they are not logged according to those session variables, they will be shown the unlogged_user.php page. Assuming they have logged in, they will be shown the logged_user.php page.

The unlogged_user.php page is displayed if the user is not logged in and their session has not yet been created. That was checked when they visited the index.php page.

The logged_user.php page is displayed if the user is logged in and their session has been created. That was also checked when they visited the index.php page. Also, it displays the username that they used to log in with in the welcome message. The $_SESSION['user_logged'] is the user's username from the database.

Here's a quick recap of what you've done:

❑   You have an index page that checks whether or not a user is logged in.

❑   Based on that check, it either tells the user to log in or register to allow access to his or her personal information area.

❑   You have the registration area covered, along with the login process, and are keeping users tracked with their session information.

Try It Out   **Authorizing Users to Edit Their Accounts**

Now you can create the area where users are allowed to change their information or delete their account. Call this page `user_personal.php`, but first you will create a slightly modified authorization page, which checks whether or not users are logged in and, if they are not, redirects them to your also slightly modified login page:

1. Enter the first set of code and call it `auth_user.inc.php`:

```php
<?php
session_start();
if ((isset($_SESSION['user_logged']) &&
      $_SESSION['user_logged'] != "") ||
    (isset($_SESSION['user_password']) &&
      $_SESSION['user_password'] != "")) {
  //Do Nothing!
} else {
  $redirect = $_SERVER['PHP_SELF'];
  header("Refresh: 5; URL=user_login.php?redirect=$redirect");
  echo "You are currently not logged in, we are redirecting you, " .
      "be patient!<br>";
  echo "(If your browser doesn't support this, " .
      "<a href=\"user_login.php?redirect=$redirect\">click here</a>)";
  die();
}
?>
```

2. Create the modified login page. Call this one `user_login.php`. The modification is in the way that you check the username and password against usernames and passwords stored in the MySQL database. Previously, you just hard-coded a username and password in the code.

```php
<?php
session_start();
include "conn.inc.php";

if (isset($_POST['submit'])) {
  $query = "SELECT username, password FROM user_info " .
          "WHERE username = '" . $_POST['username'] . "' " .
          "AND password = (PASSWORD('" . $_POST['password'] . "'))";
  $result = mysql_query($query)
    or die(mysql_error());

  if (mysql_num_rows($result) == 1) {
    $_SESSION['user_logged'] = $_POST['username'];
    $_SESSION['user_password'] = $_POST['password'];
    header ("Refresh: 5; URL=" . $_POST['redirect'] . "");
    echo "You are being redirected to your original page request!<br>";
    echo "(If your browser doesn't support this, " .
        "<a href=\"" . $_POST['redirect']. "\">click here</a>)";
  } else {
?>
<html>
<head>
<title>Beginning PHP5, Apache and MySQL</title>
```

```
    </head>
    <body>
    <p>
      Invalid Username and/or Password<br>
      Not registered?
      <a href="register.php">Click here</a> to register.<br>
      <form action="user_login.php" method="post">
        <input type="hidden" name="redirect"
          value="<?php echo $_POST['redirect']; ?>">
        Username: <input type="text" name="username"><br>
        Password: <input type="password" name="password"><br><br>
        <input type="submit" name="submit" value="Login">
      </form>
    </p>
    </body>
    </html>
    <?php
      }
    } else {
      if (isset($_GET['redirect'])) {
        $redirect = $_GET['redirect'];
      } else {
        $redirect = "index.php";
      }
    ?>
    <html>
    <head>
    <title>Beginning PHP5, Apache and MySQL</title>
    </head>
    <body>
    <p>
      Login below by supplying your username/password...<br>
      Or <a href="register.php">click here</a> to register.<br><br>
      <form action="user_login.php" method="post">
        <input type="hidden" name="redirect"
          value="<?php echo $redirect; ?>">
        Username: <input type="text" name="username"><br>
        Password: <input type="password" name="password"><br><br>
        <input type="submit" name="submit" value="Login">
      </form>
    </p>
    </body>
    </html>
    <?php
    }
    ?>
```

3. Create the `user_personal.php` page with the following code:

```
<?php
include "auth_user.inc.php";
include "conn.inc.php";
?>
<html>
<head>
```

```
<title>Beginning PHP5, Apache and MySQL</title>
</head>
<body>
<h1>Welcome to your personal information area</h1>
<p>
  Here you can update your personal information,
  or delete your account.<br>
  Your information as you currently have it is shown below:<br>
  <a href="index.php">Click here</a> to return to the home page<br><br>
<?php
$query = "SELECT * FROM user_info " .
         "WHERE username = '" . $_SESSION['user_logged'] . "' " .
         "AND password = (PASSWORD('" .
         $_SESSION['user_password'] . "'))";
$result = mysql query($query)
  or die(mysql_error());

$row = mysql_fetch_array($result);
?>
  First Name: <?php echo $row['first_name']; ?><br>
  Last Name: <?php echo $row['last_name']; ?><br>
  City: <?php echo $row['city']; ?><br>
  State: <?php echo $row['state']; ?><br>
  Email: <?php echo $row['email']; ?><br>
  Hobbies/Interests: <?php echo $row['hobbies']; ?><br><br>
  <a href="update_account.php">Update Account</a> |
  <a href="delete_account.php">Delete Account</a>
</p>
</body>
</html>
```

How It Works

How it works isn't that much different than anything you've done so far in this book. You've made calls to the database, pulled information, displayed information, and used that information. The only difference here is the use of the sessions, once again. The session is used to track users so they are not allowed to access someone else's account.

You make a call to the table to pull up the account, according to the user's supplied username and password. This way there is no confusion as to whose account they should be in; that is, if they were able to log in to the system, then they are using their own account. This section is dependent on the login process. If users fail the login process, they won't be able to use this system to update or delete their account as they see fit.

Displaying, modifying, and deleting the information from MySQL is no different than what you have done thus far, but now you've used the session security.

Try It Out	Editing User Accounts

You may have noticed in the previous exercise that there are links to pages that you haven't created yet. Let's do that now. One page will allow a logged-in user to update his or her account. The other will allow the user to delete the account upon confirming that that is the intention.

1. Create the first page, `update_account.php`, with the following code:

```php
<?php
include "auth_user.inc.php";
include "conn.inc.php";
?>
<html>
<head>
<title>Beginning PHP5, Apache and MySQL</title>
</head>
<body>
<h1>Update Account Information</h1>
<p>
  Here you can update your account information for viewing in your
  profile.<br><br>
<?php
if (isset($_POST['submit']) && $_POST['submit'] == "Update") {
  $query_update = "UPDATE user_info SET " .
                  "email = '" . $_POST['email'] . "', " .
                  "city = '" . $_POST['city'] . "', " .
                  "state = '" . $_POST['state'] . "', " .
                  "hobbies = '" . implode(", ",$_POST['hobbies']) .
                  "' WHERE username = '" . $_SESSION['user_logged'] .
                  "' AND password = (PASSWORD('" .
                  $_SESSION['user_password'] . "'))";
  $result_update = mysql_query($query_update)
    or die(mysql_error());

  $query = "SELECT * FROM user_info " .
           "WHERE username = '" . $_SESSION['user_logged'] . "' " .
           "AND password = (PASSWORD('" .
           $_SESSION['user_password'] . "'))";
  $result = mysql_query($query)
    or die(mysql_error());

  $row = mysql_fetch_array($result);
  $hobbies = explode(", ", $row['hobbies'])
?>
  <b>Your account information has been updated.</b><br>
  <a href="user_personal.php">Click here</a> to return to your account.
  <form action="update_account.php" method="post">
    Email: <input type="text" name="email"
            value="<?php echo $row['email']; ?>"><br>
    City: <input type="text" name="city"
            value="<?php echo $row['city']; ?>"><br>
    State: <input type="text" name="state"
            value="<?php echo $row['state']; ?>"><br>
    Hobbies/Interests: (choose at least one)<br>
    <select name="hobbies[]" size="10" multiple>
      <option value="Golfing"<?php
        if (in_array("Golfing", $hobbies)) {
          echo " selected";
        } ?>>Golfing</option>
      <option value="Hunting"<?php
        if (in_array("Hunting", $hobbies)) {
          echo " selected";
```

```
          } ?>>Hunting</option>
        <option value="Reading"<?php
          if (in_array("Reading", $hobbies)) {
            echo " selected";
          } ?>>Reading</option>
        <option value="Dancing"<?php
          if (in_array("Dancing", $hobbies)) {
            echo " selected";
          } ?>>Dancing</option>
        <option value="Internet"<?php
          if (in_array("Internet", $hobbies)) {
            echo " selected";
          } ?>>Internet</option>
        <option value="Flying"<?php
          if (in_array("Flying", $hobbies)) {
            echo " selected";
          } ?>>Flying</option>
        <option value="Traveling"<?php
          if (in_array("Traveling", $hobbies)) {
            echo " selected";
          } ?>>Traveling</option>
        <option value="Exercising"<?php
          if (in_array("Exercising", $hobbies)) {
            echo " selected";
          } ?>>Exercising</option>
        <option value="Computers"<?php
          if (in_array("Computers", $hobbies)) {
            echo " selected";
          } ?>>Computers</option>
        <option value="Other Than Listed"<?php
          if (in_array("Other Than Listed", $hobbies)) {
            echo " selected";
          } ?>>Other Than Listed</option>
      </select><br><br>
      <input type="submit" name="submit" value="Update">  
      <input type="button" value="Cancel" onclick="history.go(-1);">
    </form>
</p>
<?php
} else {
  $query = "SELECT * FROM user_info " .
           "WHERE username = '" . $_SESSION['user_logged']. "' " .
           "AND password = (PASSWORD('" .
           $_SESSION['user_password'] . "'));";
  $result = mysql_query($query)
    or die(mysql_error());

  $row = mysql_fetch_array($result);
  $hobbies = explode(", ", $row['hobbies'])
?>
<p>
  <form action="update_account.php" method="post">
    Email: <input type="text" name="email"
            value="<?php echo $row['email']; ?>"><br>
    City: <input type="text" name="city"
```

```
                       value="<?php echo $row['city']; ?>"><br>
         State: <input type="text" name="state"
                       value="<?php echo $row['state']; ?>"><br>
         Hobbies/Interests: (choose at least one)<br>
         <select name="hobbies[]" size="10" multiple>
           <option value="Golfing"<?php
             if (in_array("Golfing", $hobbies)) {
               echo " selected";
             } ?>>Golfing</option>
           <option value="Hunting"<?php
             if (in_array("Hunting", $hobbies)) {
               echo " selected";
             } ?>>Hunting</option>
           <option value="Reading"<?php
             if (in_array("Reading", $hobbies)) {
               echo " selected";
             } ?>>Reading</option>
           <option value="Dancing"<?php
             if (in_array("Dancing", $hobbies)) {
               echo " selected";
             } ?>>Dancing</option>
           <option value="Internet"<?php
             if (in_array("Internet", $hobbies)) {
               echo " selected";
             } ?>>Internet</option>
           <option value="Flying"<?php
             if (in_array("Flying", $hobbies)) {
               echo " selected";
             } ?>>Flying</option>
           <option value="Traveling"<?php
             if (in_array("Traveling", $hobbies)) {
               echo " selected";
             } ?>>Traveling</option>
           <option value="Exercising"<?php
             if (in_array("Exercising", $hobbies)) {
               echo " selected";
             } ?>>Exercising</option>
           <option value="Computers"<?php
             if (in_array("Computers", $hobbies)) {
               echo " selected";
             } ?>>Computers</option>
           <option value="Other Than Listed"<?php
             if (in_array("Other Than Listed", $hobbies)) {
               echo " selected";
             } ?>>Other Than Listed</option>
         </select><br><br>
         <input type="submit" name="submit" value="Update">  
         <input type="button" value="Cancel" onclick="history.go(-1);">
       </form>
   </p>
   <?php
   }
   ?>
   </body>
   </html>
```

2. Create the next page (call it `delete_account.php`) to allow users to delete their accounts, using the following code:

```php
<?php
include "auth_user.inc.php";
include "conn.inc.php";

if (isset($_POST['submit']) && $_POST['submit'] == "Yes") {
  $query_delete = "DELETE FROM user_info " .
                  "WHERE username = '" . $_SESSION['user_logged'] .
                  "' AND password = (PASSWORD('" .
                  $_SESSION['user_password'] . "'))";
  $result_delete = mysql_query($query_delete)
    or die(mysql_error());

  $_SESSION['user_logged'] = "";
  $_SESSION['user_password'] = "";

  header("Refresh: 5; URL=index.php");
  echo "Your account has been deleted! You are being sent to the " .
       "home page!<br>";
  echo "(If you're browser doesn't support this, " .
       "<a href=\"index.php\">click here</a>)";
  die();
} else {
?>
<html>
<head>
<title>Beginning PHP5, Apache and MySQL</title>
</head>
<body>
<p>
  Are you sure you want to delete your account?<br>
  There is no way to retrieve your account once you confirm!<br>
  <form action="delete_account.php" method="post">
    <input type="submit" name="submit" value="Yes">  
    <input type="button" value=" No " onclick="history.go(-1);">
  </form>
</p>
</body>
</html>
<?php
}
?>
```

That's all the code for now. It was a lot to absorb all at once, but it will make more sense when you see what it is doing in the next section.

How It Works

Imagine new users coming to this section of the site for the first time. They navigate to the `index.php` page and initially see a screen similar to the one shown in Figure 12-6.

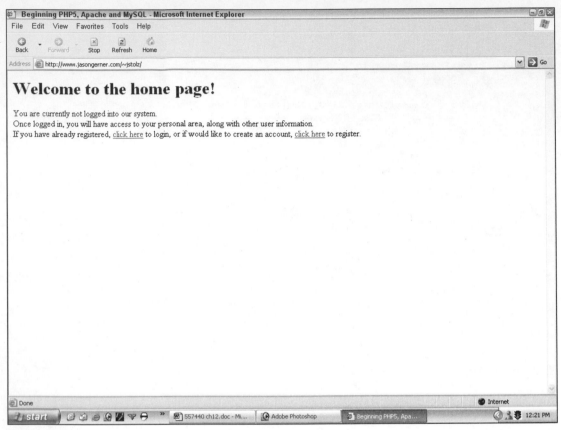

Figure 12-6

The users obviously haven't logged in yet, so they are not allowed to do anything else here. They are given the choice to log in if they have registered before, or they can register to activate an account.

Should the users decide to log in, they will be presented with the same options as when you created the previous login pages. The page should look like the one in Figure 12-7.

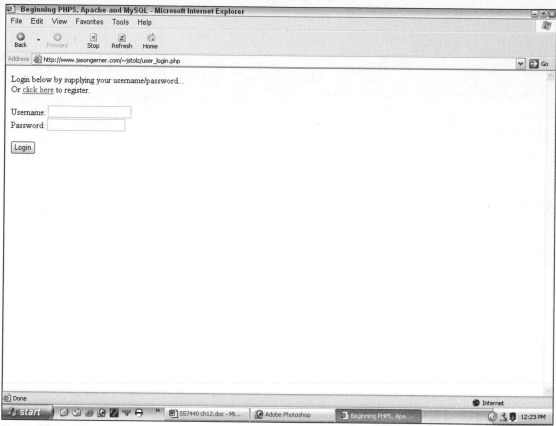

Figure 12-7

Users will be required to supply the usernames and passwords they chose for themselves. The only difference between this login page and the previous one you created is that the authorization is coming from a MySQL database, rather than hard coding of the authorization into the pages themselves. If users don't enter the information correctly, they will be asked for the information again, and have the option to register from that page as well.

If a user chooses to register, he or she will see a page similar to the one in Figure 12-8.

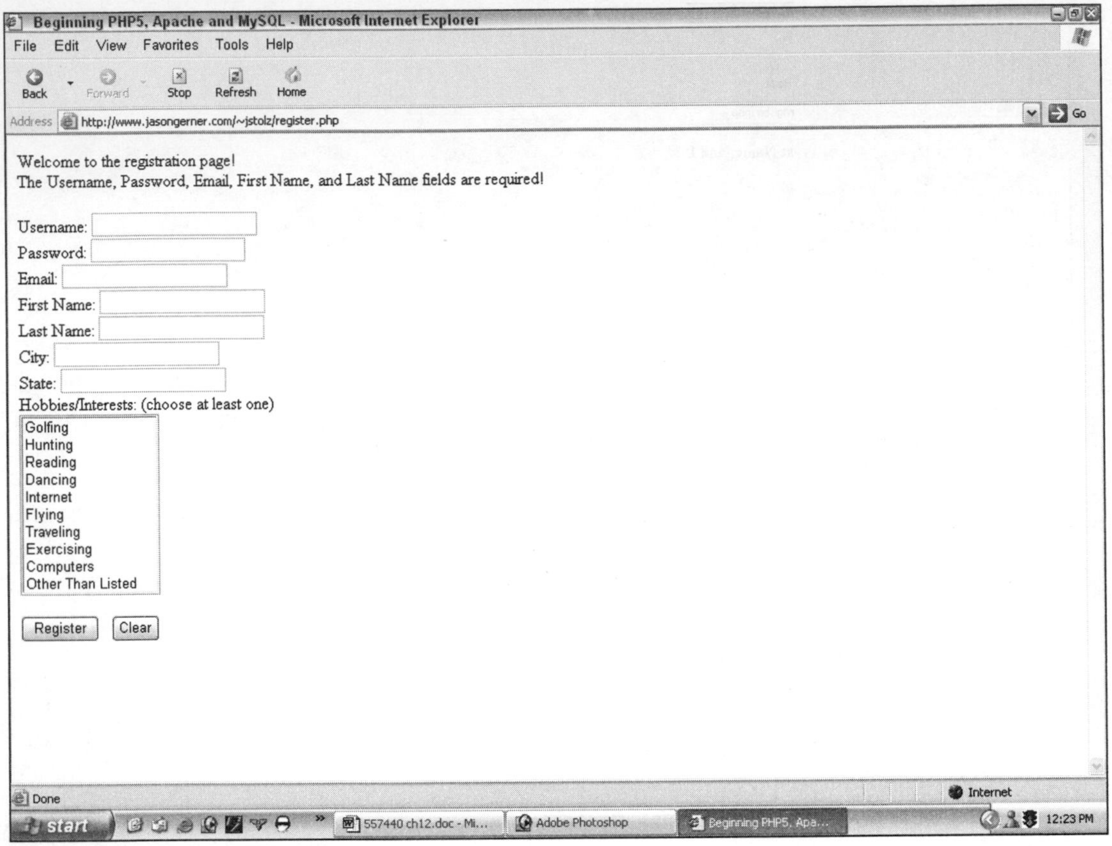

Figure 12-8

Now users can fill in their information and register to be a user of this site. Once the user fills in the information and hits the register button, the code checks whether or not the required fields have been filled out. If one (or more) of the required fields is not filled out, the form appears again with the information entered still in the form and an error message stating the problem. The page will look similar to the one shown in Figure 12-9.

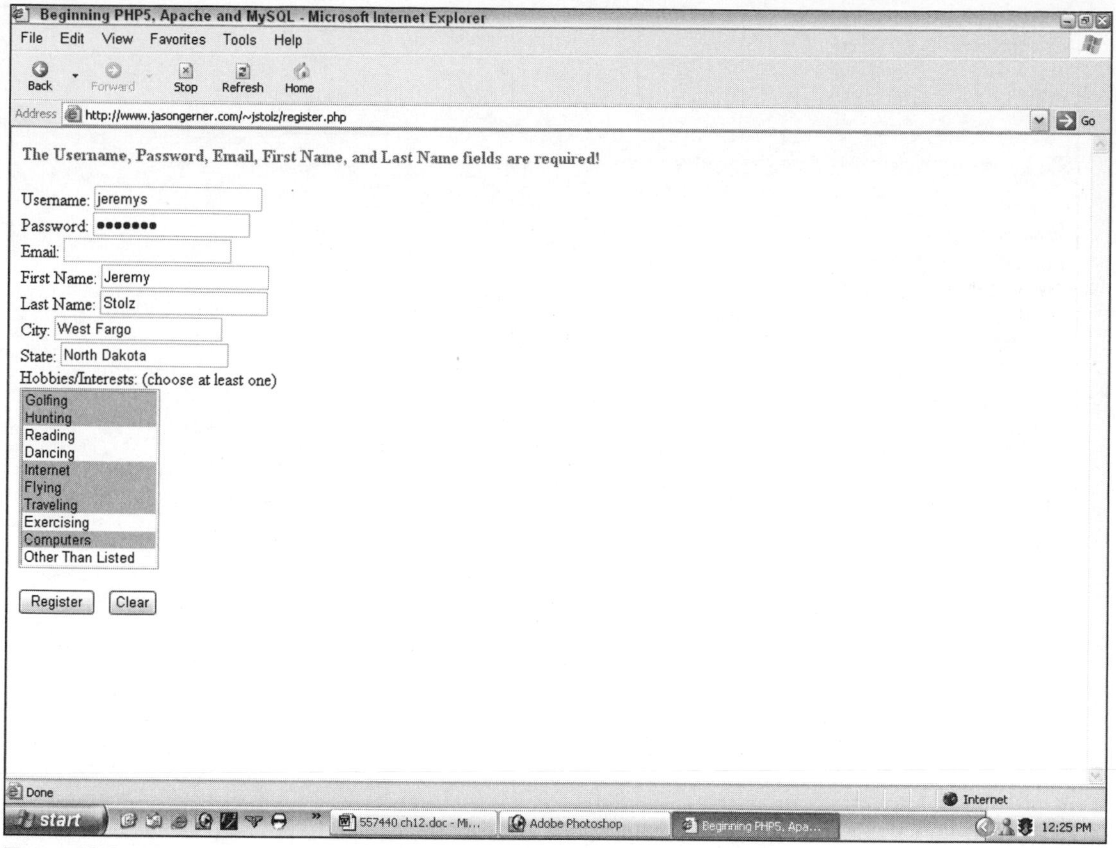

Figure 12-9

Users can now fill in the missing information and continue. A check is performed after the required fields are satisfied to see if the username chosen is already taken. Should that be the case, the form again retains any information that has been filled out, and a different error message appears on the screen stating that the username is taken. The username field is erased so users know that they need to choose another username. The screen will look like that in Figure 12-10.

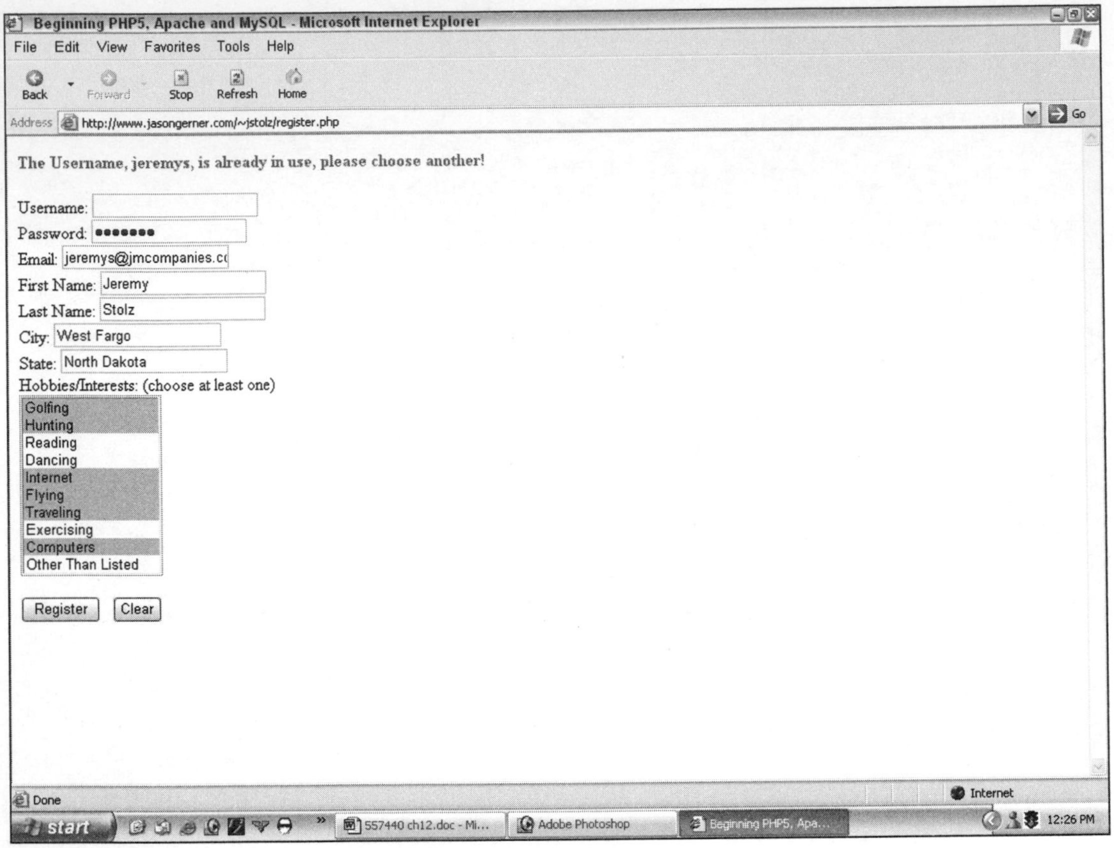

Figure 12-10

Now users can choose another username and complete the registration process. Once the user chooses a username that is *not* already taken, the registration is complete. Once the registration is complete, the user is automatically logged in for this session using the username and password as the session values, and he or she will be redirected to the home page. After being redirected, the user's screen should look similar to Figure 12-11.

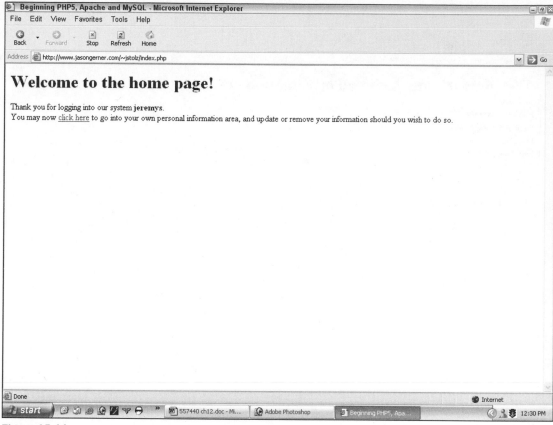

Figure 12-11

Now the logged-in users are able to navigate to their own personal information pages where they can update their information at any time and are also allowed to delete their account from this location.

The beauty of sessions and keeping track of users is that you don't have to worry about passing information about the users with form data, or passing it through the query string or address bar. All the data is stored temporarily on the server where the Web site resides. You also don't have to worry about people trying to put parameters into the address bar to fake the identity of another user. The session data is unavailable to users on the site, so only if they had access to the server itself would they be able to obtain the user-supplied data.

Now you will look at the pages where the user's information is displayed, and where a user can update or delete his or her account. The display page simply displays the previously entered user information. The update page is also straightforward: It shows a form with the user's previously entered data and gives the user the ability to update it if he or she wishes or simply cancel the update and return to the previous screen. The delete page merely asks if the user is sure he or she wants to delete the account and gives the option of returning to the previous screen. The user's information display page should look something like the one shown in Figure 12-12.

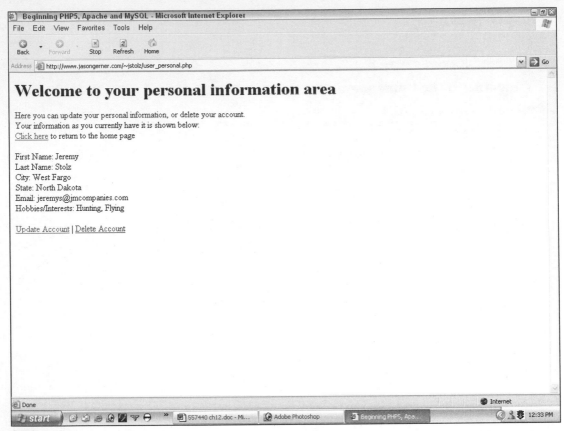

Figure 12-12

When users choose to update their accounts, they will see a screen similar to Figure 12-13.

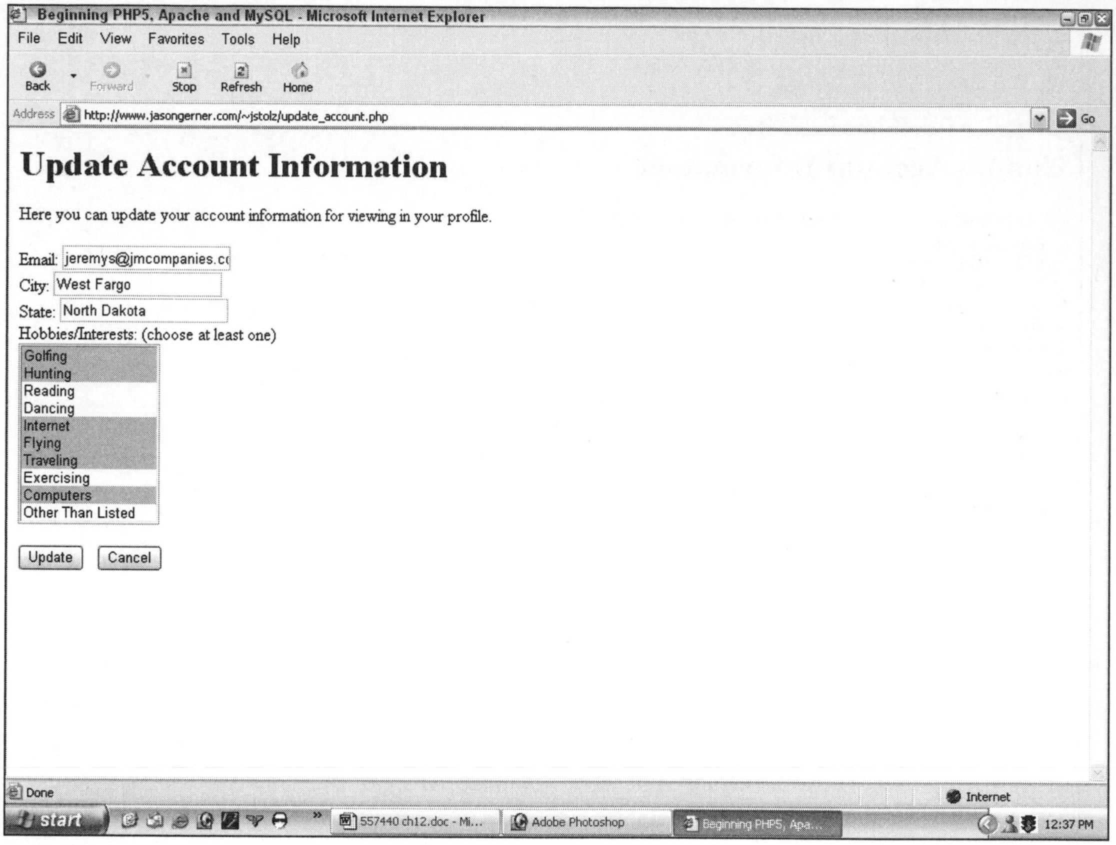

Figure 12-13

Should they update their information, users will be told that the information was indeed updated and they will be allowed to update the information again if they wish (for example, if on review they realize they input something incorrectly). That page will look like the one in Figure 12-14.

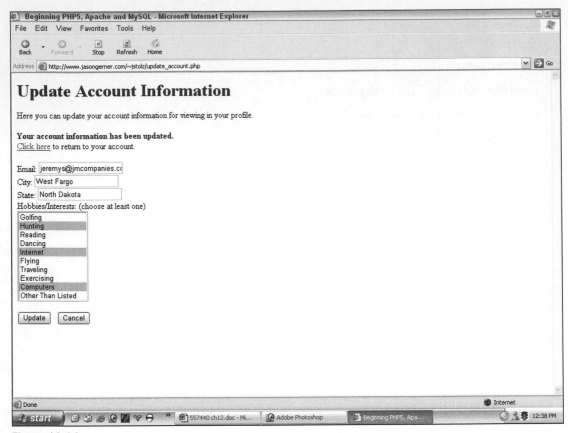

Figure 12-14

Finally, the delete page looks similar to the one shown in Figure 12-15. This appears once users choose the Delete Account link on the display page. From here, if users choose Yes, their account is deleted, their logged-in session will be destroyed, and they will be redirected to the index page.

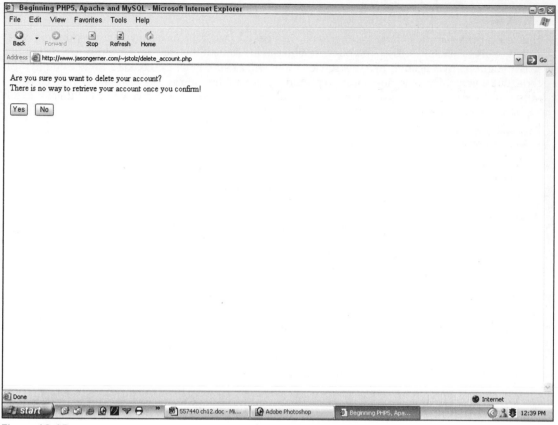

Figure 12-15

That's it for the user portion of the registration system. You'll create an administration section later in the chapter, where you can allow certain levels of admins to have different privileges from others. But now, let's move on to a quick cookie example, which you can implement into the previous registration system.

Using Cookies in PHP

Cookies are used much like sessions, as explained previously. The main difference between sessions and cookies is you can control the amount of time the cookie is available for, unlike sessions, which disappear when users close their browser.

Cookies are used to store information about a user's logins, preferences, or anything else you want to store there that you want to retrieve when a user revisits your site.

Try It Out   Cookie Tracking with PHP

Here's a quick example of how to use a cookie in a page to see if the users have a corresponding cookie stored on their machines. Then, if you want, you can implement this into your login system to allow persistent logins between single browser sessions. You will be supplying the cookie's value through the code, but if you were to implement it, you could replace all the code you've done so far with cookies rather than sessions. You'll use five small pages for this example. We will give you all of them and then explain how they work.

1. Create the first file, `setcookie.php`:

```
<html>
<head>
<title>Beginning PHP5, Apache and MySQL</title>
</head>
<body>
<h1>This is the Set Cookie Page</h1>
<p>
  <a href="setcookie_un.php">Click here</a> to set your cookies.
</p>
</body>
</html>
```

2. Create the second file, `setcookie_un.php`:

```
<?php
$username = "bp5am";
setcookie('username', $username, time() + 60 * 60 * 24 * 30);
// * sets cookie for 30 days *
header("Location: setcookie_pw.php");
?>
```

3. Create the third file, `setcookie_pw.php`:

```
<?php
$password = "bp5ampass";
setcookie('password', $password, time() + 60 * 60 * 24 * 30);
// * sets cookie for 30 days *
header("Location: cookies_set.php");
?>
```

4. Create the fourth file, `cookies_set.php`:

```
<html>
<head>
<title>Beginning PHP5, Apache and MySQL</title>
</head>
<body>
<h1>This is the Set Cookie Page</h1>
<p>
  Your cookies have been set.<br>
  <a href="testcookie.php">Click here</a> to test your cookies.
</p>
</body>
</html>
```

5. Finally, create the fifth file, `testcookie.php`:

```html
<html>
<head>
<title>Beginning PHP5, Apache and MySQL</title>
</head>
<body>
<h1>This is the Test Cookie Page</h1>
<p>
<?php
if ($_COOKIE['username'] == "" || $_COOKIE['password'] == "") {
?>
  No cookie was set.<br>
  <a href="setcookie.php">Click here</a> to set your cookie.
<?php
} else {
?>
  Your cookies were set:<br>
  Username cookie value: <b><?php echo $_COOKIE['username']; ?></b><br>
  Password cookie value: <b><?php echo $_COOKIE['password']; ?></b><br>
<?php
}
?>
</p>
</body>
</html>
```

How It Works

We ran through this cookie example to show you how you can keep persistent logins between single browser sessions. As you may have noticed, some of the pages are just display or navigation pages. For that reason, we won't explain those. We will focus instead on `setcookie_un.php`, `setcookie_pw.php`, and `testcookie.php`.

The `setcookie_un.php` page does just what the name says: It sets the cookie for the username, which is just hard-coded for this example. It then uses a header redirect to send you to the next page.

That next page is `setcookie_pw.php`, which does the same as `setcookie_un.php`, except that it is setting the cookie for the password. Then you're redirected to a simple display page that tells you your cookies have been set.

You can then navigate to `testcookie.php`. This page checks to see if the cookie values are valid. If they are not, it says "No cookies were set," and you can try to set the cookies again. If you are successful in your login, the screen will look like the one in Figure 12-16.

If you need to delete or end a cookie, simply run some code (such as the code that follows) to end the cookie from the user's browser.

```
setcookie('username', "", time() - 3600);
```

This sets the username cookie for one hour ago and sets the username value to an empty string, thereby making the username cookie unavailable to the Web site the user is logged into.

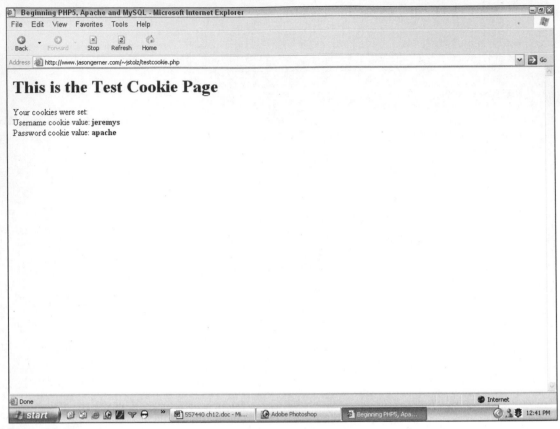

Figure 12-16

Now that you have some cookie knowledge, you can use it in the login system if you want. Although cookies are a good way to keep persistent logins between browser sessions, they can be altered or spoofed by a user because the cookie is stored on the client machine. That is generally why many systems house their main login information with sessions and use cookies as a subfeature only.

Administrator Registration

In this last portion of this chapter, you learn how logged-in admins can change information and delete information based on their access privileges. You may notice similarities between this system and the user login system, and you'd be right. Remember that the more you practice, the easier this will be when you are writing systems like this for your clients.

In this section, administrators are required to log in before they can view the users signed up in the user registration database. Once they are logged in, only certain privileged admins will be allowed to perform certain operations. For this example, admins with a privilege level of 1 are allowed to update user accounts and delete user accounts. Admins with a privilege level of 2 are allowed to update user information, but they will not be allowed to delete a user's account. This would be useful if a user was, for some reason, unable to log in to the site and the administrator needed to reset passwords, change usernames, and so on, but you don't want just any administrator to be allowed to do everything the main administrator does.

Try It Out   **Administration Section**

The code for all the pages follows. Key the pages in, and save them in a folder called `admin` in your Web directory. We will explain how they work in a bit.

1.   Create the first file, `conn.inc.php`:

```php
<?php
$conn = mysql_connect("localhost", "bp5am", "bp5ampass")
  or die(mysql_error());
$db = mysql_select_db("registration")
  or die(mysql_error());
?>
```

2.   Create the second file, `auth_admin.inc.php`:

```php
<?php
if ((isset($_SESSION['admin_logged']) &&
    $_SESSION['admin_logged']) != "" ||
  (isset($_SESSION['admin_password']) &&
    $_SESSION['admin_password'] != "")) {
//Do Nothing!
} else {
  $redirect = $_SERVER['PHP_SELF'];
  header("Refresh: 5; URL=admin_login.php?redirect=$redirect");
  echo "You are currently not logged in, we are redirecting you, " .
      "be patient!<br>";
  echo "(If your browser doesn't support this, " .
      "<a href=\"admin_login.php?redirect=$redirect\">click here</a>)";
  die();
}
?>
```

3.   Create the third file and save it as `index.php`:

```php
<?php
session_start();
if ((isset($_SESSION['admin_logged']) &&
    $_SESSION['admin_logged'] != "") ||
  (isset($_SESSION['admin_password']) &&
    $_SESSION['admin_password'] != "")) {
  include "logged_admin.php";
} else {
  include "unlogged_admin.php";
}
?>
```

4. Create the fourth file, `logged_admin.php`:

```
<html>
<head>
<title>Beginning PHP5, Apache and MySQL</title>
</head>
<body>
<h1>Welcome to the Admin Area!</h1>
<p>
  You are currently logged in.<br>
  <a href="admin_area.php">Click here</a>
  to access your administrator tools.
</p>
</body>
</html>
```

5. Create and save the fifth file as `unlogged_admin.php`:

```
<html>
<head>
<title>Beginning PHP5, Apache and MySQL</title>
</head>
<body>
<h1>Welcome to the Admin Area!</h1>
<p>
  You are currently not logged in.<br>
  Once logged in, you will have access to your administrator tools.<br>
  <a href="admin_login.php">Click here</a> to login.
</p>
</body>
</html>
```

6. Create the sixth file, `admin_login.php`:

```
<?php
session_start();
include "conn.inc.php";

if (isset($_POST['submit'])) {
  $query = "SELECT username, password, admin_level FROM admin " .
           "WHERE username = '" . $_POST['username'] . "' " .
           "AND password = (password('" . $_POST['password'] . "'))";
  $result = mysql_query($query)
    or die(mysql_error());

  $row = mysql_fetch_array($result);

  if (mysql_num_rows($result) == 1) {
    $_SESSION['admin_logged'] = $_POST['username'];
    $_SESSION['admin_password'] = $_POST['password'];
    $_SESSION['admin_level'] = $row['admin_level'];
    header ("Refresh: 5; URL=" . $_POST['redirect'] . "");
    echo "You are being redirected to your original page request!<br>";
    echo "(If your browser doesn't support this, " .
         "<a href=\"" . $_POST['redirect']. "\">click here</a>)";
  } else {
```

```
?>
<html>
<head>
<title>Beginning PHP5, Apache and MySQL</title>
</head>
<body>
<p>
  Invalid Username and/or Password<br>
  <form action="admin_login.php" method="post">
    <input type="hidden" name="redirect"
      value="<?php echo $_POST['redirect']; ?>">
    Username: <input type="text" name="username"><br>
    Password: <input type="password" name="password"><br><br>
    <input type="submit" name="submit" value="Login">
  </form>
</p>
</body>
</html>
<?php
  }
} else {
  if (isset($_GET['redirect'])) {
    $redirect = $_GET['redirect'];
  } else {
    $redirect = "index.php";
  }
?>
<html>
<head>
<title>Beginning PHP5, Apache and MySQL</title>
</head>
<body>
<p>
  Login below by supplying your username/password...<br>
  <form action="admin_login.php" method="post">
    <input type="hidden" name="redirect"
      value="<?php echo $redirect; ?>">
    Username: <input type="text" name="username"><br>
    Password: <input type="password" name="password"><br><br>
    <input type="submit" name="submit" value="Login">
  </form>
</p>
</body>
</html>
<?php
}
?>
```

7. Create the seventh file and save it as `admin_area.php`:

```
<?php
session_start();
include "auth_admin.inc.php";
include "conn.inc.php";
?>
```

```
<html>
<head>
<title>Beginning PHP5, Apache and MySQL</title>
</head>
<body>
<h1>Admin Area</h1>
<p>
  Below is a list of users and your available administrator
  privileges.<br><br>
<?php
if (isset($_SESSION['admin_level']) &&
    $_SESSION['admin_level'] != "1") {
  $query = "SELECT first_name, last_name, id FROM user_info " .
           "ORDER BY last_name";
  $result = mysql_query($query)
    or die(mysql_error());

  while ($row = mysql_fetch_array($result)) {
    echo $row['first_name'] . " " . $row['last_name'];
?>
    <a href="update_user.php?id=<?php
    echo $row['id']; ?>">Update User</a><br>
<?php
  }
} else {
  $query = "SELECT first_name, last_name, id FROM user_info " .
           "ORDER BY last_name";
  $result = mysql_query($query)
    or die(mysql_error());

  while ($row = mysql_fetch_array($result)) {
    echo $row['first_name'] . " " . $row['last_name'];
?>
    <a href="update_user.php?id=<?php
    echo $row['id']; ?>">Update User</a> |
  <a href="delete_user.php?id=<?php echo $row['id'];?>">Delete User</a><br>
<?php
  }
}
?>
</body>
</html>
```

8. Create the eighth file, `update_user.php`:

```
<?php
session_start();
include "auth_admin.inc.php";
include "conn.inc.php";
?>
<html>
<head>
<title>Beginning PHP5, Apache and MySQL</title>
</head>
<body>
```

```php
<h1>Update User Information</h1>
<p>
<?php
if (isset($_POST['submit']) && $_POST['submit'] == "Update") {
  $query_update = "UPDATE user_info SET username = '" .
                  $_POST['username'] . "', password = (PASSWORD('" .
                  $_POST['password'] . "')), first_name = '" .
                  $_POST['first_name'] . "', last_name = '" .
                  $_POST['last_name'] . "', email = '" .
                  $_POST['email'] . "', city = '" .
                  $_POST['city'] . "', state = '" .
                  $_POST['state'] . "', hobbies = '" .
                  implode(", ", $_POST['hobbies']) . "' " .
                  "WHERE id = '" . $_POST['id'] . "'";
  $result_update = mysql_query($query_update)
    or die(mysql_error());

  $query = "SELECT * FROM user_info WHERE id = '" . $_POST['id'] . "'";
  $result = mysql_query($query)
    or die(mysql_error());

  $row = mysql_fetch_array($result);
  $hobbies = explode(", ", $row['hobbies'])
?>
  <b>User information has been updated.</b><br>
  <a href="admin_area.php">Click here</a> to return to the admin area.
  <form action="update_user.php" method="post">
    <input type="hidden" name="id" value="<?php echo $_POST['id']; ?>">
    Username: <input type="text" name="username"
              value="<?php echo $row['username']; ?>"><br>
    Password: <input type="password" name="password"
              value=""> Not displayed<br>
    First Name: <input type="text" name="first_name"
                value="<?php echo $row['first_name']; ?>"><br>
    Last Name: <input type="text" name="last_name"
               value="<?php echo $row['last_name']; ?>"><br>
    Email: <input type="text" name="email"
           value="<?php echo $row['email']; ?>"><br>
    City: <input type="text" name="city"
          value="<?php echo $row['city']; ?>"><br>
    State: <input type="text" name="state"
           value="<?php echo $row['state'];?>"><br>
    Hobbies/Interests: (choose at least one)<br>
    <select name="hobbies[]" size="10" multiple>
      <option value="Golfing"<?php
        if (in_array("Golfing", $hobbies)) {
          echo " selected";
        } ?>>Golfing</option>
      <option value="Hunting"<?php
        if (in_array("Hunting", $hobbies)) {
          echo " selected";
        } ?>>Hunting</option>
      <option value="Reading"<?php
        if (in_array("Reading", $hobbies)) {
          echo " selected";
```

```
      } ?>>Reading</option>
    <option value="Dancing"<?php
      if (in_array("Dancing", $hobbies)) {
        echo " selected";
      } ?>>Dancing</option>
    <option value="Internet"<?php
      if (in_array("Internet", $hobbies)) {
        echo " selected";
      } ?>>Internet</option>
    <option value="Flying"<?php
      if (in_array("Flying", $hobbies)) {
        echo " selected";
      } ?>>Flying</option>
    <option value="Traveling"<?php
      if (in_array("Traveling", $hobbies)) {
        echo " selected";
      } ?>>Traveling</option>
    <option value="Exercising"<?php
      if (in_array("Exercising", $hobbies)) {
        echo " selected";
      } ?>>Exercising</option>
    <option value="Computers"<?php
      if (in_array("Computers", $hobbies)) {
        echo " selected";
      } ?>>Computers</option>
    <option value="Other Than Listed"<?php
      if (in_array("Other Than Listed", $hobbies)) {
        echo " selected";
      } ?>>Other Than Listed</option>
  </select><br><br>
  <input type="submit" name="submit" value="Update">
</form>
<?php
} else {
  $query = "SELECT * FROM user_info WHERE id = '" . $_GET['id'] . "'";
  $result = mysql_query($query)
    or die(mysql_error());

  $row = mysql_fetch_array($result);
  $hobbies = explode(", ", $row['hobbies'])
?>
  <form action="update_user.php" method="post">
    <input type="hidden" name="id" value="<?php echo $_GET['id']; ?>">
    Username: <input type="text" name="username"
              value="<?php echo $row['username']; ?>"><br>
    Password: <input type="password" name="password"
              value=""> Not displayed<br>
    First Name: <input type="text" name="first_name"
                value="<?php echo $row['first_name']; ?>"><br>
    Last Name: <input type="text" name="last_name"
                value="<?php echo $row['last_name']; ?>"><br>
    Email: <input type="text" name="email"
            value="<?php echo $row['email']; ?>"><br>
    City: <input type="text" name="city"
            value="<?php echo $row['city']; ?>"><br>
```

```
      State: <input type="text" name="state"
             value="<?php echo $row['state']; ?>"><br>
      Hobbies/Interests: (choose at least one)<br>
      <select name="hobbies[]" size="10" multiple>
        <option value="Golfing"<?php
          if (in_array("Golfing", $hobbies)) {
            echo " selected";
          } ?>>Golfing</option>
        <option value="Hunting"<?php
          if (in_array("Hunting", $hobbies)) {
            echo " selected";
          } ?>>Hunting</option>
        <option value="Reading"<?php
          if (in_array("Reading", $hobbies)) {
            echo " selected";
          } ?>>Reading</option>
        <option value="Dancing"<?php
          if (in_array("Dancing", $hobbies)) {
            echo " selected";
          } ?>>Dancing</option>
        <option value="Internet"<?php
          if (in_array("Internet", $hobbies)) {
            echo " selected";
          } ?>>Internet</option>
        <option value="Flying"<?php
          if (in_array("Flying", $hobbies)) {
            echo " selected";
          } ?>>Flying</option>
        <option value="Traveling"<?php
          if (in_array("Traveling", $hobbies)) {
            echo " selected";
          } ?>>Traveling</option>
        <option value="Exercising"<?php
          if (in_array("Exercising", $hobbies)) {
            echo " selected";
          } ?>>Exercising</option>
        <option value="Computers"<?php
          if (in_array("Computers", $hobbies)) {
            echo " selected";
          } ?>>Computers</option>
        <option value="Other Than Listed"<?php
          if (in_array("Other Than Listed", $hobbies)) {
            echo " selected";
          } ?>>Other Than Listed</option>
      </select><br><br>
      <input type="submit" name="submit" value="Update">  
      <input type="button" value="Cancel" onclick="history.go(-1);">
    </form>
<?php
}
?>
</p>
</body>
</html>
```

9. Finally, create the ninth file, `delete_user.php`:

```php
<?php
session_start();
include "auth_admin.inc.php";
include "conn.inc.php";
if ($_SESSION['admin_level'] == "1") {
  if (isset($_POST['submit']) && $_POST['submit'] == "Yes") {
    $query_delete = "DELETE FROM user_info " .
                    "WHERE id = '" . $_POST['id'] . "'";
    $result_delete = mysql_query($query_delete)
      or die(mysql_error());

    $_SESSION['user_logged'] = "";
    $_SESSION['user_password'] = "";

    header("Refresh: 5; URL=admin_area.php");
    echo "Account has been deleted! " .
        "You are being sent to the admin area!<br>";
    echo "(If you're browser doesn't support this, " .
        "<a href=\"admin_area.php\">click here</a>)";
    die();
  } else {
?>
<html>
<head>
<title>Beginning PHP5, Apache and MySQL</title>
</head>
<body>
<h1>Admin Area</h1>
<p>
  Are you sure you want to delete this user's account?<br>
  There is no way to retrieve your account once you confirm!<br>
  <form action="delete_user.php" method="post">
    <input type="hidden" name="id" value="<?php echo $_GET['id']; ?>">
    <input type="submit" name="submit" value="Yes">  
    <input type="button" value=" No " onclick="history.go(-1);">
  </form>
</p>
</body>
</html>
<?php
  }
} else {
?>
  You don't have a high enough privilege to delete a user.<br>
  <a href="admin_area.php">Click here</a> to go back.
<?php
}
?>
```

How It Works

This whole section is merely a rework of the user section built specifically for administrators only. The pages work the same, the sessions are used in the exact same manner, and all in all, it acts and works the same.

Now we'll explain how a typical run through with an admin (we'll call him Joe) works. Some of the pages you keyed in don't really need explaining since they are very similar in the user's section, so we won't discuss those.

When your administrator goes to the admin area, Joe is told whether or not he is logged in. If he is, he can go to his personal administration area where he is able to do whatever he is allowed to do.

The authorization is the same as the previous exercise so you can refer to previous figures for examples of how those pages look. We will show you what screens look like when administrators with different levels log in and go to the admin area.

You keyed in all the code needed to do every aspect of the admin section, but this functionality is very similar to the update and delete aspects of the user section so we won't cover those.

When an admin with a privilege level of 2 logs in, the screen should look like the one in Figure 12-17.

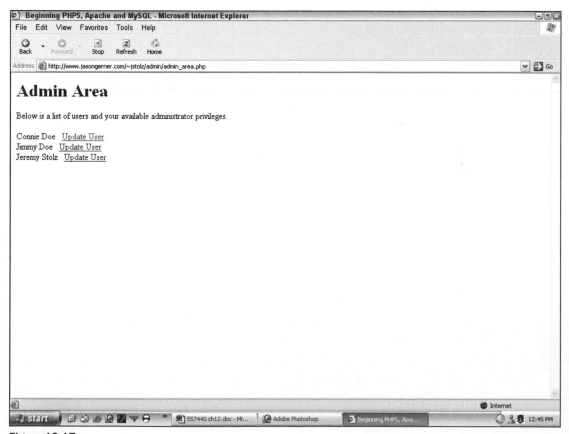

Figure 12-17

Now notice in Figure 12-17 that the admin logged in here is able to update the user but is not allowed to delete the user because you did a check with the first `if` statement to see what the admin's level is. Should Joe log in with a level of 1, he would see something similar to Figure 12-18.

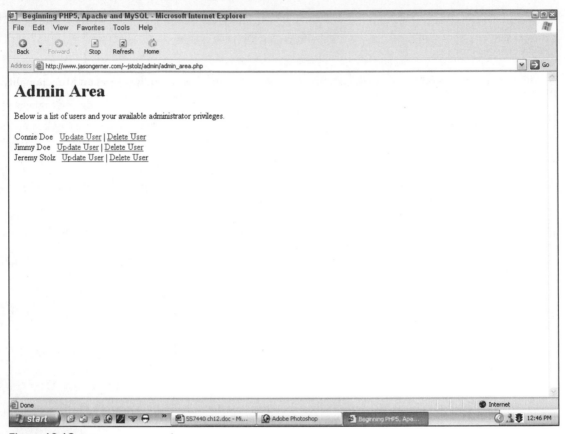

Figure 12-18

Depending on what link he chooses and whether he has a high enough admin level, the admin will be able to update or delete the user's account. To guard against an admin of lower level trying to navigate to the delete page and supply a user ID through the query string, you inserted this line of code:

```
if ($_SESSION['admin_level'] == "1")
```

This checks the admin level and notifies the admin that he or she doesn't have privileges to delete a user's account. You then provide a link back to the admin area.

Now that you have learned how to use database-driven information with an administration section, you should be on your way to creating login systems for your own personal site or for your clients.

Summary

By now, you have a good understanding of the power of PHP and its session and cookie functions, along with MySQL and database-driven information. With these two powerful programs, along with Apache, you have some great tools to further your Web development skills. Just think about the possibilities you can explore with all you learned in this chapter:

❑ You can restrict access to files/directories via htaccess.

❑ You can use PHP to accomplish the same as htaccess but with more control and functionality.

❑ You can store user and admin information in a database to utilize database-driven logins.

❑ You can create a registration system for users to sign up with the required and optional fields.

❑ You can use cookies to retain login information between sessions.

❑ You can create a navigation system dependent on whether or not a user has logged in.

Exercises

Use these exercises to sharpen your PHP session and cookie handling skills.

1. Create a "hidden" area that is only displayed to users that are logged in to your system.

2. Use cookies to retain some information for 30 minutes, dependent on logged users.

3. Create a system where certain users only have certain options, dependent on their user level.

13

Building a Content Management System

Whatever the reason, people these days seem to get bored easily. One of your jobs as the Web site administrator is not only to figure out how to get as many people to visit your site as possible, but how to keep them there and keep them coming *back*.

You can focus on many things to get the masses to your site, such as word of mouth, advertising, and search engines. To keep your users at your site, the experts give plenty of hints, such as making your site easy to navigate, making sure your pages load quickly, and giving users a personal experience. Getting your users to return, however, is how you keep your site going over time.

Getting Your Users to Return

Take a moment to think about all the sites you return to. You know . . . the ones you have saved in your bookmark list in your browser. With the exception of sites you have to visit, such as those in the "research" folder, what do most of those sites have in common?

Most likely, each site periodically has new information. You might visit a news site each day or look up the weather in your area. Perhaps you are interested in your daily horoscope, or maybe you belong to an online message board and would like to read new posts. In each case, the content gets updated on a regular basis — sometimes daily, sometimes weekly, and sometimes even hourly. Can you imagine how much work the Web site developers must have to do to update the content every day?

Content

No matter what the subject of your Web site is, it probably contains lots of content — news, images, user comments, and more. You don't want to have to maintain all that content, do you? It would be very nice to offload some of that work to others.

In fact, all a Web site developer should ever have to do is maintain the site design itself (update some HTML, change a background color, fix a bug in the PHP code, for example). The content should be completely separate from the design of the site, and should be maintained by other people. Because the content is separate from the design, those content people don't have to know anything about Web site design! But once you have your content separated, you need to figure out how to manage it.

Management

Assuming you have a lot of content, entering it into your site will most likely take a lot of work. What you need to do is come up with a way to organize it, categorize it, and push the content to your Web site. You will need a number of people, each assigned a certain role, working together to create the content and mold it into the appropriate form for presentation on the Web site. Of course, you want this process to be efficient, and you definitely need to have the appropriate tools to do the job.

System

Chapter 10 showed you how to create your own databases and tables and how to create Web pages used to insert, delete, update, and retrieve the information in those tables. In Chapter 12, you learned how to authenticate and recognize your users by making them log in to your Web site. Armed with this knowledge, you could create a system of Web pages designed to allow users to create new content (authors), edit that content (editors), and publish it. By assigning users to certain roles, you can manage who has access to certain functions within the site.

Putting It All Together

So, it seems that you need a group of Web site pages and tables, and an organized set of rules, that will give you the means to gather information, format it, and present it to the world for its enjoyment. In other words, you need a *system* in place to allow you to *manage* your Web site *content* (separately from the site design).

You need a Content Management System (or CMS, as we'll refer to it from now on).

There are many degrees of content management. On some sites, this might simply refer to a message board, where users sign up to post messages to each other about their favorite color of lint. Another site might have reporters in the field writing news stories and sending them in to be published online. Yet another site might not only allow users to update content, but will allow administrators to change the layout of the site, including colors and images.

As you have no doubt figured out, the term *CMS* refers not only to the application used to enter content, but to the people responsible for entering content, and to the rules they must follow. Without proper rules, and without the people to make it happen, no CMS application in the world is going to help you.

It's up to you to find the people. We'll help you establish the rules. Are you ready? Good, let's get started.

The CMS application you are going to build will allow registered users to post articles. Those articles will be labeled "pending" until a user with the proper permissions publishes the article. Once it's published, it will show up as the newest article on the home page. Unregistered users will be able to read articles but will not be able to post new ones.

Registered users will also be able to post comments about an article. When a visitor views a full article, all comments will be displayed below it. Sound simple? You're going to do it with about 20 PHP pages. That may sound like a lot, but it's fairly typical of a standard Web application such as this. There are pages for display (index, admin, pending articles, article review, and so on), editing (compose, user account, control panel), and transaction files (for users and articles). There are also some files used as includes (such as header and footer). Don't worry — some are only a few lines long. The whole application contains around 1,000 lines of code, which is pretty short by many application standards.

Preparing the Database

As mentioned, you'll have around 20 PHP pages. Enter each of these files in your favorite PHP editor, and save them with the given filename. We're going to give you the filename of each one, and introductions whenever necessary. Make sure all files are saved in the same directory on your Web server.

The first thing you're going to do is create a database connection script, and then use that script to create your initial database structure. Let's do some coding.

Try It Out   **Creating the Database Structure**

1.   The first file is conn.php. This file will go at the top of each page in the application where you need to connect to the database.

Be sure to enter in your own host, username, password, and database. (If you don't have a database created yet, you'll need to create one first. Chapter 10 helps you with that if you need it.)

```php
<?php

define('SQL_HOST','localhost');
define('SQL_USER','bp5am');
define('SQL_PASS','bp5ampass');
define('SQL_DB','comicsite');

$conn = mysql_connect(SQL_HOST, SQL_USER, SQL_PASS)
   or die('Could not connect to the database; ' . mysql_error());

mysql_select_db(SQL_DB, $conn)
   or die('Could not select database; ' . mysql_error());

?>
```

2.   Now you need to create your database tables. You can do this on your MySQL server, or you can simply use the following file, named cmstables.php. It will create your tables, as well as insert your first user so that you can begin administering the site immediately.

```php
<?php
require_once 'conn.php';

$sql = <<<EOS
CREATE TABLE IF NOT EXISTS cms_access_levels (
  access_lvl tinyint(4) NOT NULL auto_increment,
  access_name varchar(50) NOT NULL default '',
  PRIMARY KEY (access_lvl)
```

```
)
EOS;
$result = mysql_query($sql)
  or die(mysql_error());

$sql = "INSERT IGNORE INTO cms_access_levels " .
       "VALUES (1,'User'), " .
       "(2,'Moderator'), " .
       "(3,'Administrator')";
$result = mysql_query($sql)
  or die(mysql_error());

$sql = <<<EOS
CREATE TABLE IF NOT EXISTS cms_articles (
  article_id int(11) NOT NULL auto_increment,
  author_id int(11) NOT NULL default '0',
  is_published tinyint(1) NOT NULL default '0',
  date_submitted datetime NOT NULL default '0000-00-00 00:00:00',
  date_published datetime NOT NULL default '0000-00-00 00:00:00',
  title varchar(255) NOT NULL default '',
  body mediumtext NOT NULL,
  PRIMARY KEY (article_id),
  KEY IdxArticle (author_id,date_submitted),
  FULLTEXT KEY IdxText (title,body)
)
EOS;
$result = mysql_query($sql)
  or die(mysql_error());

$sql = <<<EOS
CREATE TABLE IF NOT EXISTS cms_comments (
  comment_id int(11) NOT NULL auto_increment,
  article_id int(11) NOT NULL default '0',
  comment_date datetime NOT NULL default '0000-00-00 00:00:00',
  comment_user int(11) NOT NULL default '0',
  comment text NOT NULL,
  PRIMARY KEY (comment_id),
  KEY IdxComment (article_id)
)
EOS;
$result = mysql_query($sql)
  or die(mysql_error());

$sql = <<<EOS
CREATE TABLE IF NOT EXISTS cms_users (
  user_id int(11) NOT NULL auto_increment,
  email varchar(255) NOT NULL default '',
  passwd varchar(50) NOT NULL default '',
  name varchar(100) NOT NULL default '',
  access_lvl tinyint(4) NOT NULL default '1',
  PRIMARY KEY (user_id),
  UNIQUE KEY uniq_email (email)
)
EOS;
$result = mysql_query($sql)
  or die(mysql_error());
```

```
$adminemail = "admin@yoursite.com";
$adminpass = "admin";
$adminname = "Admin";

$sql = "INSERT IGNORE INTO cms_users " .
       "VALUES (NULL, '$adminemail', '$adminpass', '$adminname', 3)";
$result = mysql_query($sql)
  or die(mysql_error());

echo "<html><head><title>CMS Tables Created</title></head><body>";
echo "CMS Tables created. Here is your initial login information:\n";
echo "<ul><li><strong>login</strong>: " . $adminemail . "</li>\n";
echo "<li><strong>password</strong>: " . $adminpass . "</li></ul>\n";
echo "<a href=\"login.php\">Login</a> to the site now.";
echo "</body></html>"
?>
```

3. If you have not already done so, load `cmstables.php` in your browser. If it runs with no errors, you should see a screen similar to Figure 13-1. It will look a little different, of course, if you used your own e-mail and password values.

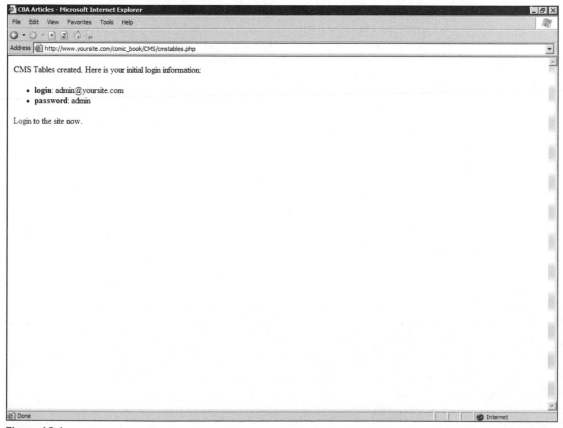

Figure 13-1

Once you have run the file, we recommend that you immediately remove it from your server. You don't want anyone getting hold of your password. We also recommend that you change your password immediately.

How It Works

Your first step in creating this application is to connect to the database. Most of your pages will require this connection, so putting it in a separate included file is the best solution. The code in `conn.php` simply defines the constants, connects to the server, and then selects the database to be used. If you are using more than one database, then you simply need to change the `mysql_select_db` command to access the appropriate database before running any SQL commands.

Take a look inside `cmstables.php`. First, you connect to the database.

```
require_once 'conn.php';
```

Next, you create the table needed for access levels. All of the fields, their datatypes, and other parameters are defined in this SQL statement. You use `IF NOT EXISTS` so that the `CREATE` command does nothing if the table already exists. If you wanted `CMStables.php` to always create a new, clean version of the app, then you could remove the `IF NOT EXISTS` and run the SQL command `DROP TABLE tablename` before re-creating the table.

```
$sql = <<<EOS
CREATE TABLE IF NOT EXISTS cms_access_levels (
   access_lvl tinyint(4) NOT NULL auto_increment,
   access_name varchar(50) NOT NULL default '',
   PRIMARY KEY (access_lvl)
)
EOS;
$result = mysql_query($sql)
   or die(mysql_error());
```

The next lines insert data into your newly created `cms_access_levels` table. These access levels are used throughout the CMS application to determine what different users have access to.

```
$sql = "INSERT IGNORE INTO cms_access_levels " .
       "VALUES (1,'User'), " .
       "(2,'Moderator'), " .
       "(3,'Administrator')";
$result = mysql_query($sql)
   or die(mysql_error());
```

We won't include every SQL statement from `CMStables.php`. If you are knowledgeable enough to read this book, then you can figure out the rest of the SQL commands. However, we are showing you the following command to illustrate the use of keys:

```
$sql = <<<EOS
CREATE TABLE IF NOT EXISTS cms_articles (
   article_id int(11) NOT NULL auto_increment,
   author_id int(11) NOT NULL default '0',
```

```
    is_published tinyint(1) NOT NULL default '0',
    date_submitted datetime NOT NULL default '0000-00-00 00:00:00',
    date_published datetime NOT NULL default '0000-00-00 00:00:00',
    title varchar(255) NOT NULL default '',
    body mediumtext NOT NULL,
    PRIMARY KEY (article_id),
    KEY IdxArticle (author_id,date_submitted),
    FULLTEXT KEY IdxText (title,body)
)
EOS;
$result = mysql_query($sql)
  or die(mysql_error());
```

The PRIMARY KEY, you may remember from Chapter 10, is what ensures that each row is unique because it is the unique identifier for each row in the table.

The keyword KEY is similar to PRIMARY KEY, and in fact can be substituted for PRIMARY KEY in most cases. In this particular case, KEY is used as a synonym for INDEX, which allows subsequent SQL statements to find data very quickly. Because you will be looking for articles by author and by date, those are the fields used to create the index.

> For more information on how MySQL uses indexes, visit
> dev.mysql.com/doc/mysql/en/MySQL_indexes.html.

You also allow users of the CMS application to search for articles based on text entered in a search string. To perform such a search (which you allow for the title and body fields), you use the FULLTEXT KEY keyword when creating your table. This is identical to using FULLTEXT INDEX.

When creating the cms_users table, you use the previous keywords to create both PRIMARY KEY to uniquely identify table rows, and UNIQUE KEY to ensure that each user's e-mail address is unique.

```
    PRIMARY KEY (user_id),
    UNIQUE KEY uniq_email (email)
```

After creating the cms_users table, you insert one record so that the administrator is able to log in with Admin permissions. This allows you to immediately administer the site as needed. This data is echoed to the screen to provide you with some feedback that everything has worked as you expected.

```
$sql = "INSERT IGNORE INTO cms_users " .
       "VALUES (NULL, '$adminemail', '$adminpass', '$adminname', 3)";
$result = mysql_query($sql)
  or die(mysql_error());

echo "<html><head><title>CMS Tables Created</title></head><body>";
echo "CMS Tables created. Here is your initial login information:\n";
echo "<ul><li><strong>login</strong>: " . $adminemail . "</li>\n";
echo "<li><strong>password</strong>: " . $adminpass . "</li></ul>\n";
echo "<a href=\"login.php\">Login</a> to the site now.";
```

Coding for Reusability

To save time and effort, most seasoned programmers will notice oft-repeated bits of code in their applications and store said code in small libraries. When the code is needed, it is included or referenced in the dependent files, instead of forcing the programmer to retype the same code over and over in each file.

In your CMS application, some core functions are used on many different pages. It would make the most sense to include those functions in a single file and include it at the top of each appropriate page.

Try It Out   Creating Reusable Scripts

1. Enter the following code, and save it as `outputfunctions.php`. This file is going to contain functions to generate different page elements throughout the CMS.

```php
<?php

function trimBody($theText, $lmt=500, $s_chr="\n", $s_cnt=2) {
  $pos = 0;
  $trimmed = FALSE;
  for ($i = 1; $i <= $s_cnt; $i++) {
    if ($tmp = strpos($theText, $s_chr, $pos+1)) {
      $pos = $tmp;
      $trimmed = TRUE;
    } else {
      $pos = strlen($theText) - 1;
      $trimmed = FALSE;
      break;
    }
  }
  $theText = substr($theText, 0, $pos);

  if (strlen($theText) > $lmt) {
    $theText = substr($theText, 0, $lmt);
    $theText = substr($theText, 0, strrpos($theText,' '));
    $trimmed = TRUE;
  }
  if ($trimmed) $theText .= '...';
  return $theText;
}

function outputStory($article, $only_snippet=FALSE) {
  global $conn;

  if ($article) {
    $sql = "SELECT ar.*, usr.name " .
           "FROM cms_articles ar " .
           "LEFT OUTER JOIN cms_users usr " .
           "ON ar.author_id = usr.user_id " .
           "WHERE ar.article_id = " . $article;
    $result = mysql_query($sql,$conn);

    if ($row = mysql_fetch_array($result)) {
      echo "<h3>" . htmlspecialchars($row['title']) . "</h3>\n";
```

```php
      echo "<h5><div class=\"byline\">By: " .
           htmlspecialchars($row['name']) .
           "</div>";
      echo "<div class=\"pubdate\">";
      if ($row['is_published'] == 1) {
        echo date("F j, Y",strtotime($row['date_published']));
      } else {
        echo "not yet published";
      }
      echo "</div></h5>\n";
      if ($only_snippet) {
        echo "<p>\n";
        echo nl2br(htmlspecialchars(trimBody($row['body'])));
        echo "</p>\n";
        echo "<h4><a href=\"viewarticle.php?article=" .
             $row['article_id'] . "\">Full Story...</a></h4><br>\n";
      } else {
        echo "<p>\n";
        echo nl2br(htmlspecialchars($row['body']));
        echo "</p>\n";
      }
    }
  }
}

function showComments($article, $showLink=TRUE) {
  global $conn;
  if ($article) {
    $sql = "SELECT is_published " .
           "FROM cms_articles " .
           "WHERE article_id=" . $article;
    $result = mysql_query($sql,$conn)
      or die('Could not look up comments; ' . mysql_error());

    $row = mysql_fetch_array($result);
    $is_published = $row['is_published'];

    $sql = "SELECT co.*, usr.name, usr.email " .
           "FROM cms_comments co " .
           "LEFT OUTER JOIN cms_users usr " .
           "ON co.comment_user = usr.user_id " .
           "WHERE co.article_id=" . $article .
           " ORDER BY co.comment_date DESC";
    $result = mysql_query($sql, $conn)
      or die('Could not look up comments; ' . mysql_error());

    if ($showLink) {
      echo "<h4>" . mysql_num_rows($result) . " Comments";
      if (isset($_SESSION['user_id']) and $is_published) {
        echo " / <a href=\"comment.php?article=" . $_GET['article'] .
             "\">Add one</a>";
      }
      echo "</h4>\n";
    }
```

423

```
      if (mysql_num_rows($result)) {
        echo "<div class=\"scroller\">\n";
        while ($row = mysql_fetch_array($result)) {
          echo "<span class=\"commentName\">" .
               htmlspecialchars($row['name']) .
               "</span><span class=\"commentDate\"> (" .
               date("l F j, Y H:i", strtotime($row['comment_date'])) .
               ")</span>\n";
          echo "<p class=\"commentText\">\n" .
               nl2br(htmlspecialchars($row['comment'])) .
               "\n</p>\n";
        }
        echo "</div>\n";
      }
      echo "<br>\n";
    }
}
?>
```

2.   Three more files are included in various pages, header.php and footer.php, which do what they imply, and also http.php, which is used to redirect the user. You'll enter those next.

Enter this code and save it as header.php:

```
<?php session_start(); ?>
<html>
<head>
<title>CMS</title>
</head>
<body>
<div id="logobar">
  <div id="logoblob">
    <h1>Comic Book Appreciation</h1>
  </div>
<?php
if (isset($_SESSION['name'])) {
  echo ' <div id="logowelcome">';
  echo '  Currently logged in as: ' . $_SESSION['name'];
  echo ' </div>';
}
?>

</div>
<div id="navright">
  <form method="get" action="search.php">
  <p class="head">Search</p>
  <p>
    <input id="searchkeywords" type="text" name="keywords"
<?php
if (isset($_GET['keywords'])) {
  echo ' value="' . htmlspecialchars($_GET['keywords']) . '" ';
}
?>
```

```
      >
      <input id="searchbutton" class="submit" type="submit"
        value="Search">
    </p>
    </form>
  </div>
<div id="maincolumn">
  <div id='navigation'>
<?php
echo '<a href="index.php">Articles</a>';
if (!isset($_SESSION['user_id'])) {
  echo ' | <a href="login.php">Login</a>';
} else {
  echo ' | <a href="compose.php">Compose</a>';

  if ($_SESSION['access_lvl'] > 1) {
    echo ' | <a href="pending.php">Review</a>';
  }

  if ($_SESSION['access_lvl'] > 2) {
    echo ' | <a href="admin.php">Admin</a>';
  }
  echo ' | <a href="cpanel.php">Control Panel</a>';
  echo ' | <a href="transact-user.php?action=Logout">Logout</a>';
}
?>
  </div>
  <div id="articles">
```

3.   And now enter `footer.php`. (This one's a toughie. You might want to take a break first.)

```
  </div>
</div>
</body>
</html>
```

4.   Now another big one, `http.php`. This one is used for redirections:

```php
<?php
function redirect($url) {
  if (!headers_sent()) {
    header('Location: http://' . $_SERVER['HTTP_HOST'] .
        dirname($_SERVER['PHP_SELF']) . '/' . $url);
  } else {
    die('Could not redirect; Headers already sent (output).');
  }
}
?>
```

How It Works

Many of the pages require output functions that can be used over and over again. Because of this, you will include these reusable functions in the `outputfunctions.php` file.

outputfunctions.php

```
function trimBody($theText, $lmt=500, $s_chr="\n", $s_cnt=2) {
```

The function `trimBody()` will take a text input and return a shortened (trimmed) version for display on a page. If an article is very long, you might want to show only the first couple of sentences, or only the first paragraph. If the article is trimmed, you should end the trimmed text with ellipses (. . .).

The first parameter, `$theText`, is the text you want trimmed. The second parameter (`$lmt`) is the absolute longest text string you want returned, expressed in number of characters. The default value, if none is supplied, is 500 characters. The third parameter (`$s_chr`) is the "stop character." You will trim the document to this character. The default value is a newline (`\n`). The last parameter is `$s_cnt`, or "stop count." Given the stop character (in this case `\n`), you will trim after you reach the number designated by `$s_cnt`. In this case you default to 2, so you will trim the text after the second newline character.

You must first initialize the variables. The variable `$pos` keeps track of the current position of the character you are examining. The variable `$trimmed` tells you whether or not the text has been trimmed.

```
$pos = 0;
$trimmed = FALSE;
```

You then loop through the text `$s_cnt` times. If you find the character within the text on the last cycle through, then `$trimmed` will be true, and `$theText` will be trimmed to that character. If not, `$trimmed` will be false, and `$theText` will contain the full text string. (This might happen if you were trimming the string to the third newline and it was only two paragraphs long, for example.)

```
for ($i = 1; $i <= $s_cnt; $i++)
  if ($tmp = strpos($theText, $s_chr, $pos+1)) {
    $pos = $tmp;
    $trimmed = TRUE;
  } else {
    $pos = strlen($theText) - 1;
    $trimmed = FALSE;
    break;
  }
}
$theText = substr($theText, 0, $pos);
```

If the returned string is now longer than your limit, you trim it to the exact length of the limit.

```
if (strlen($theText) > $lmt)
  $theText = substr($theText, 0, $lmt);
```

After doing this, you might have cut off part of a word. In the interest of keeping your trimmed text clean, you trim back to the last space, and then set `$trimmed` to true.

```
$theText = substr($theText, 0, strrpos($theText,' '));
$trimmed = TRUE;
}
```

If you have trimmed the text at all, you add the ellipsis, and return the trimmed text back to where the function was called.

```
        if ($trimmed) $theText .= '...';
        return $theText;
}
```

The trimBody function is quite flexible. You can trim text to 500 characters (by setting $s_chr = "xyz" and $s_cnt = 999), or trim it to the first sentence (setting $s_chr = "." and $s_cnt = 1). You can also set the default values to anything you want.

The next function, outputStory(), takes two arguments. The argument $article is the ID of the article you want to display, and $only_snippet is either TRUE or FALSE to indicate whether you should trim it using the trimBody() function you just created. You will not be returning a value to the calling script. Instead, you send the results directly to the screen. Because of this, outputStory() should be used in the location where you want the story echoed.

```
    function outputStory($article, $only_snippet=FALSE) {
```

In order for the function to access the $conn variable, you have to declare it global. Otherwise, it will use its own $conn variable, which currently does not contain anything. Essentially, you are saying "Use the $conn variable that was declared outside of this function." Remember that $conn is created in conn.php, which is included at the top of outputfunctions.php.

```
    global $conn;
```

If the article ID was passed as expected, then you run the rest of the function. The first step is to select the article from the database, including all the author data for that article:

```
    if ($article) {
        $sql = "SELECT ar.*, usr.name " .
                "FROM cms_articles ar " .
                "LEFT OUTER JOIN cms_users usr " .
                "ON ar.author_id = usr.user_id " .
                "WHERE ar.article_id = " . $article;
        $result = mysql_query($sql, $conn);
```

The rest of the function is fairly straightforward. It combines the data retrieved from the database with HTML to format it for the screen. There are a few things we want to point out, however.

First, notice that you use the trimBody() function you just wrote, but only if you passed TRUE in as the second parameter of the outputStory() function. Second, you use the htmlspecialchars() PHP function to convert any text in your article that might cause HTML problems (such as <, >, &, and so on) to their entity equivalents (<, >, and &, respectively, and so on). Third, newline characters in HTML are essentially ignored. For HTML to properly display text with newlines, you need to insert <br /> for every newline in the text. PHP provides a neat function to do this: nl2br(), which you use here:

```
    if ($only_snippet) {
        ...
        echo nl2br(htmlspecialchars(trimBody($row['body'])));
        ...
    } else {
        ...
        echo nl2br(htmlspecialchars($row['body']));
        ...
    }
```

The end result is that the article gets displayed on the page just as intended when it was entered and is trimmed if specified.

The last function in `outputFunctions()` is `showComments()`. You pass the article ID and a Boolean value that determines whether or not to show a link to allow users to add their own comments:

```
function showComments($article, $showLink=TRUE) {
```

Declare `$conn` to be global, so you can access it within the function: `global $conn;`.

You will need to know later whether or not this article has been published. So, you grab the value of the field `is_published` from the article for use later:

```
$sql = "SELECT is_published " .
       "FROM cms_articles " .
       "WHERE article_id=" . $article;
$result = mysql_query($sql, $conn)
  or die('Could not look up comments; ' . mysql_error());

$row = mysql_fetch_array($result);
$is_published = $row['is_published'];
```

Next, you grab all of the comments associated with this article, including the user's name and e-mail address for each comment:

```
$sql = "SELECT co.*, usr.name, usr.email " .
       "FROM cms_comments co " .
       "LEFT OUTER JOIN cms_users usr " .
       "ON co.comment_user = usr.user_id " .
       "WHERE co.article_id=" . $article .
       " ORDER BY co.comment_date DESC";
$result = mysql_query($sql, $conn)
  or die('Could not look up comments; ' . mysql_error());
```

As with the `outputStory()` function, you just want to output out HTML whenever the `outputComments` function is called. If you passed TRUE as the second parameter to this function, then you put a header on the page that says "Comments," along with a link for the user to add his or her own comment (if this is a registered user and the article is published). If there are no comments, this is all the user will see, and he or she will still be able to add a new comment.

```
if ($showLink) {
  echo "<h4>" . mysql_num_rows($result) . " Comments";
  if (isset($_SESSION['user_id']) and $is_published) {
    echo " / <a href=\"comment.php?article=" . $_GET['article'] .
         "\">Add one</a>";
  }
  echo "</h4>\n";
}
```

If there are comments, loop through each comment and display the comments below the article, with the newest comments first.

```
if (mysql_num_rows($result)) {
  echo "<div class=\"scroller\">\n";
  while ($row = mysql_fetch_array($result)) {
```

Notice the `<span>` and `</span>` tags, as well as `<div>` tags. These are not currently being used, but they will allow you to use CSS (cascading style sheets) to change how your pages are displayed. We may include a CSS file or two on the Web site to demonstrate this, but for now, describing CSS is beyond the scope of this book.

```
echo "<span class=\"commentName\">" .
     htmlspecialchars($row['name']) .
     "</span><span class=\"commentDate\"> (" .
     date("l F j, Y H:i", strtotime($row['comment_date'])) .
     ")</span>\n";
echo "<p class=\"commentText\">\n" .
     nl2br(htmlspecialchars($row['comment'])) .
     "\n</p>\n";
}
```

Again, notice the use of `htmlspecialchars()` and `nl2br()` in the preceding code. Get used to using them; they are very important for converting text entered in a text box into readable text on an HTML page.

The date function is quite powerful. It allows you to take the standard date value entered in a datetime field in MySQL and format it in many ways. In this case, the datetime of 2003-09-19 17:39:24 will be displayed as Friday September 19, 2003 17:39. Many options are available for displaying dates. For more information about this, visit www.php.net/date.

The `outputFunctions.php` file is included on each page that needs one of its functions. If you have any other functions that you might want to add to your application, simply add it to this file, and make sure this file is included in the page.

header.php

Two additional files are included on every page that displays information on the Web: `header.php` and `footer.php`. Let's look at `header.php` now. (We won't look at `footer.php`, which should be self-explanatory.)

```
<?php session_start(); ?>
```

This is the very first line of your page, and a very important one. Login information is stored using sessions. As you might remember from previous chapters, sessions allow you to store values to be used elsewhere on the site. This makes sessions ideal for storing login data. By using `session_start()` at the beginning of your page, you are telling the application to allow you access to `$_SESSION` variables. Now you can set and retrieve session variables.

For a more detailed discussion of sessions, visit www.php.net/session.

Here's the first example of session variables. Once `session_start()` has been initialized, the variable `$_SESSION['name']` should be available to you, as long as the user has logged in. So, if `isset($_SESSION['name'])` returns FALSE, you know the user is not logged in.

```
if (isset($_SESSION['name'])) {
  echo ' <div id="logowelcome">';
  echo ' Currently logged in as: ' . $_SESSION['name'];
  echo ' </div>';
}
```

The following is the search form, displayed on every page. We did not discuss this functionality earlier; we hope you discovered this little gem in your explorations of the application. Now you get to see how it works. Note that there really isn't anything special going on here; it is a standard form that posts the keywords field to search.php. If there are keywords in the URL, they will be prefilled in the keywords field. We look at the search results page a little later.

```
<form method="get" action="search.php">
<p class="head">Search</p>
<p>
  <input id="searchkeywords" type="text" name="keywords"
<?php
if (isset($_GET['keywords'])) {
  echo ' value="' . htmlspecialchars($_GET['keywords']) . '" ';
}
?>
   >
  <input id="searchbutton" class="submit" type="submit"
    value="Search">
</p>
</form>
```

In most cases, there are three values you save as session variables: the user's name, login ID, and access level. You use those values to determine what menu items to display. Here are the options:

❑   **Article:** All users

❑   **Login:** All users *not* logged in

❑   **Compose:** All logged-in users

❑   **Review:** All logged-in users with access level 2 or more

❑   **Admin:** All logged-in users with access level 3 or more

❑   **Control Panel:** All logged-in users

❑   **Logout:** All logged-in users

```
echo '<a href="index.php">Articles</a>';
if (!isset($_SESSION['user_id'])) {
  echo ' | <a href="login.php">Login</a>';
} else {
  echo ' | <a href="compose.php">Compose</a>';

  if ($_SESSION['access_lvl'] > 1) {
    echo ' | <a href="pending.php">Review</a>';
  }

  if ($_SESSION['access_lvl'] > 2) {
    echo ' | <a href="admin.php">Admin</a>';
```

```
    }
    echo ' | <a href="cpanel.php">Control Panel</a>';
    echo ' | <a href="transact-user.php?action=Logout">Logout</a>';
}
```

So, that's `header.php`. It displays the title, login status, and appropriate menu items based on the user level.

http.php

Next, take a look at `http.php`, the last of your included files:

```
function redirect($url) {
  if (!headers_sent()) {
    header('Location: http://' . $_SERVER['HTTP_HOST'] .
           dirname($_SERVER['PHP_SELF']) . '/' . $url);
  } else {
    die('Could not redirect; Headers already sent (output).');
  }
}
```

You may have noticed that this is another function and wondered why we didn't include it in the `outputFunctions.php` file. We certainly could have, but we made the choice to separate them for two reasons. First, `outputFunctions.php` is for functions that output data to be displayed on the screen, either directly or indirectly (as with `trimBody()`). The `http.php` file is used for browser functions; in this case, we have only one of those—redirection. Second, the redirection function and the output functions are used at different times. By grouping functions with similar functionality, we minimize the size of included files.

Whew. All this coding, and nothing yet to show on the screen! There are two more files to go that don't output anything. These are the workhorses of the application, so they are a bit longer than the rest.

Transaction Pages

So now you come to the tasty, gooey center of your application: the transaction pages. Any time data is posted from a form, it's handled by either the `transact-user.php` or `transact-article.php` page. Keeping all the data-manipulating code in a centralized place, such as transaction files, makes maintenance down the line easier—you'd know exactly where to go hunting for bugs. In this case, you use two different files simply to make the code more manageable.

Try It Out	User Transactions

In your first transaction file, you're going to be creating the code that performs all user data manipulation, including login, account maintenance, and access control.

1. Enter this code, and save it as `transact-user.php`:

```
<?php
require_once 'conn.php';
require_once 'http.php';
```

```php
if (isset($_REQUEST['action'])) {
  switch ($_REQUEST['action']) {
    case 'Login':
      if (isset($_POST['email'])
          and isset($_POST['passwd']))
      {
        $sql = "SELECT user_id, access_lvl,name " .
               "FROM cms_users " .
               "WHERE email='" . $_POST['email'] . "' " .
               "AND passwd='" . $_POST['passwd'] . "'";
        $result = mysql_query($sql, $conn)
          or die('Could not look up user information; ' .
                 mysql_error());

        if ($row = mysql_fetch_array($result)) {
          session_start();
          $_SESSION['user_id'] = $row['user_id'];
          $_SESSION['access_lvl'] = $row['access_lvl'];
          $_SESSION['name'] = $row['name'];
        }
      }
      redirect('index.php');
      break;

    case 'Logout':
      session_start();
      session_unset();
      session_destroy();

      redirect('index.php');
      break;

    case 'Create Account':
      if (isset($_POST['name'])
          and isset($_POST['email'])
          and isset($_POST['passwd'])
          and isset($_POST['passwd2'])
          and $_POST['passwd'] == $_POST['passwd2'])
      {
        $sql = "INSERT INTO cms_users (email, name, passwd) " .
               "VALUES ('" . $_POST['email'] . "','" .
               $_POST['name'] . "','" . $_POST['passwd'] . "')";

        mysql_query($sql, $conn)
          or die('Could not create user account; ' . mysql_error());

        session_start();
        $_SESSION['user_id'] = mysql_insert_id($conn);
        $_SESSION['access_lvl'] = 1;
        $_SESSION['name'] = $_POST['name'];
      }
      redirect('index.php');
      break;
```

```
      case 'Modify Account':
        if (isset($_POST['name'])
            and isset($_POST['email'])
            and isset($_POST['accesslvl'])
            and isset($_POST['userid']))
        {
          $sql = "UPDATE cms_users " .
                 "SET email='" . $_POST['email'] .
                 "', name='" . $_POST['name'] .
                 "', access_lvl=" . $_POST['accesslvl'] . " " .
                 " WHERE user_id=" . $_POST['userid'];

          mysql_query($sql, $conn)
            or die('Could not update user account; ' . mysql_error());
        }
        redirect('admin.php');
        break;

      case 'Send my reminder!':
        if (isset($_POST['email'])) {
          $sql = "SELECT passwd FROM cms_users " .
                 "WHERE email='" . $_POST['email'] . "'";

          $result = mysql_query($sql, $conn)
            or die('Could not look up password; ' . mysql_error());

          if (mysql_num_rows($result)) {
            $row = mysql_fetch_array($result);

            $subject = 'Comic site password reminder';
            $body = "Just a reminder, your password for the " .
                    "Comic Book Appreciation site is: " .
                    $row['passwd'] .
                    "\n\nYou can use this to log in at http://" .
                    $_SERVER['HTTP_HOST'] .
                    dirname($_SERVER['PHP_SELF']) . '/';

            mail($_POST['email'], $subject, $body)
              or die('Could not send reminder email.');
          }
        }
        redirect('login.php');
        break;

      case 'Change my info':
        session_start();

        if (isset($_POST['name'])
            and isset($_POST['email'])
            and isset($_SESSION['user_id']))
        {
          $sql = "UPDATE cms_users " .
                 "SET email='" . $_POST['email'] .
```

```
                  "', name='" . $_POST['name'] . "' " .
                  "WHERE user_id=" . $_SESSION['user_id'];

        mysql_query($sql, $conn)
            or die('Could not update user account; ' . mysql_error());
      }
      redirect('cpanel.php');
      break;
  }
}
?>
```

How It Works

The application needs to access the database and to redirect users to various pages after completing transactions. You take care of the former with conn.php, and the latter with http.php. Because transaction
pages don't display anything on the screen, you don't need to include the header.php, footer.php, or
outputFunctions.php files.

```
require_once 'conn.php';
require_once 'http.php';
```

The $_REQUEST['action'] variable contains either the name of the button you clicked on the previous
page, or a GET request in the URL (such as ?action=delete). If $_REQUEST['action'] is empty, then
you don't do any transactions, and simply redirect the user to the index.php page:

```
if (isset($_REQUEST['action'])) {
```

You use switch() in what follows because of its flexibility. If you expand the functionality of this application, you could end up adding many more "actions." In this transact-user.php page, it is a simple
matter of adding a new case condition. You could certainly use if/else statements instead of switch,
but in the long run they can be cumbersome to work with.

```
switch ($_REQUEST['action']) {
```

The e-mail and password are what you use to log in. If both are not passed, the user will not be logged in.

```
case 'Login':
  if (isset($_POST['email'])
      and isset($_POST['passwd']))
  {
```

This gets the user's information. If a row is returned, it verifies that the login e-mail address and password
supplied are correct.

```
$sql = "SELECT user_id, access_lvl,name " .
       "FROM cms_users " .
       "WHERE email='" . $_POST['email'] . "' " .
       "AND passwd='" . $_POST['passwd'] . "'";
$result = mysql_query($sql, $conn)
  or die('Could not lookup user information; ' .
         mysql_error());

if ($row = mysql_fetch_array($result)) {
```

Again, in order to retrieve or set session variables, you must first use the command `session_start()`. Once you do, you set three variables to be used throughout the application: user ID, access level, and user name:

```
    session_start();
    $_SESSION['user_id'] = $row['user_id'];
    $_SESSION['access_lvl'] = $row['access_lvl'];
    $_SESSION['name'] = $row['name'];
  }
}
```

Next, you redirect the user back to the home page (`index.php`). The `break` function is required at the end of each case statement. Otherwise, the code in the next case runs as well, and you don't want that because it logs the user out!

```
redirect('index.php');
break;
```

Logout is quite simple, really. If no session variables exist with the user ID, access level, and user name, then the application knows you are not logged in. Therefore, you first use `session_start()` to tell PHP you are accessing session variables. Then, you unset the session, which clears all the session variables, and finally you destroy the session, which destroys all of the data registered to a session. Both `session_unset()` and `session_destroy()` are used to completely remove all login data.

```
case 'Logout':
  session_start();
  session_unset();
  session_destroy();

  redirect('index.php');
  break;
```

To create an account, all of the fields must be filled in, and the two password fields must match.

```
case 'Create Account':
  if (isset($_POST['name'])
    and isset($_POST['email'])
    and isset($_POST['accesslvl'])
    and isset($_POST['passwd'])
    and isset($_POST['passwd2'])
    and $_POST['passwd'] == $_POST['passwd2']))
  {
```

You insert the user's information into the database.

```
$sql = "INSERT INTO cms_users (email, name, passwd) " .
      "VALUES ('" . $_POST['email'] . "','" .
      $_POST['name'] . "','" . $_POST['passwd'] . "')";

mysql_query($sql, $conn)
  or die('Could not create user account; ' . mysql_error());
```

Then set the appropriate session variables. This has the effect of logging in the user after he or she registers.

```
      session_start();
      $_SESSION['user_id'] = mysql_insert_id($conn);
      $_SESSION['access_lvl'] = 1;
      $_SESSION['name'] = $_POST['name'];
   }
   redirect('index.php');
   break;
```

When an account is modified, all of the fields must have data. As long as they do, the user's account is updated in the database, and the user is redirected to the admin.php page:

```
case 'Modify Account':
  if (isset($_POST['name'])
      and isset($_POST['email'])
      and isset($_POST['accesslvl'])
      and isset($_POST['userid']))
  {
    $sql = "UPDATE cms_users " .
           "SET email='" . $_POST['email'] .
           "', name='" . $_POST['name'] .
           "', access_lvl=" . $_POST['accesslvl'] . " " .
           " WHERE user_id=" . $_POST['userid'];

    mysql_query($sql, $conn)
      or die('Could not update user account; ' . mysql_error());
  }
  redirect('admin.php');
  break;
```

It's time to revisit the mail() function we introduced in Chapter 11. This will be a simple e-mail, but there is no reason you can't take your wealth of knowledge from Chapter 11 and send an HTML-enabled e-mail to your users. It's not necessary, of course, but it's your application. Do what you will!

```
case 'Send my reminder!':
  if (isset($_POST['email'])) {
    $sql = "SELECT passwd FROM cms_users " .
           "WHERE email='" . $_POST['email'] . "'";

    $result = mysql_query($sql,$conn)
      or die('Could not look up password; ' . mysql_error());
```

If you find a record, you get it, create a subject and body for your e-mail message (including the long lost password), and send it on its merry way.

```
if (mysql_num_rows($result)) {
  $row = mysql_fetch_array($result);

  $subject = 'Comic site password reminder';
  $body = "Just a reminder, your password for the " .
          "Comicbook appreciation site is: " .
          $row['passwd'] .
          "\n\nYou can use this to log in at http://" .
          $_SERVER['HTTP_HOST'] .
          dirname($_SERVER['PHP_SELF']) . '/';
```

```
mail($_POST['email'],$subject,$body)
  or die('Could not send reminder email.');
}
```

You assume, of course, that the user will immediately open his or her e-mail to read the password. You conveniently deposit users in the login page so they can enter their e-mail address and password.

```
}
redirect('login.php');
break;
```

The following code may look *very* familiar. It is virtually identical to the previous Modify Account case, except this time, the user is changing his or her own data. Because of this, the access level does not get updated.

```
case 'Change my info':
  session_start();

  if (isset($_POST['name'])
      and isset($_POST['email'])
      and isset($_SESSION['user_id']))
  {
    $sql = "UPDATE cms_users " .
           "SET email='" . $_POST['email'] .
           "', name='" . $_POST['name'] . "' " .
           "WHERE user_id=" . $_SESSION['user_id'];

    mysql_query($sql, $conn)
      or die('Could not update user account; ' . mysql_error());
  }
  redirect('cpanel.php');
  break;
```

The following is the end of your switch statement. It's easy to forget to close it, which can be the cause of much debugging grief. We are here to remind you to close your switch!

```
}
```

That wasn't so bad, was it? It's a lot of code, but much of it is fairly similar. Check some variables, run some SQL code, redirect the user. That's pretty much how most transactions work.

Article Transactions

It's time for another transaction file, this time dealing with articles. As you might have guessed, it will be controlling article submittal, publishing, and removal.

1. Now enter `transact-article.php`:

```
<?php
session_start();
require_once 'conn.php';
require_once 'http.php';
```

```php
if (isset($_REQUEST['action'])) {
  switch ($_REQUEST['action']) {
    case 'Submit New Article':
      if (isset($_POST['title'])
          and isset($_POST['body'])
          and isset($_SESSION['user_id']))
      {
        $sql = "INSERT INTO cms_articles " .
               "(title,body, author_id, date_submitted) " .
               "VALUES ('" . $_POST['title'] .
               "','" . $_POST['body'] .
               "'," . $_SESSION['user_id'] . ",'" .
               date("Y-m-d H:i:s", time()) . "')";

        mysql_query($sql, $conn)
          or die('Could not submit article; ' . mysql_error());
      }
      redirect('index.php');
      break;

    case 'Edit':
      redirect('compose.php?a=edit&article=' . $_POST['article']);
      break;

    case 'Save Changes':
      if (isset($_POST['title'])
          and isset($_POST['body'])
          and isset($_POST['article']))
      {
        $sql = "UPDATE cms_articles " .
               "SET title='" . $_POST['title'] .
               "', body='" . $_POST['body'] . "', date_submitted='" .
               date("Y-m-d H:i:s", time()) . "' " .
               "WHERE article_id=" . $_POST['article'];
               if (isset($_POST['authorid'])) {
                 $sql .= " AND author_id=" . $_POST['authorid'];
               }

        mysql_query($sql, $conn)
          or die('Could not update article; ' . mysql_error());
      }

      if (isset($_POST['authorid'])) {
        redirect('cpanel.php');
      } else {
        redirect('pending.php');
      }
      break;

    case 'Publish':
      if ($_POST['article']) {
        $sql = "UPDATE cms_articles " .
               "SET is_published=1, date_published='" .
               date("Y-m-d H:i:s",time()) . "' " .
```

```php
                "WHERE article_id=" . $_POST['article'];
        mysql_query($sql, $conn)
            or die('Could not publish article; ' . mysql_error());
      }
      redirect('pending.php');
      break;

    case 'Retract':
      if ($_POST['article']) {
        $sql = "UPDATE cms_articles " .
                "SET is_published=0, date_published='' " .
                "WHERE article_id=" . $_POST['article'];
        mysql_query($sql, $conn)
            or die('Could not retract article; ' . mysql_error());
      }
      redirect('pending.php');
      break;

    case 'Delete':
      if ($_POST['article']) {
        $sql = "DELETE FROM cms_articles " .
                "WHERE is_published=0 " .
                "AND article_id=" . $_POST['article'];
        mysql_query($sql, $conn)
            or die('Could not delete article; ' . mysql_error());
      }
      redirect('pending.php');
      break;

    case 'Submit Comment':
      if (isset($_POST['article'])
          and $_POST['article']
          and isset($_POST['comment'])
          and $_POST['comment'])
      {
        $sql = "INSERT INTO cms_comments " .
                "(article_id,comment_date,comment_user,comment) " .
                "VALUES (" . $_POST['article'] . ",'" .
                date("Y-m-d H:i:s", time()) .
                "'," . $_SESSION['user_id'] .
                ",'" . $_POST['comment'] . "')";
        mysql_query($sql, $conn)
            or die('Could add comment; ' . mysql_error());
      }
      redirect('viewarticle.php?article=' . $_POST['article']);
      break;

    case 'remove':
      if (isset($_GET['article'])
          and isset($_SESSION['user_id']))
      {
        $sql = "DELETE FROM cms_articles " .
                "WHERE article_id=" . $_GET['article'] .
                " AND author_id=" . $_SESSION['user_id'];
```

```
        mysql_query($sql, $conn)
            or die('Could not remove article; ' . mysql_error());
        }
        redirect('cpanel.php');
        break;
    }
} else {
    redirect('index.php');
}
?>
```

How It Works

Want to look at some more code? Great! Let's take a look at `transact-article.php`. This time, we'll simply point out some of the more interesting things we might not have covered yet, or things that bear repeating.

Yes, this bears repeating. You know what the following does, right? It registers the session variables that invariably will need to be set in order to run some of these transactions. This gives you access to the data for the currently logged-in user:

```
session_start();
```

The `transact-article.php` page requires connection to the database, and redirects users to various pages using the `redirect()` function. The following two include files provide this functionality, respectively.

```
require_once 'conn.php';
require_once 'http.php';
```

You need to make sure that a button was pressed, or an action is specified in the URL (such as `?action=twiddleThumbs`).

```
if (isset($_REQUEST['action'])) {
```

A lot of actions can happen in this file. The `switch()` statement is a more elegant way of choosing your transactions than `if/else`.

```
switch ($_REQUEST['action']) {
```

You first ensure that the title and body were both entered and that the user is logged in (tested by the presence of the `user_id` session variable).

```
case 'Submit New Article':
    if (isset($_POST['title'])
        and isset($_POST['body'])
        and isset($_SESSION['user_id']))
    {
```

You insert the article into the database, including the user ID and the date. The datetime is formatted in a standard MySQL datetime format that can be stored in a datetime column. When you retrieve that datetime to be displayed on the Web, you can format it any way that you want. The standard datetime format for September 21, 2003, 12:42 a.m. is 2003-09-21 00:42:00.

```
    $sql = "INSERT INTO cms_articles " .
            "(title,body, author_id, date_submitted) " .
            "VALUES ('" . $_POST['title'] . "','" . $_POST['body'] .
            "'," . $_SESSION['user_id'] . ",'" .
            date("Y-m-d H:i:s",time()) . "')";

    mysql_query($sql, $conn)
        or die('Could not submit article; ' . mysql_error());
}
redirect('index.php');
break;
```

The Edit case is simple. The compose.php page is set up to retrieve an article and preload it into the title and body fields if the appropriate data is entered in the URL. You simply need to add a=edit and article=xx to the URL and redirect the user to that URL.

```
case 'Edit':
    redirect('compose.php?a=edit&article=' . $_POST['article']);
    break;
```

Make sure the title and body fields have been filled in, and that the hidden field "article" contains a value. If you were composing a new document, the hidden field would not contain anything, and you'd know something was wrong. (You can't use the Save Changes feature for a new document.)

```
case 'Save Changes':
    if (isset($_POST['title'])
        and isset($_POST['body'])
        and isset($_POST['article']))
    {
```

Next you send the article to the database. If the hidden field authorid has a value, then a user is editing her or his own document, and you must add the condition to match the author_id to the SQL statement.

```
$sql = "UPDATE cms_articles " .
        "SET title='" . $_POST['title'] .
        "', body='" . $_POST['body'] . "', date_submitted='" .
        date("Y-m-d H:i:s", time()) . "' " .
        "WHERE article_id=" . $_POST['article'];

if (isset($_POST['authorid'])) {
    $sql .= " AND author_id=" . $_POST['authorid'];
}

mysql_query($sql, $conn)
    or die('Could not update article; ' . mysql_error());
}
```

You then redirect the user to either the control panel, if the user is editing his or her own document, or the review page, if the user is a moderator or admin editing someone else's document.

```
    if (isset($_POST['authorid'])) {
      redirect('cpanel.php');
    } else {
      redirect('pending.php');
    }
    break;
```

Next you make sure the article ID was passed. If it was, modify the article in the database to set the is_published column to 1, and set the date_published datetime column to the current date and time (formatted in MySQL datetime format).

```
case 'Publish':
  if ($_POST['article']) {
    $sql = "UPDATE cms_articles " .
        "SET is_published=1, date_published='" .
        date("Y-m-d H:i:s",time()) . "' " .
        "WHERE article_id=" . $_POST['article'];

    mysql_query($sql, $conn)
      or die('Could not publish article; ' . mysql_error());
  }
  redirect('pending.php');
  break;
```

This next case is actually quite similar to the Publish case, only this time, after checking the article ID, you set is_published to 0 and erase the date_published field. Retracting an article in this case simply returns it to its pre-published state, but you might think of better ways to retract an article. Perhaps you could have separate columns for is_retracted and retract_date. There is no right or wrong way to do it, and, of course, it depends on the needs of your own site.

```
case 'Retract':
  if ($_POST['article']) {
    $sql = "UPDATE cms_articles " .
          "SET is_published=0, date_published='' " .
          "WHERE article_id=" . $_POST['article'];

    mysql_query($sql, $conn)
      or die('Could not retract article; ' . mysql_error());
  }
  redirect('pending.php');
  break;
```

Check to see that an article ID was passed, and simply delete the record.

```
case 'Delete':
  if ($_POST['article']) {
    $sql = "DELETE FROM cms_articles " .
          "WHERE is_published=0 " .
          "AND article_id=" . $_POST['article'];

    mysql_query($sql, $conn)
      or die('Could not delete article; ' . mysql_error());
  }
```

```
      redirect('pending.php');
      break;
```

If the article ID was passed, and the comment field is filled in, process this transaction.

```
case 'Submit Comment':
  if (isset($_POST['article'])
      and $_POST['article']
      and isset($_POST['comment'])
      and $_POST['comment'])
  {
```

Insert the article ID, the comment date (in MySQL datetime format), the user ID, and the actual comment into the database. When this has been accomplished, redirect the user to the article so he or she can see the newly saved comment.

```
    $sql = "INSERT INTO cms_comments " .
           "(article_id,comment_date,comment_user,comment) " .
           "VALUES (" . $_POST['article'] . ",'" .
           date("Y-m-d H:i:s",time()) .
           "'," . $_SESSION['user_id'] .
           ",'" . $_POST['comment'] . "')";

    mysql_query($sql, $conn)
      or die('Could add comment; ' . mysql_error());
  }
  redirect('viewarticle.php?article=' . $_POST['article']);
  break;
```

This is a case where the action is passed in the URL (?action=remove&article=123). Verify that the article ID was passed and that the user is logged in.

```
case 'remove':
  if (isset($_GET['article'])
      and isset($_SESSION['user_id']))
  {
```

You currently allow only users to delete their own articles. You might modify this transaction to allow moderators and admins to delete any article, but for now only users can delete the articles they have written.

```
    $sql = "DELETE FROM cms_articles " .
           "WHERE article_id=" . $_GET['article'] .
           " AND author_id=" . $_SESSION['user_id'];

    mysql_query($sql, $conn)
      or die('Could not remove article; ' . mysql_error());
  }
  redirect('cpanel.php');
  break;
```

Once again, don't forget to close your switch statement:

```
  }
```

And again, if a user has somehow loaded this page without any posted variables, he or she is immediately redirected to the home page.

```
} else {
  redirect('index.php');
}
```

User Interface

So you've created your transaction pages, and your reusable functions, but haven't yet actually seen any real on-screen functionality. Well now's your chance! In this section, we're going to be creating the scripts that make up the various user interface screens. Dust off your browser, and let's get started!

General Functionality

The first group of files you'll be dealing with are going to provide general user access to the site. Scripts similar to these are found on many sites across the Internet, so you'll probably be familiar with their functionality.

Try It Out   **Main Index/Login Screen**

The first scripts you're going to create will deal with the action of a user coming to the site, logging in, requesting aide due to a forgotten password, and new account creation.

1.   Create login.php:

```
<?php require_once 'header.php'; ?>

<form method="post" action="transact-user.php">

<h1>Member Login</h1>

<p>
  Email Address:<br>
  <input type="text" name="email" maxlength="255" value="">
</p>
<p>
  Password:<br>
  <input type="password" name="passwd" maxlength="50">
</p>
<p>
  <input type="submit" class="submit" name="action" value="Login">
</p>

<p>
  Not a member yet? <a href="useraccount.php">Create a new account!</a>
</p>
<p>
  <a href="forgotpass.php">Forgot your password?</a>
</p>
```

```
</form>

<?php require_once 'footer.php'; ?>
```

2. Next, create `forgotpass.php`:

```php
<?php require_once 'header.php'; ?>

<form method="post" action="transact-user.php">

<h1>Email Password Reminder</h1>

<p>
  Forgot your password? Just enter your email address, and we'll
  email your password to you!
</p>

<p>
  Email Address:<br>
  <input type="text" id="email" name="email">
</p>

<p>
  <input type="submit" class="submit" name="action"
    value="Send my reminder!">
</p>
</form>

<?php require_once 'footer.php'; ?>
```

3. Create `index.php`:

```php
<?php
require_once 'conn.php';
require_once 'outputfunctions.php';
require_once 'header.php';

$sql = "SELECT article_id FROM cms_articles WHERE is_published=1 " .
       "ORDER BY date_published DESC";

$result = mysql_query($sql, $conn);

if (mysql_num_rows($result) == 0) {
  echo "  <br>\n";
  echo "  There are currently no articles to view.\n";
} else {
  while ($row = mysql_fetch_array($result)) {
    outputStory($row['article_id'], TRUE);
  }
}

require_once 'footer.php';
?>
```

4. Load `index.php` in your browser.

5. Click the Login link on the page, or open `login.php` in your browser. Enter the e-mail address and password you previously stored in the database, and click the Login button (see Figure 13-2). Don't remember the login/password combination? Try `admin@yoursite.com` for the e-mail address, and `admin` for the password.

You should now see a simple screen similar to Figure 13-3. There is not much to see yet, because you haven't written any articles. You should, however, see a handful of menu options.

Figure 13-2

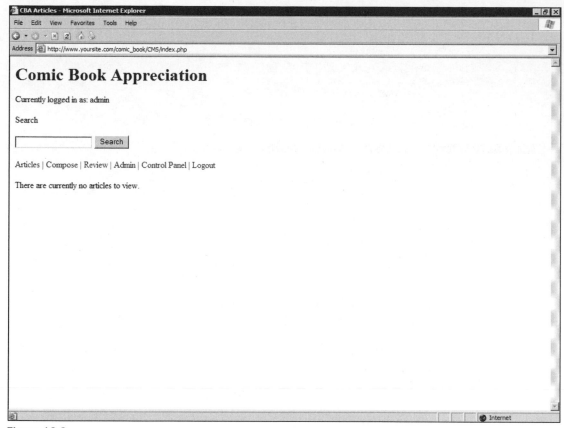

Figure 13-3

How It Works

Let's look at index.php. Include the standard files:

```php
<?php
require_once 'conn.php';
require_once 'outputfunctions.php';
require_once 'header.php';
```

Retrieve all published articles, with the most recent articles listed first:

```php
$sql = "SELECT article_id FROM cms_articles WHERE is_published=1 " .
       "ORDER BY date_published DESC";

$result = mysql_query($sql, $conn);
```

If no articles are published, let the user know. This is optional, of course. If this were part of a larger page, such as a portal application, then you might simply want to put something else in place of the article list.

```
if (mysql_num_rows($result) == 0) {
  echo "  <br>\n";
  echo "  There are currently no articles to view.\n";
```

Go through each article ID retrieved, and display the articles (trimmed) on the page:

```
} else {
  while ($row = mysql_fetch_array($result)) {
   outputStory($row['article_id'], TRUE);
  }
}
```

Then you can tidy up afterward:

```
require_once 'footer.php';
?>
```

You may have noticed that we left out two pages, `login.php` and `forgotpass.php`. They are important pages, of course, but are mostly simple HTML. The includes at the top and bottom for `header.php` and `footer.php` are the only PHP. We're sure you can figure out how those two pages work.

Try It Out   Account Creation

Now you are going to create a script that will allow guests to your CMS to create new accounts for themselves.

1. Create this new file, and save it as `useraccount.php`:

```php
<?php
require_once 'conn.php';

$userid = '';
$name = '';
$email = '';
$password = '';
$accesslvl = '';
if (isset($_GET['userid'])) {
  $sql = "SELECT * FROM cms_users WHERE user_id=" . $_GET['userid'];
  $result = mysql_query($sql, $conn)
    or die('Could not look up user data; ' . mysql_error());

  $row = mysql_fetch_array($result);
  $userid = $_GET['userid'];
  $name = $row['name'];
  $email = $row['email'];
  $accesslvl = $row['access_lvl'];
}
```

```php
require_once 'header.php';

echo "<form method=\"post\" action=\"transact-user.php\">\n";

if ($userid) {
  echo "<h1>Modify Account</h1>\n";
} else {
  echo "<h1>Create Account</h1>\n";
}
?>

<p>
  Full name:<br>
  <input type="text" class="txtinput" name="name" maxlength="100"
    value="<?php echo htmlspecialchars($name); ?>">
</p>
<p>
  Email Address:<br>
  <input type="text" class="txtinput" name="email" maxlength="255"
    value="<?php echo htmlspecialchars($email); ?>">
</p>
<?php

if (isset($_SESSION['access_lvl'])
    and $_SESSION['access_lvl'] == 3)
{
  echo "<fieldset>\n";
  echo "<legend>Access Level</legend>\n";

  $sql = "SELECT * FROM cms_access_levels ORDER BY access_lvl DESC";
  $result = mysql_query($sql, $conn)
    or die('Could not list access levels; ' . mysql_error());

  while ($row = mysql_fetch_array($result)) {
    echo ' <input type="radio" class="radio" id="acl_' .
        $row['access_lvl'] . '" name="accesslvl" value="' .
        $row['access_lvl'] . '" ';

    if ($row['access_lvl'] == $accesslvl) {
      echo 'checked="checked" ';
    }
    echo '>' . $row['access_name'] . "<br>\n";
  }
?>
</fieldset>
<p>
  <input type="hidden" name="userid" value="<?php echo $userid; ?>">
  <input type="submit" class="submit" name="action"
    value="Modify Account">
</p>
<?php } else { ?>
<p>
```

```
   Password:<br>
   <input type="password" id="passwd" name="passwd" maxlength="50">
</p>
<p>
   Password (again):<br>
   <input type="password" id="passwd2" name="passwd2" maxlength="50">
</p>
<p>
   <input type="submit" class="submit" name="action"
     value="Create Account">
</p>
<?php } ?>
</form>

<?php require_once 'footer.php'; ?>
```

2. If you're still logged in to the CMS, click the Logout link.

3. Next, click Login, and then click "Create a new account!" You should see a screen similar to Figure 13-4.

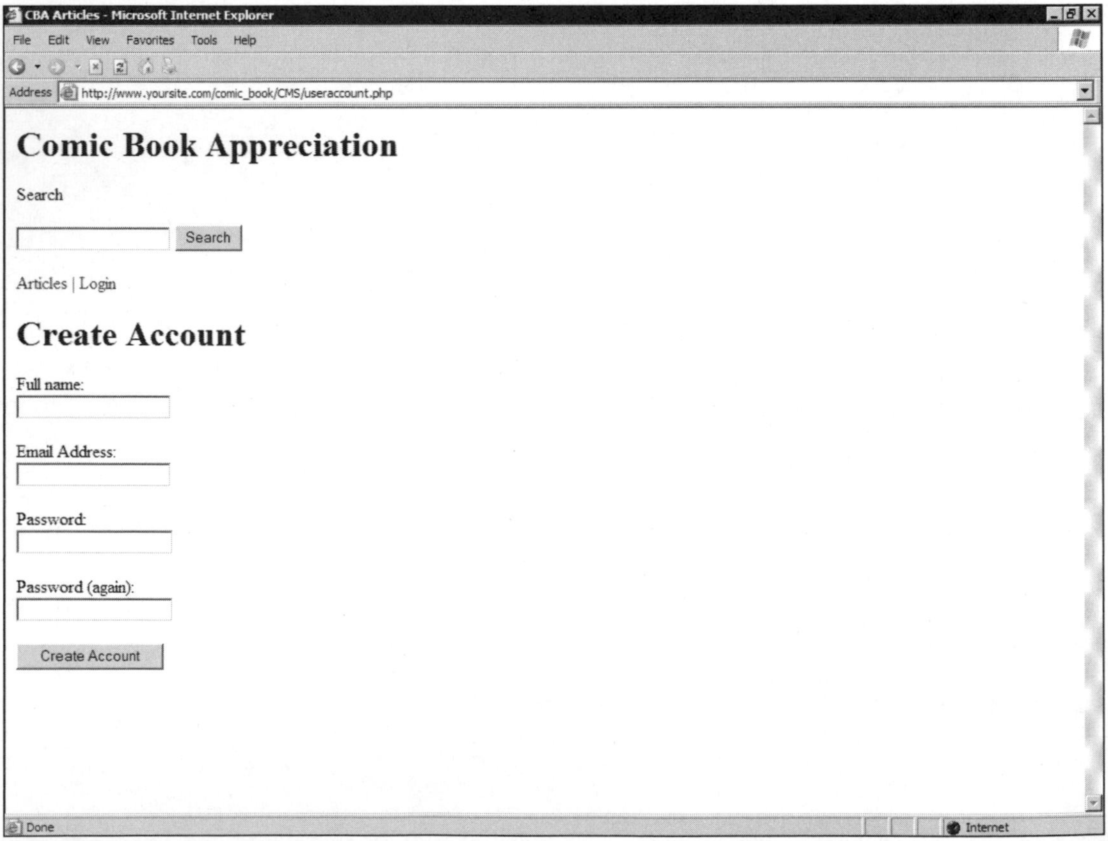

Figure 13-4

4. Enter data into each field and click Create Account. For this example, enter the following:

- ❏ Full Name: George Smith
- ❏ E-mail Address: gsmith05523@hotmail.com
- ❏ Password: phprocks
- ❏ Password (again): phprocks

Once you create a new user, you will be automatically logged in as that user. You should notice that you cannot see the Review or Admin menu items, which you might have noticed when previously logged in as Admin. Review is available to Moderators or Admins (levels 2 or 3) only, and Admin is available to Admins only (level 3). Your initial account was created at level 3, but the account you just created defaulted to level 1 (User).

How It Works

Now let's take a look at useraccount.php. First thing you'll notice is your old friend conn.php. But where is header.php? No worries—it will show up soon. As long as you don't echo anything to the page yet, you're okay.

```php
<?php
require_once 'conn.php';
```

You need to retrieve all of the data for this user. Set all the variables to empty to ensure the values you retrieve are "fresh." As long as the user is logged in, those variables will fill up with the appropriate data. If there is no user logged in, this page will create a new user. Neato, huh?

```php
$userid = '';
$name = '';
$email = '';
$password = '';
$accesslvl = '';
if (isset($_GET['userid'])) {
  $sql = "SELECT * FROM cms_users WHERE user_id=" . $_GET['userid'];
  $result = mysql_query($sql, $conn)
    or die('Could not look up user data; ' . mysql_error());

  $row = mysql_fetch_array($result);
  $userid = $_GET['userid'];
  $name = $row['name'];
  $email = $row['email'];
  $accesslvl = $row['access_lvl'];
}
```

Here's the header! We told you not to worry.

```php
require_once 'header.php';
```

What follows is no different from that last page you looked at, but you're using PHP to echo it to the page.

```php
echo "<form method=\"post\" action=\"transact-user.php\">\n";
```

You could have just as easily written this as

```
?>
<form method="post" action="transact-user.php">
<?php
```

If the user is logged in, then this page contains the user's current data. Therefore, you need to modify his account. Otherwise, it's a new user, and you need to *create* an account. The title reflects this.

```
if ($userid) {
  echo "<h1>Modify Account</h1>\n";
} else {
  echo "<h1>Create Account</h1>\n";
}
?>
```

Here's some more boring HTML. Once again, note the use of `htmlspecialchars()` to prevent weird symbols from messing up the page.

```
<p>
  Full name:<br>
  <input type="text" class="txtinput" name="name" maxlength="100"
    value="<?php echo htmlspecialchars($name); ?>">
<p>
</p>
  Email Address:<br>
  <input type="text" class="txtinput" name="email" maxlength="255"
    value="<?php echo htmlspecialchars($email); ?>">
</p>
```

If the user has Admin access, do the following:

```
<?php
if (isset($_SESSION['access_lvl'])
  and $_SESSION['access_lvl'] == 3)
{
```

While we do assume that you have a fundamental knowledge of HTML, you may not be familiar with `<fieldset>` and `<legend>`. We simply suggest you enter them and see how they are displayed on the page; using `<fieldset>` and `<legend>` is a great way to group many of your form fields.

We recommend you visit `www.w3.org/TR/REC-html40/interact/forms.html#h-17.10` *for more information.*

```
echo "<fieldset>\n";
echo " <legend>Access Level</legend>\n";
```

First, go get all of the access levels from the database:

```
$sql = "SELECT * FROM cms_access_levels ORDER BY access_lvl DESC";
$result = mysql_query($sql, $conn)
  or die('Could not list access levels; ' . mysql_error());
```

Then cycle through each one, displaying them as radio buttons on the page.

```
while ($row = mysql_fetch_array($result)) {
  echo ' <input type="radio" class="radio" id="acl_' .
      $row['access_lvl'] . '" name="accesslvl" value="' .
      $row['access_lvl'] . '" ';

  if ($row['access_lvl'] == $accesslvl) {
    echo 'checked="checked" ';
  }
  echo '>' . $row['access_name'] . "<br>\n";
}
```

The next page requires the user ID. Because this is not entered in a form field, create a hidden field to carry the data over to the transaction page.

```
?>
</fieldset>
<p>
  <input type="hidden" name="userid" value="<?php echo $userid; ?>">
  <input type="submit" class="submit" name="action"
    value="Modify Account">
</p>
```

A short but sweet PHP tag ends the first part of the if statement and adds an else clause. This is a very flexible way of using if...else commands with standard HTML. Because you can enter and exit PHP at any time, your pages are very flexible and easy to read.

The rest of this code is loaded if you are *not* an admin type.

```
<?php } else { ?>
```

If you are not an admin, you must be here to create a new account. Therefore, it asks you for your password:

```
<p>
  Password:<br>
  <input type="password" id="passwd" name="passwd" maxlength="50">
</p>
<p>
  Password (again):<br>
  <input type="password" id="passwd2" name="passwd2" maxlength="50">
</p>
<p>
  <input type="submit" class="submit" name="action"
    value="Create Account">
</p>
```

Then comes the end of the if statement and the end of the form:

```
<?php } ?>
</form>
```

And there is your footer page again, closing things off neatly:

```php
<?php require_once 'footer.php'; ?>
```

User Management

You may be wondering, "How does the administrator create other administrators or moderators to help manage the site?" Well, now we're going to give you the scripts to do just that.

Try It Out   **Administration Page**

In this exercise, you'll create the pages necessary for administrators to manage the site.

1. Create `admin.php`:

```php
<?php

require_once 'conn.php';
require_once 'header.php';

$a_users = array(1 => "Users","Moderators","Admins");

function echoUserList($lvl) {
  global $a_users;
  $sql = "SELECT user_id, name, email FROM cms_users " .
         "WHERE access_lvl = $lvl ORDER BY name";

  $result = mysql_query($sql)
    or die(mysql_error());

  if (mysql_num_rows($result) == 0) {
    echo "<em>No " . $a_users[$lvl] . " created.</em>";
  } else {
    while ($row = mysql_fetch_array($result)) {
      if ($row['user_id'] == $_SESSION['user_id']) {
        echo htmlspecialchars($row['name']) . "<br>\n";
      } else {
        echo '<a href="useraccount.php?userid=' . $row['user_id'] .
             '" title="' . htmlspecialchars($row['email']) . '">' .
             htmlspecialchars($row['name']) . "</a><br>\n";
      }
    }
  }
}
?>
<h2>User Administration</h2>
<?php
for($i=1; $i<=3; $i++) {
  echo "<h3>". $a_users[$i] . "</h3>\n" .
       "<div class=\"scroller\">\n";
```

```
    echoUserList($i);
    echo "\n</div>\n";
}
?>
<br>
<?php require_once 'footer.php'; ?>
```

2. Go ahead and log out, and then log back in using your admin account. When you are logged in, click the Admin link. You should see a screen similar to Figure 13-5.

You should see George Smith (or whatever name you used) under Users. You will notice your Admin name under Admins, but it is not a link. You can alter your own account from your Control Panel.

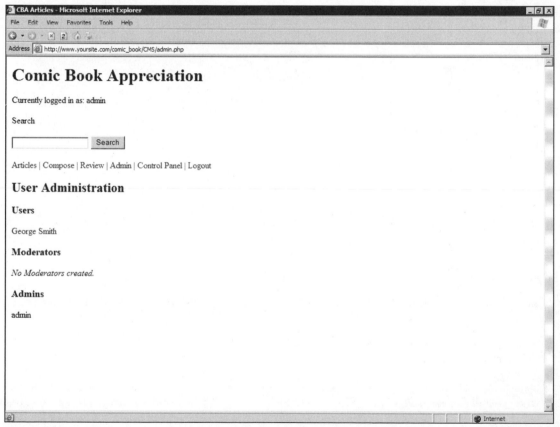

Figure 13-5

3. Click the user listed under Users. You should see a page similar to that in Figure 13-6. Notice that you can change the user's name and password. Also notice the Access Level option. You can set any user to be a User, Moderator, or Admin. User is the default for new users.

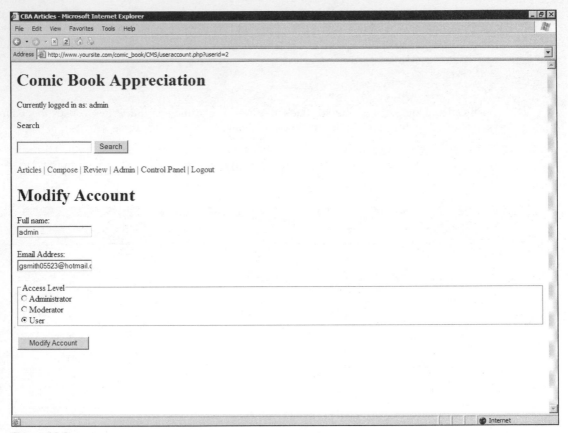

Figure 13-6

How It Works

Guess what? You guessed it. Our good friends conn.php and header.php are back. Okay, let's move on.

```
<?php
require_once 'conn.php';
require_once 'header.php';
```

Is this an associative array? Actually, it is a normal array, but it is not zero-based. The way PHP works when creating arrays is ingenious. What this line tells PHP is "Create a normal array, but start the number index at 1." You could have assigned indices to the other values as well, but this is not necessary. PHP knows that "Moderators" has an index of 2, and "Admins" has an index of 3. Now how cool is that?

```
$a_users = array(1 => "Users","Moderators","Admins");
```

Hey, a function. Shouldn't this go in an include file, such as outputfunctions.php? Perhaps, and you could certainly do that if you wanted to. However, this function is very specific to this file, so it really doesn't need to go in an include file. It's up to you, really.

```
function echoUserList($lvl) {
```

To use the array you created earlier within this function, you must declare it global. Now the function can access the data in the array.

```
global $a_users;
```

This function will be called more than once. Each time, a different value will be contained in the $lvl variable. The following SQL pulls the appropriate data according to the $lvl value:

```
$sql = "SELECT user_id, name, email FROM cms_users " .
    "WHERE access_lvl = $lvl ORDER BY name";

$result = mysql_query($sql)
  or die(mysql_error());
```

If no users are found in the database for this access level, you display a message explaining that those users were not found. You do this by using the array you created earlier:

```
if (mysql_num_rows($result) == 0) {
  echo "<em>No " . $a_users[$lvl] . " created.</em>";
```

A user cannot modify his or her own record. Instead, his or her name is shown in plain text, with no link.

```
} else {
  while ($row = mysql_fetch_array($result)) {
    if ($row['user_id'] == $_SESSION['user_id']) {
      echo htmlspecialchars($row['name']) . "<br>\n";
```

Otherwise, the user's name is displayed on the screen, as a link that loads useraccount.php.

```
    } else {
      echo '<a href="useraccount.php?userid=' . $row['user_id'] .
          '" title="' . htmlspecialchars($row['email']) . '">' .
          htmlspecialchars($row['name']) . "</a><br>\n";
    }
```

Here's the end of the function. Note that nothing has been output to the screen yet.

```
    }
  }
}
```

First you display the page title:

```
?>
<h2>User Administration</h2>
```

Then you loop through the code three times, running the function each time with a different level value:

```php
<?php
for($i=1;$i<=3;$i++) {
  echo "<h3>". $a_users[$i] . "</h3>\n" .
       "<div class='scroller'>\n";
  echoUserList($i);
  echo "\n</div>\n";
}
?>
```

And then you're done.

```
<br>
<?php require_once 'footer.php'; ?>
```

Article Publishing

You have all these transaction pages and user account maintenance so far, but nothing that would put your application squarely into the "CMS" category. Well that's all about to change! In this section you'll be creating the pages that allow you to create, review, read, and comment on articles. On to the articles!

Try It Out   Creating an Article

In your first step toward having content, you're going to create the page that allows you to actually write out the articles and save them to the database.

1.   Create a new file and name it `compose.php`:

```php
<?php

require_once 'conn.php';

$title = '';
$body = '';
$article = '';
$authorid = '';
if (isset($_GET['a'])
    and $_GET['a'] == 'edit'
    and isset($_GET['article'])
    and $_GET['article']) {
  $sql = "SELECT title,body,author_id FROM cms_articles " .
         "WHERE article_id=" . $_GET['article'];
  $result = mysql_query($sql, $conn)
    or die('Could not retrieve article data; ' . mysql_error());

  $row = mysql_fetch_array($result);
```

```php
    $title = $row['title'];
    $body = $row['body'];
    $article = $_GET['article'];
    $authorid = $row['author_id'];
}
require_once 'header.php';
?>

<form method="post" action="transact-article.php">

<h2>Compose Article</h2>

<p>
  Title:<br>
  <input type="text" class="title" name="title" maxlength="255"
    value="<?php echo htmlspecialchars($title); ?>">
</p>
<p>
  Body:<br>
  <textarea class="body" name="body" rows="10" cols="60"><?php
    echo htmlspecialchars($body); ?></textarea>
</p>
<p>
<?php
echo '<input type="hidden" name="article" value="' .
    $article . "\">\n";

if ($_SESSION['access_lvl'] < 2) {
  echo '<input type="hidden" name="authorid" value="' .
      $authorid . "\">\n";
}

if ($article) {
  echo '<input type="submit" class="submit" name="action" ' .
      "value=\"Save Changes\">\n";
} else {
  echo '<input type="submit" class="submit" name="action" ' .
      "value=\"Submit New Article\">\n";
}
?>
</p>
</form>

<?php require_once 'footer.php'; ?>
```

2. Click the Compose link to load `compose.php` (see Figure 13-7).

3. Enter a title and some text for the article. When you are done, click Submit New Article. You will be taken back to the index page, but there will still be no article. The article you just wrote is pending review.

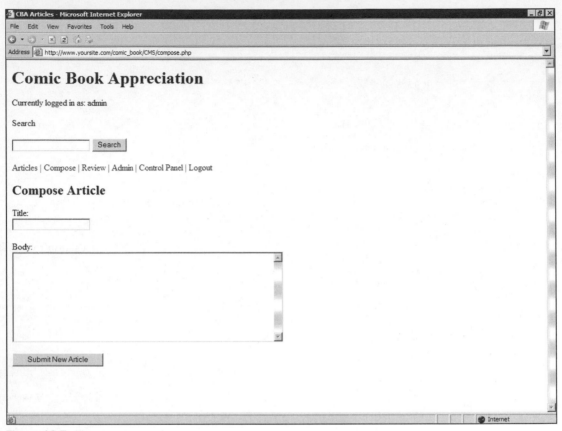

Figure 13-7

How It Works

You're almost there. Next, you tackle compose.php, the page where you create new articles. First, initialize the variables you are going to be using:

```php
<?php
require_once 'conn.php';

$title = '';
$body = '';
$article = '';
$authorid = '';
```

If you are editing an article, instead of composing a brand new one, you must go out to the database and retrieve the article.

```php
if (isset($_GET['a'])
    and $_GET['a'] == 'edit'
    and isset($_GET['article'])
    and $_GET['article']) {
  $sql = "SELECT title,body,author_id FROM cms_articles " .
```

```
                "WHERE article_id=" . $_GET['article'];

    $result = mysql_query($sql, $conn)
      or die('Could not retrieve article data; ' . mysql_error());

    $row = mysql_fetch_array($result);

    $title = $row['title'];
    $body = $row['body'];
    $article = $_GET['article'];
    $authorid = $row['author_id'];
}
```

Load the prerequisite `header.php`:

```
require_once 'header.php';
```

What follows is more standard HTML stuff. You know what `htmlspecialchars()` does, don't you? Of course you do. If not, go back a page or two and review.

```
?>

<form method="post" action="transact-article.php">

<h2>Compose Article</h2>

<p>
  Title:<br>
  <input type="text" class="title" name="title" maxlength="255"
    value="<?php echo htmlspecialchars($title); ?>">
</p>
<p>
  Body:<br>
  <textarea class="body" name="body" rows="10" cols="60"><?php
    echo htmlspecialchars($body); ?></textarea>
</p>
<p>
```

The article ID must be carried over to the transaction page if you are modifying an existing article. The following hidden input field will do this for you.

```
<?php
echo '<input type="hidden" name="article" value="' .
    $article . "\">\n";
```

You also need to pass the author ID if the original author is editing his or her own document.

```
if ($_SESSION['access_lvl'] < 2) {
  echo '<input type="hidden" name="authorid" value="' .
      $authorid . "\">\n";
}
```

If the article is being modified, display the Save Changes submit button. If it's a new article, display the Submit New Article button.

```
      if ($article) {
        echo '<input type="submit" class="submit" name="action" ' .
             "value=\"Save Changes\">\n";
      } else {
        echo '<input type="submit" class="submit" name="action" ' .
             "value=\"Submit New Article\">\n";
      }
```

And so it ends, footer and all. Clean and simple.

```
    ?>
    </p>
    </form>
    <?php require_once 'footer.php'; ?>
```

If you've looked around your Web site, you might have noticed that the article you just created doesn't show up yet. That's because you've set up a review system wherein an administrator or moderator must approve an article before it is published to the public view. This sort of control is found on many CMS-based sites on the Web and is a good way to keep an eye on quality and duplicate stories.

Try It Out   Reviewing New Articles

In this exercise, you'll create the reviewing system that lets you approve your articles.

1. Create pending.php:

```
<?php
require_once 'conn.php';
require_once 'header.php';

$a_artTypes = array(
  "Pending" => "submitted",
  "Published" => "published"
);

echo "<h2>Article Availability</h2>\n";
$i = -1;
foreach ($a_artTypes as $k => $v) {
  $i++;
  echo "<h3>" . $k . " Articles</h3>\n";
  echo "<p>\n";
  echo " <div class=\"scroller\">\n";

  $sql = "SELECT article_id, title, date_". $v .
         " FROM cms_articles " .
         "WHERE is_published=" . $i .
         " ORDER BY title";

  $result = mysql_query($sql, $conn)
    or die('Could not get list of pending articles; ' . mysql_error());
  if (mysql_num_rows($result) == 0) {
    echo " <em>No " . $k . " articles available</em>";
  } else {
    while ($row = mysql_fetch_array($result)) {
```

```
        echo '  <a href="reviewarticle.php?article=' .
             $row['article_id'] . '">' .
             htmlspecialchars($row['title']) .
             "</a> ($v " . date("F j, Y", strtotime($row['date_'.$v])) .
             ")<br>\n";
      }
  }
  echo "  </div>\n";
  echo "</p>\n";
}

require_once 'footer.php';
?>
```

2. Next, create `reviewarticle.php`:

```php
<?php
require_once 'conn.php';
require_once 'outputfunctions.php';
require_once 'header.php';
?>

<form method="post" action="transact-article.php">

<h2>Article Review</h2>
<?php

outputStory($_GET['article']);

$sql = "SELECT ar.*, usr.name, usr.access_lvl " .
       "FROM cms_articles ar INNER JOIN cms_users usr " .
       "ON ar.author_id = usr.user_id " .
       "WHERE article_id=" . $_GET['article'];

$result = mysql_query($sql, $conn)
  or die('Could not retrieve article info; ' . mysql_error());

$row = mysql_fetch_array($result);

if ($row['date_published'] and $row['is_published']) {
  echo '<h4>Published: ' .
       date("l F j, Y H:i", strtotime($row['date_published'])) .
       "</h4>\n";
}
echo "<p><br>\n";
if ($row['is_published']) {
  $buttonType = "Retract";
} else {
  $buttonType = "Publish";
}
echo "<input type=\"submit\" class=\"submit\" " .
     "name=\"action\" value=\"Edit\"> ";
if (($row['access_lvl'] > 1) or ($_SESSION['access_lvl'] > 1)) {
  echo "<input type=\"submit\" class=\"submit\" " .
       "name=\"action\" value=\"$buttonType\"> ";
```

```
}
echo "<input type=\"submit\" class=\"submit\" " .
    "name=\"action\" value=\"Delete\"> ";
?>

<input type="hidden" name="article"
  value="<?php echo $_GET['article'] ?> ">
</p>

</form>

<?php require_once 'footer.php'; ?>
```

3. Click the Review link. The Review page pending.php loads (see Figure 13-8) with a list of all pending and published articles. Right now, there is only one pending article — the one you just wrote.

4. Click the article. You will be taken to reviewarticle.php. It should look similar to Figure 13-9. You have the option to edit, publish, or delete the article.

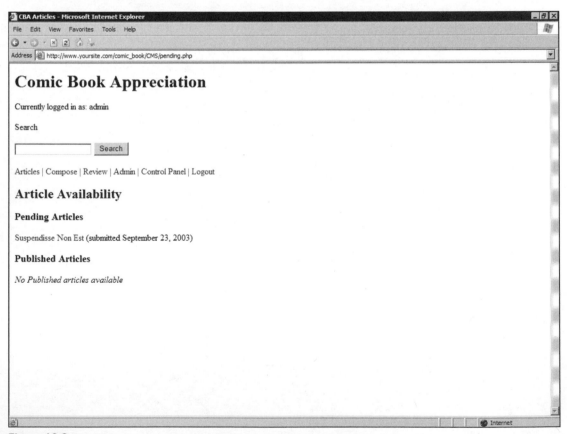

Figure 13-8

Figure 13-9

5. Click the Publish button. You will be taken back to `pending.php`, and the article will now be listed under Published Articles.

6. Click the Articles link, and you will be taken back to the index page. This time, the article should appear on the page (see Figure 13-10).

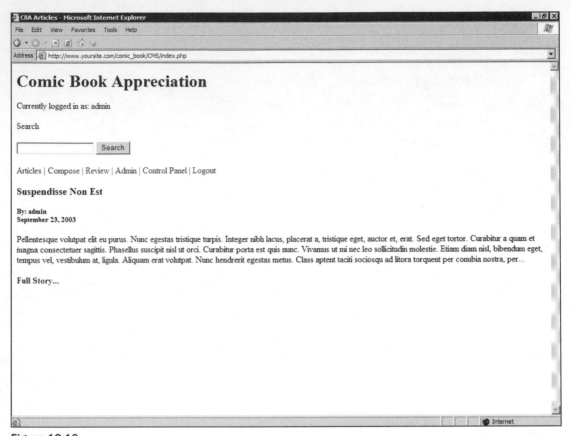

Figure 13-10

How It Works

Next comes `pending.php`:

```php
<?php
require_once 'conn.php';
require_once 'header.php';
```

Oooh . . . an associative array. This is one of PHP's advantages. Other server-side scripting languages such as ASP/VBScript do not use associative arrays, and we think they are very useful little things. What are you going to use this one for? Read on, dear reader, and we'll show you.

```php
$a_artTypes = array(
  "Pending" => "submitted",
  "Published" => "published"
);
```

The following is where you use your associative array. You are displaying pending, or submitted, articles, and then displaying published ones. In the interests of conserving code (because we're lazy, remember?), you loop through the array and substitute the appropriate values where necessary. The variable $k holds the array key, and $v holds the array value. You also set $i to –1 because it will be incremented immediately inside the loop:

```
echo "<h2>Article Availability</h2>\n";
$i = -1;
foreach ($a_artTypes as $k => $v) {
  $i++;
```

Here's your first use of the array key. The first pass through, this will read "Pending Articles." Next time through, it will read "Published Articles." Clever?

```
echo "<h3>" . $k . " Articles</h3>\n";
```

Notice that you are using $v in what follows to create the field date_submitted in the first loop, and date_published in the second. You are also using $i to first compare is_published to 0, and then to 1 in the next loop.

```
echo "<p>\n";
echo " <div class=\"scroller\">\n";

$sql = "SELECT article_id, title, date_". $v .
       " FROM cms_articles " .
       "WHERE is_published=" . $i .
       " ORDER BY title";

$result = mysql_query($sql, $conn)
  or die('Could not get list of pending articles; ' . mysql_error());
```

Again, the array key is used, if no articles are returned. Now you can see why you used an associative array.

```
if (mysql_num_rows($result) == 0) {
  echo " <em>No " . $k . " articles available</em>";
```

If rows are returned, you then loop through each article and display the title (linked to reviewarticle. php) and the date it was either submitted (pass one) or published (pass two).

```
} else {
  while ($row = mysql_fetch_array($result)) {
    echo ' <a href="reviewarticle.php?article=' .
         $row['article_id'] . '">' .
         htmlspecialchars($row['title']) .
         "</a> ($v " . date("F j, Y",strtotime($row['date_'.$v])) .
         ")<br>\n";
  }
}
echo " </div>\n";
echo "</p>\n";
}

require_once 'footer.php';
?>
```

And so ends another exciting day in the CMS saga. Stay tuned while we look at your next file, `reviewarticle.php`.

This time, you need to use one of the functions in `outputfunctions.php`, so you include it at the top of your page.

```php
<?php
require_once 'conn.php';
require_once 'outputfunctions.php';
require_once 'header.php';
?>
```

First, you display the title of the page, and then use the `outputStory()` function to display the article on the page.

```php
<form method="post" action="transact-article.php">

<h2>Article Review</h2>
<?php

outputStory($_GET['article']);
```

It is important to note that you passed only one variable to the function `outputStory()`, even though `outputStory()` takes two arguments. The second argument is `$only_snippet`, which defaults to `FALSE`. Because you did not use the second parameter, PHP automatically uses its default value. If there were no default value assigned, then attempting to call `outputStory()` with only one argument would result in a PHP warning telling you that you are missing an argument. This allows for more flexible functions.

In this Web page, you want to display additional data about the document, such as when it was published, and who wrote it. You used the previous SQL statement to retrieve this additional information. Yes, `outputStory()` retrieves this data, too, but if you modified `outputStory()` so that articles did not display their author or publish date, you would still want it displayed on this review page.

```php
$sql = "SELECT ar.*, usr.name, usr.access_lvl " .
       "FROM cms_articles ar INNER JOIN cms_users usr " .
       "ON ar.author_id = usr.user_id " .
       "WHERE article_id=" . $_GET['article'];

$result = mysql_query($sql, $conn)
  or die('Could not retrieve article info; ' . mysql_error());

$row = mysql_fetch_array($result);

if ($row['date_published'] and $row['is_published']) {
  echo '<h4>Published: ' .
       date("l F j, Y H:i", strtotime($row['date_published'])) .
       "</h4>\n";
}
```

If the document is published, you have an option to retract the article. If it is still pending, then you can publish it.

```php
echo "<p><br>\n";
if ($row['is_published']) {
  $buttonType = "Retract";
} else {
  $buttonType = "Publish";
}
```

Now add the edit button. This allows the user to edit the article:

```php
echo "<input type=\"submit\" class=\"submit\" " .
    "name=\"action\" value=\"Edit\"> ";
```

Add the Retract or Publish button, used to retract a published article, or publish a pending article. Only moderators and admins are allowed to retract and publish articles.

```php
if (($row['access_lvl'] > 1) or ($_SESSION['access_lvl'] > 1)) {
  echo "<input type=\"submit\" class=\"submit\" " .
      "name=\"action\" value=\"$buttonType\"> ";
}
```

Next insert the Delete button, used to remove articles. The Delete code in `transact-article.php` currently allows only pending articles to be deleted.

```php
echo "<input type=\"submit\" class=\"submit\" " .
    "name=\"action\" value=\"Delete\"> ";
?>
```

And they all lived happily ever after. The End.

```php
<input type="hidden" name="article"
  value="<?php echo $_GET['article'] ?> ">
</p>

</form>

<?php require_once 'footer.php'; ?>
```

Feeling a little *déjà vu?* Good.

Try It Out   Article Pages

So you've created an article, reviewed it, and published it. Now it's time to give the public a way to view the article and provide feedback.

1. Create `viewarticle.php`:

```php
<?php
require_once 'conn.php';
require_once 'outputfunctions.php';
require_once 'header.php';
```

```php
outputStory($_GET['article']);

showComments($_GET['article'], TRUE);

require_once 'footer.php';
?>
```

2. Now, create `comment.php`:

```php
<?php

require_once 'conn.php';
require_once 'outputfunctions.php';
require_once 'header.php';

outputStory($_GET['article']);

?>

<h1>Add a comment</h1>

<form method="post" action="transact-article.php">

<p>
  Comment:<br>
  <textarea id="comment" name="comment" rows="10" cols="60"></textarea>
</p>

<p>
  <input type="submit" class="submit" name="action"
    value="Submit Comment">
  <input type="hidden" name="article"
    value="<?php echo $_GET['article']; ?>">
</p>

</form>

<?php

showComments($_GET['article'], FALSE);

require_once 'footer.php';

?>
```

3. Go back to the index by clicking the Articles link. Click the "Full Story" link below the snippet of the article you want to view. The full article should appear, complete with a link to add comments.

How It Works

The first page, `viewarticle.php`, is very short, yet it illustrates the nature of included files and functions wonderfully.

As you can see, there is no content displayed directly with `viewarticle`. It simply includes the necessary files and uses two functions to display the article and all of the comments.

```php
<?php
require_once 'conn.php';
require_once 'outputfunctions.php';
require_once 'header.php';

outputStory($_GET['article']);

showComments($_GET['article'], TRUE);

require_once 'footer.php';
?>
```

You may notice that you don't worry about the situation in which an article is not passed. As it stands, if you load `viewarticle.php` without the `"article"` parameter in the URL, you will simply get a page that consists of the site title, search, and a menu (all included in `header.php`). The rest will be blank. If that's the desired result, then that's fine. You may decide to redirect the user back to the home page if `$_GET['article']` is empty. If you do, don't forget to include `http.php` and use `redirect()` *before* `header.php`.

The next page is `comment.php`. Include the necessary files:

```php
<?php
require_once 'conn.php';
require_once 'outputfunctions.php';
require_once 'header.php';
```

Then display the appropriate article at the top of the page:

```php
outputStory($_GET['article']);
```

Then add the page title:

```php
?>
<h1>Add a comment</h1>
```

A simple text area is used to enter a new comment:

```html
<form method="post" action="transact-article.php">

<p>
  Comment:<br>
  <textarea id="comment" name="comment" rows="10" cols="60"></textarea>
</p>
```

The next bit deals with the submit button and a hidden field for the article ID. This is needed to send the article ID to the next page:

```html
<p>
  <input type="submit" class="submit" name="action"
    value="Submit Comment">
  <input type="hidden" name="article"
    value="<?php echo $_GET['article']; ?>">
</p>
```

Display all the current comments for this article on this page:

```
</form>

<?php

showComments($_GET['article'], FALSE);

require_once 'footer.php';
?>
```

And that's it! They're getting easier, aren't they? Stay with us — only a couple more short ones. That last one was a doozy, huh?

Additional CMS Features

So far, you've created a system to create and manage users, and publish articles, but there are a couple additional features that can help make your CMS a lot more usable and manageable. What you're going to add is the ability for users to update their information, and the ability to search published articles by keyword.

Try It Out   User Control Panel

In this exercise, you're going to create a page so users can maintain their own information.

1.   Enter the following code, and save it as `cpanel.php`:

```
<?php
require_once 'conn.php';
require_once 'header.php';

$sql = "SELECT name, email " .
       "FROM cms_users " .
       "WHERE user_id=" . $_SESSION['user_id'];
$result = mysql_query($sql, $conn)
  or die('Could not look up user data; ' . mysql_error());

$user = mysql_fetch_array($result);
?>
<form method="post" action="transact-user.php">

<p>Name:<br>
  <input type="text" id="name" name="name"
    value="<?php echo htmlspecialchars($user['name']); ?>"></p>

<p>Email:<br>
  <input type="text" id="email" name="email"
    value="<?php echo htmlspecialchars($user['email']); ?>"></p>

<p><input type="submit" class="submit" name="action"
     value="Change my info"></p>
```

```
</form>

<h2>Pending Articles</h2>
<div class="scroller">
  <table>
<?php

$sql = "SELECT article_id, title, date_submitted " .
       "FROM cms_articles " .
       "WHERE is_published=0 " .
       "AND author_id=" . $_SESSION['user_id'] . " " .
       "ORDER BY date_submitted";
$result = mysql_query($sql, $conn)
  or die('Could not get list of pending articles; ' . mysql_error());

if (mysql_num_rows($result) == 0) {
  echo "  <em>No pending articles available</em>";
} else {
  while ($row = mysql_fetch_array($result)) {
    echo "<tr>\n";
    echo '<td><a href="reviewarticle.php?article=' .
         $row['article_id'] . '">' . htmlspecialchars($row['title']) .
         "</a> (submitted " .
         date("F j, Y", strtotime($row['date_submitted'])) .
         ")</td>\n";
    echo "</tr>\n";
  }
}
?>
  </table>
</div>
<br>

<h2>Published Articles</h2>
<div class="scroller">
  <table>
<?php

$sql = "SELECT article_id, title, date_published " .
       "FROM cms_articles " .
       "WHERE is_published=1 " .
       "AND author_id=" . $_SESSION['user_id'] . " " .
       "ORDER BY date_submitted";
$result = mysql_query($sql, $conn)
  or die('Could not get list of pending articles; ' . mysql_error());

if (mysql_num_rows($result) == 0) {
  echo "  <em>No published articles available</em>";
} else {
  while ($row = mysql_fetch_array($result)) {
    echo "<tr>\n";
    echo '<td><a href="viewarticle.php?article=' .
```

```
        $row['article_id'] . '">' . htmlspecialchars($row['title']) .
        "</a> (published " .
        date("F j, Y", strtotime($row['date_published'])) .
        ")</td>\n";
    echo "</tr>\n";
  }
}
?>
  </table>
</div>
<br>
<?php require_once 'footer.php'; ?>
```

2. On the navigation links, click Control Panel. You should see a screen similar to the one shown in Figure 13-11. Here you can change your user information (user name and e-mail), and see what articles you have written for the site.

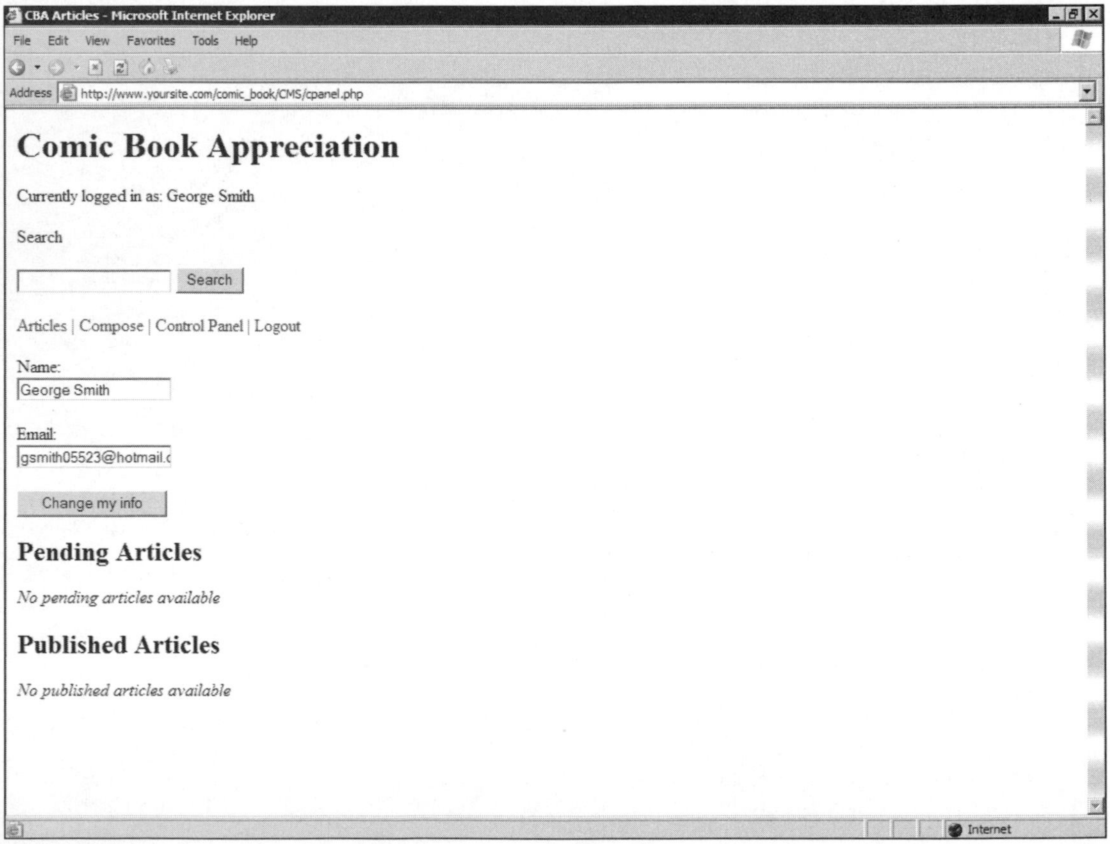

Figure 13-11

How It Works

Now let's take a look at `cpanel.php`. The Control Panel page `cpanel.php` is used to allow users to change their usernames and e-mail addresses. They can also see all of the articles they have written, categorized by Pending and Published articles.

As always, you need to connect to the database. And, as always, `conn.php` takes care of that. This time, you are displaying a Web page. You load up `header.php`, which is your standard header for all Web display pages.

```php
require_once 'conn.php';
require_once 'header.php';
```

You first go out to the database and get the user's name and e-mail address.

```php
$sql = "SELECT name, email " .
       "FROM cms_users " .
       "WHERE user_id=" . $_SESSION['user_id'];
$result = mysql_query($sql, $conn)
  or die('Could not look up user data; ' . mysql_error());

$user = mysql_fetch_array($result);
```

You will be entering and exiting PHP mode throughout this file and in the other Web pages. This gives you great flexibility and makes the page a lot easier to read. The next line exits PHP code:

```php
?>
```

The following form uses the `post` method. Notice the action. You already created that file. You know that when a submit button is clicked on this page, `transact-user.php` loads, the appropriate code runs, and the user is redirected to the control panel.

```html
<form method="post" action="transact-user.php">
```

Note the use of `htmlspecialchars()`. This prevents strange characters such as < or > from messing up the page. These characters will be displayed using their entity equivalents (such as `&lt;` and `&gt;`).

```php
<p>Name:<br>
  <input type="text" id="name" name="name"
    value="<?php echo htmlspecialchars($user['name']); ?>"></p>
```

The rest of the form is standard HTML. Now you need to display Pending and Published articles. Time to drop back into PHP:

```php
<p>Email:<br>
  <input type="text" id="email" name="email"
    value="<?php echo htmlspecialchars($user['email']); ?>"></p>

<p><input type="submit" class="submit" name="action"
    value="Change my info"></p>
```

```
</form>

<h2>Pending Articles</h2>
<div class="scroller">
  <table>
```

This code gets all pending articles written by this user. They are ordered by `date_submitted`, with the oldest being first. Please note that if there are no pending articles, this will *not* return a MySQL error. You will still get a result set, but there won't be any rows. You handle that contingency next.

```php
<?php

$sql = "SELECT article_id, title, date_submitted " .
       "FROM cms_articles " .
       "WHERE is_published=0 " .
       "AND author_id=" . $_SESSION['user_id'] . " " .
       "ORDER BY date_submitted";
$result = mysql_query($sql, $conn)
  or die('Could not get list of pending articles; ' . mysql_error());
```

If there are no pending articles, you simply state so and move on. Otherwise . . .

```php
if (mysql_num_rows($result) == 0) {
  echo "  <em>No pending articles available</em>";
} else {
```

You loop through each pending article and display the title (with a link to the article), along with the date/time it was submitted.

```php
while ($row = mysql_fetch_array($result)) {
  echo "<tr>\n";
  echo '<td><a href="reviewarticle.php?article=' .
       $row['article_id'] . '">' . htmlspecialchars($row['title']) .
       "</a> (submitted " .
       date("F j, Y", strtotime($row['date_submitted'])) .
       ")</td>\n";
  echo "</tr>\n";
}
}
```

Okay, this next code is almost identical to the code used to display pending articles. This time, display them using the `date_published` column.

```php
<?php

$sql = "SELECT article_id, title, date_published " .
       "FROM cms_articles " .
       "WHERE is_published=1 " .
       "AND author_id=" . $_SESSION['user_id'] . " " .
       "ORDER BY date_submitted";
$result = mysql_query($sql, $conn)
  or die('Could not get list of pending articles; ' . mysql_error());
```

```php
if (mysql_num_rows($result) == 0) {
  echo "  <em>No published articles available</em>";
} else {
  while ($row = mysql_fetch_array($result)) {
    echo "<tr>\n";
    echo '<td><a href="viewarticle.php?article=' .
        $row['article_id'] . '">' . htmlspecialchars($row['title']) .
        "</a> (published " .
        date("F j, Y",strtotime($row['date_published'])) .
        ")</td>\n";
    echo "</tr>\n";
  }
}
```

Then load the footer. It is only a few lines of HTML for now, but some day you will want to put a menu, or perhaps a copyright line. The great thing is, even if your site uses 300 pages, you will have to add that information in only one place: footer.php.

```php
?>
  </table>
</div>
<br>
<?php require_once 'footer.php'; ?>
```

Try It Out Search

The final thing you are going to add is a simple search feature. Using the power of the full-text searching in MySQL, you can easily put a keyword search field on each page, and show the results here.

1. Create search.php:

```php
<?php
require_once 'conn.php';
require_once 'outputfunctions.php';
require_once 'header.php';

$result = NULL;
if (isset($_GET['keywords'])) {
  $sql = "SELECT article_id FROM cms_articles " .
        "WHERE MATCH (title,body) " .
        "AGAINST ('" . $_GET['keywords'] . "' IN BOOLEAN MODE) " .
        "ORDER BY MATCH (title,body) " .
        "AGAINST ('" . $_GET['keywords'] . "' IN BOOLEAN MODE) DESC";

  $result = mysql_query($sql, $conn)
    or die('Could not perform search; ' . mysql_error());
}

echo "<h1>Search Results</h1>\n";

if ($result and !mysql_num_rows($result)) {
  echo "<p>No articles found that match the search terms.</p>\n";
} else {
  while ($row = mysql_fetch_array($result)) {
```

```
        outputStory($row['article_id'], TRUE);
    }
}

require_once 'footer.php';
?>
```

2. On any page with a search box on the top, enter a word that existed in the article you created. Once you submit the form, search.php will appear, and any matches should be shown.

How It Works

First, you include the necessary files:

```
<?php
require_once 'conn.php';
require_once 'outputfunctions.php';
require_once 'header.php';
```

As long as you passed keywords, you do a search. In the following SQL statement, you'll notice the MATCH and AGAINST keywords. This is the syntax used to do a text search in those fields. They must be full-text indexed fields in order to perform this search. Visit dev.mysql.com/doc/mysql/en/Fulltext_Search.html for more information on full-text indexed fields.

```
$result = NULL;
if (isset($_GET['keywords'])) {
    $sql = "SELECT article_id FROM cms_articles " .
           "WHERE MATCH (title,body) " .
           "AGAINST ('" . $_GET['keywords'] . "' IN BOOLEAN MODE) " .
           "ORDER BY MATCH (title,body) " .
           "AGAINST ('" . $_GET['keywords'] . "' IN BOOLEAN MODE) DESC";

    $result = mysql_query($sql, $conn)
      or die('Could not perform search; ' . mysql_error());
}
```

If you didn't find a match, say so:

```
echo "<h1>Search Results</h1>\n";

if ($result and !mysql_num_rows($result)) {
    echo "<p>No articles found that match the search terms.</p>\n";
```

Otherwise, loop through the results and display them as snippets on the screen:

```
} else {
    while ($row = mysql_fetch_array($result)) {
        outputStory($row['article_id'], TRUE);
    }
}

require_once 'footer.php';
?>
```

Summary

Well, if you didn't have writer's cramp before, you probably do now. We hope this application has given you some insight into the separation of content and design. Because of the way the application was designed, you can easily modify the look and feel of the application by either directly altering your header and footer files, or using a CSS file to set up different styles. This won't matter to your users; they will still be able to enter articles without ever having to worry about what the article will look like on the Web when it's published.

We also hope that you understand the importance of updating your site often enough to draw users back again and again. By adding an application like this to your site, and allowing users to add content for you, you create a dynamically changing site with fresh information. Just think about all the ways you could implement such a design:

❑ Create a message board. (This is examined in more detail in Chapter 16.)

❑ Add a daily comic. Perhaps you have an artist who can draw you a comic every day. You could create an application that allows him or her to upload comic strips and allows users to comment on them.

❑ Compile photo journals. A while back, there was a project in which photographers went all over the world, and in a 24-hour period, they took their pictures and uploaded the digital images, and people in the central office typed up descriptions and allowed people to view them online. It was a very ambitious project and a perfect example of a CMS application.

The bottom line is that if you have content that you want to be able to update on a regular basis, you definitely want to implement a CMS application. And now, you have the basic tools to build one on your own!

Perhaps you should send your users an e-mail to tell them of your improved functionality. You'll do that in Chapter 14.

Exercises

After all that typing, are we so cruel that we'd include more work at the end? Yes. Yes we are.

See how you might accomplish the following tasks:

1. **Delete when appropriate.** When reviewing an article, the delete button always shows up, regardless of what happens in the transaction page. Alter the code so the Delete button only shows up when the article is pending.

2. **Find out about the author.** Authors of articles might want the readers to know a little more about them. Add the ability to enter extra fields in a user's profile, and provide a link on the article full-view page to the author's information.

3. **Notify the author.** Authors might want to be automatically notified when their stories have been approved. Add an e-mail notification upon approval, and give the user the ability to toggle their notification on and off.

Mailing Lists

Ah, yes. Mailing Lists. Two simple, innocent words that never meant anyone any harm. That is, until a few years ago, when someone decided to put the two together, and junk mail was born. Oh sure, mailing lists are used for more than junk mail. After all, how else are you going to receive your Quilting Monthly magazine unless your name and address are on a list? What does this have to do with PHP? In the world of e-mail and your incredible new Web site, a mailing list is a perfect way for you to communicate with all of your users. You might need to let every user know that your site has moved to a new address. Maybe you want to send out a monthly newsletter. Whatever the reason, you will occasionally need to send e-mails to many people, and you will need a relatively easy way to do so.

Specifically, this chapter discusses the following:

❑ Administering a mailing list

❑ Creating a mailing list

❑ Spam

❑ Opt-in and opt-out

So, are you ready to learn how to spam your Web site users? We hope not, because that is not what you are going to do. Yes, you are going to use mailing lists. And yes, you are going to send out "mass" e-mails. However, you are going to be responsible, and send e-mails only to those people who have agreed to be recipients. Right? Let's get started.

What Do You Want to Send Today?

Before you actually create the mailing list, you must have something that you intend to send to your recipients. The train of thought usually goes like this: You decide that you have some information you want to share with your users. Here are a few possibilities:

❑ **Web site notifications:** These are important tidbits of information about your Web site. You will want to let your users know you've improved the level of security for online transactions on your site, for example.

❑ **Newsletters:** If you had a family Web site, for example, and wanted to let your whole family know about the new addition to your family, you could send them a newsletter.

❑ **Important announcements:** "Our site will be down for 5 days. Sorry for the inconvenience. We'll let you know when it is back up." (Oooh . . . an opportunity for *two* mailings!)

❑ **Advertising:** Perhaps you've partnered with an online comic book store to offer deals on rare comics to your members.

Once you know what you want to say, you format the information you wish to share, using plain text or HTML. You try to figure out how you are going to e-mail this information to *every* member of your Web site. If you can figure out how to send it, you hope that your users will be able to read and appreciate what you sent with their many types of e-mail clients.

In this chapter's project, you are going to send out two different e-mails: Web site change notifications and a newsletter. The former will be sent to all members of the Web site. The latter will be sent to those who subscribe to the newsletter only.

You are going to use HTML in your mass e-mail, of course. Because Chapter 11 taught you how to send HTML in an e-mail, this should pose no problem at all. You can also e-mail links to an online version of the HTML you are sending, so that those with text e-mail clients can see your hard work, as well.

Coding the Administration Application

The first thing you're going to do is to create the administration page, where you can add and remove mailing lists. There are a few scripts to tackle, but because they all rely on each other to work, you need to enter them all now. Hey . . . you're the one who wanted to write some code. Let's get cracking!

Try It Out Preparing the Database

First, you're going to create the file that will hold the server, username, password, and database values.

1. Open your favorite text editor, and enter the following code, making sure you use the proper values for your server:

```php
<?php

define('SQL_HOST','localhost');
define('SQL_USER','bp5am');
define('SQL_PASS','bp5ampass');
define('SQL_DB','comicsite');
define('ADMIN_EMAIL', 'your@emailaddress.com');

?>
```

2. Save the file as config.php.

3. Now you're going to create the tables. You can create them with your MySQL tool (such as PHPMyAdmin), or you can simply enter the following code, save it as `sql.php` on your server, and load it in your browser:

```php
<?php
require('config.php');

$conn = mysql_connect(SQL_HOST, SQL_USER, SQL_PASS)
  or die('Could not connect to MySQL database. ' . mysql_error());

$sql = "CREATE DATABASE IF NOT EXISTS " . SQL_DB;

$res = mysql_query($sql) or die(mysql_error());

mysql_select_db(SQL_DB, $conn);

$sql1 = <<<EOS
  CREATE TABLE IF NOT EXISTS ml_lists (
    ml_id int(11) NOT NULL auto_increment,
    listname varchar(255) NOT NULL default '',
    PRIMARY KEY (ml_id)
  )
EOS;

$sql2 = <<<EOS
 CREATE TABLE IF NOT EXISTS ml_subscriptions (
  ml_id int(11) NOT NULL default '0',
  user_id int(11) NOT NULL default '0',
  pending tinyint(1) NOT NULL default '1',
  PRIMARY KEY (ml_id,user_id)
 )
EOS;

$sql3 = <<<EOS
 CREATE TABLE IF NOT EXISTS ml_users (
  user_id int(11) NOT NULL auto_increment,
  firstname varchar(255) default '',
  lastname varchar(255) default '',
  email varchar(255) NOT NULL default '',
  PRIMARY KEY (user_id)
 )
EOS;

$res = mysql_query($sql1) or die(mysql_error());
$res = mysql_query($sql2) or die(mysql_error());
$res = mysql_query($sql3) or die(mysql_error());

echo "Done.";
?>
```

4. If you ran `sql.php` in your browser, it should display a "Done." message, indicating the database tables were created.

How It Works

Your first file, `config.php`, contains just five lines:

```
define('SQL_HOST','localhost');
define('SQL_USER','bp5am');
define('SQL_PASS','bp5ampass');
define('SQL_DB','comicsite');
define('ADMIN_EMAIL', 'your@emailaddress.com');
```

These constants are created separately so that in the event that you make a change such as moving the application to another server, or changing the password, it can be done in only one location. If this data were in each file, any change would require modification of several files.

Include `config.php` in each file that requires access to MySQL like so:

```
require('config.php');
```

You use `require()` instead of `include()` because if the file is not loaded, you want to halt loading of the page. Another option would be to use `include()`, and then immediately test for the existence of one of the constants. If it does not exist, you could then redirect the user to another page, which makes for a more user-friendly experience.

As you can see here, the constants from `config.php` are used to make your connection:

```
$conn = mysql_connect(SQL_HOST, SQL_USER, SQL_PASS)
    or die('Could not connect to MySQL database. ' . mysql_error());

$sql = "CREATE DATABASE IF NOT EXISTS" . SQL_DB;

$res = mysql_query($sql) or die(mysql_error());

mysql_select_db(SQL_DB, $conn);
```

Take notice of the CREATE DATABASE statement. There are a couple of things you should be aware of about creating databases. If you already have a database (one that you created in another chapter, or if your site is already using a database), it's better to keep your mailing list tables in that database. You don't need extra databases because if your Web site spans multiple databases, you will need to create multiple connections to those databases, and that is extra overhead that is just not necessary.

In addition, if there are any relationships between your tables from this application and tables from other apps, they need to be in the same database. For example, if you have a user table that stores your registered users for all applications, all of the applications that rely on that user table should reside in the same database.

If you do need to create a new database, the CREATE DATABASE command may still not work if your site is hosted by an Internet service provider (ISP). Some ISPs don't allow programmed creation of databases. If this is the case, you may need to go through your ISP to create the database (through PHPMyAdmin, for example) and run `sql.php`. Just be sure to put the proper database name in the code. See Chapter 10 for more information about creating databases.

This SQL is used to create the tables in your database:

```
$sql1 = <<<EOS
  CREATE TABLE IF NOT EXISTS ml_lists (
    ml_id int(11) NOT NULL auto_increment,
    listname varchar(255) NOT NULL default '',
    PRIMARY KEY (ml_id)
  )
EOS;

$sql2 = <<<EOS
  CREATE TABLE IF NOT EXISTS ml_subscriptions (
    ml_id int(11) NOT NULL default '0',
    user_id int(11) NOT NULL default '0',
    pending tinyint(1) NOT NULL default '1',
    PRIMARY KEY (ml_id,user_id)
  )
EOS;

$sql3 = <<<EOS
  CREATE TABLE IF NOT EXISTS ml_users (
    user_id int(11) NOT NULL auto_increment,
    firstname varchar(255) default '',
    lastname varchar(255) default '',
    email varchar(255) NOT NULL default '',
    PRIMARY KEY (user_id)
  )
EOS;
```

Note there are three tables: ml_lists, ml_users, and ml_subscriptions. The ml_lists table contains two columns: the unique ID (ml_id) and the name of the mailing list (listname). The ml_users table contains four columns: the unique ID (user_id), first and last name (firstname, lastname), and e-mail address (email).

The ml_subscriptions table is where most of the "work" is done when it comes to mailing lists. It contains three columns: ml_id, user_id, and pending. The combination of ml_id and user_id must be unique. (You don't want to have the same user subscribed to the same mailing list more than once, right?) The pending column is used to determine whether or not a user has confirmed his or her subscription. Use of the pending column is discussed later in this chapter.

The following lines simply run the SQL queries to create the tables. As long as all three tables are created (or already exist), you will see "Done" echoed to the screen. Otherwise, you will see an error message.

```
$res = mysql_query($sql1) or die(mysql_error());
$res = mysql_query($sql2) or die(mysql_error());
$res = mysql_query($sql3) or die(mysql_error());
echo "Done.";
```

Try It Out   Mailing List Administration

Next, you will create the admin page, where the administrator (that's you!) can create, delete, and rename mailing lists.

1.   Create the following code, and save it as `admin.php`:

```php
<?php
require('config.php');
?>
<html>
<head>
<title>Mailing List Administration</title>
</head>
<body>

<form method="post" action="admin_transact.php">

<p>
  Add Mailing List:<br />
  <input type="text" name="listname" maxlength="255" />
  <input type="submit" name="action" value="Add New Mailing List" />
</p>

<p>
  Delete Mailing List:<br />
  <select name="ml_id">
<?php

$conn = mysql_connect(SQL_HOST, SQL_USER, SQL_PASS)
  or die('Could not connect to MySQL database. ' . mysql_error());

mysql_select_db(SQL_DB, $conn);

$sql = "SELECT * FROM ml_lists ORDER BY listname";
$result = mysql_query($sql)
  or die('Invalid query: ' . mysql_error());

while ($row = mysql_fetch_array($result)) {
  echo "    <option value=\"" . $row['ml_id'] . "\">" . $row['listname'] .
      "</option>\n";
}

?>
  </select>
  <input type="submit" name="action" value="Delete Mailing List" />
</p>

</form>

<p>
  <a href="quickmsg.php">Send a quick message to users</a>
</p>

</body>
</html>
```

2. The administrator needs the ability to send e-mails to the members of various mailing lists. Otherwise, what was the point of creating the mailing lists in the first place? Okay, you know the routine. Enter the following code, and save it as `quickmsg.php`:

```php
<?php
require('config.php');
?>
<html>
<head>
<title>Quick Message</title>
</head>
<body>

<form method="post" action="admin_transact.php">

<p>
  Choose Mailing List:<br />
  <select name="ml_id">
    <option value="all">All</option>
<?php

$conn = mysql_connect(SQL_HOST, SQL_USER, SQL_PASS)
  or die('Could not connect to MySQL database. ' . mysql_error());

mysql_select_db(SQL_DB, $conn);

$sql = "SELECT * FROM ml_lists ORDER BY listname";
$result = mysql_query($sql)
  or die('Invalid query: ' . mysql_error());

while ($row = mysql_fetch_array($result)) {
  echo "    <option value=\"" . $row['ml_id'] . "\">" . $row['listname'] .
      "</option>\n";
}

?>
  </select>
</p>

<p>Compose Message:</p>

<p>
  Subject:<br />
  <input type="text" name="subject" />
</p>

<p>
  Message:<br />
  <textarea name="msg" rows="10" cols="60"></textarea>
</p>

<p>
  <input type="submit" name="action" value="Send Message" />
</p>

</form>
```

```
<p>
  <a href="admin.php">Back to mailing list administration</a>
</p>

</body>
</html>
```

3. This next script should look a bit familiar. If you remember, this is exactly the same `SimpleMail` class you used in Chapter 11. Save this as `class.SimpleMail.php`. If you still have the original `class.SimpleMail.php` from Chapter 11, you can simply copy it to the directory you're working in — it's identical to the following:

```php
<?php

class SimpleMail {
  public $to = NULL;
  public $cc = NULL;
  public $bcc = NULL;
  public $from = NULL;
  public $subject = '';
  public $body = '';
  public $htmlbody = '';
  public $send_text = TRUE;
  public $send_html = FALSE;
  private $message = '';
  private $headers = '';

  public function send($to = NULL,
                       $subject = NULL,
                       $message = NULL,
                       $headers = NULL) {
    if (func_num_args() >= 3) {
      $this->to = $to;
      $this->subject = $subject;
      $this->message = $message;
      if ($headers) {
        $this->headers = $headers;
      }

    } else {

      if ($this->from) {
        $this->headers .= "From: " . $this->from . "\r\n";
      }
      if ($this->cc) {
        $this->headers .= "Cc: " . $this->cc . "\r\n";
      }
      if ($this->bcc) {
        $this->headers .= "Bcc: " . $this->bcc . "\r\n";
      }

      if ($this->send_text and !$this->send_html) {
        $this->message = $this->body;
```

```
        } elseif ($this->send_html and !$this->send_text) {
            $this->message = $this->htmlbody;
            $this->headers .= "MIME-Version: 1.0\r\n";
            $this->headers .= "Content-type: text/html; " .
                                "charset=iso-8859-1\r\n";
        } else {
            $_boundary = "==MP_Bound_xyccr948x==";

            $this->headers = "MIME-Version: 1.0\r\n";
            $this->headers .= "Content-type: multipart/alternative; " .
                                "boundary=\"$_boundary\"\r\n";

            $this->message = "This is a Multipart Message in " .
                              "MIME format\n";
            $this->message .= "--$_boundary\n";
            $this->message .= "Content-Type: text/plain; " .
                                "charset=\"iso-8859-1\"\n";
            $this->message .= "Content-Transfer-Encoding: 7bit\n\n";
            $this->message .= $this->body . "\n";
            $this->message .= "--$_boundary\n";
            $this->message .= "Content-type: text/html; " .
                                "charset=\"iso-8859-1\"\n";
            $this->message .= "Content-Transfer-Encoding: 7bit\n\n";
            $this->message .= $this->htmlbody . "\n";
            $this->message .= "--$_boundary--";
        }
    }

    if (!mail($this->to,$this->subject,$this->message,$this->headers)) {
      throw new Exception('Sending mail failed.');
      return FALSE;
    } else {
      return TRUE;
    }
  }
}

?>
```

4. Okay, one more script. When the administrator clicks a button, you need to have a page that handles the transactions. Enter the following, and save it as `admin_transact.php`:

```
<?php
require('config.php');
require('class.SimpleMail.php');

$conn = mysql_connect(SQL_HOST, SQL_USER, SQL_PASS)
  or die('Could not connect to MySQL database. ' . mysql_error());

mysql_select_db(SQL_DB, $conn);

if (isset($_POST['action'])) {
```

```
switch ($_POST['action']) {
  case 'Add New Mailing List':
    $sql = "INSERT INTO ml_lists (listname) " .
           "VALUES ('" . $_POST['listname'] . "')";
    mysql_query($sql)
      or die('Could not add mailing list. ' . mysql_error());
    break;

  case 'Delete Mailing List':
    $sql = "DELETE FROM ml_lists WHERE ml_id=" . $_POST['ml_id'];
    mysql_query($sql)
      or die('Could not delete mailing list. ' . mysql_error());
    $sql = "DELETE FROM ml_subscriptions " .
           "WHERE ml_id=" . $_POST['ml_id'];
    mysql_query($sql)
      or die('Could not delete mailing list subscriptions. ' .
        mysql_error());
    break;

  case 'Send Message':
    if (isset($_POST['msg'], $_POST['ml_id'])) {
      if (is_numeric($_POST['ml_id'])) {
        $sql = "SELECT listname FROM ml_lists " .
               "WHERE ml_id='" . $_POST['ml_id'] . "'";
        $result = mysql_query($sql, $conn)
          or die(mysql_error());
        $row = mysql_fetch_array($result);
        $listname = $row['listname'];
      } else {
        $listname = "Master";
      }

      $sql = "SELECT DISTINCT usr.email, usr.firstname, usr.user_id " .
             "FROM ml_users usr " .
             "INNER JOIN ml_subscriptions mls " .
             "ON usr.user_id = mls.user_id " .
             "WHERE mls.pending=0";
      if ($_POST['ml_id'] != 'all') {
        $sql .= " AND mls.ml_id=" . $_POST['ml_id'];
      }

      $result = mysql_query($sql)
        or die('Could not get list of email addresses. ' . mysql_error());

      $headers = "From: " . ADMIN_EMAIL . "\r\n";

      while ($row = mysql_fetch_array($result)) {
        if (is_numeric($_POST['ml_id'])) {
          $ft = "You are receiving this message as a member of the ";
          $ft .= $listname . "\n mailing list. If you have received ";
          $ft .= "this email in error, or would like to\n remove your ";
          $ft .= "name from this mailing list, please visit the ";
```

```
                    $ft .= "following URL:\n";
                    $ft .= "http://" . $_SERVER['HTTP_HOST'] .
                            dirname($_SERVER['PHP_SELF']) . "/remove.php?u=" .
                            $row['user_id'] . "&ml=" . $_POST['ml_id'];
                } else {
                    $ft = "You are receiving this email because you subscribed ";
                    $ft .= "to one or more\n mailing lists. Visit the following ";
                    $ft .= "URL to change your subscriptions:\n";
                    $ft .= "http://" . $_SERVER['HTTP_HOST'] .
                            dirname($_SERVER['PHP_SELF']) . "/user.php?u=" .
                            $row['user_id'];
                }

                $msg = stripslashes($_POST['msg']) . "\n\n";
                $msg .= "--------------\n";
                $msg .= $ft;

                $email = new SimpleMail();

                $email->send($row['email'],
                            stripslashes($_POST['subject']),
                            $msg,
                            $headers)
                    or die('Could not send email.');
            }
        }
        break;
    }
}

header('Location: admin.php');

?>
```

That's it for now. You still have the user functions to worry about, but you'll tackle those in a bit. For now, load a few of these pages in your browser to see them in action; then we'll figure out how they work.

5. The first page of the mailing list application you want to take a look at is the Mailing List Administrator page. Load admin.php in your browser. As you can see in Figure 14-1, you can create a new mailing list, delete an existing mailing list, or send a quick message to users. Feel free to create a couple of new mailing lists. Go crazy, have fun, get wacky. Good. Let's move on.

6. Click the link at the bottom of the Mailing List Administrator page, "Send a quick message to users." A new page appears where you can compose a new message and send it to either a single mailing list, or all users (see Figure 14-2). If you just created these pages, you don't have any users yet. You can compose a message, but it won't go to anyone. You'll need to create the user pages first, which you'll do shortly.

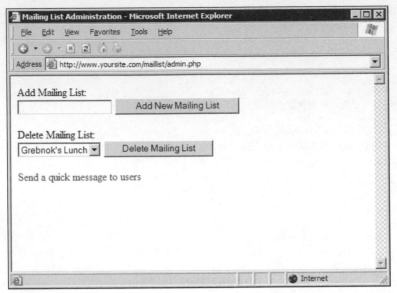

Figure 14-1

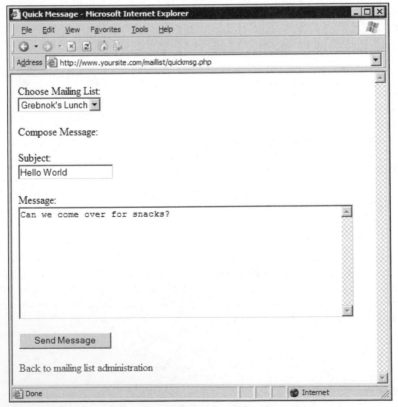

Figure 14-2

How It Works

Let's take a look at admin.php:

```
require('config.php');
```

Now you should see why you put the connection values in a separate file. By doing this, all you need is a single line to include the constants, and you can use them in this page.

Let's pause here for a moment and talk about form submittal. A common practice is to post a form back to itself, and you certainly could have done that here. When your page contains data that needs to be inserted into a database, however, you need to think twice about a self-posting form. If the user were to refresh or reload the page, all of your database functions would run again, and that could be disastrous. You would end up with duplicate data, or delete records you didn't mean to delete.

Obviously, you don't want anything like that to happen, so to minimize the probability, you post to a separate form called admin_transact.php. This page handles all of the necessary database transactions, and then redirects back to the page from which you came. If the user reloads the page at that point, no harm will come to your database.

```
<form method="post" action="admin_transact.php">
```

You might notice that all of your buttons have the same name, "action," each with a different value. When posting the form, you will be accessing the $_POST['action'] variable to see which button was pressed, and perform the appropriate actions. This allows you to use one script for multiple transactions, rather than having to create a page with multiple forms, each posting to a different transaction page.

```
<input type="submit" name="action" value="Add New Mailing List" />
```

Now you get all of the mailing lists available and wrap them in option tags so that they will appear on your page in a drop-down select box.

```php
<select name="ml_id">
<?php

$conn = mysql_connect(SQL_HOST, SQL_USER, SQL_PASS)
  or die('Could not connect to MySQL database. ' . mysql_error());

mysql_select_db(SQL_DB, $conn);

$sql = "SELECT * FROM ml_lists ORDER BY listname";
$result = mysql_query($sql)
  or die('Invalid query: ' . mysql_error());

while ($row = mysql_fetch_array($result)) {
  echo "    <option value=\"" . $row['ml_id'] . "\">" . $row['listname'] .
      "</option>\n";
}

?>
</select>
```

This is the link to the e-mail portion of the admin's functions, which is pretty self-explanatory:

```
<a href="quickmsg.php">Send a quick message to users</a>
```

You should be able to figure out `quickmsg.php` fairly easily. Most of it is HTML, and the PHP code is practically identical to the code used to build the select in `admin.php`. Feel free to cannibalize your own code as often as you need.

If you are scratching your head and trying to remember exactly how `class.SimpleMail.php` works, now would be a good time to take a break and go check out Chapter 11. There's an analysis of the script toward the end of the chapter.

Finally, you come to the real workhorse of the Mailing List Administrator application, `admin_transact.php`. This page is the one to which you post your forms, and it will process that information, update the database tables, and send out e-mails as required. Let's take a look under the hood:

```
require('config.php');
require('class.SimpleMail.php');
```

Remember seeing the preceding line in `admin.php`? Having your connection data in one file and including it in each page makes your code much more efficient. The same applies to the SimpleMail include. Of course, you already knew that. Let's move on to create the connection to the database, and select it so that you can work with it:

```
$conn = mysql_connect(SQL_HOST, SQL_USER, SQL_PASS)
  or die('Could not connect to MySQL database. ' . mysql_error());

mysql_select_db(SQL_DB, $conn);
```

Did the user click an "action" button?

```
if (isset($_POST['action'])) {
```

Depending on which button was clicked, you're going to perform one of three actions: create a new mailing list, delete an old mailing list, or send a message to the users subscribing to a mailing list:

```
switch ($_POST['action']) {
```

Not only must you delete the mailing list, like this:

```
case 'Add New Mailing List':
  $sql = "INSERT INTO ml_lists (listname) " .
          "VALUES ('" . $_POST['listname'] . "')";
  mysql_query($sql)
    or die('Could not add mailing list. ' . mysql_error());
  break;

case 'Delete Mailing List':
  $sql = "DELETE FROM ml_lists WHERE ml_id=" . $_POST['ml_id'];
  mysql_query($sql)
    or die('Could not delete mailing list. ' . mysql_error());
```

If anyone was subscribed to that mailing list, you must delete those subscriptions, too:

```
$sql = "DELETE FROM ml_subscriptions " .
       "WHERE ml_id=" . $_POST['ml_id'];
mysql_query($sql)
  or die('Could not delete mailing list subscriptions. ' .
    mysql_error());
break;
```

When you send a message, you want to let the user know which mailing list you are referring to. If the mailing list ID (ml_id) is "all" instead of a number, you will want to reflect that as well:

```
case 'Send Message':
  if (isset($_POST['msg'], $_POST['ml_id'])) {
    if (is_numeric($_POST['ml_id'])) {
      $sql = "SELECT listname FROM ml_lists " .
             "WHERE ml_id='" . $_POST['ml_id'] . "'";
      $result = mysql_query($sql, $conn)
        or die(mysql_error());
      $row = mysql_fetch_array($result);
      $listname = $row['listname'];
    } else {
      $listname = "Master";
    }
```

What follows is a more complicated SQL statement than you've written thus far, but not too difficult. What's happening here is that you are grabbing the e-mails, first names, and user IDs from the ml_users table where the mailing list ID (ml_id) matches their user ID in the ml_subscriptions table. You do this by using the INNER JOIN command in SQL. You also *must not* send any e-mails or newsletters to those that are awaiting subscription confirmation, so select only those where pending = 0, or false. If pending = 1 (true), then that row is ignored.

```
$sql = "SELECT DISTINCT usr.email, usr.firstname, usr.user_id" .
       "FROM ml_users usr " .
       "INNER JOIN ml_subscriptions mls " .
       "ON usr.user_id = mls.user_id " .
       "WHERE mls.pending=0";
```

If the administrator did not choose "all" in the select list, you must limit your selection to the specific users that are subscribed to the mailing list the administrator selected. You do this by tacking on the AND condition:

```
if ($_POST['ml_id'] != 'all') {
  $sql .= " AND mls.ml_id=" . $_POST['ml_id'];
}
```

Now execute the previous SQL statement, and return the results:

```
$result = mysql_query($sql)
  or die('Could not get list of email addresses. ' . mysql_error());
```

You may remember the next step from Chapter 11. This is how you add the From: header to an e-mail. It is fairly self-explanatory:

```
$headers = "From: " . ADMIN_EMAIL . "\r\n";
```

The following pretty piece of work is nothing more than a way to build up a custom message, depending on whether the administrator is sending the e-mail to *all* mailing lists, or to a specific one:

```
while ($row = mysql_fetch_array($result)) {
  if (is_numeric($_POST['ml_id'])) {
    $ft = "You are receiving this message as a member of the ";
    $ft .= $listname . "\n mailing list. If you have received ";
    $ft .= "this email in error, or would like to\n remove your ";
    $ft .= "name from this mailing list, please visit the ";
    $ft .= "following URL:\n";
    $ft .= "http://" . $_SERVER['HTTP_HOST'] .
           dirname($_SERVER['PHP_SELF']) . "/remove.php?u=" .
           $row['user_id'] . "&ml=" . $_POST['ml_id'];
  } else {
    $ft = "You are receiving this email because you subscribed ";
    $ft .= "to one or more\n mailing lists. Visit the following ";
    $ft .= "URL to change your subscriptions:\n";
    $ft .= "http://" . $_SERVER['HTTP_HOST'] .
           dirname($_SERVER['PHP_SELF']) . "/user.php?u=" .
           $row['user_id'];
  }
```

Wrap the message entered on the `quickmsg.php` form inside some extra disclaimer text before you send it off to SimpleMail's `send()` method:

```
$msg = stripslashes($_POST['msg']) . "\n\n";
$msg .= "--------------\n";
$msg .= $ft;
$email = new SimpleMail();

$email->send($row['email'],
             stripslashes($_POST['subject']),
             $msg,
             $headers)
  or die('Could not send email.');
}
```

And away it goes, before you loop back to the top of your `while` loop and do it again with the next user. Notice that you are looping through *each* e-mail address you have and sending an e-mail to each one using the `$email->send()` method. It is important to note that the page will not finish loading until it has sent every e-mail. This works fine if you have a few e-mail addresses (a hundred or less). It has the added benefit of allowing you (with slight modifications to the code) to personalize each e-mail with the person's first name ("Dear Billy-Bob,").

If you need to send to more people and don't want to deal with the long wait time, we recommend putting all of your e-mail addresses in the BCC: field of the mail, using headers (as discussed in Chapter 11). You can't personalize the e-mail, but the page will load much faster.

Of course, some day your site will be extremely popular, and you might have thousands of e-mails to send. At that point, it might be time to start looking at a professional mailing list management application. That, however, is beyond the scope of this book.

After the page is done with its transactions, redirect the user to the `admin.php` page. Most of the time, this happens so quickly that you don't notice the redirection at all.

```php
header('Location: admin.php');
```

Sign Me Up!

Now it's time to look at the other half of the application, the Mailing List Signup form. This is the page you send your users to that enables them to sign up for any of the mailing lists that you have created. This application consists of `user.php`, `user_transact.php`, `thanks.php`, and `remove.php`. As always, you'll also be using the `config.php` file that you already created.

On the surface, when you view the page from the Web, it looks like a simple application. However, there's a lot going on inside. So let's open it up and see what's under the hood!

Try It Out   Mailing List Signup

The first page you are going to create is the actual signup form.

1.   Enter the following code in your favorite PHP editor and save it as `user.php`:

```php
<?php
require('config.php');
?>
<html>
<head>
<title>Mailing List Signup</title>
</head>
<body>

<form method="post" action="user_transact.php">

<p>
  Sign up for Mailing List:<br />
</p>

<?php

$conn = mysql_connect(SQL_HOST, SQL_USER, SQL_PASS)
  or die('Could not connect to MySQL database. ' . mysql_error());

mysql_select_db(SQL_DB, $conn);

if (isset($_GET['u'])) {
  $uid - $_GET['u'];
  $sql = "SELECT * FROM ml_users WHERE user_id = '$uid'";
```

```
    $result = mysql_query($sql)
      or die('Invalid query: ' . mysql_error());
    if (mysql_num_rows($result)) {
      $row = mysql_fetch_array($result);
      $email = $row['email'];
    } else {
      $email = "";
    }
} else {
  $email = "";
}
?>

<p>
  Email Address:<br />
  <input type="text" name="email" size="40" value="<?php echo
    $email;?>"/>
</p>

<p>
  If you aren't currently a member, please provide
  your name:<br /><br />
  First Name:<br />
  <input type="text" name="firstname" /><br />
  Last Name:<br />
  <input type="text" name="lastname" /><br />
</p>

<p>
  Select the mailing lists you want to receive:<br />
  <select name="ml_id">

<?php
$result = mysql_query("SELECT * FROM ml_lists ORDER BY listname")
  or die('Invalid query: ' . mysql_error());

while ($row = mysql_fetch_array($result)) {
  echo "    <option value=\"" . $row['ml_id'] . "\">" .
      $row['listname'] . "</option>\n";
}

?>
  </select>
</p>

<p>
  <input type="submit" name="action" value="Subscribe" />
</p>

</form>

</body>
</html>
```

2. Enter the transaction page by entering the following code in your PHP editor and saving it as
user_transact.php:

```php
<?php
require('config.php');
require('class.SimpleMail.php');

$conn = mysql_connect(SQL_HOST, SQL_USER, SQL_PASS)
  or die('Could not connect to MySQL database. ' . mysql_error());

mysql_select_db(SQL_DB, $conn);

$headers = "From: " . ADMIN_EMAIL . "\r\n";

if (isset($_REQUEST['action'])) {
  switch ($_REQUEST['action']) {
    case 'Remove':
      $sql = "SELECT user_id FROM ml_users " .
             "WHERE email='" . $_POST['email'] . "'";
      $result = mysql_query($sql, $conn);

      if (mysql_num_rows($result)) {
        $row = mysql_fetch_array($result);
        $user_id = $row['user_id'];
        $url = "http://" . $_SERVER['HTTP_HOST'] .
               dirname($_SERVER['PHP_SELF']) .
               "/remove.php?u=" . $user_id .
               "&ml=" . $_POST['ml_id'];
        header("Location: $url");
        exit();
      }
      $redirect = 'user.php';
      break;

    case 'Subscribe':
      $sql = "SELECT user_id FROM ml_users " .
             "WHERE email='" . $_POST['email'] . "'";
      $result = mysql_query($sql, $conn);

      if (!mysql_num_rows($result)) {
        $sql = "INSERT INTO ml_users " .
               "(firstname,lastname,email) " .
               "VALUES ('" . $_POST['firstname'] . "'," .
               "'" . $_POST['lastname'] . "'," .
               "'" . $_POST['email'] . "')";
        $result = mysql_query($sql, $conn);
        $user_id = mysql_insert_id($conn);
      } else {
        $row = mysql_fetch_array($result);
        $user_id = $row['user_id'];
      }

      $sql = "INSERT INTO ml_subscriptions (user_id,ml_id) " .
             "VALUES ('" . $user_id . "','" . $_POST['ml_id'] . "')";
```

```
    mysql_query($sql, $conn);

    $sql = "SELECT listname FROM ml_lists " .
           "WHERE ml_id=" . $_POST['ml_id'];
    $result = mysql_query($sql, $conn);
    $row = mysql_fetch_array($result);
    $listname = $row['listname'];

    $url = "http://" . $_SERVER['HTTP_HOST'] .
           dirname($_SERVER['PHP_SELF']) .
           "/user_transact.php?u=" . $user_id .
           "&ml=" . $_POST['ml_id'] . "&action=confirm";

    $subject = 'Mailing list confirmation';
    $body = "Hello " . $_POST['firstname'] . "\n" .
            "Our records indicate that you have subscribed to " .
            "the " . $listname . " mailing list.\n\n" .
            "If you did not subscribe, please accept our " .
            "apologies. You will not be subscribed if you do " .
            "not visit the confirmation URL.\n\n" .
            "If you subscribed, please confirm this by visiting " .
            "the following URL:\n" . $url;

    $mailmsg = new SimpleMail();
    $mailmsg->send($_POST['email'],$subject,$body,$headers);

    $redirect = "thanks.php?u=" . $user_id . "&ml=" .
                $_POST['ml_id'] . "&t=s";
    break;

case 'confirm':
  if (isset($_GET['u'], $_GET['ml'])) {
    $sql = "UPDATE ml_subscriptions SET pending=0 " .
           "WHERE user_id=" . $_GET['u'] .
           " AND ml_id=" . $_GET['ml'];
    mysql_query($sql, $conn);

    $sql = "SELECT listname FROM ml_lists " .
           "WHERE ml_id=" . $_GET['ml'];
    $result = mysql_query($sql, $conn);

    $row = mysql_fetch_array($result);
    $listname = $row['listname'];

    $sql = "SELECT * FROM ml_users " .
           "WHERE user_id='" . $_GET['u'] . "'";
    $result = mysql_query($sql, $conn);
    $row = mysql_fetch_array($result);
    $firstname = $row['firstname'];
    $email = $row['email'];

    $url = "http://" . $_SERVER['HTTP_HOST'] .
           dirname($_SERVER['PHP_SELF']) .
```

```
                      "/remove.php?u=" . $_GET['u'] .
                      "&ml=" . $_GET['ml'];

            $subject = 'Mailing List Subscription Confirmed';
            $body = "Hello " . $firstname . ",\n" .
                    "Thank you for subscribing to the " .
                    $listname . " mailing list. Welcome!\n\n" .
                    "If you did not subscribe, please accept our " .
                    "apologies.\n" .
                    "You can remove this subscription immediately by " .
                    "visiting the following URL:\n" . $url;

            $mailmsg = new SimpleMail();
            $mailmsg->send($email,$subject,$body,$headers);

            $redirect = "thanks.php?u=" . $_GET['u'] . "&ml=" .
                        $_GET['ml'] . "&t=s";
        } else {
            $redirect = 'user.php';
        }
        break;

    default:
        $redirect = 'user.php';
    }
}

header('Location: ' . $redirect);

?>
```

3. You may have noticed when entering the last bit of code that you are redirecting your users to a page called thanks.php. It would probably be a good idea to create that page now by entering the following code and saving it as thanks.php:

```
<?php
require('config.php');
?>
<html>
<head>
<title>Thank You</title>
</head>
<body>

<?php
$conn = mysql_connect(SQL_HOST, SQL_USER, SQL_PASS)
  or die('Could not connect to MySQL database. ' . mysql_error());

mysql_select_db(SQL_DB, $conn);

if (isset($_GET['u'])) {
  $uid = $_GET['u'];
  $sql = "SELECT * FROM ml_users WHERE user_id = '$uid'";
```

```
    $result = mysql_query($sql)
      or die('Invalid query: ' . mysql_error());
    if (mysql_num_rows($result)) {
      $row = mysql_fetch_array($result);
      $msg = "<h2>Thank You, " . $row['firstname'] . "</h2><br /><br />";
      $email = $row['email'];
    } else {
      die("No match for user id " . $uid);
    }
  }

  if (isset($_GET['ml'])) {
    $ml_id = $_GET['ml'];
    $sql = "SELECT * FROM ml_lists WHERE ml_id = '" . $ml_id . "'";
    $result = mysql_query($sql)
      or die('Invalid query: ' . mysql_error());
    if (mysql_num_rows($result)) {
      $row = mysql_fetch_array($result);
      $msg .= "Thank you for subscribing to the <i>" .
              $row['listname'] . "</i> mailing list.<br />";
    } else {
      die ("Could not find Mailing List $ml_id");
    }
  } else {
    die ("Mailing List id missing.");
  }

  if (!isset($_GET['t'])) {
    die("Missing Type");
  }

  switch ($_GET['t']) {
    case 'c':
      $msg .= "A confirmation request has been sent " .
              "to <b>$email</b>.<br /><br />";
      break;
    case 's':
      $msg .= "A subscription notification has been " .
              "sent to you at <b>$email</b>.<br /><br />";
  }
  $msg .= "<a href='user.php?u=$uid'>" .
          "Return to Mailing List Signup page</a>";
  echo $msg;
?>

</body>
</html>
```

Excellent job! Now it's time to test your code and figure out how it works.

4. Open your browser and open user.php. You should see a form that looks very much like the one in Figure 14-3.

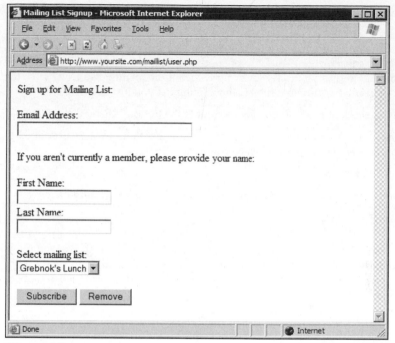

Figure 14-3

5. Enter your e-mail address and your first and last name, choose a mailing list to subscribe to, and click Subscribe.

You should see a Thank You screen (shown in Figure 14-4) and receive a confirmation e-mail at the e-mail address you entered.

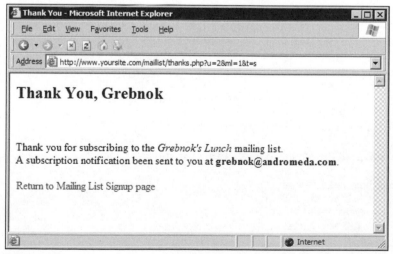

Figure 14-4

6. Open the confirmation e-mail. There will be a link at the bottom (or a nonlinked URL if you are using a text e-mail client).

7. Click the link, and it takes you back to the Thank You page, this time thanking you for confirming your subscription. You will get another e-mail informing you about your subscription, with a link that allows you to remove yourself from the mailing list. Don't click that link just yet. First you're going to send an e-mail to the mailing list you just subscribed to.

8. Open `admin.php`, and then click the link at the bottom, "Send a quick message to users."

9. In the Quick Message page, choose the mailing list that you just subscribed to in the previous steps, and enter a subject. Then type a quick message.

10. Click Send Message.

11. Open your e-mail client again, and read the message you should have received.

How It Works

By now, you know how `config.php` works. You know why you use it. We won't insult your intelligence by explaining again how it's important to use this file to hold your MySQL connection info and password. We are also going to skip over parts of the code that we've touched on before. We certainly don't want to bore you!

Let's take a look at `user.php` instead, shall we?

user.php

Typically, `user.php` loads empty, without any extra data. Occasionally, you may return to this page from elsewhere and will have the user ID of the person loading the page. In this case, you tack on `?u=x` to the end of the URL (where *x* is the user ID, such as 3). This bit of code detects the presence of that value:

```
if (isset($_GET['u']))
{
```

and then puts it into a variable:

```
$uid = $_GET['u'];
```

and finally looks up the user's e-mail address:

```
$sql = "SELECT * FROM ml_users WHERE user_id = '$uid';";
$result = mysql_query($sql)
  or die('Invalid query: ' . mysql_error());
```

If you find a row, grab the e-mail address and stick it into a variable:

```
if (mysql_num_rows($result)) {
  $row = mysql_fetch_array($result);
  $email = $row['email'];
} else {
  $email = "";
}
```

Then use that e-mail address as the default value for the e-mail field on the form. (How clever is that?)

```
Email Address:<br />
<input type="text" name="email" size="40" value="<?php echo
   $email;?>"/>
```

The following code is very similar to the code used on the admin.php page. It loops through the existing mailing lists in the database and formats them on the page as options for the select field.

```
<select name="ml_id">

<?php
$result = mysql_query("SELECT * FROM ml_lists ORDER BY listname")
   or die('Invalid query: ' . mysql_error());

while ($row = mysql_fetch_array($result)) {
  echo "    <option value=\"" . $row['ml_id'] . "\">" .
      $row['listname'] . "</option>\n";
}

?>
</select>
```

The rest of user.php is boring HTML. Let's take a look at the meat and potatoes of the user side of things next.

user_transact.php

This is where the action happens, for the most part. Let's take a look, shall we?

First, make the connection to the server, and select the database:

```
$conn = mysql_connect(SQL_HOST, SQL_USER, SQL_PASS)
   or die('Could not connect to MySQL database. ' . mysql_error());

mysql_select_db(SQL_DB, $conn);
```

You will be building the e-mail message later. The parameter $headers will be the fourth parameter of the mail() function, and will insert a From address in the e-mail.

```
$headers = "From: " . ADMIN_EMAIL . "\r\n";
```

For more information about headers, see Chapter 11. When loading user_transact.php, you either clicked a button named 'action' (POST), or action is in the URL as ?action=xyz (GET). Because it can come across as a POST or a GET, you use $_REQUEST to grab the value. The variable $_REQUEST is your "catch-all" predefined variable, which contains an associative array of all $_GET, $_POST, and $_COOKIE variables.

```
if (isset($_REQUEST['action'])) {
  switch ($_REQUEST['action']) {
```

If `'action'` = `'Remove'`, you look up the user ID in the `ml_users` database. If you find a user id, you pass that ID on to `remove.php`, along with the mailing list id. Your job is done, so you redirect the user to `remove.php`.

```
case 'Remove':
  $sql = "SELECT user_id FROM ml_users " .
         "WHERE email='" . $_POST['email'] . "'";
  $result = mysql_query($sql, $conn);

  if (mysql_num_rows($result)) {
    $row = mysql_fetch_array($result);
    $user_id = $row['user_id'];
    $url = "http://" . $_SERVER['HTTP_HOST'] .
           dirname($_SERVER['PHP_SELF']) .
           "/remove.php?u=" . $user_id .
           "&ml=" . $_POST['ml_id'];
    header("Location: $url");
    exit();
  }
  $redirect = 'user.php';
  break;
```

Note the `exit()` function immediately following `header()`. This is important, so the rest of the page is not loaded. The end of each `case` statement contains a break so that the rest of the case statements are not executed.

If the user clicks the Subscribe button, a number of things have to happen. First, you must look up the e-mail address that was provided to see if the user already exists:

```
case 'Subscribe':
  $sql = "SELECT user_id FROM ml_users " .
         "WHERE email='" . $_POST['email'] . "'";
  $result = mysql_query($sql, $conn);
```

If the user does not exist (no rows were returned from your query), you will insert a new record in the `ml_users` table. MySQL automatically assigns a user id.

```
if (!mysql_num_rows($result)) {
  $sql = "INSERT INTO ml_users " .
         "(firstname,lastname,email) " .
         "VALUES ('" . $_POST['firstname'] . "'," .
         "'" . $_POST['lastname'] . "'," .
         "'" . $_POST['email'] . "')";
  $result = mysql_query($sql, $conn);
```

To retrieve that user id, use the PHP function `mysql_insert_id`. The variable `$conn` is optional, but it's usually a good idea to include it. If you omit it, it will automatically use the last open connection. The `mysql_insert_id` function will return a valid value only if the last SQL statement run resulted in a column being automatically incremented. In this case that did happen—the column is `user_id`, which is the value you need for the next part of your code.

```
$user_id = mysql_insert_id($conn);
```

If the e-mail address was found in the database, you simply grab the user ID from the record that was returned. Either way, you now have a `$user_id`. You also have a mailing list id, retrieved from `$_POST['ml_id']`. That's all you need to create a subscription record.

```
} else {
  $row = mysql_fetch_array($result);
  $user_id = $row['user_id'];
}
```

You may recall that the `ml_subscriptions` table contains three columns: `user_id`, `ml_id`, and `pending`. The first two values you have. The last one, `pending`, should be set to 1 until the user confirms the subscription. You initially set up the table to set `pending` to 1 as a default, so that column is automatically taken care of. So you now have all the data you need to create a subscription, and just like that, you insert the appropriate data into the subscriptions table.

```
$sql = "INSERT INTO ml_subscriptions (user_id,ml_id) " .
       "VALUES ('" . $user_id . "','" . $_POST['ml_id'] . "')";
mysql_query($sql, $conn);
```

Now all that is left to do is to notify the user. You do this in two ways: with a Thank You Web page that confirms that the subscription was processed, and with an e-mail to request confirmation because you don't want people to be able to sign other people up for mail. It's not a foolproof security measure, but it will stop most abuse.

You'll send the e-mail, and then redirect the user to the Thank You page. The first thing you do is get the name of the mailing list, using the mailing list id. That's because you want to tell the user in the e-mail which mailing list he or she subscribed to, and it wouldn't be too helpful to say it was mailing list #42.

```
$sql = "SELECT listname FROM ml_lists " .
       "WHERE ml_id=" . $_POST['ml_id'];
$result = mysql_query($sql, $conn);

$row = mysql_fetch_array($result);
$listname = $row['listname'];
```

Next, you build up the URL that will be at the bottom of the e-mail message. This URL directs the user back to this same page (`user_transact.php`), this time with an `'action'` of `'confirm'` (the third "action" choice, which we'll look at shortly).

```
$url = "http://" . $_SERVER['HTTP_HOST'] .
       dirname($_SERVER['PHP_SELF']) .
       "/user_transact.php?u=" . $user_id .
       "&ml=" . $_POST['ml_id'] . "&action=confirm";
```

Then you build the subject and body of the message, concatenating the URL to the bottom, and send it off with the `mail()` command:

```
$subject = 'Mailing list confirmation';
$body = "Hello " . $_POST['firstname'] . "\n" .
        "Our records indicate that you have subscribed to " .
        "the " . $listname . " mailing list.\n\n" .
```

```
            "If you did not subscribe, please accept our " .
            "apologies. You will not be subscribed if you do " .
            "not visit the confirmation URL.\n\n" .
            "If you subscribed, please confirm this by visiting " .
            "the following URL:\n" . $url;

$mailmsg = new SimpleMail();
$mailmsg->send($_POST['email'],$subject,$body,$headers);
```

Once the mail has been sent, all that is left to do is send the user to the Thank You page. We will look at the Thank You page shortly.

```
$redirect = "thanks.php?u=" . $user_id . "&ml=" .
            $_POST['ml_id'] . "&t=s";
break;
```

When the user receives the confirmation e-mail, he or she clicks the link at the bottom, which loads `user_transact.php` again, this time with `action=confirm`. When confirming, you simply need to do one thing — change the pending flag for the appropriate subscription to 0. Once that is done, redirect the user to the Thank You page for confirmation, and send another e-mail informing the user of his or her new subscription. You will also provide an easy means of removal in the e-mail.

The first thing to do is make sure the user ID and mailing list ID were passed to the function. If not, you simply redirect the user to `user.php`.

```
case 'confirm':
  if (isset($_GET['u'], $_GET['ml'])) {

    ...

  } else {
    $redirect = 'user.php';
  }
```

Next, find the subscription that matches the user ID and mailing list ID and update the pending column to 0. Remember that the `user_id` and `ml_id` columns combined make up a primary key, so there can be just one record for each set of possible values.

```
$sql = "UPDATE ml_subscriptions SET pending=0 " .
       "WHERE user_id=" . $_GET['u'] .
       " AND ml_id=" . $_GET['ml'];
mysql_query($sql, $conn);
```

Look familiar? It should — you are grabbing the mailing list name based on the mailing list id, just as you did for the Subscribe case. Looks like this is a prime candidate for a function:

```
$sql = "SELECT listname FROM ml_lists " .
       "WHERE ml_id=" . $_GET['ml'];
$result = mysql_query($sql, $conn);

$row = mysql_fetch_array($result);
$listname = $row['listname'];
```

Now you need to retrieve the user's e-mail address based on his or her user id, so you can send him or her an e-mail. This should also look familiar:

```php
$sql = "SELECT * FROM ml_users " .
        "WHERE user_id='" . $_GET['u'] . "';";
$result = mysql_query($sql, $conn);
$row = mysql_fetch_array($result);
$firstname = $row['firstname'];
$email = $row['email'];
```

The body of this message is a little different. You are building the subject and body parameters for the `mail()` function and sending the mail to your user. Now you just need to send it on its way.

```php
$url = "http://" . $_SERVER['HTTP_HOST'] .
        dirname($_SERVER['PHP_SELF']) .
        "/remove.php?u=" . $_GET['u'] .
        "&ml=" . $_GET['ml'];

$subject = 'Mailing List Subscription Confirmed';
$body = "Hello " . $firstname . ",\n" .
        "Thank you for subscribing to the " .
        $listname . " mailing list. Welcome!\n\n" .
        "If you did not subscribe, please accept our " .
        "apologies.\n" .
        "You can remove this subscription immediately by " .
        "visiting the following URL:\n" . $url;

$mailmsg = new SimpleMail();
$mailmsg->send($email,$subject,$body,$headers);
```

Off your user goes, to the Thank You page:

```php
$redirect = "thanks.php?u=" . $_GET['u'] . "&ml=" .
            $_GET['ml'] . "&t=s";
```

Finally, if `'action'` somehow is set to something other than `Remove`, `Subscribe`, or `confirm`, you will need to redirect the user somewhere else—in this case, `user.php`. The final line handles the redirection:

```php
    default:
        $redirect = 'user.php';
    }
}

header('Location: ' . $redirect);
```

The `user_transact.php` page is not terribly complicated. However, when you have a single page performing multiple tasks, you need to be careful that all situations are handled correctly.

thanks.php

Next let's look at the code in `thanks.php`. Most of it is familiar code that you have used elsewhere. You should have no problem breezing through this one.

Connect to the database:

```
$conn = mysql_connect(SQL_HOST, SQL_USER, SQL_PASS)
  or die('Could not connect to MySQL database. ' . mysql_error());

mysql_select_db(SQL_DB, $conn);
```

Get user info based on the user id. If you find it, display the title "Thank You," followed by the user's first name. Also grab the user's e-mail address. You'll use it later.

```
if (isset($_GET['u'])) {
  $uid = $_GET['u'];
  $sql = "SELECT * FROM ml_users WHERE user_id = '$uid'";
  $result = mysql_query($sql)
    or die('Invalid query: ' . mysql_error());
  if (mysql_num_rows($result)) {
    $row = mysql_fetch_array($result);
    $msg = "<h2>Thank You, " . $row['firstname'] . "</h2><br /><br />";
    $email = $row['email'];
  } else {
    die("No match for user id " . $uid);
  }
}
```

Next, you get the listname, based on the mailing list id. If you find it, you build the message to include "Thanks for subscribing." Once you get past this point, you know you have the user ID and mailing list ID.

```
if (isset($_GET['ml'])) {
  $ml_id = $_GET['ml'];
  $sql = "SELECT * FROM ml_lists WHERE ml_id = '" . $ml_id . "'";
  $result = mysql_query($sql)
    or die('Invalid query: ' . mysql_error());
  if (mysql_num_rows($result)) {
    $row = mysql_fetch_array($result);
    $msg .= "Thank you for subscribing to the <i>" .
            $row['listname'] . "</i> mailing list.<br />";
  } else {
    die ("Could not find Mailing List $ml_id");
  }
} else {
  die ("Mailing List id missing.");
}
```

Now all you have to do is determine the type of message you're displaying.

```
if (!isset($_GET['t'])) {
  die("Missing Type");
}
```

It is crucial that the type be set. If not, stop processing this page. You don't know what to thank the user for.

Then comes the custom part of the message. Currently, there are two types of Thank You messages: "A confirmation request has been sent to . . .", and "A subscription notification has been sent . . ."

```
switch ($_GET['t']) {
  case 'c':
    $msg .= "A confirmation request has been sent " .
            "to <b>$email</b>.<br /><br />";
    break;
  case 's':
    $msg .= "A subscription notification has been " .
            "sent to you at <b>$email</b>.<br /><br />";
}
```

Finally, you finish the page by putting a link back to user.php, and displaying the page.

```
$msg .= "<a href='user.php?u=$uid'>" .
        "Return to Mailing List Signup page</a>";
echo $msg;
```

Try It Out   Removing Your Subscription

Now that you've given users the ability to add themselves to your mailing lists, you need to give them the ability to remove themselves when they want.

1.   The e-mail that you sent yourself has a link on it allowing your users to remove themselves from the mailing list, if they desire. Enter that file now, and save it as remove.php:

```
<?php
require('config.php');

$conn = mysql_connect(SQL_HOST, SQL_USER, SQL_PASS)
  or die('Could not connect to MySQL database. ' . mysql_error());

mysql_select_db(SQL_DB, $conn);

if (isset($_GET['u'], $_GET['ml'])) {
  $sql = "DELETE FROM ml_subscriptions " .
         "WHERE user_id=" . $_GET['u'] .
         " AND ml_id=" . $_GET['ml'];
  $result = mysql_query($sql, $conn);
} else {
  die("Incorrect parameters passed for deletion");
}

if ($result) {
  $msg = "<h2>Removal Successful</h2>";
} else {
  $msg = "<h2>Removal Failed</h2>";
}

$ml_id = $_GET['ml'];
$sql = "SELECT * FROM ml_lists WHERE ml_id = '" . $ml_id . "'";
```

```
$result = mysql_query($sql)
  or die('Invalid query: ' . mysql_error());
if (mysql_num_rows($result)) {
  $row = mysql_fetch_array($result);
  $msg .= "You have been removed from the <i>" .
          $row['listname'] . "</i> mailing list.<br />";
} else {
  $msg .= "Sorry, could not find Mailing List id#{$ml_id}";
}

$msg .= "<a href='user.php?u=" . $_GET['u'] .
        "'>Return to Mailing List Signup page</a>";
echo $msg;
?>
```

2. At the bottom of the e-mail you sent yourself is a link you can click to remove yourself from the mailing list.

Now, click the link. You should see the Removal page (see Figure 14-5), with a message of success. If you send another message to that mailing list, the message should not be sent to your e-mail address.

Figure 14-5

How It Works

A user can remove him- or herself from a mailing list in two ways. The first way is for the user to go to user.php, enter the e-mail address, choose the mailing list, and click the Remove button. The second way is via a link that you conveniently include at the end of e-mails that are sent to the mailing list recipients.

The remove.php page requires two parameters, user ID and mailing list ID. You are removing a database record from the ml_subscriptions table, and you will recall that those two values are what make each record unique. You can easily get that data from the e-mail link; it's embedded as part of the URL.

However, the user.php form forces you to take one extra step. You get the mailing list ID from the mailing list choice, but you have only an e-mail address for the user. Therefore, you will need to do a lookup with that e-mail address. As you'll no doubt recall, the Remove button on user.php loads the user_transact.php page, and when the 'action' is Remove, you do a lookup for user_id based on the e-mail address, and build the URL for remove.php. You then redirect the user to remove.php with the correct parameters. Time for remove.php to do its job!

You can't just assume that remove.php received the appropriate variables. You test to ensure they are set and run the DELETE query.

```
if (isset($_GET['u'], $_GET['ml'])) {
  $sql = "DELETE FROM ml_subscriptions " .
         "WHERE user_id=" . $_GET['u'] .
         " AND ml_id=" . $_GET['ml'];
  $result = mysql_query($sql, $conn);
} else {
  die("Incorrect parameters passed for deletion");
}
```

That was easy, but you still need to do a couple of things, like build the page. Don't quit on us now. Of course, first, you must make sure the deletion worked. Announce the results in big letters!

```
if ($result) {
  $msg = "<h2>Removal Successful</h2>";
} else {
  $msg = "<h2>Removal Failed</h2>";
}
```

Using the mailing list id, you do a lookup for the name of the mailing list and build the page's message:

```
$ml_id = $_GET['ml'];
$sql = "SELECT * FROM ml_lists WHERE ml_id = '" . $ml_id . "'";
$result = mysql_query($sql)
  or die('Invalid query: ' . mysql_error());
if (mysql_num_rows($result)) {
  $row = mysql_fetch_array($result);
  $msg .= "You have been removed from the <i>" .
          $row['listname'] . "</i> mailing list.<br />";
} else {
  $msg .= "Sorry, could not find Mailing List id#{$ml_id}";
}
```

Finally, you add a link back to user.php at the bottom of the page and echo it to the screen.

```
$msg .= "<a href='user.php?u=" . $_GET['u'] .
        "'>Return to Mailing List Signup page</a>";
echo $msg;
```

Mailing List Ethics

You should know about a couple of ethical issues when dealing with the world of mailing lists, namely spam and opt-in/opt-out. This section represents our personal soap box for airing our opinions about them.

A Word About Spam

With the advent of the computer, mailing lists have been brought to a whole new level. Now you can be (and no doubt are) told on a daily basis that Candy really wants you to visit her Web site, and that a little blue pill will solve all of your personal problems. Yes, occasionally an e-mail sits in your Inbox informing you of new job postings, new posts on PHPBuilder.com, or tour dates for Jimmy Buffett. But we think you know what mailing lists are primarily used for: spam!

For those of you just crawling out of a suspended animation chamber, *spam* is a term used to describe a "shotgun" approach to advertising. You simply send your e-mail advertisement to as many people as you possibly can, in the hopes that a certain small percentage of them will actually respond.

What is our point? SPAM is a luncheon meat. You spell it in all capital letters, and you enjoy it on your sandwiches. Spam is another name for UCE, or unsolicited commercial e-mail. It is spelled in all lower-case, and we shun it.

The bottom line: Don't use mailing lists to send spam. Your mother would be *very* disappointed.

Opt-In versus Opt-Out

You may have heard these terms before. What do they mean? To most of your users, probably not much. They simply answer the questions on your registration, read the fine print (as all users do, of course), and click the Submit button.

However, you aren't a user any more. At least, not on your own site. You are the administrator. You need to understand the difference between opt-in and opt-out because it may mean the difference between annoyance and acceptance for your users.

Opt-in and opt-out are fancy ways of saying "What is the default choice for your users?" Opt-in means the user is not currently scheduled to receive a specific newsletter, but he or she may *opt* to subscribe. Obviously, opt-out is the opposite — your user will automatically receive notifications unless he or she *opts* to remove him- or herself from that mailing list.

Why the difference? As the administrator, you may sometimes have to walk a fine line between satisfying your advertisers (the ones giving you money to keep your site alive) and your users (the ones visiting your site, keeping your advertisers happy by driving up the number of hits). If an advertiser pays you enough, you might agree to automatically send advertisements from that company unless the user explicitly chooses not to receive them (opt-out).

However, you might have a newsletter you send once per week that contains, for example, details of comic conventions throughout the country (or even the world). Not all visitors to your site will be interested in that, but if any are, they can subscribe to the newsletter so they will always be notified (opt-in).

As we mentioned, you walk a fine line when choosing between the two. Because this is a new Web site for you, the decision might not be that difficult. But as your site grows, interest increases, and companies want to advertise with you, you'll need to make these important decisions. For now, we suggest you make all mailing lists opt-in, with the exception of important site announcements.

Summary

You have just created a nice, relatively simple mailing list subscription application. You have the ability to create new mailing lists, delete old ones, and send e-mails to multiple recipients. Users can subscribe and unsubscribe to any mailing lists, and you added a step for confirmation to help stamp out abuse.

We hope you come away from this chapter with an understanding of the difference between good, informative mass e-mails and spam.

Mailing lists are good. Spam is bad. Any questions? Good. Next we'll take a look at how to sell your SPAM collection on your Web site.

Exercises

1. **Hide your users' addresses.** Modify the send message functionality to send the e-mails to your users using the "Bcc:" e-mail field, instead of the usual "To:" field.

2. **Reduce sending.** Modify the send message functionality to send e-mails to your users in groups of 10. That is, every e-mail that is sent should be sent to 10 users at a time (when possible), instead of one e-mail per user.

3. **Let the administrator know.** Add functionality to send an e-mail to an administrator when new users confirm their subscription to the mailing list.

4. **Clean up any leftovers.** Add functionality to the administration page to allow an admin to purge the database of any subscriptions that haven't yet been confirmed.

Online Stores

Some of us cringe when we hear the word "e-commerce" and the phrase "selling over the Internet." Perhaps we've had a bad experience ourselves, or the thought of opening an online store is just too overwhelming. Even though this is the part of the book that all geeks out there probably dread reading, we're here to show you that e-commerce is really not so bad, and that pretty much anyone can do it.

However, just because anyone can do it doesn't mean it's always done the right way. Done the wrong way, your site can look downright cheesy, but done the right way, your site can look professional and inviting, and become an excellent resource for your visitors and potential customers. There are definite, if unwritten, guidelines for selling things over the Web and we want to make sure you do things the right way.

Selling things from your Web site can not only make you some extra cash; it can enhance your relationship with your Web site visitors (if e-commerce is not your site's primary function). In the case of your comic book fan site, offering pertinent items can make your site more interactive and interesting and bring visitors back again to see what new items you have for sale. True comic book fans will appreciate the niche of items you are providing, especially if some of the items are unique or hard to come by.

This chapter discusses the following:

- ❑ Creating a simple shopping cart script
- ❑ Other ideas to improve your script
- ❑ E-commerce basics

Adding E-Commerce to the Comic Book Fan Site

It's time to show you how you can easily incorporate an e-commerce section on your Comic Book Appreciation fan site. You will need a few things to get started:

❑   Something to sell

❑   Some mechanism for your customers to pick what they want to buy

❑   Some way for your customers to pay for what they want to buy

❑   Some process to get the merchandise to your customers

Let's break it down (break dancing gear optional) and talk about each of these things individually. The first two we can help you with; the second two are really outside the scope of this book, beyond a general discussion.

Something to Sell

Before you can sell something, you have to have something to sell. Duh. Next topic. No, seriously, retailers spend millions researching what will sell and what won't, what the hottest trends are, and what the latest technology has to offer. All that being said, your ideas for products will probably come from one or more of the following categories:

❑   **Your own knowledge:** You will most likely know what your customers want based on your inherent knowledge of the focus of your Web site. For example, if you have a site for collectors of old tractors, you probably know what products would appeal to your typical customer because *you* are the typical customer.

❑   **Something you yourself couldn't easily find:** You also may have been looking for a specific product or group of products, only to find that they do not exist on one particular site until you create it and pull them all together. (For example, www.giftsforengineers.com was created to be a compilation of products that appeal to engineers.)

❑   **Your own inventions:** Another item you might sell from your site is a new invention or design you have created from your little old brain. Many budding artists and inventors sell their stuff on the Web, where they can reach a multitude of potential buyers.

❑   **Promotion of your site:** Many other Web sites offer promotional items for sale that tout the URL of their site. This acts as a "win-win" for both parties; the customers can proclaim their support for a cool site and the site makes a few bucks and gets its name out there for all to see.

So whether you're reinventing the wheel, selling specific types of wheels, taking a bunch of wheels and putting them together, or selling wheels with your name on them, you must create a product base, and it may not be as easy as it looks.

For your CBA site, you will be selling items from a few different categories. To spice things up a bit, we decided it would be great to have some fun with this:

❑   T-shirts, bumper stickers, and coffee mugs with the CBA logo, from the promotional category

❑ Superhero suits customizable with color schemes and monogrammed torso letters

❑ Two different types of grappling hooks for all our superheroes' needs

You will be expanding on these products later and adding them to your product catalog (that is, the `products` table in your database).

A Shopping Cart

Now that you know what you are going to sell, you have to have some way for your customers to choose the specific products they want to buy; this involves a shopping cart. You can hook yourself up with ready-made shopping cart software, or you can use a cart straight from a programming script, such as PHP (or CGI, or whatever). Because we're on this topic, we may as well get a little crazy and talk a little bit about the pros and cons of each.

Shopping Cart Software

Numerous shopping cart software programs are available that can easily hook your customers up and make it easy for them to pick what they want. Although these programs can be expensive, they can also take care of things such as security, complex product option selection, maintaining customer information, and keeping track of previously placed orders.

An example of shopping cart software is Cart32. Available at `www.cart32.com`, this is a widely used shopping cart program that provides numerous configuration options for a Webmaster. Features include Web-based administration of your cart and pending/sent orders, the ability to use your own database or theirs to store product and customer information, automatic credit card processing and e-mail confirmations, complex product options and discount structures, online tracking through the major shipping carriers for your customers to track their orders, inventory management, and customization of the look of your cart. The costs are $29.95 to set up and $29.95 per month if you have Cart32 host the cart portion of your site for you. Many Web hosting companies have chosen Cart32 for the cart they offer to their customers.

These types of software programs are popular because they enable you to get your store up and running with relative ease and because they take care of the security issues for you.

Your Own Cart Software Code

Remember that whenever you depend on someone else to supply a portion of your site, you are at the mercy of their servers and their software. If they are hosting your shopping cart for you, when their site is down, so is yours. If their servers catch a virus, it affects you and your customers, too. Plus, there may be a function you need that they don't offer, or the cost may be prohibitive for your newly created site. Whatever the reason, you may want to code your own script, and if you are brave enough to tread these waters, let's go!

You'll start with a very simple shopping cart system that will consist of several files:

❑ `create.php`: Creates the main database and the necessary tables.

❑ `createtemp.php`: Creates a temporary table to store shopping cart information before the customer actually checks out.

❑ `products.php`: Populates the database with product information.

- cbashop.php: Acts as the home page for your little store and lists your available products.

- getprod.php: Retrieves detailed information about a single product.

- modcart.php: Adds, deletes, or changes quantities of a product to your shopping cart. Also empties the shopping cart completely.

- cart.php: Displays the contents of your shopping cart.

- checkout.php: The first step in the checkout process; this is where the customer enters billing and shipping information.

- checkout2.php: The second step in the checkout process; this is where customers verify the accuracy of their orders and make any last-minute changes.

- checkout3.php: The final step of the checkout process, where the customer actually sends the order to you, and receives an order number and confirmation. The information is put into the database and deleted from the temporary table, a customer number is assigned (if it's a new customer), and an order number is assigned, as well. E-mail confirmations are sent to the customer and to you.

Try It Out   Defining the Database and Tables

In this exercise you'll create a run-once script that creates the database and tables for this chapter's project.

1. Open your text editor and type the following code:

```php
<?php
//connect to the database - either include a connection variable file or
//type the following lines:
$connect = mysql_connect("localhost", "bp5am", "bp5ampass") or
  die ("Hey loser, check your server connection.");

//Create the ecommerce database
if (mysql_query("CREATE DATABASE ecommerce")) {
  echo "Woo hoo! Database created! <br>";
} else {
  echo "Sorry, try creating the database again.";
}
mysql_select_db("ecommerce");

//Define the product table
$query = "CREATE TABLE products (
        products_prodnum CHAR(5) NOT NULL,
        products_name VARCHAR(20) NOT NULL,
        products_proddesc TEXT NOT NULL,
        products_price DEC (6,2) NOT NULL,
        products_dateadded DATE NOT NULL,
        PRIMARY KEY(products_prodnum))";

$product = mysql_query($query)
  or die(mysql_error());

//Define the customer table
$query2 = "CREATE TABLE customers (
```

```
                customers_custnum INT(6) NOT NULL AUTO_INCREMENT,
                customers_firstname VARCHAR (15) NOT NULL,
                customers_lastname VARCHAR (50) NOT NULL,
                customers_add1 VARCHAR (50) NOT NULL,
                customers_add2 VARCHAR (50),
                customers_city VARCHAR (50) NOT NULL,
                customers_state CHAR (2) NOT NULL,
                customers_zip CHAR (5) NOT NULL,
                customers_phone CHAR (12) NOT NULL,
                customers_fax CHAR (12),
                customers_email VARCHAR (50) NOT NULL,
                PRIMARY KEY (customers_custnum))";

$customers = mysql_query($query2)
  or die(mysql_error());

//Define the general order table
$query3 = "CREATE TABLE ordermain (
                ordermain_ordernum INT(6) NOT NULL AUTO_INCREMENT,
                ordermain_orderdate DATE NOT NULL,
                ordermain_custnum INT(6) NOT NULL,
                ordermain_subtotal DEC (7,2) NOT NULL,
                ordermain_shipping DEC (6,2),
                ordermain_tax DEC(6,2),
                ordermain_total DEC(7,2) NOT NULL,
                ordermain_shipfirst VARCHAR(15) NOT NULL,
                ordermain_shiplast VARCHAR(50) NOT NULL,
                ordermain_shipcompany VARCHAR (50),
                ordermain_shipadd1 VARCHAR (50) NOT NULL,
                ordermain_shipadd2 VARCHAR(50),
                ordermain_shipcity VARCHAR(50) NOT NULL,
                ordermain_shipstate CHAR(2) NOT NULL,
                ordermain_shipzip CHAR(5) NOT NULL,
                ordermain_shipphone CHAR(12) NOT NULL,
                ordermain_shipemail VARCHAR(50),
                PRIMARY KEY(ordermain_ordernum)) ";

$ordermain = mysql_query($query3)
  or die(mysql_error());

//Define the order details table
$query4 = "CREATE TABLE orderdet (
                orderdet_ordernum INT (6) NOT NULL,
                orderdet_qty INT(3) NOT NULL,
                orderdet_prodnum CHAR(5) NOT NULL,
                KEY(orderdet_ordernum))";

$orderdet = mysql_query($query4)
  or die(mysql_error());

echo "Tables created successfully.";
?>
```

2. Save this as create.php.

3. Run the file from your browser. You should get confirmation that the database and all the tables have been successfully created.

How It Works

You can see that several things are accomplished in this script. You now have a new database called ecommerce with four tables in it. The first table is named products and contains the list of products available:

Fieldname	Type	Description of What It Stores
products_prodnum	CHAR(5)	The individual product number assigned to each product.
products_name	VARCHAR(20)	A brief title for the product, such as "CBA Logo T-shirt."
products_proddesc	TEXT	A longer description you can use on the individual page for that product. May contain HTML code.
products_price	DEC(6,2)	Price of the product up to 999.99.
products_dateadded	DATE	Date the product was added to the site.

The next table is named customers and contains the list of customers and their information:

Fieldname	Type	Description of What It Stores
customers_custnum	INT(6)	The individual customer number assigned to each customer. This will auto-increment.
customers_firstname	VARCHAR(15)	Customer's first name.
customers_lastname	VARCHAR(50)	Customer's last name.
customers_add1	VARCHAR(50)	Customer's address: line 1.
customers_add2	VARCHAR(50)	Customer's address: line 2 (can be null).
customers_city	VARCHAR(50)	Customer's city.
customers_state	CHAR(2)	Customer's state.
customers_zip	CHAR(5)	Customer's zip code.
customers_phone	CHAR(12)	Customer's phone number (in xxx-xxx-xxxx format).
customers_fax	CHAR(12)	Customer's fax number (same format as phone number, can be null).
customers_email	VARCHAR(50)	Customer's e-mail address.

The next table you create is called `ordermain` and contains the main order information:

Fieldname	Type	Description of What It Stores
ordermain_ordernum	INT(6)	The individual number assigned to each order. This will auto-increment and is the primary key.
ordermain_orderdate	DATE	Date the order was placed.
ordermain_custnum	INT(6)	Number of the customer who placed the order.
ordermain_subtotal	DEC(7,2)	Subtotal of the order before tax and shipping, up to 9999.99.
ordermain_shipping	DEC(6,2)	Shipping costs for the order, up to 999.99.
ordermain_tax	DEC(6,2)	Tax on the order, up to 999.99.
ordermain_total	DEC(7,2)	Total of the order, up to 9999.99.
ordermain_shipfirst	VARCHAR(15)	First name of the shipping contact for this order.
ordermain_shiplast	VARCHAR(50)	Last name of the shipping contact.
ordermain_shipadd1	VARCHAR(50)	Shipping contact's address: line 1.
ordermain_shipadd2	VARCHAR(50)	Shipping contact's address: line 2 (can be null).
ordermain_shipcity	VARCHAR(50)	Shipping contact's city.
ordermain_shipstate	CHAR(2)	Shipping contact's state.
ordermain_shipzip	CHAR(5)	Shipping contact's zip code.
ordermain_shipphone	CHAR(12)	Shipping contact's phone number (in xxx-xxx-xxxx format).
ordermain_shipemail	VARCHAR(50)	Shipping contact's e-mail address.

The fourth and final table is named `orderdet` and contains a detailed list of the products in each order:

Fieldname	Type	Description of What It Stores
orderdet_ordernum	INT(6)	The order number (note this is designated a "key" and not "primary key."
orderdet_qty	INT (3)	How many of the item the customer wants.
orderdet_productnum	CHAR(5)	The product associated with this order.

You now have a mechanism set up so that you can store all your products, all your customers, and all the information associated with the orders they place.

Try It Out Adding Your Products

Begin by filling the `products` database (which you can also do with phpMyAdmin, if you have it available).

1. Open your text editor and type the following program:

```php
<?php
//connect to the database - either include a connection variable file
//or type the following lines:
$connect = mysql_connect("localhost", "bp5am", "bp5ampass")
  or die ("Hey loser, check your server connection.");

mysql_select_db("ecommerce");

$query = "INSERT INTO products VALUES (
        '00001', 'CBA Logo T-shirt',
        'This T-shirt will show off your CBA connection.
        Our t-shirts are high quality and 100% preshrunk cotton.',
        17.95, '2004-08-01'),
        ('00002','CBA Bumper Sticker',
        'Let the world know you are a proud supporter of the
        CBA Web site with this colorful bumper sticker.',
        5.95, '2004-08-01'),
        ('00003', 'CBA Coffee Mug',
        'With the CBA logo looking back at you over your
        morning cup of coffee, you\'re sure to have a great
        start to your day. Our mugs are microwave and dishwasher
        safe.',
        8.95, '2004-08-01'),
        ('00004', 'Superhero Body Suit',
        'We have a complete selection of colors and sizes for you
        to choose from. This body suit is sleek, stylish, and
        won\'t hinder your crime-fighting or evil scheming abilities.
        We also offer your choice in monogrammed letter applique.',
        99.95, '2004-08-01'),
        ('00005', 'Small Grappling Hook',
        'This specialized hook will get you out of the tightest
        places. Specially designed for portability and stealth,
        please be aware that this hook does come with
        a weight limit.',
        139.95, '2004-08-01'),
        ('00006', 'Large Grappling Hook',
        'For all your heavy-duty building-to-building swinging needs,
        this large version of our grappling hook will safely transport
        you throughout the city. Please be advised however that at
        50 pounds, this is hardly the hook to use if you\'re a
        lightweight.',
        199.95, '2004-08-01')";
```

```
$result = mysql_query($query)
  or die(mysql_error());
echo "Products added successfully!";

?>
```

2. Save it as `products.php`.

3. Open the file in your browser. You should see confirmation that the products were successfully loaded into the table.

How It Works

You started your script with a connection to the MySQL server; then you made sure your database was the "active" one.

You then inserted each of your products into the `products` table, while keeping the values in the same order as you used when creating the table:

- ❏ `prodnum`
- ❏ `name`
- ❏ `proddesc`
- ❏ `price`
- ❏ `dateadded`

By keeping the values in the same order, you don't need to spell out the names of the columns themselves, as you usually would in the MySQL query syntax for `INSERT`.

Notice that although you assigned sequential numbers to your products, you are not using the auto-increment feature, because in the real world, you may wish to assign product numbers based on category, distributor/manufacturer, or other numbering scheme; these product IDs may include letters and numbers.

Because you had no errors and your query didn't die, you should have seen the "Products added successfully" statement, and your products should now be in the database.

If you don't have faith and believe that they're really in there, you can reaffirm your query with this small test program (save this as `producttest.php` and run it from your browser):

```php
<?php
//connect to the database - either include a connection variable file or
//type the following lines:
$connect = mysql_connect("localhost", "bp5am", "bp5ampass") or
  die ("Hey loser, check your server connection.");
mysql_select_db("ecommerce");
$query = "SELECT * FROM products";
```

```
$results = mysql_query($query)
  or die(mysql_error());

?>
<html>
<head>
<title>Product List</title>
</head>
<body>
<table>
  <tr>
    <td width="10%">Product Number</td>
    <td width="20%">Name</td>
    <td width="50%">Description</td>
    <td width="10%">Price</td>
    <td width="10%">Date Added</td>
  </tr>
<?php
while ($row = mysql_fetch_array($results)) {
  extract($row);
  echo "<tr><td width=\"10%\">";
  echo $products_prodnum;
  echo "</td><td width=\"20%\">";
  echo $products_name;
  echo "</td><td width=\"50%\">";
  echo $products_proddesc;
  echo "</td><td width=\"10%\">";
  echo $products_price;
  echo "</td><td width=\"10%\">";
  echo $products_dateadded;
  echo "</td></tr>";
}
?>
</table>
</body>
</html>
```

This program asks MySQL to give you all the products from the products table and populate an HTML table with the results. Each row is created while the rows are still being fetched. When it's complete, you should see the screen depicted in Figure 15-1.

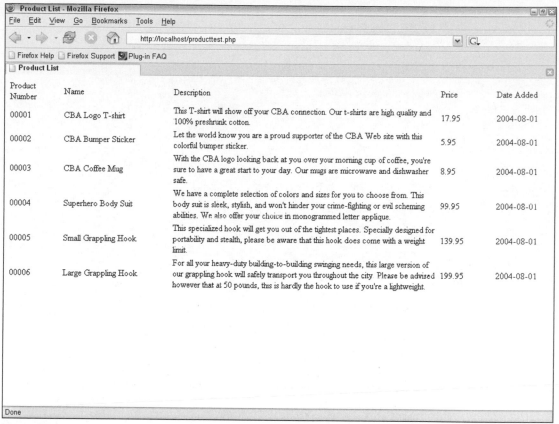

Figure 15-1

Now that you have everything ready to go, write the code that shows you more information about a specific product.

Creating the Store Home Page

In this exercise, you'll create the home page that all users will see when they start to shop at your site, listing all the available products you have for sale.

1. Open your text editor and save the following as `cbashop.php`. Unfortunately, we can't give you the images through this book, but you can download them from our source Web site, `www.wrox.com`.

```php
<?php
//connect to the database - either include a connection variable file
//or type the following lines:
$connect = mysql_connect("localhost", "bp5am", "bp5ampass")
  or die ("Hey loser, check your server connection.");
mysql_select_db ("ecommerce");
$query = "SELECT * FROM products";
$results = mysql_query($query)
  or die(mysql_error());

?>
<html>
<head>
<title>Comic Book Appreciation Site Product List</title>
</head>
<body>
<div align="center">
Thanks for visiting our site! Please see our list of awesome
products below, and click on the link for more information:
<br><br>
<table width="300">
<?php

// Show only Name, Price and Image
while ($row = mysql_fetch_array($results)) {
  extract($row);
  echo "<tr><td align=\"center\">";
  echo "<a href=\"getprod.php?prodid=" . $products_prodnum . "\">";
  echo "<em>THUMBNAIL<br>IMAGE</em></a></td>";
  echo "<td>";
  echo "<a href=\"getprod.php?prodid=" . $products_prodnum . "\">";
  echo $products_name;
  echo "</td></a>";
  echo "<td align=\"right\">";
  echo "<a href=\"getprod.php?prodid=" . $products_prodnum . "\">";
  echo "$" . $products_price;
  echo "</a></td></tr>";
}

?>
</table>
</div>
</body>
</html>
```

2.   Your screen should now look like Figure 15-2.

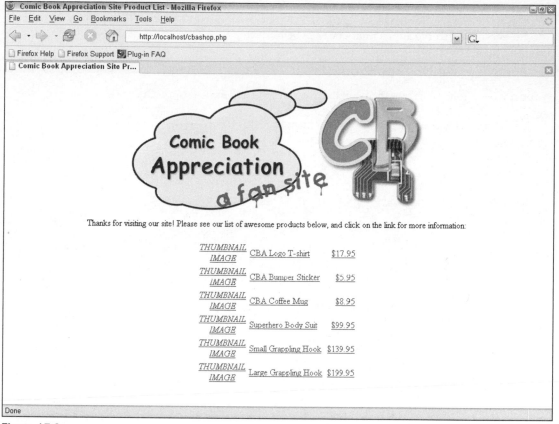

Figure 15-2

How It Works

First, you connected to the database just like you do every time. You might consider putting this info in an `include` file for simplicity's sake. Then you listed your intro information, "welcome to our site," blah blah blah — you know the routine. We've tried to keep it simple here, but in the real world this would look a lot fancier.

Then you got to the meat of the page, the actual products. You had your table populate a new row so long as there were results still being retrieved from the database with your `while` statements. When the query was finished getting results, you ended the table.

You also included a link to each of your products from either the picture of the item, the name of the item, or the price of the item. You can see an example in these lines:

```
echo "<a href=\"getprod.php?prodid=" . $products_prodnum . "\">";
echo "<em>THUMBNAIL<br>IMAGE</em></a></td>";
```

The URL then becomes `http://localhost/getprod.php?prodid=0001`, or something similar, depending on what product the user clicks. The program inserts the product ID number and sends it to the server so that the appropriate data can be retrieved.

Try It Out **Viewing the Products**

You are now going to create the page that displays the details of each product.

1. Enter this code in your text editor, then save this file as `getprod.php`.

```php
<?php
session_start();
//connect to the database - either include a connection variable file
//or type the following lines:
$connect = mysql_connect("localhost", "bp5am", "bp5ampass")
  or die("Hey loser, check your server connection.");
//make our database active
mysql_select_db("ecommerce");

//get our variable passed through the URL
$prodid = $_REQUEST['prodid'];

//get information on the specific product we want
$query = "SELECT * FROM products WHERE products_prodnum='$prodid'";
$results = mysql_query($query)
  or die(mysql_error());
$row = mysql_fetch_array($results);
extract($row);

?>
<html>
<head>
<title><?php echo $products_name; ?></title>
</head>
<body>
<div align="center">
<table cellpadding="5" width="80%">
  <tr>
    <td>PRODUCT IMAGE</td>
    <td><strong><?php echo $products_name; ?></strong><br>
      <?php echo $products_proddesc; ?><br \>
      <br>Product Number: <?php echo $products_prodnum; ?>
      <br>Price: $<?php echo $products_price; ?><br>
      <form method="POST" action="modcart.php?action=add">
        Quantity: <input type="text" name="qty" size="2"><br>
        <input type="hidden" name="products_prodnum"
          value="<?php echo $products_prodnum ?>">
        <input type="submit" name="Submit" value="Add to cart">
      </form>
```

```
            <form method="POST" action="cart.php">
              <input type="submit" name="Submit" value="View cart">
            </form>
        </td>
    </tr>
</table>
<hr width="200">
<p><a href="cbashop.php">Go back to the main page</a></p>
</div>
</body>
</html>
```

2. Run the script, and click the Superhero Body Suit. Your screen should look like that shown in Figure 15-3 (again, the images would be shown in place of the "IMAGE" marker there).

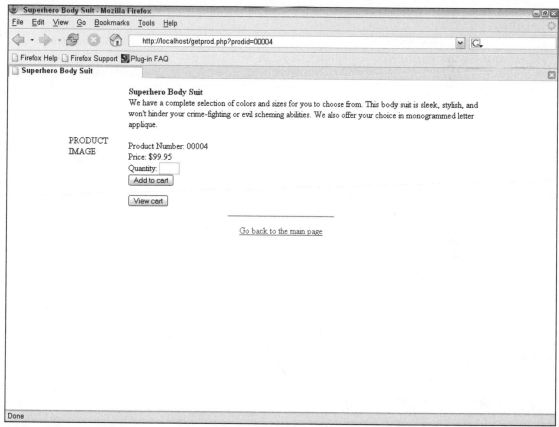

Figure 15-3

How It Works

First, you start a session for the customer. Then you again connect to the database. From there you have the following:

```
//get our variable passed through the URL
$prodid = $_REQUEST['prodid'];

//get information on the specific product we want
$query = "SELECT * FROM products WHERE products_prodnum='$prodid'";
$results = mysql_query($query)
  or die(mysql_error());
$row = mysql_fetch_array($results);
extract($row);

?>
```

In this block of code, you first take `products_prodid`, which came from the URL, and rename it so you can easily use it in your MySQL queries. In the next line, you query the `products` table for the appropriate product ID. You then run the query and extract the results so you can use them.

In the next several lines, you build a table and display the information straight from the database. Then you have the following:

```
<form method="POST" action="modcart.php?action=add">
  Quantity: <input type="text" name="qty" size="2"><br>
  <input type="hidden" name="products_prodnum"
    value="<?php echo $products_prodnum; ?>">
  <input type="submit" name="Submit" value="Add to cart">
</form>
```

Here you have created a form that calls to action the `modcart.php` file (which you'll create in a moment) and passes the only real variables you care about: the product number (`products_prodnum`) and the quantity (`qty`).

The following gives the customer the option of viewing the current contents of the shopping cart. You can also supply this in the form of a link, but we chose to offer it as a button in this case.

```
<form method="POST" action="cart.php">
  <input type="submit" name="Submit" value="View cart">
</form>
</td>
```

You also gave your customers the option to return to the main page.

Try It Out   Creating a Table for the Shopping Cart

In this exercise, you'll create a temporary table to store the items in the customer's cart before he or she checks out.

1.   Create this file, and save it as `createtemp.php`:

```php
<?php
//connect to the database - either include a connection variable file
//or type the following lines:
$connect = mysql_connect("localhost", "bp5am", "bp5ampass")
  or die("Hey loser, check your server connection.");

mysql_select_db("ecommerce");

//Define the temp table
$query = "CREATE TABLE carttemp(
        carttemp_hidden INT(10) NOT NULL AUTO_INCREMENT,
        carttemp_sess CHAR(50) NOT NULL,
        carttemp_prodnum CHAR(5) NOT NULL,
        carttemp_quan INT(3) NOT NULL,
        PRIMARY KEY (carttemp_hidden),
        KEY(carttemp_sess))";

$temp = mysql_query($query)
  or die(mysql_error());
echo "Temporary cart table created successfully!";
?>
```

How It Works

Hey, guess what? You're right: You had to connect to the database again.

Then you created a temporary table that will "hold" the items while the customer continues browsing and before they actually check out. You didn't want to populate the other tables with this information yet because your customers may decide not to go through with the order and you would have assigned them order numbers for orders that are never sent. This can really mess up your accounting and tracking systems.

Also, because shopping cart "abandonment," as it's called, is one of the major obstacles e-commerce ventures face, data in this temporary cart can really help you glean information about your customers. For example, by viewing this table:

❑   You can gauge what percentage of customers are abandoning their carts. If it's exceedingly high, then your checkout procedure may be too complicated or convoluted for them to finish the process, or perhaps your shipping costs are not made clear up-font and people are forced into faking their shopping carts to determine shipping costs.

❑   You can track any trends in what items are consistently being left in the cart. If one or two items stick out, perhaps there is something wrong with your checkout procedure for these items, or the shipping costs come up exceedingly high, or something to that effect. This would require greater analysis of your setup of the flagged items.

❑   You can track any trends in when your customers are leaving items in the cart. If you find a large number of customers are abandoning their carts during your Website or server maintenance, perhaps the workload on the server is causing your site to load slowly and your customers are losing patience and leaving their cart. In this instance, you would want to time such maintenance with when your site has the fewest number of shoppers online. As you can see, what people *don't* buy can be just as informative as what they *do* buy.

In your temporary cart table, you want to keep each entry separate, so you create a `carttemp_hidden` field that will simply act as a primary key and allow you to later delete only one row from your shopping cart. The `carttemp_sess` field is used to temporarily store your session ID (which is assigned by the browser) to allow you to link the information from this particular shopping session, and keep it all together.

Try It Out   Viewing the Shopping Cart

In this exercise, you'll create the actual shopping cart.

1.   Same drill as usual. Enter this code, and save it as `cart.php`:

```php
<?php
if (!session_id()) {
  session_start();
}//connect to the database
$connect = mysql_connect("localhost", "bp5am", "bp5ampass")
  or die ("Hey loser, check your server connection.");
mysql_select_db("ecommerce");
?>
<html>
<head>
<title>Here is Your Shopping Cart!</title>
</head>
<body>
<div align="center">
You currently have

<?php
$sessid = session_id();

//display number of products in cart
$query = "SELECT * FROM carttemp WHERE carttemp_sess = '$sessid'";
$results = mysql_query($query)
  or die (mysql_query());
$rows = mysql_num_rows($results);
echo $rows;
?>

product(s) in your cart.<br>

<table border="1" align="center" cellpadding="5">
  <tr>
    <td>Quantity</td>
    <td>Item Image</td>
    <td>Item Name</td>
    <td>Price Each</td>
    <td>Extended Price</td>
    <td></td>
    <td></td>
<?php
$total = 0;
while ($row = mysql_fetch_array($results)) {
  echo "<tr>";
```

```php
        extract($row);
        $prod = "SELECT * FROM products " .
                "WHERE products_prodnum='$carttemp_prodnum'";
        $prod2 = mysql_query($prod);
        $prod3 = mysql_fetch_array($prod2);
        extract($prod3);
        echo "<td
                <form method=\"POST\" action=\"modcart.php?action=change\">
                    <input type=\"hidden\" name=\"modified_hidden\"
                      value=\"$carttemp_hidden\">
                    <input type=\"text\" name=\"modified_quan\" size=\"2\"
                      value=\"$carttemp_quan\">";
        echo "</td>";
        echo "<td>";
        echo "<a href=\"getprod.php?prodid=" . $products_prodnum . "\">";
        echo "THUMBNAIL<br>IMAGE</a></td>";
        echo "<td>";
        echo "<a href=\"getprod.php?prodid=" . $products_prodnum . "\">";
        echo $products_name;
        echo "</a></td>";
        echo "<td align=\"right\">";
        echo $products_price;
        echo "</td>";
        echo "<td align=\"right\">";
        //get extended price
        $extprice = number_format($products_price * $carttemp_quan, 2);
        echo $extprice;
        echo "</td>";
        echo "<td>";
        echo "<input type=\"submit\" name=\"Submit\"
                value=\"Change Qty\">
              </form></td>";
        echo "<td>";
        echo "<form method=\"POST\" action=\"modcart.php?action=delete\">
                <input type=\"hidden\" name=\"modified_hidden\"
                  value=\"$carttemp_hidden\">";
        echo "<input type=\"submit\" name=\"Submit\"
                value=\"Delete Item\">
              </form></td>";
        echo "</tr>";
        //add extended price to total
        $total = $extprice + $total;

}
?>
    <tr>
      <td colspan=\"4\" align=\"right\">
        Your total before shipping is:</td>
      <td align=\"right\"> <?php echo number_format($total, 2); ?></td>
      <td></td>
      <td>
<?php
echo "<form method=\"POST\" action=\"modcart.php?action=empty\">
        <input type=\"hidden\" name=\"carttemp_hidden\"
```

```
            value=\"";
if (isset($carttemp_hidden)) {
  echo $carttemp_hidden;
}
echo "\">";
echo "<input type=\"submit\" name=\"Submit\" value=\"Empty Cart\">
      </form>";
?>


</td>
</tr>
</table>
<form method="POST" action="checkout.php">
<input type="submit" name="Submit" value="Proceed to Checkout">
</form>
<a href="cbashop.php">Go back to the main page</a>
</div>
</body>
</html>
```

How It Works

Now, looking at your code, you can see the following:

```
<div align="center">
You currently have

<?php
$sessid = session_id();

//display number of products in cart
$query = "SELECT * from carttemp WHERE carttemp_sess = '$sessid'";
$results = mysql_query($query)
  or die (mysql_query());
$rows = mysql_num_rows($results);
echo $rows;
?>


product(s) in your cart.<br>
```

You want to display the total number of items in your cart, so you start in HTML and flip over to PHP where you query your temporary table to see what is in there for the current session. You get the total number of rows and that tells you how many entries are in your cart. Of course, this doesn't check for duplicates—it's only a start. You then flip back over to HTML to finish your sentence, and the result is:

```
You currently have 1 product(s) in your cart.
```

You then populate your table much in the same way you did in cbashop.php, except this time you're pulling the information from your temporary table. Because you also wanted to provide a link to the product detail page for each product (in case your customers forgot what they ordered), you had to also grab info from your products table.

You then come to these lines:

```
//get extended price
$extprice = number_format($products_price * $carttemp_quan, 2);
echo $extprice;
```

This is where you show your customers the extended price for each item based on how many they are ordering.

Likewise, you keep a tally of their order with these lines:

```
//add extended price to total
$total = $extprice + $total;
```

You also allow them to change the quantities, delete an item altogether, or empty their cart with one more file, modcart.php. Notice that it is the same file you used to add an item to the cart as well. You use this file as the "actions" in your HTML forms, and pass the variables as needed, as in these lines, for example:

```
echo "<td>";
echo "<form method=\"POST\" action="modcart.php?action=delete\">
      <input type=\"hidden\" name=\"modified_hidden\"
        value=\"$carttemp_hidden\">";
echo "<input type=\"submit\" name=\"Submit\"
        value=\"Delete Item\">
</form></td>";
```

You then give customers the option of proceeding to the checkout or going back to the main page for more shopping with these lines:

```
<form method="POST" action="checkout.php">
<input type="submit" name="Submit" value="Proceed to Checkout">
</form>
<a href="cbashop.php">Go back to the main page</a>
```

Try It Out   Adding, Changing, and Deleting Items in the Cart

In this exercise, you'll write the script that updates the contents of the cart.

1.   Type in this code, and save it as modcart.php:

```
<?php
session_start();
$connect = mysql_connect("localhost", "bp5am", "bp5ampass")
   or die("Hey loser, check your server connection.");
mysql_select_db("ecommerce");
if (isset($_POST['qty'])) {
  $qty = $_POST['qty'];
}
if (isset($_POST['products_prodnum'])) {
```

```php
      $prodnum = $_POST['products_prodnum'];
}
if (isset($_POST['modified_hidden'])) {
    $modified_hidden = $_POST['modified_hidden'];
}
if (isset($_POST['modified_quan'])) {
  $modified_quan = $_POST['modified_quan'];
}
$sess = session_id();
$action = $_REQUEST['action'];

switch ($action) {
  case "add":
    $query = "INSERT INTO carttemp (
              carttemp_sess,
              carttemp_quan,
              carttemp_prodnum)
              VALUES ('$sess','$qty','$prodnum')";
    $message = "<div align=\"center\"><strong>Item
                added.</strong></div>";
    break;

  case "change":
    $query = "UPDATE carttemp
              SET carttemp_quan = '$modified_quan'
              WHERE carttemp_hidden = '$modified_hidden'";
    $message = "<div align='center'><strong>Quantity
                changed.</strong></div>";
    break;

  case "delete":
    $query = "DELETE FROM carttemp
              WHERE carttemp_hidden = '$modified_hidden'";
    $message = "<div align='center'><strong>Item
                deleted.</strong></div>";
    break;

  case "empty":
    $query = "DELETE FROM carttemp WHERE carttemp_sess = '$sess'";
    $message = "<div align='center'><strong>Cart
                emptied.</strong></div>";
    break;

}

$results = mysql_query($query)
  or die(mysql_error());

echo $message;

include("cart.php");
?>
```

2. Enter the site and add an item to the cart. You should see the result as shown in Figure 15-4.

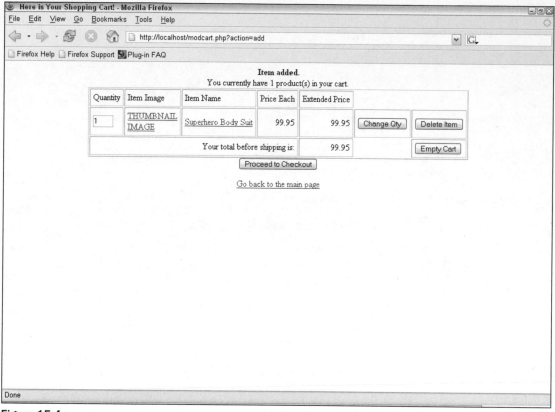

Figure 15-4

How It Works

You basically only need one file that will modify your current shopping cart however you need. This is dictated with the variable $action, which is passed through your URL. First, you keep your session going and then you connect to the database.

Then, based on what action you are currently requesting, you use the switch() function to set up the correct query. If you want to add an item to the cart, you use the INSERT MySQL function, the UPDATE function to change, and the DELETE function to delete an item or empty the cart.

You then send a message to your customer using $message to confirm the action they requested and show them the current contents of the cart. For simplicity's sake of the cart example here, you simply included the cart.php file, but there are several other ways of doing this.

Try It Out   Checking Out: Step One

In this exercise, you'll create the first of three checkout files. This is one hefty file, so get your typing fingers ready.

1.   As usual, enter this code, and then save it as checkout.php:

```php
<?php
session_start();
?>
<html>
<head>
<title>Step 1 of 3 - Billing and Shipping Information</title>
</head>
<body>
<strong>Order Checkout</strong><br>
<strong>Step 1 - Please Enter Billing and Shipping
  Information</strong><br>
Step 2 - Please Verify Accuracy of Order Information and Send Order<br>
Step 3 - Order Confirmation and Receipt<br>

<form method="post" action="checkout2.php">

<table width="300" border="1" align="left">
  <tr>
    <td colspan="2" bgcolor="#0000FF">
      <div align="center"><strong>Billing Information</strong></div>
    </td>
  </tr>
  <tr>
    <td width="50%">
      <div align="right">First Name</div>
    </td>
    <td width="50%">
      <input type="text" name="firstname" maxlength="15">
    </td>
  </tr>
  <tr>
    <td width="50%">
      <div align="right">Last Name</div>
    </td>
    <td width="50%">
      <input type="text" name="lastname" maxlength="50">
    </td>
  </tr>
  <tr>
    <td width="50%">
      <div align="right">Billing Address</div>
    </td>
    <td width="50%">
      <input type="text" name="add1" maxlength="50">
    </td>
  </tr>
  <tr>
    <td width="50%">
      <div align="right">Billing Address 2</div>
    </td>
    <td width="50%">
      <input type="text" name="add2" maxlength="50">
```

```
      </td>
    </tr>
    <tr>
      <td width="50%">
        <div align="right">City</div>
      </td>
      <td width="50%">
        <input type="text" name="city" maxlength="50">
      </td>
    </tr>
    <tr>
      <td width="50%">
        <div align="right">State</div>
      </td>
      <td width="50%">
        <input type="text" name="state" size="2" maxlength="2">
      </td>
    </tr>
    <tr>
      <td width="50%">
        <div align="right">Zip</div>
      </td>
      <td width="50%">
        <input type="text" name="zip" maxlength="5" size="5">
      </td>
    </tr>
    <tr>
      <td width="50%">
        <div align="right">Phone Number</div>
      </td>
      <td width="50%">
        <input type="text" name="phone" size="12" maxlength="12">
      </td>
    </tr>
    <tr>
      <td width="50%">
        <div align="right">Fax Number</div>
      </td>
      <td width="50%">
        <input type="text" name="fax" maxlength="12" size="12">
      </td>
    </tr>
    <tr>
      <td width="50%">
        <div align="right">E-Mail Address</div>
      </td>
      <td width="50%">
        <input type="text" name="email" maxlength="50">
      </td>
    </tr>
</table>
<table width="300" border="1">
```

```
<tr bgcolor="#990000">
  <td colspan="2">
    <div align="center"><strong>Shipping Information</strong></div>
  </td>
</tr>
<tr>
  <td width="50%">
    <div align="right">Shipping Info same as Billing</div>
  </td>
  <td width="50%">
    <input type="checkbox" name="same">
  </td>
</tr>
<tr>
  <td width="50%">
    <div align="right">First Name</div>
  </td>
  <td width="50%">
    <input type="text" name="shipfirst" maxlength="15">
  </td>
</tr>
<tr>
  <td width="50%">
    <div align="right">Last Name</div>
  </td>
  <td width="50%">
    <input type="text" name="shiplast" maxlength="50">
  </td>
</tr>
<tr>
  <td width="50%">
    <div align="right">Shipping Address</div>
  </td>
  <td width="50%">
    <input type="text" name="shipadd1" maxlength="50">
  </td>
</tr>
<tr>
  <td width="50%">
    <div align="right">Shipping Address 2</div>
  </td>
  <td width="50%">
    <input type="text" name="shipadd2" maxlength="50">
  </td>
</tr>
<tr>
  <td width="50%">
    <div align="right">City</div>
  </td>
  <td width="50%">
    <input type="text" name="shipcity" maxlength="50">
```

```
      </td>
    </tr>
    <tr>
      <td width="50%">
        <div align="right">State</div>
      </td>
      <td width="50%">
        <input type="text" name="shipstate" size="2" maxlength="2">
      </td>
    </tr>
    <tr>
      <td width="50%">
        <div align="right">Zip</div>
      </td>
      <td width="50%">
        <input type="text" name="shipzip" maxlength="5" size="5">
      </td>
    </tr>
    <tr>
      <td width="50%">
        <div align="right">Phone Number</div>
      </td>
      <td width="50%">
        <input type="text" name="shipphone" size="12" maxlength="12">
      </td>
    </tr>
    <tr>
      <td width="50%">
        <div align="right">E-Mail Address</div>
      </td>
      <td width="50%">
        <input type="text" name="shipemail" maxlength="50">
      </td>
    </tr>
  </table>
  <p>
    <input type="submit" name="Submit"
      value="Proceed to Next Step --&gt;">
  </p>
</form>

</body>
</html>
```

2. Now to test it. Enter the site, put one Superhero Body Suit in your cart, and then choose to check out. You should see something that looks like Figure 15-5.

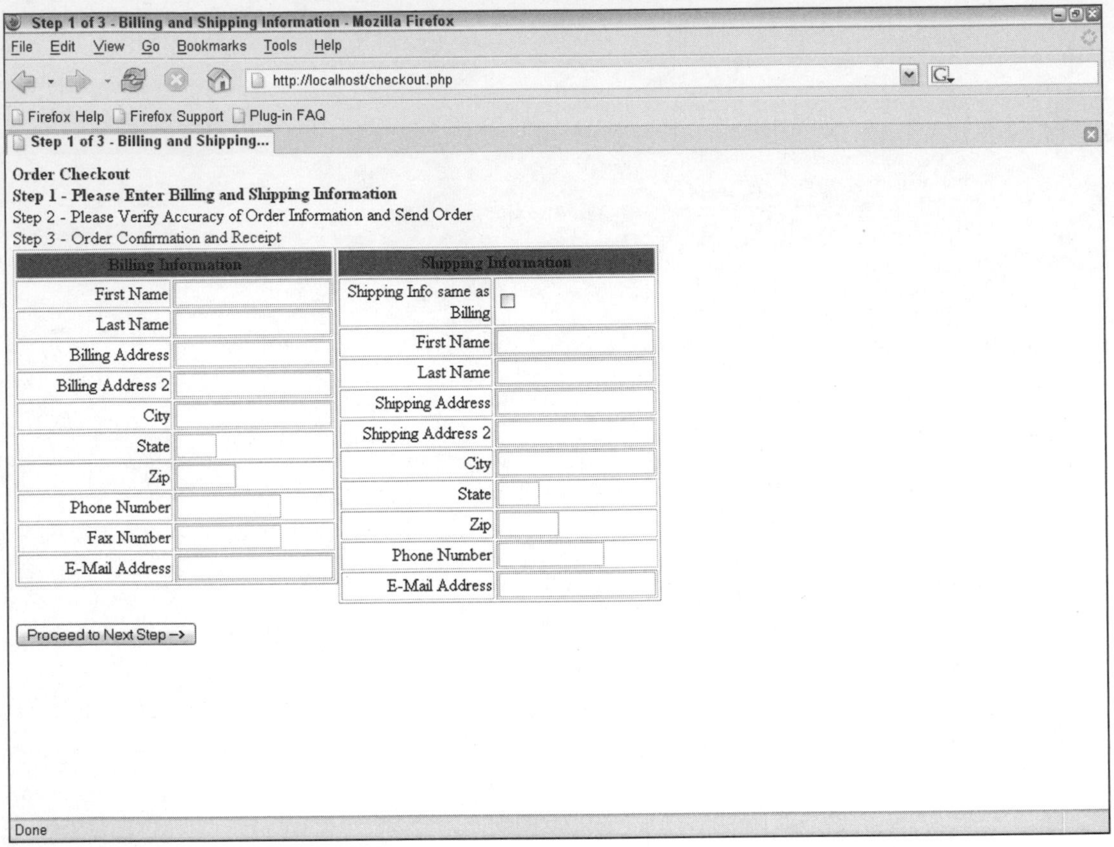

Figure 15-5

How It Works

The following is the step that asks for your customer's billing and shipping information. You start with a little intro, and you let the customer know what step he or she is currently on. Then you set up the form that will collect all the information and submit it to the next page of the checkout process:

```
<form method="post" action="checkout2.php">
```

The rest is pretty much no-brainer type stuff, just getting the variables and passing them along to checkout2.php.

Try It Out   **Checking Out: Step Two**

In this exercise, you'll create the file that lets customers verify that all the information is accurate, and gives customers a chance to make any last minute changes.

1.   Enter the following code, and save the file as checkout2.php:

```
<?php
session_start();
```

```
//connect to the database
$connect = mysql_connect("localhost", "bp5am", "bp5ampass")
  or die ("Hey loser, check your server connection.");
mysql_select_db("ecommerce");
if ($_POST['same'] == 'on') {
  $_POST['shipfirst'] = $_POST['firstname'];
  $_POST['shiplast'] = $_POST['lastname'];
  $_POST['shipadd1'] = $_POST['add1'];
  $_POST['shipadd2'] = $_POST['add2'];
  $_POST['shipcity'] = $_POST['city'];
  $_POST['shipstate'] = $_POST['state'];
  $_POST['shipzip'] = $_POST['zip'];
  $_POST['shipphone'] = $_POST['phone'];
  $_POST['shipemail'] = $_POST['email'];
}
?>
<html>
<head>
<title>Step 2 of 3 - Verify Order Accuracy</title>
</head>
<body>
Step 1 - Please Enter Billing and Shipping Information<br>
<strong>Step 2 - Please Verify Accuracy and Make Any Necessary
     Changes</strong><br>
Step 3 - Order Confirmation and Receipt<br>

<form method="post" action="checkout3.php">
<table width="300" border="1" align="left">
  <tr>
    <td colspan="2" bgcolor="#0000FF">
      <div align="center"><strong>Billing Information</strong></div>
    </td>
  </tr>
  <tr>
    <td width="50%">
      <div align="right">First Name</div>
    </td>
    <td width="50%">
      <input type="text" name="firstname" maxlength="15"
        value="<?php echo $_POST['firstname']; ?> ">
    </td>
  </tr>
  <tr>
    <td width="50%">
      <div align="right">Last Name</div>
    </td>
    <td width="50%">
      <input type="text" name="lastname" maxlength="50"
        value="<?php echo $_POST['lastname']; ?>">
    </td>
  </tr>
  <tr>
    <td width="50%">
      <div align="right">Billing Address</div>
    </td>
```

```
      <td width="50%">
        <input type="text" name="add1" maxlength="50"
          value="<?php echo $_POST['add1']; ?>">
      </td>
    </tr>
    <tr>
      <td width="50%">
        <div align="right">Billing Address 2</div>
      </td>
      <td width="50%">
        <input type="text" name="add2" maxlength="50"
          value="<?php echo $_POST['add2']; ?>">
      </td>
    </tr>
    <tr>
      <td width="50%">
        <div align="right">City</div>
      </td>
      <td width="50%">
        <input type="text" name="city" maxlength="50"
          value="<?php echo $_POST['city']; ?> ">
      </td>
    </tr>
    <tr>
      <td width="50%">
        <div align="right">State</div>
      </td>
      <td width="50%">
        <input type="text" name="state" size="2" maxlength="2"
          value="<?php echo $_POST['state']; ?>">
      </td>
    </tr>
    <tr>
      <td width="50%">
        <div align="right">Zip</div>
      </td>
      <td width="50%">
        <input type="text" name="zip" maxlength="5" size="5"
          value="<?php echo $_POST['zip']; ?>">
      </td>
    </tr>
    <tr>
      <td width="50%">
        <div align="right">Phone Number</div>
      </td>
      <td width="50%">
        <input type="text" name="phone" size="12" maxlength="12"
          value="<?php echo $_POST['phone']; ?>">
      </td>
    </tr>
    <tr>
      <td width="50%">
        <div align="right">Fax Number</div>
      </td>
      <td width="50%">
```

```
        <input type="text" name="fax" maxlength="12" size="12"
          value="<?php echo $_POST['fax']; ?>">
      </td>
    </tr>
    <tr>
      <td width="50%">
        <div align="right">E-Mail Address</div>
      </td>
      <td width="50%">
        <input type="text" name="email" maxlength="50"
          value="<?php echo $_POST['email']; ?>">
      </td>
    </tr>
</table>
<table width="300" border="1">
  <tr bgcolor="#990000">
    <td colspan="2">
      <div align="center"><strong>Shipping Information</strong></div>
    </td>
  </tr>
  <tr>
    <td width="50%">
      <div align="right">Shipping Info same as Billing</div>
    </td>
    <td width="50%">
      <input type="checkbox" name="same"></td>
  </tr>
  <tr>
    <td width="50%">
      <div align="right">First Name</div>
    </td>
    <td width="50%">
      <input type="text" name="shipfirst" maxlength="15"
        value="<?php echo $_POST['shipfirst']; ?>">
    </td>
  </tr>
  <tr>
    <td width="50%">
      <div align="right">Last Name</div>
    </td>
    <td width="50%">
      <input type="text" name="shiplast" maxlength="50"
        value="<?php echo $_POST['shiplast']; ?>">
    </td>
  </tr>
  <tr>
    <td width="50%">
      <div align="right">Shipping Address</div>
    </td>
    <td width="50%">
      <input type="text" name="shipadd1" maxlength="50"
        value="<?php echo $_POST['shipadd1']; ?>">
    </td>
  </tr>
  <tr>
```

```
      <td width="50%">
        <div align="right">Shipping Address 2</div>
      </td>
      <td width="50%">
        <input type="text" name="shipadd2" maxlength="50"
          value="<?php echo $_POST['shipadd2']; ?>">
      </td>
    </tr>
    <tr>
      <td width="50%">
        <div align="right">City</div>
      </td>
      <td width="50%">
        <input type="text" name="shipcity" maxlength="50"
          value="<?php echo $_POST['shipcity']; ?>">
      </td>
    </tr>
    <tr>
      <td width="50%">
        <div align="right">State</div>
      </td>
      <td width="50%">
        <input type="text" name="shipstate" size="2" maxlength="2"
          value="<?php echo $_POST['shipstate']; ?>">
      </td>
    </tr>
    <tr>
      <td width="50%">
        <div align="right">Zip</div>
      </td>
      <td width="50%">
        <input type="text" name="shipzip" maxlength="5" size="5"
          value="<?php echo $_POST['shipzip']; ?>">
      </td>
    </tr>
    <tr>
      <td width="50%">
        <div align="right">Phone Number</div>
      </td>
      <td width="50%">
        <input type="text" name="shipphone" size="12" maxlength="12"
          value="<?php echo $_POST['shipphone']; ?>">
      </td>
    </tr>
    <tr>
      <td width="50%">
        <div align="right">E-Mail Address</div>
      </td>
      <td width="50%">
        <input type="text" name="shipemail" maxlength="50"
          value="<?php echo $_POST['shipemail']; ?>">
      </td>
    </tr>
</table>
```

```
<hr>
<table border="1" align="left" cellpadding="5">
  <tr>
    <td>Quantity</td>
    <td>Item Image</td>
    <td>Item Name</td>
    <td>Price Each</td>
    <td>Extended Price</td>
    <td></td>
    <td></td>
  </tr>
<?php

$sessid = session_id();

$query = "SELECT * FROM carttemp WHERE carttemp_sess = '$sessid'";
$results = mysql_query($query)
  or die (mysql_query());

$total = 0;
while ($row = mysql_fetch_array($results)) {
  extract($row);
  $prod = "SELECT * FROM products WHERE
          products_prodnum = '$carttemp_prodnum'";
  $prod2 = mysql_query($prod);
  $prod3 = mysql_fetch_array($prod2);
  extract($prod3);
  echo "<tr><td>";
  echo $carttemp_quan;
  echo "</td>";
  echo "<td>";
  echo "<a href=\"getprod.php?prodid=" .
       $products_prodnum . "\">";
  echo "THUMBNAIL<br>IMAGE</td></a>";
  echo "<td>";
  echo "<a href=\"getprod.php?prodid=" .
       $products_prodnum . "\">";
  echo $products_name;
  echo "</td></a>";
  echo "<td align=\"right\">";
  echo $products_price;
  echo "</td>";
  echo "<td align=\"right\">";
  //get extended price
  $extprice = number_format($products_price * $carttemp_quan, 2);
  echo $extprice;
  echo "</td>";
  echo "<td>";
  echo "<a href=\"cart.php\">Make Changes to Cart</a>";
  echo "</td>";
  echo "</tr>";
  //add extended price to total
  $total = $extprice + $total;
```

```
}
?>
<tr>
<td colspan="4" align="right">Your total before shipping is:</td>
<td align="right"> <?php echo number_format($total, 2); ?></td>
<td></td>
<td></td>
</tr>
</table>
<input type="hidden" name="total" value="<?php echo $total; ?>">
<p>
  <input type="submit" name="Submit" value="Send Order --&gt;">
</p>
</form>

</body>
</html>
```

2. Time to test the code again. Enter the site again, select the Superhero Body Suit again, and check out. This time, enter your information in the form, and click the Proceed to Next Step button. Your screen should look like that in Figure 15-6.

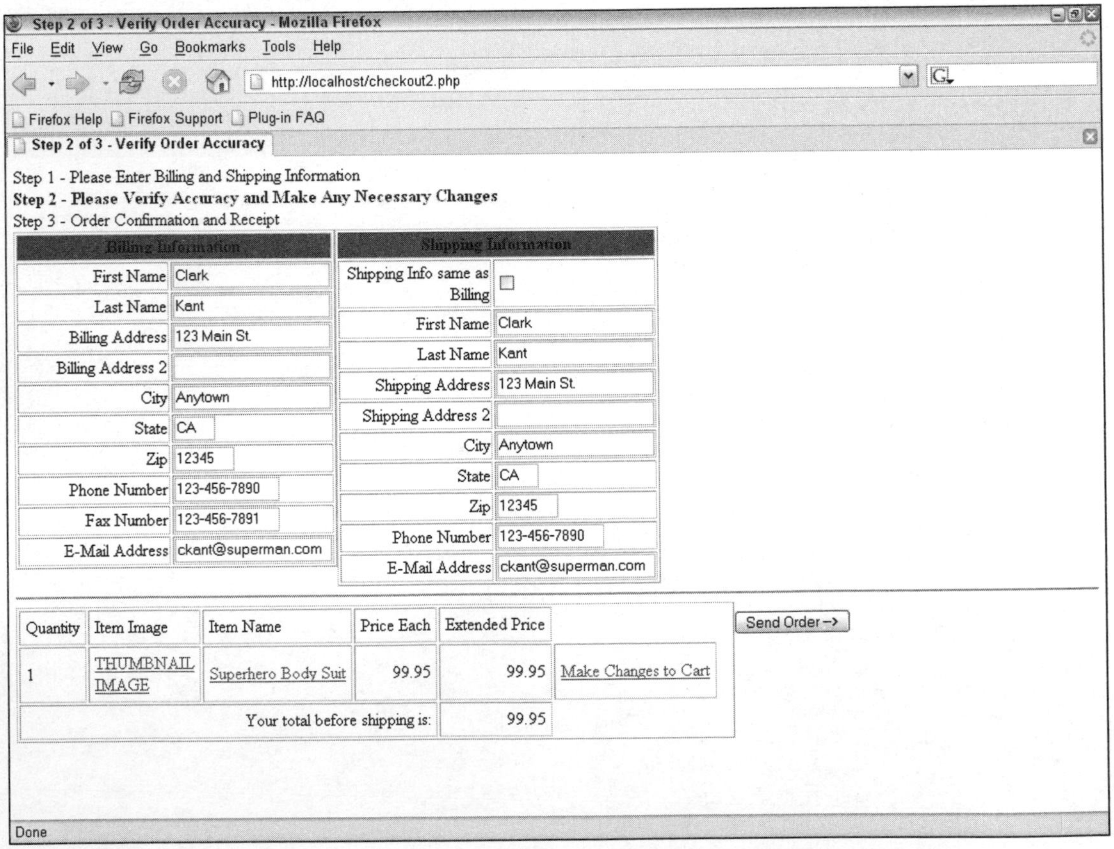

Figure 15-6

How It Works

In the code, you see the standard connection lines and your session lines. Then you check to see if the billing info is the same as the shipping info, and, if so, you populate the shipping table with the billing information, as follows:

```
if ($_POST['same'] == 'on') {
  $_POST['shipfirst'] = $_POST['firstname'];
  $_POST['shiplast'] = $_POST['lastname'];
  $_POST['shipadd1'] = $_POST['add1'];
  $_POST['shipadd2'] = $_POST['add2'];
  $_POST['shipcity'] = $_POST['city'];
  $_POST['shipstate'] = $_POST['state'];
  $_POST['shipzip'] = $_POST['zip'];
  $_POST['shipphone'] = $_POST['phone'];
  $_POST['shipemail'] = $_POST['email'];
}
```

The rest of the script is pretty similar to previous pages. You show the billing and shipping information as you did in checkout.php and you show your cart contents as you did in cart.php. You decided in this case to keep your shopping cart changes in the cart.php file itself, so you provided a link to cart.php.

Just another point worth mentioning: You passed the $total variable in a hidden field instead of retabulating it in the next page; you needed to access it early on in the code. This just makes life a lot easier.

You also set your form action to be checkout3.php, where it all happens.

Try It Out   Checking Out: Step Three

For your final file, you want to complete checkout3.php. Numerous things will be going on in this file, and we'll talk about them in a minute.

1. Enter this code, and save the file as checkout3.php:

```
<?php
session_start();
//connect to the database - either include a connection variable file
//or type the following lines:
$connect = mysql_connect("localhost", "bp5am", "bp5ampass")
  or die ("Hey loser, check your server connection.");
mysql_select_db("ecommerce");

//Let's make the variables easy to access in our queries
$firstname = $_POST['firstname'];
$lastname = $_POST['lastname'];
$firstname = $_POST['firstname'];
$add1 = $_POST['add1'];
$add2 = $_POST['add2'];
$city = $_POST['city'];
$state = $_POST['state'];
$zip = $_POST['zip'];
$phone = $_POST['phone'];
$fax = $_POST['fax'];
$email = $_POST['email'];
$shipfirst = $_POST['shipfirst'];
```

```php
$shiplast = $_POST['shiplast'];
$shipadd1 = $_POST['shipadd1'];
$shipadd2 = $_POST['shipadd2'];
$shipcity = $_POST['shipcity'];
$shipstate = $_POST['shipstate'];
$shipzip = $_POST['shipzip'];
$shipstate = $_POST['shipstate'];
$shipphone = $_POST['shipphone'];
$shipemail = $_POST['shipemail'];
$total = $_POST['total'];
$sessid = session_id();
$today = date("Y-m-d");

//1) Assign Customer Number to new Customer, or find existing customer number
$query = "SELECT * FROM customers WHERE
          (customers_firstname = '$firstname' AND
          customers_lastname = '$lastname' AND
          customers_add1 = '$add1' AND
          customers_add2 = '$add2' AND
          customers_city = '$city')";
$results = mysql_query($query)
  or (mysql_error());
$rows = mysql_num_rows($results);

if ($rows < 1) {
  //assign new custnum
  $query2 = "INSERT INTO customers (
             customers_firstname, customers_lastname, customers_add1,
             customers_add2, customers_city, customers_state,
             customers_zip, customers_phone, customers_fax,
             customers_email)
             VALUES (
             '$firstname',
             '$lastname',
             '$add1',
             '$add2',
             '$city',
             '$state',
             '$zip',
             '$phone',
             '$fax',
             '$email')";
  $insert = mysql_query($query2)
    or (mysql_error());
  $custid = mysql_insert_id();
}

//If custid exists, we want to make it equal to custnum
//Otherwise we will use the existing custnum
if ($custid) {
  $customers_custnum = $custid;
}

//2) Insert Info into ordermain
//determine shipping costs based on order total (25% of total)
```

```
$shipping = $total * 0.25;

$query3 = "INSERT INTO ordermain (
          ordermain_orderdate, ordermain_custnum,
          ordermain_subtotal,ordermain_shipping,
          ordermain_shipfirst, ordermain_shiplast,
          ordermain_shipadd1, ordermain_shipadd2,
          ordermain_shipcity, ordermain_shipstate,
          ordermain_shipzip, ordermain_shipphone,
          ordermain_shipemail)
          VALUES (
          '$today',
          '$customers_custnum',
          '$total',
          '$shipping'
          '$shipfirst',
          '$shiplast',
          '$shipadd1',
          '$shipadd2',
          '$shipcity',
          '$shipstate',
          '$shipzip',
          '$shipphone',
          '$shipemail')";
$insert2 = mysql_query($query3)
  or (mysql_error());
$orderid = mysql_insert_id();

//3) Insert Info into orderdet
//find the correct cart information being temporarily stored
$query = "SELECT * FROM carttemp WHERE carttemp_sess='$sessid'";
$results = mysql_query($query)
  or (mysql_error());

//put the data into the database one row at a time
while ($row = mysql_fetch_array($results)) {
  extract($row);
  $query4 = "INSERT INTO orderdet (
            orderdet_ordernum, orderdet_qty, orderdet_prodnum)
            VALUES (
            '$orderid',
            '$carttemp_quan',
            '$carttemp_prodnum')";
  $insert4 = mysql_query($query4)
    or (mysql_error());
}

//4)delete from temporary table
$query = "DELETE FROM carttemp WHERE carttemp_sess='$sessid'";
$delete = mysql_query($query);


//5)email confirmations to us and to the customer
/* recipients */
$to = "<" . $email .">";
```

```
/* subject */
$subject = "Order Confirmation";

/* message */
  /* top of message */
  $message = "
    <html>
    <head>
    <title>Order Confirmation</title>
    </head>
    <body>
    Here is a recap of your order:<br><br>
    Order date: ";
  $message .= $today;
  $message .= "
    <br>
    Order Number: ";
  $message .= $orderid;
  $message .= "
    <table width=\"50%\" border=\"0\">
      <tr>
        <td>
          <p>Bill to:<br>";
  $message .= $firstname;
  $message .= " ";
  $message .= $lastname;
  $message .= "<br>";
  $message .= $add1;
  $message .= "<br>";
  if ($add2) {
    $message .= $add2 . "<br>";
  }
  $message .= $city . ", " . $state . " " . $zip;
  $message .= "</p></td>
    <td>
      <p>Ship to:<br>";
  $message .= $shipfirst . " " . $shiplast;
  $message .= "<br>";
  $message .= $shipadd1 . "<br>";
  if ($shipadd2) {
    $message .= $shipadd2 . "<br>";
  }
  $message .= $shipcity . ", " . $shipstate . " " . $shipzip;
  $message .= "</p>
        </td>
      </tr>
    </table>
    <hr width=\"250px\" align=\"left\">
    <table cellpadding=\"5\">";

//grab the contents of the order and insert them
//into the message field

$query = "SELECT * FROM orderdet WHERE orderdet_ordernum = '$orderid'";
$results = mysql_query($query)
  or die (mysql_query());
```

```php
while ($row = mysql_fetch_array($results)) {
   extract($row);
   $prod = "SELECT * FROM products
            WHERE products_prodnum = '$orderdet_prodnum'";
   $prod2 = mysql_query($prod);
   $prod3 = mysql_fetch_array($prod2);
   extract($prod3);
   $message .= "<tr><td>";
   $message .= $orderdet_qty;
   $message .= "</td>";
   $message .="<td>";
   $message .= $products_name;
   $message .= "</td>";
   $message .= "<td align=\"right\">";
   $message .= $products_price;
   $message .= "</td>";
   $message .= "<td align=\"right\">";
   //get extended price
   $extprice = number_format($products_price * $orderdet_qty, 2);
   $message .= $extprice;
   $message .= "</td>";
   $message .= "</tr>";
}

   $message .= "<tr>
     <td colspan=\"3\" align=\"right\">
       Your total before shipping is:
     </td>
     <td align=\"right\">";
   $message .= number_format($total, 2);
   $message .= "
       </td>
     </tr>
     <tr>
       <td colspan=\"3\" align=\"right\">
         Shipping Costs:
       </td>
       <td align=\"right\">";
   $message .= number_format($shipping, 2);
   $message .= "
       </td>
     </tr>
     <tr>
       <td colspan=\"3\" align=\"right\">
         Your final total is:
       </td>
       <td align=\"right\"> ";
   $message .= number_format(($total + $shipping), 2);
   $message .= "
         </td>
       </tr>
     </table>
     </body>
     </html>";

/* headers */
```

```
$headers = "MIME-Version: 1.0\r\n";
$headers .= "Content-type: text/html; charset=iso-8859-1\r\n";
$headers .= "From: <storeemail@email.com>\r\n";
$headers .= "Cc: <storeemail@email.com>\r\n";
$headers .= "X-Mailer: PHP / ".phpversion()."\r\n";

/* mail it */
mail($to, $subject, $message, $headers);


//6)show them their order & give them an order number

echo "Step 1 - Please Enter Billing and Shipping Information<br>";
echo "Step 2 - Please Verify Accuracy and Make Any Necessary Changes<br>";
echo "<strong>Step 3 - Order Confirmation and Receipt</strong><br><br>";

echo $message;

?>
```

2. Finally, it's time to test. Enter the site, select your item, check out, enter your information, and finally, place the order. Figure 15-7 shows the confirmation of your order.

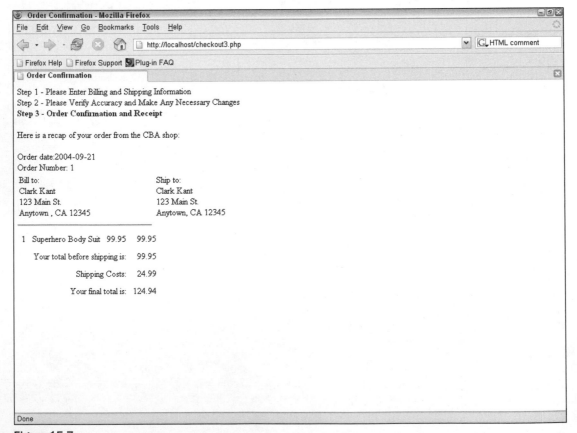

Figure 15-7

How It Works

Of course, there are comments throughout the code, but here is a rundown of what this script accomplishes.

Before you can enter anything else, you have to determine whether or not your customer is new or returning. You accomplish this in the following lines:

```
$query = "SELECT * FROM customers WHERE
            (customers_firstname = '$firstname' AND
            customers_lastname = '$lastname' AND
            customers_add1 = '$add1' AND
            customers_add2 = '$add2' AND
            customers_city = '$city')";
$results = mysql_query($query)
  or (mysql_error());
$rows = mysql_num_rows($results);
```

If he or she is a returning customer, you want to keep the existing customer number, and if new, he or she will be assigned the next customer number in line. You do this in the following lines:

```
if ($rows < 1) {
  //assign new custnum
  $query2 = "INSERT INTO customers (
            customers_firstname, customers_lastname, customers_add1,
            customers_add2, customers_city, customers_state,
            customers_zip, customers_phone, customers_fax,
            customers_email)
            VALUES (
            '$firstname',
            '$lastname',
            '$add1',
            '$add2',
            '$city',
            '$state',
            '$zip',
            '$phone',
            '$fax',
            '$email')";
  $insert = mysql_query($query2)
    or (mysql_error());
  $custid = mysql_insert_id();
}
```

Of course, this is not a fail-safe plan: You check for the same first name, last name, two lines of address, and city. A returning customer would just have to abbreviate something differently to be considered "new." We talk more about this later in this chapter.

You use the PHP function `mysql_insert_id()` to get the auto-increment value that was just added into the database. This helps you make sure you are keeping all the information from the same order together. Once you have the customer information entered in the database, you can then enter the order-specific information. This includes the date and order number, as well as the shipping information associated with this order. You also tabulated the shipping costs as a percentage of total cost of the order (25 percent), but obviously you can set your shipping costs to be whatever you like. You can see all of this in the following lines:

```
//2) Insert Info into ordermain
//determine shipping costs based on order total (25% of total)
$shipping = $total * 0.25;

$query3 = "INSERT INTO ordermain (
            ordermain_orderdate, ordermain_custnum,
            ordermain_subtotal,ordermain_shipping,
            ordermain_shipfirst, ordermain_shiplast,
            ordermain_shipadd1, ordermain_shipadd2,
            ordermain_shipcity, ordermain_shipstate,
            ordermain_shipzip, ordermain_shipphone,
            ordermain_shipemail)
            VALUES (
            '$today',
            '$customers_custnum',
            '$total',
            '$shipping'
            '$shipfirst',
            '$shiplast',
            '$shipadd1',
            '$shipadd2',
            '$shipcity',
            '$shipstate',
            '$shipzip',
            '$shipphone',
            '$shipemail')";
$insert2 = mysql_query($query3)
  or (mysql_error());
$orderid = mysql_insert_id();
```

You can then enter the order detail information with all the specific items that have been placed in the shopping cart, as such:

```
 //3) Insert Info into orderdet
//find the correct cart information being temporarily stored
$query = "SELECT * FROM carttemp WHERE carttemp_sess='$sessid'";
$results = mysql_query($query)
  or (mysql_error());

//put the data into the database one row at a time
while ($row = mysql_fetch_array($results)) {
  extract($row);
  $query4 = "INSERT INTO orderdet (
              orderdet_ordernum, orderdet_qty, orderdet_prodnum)
              VALUES (
              '$orderid',
              '$carttemp_quan',
              '$carttemp_prodnum')";
  $insert4 = mysql_query($query4)
    or (mysql_error());
}
```

You then delete the temporary information, because you don't need it anymore:

```
//4)delete from temporary table
$query = "DELETE FROM carttemp WHERE carttemp_sess='$sessid'";
$delete = mysql_query($query);
```

You also send a confirmation e-mail to your customer, and one to yourself to let you know an order was placed. E-mail was discussed in depth in Chapter 13, so we won't go into detail about this code.

Lastly, you display the order confirmation on the page to let the customer know immediately that the order was received and to give him or her an order number. Since you have already created an HTML page for e-mailing purposes, you simply output the message as it would show up in the confirmation e-mail, as can be seen in the following lines:

```
//6)show them their order & give them an order number

echo "Step 1 - Please Enter Billing and Shipping Information<br>";
echo "Step 2 - Please Verify Accuracy and Make Any Necessary Changes<br>";
echo "<strong>Step 3 - Order Confirmation and Receipt</strong><br><br>";

echo $message;

?>
```

This is the end of your simple shopping cart script.

E-Commerce, Any Way You Slice It

As we briefly mentioned before, you can integrate e-commerce into your site the right way and you can do it the wrong way. To prevent yourself from looking like a complete idiot and virtually ensuring e-commerce failure, we highly recommend doing things the right way. Good word-of-mouth travels slowly, but we all know how quickly bad word-of-mouth spreads. Also, with so many millions of Web sites out there competing for attention, we want to elevate yours above the rest.

This may sound harsh, but here are some things to remember about some of the more challenging characteristics of your potential customers:

❑ **Your customers are impatient.** They don't want to have to wait for your pages to load or for answers to their questions. They are busy people, just like you, and if they don't find what they need right away, they're outta there and on to something else.

❑ **Your customers are distrustful.** Who wants their personal information strewn about all over the Web? You certainly don't, and they don't either. They don't want their credit card number to be used by every geek in your office, and they don't want to give you tons of money and never see the product they purchased. They don't want to order from you one week and have you go bankrupt the next.

❑ **Your customers want a lot for a little.** In this age of Web site competition, where people can compare prices with a few mouse clicks, they are striving to get the best deal they can. They want to make sure they are getting the best deal, but they also appreciate the value-added services of a high-quality Web site.

❑ **Your customers are generally lazy.** They don't want to have to put any effort into trying to find the right product on your site or figuring out what you're trying to say or what your policies are. They don't want to work at trying to get the checkout process to work, and they don't want to have to filter through pages and pages of text to glean information.

❑ **Your customers aren't very forgiving.** You basically have one chance to make a good first impression on your customers. Nothing can eliminate a sale (and future sales for that matter) faster than a bad experience. Whether it is something minor such as spelling mistakes and broken images on your site or something major such as selling faulty merchandise, your customers are likely to remember something bad a lot longer than something good. They will also be more likely to share a bad experience more quickly than they will a good one.

❑ **Your customers may not be as technically savvy as you are.** Yes, there are actually people out there who still use dial-up with 56K. There are people out there who still use 14-inch monitors and there are people out there who have never made an online purchase in their lives. Remember these people and don't leave them behind totally when designing your site. If you do, you are alienating a huge percentage of the population.

Don't worry: Satisfying e-commerce customers is not hard, but a little effort can really go a long way. We've included some general guidelines to follow. After reading them, you may think, "Well, duh, no kidding," but you'd be surprised at how many big, well-known companies don't follow them.

Information Is Everything

Your customers have to get as much information as possible about your product because they can't actually see, feel, touch, and smell what you have to offer. Your site is your window to your customers, and they have to depend on what you're telling them to make their purchasing decision. Whatever blanks you leave in your product description, policies, company history, or checkout process will have to be filled in by the customer's imagination. While that may be good in certain circumstances, you do not want your customers to make incorrect assumptions that leave them dissatisfied after the fact, or for their uncertainty to prevent the sale altogether.

Besides textual information, graphics are a very important part of the sale. There is a fine balance between adding too many graphics to your site, which causes your potential patrons to wait longer than they need to, and providing enough high-quality pictures so they can actually see what they're getting.

Importance of Trust

Let's talk for a minute about trust over the Web. We all know that most of the proclaimed 14-year-old females in those online chat rooms are really 40-year-old fat guys sitting in their living rooms. Things are not always as they seem in the online world, and because of that, as an e-commerce retailer, you are at a disadvantage over those with a physical storefront and salespeople. And then there's the old saying "caveat emptor" ("buyer beware") that goes along with any purchase/sales transaction. "Trust" must be established and it certainly is an uphill battle. If you're an established business already, and you have spent years building product or brand name recognition, don't think that switching to e-commerce will be so easy. Yes, if your business has an established reputation you may have an easier time than some unknown entity, like "Joe's House of Beauty," but people still want to know what they're getting and be assured that they're not going to get ripped off.

Privacy Policy

Users want to know that their personal information will not be sold and they won't end up on 47 spam e-mail lists. They also want to make sure they won't be on an annoying telemarketing phone list or receive junk snail mail. The only way they can be assured this won't happen is if you provide a clear, concise privacy policy in an easy-to-find place on your site.

Return Policy

Returns are a sometimes overlooked part of a company's e-commerce venture. There have to be processes in place for accepting returns, shipping out replacement merchandise, or issuing credits in exchange. Your users will need to know where you stand on returns, what your requirements are for accepting them, and how they will be handled once they reach your warehouse (or basement).

If you are a relatively (or completely) unknown entity, you may want to consider providing a 100 percent money back guarantee or something similar to try and build trust with your potential customers. You may get burned once or twice on this and it may require more work from you, but overall it can be a very beneficial asset to you, especially if your customers are riding the fence on a potential purchase.

Whatever you decide, you should think long and hard about how you want to handle returned merchandise, and then make sure your customers understand your decisions in order to avoid misunderstandings later on.

Warm Bodies

Who doesn't love a nice, warm body? In this age of technology, sometimes it's nice just to talk to an actual living, breathing person who can help you answer a question or find what you are looking for. If you can manage this in your e-commerce business, it is another great feature that will undoubtedly pay for itself in those "on the fence" purchasing decisions. You can provide personal customer service in a few ways:

- ❑ Give your customers a phone number (preferably toll-free) where they can have access to your customer service staff, or just you, if you're a one-man show.

- ❑ Offer online customer service chat for your customers, where you can address customer questions or concerns without having to pay someone to wait for the phone to ring.

- ❑ Provide a customer service e-mail address for questions and problems. Although this isn't the optimal solution, because many people don't want to wait for answers to their questions, at least this gives customers an outlet to vent their frustrations and then move on to something else. It also gives you a chance to prepare a proper reply and respond accordingly.

Secure Credit Card Processing

Nothing will make your customers feel better than knowing their credit card information is safe and won't get stolen along the way. Make sure you are using a secure encryption method to transfer sensitive information, such as SSL, and make sure your customers understand how safe their information is. It's a good idea to not get too technical; just explain the security process in layman's terms.

If it's possible, it's a good idea to have a third party (such as Verisign) verify that your site is secure and prominently display its seal somewhere on your site.

Professional Look

When designing your site, you want to make sure it doesn't look "homemade" and that it appears as professional as possible. Professional equals credible in the minds of your customers, and it helps to build that elusive trusting relationship.

Here are some ways to improve the look of your site:

❏ Spend some time viewing other e-commerce sites. What do you personally like about them? What don't you like? By emulating the big guys, you can look big, too.

❏ Invest in a few Web site design books or do some online research. Numerous articles and books have been written on the topic, and you may as well not reinvent the wheel.

❏ If you use a template of some sort, please, please, please do yourself a favor and make sure you remove all generic instances. We've seen sites with a title bar that reads "Insert Description Here." This is not a good look, trust us.

❏ *Spell check* your document. Spell checkers are available in nearly all text editors, so spelling mistakes are pretty much unacceptable and can really undermine your professional look.

Easy Navigation

You want to make sure your customers are able to move around your site and find what they need. Remember the rule from earlier in this section: They do not want to work too hard, or they will lose interest and go somewhere else.

Common Links

Make sure you have clear links to every area of your site, and put the common links near the top where they can be seen easily. Common links include a customer's shopping cart, customer service, or user login.

Search Function

You should give your customers a way to easily find what they're looking for. An accurate and quick search engine is essential to accomplish this. There are many ways to add this feature to your site, either through coding it by hand in PHP or hooking up with third-party software. Another way to improve your search engine is to make sure you include misspellings and not-so-common terms to give your customers the best results possible.

Typical Design

It's been long enough now that most people are accustomed to seeing navigation links either at the top or to the left side of a page. By keeping with this general scheme, you can ensure that your customers will know where to look to find what they need.

Competitive Pricing

If you are selling items that are available from other sources, it's important to remember that your store can easily be compared with numerous other stores selling the same thing. If your prices are way out of line, your customers will get a good chuckle and then promptly click back to their Google search. Do your research, and make sure you are in line with similar products being sold on the Web. Not all customers base their decision solely on price, but they definitely don't want to be taken for a ride, unless you have a Lamborghini Diablo, and that's a different story.

Appropriate Merchandise

Only a handful of stores on the Web can get away with carrying a wide range of unrelated products, and, no offense, chances are you aren't one of them. Be sure you are carrying items that are related to your overall site and to each other, or you will confuse your customers and detract from your look and focus.

Timely Delivery

In this world of "overnight this" and "immediately download that," it is no longer acceptable to ask for six to eight weeks to deliver your merchandise to your customers. The only exception is if you are creating something custom made or if your customers are preordering something that hasn't been officially released yet. The typical lead time for standard products to ship to a customer is roughly two to three business days. If you can do better than that, your customers will be happy, and if not, you need to make sure your customer realizes it will take longer and give an explanation.

It is also important to provide numerous shipping options to your customers and let them decide how quickly they need your products and how much they are willing to spend to get them faster.

Communication

Because you are isolated from your customers, communication is essential to building strong relationships. Your customers want to know that you received their order, when the order is ready to ship, and when it ships. They appreciate getting a tracking number so they can see where their package is every step of the way. Some companies even track each outgoing package and let their customers know when they think the package has been delivered, in case there are any misunderstandings. All of this can be communicated via e-mail. Your customers will definitely appreciate being kept in the loop, and knowing that their order has not been lost somewhere along the order fulfillment and delivery chain.

Customer Feedback

The online world presents an interesting dilemma for e-commerce retailers in that you must operate your store in a bubble. You can't tell what your customers are thinking or how they react to your site. You know you're relatively successful at something only if you have sales and relatively unsuccessful if you don't. Figuring out which of our rules you're breaking can be a tricky endeavor. That's when your customer feedback can make or break you.

You always want to give your customers an outlet to express their concerns or problems, and it can give you a warm fuzzy feeling to get some positive feedback once in a while. To encourage your customers to provide you with feedback you should do two things:

❑ Give them an incentive to complete a survey or provide some sort of feedback. Free shipping, a discount on their next order, or a free gift of some sort are some good possibilities.

❑ Make it easy for your customers to complete a survey, but make sure it provides you with valuable feedback. Don't just ask for their comments; ask them to rate certain areas of your site. Also, don't give them 100 questions, but a maximum of 15 to 20. After that, people lose interest and their special gift isn't worth it.

By sticking to the preceding guidelines and advice, you will increase the quality and quantity of your customer feedback and increase your ability to tap into one of your most valuable resources.

Summary

Now that you have the know-how to add e-commerce to your site, you should feel comfortable making your site as competitive and professional as any other site out there. You should be able to set up a simple shopping cart, and, with time, you will be able to continue to add features to really enhance your cart and your site in general. E-commerce concepts aren't difficult to comprehend, and by following the simple guidelines we've outlined, you will be well on your way. Although e-commerce retailers don't typically enjoy overnight success, adding e-commerce to your site can really augment what you're currently doing and may grow to something big over time.

Exercises

We know we're not perfect, so before you start naming all the things we didn't accomplish in our shopping cart scripts, we'll save you the trouble and list them for you. As a matter of fact, we did these things on purpose because we wanted to give you some homework.

Here are the things you can work on, and hints are in Appendix A in case you want some help:

1. **Allow for tax.** Many states require that you charge sales tax on the orders shipped to the state where you have a physical presence, and some states require sales tax on all online orders. Set your code to check for customers in your own state and add the appropriate sales tax to those orders only.

2. **Allow for inventory control.** Your shopping cart script can keep track of how many items you have in stock and display that to your customers. You can also show an "out of stock" message to your customers letting them know that a particular item is temporarily out of stock, but still available for purchase if they like.

3. **Show your customers your most popular items.** Which of your items are purchased the most? If an item is in the top 5 on your bestseller list, show a "bestseller" icon in the description of that item.

Other things you can add to your shopping cart script include:

❑ **Allow for options.** You may have noticed that you didn't let your customers pick the size of their T-shirt or size and color of the Superhero Body Suit. Alter the codes to allow for these options.

❑ **Allow for payment.** Because of copyright issues, we weren't able to actually hook you up with Paypal or one of the other payment processors available. Decide how you want to accept payment, and then alter the code accordingly.

❑ **Check for mistakes.** We have not included any mechanism to check for required fields or for mismatched types (such as a bogus e-mail address). Add these checks in your code.

❑ **Perform a cart-abandonment analysis.** Numerous studies have shown that online shoppers abandon their carts roughly 75% of the time. How does your site stack up?

❑ **Make add-on purchase recommendations.** Once customers place an item in their cart, you might make suggestions for related items or items that customers have bought in addition to the current item.

❑ **Allow for registering, login, and order tracking.** Some customers like to check the status of their orders.

Creating a Bulletin Board System

People don't like to be alone because we are social animals. Throughout our brief history as civilized human beings, we have consistently maintained some sort of connection to other people, whether it be the family unit, clans, chess clubs, or AA meetings. With the advent of the computer, many geeks found themselves shut in a room for long periods, becoming the modern equivalent of the social outcast. (How many of us have joked about not knowing what the sun looks like?) The development of the electronic bulletin board made it possible for computer geeks to communicate without ever having to look at each other's faces.

Many Bulletin Board Systems, or BBS, refer to themselves as *forums*. By definition, a forum is a gathering place where people can meet and discuss different topics. That is a very apt definition for a BBS. However, we are going to clarify it a little further, for use in the computer world. By our definition (and the way we'll use it in this chapter), a forum is a place to talk to other people about a common interest. A bulletin board is the location in which the forum exists, which may house multiple forums. Therefore, you might visit a book BBS to find different forums for science fiction, nonfiction, authors, and more.

Your Bulletin Board

This brings us to the reason for this chapter. You are going to create a Bulletin Board System. Once you create the BBS, it will be up to you to create any type of forums within it that you need.

No doubt, you have visited many bulletin boards by now and are aware of the different features they have to offer. Some of them have many bells and whistles, and are very slick programs. PHPBB and Vbulletin are two of those very nice applications. Yours will not have quite the feature set these offer (unless you are ambitious and decide to expand the app you write).

You have probably seen some very simple boards out there, too. Some are nothing more than a couple of input boxes for Subject and Body, with no authentication. Those are fine for some Web sites, but not for you. This is the last application of the book, and you're going to put a few features in this thing. You are also going to use cascading style sheets (CSS) to alter the look of the page because, let's face it, the apps up to now have been fairly plain. Because of the extended feature set of this app, CSS will help you position things on the page a little better.

Don't worry if you don't know CSS; it's not a requirement. We will provide you with a CSS file, down-loadable from the Web site. If you know how, you can write your own style sheet, or modify the one we provide. Otherwise, simply use the one we give you and you'll be fine. The application will work fine without the CSS, but as you will see, it will be much prettier and better laid out with it.

If you want to know more about CSS, we recommend getting a book or reading an online tutorial. Some excellent sites are dedicated to teaching people how to make their Web pages CSS-compliant. We recommend you take a look at the following pages:

❑ `www.w3schools.com/css/default.asp`: A great site at which to start learning the basics of CSS.

❑ `http://webmonkey.wired.com/webmonkey/authoring/stylesheets/tutorials/tutorial1.html`: A long URL, yes, but an excellent tutorial. It's very funny, too. We strongly recommend you check this one out. In fact, put `webmonkey.wired.com/webmonkey` in your favorites list. There are many articles there you will want to read.

❑ `www.zeldman.com`: Jeffrey Zeldman's very informative site. If you get into CSS and XHTML compliance, you will hear his name *many* times.

❑ `www.alistapart.com`: Many very informative articles on everything from CSS to XML to typography. The authors of these articles are considered by some to be the masters of CSS and XHTML compliance.

So there you have it. You do not need to know a single bit of CSS to do every example in this book, including this chapter. But if you are ambitious enough to have read this far and have written most of the applications in the book, we are sure a little thing like CSS will be no problem for you.

Here is a list of some of the more prominent features of the bulletin board you will build:

❑ **User authentication:** You want to keep track of who is posting what. You can certainly allow anonymous access but this application will require users to log in before they can post. Users will *not* have to log in to read posts, however.

❑ **Search:** This is the key to any good board, in our opinion. Searching allows users to see if their question has already been answered, as well as enable people to find posts that discuss the topic they want to talk about.

❑ **Admin screen:** There will be a few features of the site that can be modified in the admin screen. These will be fairly limited, but we hope that the implementation will inspire you to figure out what other parts of the bulletin board you can include in the Admin section.

❑ **Regular expressions:** We include BBcodes in the application. If you have never seen them, these are special codes that give users a limited ability to format their posts. For example, by placing [b] and [/b] around words they will become bold (for example, [b]some words[/b] will become **some words**). You will be using regular expressions for this feature.

❑ **Pagination:** You don't want to have 328 posts on a single page. For one, it's a bit long for users to read. Second, PHP takes a while to render such a page, especially if the posts contain images. For this reason, you offer page links at the bottom to load different pages. To enable this, you will be creating a pagination function.

These are most of the major features of the board. You will add a few more bells and whistles, but we won't spoil the surprise yet. We want to give you plenty of "ooh," "aah," and "You're a genius!" moments later.

In this chapter, you'll work your way through a fresh installation of the Comic Book Appreciation Bulletin Board System. (That is a mouthful, so from now on, we'll refer to it as the "CBA board.")

Note that many screens are involved in this application. You have probably seen a bulletin board application before, so we are not going to show you each and every screen as we describe the application, just some of the more important screens.

Preparing the Database

This is a large application—the biggest in the book. It consists of about 1,800 lines of code. Are you scared yet? Well, don't be. The hardest part is the typing, and if you want to avoid that, you can always download the code from the Web site:

www.wrox.com

The first thing you will need to do is create a database. If you have already created a database for the other apps in this book, we recommend you use the same database. There is no need to create a new one. This app uses the prefix forum_ for its tables, so there should be no conflict.

If you do not have a database created, then Chapter 10 will help you create one. Do that, and then come back. We'll wait . . . .

Try It Out   **Preparing the Database**

You have around 20 PHP files to enter. We are simply going to list them one after another, giving you the filename of each, and a short explanation of what the file is for. Save each file in the same folder.

Do your typing finger warm-ups, and let's get started!

1. Open your favorite PHP editor. Remember to save early, and save often!

2. Create conn.php: This is the file that connects the application to the database. This file will be included at the top of almost every other page, and contains all of your connection information. Substitute the appropriate data for your host, username, password, and database.

```php
<?php
define('SQL_HOST','localhost');
define('SQL_USER','bp5am');
define('SQL_PASS','bp5ampass');
define('SQL_DB','comicsite');

$conn = mysql_connect(SQL_HOST, SQL_USER, SQL_PASS)
   or die('Could not connect to the database; ' . mysql_error());

mysql_select_db(SQL_DB, $conn)
   or die('Could not select database; ' . mysql_error());
?>
```

3. Enter `setup.php`. Once you have your database created, and `conn.php` saved, this file creates all of the necessary tables in your database.

```php
<?php
require_once "conn.php";
$adminemail = "admin@yoursite.com";
$adminpass = "admin";
$adminname = "Admin";

/******* Access Levels Table ****************************************/
$sql = <<<EOS
CREATE TABLE forum_access_levels (
  access_lvl tinyint(4) NOT NULL auto_increment,
  access_name varchar(50) NOT NULL default '',
  PRIMARY KEY (access_lvl)
)
EOS;
$result = mysql_query($sql);
switch(mysql_errno()) {
  case 1050:
    break;

  case 0:
    $sql = "INSERT IGNORE INTO forum_access_levels " .
           "VALUES (1,'User')";
    $result = mysql_query($sql)
      or die(mysql_error());
    $sql = "INSERT IGNORE INTO forum_access_levels " .
           "VALUES (2,'Moderator')";
    $result = mysql_query($sql)
      or die(mysql_error());
    $sql = "INSERT IGNORE INTO forum_access_levels " .
           "VALUES (3,'Administrator')";
    $result = mysql_query($sql)
      or die(mysql_error());
    break;

  default:
    die(mysql_error());
    break;
}
$a_tables[] = "forum_access_levels";

/******* Admin Table ***********************************************/
$sql = <<<EOS
CREATE TABLE  forum_admin (
  id int(11) NOT NULL auto_increment,
  title varchar(100) NOT NULL default '',
  value varchar(255) NOT NULL default '',
  constant varchar(100) NOT NULL default '',
  PRIMARY KEY  (id)
)
EOS;
$result = mysql_query($sql);
switch(mysql_errno()) {
```

```
      case 1050:
        break;

      case 0:
        $sql = "INSERT INTO forum_admin " .
               "VALUES (NULL, 'Board Title', " .
               "'Comic Book Appreciation Forums', 'title')";
        $result = mysql_query($sql)
          or die(mysql_error());
        $sql = "INSERT INTO forum_admin " .
               "VALUES (NULL, 'Board Description', " .
               "'The place to discuss your favorite " .
               "comic books, movies, and more!', 'description')";
        $result = mysql_query($sql)
          or die(mysql_error());
        $sql = "INSERT INTO forum_admin " .
               "VALUES (NULL,'Admin Email', '$adminemail', 'admin_email')";
        $result = mysql_query($sql)
          or die(mysql_error());
        $sql = "INSERT INTO forum_admin " .
               "VALUES (NULL, 'Copyright', ".
               "'&copy;2003 CBA Inc.  All rights reserved.', 'copyright')";
        $result = mysql_query($sql)
          or die(mysql_error());
        $sql = "INSERT INTO forum_admin " .
               "VALUES (NULL, 'Board Titlebar', 'CBA Forums', 'titlebar')";
        $result = mysql_query($sql)
          or die(mysql_error());
        $sql = "INSERT INTO forum_admin " .
               "VALUES (NULL, 'Pagination Limit', '10', 'pageLimit')";
        $result = mysql_query($sql)
          or die(mysql_error());
        $sql = "INSERT INTO forum_admin " .
               "VALUES (NULL, 'Pagination Range', '7', 'pageRange')";
        $result = mysql_query($sql)
          or die(mysql_error());
        break;

      default:
        die(mysql_error());
        break;
    }
    $a_tables[] = "forum_admin";

/******* BBcode Table ***********************************************/
$sql = <<<EOS
CREATE TABLE IF NOT EXISTS forum_bbcode (
  id int(11) NOT NULL auto_increment,
  template varchar(255) NOT NULL default '',
  replacement varchar(255) NOT NULL default '',
  PRIMARY KEY  (id)
)
EOS;
$result = mysql_query($sql)
  or die(mysql_error());
```

```
$a_tables[] = "forum_bbcode";

/******* Forum Table ***************************************************/
$sql = <<<EOS
CREATE TABLE  forum_forum (
  id int(11) NOT NULL auto_increment,
  forum_name varchar(100) NOT NULL default '',
  forum_desc varchar(255) NOT NULL default '',
  forum_moderator int(11) NOT NULL default '0',
  PRIMARY KEY  (id)
)
EOS;
$result = mysql_query($sql);
switch(mysql_errno()) {
  case 1050:
    break;

  case 0:
    $sql = "INSERT INTO forum_forum VALUES (NULL, 'New Forum', " .
           "'This is the initial forum created when installing the " .
           "database.  Change the name and the description after " .
           "installation.', 1)";
    $result = mysql_query($sql)
      or die(mysql_error());
    break;

  default:
    die(mysql_error());
    break;
}
$a_tables[] = "forum_forum";

/******* Post Count Table ***********************************************/
$sql = <<<EOS
CREATE TABLE forum_postcount (
  user_id int(11) NOT NULL default '0',
  count int(9) NOT NULL default '0',
  PRIMARY KEY  (user_id)
)
EOS;
$result = mysql_query($sql);
switch(mysql_errno()) {
  case 1050:
    break;

  case 0:
    $sql = "INSERT INTO forum_postcount VALUES (1,1)";
    $result = mysql_query($sql)
      or die(mysql_error());
    break;

  default:
    die(mysql_error());
    break;
}
```

```
$a_tables[] = "forum_postcount";

/******* Posts Table **************************************************/
$sql = <<<EOS
CREATE TABLE  forum_posts (
  id int(11) NOT NULL auto_increment,
  topic_id int(11) NOT NULL default '0',
  forum_id int(11) NOT NULL default '0',
  author_id int(11) NOT NULL default '0',
  update_id int(11) NOT NULL default '0',
  date_posted datetime NOT NULL default '0000-00-00 00:00:00',
  date_updated datetime NOT NULL default '0000-00-00 00:00:00',
  subject varchar(255) NOT NULL default '',
  body mediumtext NOT NULL,
  PRIMARY KEY  (id),
  KEY IdxArticle (forum_id,topic_id,author_id,date_posted),
  FULLTEXT KEY IdxText (subject,body)
)
EOS;
$result = mysql_query($sql);
switch(mysql_errno()) {
  case 1050:
    break;

  case 0:
    $sql = "INSERT INTO forum_posts VALUES (NULL, 0, 1, 1, 0, '" .
           date("Y-m-d H:i:s", time())."', 0, 'Welcome', 'Welcome " .
           "to your new Bulletin Board System. Do not forget to " .
           "change your admin password after installation. " .
           "Have fun!')";
    $result = mysql_query($sql)
      or die(mysql_error());
    break;

  default:
    die(mysql_error());
    break;
}
$a_tables[] = "forum_posts";

/******* Users Table **************************************************/
$sql = <<<EOS
CREATE TABLE  forum_users (
  id int(11) NOT NULL auto_increment,
  email varchar(255) NOT NULL default '',
  passwd varchar(50) NOT NULL default '',
  name varchar(100) NOT NULL default '',
  access_lvl tinyint(4) NOT NULL default '1',
  signature varchar(255) NOT NULL default '',
  date_joined datetime NOT NULL default '0000-00-00 00:00:00',
  last_login datetime NOT NULL default '0000-00-00 00:00:00',
  PRIMARY KEY  (id),
  UNIQUE KEY uniq_email (email)
)
```

```
EOS;
$result = mysql_query($sql);
switch(mysql_errno()) {
  case 1050:
    break;

  case 0:
    $datetime = date("Y-m-d H:i:s",time());
    $sql = "INSERT IGNORE INTO forum_users VALUES (NULL, " .
           "'$adminemail', '$adminpass', '$adminname', 3, '', " .
           "'$datetime', 0)";
    $result = mysql_query($sql)
      or die(mysql_error());
    break;

  default:
    die(mysql_error());
    break;
}
$a_tables[] = "forum_users";

/******* Display Results **********************************************/
echo "<html><head><title>Forum Tables Created</title>";
echo "<link rel=\"stylesheet\" type=\"text/css\" ";
echo "href=\"forum_styles.css\">";
echo "</head><body>";
echo "<div class=\"bodysmall\">";
echo "<h1>Comic Book Appreciation Forums</h1>";
echo "<h3>Forum Tables created:</h3>\n<ul>";
foreach ($a_tables as $table) {
  $table = str_replace("forum_","",$table);
  $table = str_replace("_", " ",$table);
  $table = ucWords($table);
  echo "<li>$table</li>\n";
}
echo "</ul>\n<h3>Here is your initial login information:</h3>\n";
echo "<ul><li><strong>login</strong>: " . $adminemail . "</li>\n";
echo "<li><strong>password</strong>: " . $adminpass . "</li></ul>\n";
echo "<h3><a href=\"login.php?e=" . $adminemail . "\">Log In</a> ";
echo "to the site now.</h3></div>";
echo "</body></html>";
?>
```

4. Load setup.php in your browser. You should see a screen similar to Figure 16-1, informing you that the databases have been created and reminding you of your initial login e-mail and password.

If you downloaded the application from the Web site, your screen should look very similar to Figure 16-1. However, if you entered the code from the book, it will look quite different. The reason for this is that you are missing a file, forum_styles.css, that modifies the way the page looks. You can download this file from the Web site if you would like to use it, although it is not required. All screenshots in this chapter utilize the forum_styles.css style sheet mentioned previously.

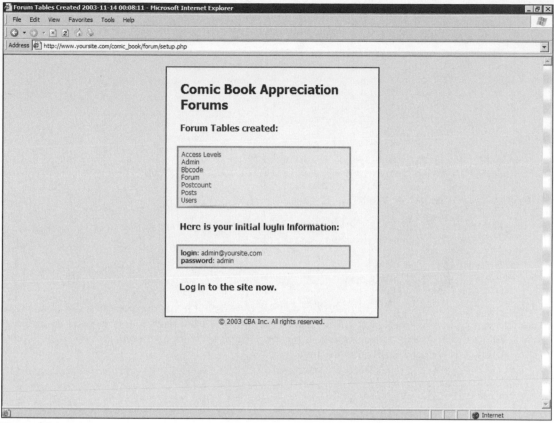

Figure 16-1

How It Works

Unlike some previous chapters, we are not going to show you how the app works page by page, line by line. Not only is it a very large application that would take too many pages to explain, but most of the code of the Bulletin Board application has been explained in previous chapters. So far, we have shown you how to write a SQL statement, how to work with arrays, and how to create reusable functions and classes.

You're doing things a little differently here from the way you did them in other chapters. Previously, when creating a database, you used CREATE TABLE IF NOT EXISTS. That is a good way to create a new table yet avoid errors if the table already exists. But what if data needs to be inserted into the table? How do you know whether the table was just created or already existed? By using the CREATE TABLE command, you can't know.

Instead, you are going to trap the error caused by creating an existing table. If the error occurs, then you know the table already exists, and you will skip over the data insertions and continue with the next table. If any other error occurs, you will halt execution with the die() command, as usual.

First, you create your SQL statement and then run it with the `mysql_query` command. Note the creation of a full text index for the subject and body fields. This makes searches easier (which we will cover shortly). Also note the absence of the "IF NOT EXISTS" keywords.

```
$sql = <<<EOS
CREATE TABLE forum_posts (
  id int(11) NOT NULL auto_increment,
  topic_id int(11) NOT NULL default '0',
  forum_id int(11) NOT NULL default '0',
  author_id int(11) NOT NULL default '0',
  update_id int(11) NOT NULL default '0',
  date_posted datetime NOT NULL default '0000-00-00 00:00:00',
  date_updated datetime NOT NULL default '0000-00-00 00:00:00',
  subject varchar(255) NOT NULL default '',
  body mediumtext NOT NULL,
  PRIMARY KEY  (id),
  KEY IdxArticle (forum_id,topic_id,author_id,date_posted),
  FULLTEXT KEY IdxText (subject,body)
)
EOS;
$result = mysql_query($sql);
```

Next, you test for the error condition caused by the table existing in the database. The error code is 1050 and is returned by the function `mysql_errno()`. If you receive that particular error code, everything is okay, but no insert will take place. If there is no error, the table creation worked, and you insert your new data. Any other error code halts the program.

```
switch(mysql_errno()) {
  case 1050:
    break;

  case 0:
    $sql = "INSERT INTO forum_posts VALUES (NULL, 0, 1, 1, 0, '" .
             date("Y-m-d H:i:s", time())."'", 0, 'Welcome', 'Welcome " .
             "to your new Bulletin Board System. Do not forget to " .
             "change your admin password after installation. " .
             "Have fun!')";
    $result = mysql_query($sql)
      or die(mysql_error());
    break;

  default:
    die(mysql_error());
    break;
}
```

You may assume we have a vast knowledge of MySQL just because we know that the error code for creating a table that already exists is 1050. The fact is, we did *not* know the code: We simply ran a CREATE query on a table we knew already existed and echoed the resulting `mysql_errno()` to the screen. We then knew the code and could trap for it.

Why do we give away such a secret? Some day you may find yourself trying to trap a particular error condition in your code, and you won't know the code you are looking for. Rather than scouring the Internet hoping to find the code, you can usually induce the error yourself and echo the resulting code number to the screen. Once you have the code number, you can trap for it, just as we did in the preceding code.

One last comment about setup.php before we move on: You may notice that in some cases you *did* use IF NOT EXISTS. If you do not need to know whether you are duplicating a table, then IF NOT EXISTS will work nicely.

Reusable Code

The next thing you're going to do is create reusable functions to be included in your forum scripts. Some of these may look familiar — they are similar or in some cases, exactly the same, as some of the reusable functions from your Chapter 13 CMS application.

Try It Out   Creating Reusable Scripts

In this exercise, the reusable scripts you are creating don't have any standalone purpose. Even though they don't show anything on the screen, you must pay careful attention when typing them, because they form the backbone of the user interface pages later on.

1. Create functions.php. Okay, this is a big one. This file contains most of the major functions that the board uses.

```php
<?php
function trimBody($theText, $lmt=100, $s_chr="@@@", $s_cnt=1) {
  $pos = 0;
  $trimmed = FALSE;
  for ($i = 1; $i <= $s_cnt; $i++) {
    if ($tmp = strpos($theText, $s_chr, $pos)) {
      $pos = $tmp;
      $trimmed = TRUE;
    } else {
      $pos = strlen($theText);
      $trimmed = FALSE;
      break;
    }
  }
  $theText = substr($theText, 0, $pos);

  if (strlen($theText) > $lmt) {
    $theText = substr($theText, 0, $lmt);
    $theText = substr($theText, 0, strrpos($theText,' '));
    $trimmed = TRUE;
  }
  if ($trimmed) $theText .= '...';
  return $theText;
}
```

```php
function msgBox($m, $t, $d="index.php", $s="Info") {
  $theMsg = "<div id=\"requestConfirm" . $s . "\">";
  $theMsg .= "<h2>" . $t . "</h2>\n";
  $theMsg .= "<p>" . $m . "</p>";
  $theMsg .= "<p><a href=\"" . $d . "\" ";
  $theMsg .= "class=\"buttonlink\">";
  $theMsg .= "Yes</a>";
  $theMsg .= "<a href=\"index.php\" class=\"buttonlink\">";
  $theMsg .= "No</a></p>";
  $theMsg .= "</div>";
  return $theMsg;
}

function getForum($id) {
  $sql = "SELECT forum_name as name, forum_desc as description, " .
         "forum_moderator as mod ".
         "FROM forum_forum ".
         "WHERE id = " . $id;
  $result = mysql_query($sql)
    or die(mysql_error() . "<br>" . $sql);
  $row = mysql_fetch_array($result);
  return $row;
}

function getForumID($topicid) {
  $sql = "SELECT forum_id FROM forum_posts WHERE id=$topicid";
  $result = mysql_query($sql)
    or die(mysql_error() . "<br>" . $sql);
  $row = mysql_fetch_array($result);
  return $row['forum_id'];
}

function breadcrumb($id, $getfrom="F") {
  $sep = "<span class=\"bcsep\">";
  $sep .= " &middot; ";
  $sep .= "</span>";
  if ($getfrom == "P") {
    $sql = "SELECT forum_id, subject FROM forum_posts " .
           "WHERE id = " . $id;
    $result = mysql_query($sql)
      or die(mysql_error() . "<br>" . $sql);
    $row = mysql_fetch_array($result);
    $id = $row['forum_id'];
    $topic = $row['subject'];
  }
  $row = getForum($id);
  $bc = "<a href=\"index.php\">Home</a>$sep";
  switch ($getfrom) {
    case "P":
      $bc .= "<a href=\"viewforum.php?f=$id\">".$row['name'] .
             "</a>$sep" . $topic;
      break;

    case "F":
      $bc .= $row['name'];
```

```
        break;
    }
  return "<h4 class=\"breadcrumb\">" . $bc . "</h4>";
}

function showTopic($topicid, $showfull=TRUE) {
  global $conn;
  global $userid;
  global $limit;

  echo breadcrumb($topicid, "P");
  if (isset($_GET['page'])) {
    $page = $_GET['page'];
  } else {
    $page = 1;
  }
  if ($limit == "") $limit = 25;
  $start = ($page - 1) * $limit;
  if (isset($_SESSION['user_id'])) {
    echo topicReplyBar($topicid, getForumID($topicid), "right");
  }
  $sql = "SELECT SQL_CALC_FOUND_ROWS " .
          "p.id, p.subject, p.body, p.date_posted, " .
          "p.date_updated, u.name as author, u.id as author_id, " .
          "u.signature as sig, c.count as postcount, " .
          "p.forum_id as forum_id, f.forum_moderator as mod, " .
          "p.update_id, u2.name as updated_by " .
        "FROM forum_forum f " .
        "JOIN forum_posts p " .
        "ON f.id = p.forum_id " .
        "JOIN forum_users u " .
        "ON u.id = p.author_id " .
        "LEFT JOIN forum_users u2 " .
        "ON u2.id = p.update_id " .
        "LEFT JOIN forum_postcount c " .
        "ON u.id = c.user_id " .
        "WHERE (p.topic_id = $topicid OR p.id = $topicid) " .
        "ORDER BY p.topic_id, p.date_posted " .
        "LIMIT $start,$limit";
  $result = mysql_query($sql, $conn)
    or die(mysql_error() . "<br>" . $sql);
  $pagelinks = paginate($limit);
  if (mysql_num_rows($result) == 0) {
    $msg = "There are currently no posts.  Would you " .
          "like to be the first person to create a thread?";
    $title = "No Posts...";
    $dest = "compose.php?forumid=" . $forumid;
    $sev = "Info";
    $message = msgBox($msg,$title,$dest,$sev);
    echo $message;
  } else {
    echo "<table class=\"forumtable\" cellspacing=\"0\" ";
    echo "cellpadding=\"2\"><tr>";
    echo "<th class=\"author\">Author</th>";
```

```php
      echo "<th class=\"post\">Post</th>";
    echo "</tr>";
$rowclass = "";
while ($row = mysql_fetch_array($result)) {
  $lastupdate = "";
  $editlink = "";
  $dellink = "";
  $replylink = " ";
  $pcount = "";
  $pdate = "";
  $sig = "";
  if ($showfull) {
    $body = $row['body'];
    if (isset($_SESSION['user_id'])) {
      $replylink = "<a href=\"compose.php?forumid=" .
        $row['forum_id'] . "&topicid=$topicid&reid=" . $row['id'] .
        "\" class=\"buttonlink\">REPLY</a> ";
    } else {
      $replylink = "";
    }
    if ($row['update_id'] > 0) {
    $lastupdate = "<p class=\"smallNote\">Last updated: " .
        $row['date_updated'] . " by " .
        $row['updated_by'] . "</p>";
    }
    if (($userid == $row['author_id']) or
        ($userid == $row['mod']) or
        ($_SESSION['access_lvl'] > 2)) {
      $editlink = "<a href=\"compose.php?a=edit&post=".$row['id'].
        "\" class=\"buttonlink\">EDIT</a> ";
      $dellink = "<a href=\"transact-affirm.php?action=deletepost&".
        "id=" . $row['id'] .
        "\" class=\"buttonlink\">DELETE</a> ";
    }
    $pcount = "<br><span class=\"textsmall\">Posts: " .
      ($row['postcount']==""?"0":$row['postcount']) . "</span>";
    $pdate = $row['date_posted'];
    $sig = ($row['sig'] != ""?"<p class=\"sig\">".
        bbcode(nl2br($row['sig'])):"")."</p>";
  } else {
    $body = trimBody($body);
  }
  $rowclass = ($rowclass == "row1"?"row2":"row1");
  echo "<tr class=\"$rowclass\">";
  echo "<td class=\"author\">" . $row['author'];
  echo $pcount;
  echo "</td><td class=\"post\"><p>";
  if (isset($_SESSION['user_id'])
      and ($_SESSION['last_login'] < $row['date_posted'])) {
    echo NEWPOST . " ";
  }
  if (isset($_GET['page'])) {
    $pagelink = "&page=" . $_GET['page'];
  } else {
    $pagelink = "";
```

```php
      }
      echo "<a name=\"post" . $row['id'] .
          "\" href=\"viewtopic.php?t=" . $topicid .$pagelink ."#post".
          $row['id'] . "\">".POSTLINK."</a>";
      if (isset($row['subject'])) {
        echo " <strong>" . $row['subject'] . "</strong>";
      }
      echo "</p><p>" . bbcode(nl2br(htmlspecialchars($body))) . "</p>";
      echo $sig;
      echo $lastupdate;
      echo "</td></tr>";
      echo "<tr class=\"$rowclass\"><td class=\"authorfooter\">";
      echo $pdate . "</td><td class=\"threadfooter\">";
      echo $replylink;
      echo $editlink;
      echo $dellink;
      echo "</td></tr>\n";
    }
    echo "</table>";
    echo $pagelinks;
    echo "<p>".NEWPOST." = New Post     ";
    echo POSTLINK." = Post link (use to bookmark)</p>";
  }
}

function isParent($page) {
  $currentpage = $_SERVER['PHP_SELF'];
  if (strpos($currentpage, $page) === false) {
    return FALSE;
  } else {
    return TRUE;
  }
}

function topicReplyBar($topicid,$forumid,$pos="right") {
  $html = "<p class=\"buttonBar" . $pos . "\">";
  if ($topicid > 0) {
    $html .= "<a href=\"compose.php?forumid=$forumid" .
             "&topicid=$topicid&reid=$topicid\" " .
             "class=\"buttonlink\">Reply to Thread</a>";
  }
  if ($forumid > 0) {
    $html .= "<a href=\"compose.php?forumid=$forumid\" " .
             "class=\"buttonlink\">New Thread</a>";
  }
  $html .= "</p>";
  return $html;
}

function userOptionList($level) {
  $sql = "SELECT id, name, access_lvl " .
         "FROM forum_users " .
         "WHERE access_lvl=" . $level . " " .
         "ORDER BY name";
  $result = mysql_query($sql)
```

```php
      or die(mysql_error());

  while ($row = mysql_fetch_array($result)) {
    echo "<option value=\"". $row['id'] . "\">" .
         htmlspecialchars($row['name']) . "</option>";
  }
}

function paginate($limit=10) {
  global $admin;

  $sql = "SELECT FOUND_ROWS();";
  $result = mysql_query($sql)
    or die(mysql_error());
  $row = mysql_fetch_array($result);
  $numrows = $row[0];
  $pagelinks = "<div class=\"pagelinks\">";
  if ($numrows > $limit) {
    if(isset($_GET['page'])){
      $page = $_GET['page'];
    } else {
      $page = 1;
    }
    $currpage = $_SERVER['PHP_SELF'] . "?" . $_SERVER['QUERY_STRING'];
    $currpage = str_replace("&page=".$page,"",$currpage);

    if($page == 1){
      $pagelinks .= "<span class=\"pageprevdead\">&lt; PREV</span>";
    }else{
      $pageprev = $page - 1;
      $pagelinks .= "<a class=\"pageprevlink\" href=\"" . $currpage .
                    "&page=" . $pageprev . "\">&lt; PREV</a>";
    }

    $numofpages = ceil($numrows / $limit);
    $range = $admin['pageRange']['value'];
    if ($range == "" or $range == 0) $range = 7;
    $lrange = max(1,$page-(($range-1)/2));
    $rrange = min($numofpages,$page+(($range-1)/2));
    if (($rrange - $lrange) < ($range - 1)) {
      if ($lrange == 1) {
        $rrange = min($lrange + ($range-1), $numofpages);
      } else {
        $lrange = max($rrange - ($range-1), 0);
      }
    }

    if ($lrange > 1) {
      $pagelinks .= "..";
    } else {
      $pagelinks .= "  ";
    }
    for($i = 1; $i <= $numofpages; $i++){
      if ($i == $page) {
```

```php
          $pagelinks .= "<span class=\"pagenumdead\">$i</span>";
        } else {
          if ($lrange <= $i and $i <= $rrange) {
            $pagelinks .= "<a class=\"pagenumlink\" " .
                          "href=\"" . $currpage . "&page=" . $i .
                          "\">" . $i . "</a>";
          }
        }
      }
      if ($rrange < $numofpages) {
        $pagelinks .= "..";
      } else {
        $pagelinks .= "  ";
      }

      if(($numrows - ($limit * $page)) > 0){
        $pagenext = $page + 1;
        $pagelinks .= "<a class=\"pagenextlink\" href=\"" . $currpage .
                      "&page=" . $pagenext . "\">NEXT &gt;</a>";
      } else {
        $pagelinks .= "<span class=\"pagenextdead\">NEXT &gt;</span>";
      }
    } else {
      $pagelinks .= "<span class=\"pageprevdead\">&lt; " .
                    "PREV</span>  ";
      $pagelinks .= "<span class=\"pagenextdead\"> " .
                    "NEXT &gt;</span>  ";
    }
    $pagelinks .= "</div>";
    return $pagelinks;
}

function bbcode($data) {
  $sql = "SELECT * FROM forum_bbcode";
  $result = mysql_query($sql);
  if (mysql_num_rows($result) > 0) {
    while($row = mysql_fetch_array($result)) {
      $bbcode['tpl'][] =
        "/" . html_entity_decode($row['template'],ENT_QUOTES). "/i";
      $bbcode['rep'][] =
        html_entity_decode($row['replacement'],ENT_QUOTES);
    }
    $data1 = preg_replace($bbcode['tpl'],$bbcode['rep'],$data);
    $count = 1;
    while (($data1 != $data) and ($count < 4)) {
      $count++;
      $data = $data1;
      $data1 = preg_replace($bbcode['tpl'],$bbcode['rep'],$data);
    }
  }

  return $data;
}
?>
```

2. Enter `http.php`. This is for various functions used for navigating around the site. It contains the `redirect()` function.

```php
<?php
function redirect($url) {
  if (!headers_sent()) {
    header('Location: http://' . $_SERVER['HTTP_HOST'] .
           dirname($_SERVER['PHP_SELF']) . '/' . $url);
  } else {
    die('Could not redirect; Headers already sent (output).');
  }
}
?>
```

3. Create `config.php`. This sets up any constants or variables you may need in the app. It loads admin settings and BBcodes into arrays to be used by the board.

```php
<?php
require_once 'conn.php';
require_once 'functions.php';

$sql = 'SELECT * FROM forum_admin';
$result = mysql_query($sql)
  or die(mysql_error());

while ($row = mysql_fetch_array($result)) {
  $admin[$row['constant']]['title'] = $row['title'];
  $admin[$row['constant']]['value'] = $row['value'];
}

$sql = 'SELECT * FROM forum_bbcode';
$result = mysql_query($sql)
  or die(mysql_error());

while ($row = mysql_fetch_array($result)) {
  $bbcode[$row['id']]['template'] = $row['template'];
  $bbcode[$row['id']]['replacement'] = $row['replacement'];
}

// define constants here:
define("NEWPOST",
       "<span class=\"newpost\">&raquo;</span>");
define("POSTLINK",
       "<span class=\"postlink\">&diams;</span>");
?>
```

4. Create `header.php`. This goes at the top of each page that gets displayed.

```php
<?php
session_start();
require_once 'config.php';
$title = $admin['titlebar']['value'];
if (isset($pageTitle) and $pageTitle != "") {
  $title .= " :: " . $pageTitle;
}
```

```php
if (isset($_SESSION['user_id'])) {
  $userid = $_SESSION['user_id'];
} else {
  $userid = null;
}
if (isset($_SESSION['access_lvl'])) {
  $access_lvl = $_SESSION['access_lvl'];
} else {
  $access_lvl = null;
}
if (isset($_SESSION['name'])) {
  $username = $_SESSION['name'];
} else {
  $username = null;
}
?>
<html>
<head>
<title><?php echo $title; ?></title>
<link rel="stylesheet" type="text/css" href="forum_styles.css">
</head>
<body>
<div class="body">
<div id="header">
  <form method="get" action="search.php" id="searchbar">
    <input id="searchkeywords" type="text" name="keywords"
    <?php
      if (isset($_GET['keywords'])) {
        echo ' value="' . htmlspecialchars($_GET['keywords']) . '" ';
      }
    ?>>
      <input id="searchbutton" class="submit" type="submit"
      value="Search">
  </form>
  <h1 id="sitetitle"><?php echo $admin['title']['value']; ?></h1>
  <div id="login">
  <?php
    if (isset($_SESSION['name'])) {
      echo 'Welcome, ' . $_SESSION['name'];
    }
  ?>
  </div>
  <p id="subtitle"><?php echo $admin['description']['value']; ?></p>
</div>
<div id="subheader">
  <div id="navigation">
  <?php
  echo '    <a href="index.php">Home</a>';
  if (!isset($_SESSION['user_id'])) {
    echo ' | <a href="login.php">Log In</a>';
    echo ' | <a href="useraccount.php">Register</a>';
  } else {
    echo ' | <a href="transact-user.php?action=Logout">';
    echo "Log out " . $_SESSION['name'] . "</a>";
    if ($_SESSION['access_lvl'] > 2) {
```

```
      echo ' | <a href="admin.php">Admin</a>';
    }
    echo ' | <a href="useraccount.php">Profile</a>';
  }
  ?>
  </div>
</div>
```

5. Enter `footer.php`, which places a footer at the bottom of each page that gets displayed:

```
</div>
<div class="copyright">
  <?php echo $admin['copyright']['value']; ?>
</div>
</body>
</html>
```

How It Works

Most of the code in these scripts should be pretty understandable by this point. You've seen functions like `trimBody` before in similar functionality in Chapter 13's CMS application. Let's look, however, at some of the more powerful functionality that `functions.php` gives you.

Pagination

If you are not familiar with pagination, then we suggest you do a quick search on Google.com. Search for the term Spider-Man. Don't get caught up looking at the sites your search returns! When your search results are displayed, scroll to the bottom of the page. You should see some links that will take you to more pages of search results, with the option of clicking next, previous, or a specific numbered page.

That, friend, is pagination, and we are going to teach you how to do it for your own pages. (No need to thank us. Just send money.)

If you visit the PHPBuilder.com forums, you may see this question asked over and over again: "How do I add PREV/NEXT buttons to the bottom of my pages?" We have yet to see a good, comprehensive answer. Indeed, you may even run screaming after we explain it to you. But, we hope to finally clear the air, and give you a tool that will allow you to paginate almost any set of data returned from MySQL. So let's get started.

When paginating your data, there are a few things you should have. The first, of course, is a large set of data that you can't display on one page. You also need to know how many rows of data you will display per page, and how many total records you have in your result set. For the purposes of this example, you also need to know how many pages you will have access to at one time. For example, if you had 40 pages of data to display, you might want to show links only for pages 1 through 10, or 12 through 21, and so forth. This is called the *range*.

Take a look at `showTopic()` in `functions.php`. We will list the rows relevant to pagination only:

```
    global $limit;
    ...
    if (isset($_GET['page'])) {
```

```
    $page = $_GET['page'];
  } else {
    $page = 1;
  }
  if ($limit == "") $limit = 25;
  $start = ($page - 1) * $limit;
```

In a calling page, you have set a variable called $limit to a number equaling the maximum number of records per page you want to display. Declaring $limit global inside the function, you make the variable (set in viewtopic.php) available to the function. If you don't pass $page to the Web page, you assume you are on page 1. Otherwise, you set $page to the value passed to you in the URL. By knowing the page, and the limit (number of posts per page), you can calculate your $start value (which will be used by the LIMIT statement in the SQL used to retrieve rows). For example, if you are on page 3, and your limit is 25 posts per page, then the third page will display rows 51 through 75.

Here is the whole SQL statement for returning posts. It is long, but not overly complex. It is simply four tables joined by the JOIN statement. Please note the first line and the last line of the SQL statement:

```
$sql = "SELECT SQL_CALC_FOUND_ROWS ".
          "p.id, p.subject, p.body, p.date_posted, " .
          "p.date_updated, u.name as author, u.id as author_id, " .
          "u.signature as sig, c.count as postcount, " .
          "p.forum_id as forum_id, f.forum_moderator as mod, " .
          "p.update_id, u2.name as updated_by " .
        "FROM forum_forum f " .
        "JOIN forum_posts p " .
        "ON f.id = p.forum_id " .
        "JOIN forum_users u " .
        "ON u.id = p.author_id " .
        "LEFT JOIN forum_users u2 " .
        "ON u2.id = p.update_id " .
        "LEFT JOIN forum_postcount c " .
        "ON u.id = c.user_id " .
        "WHERE (p.topic_id = $topicid OR p.id = $topicid) " .
        "ORDER BY p.topic_id, p.date_posted ".
        "LIMIT $start,$limit";
  $result = mysql_query($sql, $conn)
    or die(mysql_error() . "<br>" . $sql);
  $pagelinks = paginate($limit);
```

This query will return a maximum of the number of rows in $limit. The problem is, you need to know how many rows *would have returned* if LIMIT had not been used. Fortunately, MySQL provides a means for you to find out.

In the first line, you are using the SQL command SQL_CALC_FOUND_ROWS. This doesn't do anything to the query directly. It slows it down slightly, but it does allow you to subsequently run the SQL command:

```
$sql = "SELECT FOUND_ROWS();";
```

This command, when run, returns the number of rows that SQL_CALC_FOUND_ROWS found. Although SQL_CALC_FOUND_ROWS makes the query take a little longer, it is still more efficient than running the query a second time with the COUNT(*) parameter.

Okay. You have your numbers; time to create the page links. Take a look at the `paginate()` function in the same file:

```
function paginate($limit=10) {
  global $admin;

  $sql = "SELECT FOUND_ROWS();";
  $result = mysql_query($sql)
    or die(mysql_error());
  $row = mysql_fetch_array($result);
  $numrows = $row[0];
  $pagelinks = "<div class=\"pagelinks\">";
  if ($numrows > $limit) {
    if(isset($_GET['page'])){
      $page = $_GET['page'];
    } else {
      $page = 1;
    }
...
  } else {
    $pagelinks .= "<span class=\"pageprevdead\">&lt; " .
                  "PREV</span>  ";
    $pagelinks .= "<span class=\"pagenextdead\"> " .
                  "NEXT &gt;</span>  ";
  }
```

The paginate function takes one parameter, `$limit`. If `$limit` is not passed in to the function, then you set `$limit` to a default value of 10.

Because your focus is now in a function, in order for the code to access the admin variables (such as range and limit), `$admin` must be declared global.

As you can see, by using `SELECT FOUND_ROWS()`, `$numrows` contains the number of rows your query returns. As long as the number of rows is larger than your limit, you'll generate the pagination links. Otherwise, you'll just display inactive links.

Next, you grab the page variable, if it is set. If not, you set `$page` to 1.

Your next step is to determine whether the <PREV link should be activated or not. Obviously, if you are on page 1, there is no previous page. Otherwise, the previous page is the current page number minus 1:

```
if($page == 1){
      $pagelinks .= "<span class=\"pageprevdead\">&lt; PREV</span>";
    }else{
      $pageprev = $page - 1;
      $pagelinks .= "<a class=\"pageprevlink\" href='" . $currpage .
                    "&page=" . $pageprev . "'>&lt; PREV</a>";
  }
```

The next chunk of code does a bit of math. You are determining a few things in this code block. First, the number of pages is determined by dividing the total number of rows returned by your previous SELECT FOUND_ROWS() query (`$numrows`) by the number of posts per page (`$limit`) and rounding up.

Next, the range is grabbed from a global variable $admin['pagerange']['value'] and stored in $range. You may be wondering, "where did this $admin variable come from!?" We'll explain the $admin variable shortly, but for now, all you need to know is that, in this case, it holds the range for the pagination display. If it's not available, then $range defaults to 7. This value determines how many pages are accessible via a link at the bottom of the page. For example, if the range is 5, there are 13 pages, and you are currently viewing page 6, you will have access to pages 4, 5, 6, 7, and 8:

```
< PREV .. [4] [5] 6 [7] [8] .. NEXT >
```

The ".." tells you that there are more pages in that direction (before or after).

```
$numofpages = ceil($numrows / $limit);
$range = $admin['pageRange']['value'];
if ($range == "" or $range == 0) $range = 7;
```

The next few lines determine what range of pages to show you. In the previous example, if the $range is 5, but you are viewing page 2 out of 13 pages, the code should be smart enough to allow you access to pages 1 through 5:

```
< PREV  [1] 2 [3] [4] [5] .. NEXT >
```

As you can see, you are viewing page 2, you can directly get to pages 1 through 5, and there are more pages past 5. The piece of logic that determines which pages are available is the following:

```
$lrange = max(1,$page-(($range-1)/2));
$rrange = min($numofpages,$page+(($range-1)/2));
if (($rrange - $lrange) < ($range - 1)) {
  if ($lrange == 1) {
    $rrange = min($lrange + ($range-1), $numofpages);
  } else {
    $lrange = max($rrange - ($range-1), 0);
  }
}
```

Then, the next part of the code renders the space between PREV and NEXT. If the lower range is higher than 1, put ".." in to show that there are more pages by clicking <PREV. Then, use the $lrange and $rrange values to build the page number links. If the link corresponds to the current page, don't make it a link. Next, if the high end of the range of pages is lower than the total number of pages available, put in the ".." to show that there are more pages by clicking NEXT>.

```
if ($lrange > 1) {
  $pagelinks .= "..";
} else {
  $pagelinks .= "  ";
}
for($i = 1; $i <= $numofpages; $i++){
  if($i == $page){
    $pagelinks .= "<span class=\"pagenumdead\">$i</span>";
  } else{
    if ($lrange <= $i and $i <= $rrange) {
      $pagelinks .= "<a class=\"pagenumlink\" " .
                    "href='" . $currpage . "&page=" . $i .
```

```
                                   "'>" . $i . "</a>";
            }
          }
        }
        if ($rrange < $numofpages) {
          $pagelinks .= "..";
        } else {
          $pagelinks .= "  ";
        }
```

The last part is to render NEXT> as clickable or not, depending on whether or not you are looking at the last post of the thread. Doing this is relatively simple:

```
        if(($numrows - ($limit * $page)) > 0){
          $pagenext = $page + 1;
          $pagelinks .= "<a class=\"pagenextlink\" href=\"" . $currpage .
                        "&page=" . $pagenext . "\">NEXT &gt;</a>";
        } else {
          $pagelinks .= "<span class=\"pagenextdead\">NEXT &gt;</span>";
        }
```

You may notice that this code generates simple text links for the pages. This is true. However, each element is surrounded by <span> tags, which allows you to use style sheets to easily modify the look of these links.

Voilà! You have a terrific, customizable, dynamically built pagination function.

Breadcrumbs

Once upon a time, there were two skinny little yahoos named Hansel and Gretel. They didn't want to get lost in the forest, blah blah blah, so Hansel got the bright idea of dropping crumbs of bread so that they could find their way back. Birds ate the bread, the kids got lost, and they ate a house. Hansel got fat eating German chocolates and candies while sitting in a cage, and Gretel was forced to do chores. Then one day they stuffed a little old lady in an oven and ran home. The End.

Except for the fact that the birds ate their trail, Hansel had the right idea. By placing a trail of crumbs behind them, they should have been able to navigate out of any dark forest.

Some time ago, Yahoo! came along, giving us the ability to find Web sites based on categories. Because there are so many sites out there that are very specialized, some of them might be in a sub-sub-sub-sub-category.

For example, say you wanted to view some sites in the Yahoo! directory about PHP. You click the Computers and Internet category. Hmmm. Next, click Software, then Internet, World Wide Web, Servers (ah, getting close we think), Server Side Scripting, and (yes, finally!) PHP. Or, you could have simply done a search for "PHP" and clicked the categories link near the top of the page.

Now that you have been to this page, wouldn't it be nice to remember how you got here? If you look near the top of the screen, you should see something that looks like this:

```
Directory > Computers and Internet > Software > Internet >
    World Wide Web > Servers >Server Side Scripting > PHP
```

It is a map of categories and subcategories telling you exactly how to get to the category you are looking at. Someone (probably a fan of gingerbread houses, but don't quote us on that) saw this "map" and decided to call it a breadcrumb list. The name has stuck.

The truth is, breadcrumbs are very helpful, and they make a lot of sense for a bulletin board forum. They can give you a map from the post you are reading, to the thread it was in, to the forum the thread was in, to the category the forum was in, to the home page. Perhaps it would look like this:

```
Home > Comic Book Movies > Spider-Man > This movie rocked! > I agree
```

By allowing you to click on any part of the breadcrumb, you can easily navigate to another part of the site.

We have implemented breadcrumbs for this application, and we will show you how it was done. You could implement a breadcrumb system in many different ways (such as by folder structure). This is just one, and it is relatively simple.

The function itself takes two arguments, $id and $getfrom. The argument $getfrom will either be "F" for forum or "P" for post. The default is "F."

```
function breadcrumb($id, $getfrom="F") {
```

There is usually a standard separator for crumbs. Some people use >, but we like to use a bullet, or dot. If you prefer to use >, then use the HTML entity > in place of ·:

```
$sep = "<span class=\"bcsep'>\";
$sep .= " &middot; ";
$sep .= "</span>";
```

If you are in a post, then you want your breadcrumb to include a link to the forum, along with a non-linked indication of what thread you are in. You pass in the topic_id to retrieve the right topic and get the forum_id from that topic and put it into the $id field. You also extract the name of the topic.

```
if ($getfrom == "P") {
  $sql = "SELECT forum_id, subject FROM forum_posts ".
         "WHERE id = " . $id;
  $result = mysql_query($sql)
    or die(mysql_error() . "<br>" . $sql);
  $row = mysql_fetch_array($result);
  $id = $row['forum_id'];
  $topic = $row['subject'];
}
```

Next, you run getForum on the $id that is now a forum_id. It returns a row that contains the name and description of the forum. You don't currently use the description, but you could if you wanted to use it as the alt or title attribute for the breadcrumb. At this point, you begin building the breadcrumb in the variable $bc; Home is always first, and then the separator. Next is either a link to the forum (if looking at a post), or simply the forum listed without a link. Next comes the thread title for the post you are looking at.

```
$row = getForum($id);
$bc = "<a href=\"index.php\">Home</a>$sep";
```

```
    switch ($getfrom) {
      case "P":
        $bc .= "<a href=\"viewforum.php?f=$id\">".$row['name'].
              "</a>$sep".$topic;
        break;

      case "F":
        $bc .= $row['name'];
        break;
    }
    return "<h4 class=\"breadcrumb\">" . $bc . "</h4>";
  }
```

As we said, this breadcrumb is not that difficult. We are sure that armed with all of the PHP knowledge you now have, you could come up with a very impressive breadcrumb function.

Next, take a look at your `header.php` file. There isn't much new to see here, but it gives us a chance to discuss authentication with you for a moment.

A Last Look at User Authentication

The CBA board uses user authentication, but it is by no means totally secure. For a board application, it is probably secure enough. However, if this were human resources data containing sensitive information, you might want to make it a bit more secure.

> *This book does not attempt to help you create a virtual Fort Knox. If you have such a need, we strongly suggest you look for a good book on security, and perhaps look at a few online resources. A good start is* www.w3.org/Security/Faq/.

Take a look at your security model, and see where there might be some places to improve it a bit. If you look at most of the PHP pages that make up the application, you see where you check for a user's access level before displaying certain items. For example, take a look at `header.php`.

Because `header.php` is included at the top of almost every Web page, you do most of your user authentication there. By checking for the existence of the `user_id` session variable, you know the user is logged in. By checking if `access_lvl` is greater than 2, you know whether the user has administrator access. This allows you to customize the main menu depending on whether the user is logged in, and what access level he or she possesses. It also allows you to address the user by name.

```
    echo '    <a href="index.php">Home</a>';
    if (!isset($_SESSION['user_id'])) {
      echo ' | <a href="login.php">Log In</a>';
      echo ' | <a href="useraccount.php">Register</a>';
    } else {
      echo ' | <a href="transact-user.php?action=Logout">';
      echo "Log out " . $_SESSION['name'] . "</a>";
      if ($_SESSION['access_lvl'] > 2) {
        echo ' | <a href="admin.php">Admin</a>';
      }
      echo ' | <a href="useraccount.php">Profile</a>';
    }
```

So, if users are not logged in, you give them links to log in or register as a new user. If they are logged in, they can log out or view their profile. And, if they are administrators, they will have access to the admin functions.

Transaction Pages

The next group of files you're going to create are the transaction pages. Like the reusable scripts just covered, they don't have anything pretty to show the end user, but they drive a large portion of the behind-the-scenes board operations.

Try It Out   **Admin Transactions**

The first file is responsible for all transactions related to the general administration of the board — things like creating new forums, changing the board options, text substitutions, and so on.

1. Create `transact-admin.php`, the first of four transaction pages. Admin forms post to this page, which manipulates the data and then redirects the user to another page. Transaction pages do not send any data to the client unless there is an error.

```php
<?php
session_start();
require_once 'conn.php';
require_once 'http.php';

if (isset($_REQUEST['action'])) {
  switch ($_REQUEST['action']) {
    case 'Add Forum':
      if (isset($_POST['forumname'])
          and $_POST['forumname'] != ""
          and isset($_POST['forumdesc'])
          and $_POST['forumdesc'] != "") {
        $sql = "INSERT IGNORE INTO forum_forum " .
               "VALUES (NULL, '" .
               htmlspecialchars($_POST['forumname'], ENT_QUOTES) .
               "', '" .
               htmlspecialchars($_POST['forumdesc'], ENT_QUOTES) .
               "', " . $_POST['forummod'][0] . ")";
        mysql_query($sql)
          or die(mysql_error());
      }
      redirect('admin.php?option=forums');
      break;

    case 'Edit Forum':
      if (isset($_POST['forumname'])
          and $_POST['forumname'] != ""
          and isset($_POST['forumdesc'])
          and $_POST['forumdesc'] != "") {
        $sql = "UPDATE forum_forum " .
               "SET forum_name = '" . $_POST['forumname'] .
               "', forum_desc = '" . $_POST['forumdesc'] .
```

```
          "', forum_moderator = " . $_POST['forummod'][0] .
          " WHERE id = " . $_POST['forum_id'];
    mysql_query($sql)
      or die(mysql_error());
  }
  redirect('admin.php?option=forums');
  break;

case 'Modify User':
  redirect("useraccount.php?user=" . $_POST['userlist'][0]);
  break;

case 'Update':
  foreach ($_POST as $key => $value) {
    if ($key != 'action') {
      $sql = "UPDATE forum_admin SET value='$value' " .
             "WHERE constant = '$key'";
      mysql_query($sql)
        or die(mysql_error());
    }
  }
  redirect('admin.php');
  break;

case "deleteForum":
  $sql = "DELETE FROM forum_forum WHERE id=" . $_GET['f'];
  mysql_query($sql)
    or die(mysql_error());
  $sql = "DELETE FROM forum_posts WHERE forum_id=" . $_GET['f'];
  mysql_query($sql)
    or die(mysql_error());
  redirect('admin.php?option=forums');
  break;

case "Add New":
  $sql = "INSERT INTO forum_bbcode " .
         "VALUES (NULL,'" .
         htmlentities($_POST['bbcode-tnew'],ENT_QUOTES) . "','" .
         htmlentities($_POST['bbcode-rnew'],ENT_QUOTES) . "')";
  mysql_query($sql)
    or die(mysql_error() . "<br>" . $sql);
  redirect('admin.php?option=bbcode');
  break;

case "deleteBBCode":
  if (isset($_GET['b'])) {
    $bbcodeid = $_GET['b'];
    $sql = "DELETE FROM forum_bbcode WHERE id=" . $bbcodeid;
    mysql_query($sql)
      or die(mysql_error());
  }
  redirect('admin.php?option=bbcode');
  break;
```

```
      case 'Update BBCodes':
        foreach($_POST as $key => $value) {
          if (substr($key,0,7) == 'bbcode_') {
            $bbid = str_replace("bbcode_", "", $key);
            if (substr($bbid,0,1) == 't') {
              $col = "template";
            } else {
              $col = "replacement";
            }
            $id = substr($bbid,1);
            $sql = "UPDATE forum_bbcode SET $col='" .
                    htmlentities($value,ENT_QUOTES) . "' " .
                    "WHERE id=$id";
            mysql_query($sql)
              or die(mysql_error());
          }
        }
        redirect('admin.php?option=bbcode');
        break;

    default:
      redirect('index.php');
  }
} else {
  redirect('index.php');
}
?>
```

How It Works

At this point, none of the code in transact-admin.php should be unfamiliar to you. As seen before in previous chapters, this script determines what action is to be performed in the database, executes a corresponding query, then redirects the user to the appropriate page.

One of the more important things to remember from this page is the actions it handles, as shown here:

```
switch ($_REQUEST['action']) {
    case 'Add Forum':
      . . .
    case 'Edit Forum':
      . . .
    case 'Modify User':
      . . .
    case 'Update':
      . . .
    case "deleteForum":
      . . .
    case "Add New":
      . . .
    case "deleteBBCode":
      . . .
    case 'Update BBCodes':
      . . .
}
```

You probably already understand how the switch statement works, so a key thing to keep in mind, instead, is the different cases this specific switch processes. Remembering where a certain action takes place can help you more quickly find and diagnose problems when they occur.

Try It Out   **Post Transactions**

The next transaction file controls all transactions related to forum posts — creating, editing, replying, and so on.

1.   Enter transact-post.php, the second of four transaction pages:

```php
<?php
session_start();
require_once 'conn.php';
require_once 'http.php';

if (isset($_REQUEST['action'])) {
  switch (strtoupper($_REQUEST['action'])) {
    case 'SUBMIT NEW POST':
      if (isset($_POST['subject'])
          and isset($_POST['body'])
          and isset($_SESSION['user_id'])) {
        $sql = "INSERT INTO forum_posts VALUES (" .
               "NULL," . $_POST['topic_id'] .
               "," . $_POST['forum_id'] .
               "," . $_SESSION['user_id'] .
               ",0" .
               ",'" . date("Y-m-d H:i:s",time()) .
               "',0" .
               ",'" . $_POST['subject'] .
               "','" . $_POST['body'] . "')";

        mysql_query($sql, $conn)
          or die('Could not post: ' . mysql_error() . "<br>$sql");
        $postid = mysql_insert_id();

        $sql = "INSERT IGNORE INTO forum_postcount " .
               "VALUES (" . $_SESSION['user_id'] . ",0)";
        mysql_query($sql, $conn)
          or die(mysql_error());

        $sql = "UPDATE forum_postcount SET count = count + 1 " .
               "WHERE user_id = " . $_SESSION['user_id'];
        mysql_query($sql, $conn)
          or die(mysql_error());

      }
      $topicid = ($_POST['topic_id']==0?$postid:$_POST['topic_id']);
      redirect('viewtopic.php?t=' . $topicid . '#post' . $postid);
      break;

    case 'NEW TOPIC':
      redirect('compose.php?f=' . $_POST['forum_id']);
      break;
```

```
      case 'EDIT':
        redirect('compose.php?a=edit&post=' . $_POST['topic_id']);
        break;

      case 'SAVE CHANGES':
        if (isset($_POST['subject'])
            and isset($_POST['body'])) {
          $sql = "UPDATE forum_posts " .
                 "SET subject='" . $_POST['subject'] .
                 "', update_id=" . $_SESSION['user_id'] .
                 ", body='" . $_POST['body'] . "', date_updated='" .
                 date("Y-m-d H:i:s",time()) . "' " .
                 "WHERE id=" . $_POST['post'];
          if (isset($_POST['author_id'])) {
            $sql .= " AND author_id=" . $_POST['author_id'];
          }

          mysql_query($sql, $conn)
            or die('Could not update post; ' . mysql_error());
        }
        $redirID = ($_POST['topic_id'] == 0?$_POST['post']:
          $_POST['topic_id']);
        redirect('viewtopic.php?t=' . $redirID);
        break;

    case 'DELETE':
      if ($_REQUEST['post']) {
        $sql = "DELETE FROM forum_posts " .
               "WHERE " . "id=" . $_REQUEST['post'];
        mysql_query($sql, $conn)
          or die('Could not delete post; ' . mysql_error());
      }
      redirect($_REQUEST['r']);
      break;
  }
} else {
  redirect('index.php');
}
?>
```

How It Works

Like the previous example, most of this is familiar by now. Again, it's good practice to keep in mind what actions this transaction page performs. One bit of code worth noting is the addition of a new post.

```
case 'SUBMIT NEW POST':
    if (isset($_POST['subject'])
        and isset($_POST['body'])
        and isset($_SESSION['user_id'])) {
      $sql = "INSERT INTO forum_posts VALUES (" .
             "NULL," . $_POST['topic_id'] .
             "," . $_POST['forum_id'] .
             "," . $_SESSION['user_id'] .
             ",0" .
             ",'" . date("Y-m-d H:i:s",time()) .
```

```
                "',0" .
                "','" . $_POST['subject'] .
                "','" . $_POST['body'] . "')";

        mysql_query($sql, $conn)
          or die('Could not post: ' . mysql_error() . "<br>$sql");
        $postid = mysql_insert_id();

        $sql = "INSERT IGNORE INTO forum_postcount " .
                "VALUES (" . $_SESSION['user_id'] . ",0)";
        mysql_query($sql, $conn)
          or die(mysql_error());

        $sql = "UPDATE forum_postcount SET count = count + 1 " .
                "WHERE user_id = " . $_SESSION['user_id'];
        mysql_query($sql, $conn)
          or die(mysql_error());

        }
        $topicid = ($_POST['topic_id']==0?$postid:$_POST['topic_id']);
        redirect('viewtopic.php?t=' . $topicid . '#post' . $postid);
        break;
```

Note how you first insert the post into the forum_posts table, then proceed to update the post count for the user. In this case, you add the user into the forum_postcount table, in case they don't yet exist there, and follow up by incrementing their post count by one.

Try It Out   User Transactions

Now you're going to create the file responsible for all user-related transactions. Any time a user is created or modified in the system, the database changes are performed here.

1. Create transact-user.php, the third of four transaction pages. This one handles functions related to the users (such as logging in).

```php
<?php
require_once 'conn.php';
require_once 'http.php';

if (isset($_REQUEST['action'])) {
  switch ($_REQUEST['action']) {
    case 'Login':
      if (isset($_POST['email'])
          and isset($_POST['passwd'])) {
        $sql = "SELECT id,access_lvl,name,last_login " .
                "FROM forum_users " .
                "WHERE email='" . $_POST['email'] . "' " .
                "AND passwd='" . $_POST['passwd'] . "'";
        $result = mysql_query($sql, $conn)
          or die('Could not look up user information; ' .
                  mysql_error());

        if ($row = mysql_fetch_array($result)) {
          session_start();
```

```php
          $_SESSION['user_id'] = $row['id'];
          $_SESSION['access_lvl'] = $row['access_lvl'];
          $_SESSION['name'] = $row['name'];
          $_SESSION['last_login'] = $row['last_login'];
          $sql = "UPDATE forum_users SET last_login = '" .
                 date("Y-m-d H:i:s",time()) . "' " .
                 "WHERE id = " . $row['id'];
          mysql_query($sql, $conn)
            or die(mysql_error() . "<br>" . $sql);
      }
  }
  redirect('index.php');
  break;

case 'Logout':
  session_start();
  session_unset();
  session_destroy();

  redirect('index.php');
  break;

case 'Create Account':
  if (isset($_POST['name'])
      and isset($_POST['email'])
      and isset($_POST['passwd'])
      and isset($_POST['passwd2'])
      and $_POST['passwd'] == $_POST['passwd2']) {
    $sql = "INSERT INTO forum_users " .
           "(email,name,passwd,date_joined,last_login) " .
           "VALUES ('" . $_POST['email'] . "','" .
           $_POST['name'] . "','" . $_POST['passwd'] . "','" .
           date("Y-m-d H:i:s",time()). "','" .
           date("Y-m-d H:i:s",time()). "')";

    mysql_query($sql, $conn)
      or die('Could not create user account; ' . mysql_error());

    session_start();
    $_SESSION['user_id'] = mysql_insert_id($conn);
    $_SESSION['access_lvl'] = 1;
    $_SESSION['name'] = $_POST['name'];
    $_SESSION['login_time'] = date("Y-m-d H:i:s",time());
  }
  redirect('index.php');
  break;

case 'Modify Account':
  if (isset($_POST['name'])
      and isset($_POST['email'])
      and isset($_POST['accesslvl'])
      and isset($_POST['userid'])) {
    $sql = "UPDATE forum_users " .
           "SET email='" . $_POST['email'] .
```

```
                    "', name='" . $_POST['name'] .
                    "', access_lvl=" . $_POST['accesslvl'] .
                    ", signature='" . $_POST['signature'] . "' " .
                    " WHERE id=" . $_POST['userid'];

        mysql_query($sql, $conn)
          or die('Could not update user account... ' . mysql_error() .
                 '<br>SQL: ' . $sql);
      }
      redirect('admin.php');
      break;

  case 'Edit Account':
    if (isset($_POST['name'])
        and isset($_POST['email'])
        and isset($_POST['accesslvl'])
        and isset($_POST['userid'])) {
      $chg_pw = FALSE;
      if (isset($_POST['oldpasswd'])
          and $_POST['oldpasswd'] != '') {
        $sql = "SELECT passwd FROM forum_users " .
               "WHERE id=" . $_POST['userid'];
        $result = mysql_query($sql)
          or die(mysql_error());
        if ($row = mysql_fetch_array($result)) {
          if (($row['passwd'] == $_POST['oldpasswd'])
              and (isset($_POST['passwd']))
              and (isset($_POST['passwd2']))
              and ($_POST['passwd'] == $_POST['passwd2']))
          {
            $chg_pw = TRUE;
          } else {
            redirect('useraccount.php?error=nopassedit');
            break;
          }
        }
      }
      $sql = "UPDATE forum_users " .
             "SET email='" . $_POST['email'] .
             "', name='" . $_POST['name'] .
             "', access_lvl=" . $_POST['accesslvl'] .
             ", signature='" . $_POST['signature'];
      if ($chg_pw) {
        $sql .= "', passwd='" . $_POST['passwd'];
      }
      $sql .= "' WHERE id=" . $_POST['userid'];
      mysql_query($sql, $conn)
        or die('Could not update user account... ' . mysql_error() .
               '<br>SQL: ' . $sql);
    }
    redirect('useraccount.php?blah=' . $_POST['userid']);
    break;

  case 'Send my reminder!':
    if (isset($_POST['email'])) {
```

```
            $sql = "SELECT passwd FROM forum_users " .
                   "WHERE email='" . $_POST['email'] . "'";

            $result = mysql_query($sql, $conn)
              or die('Could not look up password; ' . mysql_error());

            if (mysql_num_rows($result)) {
              $row = mysql_fetch_array($result);

              $subject = 'Comic site password reminder';
              $body = "Just a reminder, your password for the " .
                      "Comic Book Appreciation site is: " . $row['passwd'] .
                      "\n\nYou can use this to log in at http://" .
                      $_SERVER['HTTP_HOST'] .
                      dirname($_SERVER['PHP_SELF']) . '/login.php?e=' .
                      $_POST['email'];
              $headers = "From: admin@yoursite.com\r\n";

              mail($_POST['email'],$subject,$body,$headers)
                or die('Could not send reminder email.');
            }
          }
          redirect('login.php');
          break;
      }
    }
?>
```

How It Works

Like its predecessors, this transaction page follows the familiar determine action, query database, return pattern. Most of the action processing is pretty straightforward, with the exception of the account edit action. Let's take a look at that specific case.

```
case 'Edit Account':
    if (isset($_POST['name'])
        and isset($_POST['email'])
        and isset($_POST['accesslvl'])
        and isset($_POST['userid'])) {
```

This time, instead of a simple query to the database, you must do some preliminary checks. First, the script checks to see if users have elected to change their password:

```
$chg_pw = FALSE;
        if (isset($_POST['oldpasswd'])
            and $_POST['oldpasswd'] != '') {
```

If this condition is met, the script checks the old password in the database, to see if a change has truly been made. If not, the user is redirected back to the account edit page, and an error is flagged.

```
            $sql = "SELECT passwd FROM forum_users " .
                   "WHERE id=" . $_POST['userid'];
            $result = mysql_query($sql)
```

```
        or die(mysql_error());
      if ($row = mysql_fetch_array($result)) {
        if (($row['passwd'] == $_POST['oldpasswd'])
            and (isset($_POST['passwd']))
            and (isset($_POST['passwd2']))
            and ($_POST['passwd'] == $_POST['passwd2']))
        {
          $chg_pw = TRUE;
        } else {
          redirect('useraccount.php?error=nopassedit');
          break;
        }
      }
    }
```

Then the account is finally updated.

```
    $sql = "UPDATE forum_users " .
           "SET email='" . $_POST['email'] .
           "', name='" . $_POST['name'] .
           "', access_lvl=" . $_POST['accesslvl'] .
           ", signature='" . $_POST['signature'];
    if ($chg_pw) {
      $sql .= "', passwd='" . $_POST['passwd'];
    }
    $sql .= "' WHERE id=" . $_POST['userid'];
    mysql_query($sql, $conn)
      or die('Could not update user account... ' . mysql_error() .
             '<br>SQL: ' . $sql);
  }
  redirect('useraccount.php?blah=' . $_POST['userid']);
  break;
```

The rest of the actions should be pretty self-explanatory. All actions update the database with appropriate information, with the exception of the last case, where a reminder e-mail is sent to users if they forgot their password.

Try It Out   Removal Transactions

The last transaction page covers situations where forums or posts need to be deleted.

1. Create `transact-affirm.php`. This is the only "transaction page" that does send data to the client. If a function requires confirmation, the user is sent here and redirected forward.

```
<?php
require_once 'conn.php';
require_once 'functions.php';
require_once 'http.php';
require_once 'header.php';
?>
<script type="text/javascript">
<!--
function deletePost(id,redir) {
```

```
    if (id > 0) {
      window.location = "transact-post.php?action=delete&post=" +
        id + "&r=" + redir;
    } else {
      history.back();
    }
  }
  function deleteForum(id) {
    if (id > 0) {
      window.location = "transact-admin.php?action=deleteForum&f=" + id;
    } else {
      history.back();
    }
  }
  //-->
  </script>
  <?php
  switch (strtoupper($_REQUEST['action'])) {
    case "DELETEPOST":
      $sql = "SELECT * FROM forum_posts WHERE id=" . $_REQUEST['id'];
      $result = mysql_query($sql);
      $row = mysql_fetch_array($result);
      if ($row['topic_id'] > 0) {
        $msg = "Are you sure you wish to delete the post<br>" .
               "<em>" . $row['subject'] . "</em>?";
        $redir = htmlspecialchars("viewtopic.php?t=" . $row['topic_id']);
      } else {
        $msg = "If you delete this post, all replies will be deleted " .
               "as well.  Are you sure you wish to delete the entire " .
               "thread<br><em>" . $row['subject'] . "</em>?";
        $redir = htmlspecialchars("viewforum.php?f=" . $row['forum_id']);
      }
      echo "<div id=\"requestConfirmWarn\">";
      echo "<h2>DELETE POST?</h2>\n";
      echo "<p>" . $msg . "</p>";
      echo "<p><input class=\"confirm\" type=\"button\" ";
      echo "value=\"Delete\" onclick=\"deletePost(" . $row['id'] .
           ",'" . $redir . "');\">";
      echo "<input class=\"confirm\" type=\"button\" value=\"Cancel\" ";
      echo "onclick=\"history.back()\"></p>";
      echo "</div>";
      break;

    case "DELETEFORUM":
      $sql = "SELECT * FROM forum_forum WHERE id=" . $_REQUEST['f'];
      $result = mysql_query($sql);
      $row = mysql_fetch_array($result);
      $msg = "If you delete this forum, all topics and replies will " .
             "be deleted as well.  Are you sure you wish to delete " .
             "the entire forum<br><em>" . $row['forum_name'] . "</em>?";
      echo "<div id=\"requestConfirmWarn\">";
      echo "<h2>DELETE FORUM?</h2>\n";
      echo "<p>" . $msg . "</p>";
      echo "<p><input class=\"confirm\" type=\"button\" ";
```

```
        echo "value=\"Delete\" ";
        echo "onclick=\"deleteForum(" . $_REQUEST['f'] . ");\">";
        echo "<input class=\"confirm\" type=\"button\" value=\"Cancel\" ";
        echo "onclick=\"history.back()\"></p>";
        echo "</div>";


    }
    require_once 'footer.php';
    ?>
```

How It Works

An exception to the previous group of transaction pages, this script actually generates output to which the user can respond. The switch() statement determines which text to display:

```
switch (strtoupper($_REQUEST['action'])) {
  case "DELETEPOST":
    . . .
  case "DELETEFORUM":
    . . .
}
```

Each of the options outputs two buttons, one to confirm the action, and one to go back. If users choose to confirm, it calls a bit of client-side Javascript code to redirect them to the proper transaction page:

```
<script type="text/javascript">
<!--
function deletePost(id,redir) {
  if (id > 0) {
    window.location = "transact-post.php?action=delete&post=" +
      id + "&r=" + redir;
  } else {
    history.back();
  }
}
function deleteForum(id) {
  if (id > 0) {
    window.location = "transact-admin.php?action=deleteForum&f=" + id;
  } else {
    history.back();
  }
}
//-->
</script>
```

Account Functionality

The next section of your bulletin board application deals with general account functionality. Here you'll give users the ability to create their own account, request a forgotten password, and administer other users. Let's continue.

Initial Login

The first thing you need to do is create the pages to allow users to create their account and log in to the site.

1.   Enter `login.php`, the login page. (Guess what it's used for?)

```php
<?php require_once 'header.php'; ?>
<form name="theForm" method="post" action="transact-user.php">
<h3>Member Login</h3>
<p>
  Email Address:<br>
  <input type="text" name="email" maxlength="255"
    value="<?php if (isset($_GET['e'])) { echo $_GET['e']; } ?>">
</p>
<p>
  Password:<br>
  <input type="password" name="passwd" maxlength="50">
</p>
<p>
  <input type="submit" class="submit" name="action" value="Login">
</p>

<p>
  Not a member yet? <a href="useraccount.php">Create a new account!</a>
</p>
<p>
  <a href="forgotpass.php">Forgot your password?</a>
</p>
</form>
<?php require_once 'footer.php'; ?>
```

2.   Create `index.php`, the home page. This is the page users first see when they view the board.

```php
<?php
require_once 'conn.php';
require_once 'functions.php';
require_once 'header.php';

$sql = <<<EOS
  SELECT f.id as id, f.forum_name as forum,
    f.forum_desc as description,
    count(forum_id) as threads, u.name as mod
  FROM forum_forum f
  LEFT JOIN forum_posts p
  ON f.id = p.forum_id
  AND p.topic_id=0
  LEFT JOIN forum_users u
  ON f.forum_moderator = u.id
  GROUP BY f.id
EOS;
$result = mysql_query($sql)
  or die(mysql_error());
if (mysql_num_rows($result) == 0) {
  echo "    <br>\n";
  echo "    There are currently no forums to view.\n";
```

```
    } else {
      echo "<table class=\"forumtable\" cellspacing=\"0\" ";
      echo "cellspacing=\"0\"><tr>";
      echo "<th class=\"forum\">Forum</th>";
      echo "<th class=\"threadcount\">Threads</th>";
      echo "<th class=\"moderator\">Moderator</th>";
      echo "</tr>";
      $rowclass = "";
      while ($row = mysql_fetch_array($result)) {
        $rowclass = ($rowclass == "row1"?"row2":"row1");
        echo "<tr class=\"$rowclass\">";
        echo "<td class=\"firstcolumn\"><a href=\"viewforum.php?f=" .
            $row['id'] . "\">";
        echo $row['forum'] . "</a><br>";
        echo "<span class=\"forumdesc\">" . $row['description'];
        echo "</span></td>";
        echo "<td class=\"center\">" . $row['threads'] . "</td>";
        echo "<td class=\"center\">" . $row['mod'] . "</td>";
        echo "</tr>\n";
      }
      echo "</table>";
    }

    require_once 'footer.php';
    ?>
```

3. Create `forgotpass.php`. This page is displayed if the user forgets his or her password.

```
<?php require_once 'header.php'; ?>
<form method="post" action="transact-user.php">
<h3>Email Password Reminder</h3>
<p>
  Forgot your password? Just enter your email address, and we'll email
  your password to you!
</p>
<p>
  Email Address:<br>
  <input type="text" id="email" name="email">
</p>
<p>
  <input type="submit" class="submit" name="action"
    value="Send my reminder!">
</p>
</form>
<?php require_once 'footer.php'; ?>
```

4. Load `login.php`. If you are still on the `setup.php` script you ran earlier, you can simply click the Log In link at the bottom of the setup page. You are taken to the login page, and the e-mail address is filled in for you.

Observe the link at the bottom of the login screen, "Forget your password?" If a user cannot remember her password, she can click this link and submit her e-mail address. If she is verified to be a valid user, her password will be sent to the e-mail address given. You can try this out yourself if you like, assuming you are using a legitimate e-mail address (and not the admin@yoursite.com default).

5. Enter your password and click the Login button. You should now see the home page of the CBA board application (see Figure 16-2).

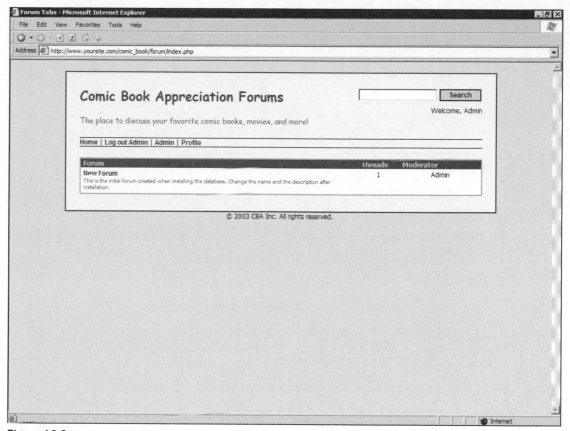

Figure 16-2

You are now logged in as the administrator of the CBA board application. As the administrator, you have complete control of your application. Three other roles apply to the board: Moderator, User, and Anonymous. Technically "Anonymous" isn't really a role, but if you are not logged in, the system does not know who you are and treats you as "anonymous."

How It Works

You may have noticed that login.php and forgotpass.php seem very similar. If you look closely, you'll notice they are very similar to the files of the same name discussed in Chapter 13. Since they are pretty much just HTML, we'll skip those for now, and talk about your home page, index.php.

At the start of the file, you include your standard three reusable scripts and then proceed to query the database. This time you use a three-table JOIN to retrieve a list of all the available forums, the number of threads per forum, and the name of the moderator for each.

```php
<?php
require_once 'conn.php';
require_once 'functions.php';
require_once 'header.php';

$sql = <<<EOS
  SELECT f.id as id, f.forum_name as forum,
    f.forum_desc as description,
    count(forum_id) as threads, u.name as mod
  FROM forum_forum f
  LEFT JOIN forum_posts p
  ON f.id = p.forum_id
  AND p.topic_id=0
  LEFT JOIN forum_users u
  ON f.forum_moderator = u.id
  GROUP BY f.id
EOS;
$result = mysql_query($sql)
  or die(mysql_error());
```

The rest of the script is all output. You check if any forums are found, and if so, you generate a table with links to each forum.

```php
if (mysql_num_rows($result) == 0) {
  echo "     <br>\n";
  echo "     There are currently no forums to view.\n";
} else {
  echo "<table class=\"forumtable\" cellspacing=\"0\" ";
  echo "cellspacing=\"0\"><tr>";
  echo "<th class=\"forum\">Forum</th>";
  echo "<th class=\"threadcount\">Threads</th>";
  echo "<th class=\"moderator\">Moderator</th>";
  echo "</tr>";
  $rowclass = "";
  while ($row = mysql_fetch_array($result)) {
    $rowclass = ($rowclass == "row1"?"row2":"row1");
    echo "<tr class=\"$rowclass\">";
    echo "<td class=\"firstcolumn\"><a href=\"viewforum.php?f=" .
        $row['id'] . "\">";
    echo $row['forum'] . "</a><br>";
    echo "<span class=\"forumdesc\">" . $row['description'];
    echo "</span></td>";
    echo "<td class=\"center\">" . $row['threads'] . "</td>";
    echo "<td class=\"center\">" . $row['mod'] . "</td>";
    echo "</tr>\n";
  }
  echo "</table>";
}

require_once 'footer.php';
?>
```

Simple enough, let's move on.

Try It Out   **User Management**

The next thing you are going to do is create the pages that allow the admin to control board settings and create user accounts.

1. Enter admin.php. This is the page used to edit different board attributes, user information, forums, and more.

```php
<?php
require_once 'header.php';
?>

<script type="text/javascript">
<!--
  function delBBCode(id) {
    window.location = "transact-admin.php?action=deleteBBCode&b=" + id;
  }
  function delForum(id) {
    window.location = "transact-affirm.php?action=deleteForum&f=" + id;
}
//-->
</script>

<?php
$sql = "SELECT access_lvl, access_name FROM forum_access_levels " .
       "ORDER by access_lvl DESC";
$result = mysql_query($sql)
  or die(mysql_error());
while ($row = mysql_fetch_array($result)) {
  $a_users[$row['access_lvl']] = $row['access_name'];
}

$menuoption = "boardadmin"; // default
if (isset($_GET['option'])) $menuoption = $_GET['option'];

$menuItems = array(
  "boardadmin" => "Board Admin",
  "edituser" => "Users",
  "forums" => "Forums",
  "bbcode" => "BBcode"
  );
echo "<p class=\"menu\">|";
foreach ($menuItems as $key => $value) {
  if ($menuoption != $key) {
    echo "<a href=\"" . $_SERVER['PHP_SELF'] . "?option=$key\">";
  }
  echo " $value ";
  if ($menuoption != $key) echo "</a>";
  echo "|";
}
echo "</p>";

switch ($menuoption) {
  case 'boardadmin':
```

```
  ?>
     <h3>Board Administration</h3>
     <form id="adminForm" method="post" action="transact-admin.php">
     <table cellspacing="0" class="forumtable">
     <tr>
       <th>Title</th><th>Value</th><th>Parameter</th>
     </tr>
<?php
     foreach ($admin as $k => $v) {
       echo "<tr><td>". $v['title'] . "</td><td>" .
         "<input type=\"text\" name=\"". $k . "\" " .
         "value=\"" . $v['value'] . "\" size=\"60\">" .
         "</td><td>$k</td></tr>\n";
     }
  ?>
     </table>
     <p class="buttonBar">
       <input class="submit" type="submit" name="action"
         id="Update" value="Update">
     </p>
     </form>
<?php
     break;

  case 'edituser':
  ?>
     <h3>User Administration</h3>
     <div id="users">
     <form name="myform" action="transact-admin.php" method="post">
     Please select a user to admin:<br>
     <select id="userlist" name="userlist[]">
<?php
     foreach ($a_users as $key => $value) {
       echo "<optgroup label=\"". $value . "\">\n";
       userOptionList($key);
       echo "\n</optgroup>\n";
     }
  ?>
     </select>
     <input class="submit"  type="submit" name="action"
       value="Modify User">
     </form>
     </div>
<?php
     break;

  case 'forums':
     ?>
     <h2>Forum Administration</h2>
     <table class="forumtable" cellspacing="0">
     <tr><th class="forum">Forum</th><th> </th><th> </th></tr>
     <?php
     $sql = "SELECT * FROM forum_forum";
     $result = mysql_query($sql)
       or die(mysql_error());
```

```php
    while ($row = mysql_fetch_array($result)) {
      echo "<tr><td><span class=\"forumname\">" . $row['forum_name'] .
        "</span><br><span class=\"forumdesc\">" .$row['forum_desc'].
        "</span></td><td>" . "<a href=\"editforum.php?forum=" .
        $row['id'] . "\">Edit</a></td><td>" .
        "<a href=\"#\" onclick=\"delForum(". $row['id'] .
        ");\">" . "Delete</a></td></tr>";
    }
    ?>
    </table>
    <p class="buttonBar">
      <a href="editforum.php" class="buttonlink">New Forum</a>
    </p>
  <?php
    break;

  case 'bbcode':
  ?>
    <h3>BBcode Administration</h3>
    <form id="bbcodeForm" method="post"
      action="transact-admin.php">
    <table cellspacing="0" class="forumtable">
    <tr>
      <th class="template">Template</th>
      <th class="replacement">Replacement</th>
      <th class="action">Action</th>
    </tr>
  <?php
    if (isset($bbcode)) {
      foreach ($bbcode as $k => $v) {
        echo "<tr class=\"row1\"><td>" .
          "<input class=\"mono\" type=\"text\" " .
          "name=\"bbcode_t" . $k . "\" " .
          "value=\"" . $v['template'] . "\" size=\"32\">" .
          "</td><td>" .
          "<input class=\"mono\" type=\"text\" " .
          "name=\"bbcode_r". $k . "\" " .
          "value=\"" . $v['replacement'] . "\" size=\"32\">" .
          "</td><td><input type=\"button\" class=\"submit\" " .
          "name=\"action\" id=\"DelBBCode\" value=\"Delete\" " .
          "onclick=\"delBBCode(".$k.");\">" .
          "</td></tr>\n";
      }
    }
  ?>
    <tr class="row2"><td colspan="3"> </td></tr>
    <tr class="row2"><td>
    <input class="mono" type="text" name="bbcode-tnew" size="32">
    </td><td>
    <input class="mono" type="text" name="bbcode-rnew" size="32">
    </td><td>
    <input type="submit" class="submit" name="action"
      id="AddBBCode" value="Add New">
    </td></tr>
    </table>
```

```
      <p class="buttonBar">
        <input class="submit" type="submit" name="action"
          id="Update" value="Update BBCodes">
      </p>
      </form>
    <?php
      break;
}
?>
</script>
<?php require_once 'footer.php'; ?>
```

2. Create `useraccount.php`. Users access this page to edit their own profiles.

```php
<?php
require_once 'header.php';

$userid = $username = $useremail = $password = $accesslvl = '';
$mode = "Create";
if (isset($_SESSION['user_id'])) {
  $userid = $_SESSION['user_id'];
  $mode = "Edit";
  if (isset($_GET['user'])) {
    if (($_SESSION['user_id'] == $_GET['user'])
        || ($_SESSION['access_lvl'] > 2)) {
      $userid = $_GET['user'];
      $mode = "Modify";
    }
  }
  $sql = "SELECT * FROM forum_users WHERE id=$userid";
  $result = mysql_query($sql)
    or die('Could not look up user data; ' . mysql_error());

  $row = mysql_fetch_array($result);
  $username = $row['name'];
  $useremail = $row['email'];
  $accesslvl = $row['access_lvl'];
  $signature = $row['signature'];
}

echo "<h3>$mode Account</h3>\n";
echo "<form method=\"post\" action=\"transact-user.php\">\n";
?>

<p>
  Full name:<br>
  <input type="text" class="txtinput" name="name" maxlength="100"
    value="<?php echo htmlspecialchars($username); ?>">
</p>
<p>
  Email Address:<br>
  <input type="text" class="txtinput" name="email" maxlength="255"
    value="<?php echo htmlspecialchars($useremail); ?>">
</p>
<?php
```

```php
if ($mode == "Modify") {
  echo "<div><fieldset>\n";
  echo "  <legend>Access Level</legend>\n";

  $sql = "SELECT * FROM forum_access_levels ORDER BY access_lvl DESC";
  $result = mysql_query($sql,$conn)
    or die('Could not list access levels; ' . mysql_error());

  while ($row = mysql_fetch_array($result)) {
    echo '  <input type="radio" class="radio" id="acl_' .
        $row['access_lvl'] . '" name="accesslvl" value="' .
        $row['access_lvl'] . '" ';

    if ($row['access_lvl'] == $accesslvl) {
      echo 'checked ';
    }
    echo '>' . $row['access_name'] . "<br>\n";
  }
  echo "</fieldset></div>";
}
if ($mode != "Modify") echo "<div id=\"passwords\">";
if ($mode == "Edit") {
  if (isset($_GET['error']) and $_GET['error'] == "nopassedit") {
    echo "<span class=\"error\">Could not modify passwords.";
    echo " Please try again.</span><br>";
  }
?>
<p>
  Old Password:<br>
  <input type="password" id="oldpasswd"
    name="oldpasswd" maxlength="50">
</p>
<?php
}
if ($mode != "Modify") {
?>
<p>
  New Password:<br>
  <input type="password" id="passwd" name="passwd" maxlength="50">
</p>
<p>
  Password Verification:<br>
  <input type="password" id="passwd2" name="passwd2" maxlength="50">
</p>
<?php }
if ($mode != "Modify") echo "</div>";
if ($mode != "Create") {
?>
<p>
  Signature:<br>
  <textarea name="signature" id="signature" cols="60" rows-"5"><?php
    echo $signature; ?></textarea>
</p>
<?php } ?>
```

```
<p>
  <input type="submit" class="submit" name="action"
    value="<?php echo $mode; ?> Account">
</p>
<?php if ($mode == "Edit") {?>
<input type="hidden" name="accesslvl"
  value="<?php echo $accesslvl; ?>">
<?php } ?>
<input type="hidden" name="userid" value="<?php echo $userid; ?>">
</form>
<?php require_once 'footer.php'; ?>
```

3. You are going to create a couple of new user identities to demonstrate the difference between the various roles.

    Log out, and click Register. You should see a screen similar to the one shown in Figure 16-3.

4. Enter a name. This name will be used for display purposes.

5. Enter your e-mail address.

6. Enter your password twice for verification.

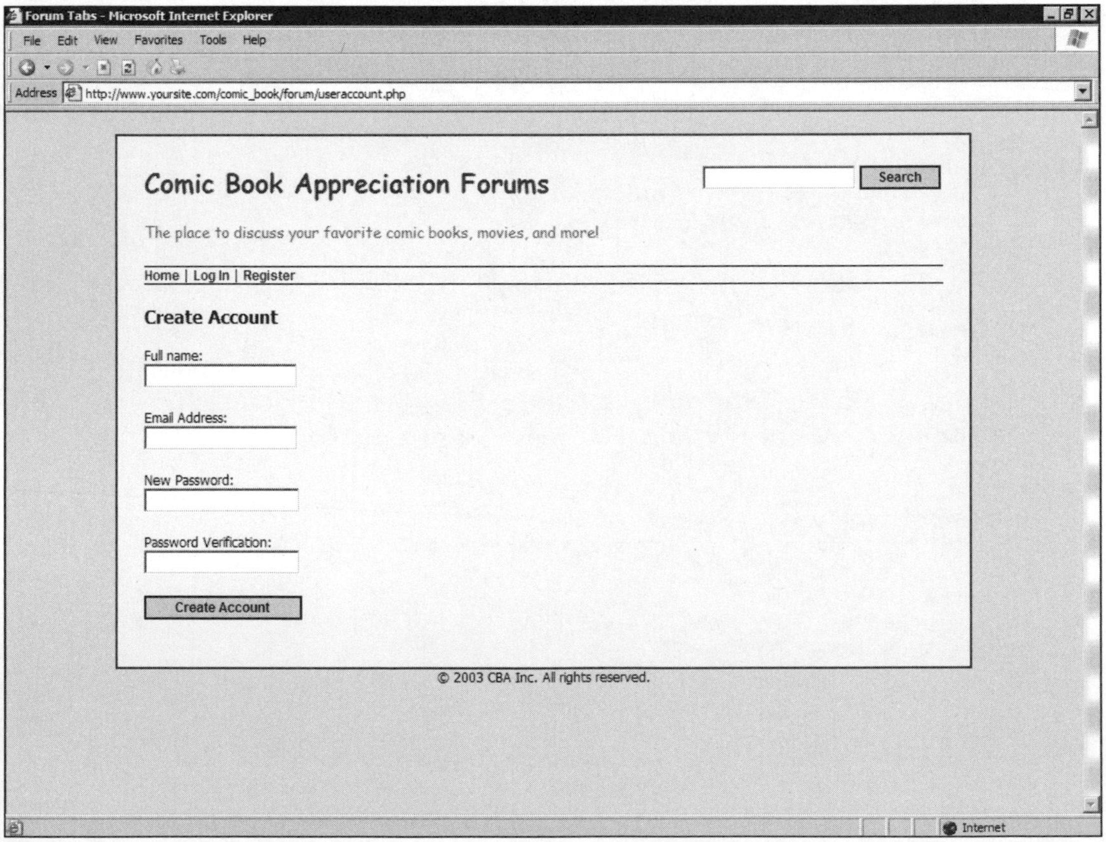

Figure 16-3

7. Click the Create Account button.

Your account will be created, and you will be automatically logged in with your new account.

8. Repeat steps 3 through 7 to create one more account.

9. Log out, and then Log back in with your original admin account.

If you don't remember the e-mail and password, just run `setup.php` again in your browser. Don't worry — your tables won't be re-created.

10. Now that you are logged in as the site administrator, you should see a menu item called "Admin." Click it.

11. Click "Users" in the Administration menu.

This displays the User Administration screen; from here you can select a user from the drop-down menu and edit user details.

12. Choose one of the user profiles you created in step 7 and click "Modify User."

From this page (see Figure 16-4), you can modify a user's name, access level, and signature.

13. Change the user's access level to Moderator and click "Modify Account."

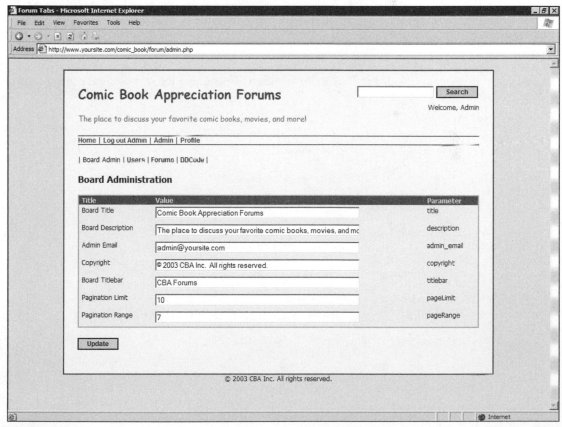

Figure 16-4

How It Works

Let's begin by looking at useraccount.php. At the beginning of the file, you check the user's credentials stored in your session variables. If the user is an admin, the form is set up to allow the admin to change his or her access level.

```
$mode = "Create";
if (isset($_SESSION['user_id'])) {
  $userid = $_SESSION['user_id'];
  $mode = "Edit";
  if (isset($_GET['user'])) {
    if (($_SESSION['user_id'] == $_GET['user'])
        || ($_SESSION['access_lvl'] > 2)) {
      $userid = $_GET['user'];
      $mode = "Modify";
    }
  }
  $sql = "SELECT * FROM forum_users WHERE id=$userid";
  $result = mysql_query($sql)
    or die('Could not look up user data; ' . mysql_error());

  $row = mysql_fetch_array($result);
  $username = $row['name'];
  $useremail = $row['email'];
  $accesslvl = $row['access_lvl'];
  $signature = $row['signature'];
}
```

Later down in the page, the determined mode toggles whether or not the Access Level controls will be displayed.

```
if ($mode == "Modify") {
  echo "<div><fieldset>\n";
  echo "  <legend>Access Level</legend>\n";

  $sql = "SELECT * FROM forum_access_levels ORDER BY access_lvl DESC";
  $result = mysql_query($sql,$conn)
    or die('Could not list access levels; ' . mysql_error());

  while ($row = mysql_fetch_array($result)) {
    echo '  <input type="radio" class="radio" id="acl_' .
        $row['access_lvl'] . '" name="accesslvl" value="' .
        $row['access_lvl'] . '" ';

    if ($row['access_lvl'] == $accesslvl) {
      echo 'checked ';
    }
    echo '>' . $row['access_name'] . "<br>\n";
  }
  echo "</fieldset></div>";
}
```

The rest of the page simply finishes out the form. Let's move on to admin.php.

You may have noticed sections of code in `admin.php` that involve forum settings, BBcode settings, and more. We're going to ignore those for now to talk about the User Administration portion of the admin area. We'll touch back on those other functions later in the chapter.

User Administration

On the User Administration page, the first thing you need to do is gather up all of the access levels, along with their names. That is done with the following code, which results in a numerical array of Access Levels:

```php
$sql = "SELECT access_lvl, access_name FROM forum_access_levels " .
       "ORDER by access_lvl DESC";
$result = mysql_query($sql)
  or die(mysql_error());
while ($row = mysql_fetch_array($result)) {
  $a_users[$row['access_lvl']] = $row['access_name'];
}
```

Next, under the "edituser" case of your `switch()` you create an HTML select field, dynamically building up the options. By looping through the access level array you just created, you can also use the `optgroup` tag to categorize the select list by access level. (Aren't you so clever?)

```php
    <select id="userlist" name="userlist[]">
<?php
    foreach ($a_users as $key => $value) {
      echo "<optgroup label=\"". $value . "\">\n";
      userOptionList($key);
      echo "\n</optgroup>\n";
    }
?>
    </select>
```

Note that you create the list of users by calling the `userOptionList()` function. This function resides in `functions.php` and is called once for each access level. A list of `<option>` tags is output, each containing the appropriate user information.

```php
function userOptionList($level) {
  $sql = "SELECT id, name, access_lvl " .
         "FROM forum_users " .
         "WHERE access_lvl=" . $level . " " .
         "ORDER BY name";
  $result = mysql_query($sql)
    or die(mysql_error());

  while ($row = mysql_fetch_array($result)) {
    echo "<option value=\"". $row['id'] . "\">" .
         htmlspecialchars($row['name']) . "</option>";
  }
}
```

That's really all there is to it. When the appropriate user is chosen, his or her ID is passed on to the `transact-admin.php` transaction page, where the admin user is redirected to the `useraccount.php` page for that user.

Forum Functionality

The last section of this application covers the actual forum-specific functionality. Up until now, everything, with the exception of some functions and transaction pages, has been pretty generic, and could really be used for almost any type of member-driven Web site. Now we're getting to the fun stuff, the reason for this chapter.

Editing Board Settings

The first thing you need to do is customize your bulletin board to your liking.

1. Enter editforum.php, which is used to edit forum details:

```php
<?php
if (isset($_GET['forum'])) {
  $action = "Edit";
} else {
  $action = "Add";
}
$pageTitle = "$action Forum";
require_once 'header.php';

$forum = 0;
$fname = '';
$fdesc = '';
$fmod = '';
$userid = 0;

if (isset($_GET['forum'])) {
  $forum = $_GET['forum'];
  $sql = "SELECT forum_name, forum_desc, u.name, u.id " .
         "FROM forum_forum f " .
         "LEFT JOIN forum_users u " .
         "ON f.forum_moderator = u.id " .
         "WHERE f.id = $forum";
  $result = mysql_query($sql)
    or die(mysql_error());
  if ($row = mysql_fetch_array($result)) {
    $fname = $row['forum_name'];
    $fdesc = $row['forum_desc'];
    $fmod = $row['name'];
    $userid = $row['id'];
  }
}
echo "<h2>$action forum</h2>";
?>
<form name="forumedit" action="transact-admin.php" method="post">
<table class="forumtable" cellspacing="0">
  <tr><th colspan="2">General Forum Settings</th></tr>
  <tr>
```

```
      <td>Forum Name</td>
      <td>
        <input type="text" name="forumname"
          value="<?php echo $fname; ?>">
      </td>
  </tr>
  <tr>
      <td>Forum Description</td>
      <td>
        <input type="text" name="forumdesc" size="75"
          value="<?php echo $fdesc; ?>">
      </td>
  </tr>
  <tr>
      <td>Forum Moderator</td>
      <td>
        <select id="moderator" name="forummod[]">
          <option value="0">unmoderated</option>
<?php
$sql = "SELECT * FROM forum_users WHERE access_lvl > 1";
$result = mysql_query($sql)
  or die(mysql_error());
while ($row = mysql_fetch_array($result)) {
  echo "<option value=\"" . $row['id'] . "\"";
  if ($userid == $row['id']) echo " selected='selected'";
  echo ">" . $row['name'] . "</option>";
}
?>
        </select>
      </td>
  </tr>
  <tr>
      <td colspan="2">
        <input class="submit" type="submit" name="action"
          value="<?php echo $action; ?> Forum">
      </td>
  </tr>
</table>
<input type="hidden" name="forum_id" value="<?php echo $forum; ?>">
</form>
<?php require_once 'footer.php'; ?>
```

2. Click the "Admin" link from the navigation menu. This brings you to the administration page (see Figure 16-5). The values in the fields you now see are used in the application. For instance, the first field, Board Title, is "Comic Book Appreciation Forums."

3. Edit the Board Title field to read "Comic Book Appreciation Bulletin Board" and click Update.

   The title at the top of the page should change accordingly.

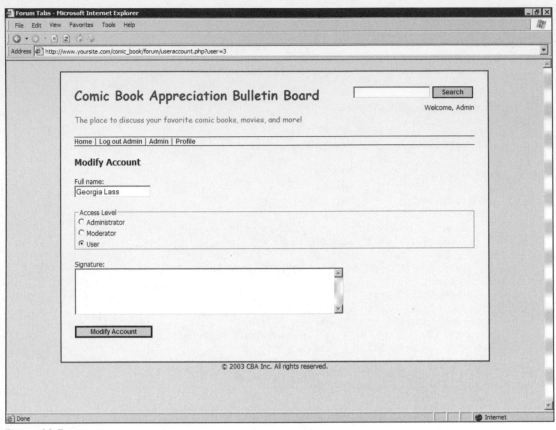

Figure 16-5

4. Complete the other fields in the administration page:

   ❏ Board Description

   ❏ Admin Email

   ❏ Copyright

   ❏ Board Titlebar

   Most of those should be fairly self-explanatory. The last two fields control how many posts you see on one page and how many pages you have access to at one time.

5. Change Pagination Limit to 3 and click the Update button.

6. Now, click "Forums" on the Administration menu. You should see a list of the forums available for your board. If this is your initial installation, you will have only one forum—called New Forum. You can edit this forum, delete it, or create a new forum. Feel free to create as many forums as you want. Note that when creating or editing a forum, you can choose a moderator. The user's account you edited earlier is now available as a choice in the Moderator field.

7. Click "BBcodes" in the Administration menu.

You will see a form where you can enter a "template" and "replacement." This allows you to designate words or phrases that will be replaced by different words or phrases. For instance, you can enter the phrase "very hard" in the template field, and "cats and dogs" in the replacement field. Once you click the Add New button, these will be added to the database. Note that the real power of this page is in the use of regular expressions. If you are not familiar with regular expressions, we explain how they work in the "How It Works" section.

8. Enter the following template and replacement values exactly as they are shown. Remember to click Add New after entering each one:

Target	Replacement
\[url\]([^[]+?)\[\/url\]	<a href="$1" target="_blank">$1</a>
\[img\]([^[]+?)\[\/img\]	<img src="$1">
\[i\]([^[]+?)\[\/i\]	<i>$1</i>
\[b\]([^[]+?)\[\/b\]	$1
\[u\]([^[]+?)\[\/u\]	<u>$1</u>
\[url=([^]]+?)\]	<a href="$1" target="_blank">
\[\/url\]	</a>
very hard	cats and dogs

That's it for the administration functions. There are not too many, but we are sure you will think of many things to add down the road.

How It Works

That brings you back to the admin.php page. You were able to get here by clicking the Admin link, which is available only if you are logged in as the administrator. So far, so good. What if the user attempts to access the admin.php page directly?

Try it yourself. Load index.php in your browser, and then make sure you are logged out. Once you are logged out, load admin.php by typing it directly in the address bar of your browser. It should load with no problem. Now, edit one of the fields on the main admin page. Again, nothing is stopping you. Indeed, when you click the Update button, the data will be saved.

But wait . . . you are not logged in! How is this possible? Simple. You have not checked the user's credentials once he or she got into the page.

Just as you are responsible for checking IDs in your bar in case underage patrons slip in, you are responsible for the users' access to your entire site. If you don't want certain people to access a page, you not only have to bar access to any link loading the page, but kick them off the page if they are successful in loading it.

Fortunately, this is easy to do. At the top of your page, simply check their credentials (those are up to you. Do they need a certain access level? Do they just need to be logged in?), and then redirect them to another page if they don't pass (shameonyou.php, or simply back to index.php).

You can do other things to make your site more secure. Most are way beyond the scope of the book. A look at the link we gave you earlier should help you if you are interested in learning more about security. Just don't ever think you are "secure enough" if you haven't considered the risk of unauthorized access.

While you are still visiting admin.php, let's take a closer look at it.

The file admin.php is set up in four different areas: board administration, user admin, forum admin, and BBcode admin. A lot is going on in this page. You've already seen User Administration, so we'll tackle the other three areas, one at a time. First let's look at board administration.

Board Administration

Looking at the code, you will see that you simply build your table of fields by looping through an array called $admin.

```
foreach ($admin as $k => $v) {
  echo "<tr><td>". $v['title'] . "</td><td>" .
    "<input type=\"text\" name=\"". $k . "\" " .
    "value=\"" . $v['value'] . "\" size=\"60\">" .
    "</td><td>$k</td></tr>\n";
}
```

The array $admin is associative. The key is a unique identifier for the data, which is associated with a value and a title. For example, the title bar's title is "Board Titlebar" and the value is "CBA Forums." It is represented in the $admin array as follows:

```
$admin['titlebar']['title'] = "Board Titlebar"
$admin['titlebar']['value'] = "CBA Forums"
```

By looping through the $admin array, you can extract each piece of data and use it to build your form. But the question is, where is $admin populated? It is certainly not created anywhere in admin.php.

If you look at the top of admin.php, you'll notice that header.php is included. The array is not built in header.php either, but looking at the top of header.php you will notice another included file, config.php. A quick look into config.php uncovers the fact that $admin is loaded there. Note that $bbcode is also being built. You'll see that used shortly.

```
$sql = 'SELECT * FROM forum_admin';
$result = mysql_query($sql)
  or die(mysql_error());

while ($row = mysql_fetch_array($result)) {
  $admin[$row['constant']]['title'] = $row['title'];
  $admin[$row['constant']]['value'] = $row['value'];
}
```

```
$sql = 'SELECT * FROM forum_bbcode';
$result = mysql_query($sql)
  or die(mysql_error());

while ($row = mysql_fetch_array($result)) {
  $bbcode[$row['id']]['template'] = $row['template'];
  $bbcode[$row['id']]['replacement'] = $row['replacement'];
}
```

Notice that $admin (and $bbcode) are built by looping through the entire admin (and BBcode) table. This is important because it illustrates how the board administration page contains every piece of data contained in the admin table. These values are available, and are used, throughout the application. For example, header.php uses some of the $admin data:

```
$title = $admin['titlebar']['value'];
  ...
<title><?php echo $title; ?></title>
  ...
  <h1 id="sitetitle"><?php echo $admin['title']['value']; ?></h1>
  ...
  <p id="subtitle"><?php echo $admin['description']['value']; ?></p>
```

You may also notice the lack of any way to add or delete admin values. There is a good reason for this. The $admin values are available at the code level. Because of this, you don't want to be able to delete a value that the code is relying on. You also don't need to create new values because the code wouldn't use the new values in any case.

However, you may find the need to create a new row of data in the admin table to be used in your board application. For example, you are using a style sheet to alter the appearance of the application. Perhaps you want the ability to dynamically change the style sheet used by changing a value in the admin page, rather than editing the header.php file.

The good news is that once you add a new row of data to the admin table, it is automatically detected by the board administration page and displayed. The bottom line? If you feel you need a new, administrator-controlled value in your application, simply add the appropriate row of data to your admin table (using phpMyAdmin, if you like), and access it in your code using the $admin['key']['value'] and $admin['key']['title'] syntax.

Let's take a gander at the forum administration page next.

Forum Administration

This part is pretty straightforward. You look up all of the forums in the forum table and then list them with their descriptions, plus a link for editing and a link for deleting. Choosing delete takes the administrator to transact-affirm.php, which prompts the user for confirmation before deleting the forum. This is a safety precaution because deleting a forum results in the deletion of all posts within that forum as well. We leave it to you to explore transact-affirm.php on your own. It is a fairly self-explanatory page, and by now you should have no problem figuring out how it works.

BBcode Administration

Now we come to the real neat stuff. This is really part of a larger topic of discussion involving regular expressions. Therefore, we believe it deserves its own heading.

Regular Expressions

If you are not familiar with regular expressions, one look at a typical regular expression might prompt you to wonder just who would consider it "regular." However, just like any language, once you learn what the syntax means, regular expressions are not that difficult. With the right combination of commands, however, regular expressions can be very powerful.

A regular expression (often abbreviated "regex" or "regexp") is a pattern of symbols and letters used to match text. Once a match is found, it can either be displayed, erased, or replaced with something else. If you have ever used *.php to list all PHP files in a directory, then you have used a regex pattern.

So, how do regular expressions apply to an application such as this one? Good question. Imagine that this site catered to children (as it might, in fact, because many children are comic book fans). You might want to prevent the usage of obscene words on your site, so that it is a friendly place that parents appreciate and allow their children to visit. By using regular expressions, you can scan a post before it gets displayed on the screen and replace any vulgarities with cleaner prose.

The topic of regular expressions could easily fill a book by itself. Indeed, there are many places to learn more about regular expressions than you will learn in this chapter. You can start with the PHP manual by visiting www.php.net/pcre.

The Two Types of regex Functions

In PHP, there are two basic types of regular expression functions: POSIX and PCRE.

POSIX stands for Portable Operating System Interface (don't ask about the X; we think geeks just like to use X wherever they can). POSIX is a set of standard operating system interfaces based on the Unix operating system. The term POSIX, therefore, does not actually refer to the regular expressions themselves, but describes the source of the regular expression syntax. It is more proper to refer to them as POSIX-style regular expressions. POSIX-style regular expressions are implemented in PHP by using the ereg() functions, such as ereg(), eregi(), and ereg_replace().

PCRE stands for Perl Compatible Regular Expressions. They are usually faster than POSIX-style regular expressions, and for that reason along with the fact that PCRE regular expressions are usually more powerful, most developers choose to use PCRE functions such as preg_match() and preg_replace().

Chapter 8 briefly introduced you to a POSIX-style regular expression. Here we show you PCRE. It is ultimately up to you which you choose to use. However, for a thorough understanding of both styles, make sure you read the PHP manual.

How to Write a PCRE regex

So, what does a regex look like? We will demonstrate different regex patterns using the `preg_replace()` function. The `preg_replace()` function takes three arguments: the search pattern (the needle), the replacement pattern, and the text to be searched (the haystack). The regex pattern is contained in `$needle`:

```
$result = preg_replace($needle, $replacement, $haystack);
```

When creating your regex pattern, you must use delimiters to define the boundaries of your regex. The delimiters can be any character except alphanumeric. Most use the forward slash character (/). This is not a requirement; use any character you are comfortable with. Just remember that if you use the same character within your pattern, it must be escaped by a preceding backslash (\ ).

You can designate search patterns in your regexp in many ways. The simplest is the literal: What you are looking for is literally entered in your pattern, usually within parentheses:

```
preg_replace('/(goose)/', 'pinch', 'Do not goose me, please');
```

If you are looking for one of a group of patterns, separate them with the pipe (|):

```
/(goose|duck|egret)/
```

To look for specific characters, put them in square brackets. All of the following are legal regex expressions:

`/[abc]/`	Matches the letter a, b, or c
`/[a-z]/`	Matches any lowercase letter
`/[a-zA-Z0-9]/`	Matches any alphanumeric character
`/[^aeiou]/`	Matches any consonant (^ means "not")

You have a few options to specify the number of times a character should or can be repeated:

`. (period)`	Matches any single character except newlines
`?`	Matches the preceding token 0 or 1 times
`*`	Matches the preceding token 0 or more times
`+`	Matches the preceding token 1 or more times
`{x}`	Matches any x times (such as {5})
`{x,y}`	Matches any x through y times (such as {2,4})

There is much more to regular expressions than this list covers. For a complete list, visit www.php.net/manual/en/reference.pcre.pattern.syntax.php.

In addition to pattern matching, modifiers exist that change the "rules" of your pattern. These go on the right side of the right-hand delimiter. For the complete list of modifiers, visit www.php.net/manual/en/reference.pcre.pattern.modifiers.php; for now, here is a partial list:

i	Caseless: Pattern matches any uppercase and lowercase.
s	Dot (.) matches all characters, *including newlines.*
e	Very powerful! After pattern matching, evaluates the result as PHP.

In step 8 of the previous "Try It Out" section, you entered a few strange patterns in the BBcode Administration page. We will clear up the mystery of those values for you, and show you how they work. Before we do that, however, let's look at how BBcodes are implemented. Once you see where the replacements take place, we will look at the actual patterns.

If you take a look at the showTopic() function defined in functions.php, you'll see a line that looks like this:

```
echo "</p><p>" . bbcode(nl2br(htmlspecialchars($body))) . "</p>";
```

The variable $body contains the text you want to display on the screen. However, before you do that, you have a couple of "cleanup" tasks to perform. First, you want to convert (and not render) any HTML that might exist in the form to the HTML equivalents, so that the HTML is displayed in the body as it was entered. This will prevent malicious users from inputting HTML that can break your page. The function htmlspecialchars() will take care of that for you.

Once all of the HTML has been converted to the HTML entity equivalents, enter <br> tags for every newline entered in the body of the post. PHP has a handy tool for that, of course: nl2br().

Finally, perform all of the replacements you have set up on the BBcode administration page. That is accomplished using the function bbcode(), which runs through each of the target/replacement pairs in the BBcode database, replacing any relevant text in the body. It does this recursively (a max of four iterations) until no more matches are found.

```
function bbcode($data) {
  $sql = "SELECT * FROM forum_bbcode";
  $result = mysql_query($sql);
  if (mysql_num_rows($result) > 0) {
    while($row = mysql_fetch_array($result)) {
      $bbcode['tpl'][] =
        "/" . html_entity_decode($row['template'],ENT_QUOTES). "/i";
      $bbcode['rep'][] =
        html_entity_decode($row['replacement'],ENT_QUOTES);
    }
    $data1 = preg_replace($bbcode['tpl'],$bbcode['rep'],$data);
    $count = 1;
    while (($data1 != $data) and ($count < 4)) {
      $count++;
      $data = $data1;
      $data1 = preg_replace($bbcode['tpl'],$bbcode['rep'],$data);
```

```
        }
    }

    return $data;
}
```

Because regex uses many odd characters in the pattern, before storing the data in your table you use `htmlentities()` to convert the data into something MySQL can safely store. For that reason, when retrieving the data, you must perform `html_entity_decode()`.

Also note the use of the *i* modifier after the right-hand modifier. This specifies that you do not care about upper- or lowercase matching. If you want to use case matching, feel free to remove this modifier.

As you can see from the code, `$row['template']` contains the regex pattern. The array variable `$row['replacement']` contains the replacement pattern. Now, let's look at some of the pattern/replacement pairs you entered earlier:

Pattern	Replacement	Explanation
`very hard`	`cats and dogs`	This is a very simple replacement, using a literal pattern match. It replaces the words "very hard" with the words "cats and dogs" in any post or signature. You saw evidence of this in one of your posts.
`\[\/url\]`	`</a>`	Replaces any instance of `[/url]` in the body with `</a>`. Note that the opening and closing square brackets and the forward slash must be delimited to show that you want to match them literally.
`\[b\]([^[]+?)\[\/b\]`	`<b>$1</b>`	Now we're getting into some interesting stuff. This pattern matches `[b]some text here[/b]` and replaces it with `<b>some text here</b>`.

The last pattern deserves a bit of explanation, because it introduces a couple of new concepts. The parentheses are there so you can use what we call *back references*. Note the `$1` in the replacement pattern. This tells the function "Take whatever you found in the first set of parentheses and put it here." If you had a more complex pattern with a second set of parentheses, you would refer to the data matched within those parentheses using `$2`.

Within those parentheses, you are matching any character at all *except* a left square bracket. The + tells the expression to match from 1 to any number of those characters. If you wanted the expression to match 0 or more, use * instead of +.

The ? can be very confusing, especially if you're not familiar with regular expressions. Because it is immediately preceded by a quantifier (+), it does not mean 0 characters or 1 character as it usually does. In this case, it is telling the regex not to be greedy.

Take the following text, for example:

```
Hello, [b]George[/b], how are [b]you[/b] doing today?
```

If you ran the regex pattern \[b\]([^[]+)\[\/b\] against that text (note the lack of ?), the regex would be "greedy" and match the maximum-sized pattern it could find by default. The result is that the preceding text would be altered like so:

```
Hello, <b>George[/b], how are [b]you</b> doing today?
```

This isn't good in this particular case because you are only trying to style "George" and "you" in bold-face. You use the ? in your pattern after the + to tell the regex pattern to be *ungreedy*, so that it finds the smallest matches. By adding in the ?, the result would be

```
Hello, <b>George</b>, how are <b>you</b> doing today?
```

which of course is the intended result.

We know regular expressions can be a bit confusing. Take the time to learn them, though. If you understand them well, they can be your biggest ally. You will be surprised at the sort of patterns you can match with regex.

For more information on PCRE regular expressions, visit the following pages in the PHP manual:

❑   http://www.php.net/manual/en/ref.pcre.php

❑   http://www.php.net/manual/en/reference.pcre.pattern.modifiers.php

❑   http://www.php.net/manual/en/reference.pcre.pattern.syntax.php

Try It Out   Using the Board

The final thing you're going to do is use the board as a normal user would. You're going to create a new post, view it, and reply to it.

1.   Create viewforum.php, which displays all of the threads (topics) for a forum:

```php
<?php
require_once 'conn.php';
require_once 'functions.php';
require_once 'http.php';
if (!isset($_GET['f'])) redirect('index.php');
require_once 'header.php';

$forumid = $_GET['f'];
$forum = getForum($forumid);

echo breadcrumb($forumid, "F");
if (isset($_GET['page'])) {
  $page = $_GET['page'];
} else {
  $page = 1;
}
```

```php
$limit = $admin['pageLimit']['value'];
if ($limit == "") $limit = 25;
$start = ($page - 1) * $admin['pageLimit']['value'];

$sql = "CREATE TEMPORARY TABLE tmp ( " .
        "topic_id INT(11) NOT NULL DEFAULT 0, " .
        "postdate datetime NOT NULL default '0000-00-00 00:00:00')";
mysql_query($sql)
  or die(mysql_error() . "<br>" . $sql);

$sql = "LOCK TABLES forum_users READ,forum_posts READ";
mysql_query($sql)
  or die(mysql_error() . "<br>" . $sql);

$sql = "INSERT INTO tmp SELECT topic_id, MAX(date_posted) " .
        "FROM forum_posts " .
        "WHERE forum_id = $forumid " .
        "AND topic_id > 0 " .
        "GROUP BY topic_id";
mysql_query($sql)
  or die(mysql_error() . "<br>" . $sql);

$sql = "UNLOCK TABLES";
mysql_query($sql)
  or die(mysql_error()."<br>".$sql);

//die('stop');
$sql = "SELECT SQL_CALC_FOUND_ROWS " .
        "t.id as topic_id, t.subject as t_subject, " .
        "u.name as t_author, count(p.id) as numreplies, " .
        "t.date_posted as t_posted, tmp.postdate as re_posted " .
        "FROM forum_users u " .
        "JOIN forum_posts t " .
        "ON t.author_id = u.id " .
        "LEFT JOIN tmp " .
        "ON t.id = tmp.topic_id " .
        "LEFT JOIN forum_posts p " .
        "ON p.topic_id = t.id " .
        "WHERE t.forum_id = $forumid " .
        "AND t.topic_id = 0 " .
        "GROUP BY t.id " .
        "ORDER BY re_posted DESC " .
        "LIMIT $start, $limit";
$result = mysql_query($sql)
  or die(mysql_error() . "<br>" . $sql);

$numrows = mysql_num_rows($result);
if ($numrows == 0) {
  $msg = "There are currently no posts.  Would you " .
        "like to be the first person to create a thread?";
  $title = "Welcome to " . $forum['name'];
  $dest = "compose.php?forumid=" . $forumid;
  $sev = "Info";
  $message = msgBox($msg,$title,$dest,$sev);
```

```
    echo $message;
} else {
  if (isset($_SESSION['user_id'])) {
    echo topicReplyBar(0, $_GET['f'], "right");
  }
  echo "<table class=\"forumtable\" cellspacing=\"0\" ";
  echo "cellpadding=\"2\"><tr>";
  echo "<th class=\"thread\">Thread</th>";
  echo "<th class=\"author\">Author</th>";
  echo "<th class=\"replies\">Replies</th>";
  echo "<th class=\"lastpost\">Last Post</th>";
  echo "</tr>";
  $rowclass = "";
  while ($row = mysql_fetch_array($result)) {
    $rowclass = ($rowclass == "row1"?"row2":"row1");
    if ($row['re_posted'] == "") {
      $lastpost = $row['t_posted'];
    } else {
      $lastpost = $row['re_posted'];
    }
    if ((isset($_SESSION['user_id'])) and
        ($_SESSION['last_login'] < $lastpost)) {
      $newpost = true;
    } else {
      $newpost = false;
    }
    echo "<tr class=\"$rowclass\">";
    echo "<td class=\"thread\">" . ($newpost?NEWPOST." ":"");
    echo "<a href=\"viewtopic.php?t=";
    echo $row['topic_id'] . "\">" . $row['t_subject'] . "</a></td>";
    echo "<td class=\"author\">" . $row['t_author'] . "</td>";
    echo "<td class=\"replies\">" . $row['numreplies'] . "</td>";
    echo "<td class=\"lastpost\">" . $lastpost . "</td>";
    echo "</tr>\n";
  }
  echo "</table>";
  echo paginate($limit);
  echo "<p>" . NEWPOST . " = New Post(s)</p>";
}
$sql = "DROP TABLE tmp";
mysql_query($sql)
  or die(mysql_error()."<br>".$sql);

require_once 'footer.php';
?>
```

2. Create `viewtopic.php`, which displays all of the posts in a thread:

```
<?php
require_once 'conn.php';
require_once 'functions.php';
require_once 'http.php';
if (!isset($_GET['t'])) redirect('index.php');
require_once 'header.php';
```

```
$topicid = $_GET['t'];
$limit = $admin['pageLimit']['value'];

showTopic($topicid, TRUE);

require_once 'footer.php';
?>
```

3. Enter `compose.php`, the form used to enter the subject and body of a post:

```
<?php
require_once 'conn.php';
require_once 'functions.php';
require_once 'header.php';

$subject = '';
if (isset($_GET['topicid'])) {
  $topicid = $_GET['topicid'];
} else {
  $topicid = "";
}
if (isset($_GET['forumid'])) {
  $forumid = $_GET['forumid'];
} else {
  $forumid = "";
}
if (isset($_GET['reid'])) {
  $reid = $_GET['reid'];
}
$body = '';
$post = '';
$authorid = $_SESSION['user_id'];
$edit_mode = FALSE;

if (isset($_GET['a'])
    and $_GET['a'] == 'edit'
    and isset($_GET['post'])
    and $_GET['post']) {
  $edit_mode = TRUE;
}

require_once 'header.php';

if (!isset($_SESSION['user_id'])) {
  echo "<div class=\"notice\">" .
      "You must be logged in to post.  Please <a href=\"" .
      "login.php\">Log in</a> before posting a message." .
      "</div>";
} elseif ($edit_mode and $_SESSION['user_id'] != $authorid) {
  echo "<div class=\"noauth\">" .
      "You are not authorized to edit this post.  Please contact " .
      "your administrator.</div>";
} else {
  if ($edit_mode) {
```

```php
    $sql = "SELECT * FROM forum_posts p, forum_forum f " .
          "WHERE p.id = " . $_GET['post'] .
          " AND p.forum_id = f.id";
    $result = mysql_query($sql,$conn)
      or die('Could not retrieve post data; ' . mysql_error());

    $row = mysql_fetch_array($result);

    $subject = $row['subject'];
    $topicid = $row['topic_id'];
    $forumid = $row['forum_id'];
    $body = $row['body'];
    $post = $_GET['post'];
    $authorid = $row['author_id'];
} else {

  if ($topicid == "") {
    $topicid = 0;
    $topicname = "New Topic";
  } else {
    if ($reid != "") {
      $sql = "SELECT subject FROM forum_posts WHERE id = " . $reid;
      $result = mysql_query($sql, $conn)
        or die('Could not retrieve topic; ' . mysql_error());
      if (mysql_num_rows($result) > 0) {
        $row = mysql_fetch_array($result);
        $re = preg_replace("/(re: )/i","",$row['subject']);
      }
    }
    $sql = "SELECT subject FROM forum_posts WHERE id = ";
    $sql .= $topicid . " AND topic_id = 0 AND forum_id = $forumid";
    $result = mysql_query($sql,$conn)
      or die('Could not retrieve topic; ' . mysql_error());
    if (mysql_num_rows($result) > 0) {
      $row = mysql_fetch_array($result);
      $topicname = "Reply to <em>" . $row['subject'] . "</em>\n";
      $subject = ($re == ""?"":"Re: " . $re);
    } else {
      $topicname = "Reply";
      $topicid = 0;
    }
  }
}
if ($forumid == "" or $forumid == 0) $forumid = 1;
$sql = "SELECT forum_name FROM forum_forum " .
      "WHERE id = '" . $forumid . "'";
$result = mysql_query($sql, $conn)
  or die('Could not retrieve forum name; ' . mysql_error());
$row = mysql_fetch_array($result);
$forumname = $row['forum_name'];

?>

<form id="forumpost" method="post" action="transact-post.php">
```

```php
  <h3><?php echo $edit_mode
                ?"Edit Post"
                :"$forumname: $topicname"; ?>
  </h3>
  <p>
    Subject:<br>
    <input type="text" class="subject" name="subject" maxlength="255"
      value="<?php echo $subject; ?>">
  </p>
  <p>
    Body:<br>
    <textarea class="body" name="body" rows="10" cols="60"><?php
      echo $body; ?></textarea>
  </p>
  <p>
  <?php

  if ($edit_mode) {
    echo '<input type="submit" class="submit" name="action" ' .
        "value=\"Save Changes\">\n";
  } else {
    echo '<input type="submit" class="submit" name="action" ' .
        "value=\"Submit New Post\">\n";
  }
?>
  </p>
<?php
  echo "<input type=\"hidden\" name=\"post\" " .
      "value=\"$post\">\n";
  echo "<input type=\"hidden\" name=\"topic_id\" " .
      "value=\"$topicid\">\n";
  echo "<input type=\"hidden\" name=\"forum_id\" " .
      "value=\"$forumid\">\n";
  echo "<input type=\"hidden\" name=\"author_id\" " .
      "value=\"$authorid\">\n";
  echo "</form>\n";
}
require_once 'footer.php';
?>
```

4. Create `search.php`, which displays the user's search results:

```php
<?php
require_once 'conn.php';
require_once 'functions.php';
require_once 'header.php';

$result = NULL;

if (isset($_GET['keywords'])) {
  $sql = "SELECT *, MATCH (subject,body) " .
      "AGAINST ('" . $_GET['keywords'] . "') AS score " .
      "FROM forum_posts " .
      "WHERE MATCH (subject,body) " .
```

```
              "AGAINST ('" . $_GET['keywords'] . "') " .
              "ORDER BY score DESC";

  $result = mysql_query($sql, $conn)
     or die('Could not perform search; ' . mysql_error());
}

echo "<table class=\"forumtable\" width=\"100%\" " .
     "cellspacing=\"0\">\n";
echo "<tr><th class=\"searchHeader\">Search Results</th></tr>\n";

if ($result and !mysql_num_rows($result)) {
  echo "<tr class=\"row1\"><td>No articles found that match the ";
  echo "search term(s) '<strong>" . $_GET['keywords'] . "</strong>'";
  if ($access_lvl > 2) echo "<p>SQL: $sql</p>";
  echo "</td></tr>\n";
} else {
  $rowclass = "";
  while ($row = mysql_fetch_array($result)) {
    $rowclass = ($rowclass == "row1"?"row2":"row1");
    echo "<tr class=\"$rowclass\">\n<td>\n";
    $topicid=($row['topic_id']==0?$row['id']:$row['topic_id']);
    echo "<p class=\"searchSubject\">\n<a href=\"viewtopic.php?t=" .
         $topicid . "#post" . $row['id'] . "\">" .
         $row['subject'] . "</a>\n";
    echo "</p>\n";
    echo "<p class=\"searchBody\">\n";
    echo htmlspecialchars(trimBody($row['body']));
    if ($access_lvl > 2) {
         echo "<p>SQL: $sql</p>";
         echo "<br><br>relevance: " . $row['score'];
    }
    echo "\n</p>\n";
    echo "</td>\n</tr>\n\n";
  }
}
echo "</table>";

require_once 'footer.php';
?>
```

5. Click the Home item on the main menu. You should now see a screen similar to Figure 16-6. If you did not make any changes to the forums, there will be just one forum called "New Forum." If you did make changes, you should see your forums listed here.

6. Click the first forum on the page.

7. If you are prompted to create a new thread, click "yes." Otherwise, click New Thread.

8. Enter any subject you like, and any text in the body. Somewhere in the body field, include the phrase "It was raining very hard today."

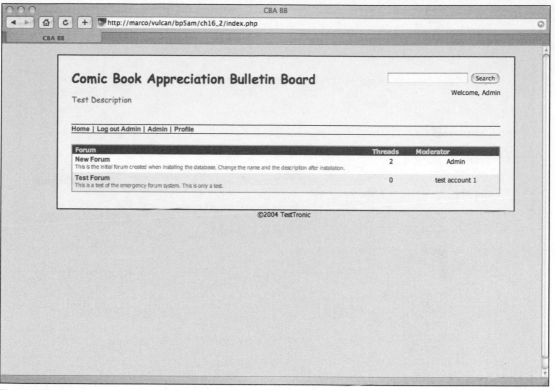

Figure 16-6

9. When you are done, click the Submit New Post button. You should now see your post on the screen (see Figure 16-7). Note that although you typed in "very hard" in your post, it now reads "cats and dogs." That is the BBcode tool at work. We'll look at that in more detail in the "How It Works" section that follows.

10. Click Reply to Thread and repeat steps 8 and 9 to create at least three more posts. After creating the last post, note that the Next/Prev buttons become available at the bottom of the thread. Because you changed your Pagination Limit to 3 in the steps, you can see only three posts on this page. You can see that you can click the number 2, or click "Next" and it will take you to the next (up to 3) posts.

11. Let's look at one more function, Search. Up at the top of the screen, you should see a text box with a button labeled "Search." Enter the word "raining" and click the Search button.

12. If you followed step 8 in the previous series of steps, you should see at least one document returned in the search results. If you are still logged in as the administrator, you should also see the SQL statement that was used to find that document, and a score value. We explain that later in "How It Works."

That's just about it for the Bulletin Board application. It's not overly complex, but it does have a few useful features. When you are done with this chapter (and the book), you should be armed with enough knowledge to add your own ideas to this and the other applications.

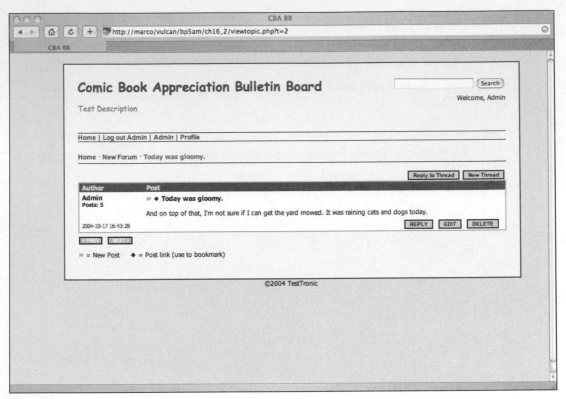

Figure 16-7

How It Works

By now, most of the code in this section should be easy for you to understand. The steps involved in creating a post, editing a post, replying to a post, and displaying a forum or post have been covered in similar applications in the previous chapters. The basics of that process being, collect information from the user, store it in a database, and display the information based on user request. Since we've covered this kind of behavior before, let's talk about something a little more powerful, searching.

Searching

A bulletin board would not be worth much in the long run unless you had the ability to search for old posts. Visit any bulletin board you might be familiar with, and most likely you will find a search function there.

There are many types of searches. The simplest requires that you enter text into an input field, and when you click the Search button, it looks for any of the text you entered. That is the search we created for this application.

Searches can get very complicated, too. You might want to search posts by the date they were entered, or by author. You might want to find a range of dates. You might even want to be able to designate how the result page is sorted. These capabilities are not currently available in the CBA Forums, but if you feel ambitious enough, feel free to beef up your search.

The actual search mechanism is fairly simple, and we quickly introduced it in Chapter 13. You have a single text field with a Search button that submits your form. The search.php page captures the search term, and builds a relatively simple SQL statement that is designed to return matching rows. You then simply iterate through those rows and display the data on the screen. It's not that much different than displaying a forum or thread on the page. The only real difference is the SQL statement.

```
if (isset($_GET['keywords'])) {
  $sql = "SELECT *, MATCH (subject,body) " .
         "AGAINST ('" . $_GET['keywords'] . "') AS score " .
         "FROM forum_posts " .
         "WHERE MATCH (subject,body) " .
         "AGAINST ('" . $_GET['keywords'] . "') " .
         "ORDER BY score DESC";

  $result = mysql_query($sql,$conn)
    or die('Could not perform search; ' . mysql_error());
}
```

The bulk of the work of a search happens in the database. It stands to reason, then, that the more efficient and well-built your database is, the faster your data will be retrieved. To maximize the efficiency, you create an index for the fields to be searched. In this case, you index the subject and body columns of your forum_posts table. You can see how this works in the CREATE TABLE command in setup.php:

```
CREATE TABLE  forum_posts (
  id int(11) NOT NULL auto_increment,
  topic_id int(11) NOT NULL default '0',
  forum_id int(11) NOT NULL default '0',
  author_id int(11) NOT NULL default '0',
  update_id int(11) NOT NULL default '0',
  date_posted datetime NOT NULL default '0000-00-00 00:00:00',
  date_updated datetime NOT NULL default '0000-00-00 00:00:00',
  subject varchar(255) NOT NULL default '',
  body mediumtext NOT NULL,
  PRIMARY KEY  (id),
  KEY IdxArticle (forum_id,topic_id,author_id,date_posted),
  FULLTEXT KEY IdxText (subject,body)
)
```

Note that after creating each of the columns, you set the Primary Key, a Key, and a Fulltext Key. Primary Keys were discussed in Chapter 10. These help you create and track unique records. The KEY is another term for INDEX. As you can see, you have created in index for forum_id, topic_id, author_id, and date_posted. An index makes searching for rows *much* faster.

For more information on keys (indexes), visit http://dev.mysql.com/doc/mysql/en/ MySQL_indexes.html.

As you can see from the last line of the SQL query, you create a Fulltext index with the subject and body columns. This allows you to quickly find the records you are searching for.

Let's take a look at the SQL statement that does the actual search. Assume you are looking for the word "Board."

```
SELECT *, MATCH (subject,body) AGAINST ('Board') AS score
FROM forum_posts
WHERE MATCH (subject,body) AGAINST ('Board')
ORDER BY score DESC
```

To understand how this returns records, you must understand the MATCH command. MATCH returns a score value that rates how relevant the match was for each and every row in the table. According to the MySQL manual, it is based on the "number of words in the row, the number of unique words in that row, the total number of words in the collection, and the number of documents (rows) that contain a particular word."

Note that the same MATCH command is used twice. Fortunately, the MySQL optimizer caches the results of the MATCH command the first time it is run and will not run it twice. Because the MATCH command returns a zero (0) for rows that do not match at all, putting MATCH in the WHERE clause prevents those rows from returning. If you do not put in the WHERE clause, all rows in the table will be returned, and they will not be sorted.

Using MATCH in the WHERE clause causes the rows to be returned sorted by relevance. This is not intuitive to all users, however, so we like to put in ORDER BY score DESC just for good measure, although it is not required.

For more information on Fulltext indexes, visit `http://dev.mysql.com/doc/mysql/en/ Fulltext_Search.html`.

Afterthoughts

Congratulations! You have just completed the creation of a fully functioning Bulletin Board System. It is more powerful than some of the simpler ones you'll find, but it is certainly not the most complex. You could still do many things to this application that could really make it sing, if you were so inclined.

What else could you add to this application? Perhaps you have a few ideas already, based on what you have seen on other forums. If you need some ideas, here is a short list to get you started:

❑ **Avatars:** Allow your users to upload (or choose from your site) a small image that can be placed under his or her username.

❑ **Smilies:** Most forums will replace smilies with a graphical representation of some sort. Create some smilies yourself (or find good ones on the Internet that are not copyrighted), store them in an images folder on your Web site, and use regular expressions to replace smilies with the appropriate images.

❑ **User profiles:** Allow users to add more information to their profiles, such as hobbies, location, age, sex, and so on. Also allow them to add their AIM, Yahoo! IM, and MSN IDs. Make their usernames into a link that allows other users to contact them via e-mail or Instant Messenger. Make sure you include a checkbox to allow users to hide their e-mail address, if they want to.

❑ **Quoting:** What is a forum without the ability to quote relevant text? Allow users to quote all or part of a post. We leave it up to you to figure out how to implement it.

❑ **Polls:** A very popular option, polls allow users to post a short questionnaire for their peers to answer. Install a poll option when posting a new topic, and display a graph of the results at the top of the thread.

Summary

Now you have created a community where your visitors can hang their hats and stay a while. Combined with all of the other applications you have built, you should no doubt have a very cool, integrated Web site up and running in no time! Congratulations on making it this far. This chapter was long, with a lot of code. Most of it was not overly difficult; indeed, most of the code was stuff you did in other chapters. But we hope that by the time you have read this whole chapter, you will feel comfortable creating a Web site from the ground up, using PHP and MySQL installed on an Apache server.

Exercises

If you would like to test out how much you have learned from this chapter, take the time to do these little exercises. Not only will they help you learn; they will allow you to add some extra features to your bulletin board application.

1. Add code to `admin.php` to prevent unauthorized users from loading the page. Redirect them back to `index.php`.

2. Create a regular expression that recognizes an e-mail address in a post and turns it into a link.

3. Add a bit of code to the pagination function to allow the user to go to the first page or last page. For example, if there are 14 pages, and the user is on page 8, and the range is 7, it should look something like this:

```
<PREV [1] .. [5] [6] [7] 8 [9] [10] [11] .. [14] NEXT >
```

Using Log Files to Improve Your Site

The cool thing about being a Web developer is that sometimes you get to act like Big Brother and keep close tabs on what your visitors are doing. Although it may seem voyeuristic to some, analyzing what goes on at your site can give you valuable information that will enable you to make your site better. To perform this analysis, you have to gather data first, and to do that, you need a log.

A *log* is a text file saved on your server. This file is updated by a logging application on the server every time something happens, such as when a file is requested by someone or when an error occurs. When something happens, a line of text is added to the end of the file, essentially "logging in" the activity. Here are three types of logs:

❑ Access Logs track every hit.

❑ Error Logs track every error or warning.

❑ Custom Logs track whatever information you tell them to.

Some examples of the types of information you can glean from logs include:

❑ What IP addresses your visitors are using, so you can get a geographical location for your most common visitors; this helps with language and international issues

❑ What browsers your visitors are using, so you can make sure your site is readable by your most common visitors

❑ What times and days your visitors are visiting, so you can schedule maintenance during slow times or special events during busier times

❑ What pages are the most popular on your site, so you can gauge the success or failure of certain pages and remove the dead weight

❑ Whether your traffic is increasing, so you can determine if your site is becoming more well-known or stagnating itself into oblivion

❑ What pages and processes are causing problems, so you can fix them — duh

❑ If you're using user authentication on your site, what users are logging in when and what their activity is, so you can see who your MVPs are and perhaps offer them special Web site features (or maybe a beer at the local bar)

This chapter is all about logs, and it covers the following:

❑ What logs look like and what information they contain

❑ Where you can find them on your system

❑ What resources you can use to help analyze your statistics

❑ How you can use the information to improve your site

Locating Your Logs

Log files are in different locations, depending on what program created them and what their function is. Most are available in a folder outside the scope of your Web site so that users don't have access to them.

Apache

Apache keeps access logs and error logs. If Apache has been installed on your server, the default location is \<apache install directory>\logs.

The typical access log entry looks like this:

```
127.0.0.1 - george [29/Aug/2003:13:55:36 -0500] "GET /index.php?xyz=123 HTTP/1.0"
200 2326 "http://www.yourserver.com/cms/index.php" "Mozilla/4.08 [en] (Win98; I
;Nav)"
```

All of this information is on one line of the log, and is built by Apache according to the LogFormat directive in the mod_log_config module. The typical configuration looks like this:

```
LogFormat "%h %l %u %t \"%r\" %>s %b" common
```

The config string that built the line you saw from the log file used the *combined format*, and looks like this:

```
LogFormat "%h %l %u %t \"%r\" %>s %b \"%{Referer}i\" \"%{User-agent}i\""
    combined
```

Although the LogFormat directive is beyond the scope of this book, we will list each parameter here so that you can understand what each piece of the log is and how it's broken down:

❑ **%h (127.0.0.1):** The address of the client currently accessing your server. This can be an IP address or a hostname (if HostNameLookups is turned on on your server).

❑ **%l (-):** The RFC 1413 identity of the client. This is usually a hyphen (-) to indicate that Apache was not able to obtain the information.

❑ **%u (george):** The username of the client. This is set if the page is using HTTP User Authentication. Otherwise, you see a hyphen (-).

- **%t ([29/Aug/2003:13:55:36 -0500]):** The date and time the client accessed your server.
    - The format for this is as follows: [day/month/year:hour:minute:second zone]
    - day = 2 digits
    - month = 3 letters
    - year = 4 digits
    - hour = 2 digits
    - minute = 2 digits
    - second = 2 digits
    - zone = (`+' | `-') 4 digits

- **\"%r\" ("GET /index.php?xyz=123 HTTP/1.0"):** The request line from the client. This is wrapped in quotes, which have to be escaped. This is actually multiple information, which could be built using other parameters:
    - %m (request method), in this case, GET
    - %U (URI), in this case, /index.php
    - %q (query string), in this case, ?xyz=123
    - %H (protocol), in this case, HTTP/1.0
    - \"%m %U%p %H\" is the functional equivalent of \"%r\"

- **%>s (200):** The status code sent back to the client. In this case, because it starts with a "2," we know it was a successful request.

- **%b (2326):** The size of the object returned to the client in bytes (not including headers). If no content is returned, the value is hyphen (-), or "0" if %B is used.

- **\"%{Referer}i\" ("http://www.yourserver.com/cms/index.php"):** The address of the page the client came from. This is useful for compiling information about where your users heard about your Web site.

- **\"%{User-agent}i\" ("Mozilla/4.08 [en] (Win98; I ;Nav)"):** User-Agent HTTP request header information. This is the information the client's browser sends about itself. This is very useful for determining how many people are using certain browsers, such as Internet Explorer.

If the preceding information looks like Greek to you, don't worry. There are ways of getting the information without understanding any programming, and methods of reading the information to build statistics, charts, graphs, and other things that are much easier to read. We'll share those methods with you shortly.

Here is what the typical error log entry looks like:

```
[Wed Aug 27 14:32:52 2003] [warning] [client 69.129.21.24] File does
    not exist: /home/grebnol/public_html/index.php
```

The information in the error log is pretty self-explanatory. It is free-form and descriptive, but typically most error logs capture the date and time, the error severity, the client IP address, the error message, and the object the client was requesting.

Because the error message is also contained in the Apache access log, it makes more sense to pull the data out of the access log. For example, the preceding error will show up in the access log with access code 404.

PHP

PHP also keeps a log of errors for you, but as we discussed in Chapter 1, the default setting for this feature is set to "off" in your php.ini file. You have to turn it on to enable error logging, which we highly recommend. Also, don't forget to tell your php.ini file where you want the error log to be saved.

The typical error log entry looks like this:

```
[01-Sep-2003 18:42:03] PHP Parse error:  parse error, unexpected '}' in
C:\Program Files\Apache Group\Apache2\test\deleteme.php on line 14
```

As in the other logs we have looked at, the logs themselves are relatively straightforward, and their purpose is to keep track of all of the errors that occurred when your PHP pages were being accessed.

In the preceding example, you can see that there was a parse error in the file deleteme.php on line 14, which merits attention. Anyone attempting to see the contents of this file will see only the parse error until it is fixed.

A regular check of the PHP error log should be on your "to-do" list, just to make sure there aren't any errors in your code.

MySQL

As if that's not enough, MySQL also logs queries and errors that pertain to database transactions. By default, the error log is stored as hostname.err in the data directory (in Windows and UNIX both). You can specify where the error log is saved by issuing the following command from the command prompt when starting the MySQL server:

```
mysqld --log-error[=filename].
```

Here is a typical entry in the error log:

```
030812  0:28:02  InnoDB: Started
MySql: ready for connections.
Version: '4.0.20-max-debug'  socket: ''  port: 3306
```

This lets you know that the MySQL server started successfully, what version is currently running, and what socket and port it is configured for. It also gives you the date and time that the server began running (in the first line). You should know that on Windows, you cannot access this log while the server is running; you need to stop the server to open this file.

MySQL also allows you to view every query that is sent to the server. To specify where the general query log is located, you would type the following command when starting the MySQL server;

```
mysqld --log[=file]
```

Again, by default, this file will be stored in the "data" directory with the name *hostname*.log file, unless you specify otherwise. An entry in the general query log looks like this:

```
 /usr/local/mysql/libexec/mysqld, Version: 4.0.16-log, started with:
Tcp port: 3306  Unix socket: /tmp/mysql.sock
Time                Id Command      Argument
031109 21:33:34      1 Connect      buzzly_comic@localhost on
                     1 Init DB      buzzly_comicsite
                     1 Query        SELECT * FROM forum_admin
                     1 Query        SELECT * FROM forum_bbcode
                     1 Quit
031109 21:33:50      2 Connect      buzzly_comic@localhost on
                     2 Init DB      buzzly_comicsite
                     2 Query        SELECT id,access_lvl,name,last_login FROM
forum_users
WHERE email='admin@yoursite.com' AND passwd='admin'
                     2 Query        UPDATE forum_users SET last_login = '2003-11-09
21:33:50'
WHERE id = 1
                     2 Quit
                     3 Connect      buzzly_comic@localhost on
                     3 Init DB      buzzly_comicsite
                     3 Query        SELECT * FROM forum_admin
                     3 Query        SELECT * FROM forum_bbcode
```

If you are interested in seeing only the queries that changed data, you should view the binary log file instead of the general query file.

This file is also saved by default in your "data" directory, with the filename of *hostname*-bin unless you specify otherwise. You activate this log by typing the following at the command prompt:

```
mysqld --log-bin[=file_name]
```

An entry in the binary log looks like this:

```
# at 4
#031109 21:29:46 server id 1  log pos 4        Start: binlog v 3, server v 4.0.16-
log created 031109 21:29:46 at startup
# at 79
#031109 21:33:50 server id 1  log_pos 79 Query        thread_id=2  exec_time=0
error_code=0
use buzzly_comicsite;
SET TIMESTAMP=1068431630;
UPDATE forum_users SET last_login = '2003-11-09 21:33:50' WHERE id = 1;
# at 196
#031109 21:34:52 server id 1  log_pos 196        Query        thread_id=8
exec_time=0
error_code=0
SET TIMESTAMP=1068431692;
UPDATE forum_users SET email='admin@yoursite.com', name='Admin', access_lvl=3,
signature='Testing, testing, 123.'  WHERE id=1;
```

Unlike the other logs in this chapter that you can access with WordPad or Notepad, you must access the binary log using the `mysqlbinlog` utility. At the command prompt, you would type **mysqlbinlog** to see the parameters for this software. Your screen will look something like the one shown in Figure 17-1.

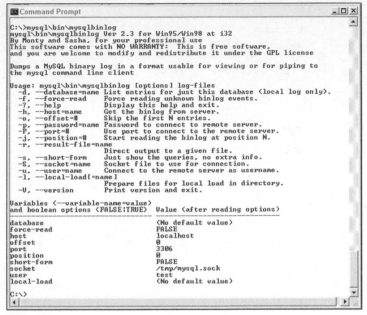

Figure 17-1

As you can see, there are many parameters you can set to glean the specific information you are looking for.

Analyzing Your Log Data

Numerous software programs are available that live to help you take this gobbledygook and make sense out of it. Although you could write your own log analysis application, there's no real reason to when there are so many alternatives available. We'll describe some of them in this section. Note that most of these programs are used for analyzing Web server activity, and not MySQL or PHP logs.

Webalizer

You can find Webalizer at www.webalizer.com and it is a proud part of the wonderful open source community we talked about in Chapter 1. It provides reports in an easy-to-read HTML format with pretty charts and such that can be read by just about anyone, including the higher-ups. Its main purpose is to produce reports on server activity, most specifically Apache. It is meant for use on Unix systems, and thus far isn't compatible with Windows. If you set your Apache config files to do DNS server lookups, then your reports with Webalizer will show those instead of simple IP addresses. This program is also known for its incredible speed, as it can process 10,000 records in a matter of one second.

You can see a sample screenshot in Figure 17-2, also available at the Webalizer Web site.

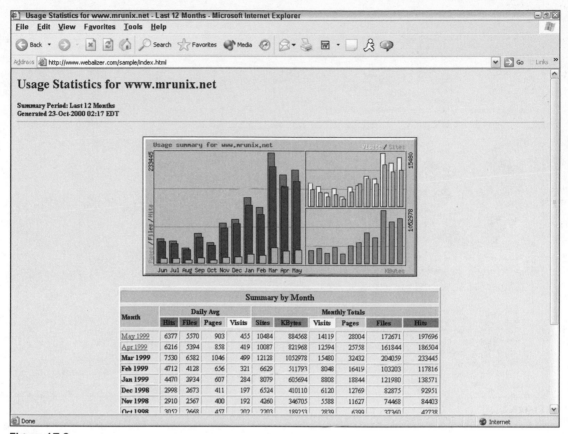

Figure 17-2

Analog

Another open source contender for helping you make sense of your log files is Analog, which you can find at www.analog.cx. Although it's a little rough around the edges, it's still a powerful tool that can be customized to show what you want to see. By using the add-on, Report Magic (available at www.reportmagic.org), you can generate all kinds of fancy 3-D charts and graphs and really impress your superiors (or your dog if you're a one-man or one-woman show).

You can see sample screenshots in Figure 17-3, also available at the Analog Web site.

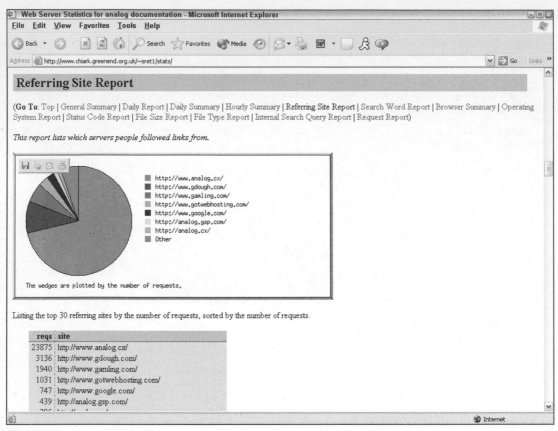

Figure 17-3

WebTrends

If you've got some money to throw around, WebTrends (www.netiq.com) is another good log analyzer program. For a mere $495 (or $35 a month for its "on demand" service) it can pretty much tell you everything you ever wanted to know about your Web site. It works on numerous platforms, including Apache, and you are really given a lot of control over what your output looks like. We recommend this type of software if you have a high-powered server and are supporting a high-powered client who wants fancy stuff like his own logo on his own reports. The customization is really a great feature.

This software also offers a SmartSource data option that allows you to track specific things about your Web site with the use of client-side server tags in your HTML. This bypasses the whole "log" step and sends the info straight to the WebTrends software. It can even perform a DNS lookup at report generation if you forget to enable this option in your config files, or if you want to reduce server activity.

Again, this powerful software is not for the faint of heart and should be reserved for the heavy-duty users.

You can see a 10-minute product demo on the WebTrends Web site.

AWStats

Another of our open source buddies, you can find AWStats at http://awstats.sourceforge.net/. Don't be fooled by its price tag—this free software provides numerous features also offered by the big guys. Unlike some of the other open source stats programs, AWStats can track the number of unique visitors; entry and exit pages; search engines and keywords used to find the site; and browser details of each visitor, such as version and screen size.

AWStats also allows the Web administrator to set up customized reports for tracking something of specific interest for his or her specific needs, which is a welcome addition to this software package.

You can see a sample screenshot in Figure 17-4, also available at the AWStats Web site.

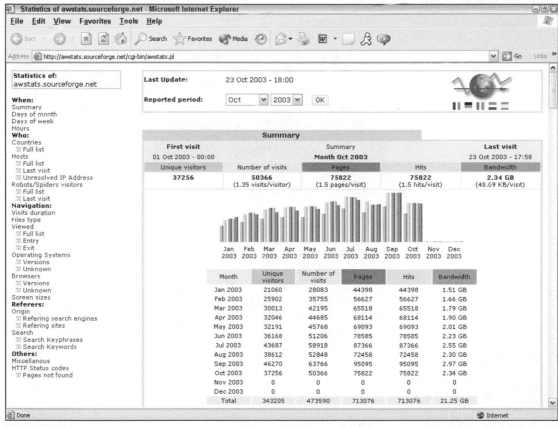

Figure 17-4

HTTP Analyze

One more stats program for you to investigate is HTTP Analyze, which you can find at www.http-analyze.org. Another open source favorite, this program works on any log file that is in the NCSA Common Logfile Format or W3C Extended File Format, and thus works great with Apache. It should be noted that HTTP Analyze is supported by both UNIX and Windows systems. It also provides several different options for viewing data, all in HTML and easy-to-read formats.

You can see a sample screenshot in Figure 17-5, also available at the HTTP Analyze Web site.

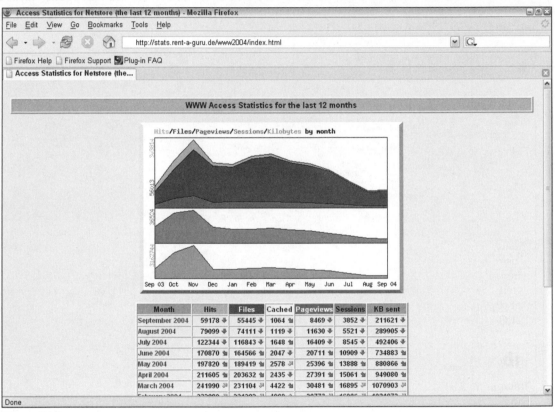

Figure 17-5

Putting the Analysis to Work

So now you have all these beautiful reports, and you go to your boss and proudly display your charts and graphs and expect a big pat on the back. But what happens when he or she says to you, "So?"

Let's talk a minute about what the reports mean to you, so you have a nice, neat, witty response.

Earlier in the chapter, we touched on how using the stats can help you improve your site. Your logs are, in many cases, your only source of feedback from your visitors. You can't know what you're doing right or wrong without any feedback, so as your only tangible evidence, these stats are really quite valuable. There are several different areas you probably want to pay attention to, depending on the specific needs of your site.

Site Health

Your error logs and Apache server logs (specifically the 404 errors) can be crucial in ensuring that your site is completely functional and has no broken links. This can be especially true if you have a large site with a lot of intertwined links and pages; it would be virtually impossible for you to manually test each link on each page of your site. Broken links can be frustrating for the user, and if it is a link to a crucial portion of your site, can have adverse affects on your site performance.

User Preferences and Information

You can't please all of the people all of the time, but you can certainly try. You care about what your users like, so you obviously want to tailor your site to the most common visitor and try to minimize the number of visitors who won't have the optimal viewing experience. You want to know what percentage of visitors are using which browsers so you can be sure to test your site against the most popular browsers of your audience. You also care about how many unique and not-so-unique visitors are coming to your site so you can tell if your site is gaining a new following, while maintaining its current one. You also want to know what screen size they are using, so you can again tailor the look of your site to be the best it can be for the most visitors.

Number of Hits and Page Views

Remember, a "hit" is any request made to the server, whereas a "page view" is a request for a page (such as an HTML page). Hits can consist of images, sound files, or anything that requires activity from the server. This number doesn't really give you an accurate count of how many people are viewing a page, so you typically go by page views.

You want to see which pages get the most page views, and which are the most popular so that if you need to make something known about your site, you can make sure it appears on those pages. For example, say you have a new product to promote—if no one ever visits the "new products" page, it won't do you much good to only post it there. If the home page of your site is the most popular, you want to also post that information on that page, so you make sure that everybody who visits your site knows about your new product.

You also want to be able to look at the pages that are doing well and compare them with the pages that aren't doing so well. Is the content of both pages clear and concise? What is it about the popular pages that makes them so great? Can you make your losers closer to the winners in page design, content, or positioning?

Trends over Time

It's rewarding to see your site become more popular as time goes on, but it creates a big pit in your stomach if things are going downhill. Tracking popularity over time can help you discern if interest in your site is waning, or if it is perhaps more popular around certain seasons of the year. If your site sells golf equipment and you notice a dip in page views during the winter months, obviously you don't have much to worry about, because your business is a seasonal business and this dip is understandable. Perhaps you notice that during the winter months your average visitor is coming from Florida (makes sense, eh?). Perhaps you can work with Marketing to develop an advertising strategy tailored to the loyal Floridians during those months. (Yes, we said "Work with Marketing." It happens, get over it!)

Referring Sites

If you can discern where people are finding your site, you will have a very valuable resource at your disposal. Are the search engines actually working in your favor? What keywords are people using to reach your site? Do you fare better with certain search engines than others? Are you getting referred from other, non-directory sites?

Perhaps you have a site that sells bowling equipment, and you notice through your stats that the Professional Bowlers Association has your site listed on its own site as a resource for its visitors, and has referred the majority of your visitors. Perhaps then you decide you want to offer a special discount to PBA members as a "thank you." Increasing your Web site traffic can be as simple as getting yourself listed on as many other sites as possible. Not only will it help people see you, but it will help increase your listing in search engines such as Google that take into account criteria such as how many other places your Web site is listed.

Summary

You should now feel comfortable looking at log files to benefit your site and your skills as a professional Web designer. You can choose to massage the data based on a program you have written yourself, or you may choose to utilize numerous other resources out there to provide you with fancy reports that let you know what is going on with your site. By paying attention to trends and popular pages in your site, you can get a better feel for who your visitor really is. This, in turn, enables you to continually improve your site.

At the very least, you will be able to speak intelligently to your boss when he or she asks "So what's going on with our Web site?"

Troubleshooting

Nothing is more frustrating than thinking you have all your "t's" crossed and your "i's" dotted, only to have your program blow up on you with a string of errors. Worse yet is having your program produce completely perplexing and unwanted results.

You may find comfort in knowing that many developers experience the same types of obstacles. With this chapter, we hope to shed light on some potential problems you may encounter and suggest a few troubleshooting strategies.

Installation Troubleshooting

You're trying to access either PHP, MySQL, or Apache and you are running into problems. Perhaps for some reason they are not playing well with others and you are getting errors, or things aren't working the way they should be based on the installation instructions.

Many times, commonly seen errors or obstacles will be discussed on the source Web sites for each of the components. The source Web sites also provide detailed instructions for the particular system you are using, and we encourage you to read through them carefully to double-check yourself. Make sure you follow the instructions to the "t."

If while configuring PHP you receive an error that tells you that the server can't find a specific library, you can do one of two things:

❑   Check to make sure you've actually installed the library on your machine.

❑   Verify that the correct path has been specified in your configure command.

Parse Errors

You've seen it many times:

```
Parse error: parse error, expecting `','' or `';'' in
/foo/public_html/forum/index.php on line 25
```

Oh, the dreaded parse error! These are quite common, even with experienced programmers. Even with the best color-coded PHP text editors that check your syntax for you, one or two parse errors undoubtedly slip through. These can be very frustrating, but they are usually the simplest to fix, because they usually occur because of mistakes in your syntax, as opposed to your logic.

Cleanup on Line 26 . . . Oops, I Mean 94

When PHP displays a parse error, it includes a line number, which provides your first clue for solving the mystery. However, don't be fooled! Sometimes the line number can be misleading; in fact, at times the mistake will have occurred several lines up from the one identified by the server as the culprit.

Take a missing semicolon, for example. Without the semicolon to signify to the server that the line has come to an end, the server will continue to string subsequent lines together. It may not realize there is a problem until several lines later, and it will issue a parse error on the wrong line. Likewise with a missing quotation mark or parenthesis. For example, let's look at the following lines of code (we have added line numbers in to prove our point):

```
1 <?php
2 $greeting1="aloha";
3 $greeting2="bon jour";
4 $greeting3="hola"
5 $greeting4="good morning";
6 ?>
```

The error you get if you run this code as-is, is as follows:

Parse error: parse error, unexpected T_VARIABLE in **C:\Program Files\Apache Group\ Apache2\htdocs\error.php** on line 5

For our purposes here, we named the above script error.php and you can see that line 5 is referenced when line 4 was actually the line with the error in it. Because we neglected to use a semicolon at the end of the line, line 5 was seen as a continuation of line 4 and the server was quite confused.

Elementary, My Dear Watson!

Sometimes the simplest answer is the right answer. Make sure you check to see that you've done all of the following:

❑ Each line ends with a semicolon.

❑ All quotes and parentheses are closed.

❑ All of your functions and control statements (if, which, and so on) end with a curly brace (}).

❑ All single and double quotes are nested properly.

If you get into the habit of checking your syntax regularly as you write your code, you will greatly decrease the risk of introducing parse errors. You may want to use an editor that is familiar with PHP and can color-code your programs. This makes it much easier to recognize when you have misspelled a function or forgotten to close your quotes. We use two programs:

❑ **UltraEdit (www.ultraedit.com):** This one is very customizable and easy to use. There is a small fee to register, but it's well worth it.

❑ **PHPEdit (www.phpedit.com):** This program is extremely powerful and free. It includes a context-sensitive manual for PHP, MySQL, and HTML. The program also has dynamic color coding, depending on whether you are currently typing in HTML or PHP. We have been using this one for a while now, and we are very impressed with it.

Empty Variables

You just built a large page that collects 50 fields of information from your users. There are no parse errors. You fill in the form online and click the submit button. The next page loads, just as it should. The only problem is that none of the variables seem to have been passed on to the new form!

This actually happens quite often. The first possible cause is that you are expecting your values to be posted, but you forgot to use `method="post"` on your form. By default, forms use the `get` method.

How do you solve this? Check the address of your second page. Are there variables in the query string? If so, then you've inadvertently used the GET method, and you need to go back and change your method to POST. Mystery solved. If there are no variables in the query string, then you need to check something else, such as your `register_globals` settings.

The Ultimate Bait-and-Switch

Another very common problem, addressed ad nauseam in this book, is a setting in your `php.ini` file called `register_globals`. If you have recently upgraded your server, or migrated your code to a different server, this just may be the reason you no longer have access to your variables.

As of PHP version 4.2.0, the PHP directive `register_globals` changed from a default value of "on" to a default value of "off." This was a controversial decision, and the cause of a lot of heartache with developers who wrote their programs on the assumption that it would always default to "on." When `register_globals` is set to "off," you must access your posted variables through the `$_POST` array.

For example, prior to 4.2.0, if you had `register_globals` set to the default of "on," you could post a form field called `first_name`, and the variable on the subsequent page could immediately be accessed as `$first_name`. It was determined that this could be a big security risk, so it was changed in PHP 4.2.0. Now, if you kept `register_globals` set to the default of "off," you'd have to access your posted form field `first_name` through the `$_POST` array, as `$_POST['first_name']`.

You can do a couple of things to fix this problem. The most obvious, of course, is to set the `register_globals` setting to "on" in your `php.ini` file. However, because of the recognized security risk, this is no longer the recommended course of action. For a more detailed discussion of this, visit the following URL:

```
www.php.net/register_globals
```

A better solution is to always access your variables via the $_POST array. If you want, you can always set your variables:

```
$first_name = $_POST['first_name'];
```

If you have a large number of $_POST variables, use this loop to convert them all to the more familiar format:

```
foreach($_POST as $key => $value) {
    $$key = $value;
}
```

If $_POST['first_name'] is set to George, the preceding code will set $key to first_name and $value to George. Then, it sets $first_name = George. It will loop through every posted field, setting each variable. This is a good temporary fix to make your pages work, but we strongly recommend that, from this point forward, you always assume that register_globals is off, and you will never run into this particular problem again.

Consistent and Valid Variable Names

First you should make sure that your variable names are appropriate and valid according to the naming rules, as outlined in Chapter 2. Make sure you aren't beginning any variable name with a number, or trying to use a predefined variable for your variable name such as $php_errormsg. You can find a complete list in the PHP manual, at http://us2.php.net/manual/en/reserved.variables.php.

Also, check the case you are using when referencing variables, because variable names are case-sensitive. The same holds true for database and table names. Make sure you are referencing them consistently, and if you make a change to a variable name after the fact, be sure to change all the instances of the variable name.

It is easier to maintain consistent variable names if you pick a naming convention and stick with it throughout your scripts. For example, if you always name your variables with a prefix of $var_, you can easily spot them in the code. This convention ties into the discussion in Chapter 2 regarding good coding practices.

Open a New Browser

Sometimes if you are working with sessions, and you are in the testing phase of your scripts, there may be an extraneous session setting hanging out there that could be preventing you from obtaining the desired results, and altering your variable values.

You can clear all session variables (provided you haven't changed your config files as we discussed in Chapter 2) by simply closing the browser and opening a new one, instead of just hitting Refresh or Reload.

"Headers Already Sent" Error

You may encounter an error message that looks like this:

Warning: Cannot modify header information - headers already sent by (output started at C:\Program Files\Apache Group\Apache2\test\headererror.php:1) in **C:\Program Files\Apache Group\Apache2\test\headererror.php** on line **2**

This is a common error when working with sessions and cookies. It can occur if you try to set them after you have sent HTML code to the server. The server has to deal with sessions and cookies before any HTML output is sent to the browser, which means that these lines must be the first in the code before any HTML code or echo statement. If you have even a trailing leading space before your first <?php line of code, you will see this error.

If you need to set cookie or session variables within the body of your code, you need to rethink your logic to accommodate this limitation. As we discussed in Chapter 2, those variables need to be addressed at the beginning of your code for them to be parsed correctly by the PHP server.

Ways exist to get around this error, using the output buffer to suppress these errors. The output buffer is used to store all HTML output in a buffer until you are ready to send it to the browser. The command ob_start is used to begin the output buffering process, and ob_end_flush will send all of the stored HTML output to the browser, empty the buffer, and end the output storing process. This will let you cheat the system and store session and cookie variables in the body of the code, as well as allow you to use the header("location:") function in the body of the code. For example, this snippet of code uses the output buffer to suppress our error. In the following example, the top.php file contains the connection variables to connect to the MySQL database, as well as some HTML code which is common to all the pages in our site.

```php
<?php
ob_start()
include "top.php";
//perform a mysql query to determine which page the user is supposed to see;

if ($userage<18) header("location:child.php");
else header("location:adult.php");
ob_end_flush();
?>
```

Without the use of the ob_start() and ob_end_flush() functions, we would have gotten the "headers already sent" error when we tried to redirect our user. This is because of the HTML code that is in the top.php file. You can see that the logic is flawed somewhat because we should keep our connection variables in a separate file away from the HTML code, but it's not such a fatal design flaw that our Web site shouldn't function. We can thus cheat the system.

Although this is not recommended for beginners, because it is more important for you to learn to code well, and according to the "rules," this can be a useful set of functions for a more experienced programmer. If you would like to learn more about the output buffer functions, you can find a complete list of them in Appendix C, or visit www.php.net.

General Debugging Tips

Following are a few tips for general debugging purposes that can help you out of many sticky spots.

Using echo

Occasionally, you might want to read the server's mind and see what it thinks is going on. One way to do this is to echo out variable names periodically in your code. This will let you verify that the server is parsing everything correctly.

You can use echo in a step-by-step process as you follow the path of your variable, to see how the server is treating the variable throughout the code. This process would help, for example, if you wanted to perform a complex mathematical equation on a variable, and all you could tell from your output was that you were getting the wrong answer. You want to find out at what point the breakdown occurs, so you insert echo statements throughout each step of the equation to verify the accuracy of your calculation as it runs through the equation. You will then see the value of the variable as it changes.

The echo command can also be useful in if statements, foreach statements, functions, and so on to ensure that these loops are being called or processed correctly.

Here's a very simple example to illustrate how echo can help you. Assume you have the following script:

```php
<?php
$curr_var = 0;

while ($curr_var < 20) {
     $abc = 2 * $curr_var;
     $curr_var ++;
}
echo $abc;
?>
```

By running this code in your browser, you get the number 38. What if you were expecting to get the number 40, or you wanted to check to see if your $abc variable was right? You could echo out the variable as it was processed to see how the program was working, as such:

```php
<?php
$curr_var = 0;

while ($curr_var < 20) {
     $abc = 2 * $curr_var;
     $curr_var ++;

     // debug lines
     echo $curr_var;
     echo "<br>";
}
echo $abc;
?>
```

You now see the numbers 1 through 20, plus your original answer of 38. It is easier for you to see that although the $curr_var goes to 20, it processes the answer only 19 times and so you get the answer of 38. Therefore, you should change the `while` statement as such:

```
while ($curr_var <= 20) {
```

Now your `while` statement will process when $curr_var = 20, and you get a result of 40 at the end. (Okay, so you probably figured that out without the `echo` statement — work with us here.) Use the comments as a reminder to yourself to delete the debugging lines when you have solved the problem, to avoid unwanted output to your browser when your page goes live.

Remember that arrays, although variables, behave a little differently. If you echo an array, all you will see on the screen is `Array()`. To view the contents of an array, instead of using `echo`, use `print_r($array)`. Even with a multidimensional array, every value in the array will be echoed to the screen.

Divide and Conquer

Another good way to tackle a huge problem is to break it down into baby steps and test each one to make sure you are getting the correct result every step of the way. One small mistake in the beginning of a complex block of statements can have a snowball effect and completely alter your results at the end. By checking each step one by one, you can iron out those small bugs and can eventually get the intended results.

Test, Test, Test!

Many coders test their program out on their own system, and as long as it works for them with their settings, they assume they are home free. To be completely thorough, you should test your code using every different environment available to you: different browsers, different preferences, different computer systems, and so on. If you have the opportunity and know-how, you should even try to hack through your own system to look for holes that might be exploited by someone a little less kind than you.

Where to Go for Help

Fortunately, the PHP, Apache, and MySQL communities are growing. Numerous sources are available online to help guide you through the murky waters should the going get tough. We have mentioned these numerous times in this book, but here they are again, one more time.

www.wrox.com

This book is specifically designed to provide help online in a companion Web site, so if you encounter trouble, we strongly encourage you to check out the book's sister site at www.wrox.com.

PHPBuilder.com

Many PHP help Web sites are out there, but our personal favorite tends to be PHPBuilder.com. You can find numerous articles, archives, snippets of useful code, and, most importantly, a well-developed and very helpful online community of fellow coders from all over the world with all levels of competency to assist you as quickly as they can. We have yet to find such a tight-knit and friendly community elsewhere, and we encourage you to post your questions in their forums.

If you are lucky, you might find one of the authors of this book lurking around at PHPBuilder.com. We are all regular contributors, and some of us are moderators. (Hint: check the Echo Lounge.)

Source Web Sites

You will see this time and time again, but like the other advice, we can't stress it enough. If you have a question about virtually anything, chances are the answer can be found at a source Web site. Each of these Web sites provides a very comprehensive manual that encompasses basically all known knowledge about the software at hand.

To refresh your memory, here they are:

❑ **PHP:** www.php.net (Useful hint: If you are looking for help with a function, such as echo, you can simply type **www.php.net/echo** in your browser and it takes you directly to the echo page. How nifty is that?)

PHP also provides the manual in a Microsoft Windows Help format (CHM), which is very useful for Windows users. You can download the manual from the php.net Web site and install it on your local machine.

❑ **Apache:** httpd.apache.org

❑ **MySQL:** www.mysql.com

Search and Rescue

If you're experiencing problems with a script, chances are you aren't the first to experience the same obstacles. Use your favorite search engine (such as Google.com) to scour the Internet for articles, discussion forum posts, tutorials, or anything that discusses the problems you're having. This can be a very quick and easy way to keep from reinventing the wheel.

IRC Channels

You may require immediate assistance with your dilemma or question, and the IRC resource may be your solution. Many PHP IRC channels are out there: irc://quakenet.org/php and irc://quakenet.org/phphelp are good ones.

Summary

We hope we have helped you trudge through the slush and muck of debugging and working out the errors in your programs. Although you may not have found your "holy grail," we hope you will at least know where to search for it.

Answers to Exercises

This appendix supplies answers to the exercises we gave you at the end of many of the chapters. Keep in mind, as is always the case in programming, there is more than one way to skin a cat, and these are just our recommendations. If you were able to accomplish the given task in another way, then pat yourself on the back and take yourself to a movie because you're on your way!

Chapter 2

1. Go back to your date.php file and instead of displaying only the number of days in the current month, add a few lines that say:

The month is _____.

There are ____ days in this month.

There are _____ months left in the current year.

A. Your date.php file should look like something like this:

```
<html>
<head>
<title>How many days in this month?</title>
</head>
<body>
<?php

$monthname = date("F");
echo "The month is: " ;
echo $monthname;
echo "<br>";

echo "There are ";
$month=date("n");
if ($month==1) echo "31";
if ($month==2) echo "28 (unless it's a leap year)";
if ($month==3) echo "31";
```

```
if ($month==4) echo "30";
if ($month==5) echo "31";
if ($month==6) echo "30";
if ($month==7) echo "31";
if ($month==8) echo "31";
if ($month==9) echo "30";
if ($month==10) echo "31";
if ($month==11) echo "30";
if ($month==12) echo "31";
echo " days in this month.";

echo "<br>";

$monthsleft = 12-$month;

echo "There are ";
echo $monthsleft;
echo " months left in the year.";

?>
</body>
</html>
```

2. On your movie Web site, write a file that displays the following line at the bottom center of every page of your site, with a link to your e-mail address. Set your font size to 1.

This site developed by: <u>ENTER YOUR NAME HERE</u>.

A. The files of your movie site should all include these lines near the bottom of the script:

```
<?php
include "footer.php";
?>
```

Then you need to create the file footer.php, which consists of these lines:

```
<div align="center">
<font size="1">This site developed by <a href="mailto:johndoe@nothing.com">John
Doe</a></font>
</div>
```

3. Write a program that displays a different message based on the time of day. For example, if it is in the morning, have the site display "Good Morning!"

A. Your header.php page should include lines that resemble something like this:

```
<br>
<font size="2">
<?php
if ((date("G") >=5) AND (date("G") <= 11 )) echo "Good Morning!";
if ((date("G") >=12) AND (date("G") <=18)) echo "Good Afternoon!";
if ((date("G") >= 19) AND (date("G") <= 4)) echo "Good Evening!";
?>
</font>
```

4. Write a program that formats a block of text (to be input by the user) based on preferences chosen by the user. Give your user options for color of text, font choice, and size. Display the output on a new page.

A. This would be most easily accomplished by CSS, but that is really beyond the scope of this book. Generally, you would include a form for your users, possibly on the login page, such as this:

```
<p>Enter your font choice:
<select name="font">
<option value="Verdana">Verdana</option>
<option value="Arial">Arial</option>
<option value="Times New Roman">Times New Roman</option>
</select>
</p>
<p>Enter your font size:
<select name="size">
<option value="1">1</option>
<option value="2">2</option>
<option value="3">3</option>
<option value="4">4</option>
</select>
</p>
<select name="menu">
<option value="black">Black</option>
<option value="red">Red</option>
<option value="green">Green</option>
<option value="purple">Purple</option>
</select>
</p>
```

If you didn't want to use CSS, you could store the variables with your session variables. You would add something like this to your `movie1.php` script, or whatever script is processing your font information:

```
$_SESSION['font']=$_POST['font'];
$_SESSION['size']=$_POST['size'];
$_SESSION['color']=$_POST['color'];
```

Then, every time you had text, you would echo in your session variable's value, like this:

```
echo "<font face='";
echo $_SESSION['font'];
echo "' size='";
echo $_SESSION['size'];
echo "' color='";
echo $_SESSION['color'];
echo "'>";
```

As you can see, this would be quite tedious to type everywhere you had text, so perhaps you would be better off putting this information in an include file, or using CSS.

5. In the program you created in step 4, allow your users the option of saving the information for the next time they visit, and if they choose "yes," save the information in a cookie.

A. You would add a line like this to the end of your font preference form, wherever you've stored it:

```
Do you want to save these preferences for the next time you log in?
<input type="checkbox" name="pref" value="y">
```

Then at the very beginning of your movie1.php script (or again, wherever your script is that is processing the form variables) you would add a statement that looks something like this:

```
if ($_POST['pref']=='y') {
    setcookie('font', '$_POST['font'], time()+60);
    setcookie('size', '$_POST['size'], time()+60);
    setcookie('color', '$_POST['color'], time ()+60);
}
```

Then instead of accessing those variables through the session, you would access them through the cookie like this:

```
echo $_COOKIE['font'];
```

6. Using functions, write a program that keeps track of how many times a visitor has loaded the page.

A. Alter the following lines in your moviesite.php file:

```
//list the movies
    echo "<table>";


    $numlist = 1;
    while ($numlist <= $_POST["num"]) {
        echo "<tr>";
        echo "<td>";
        echo pos($favmovies);
        echo "</td>";
        next($favmovies);
        $numlist = $numlist + 1;
        echo "</tr>";
        }

    echo "</table>";
```

Chapter 3

1. Create a PHP program that prints the lead actor and director for each movie in the database.

A. Your program should look something like this:

```
<?php
//connect to MySQL
$connect = mysql_connect("localhost", "root", "mysqlpass") or
    die ("Hey loser, check your server connection.");
```

```php
//make sure we're using the right database
mysql_select_db ("wiley");

//create function to get lead actor
function get_leadactor($lead_actor) {
global $actorname;
    $query2="SELECT people_fullname
        FROM people
        where people.people_id = $lead_actor";
        $results=mysql_query($query2)
            or die(mysql_error());
        $rows=mysql_fetch_array($results);
        extract ($rows);
        $actorname=$people_fullname;
}

//create a function to get director
function get_director($director) {
global $directorname;
    $query2="SELECT people_fullname
        FROM people
        where people.people_id = '$director'";
        $results=mysql_query($query2)
            or die(mysql_error());
        $rows=mysql_fetch_array($results);
        extract($rows);
        $directorname = $people_fullname;
}

//add a header row
echo "<table border='1'>\n";
echo "<tr>\n";
echo "<td><strong>Movie Name</strong></td>";
echo "<td><strong>Lead Actor</strong></td>";
echo "<td><strong>Director</strong></td>";
echo "</tr>";

//get the movies
$query="SELECT * FROM movie";
$results=mysql_query($query)
    or die(mysql_error());

while ($rows=mysql_fetch_assoc($results)) {
extract ($rows);

//call our functions to get specific info
get_leadactor($movie_leadactor);
get_director($movie_director);

//build the table
echo "<tr>\n";
    echo "<td>\n";
    echo $movie_name;
    echo "</td>\n";
    echo "<td>";
```

```
        echo $actorname;
        echo "</td>\n";
        echo "<td>\n";
        echo $directorname;
        echo "</td>\n";
echo "</tr>\n";
}
echo "</table>\n";
?>
```

2. Pick only comedies from the movie table, and show the movie name and year it was produced. Sort the list alphabetically.

A. Your code should look something like this:

```php
<?php
//connect to MySQL
$connect = mysql_connect("localhost", "root", "mysqlpass") or
     die ("Hey loser, check your server connection.");

//make sure we're using the right database
mysql_select_db ("wiley");

$query="SELECT movie_name, movie_year
     FROM movie
     WHERE movie_type = 5
     ORDER BY movie_name";
$results=mysql_query($query)
     or die(mysql_error());
echo "<table>\n";
while ($rows=mysql_fetch_assoc($results)) {
echo "<tr>\n";
     foreach($rows as $value) {
     echo "<td>\n";
     echo $value;
     echo "</td>\n";
     }
echo "</tr><br>\n";
}
echo "</table>\n";
?>
```

3. Show each movie in the database on its own page, and give the user links in a "page 1, page 2 . . . " type navigation system.

A. Although you could do this many ways, a simple way is to manipulate the LIMIT clause in your SELECT statement as we have done through the URL here:

```php
<?php
//connect to MySQL
$connect = mysql_connect("localhost", "root", "mysqlpass") or
     die ("Hey loser, check your server connection.");

//make sure we're using the right database
mysql_select_db ("wiley");
```

```
//get our starting point for the query through the URL variable "offset"
$offset=$_REQUEST['offset'];
$query="SELECT movie_name, movie_year
     FROM movie
     ORDER BY movie_name
     LIMIT $offset,1";
$results=mysql_query($query)
     or die(mysql_error());
echo "<table>\n";
while ($rows=mysql_fetch_assoc($results)) {
echo "<tr>\n";
     foreach($rows as $value) {
     echo "<td>\n";
     echo $value;
     echo "</td>\n";
     }
echo "</tr><br>\n";
}
echo "</table>\n";
echo "<a href='page.php?offset=0'>Page 1</a><br>";
echo "<a href='page.php?offset=1'>Page 2</a><br>";
echo "<a href='page.php?offset=2'>Page 3</a><br>";
?>
```

Chapter 4

1. Add a column in the top table of your `movie_details.php` file that shows the average rating given by reviewers.

A. First you need to add the column under the `movie_table_headings` variable in your `movie_details.php` file as follows:

```
$movie_table_headings=<<<EOD
  <tr>
    <th>Movie Title</th>
    <th>Year of Release</th>
    <th>Movie Director</th>
    <th>Movie Lead Actor</th>
    <th>Movie Running Time</th>
    <th>Movie Health</th>
    <th>Average Review</th>
  </tr>
EOD;
```

Then you can create a quick function to calculate the number of total reviews and the average. These lines would go near the top of your `movie_details.php` file, where the rest of the functions are defined.

```
function avgreview() {
global $avgreview;
$query = mysql_query("SELECT review_rating FROM reviews
     WHERE review_movie_id='" . $_GET['movie_id'] . "'");
$totalreviews = mysql_num_rows($query);
```

```
$current=0;
while ($rows = mysql_fetch_array($query)) {
    extract ($rows);
    $current = $current + $review_rating;
}
$avgreview = $current/$totalreviews;
}
```

Then call the function when you get the main information for the movie by adding the following lines (still to the `movie_details.php` file):

```
while ($row = mysql_fetch_array($result)) {
  $movie_name = $row['movie_name'];
  $movie_director = $row['movie_director'];
  $movie_leadactor = $row['movie_leadactor'];
  $movie_year = $row['movie_year'];
  $movie_running_time = $row['movie_running_time']." mins";
  $movie_takings = $row['movie_takings'];
  $movie_cost = $row['movie_cost'];

  //get director's name from people table
  get_director();

  //get lead actor's name from people table
  get_leadactor();

  //get the average movie rating
  avgreview();

}
```

Then echo the calculated average review by adding the following lines to the `movie_details` section of the `movie_details.php` file:

```
$movie_details =<<<EOD
<table width="70%" border="0" cellspacing="2"
      cellpadding="2" align="center">
  <tr>
    <th colspan="6"><u><h2>$movie_name: Details</h2></u></th>
  </tr>
  $movie_table_headings
  <tr>
    <td width="33%" align="center">$movie_name</td>
    <td align="center">$movie_year</td>
    <td align="center">$director</td>
    <td align="center">$leadactor</td>
    <td align="center">$movie_running_time</td>
    <td align="center">$movie_health</td>
    <td align="center">$avgreview</td>
  </tr>
</table>
<br>
<br>
EOD;
```

2. Change each column heading of the review table in your `movie_details.php` to a link that allows the user to sort by that column (i.e., the user would click on "Date of Review" to sort all the reviews by date).

A. You need to change your `movie_details.php` file as follows:

```
//pull out "GET" variable for use in EOD

$movieid = $_GET['movie_id'];
$review_table_headings=<<<EOD
  <tr>
    <th><a href="movie_details.php?movie_id=$movieid&order_by=review_date">Date of
Review</a></th>
    <th><a href="movie_details.php?movie_id=$movieid&order_by=review_name">Review
Title</a></th>
    <th><a href="movie_details.php?movie_id=$movieid&order_by=review_reviewer_name">
Reviewer Name</a></th>
    <th><a href="movie_details.php?movie_id=$movieid&order_by=review_comment">Movie
Review Comments</th>
    <th><a href="movie_details.php?movie_id=$movieid&order_by=review_rating">
Rating</th>
  </tr>
EOD;
```

Then later in the script, make the following changes:

```
//allow users to control how reviews were sorted.
//If they are coming from the main table, default sort = review date
//Otherwise, use the field they want. ASC is default.
if (!$_GET['order_by']) $order_by='review_date';
else $order_by = $_GET['order_by'];
```

```
$review_query = "SELECT * FROM reviews WHERE review_movie_id
='".$_GET['movie_id']."' ORDER BY " . $order_by . " ASC";
```

3. Alternate the background colors of each row in the review table of your `movie_details.php` file to make them easier to read. Hint: odd-numbered rows would have a background of one color, even-numbered rows would have a background of another color; check each row number to see if it is divisible by 2 to determine even/odd.

A. Your `movie_details.php` file will need these lines added in or changed:

```
$i=0;
while($i<sizeof($review))
{
    //because $i begins at "0" we will add 1 to the value
    //to truly represent the row number
    if (is_int(($i+1)/2)==TRUE) $bg = "#FFFFFF";
    else $bg = "#CCCCCC";

    $review_details .=<<<EOD
    <tr bgcolor='$bg'>
        <td width='15%' valign='top' align='center'>$review_date[$i]</td>
        <td width='15%' valign='top'>$review_title[$i]</td>
        <td width='10%' valign='top'>$reviewer_name[$i]</td>
```

```
            <td width='50%' valign='top'>$review[$i]</td>
            <td width='10%' valign='top'align='center'>$review_rating[$i]</td>
      </tr>
EOD;
      $i++;
}
```

Chapter 5

1. Create a form and processing page that let you choose a rating (stars, thumbs up, # out of 5, whatever), and provide comments for a movie.

A. All that's needed for this exercise is a simple HTML form, something similar to the following:

```
<form method="post" action="showratings.php">
<p>Movie title: <input type="text" name="movie"></p>
<p>Rating:<br>
<ul>
<?php
  for ($i = 1; $i <= 5; $i++) {
    echo "<li><input type=\"radio\" name=\"rating\"
          value=\"" . $i ."\"> " . $i . "</li>";
  }
?>
</ul></p>
<p>Comments:<br>
  <textarea name="comments" cols="40" rows="10"></textarea></p>
</form>
```

2. Create a form with several text input boxes that allow you to populate the options of a select field on a subsequent page.

A. This exercise takes the form of two pages. The first provides the form to enter the options, the latter shows the result. First, the form on the input page:

```
<form method="post" action="generateselect.php">
<p>Provide select options:<br>
  <input type="text" name="sval1"><br>
  <input type="text" name="sval2"><br>
  <input type="text" name="sval3"><br>
  <input type="text" name="sval4"><br>
  <input type="text" name="sval5"><br>
</p>
</form>
```

And then, on the second page:

```
<form>
<select name="generatedselect">
<?php

for ($i = 1; $i <= 5; $i++) {
  echo "<option value=\"" . $_POST['sval'.$i] . "\">" .
```

```
            $_POST['sval'.$i] . "</option>";
  }

?>
</select>
</form>
```

3. Create a calculator form that takes two numbers and calculates their sum.

A. This exercise is easily handled using a few form fields and some basic arithmetic:

```
<form method="post" action="#">
<p>
  Number 1: <input type="text" name="num1"><br>
  Number 2: <input type="text" name="num2"><br>
  <hr>
  Sum: <input type="text" readonly
          value="<?php echo $_POST['num1'] + $_POST['num2']; ">
</p>
</form>
```

Chapter 6

1. Create the edit/delete code for the `people` table. Use the movie code as an example.

A. One possible solution is as follows. Change `commit.php` as highlighted:

```
<?php
// COMMIT ADD AND EDITS
  $link = mysql_connect("localhost", "bp5am", "bp5ampass")
    or die("Could not connect: " . mysql_error());
  mysql_select_db('moviesite', $link)
    or die ( mysql_error());
  switch ($_GET['action']) {
    case "edit":
      switch ($_GET['type']) {
        case "movie":
          $sql = "UPDATE movie SET
                    movie_name = '" . $_POST['movie_name'] . "',
                    movie_year = '" . $_POST['movie_year'] . "',
                    movie_type = '" . $_POST['movie_type'] . "',
                    movie_leadactor = '" .$_POST['movie_leadactor']."',
                    movie_director = '" . $_POST['movie_director'] . "'
                  WHERE movie_id = '" . $_GET['id'] . "'";
          break;
        case "people":
          $sql = "UPDATE people SET
                    people_fullname = '" . $_POST['people_fullname'] . "',
                    people_isactor = '" . $_POST['people_isactor'] . "',
                    people_isdirector = '" . $_POST['people_isdirector'] . "'
                  WHERE people_id = '" . $_GET['id'] . "'";
          break;
      }
```

```
        break;
      case "add":
        switch ($_GET['type']) {
          case "movie":
            $sql = "INSERT INTO movie
                       (movie_name,
                        movie_year,
                        movie_type,
                        movie_leadactor,
                        movie_director)
                     VALUES
                       ('" . $_POST['movie_name'] . "',
                       '" . $_POST['movie_year'] . "',
                       '" . $_POST['movie_type'] . "',
                       '" . $_POST['movie_leadactor'] . "',
                       '" . $_POST['movie_director'] . "')";
            break;
          case "people":
            $sql = "INSERT INTO people
                       (people_fullname,
                        people_isactor,
                        people_isdirector)
                     VALUES
                       ('" . $_POST['people_name'] . "',
                       '" . $_POST['people_isactor'] . "',
                       '" . $_POST['people_isdirector'] . "')";
            break;
        }
        break;
    }
    if (isset($sql) && !empty($sql)) {
      echo "<!--" . $sql . "-->";
      $result = mysql_query($sql)
        or die("Invalid query: " . mysql_error());
?>
  <p align="center" style="color:#FF0000">
    Done. <a href="index.php">Index</a>
  </p>
<?php
    }
?>
```

Chapter 7

1. Create a site called a "virtual vacation." Offer different backgrounds for people to superimpose photos of themselves in, and let them send virtual postcards to their friends and family.

A. Your code would need to include a background/upload page and a result page. We cover sending e-mail postcards in Chapter 11, so you would simply use the scripts from that chapter and insert your newly created postcard.

This code comes with some caveats; of course you don't have access to the sample image files we've used, and you will have to alter your code a bit based on the sizes of your images. Also, we've not stored our image in any database, and we've only allowed for JPG images to be uploaded. Keeping those things in mind, your background/upload page should look something like this (we named our file vacation.htm):

```html
<html>
<head>
<title>Go on a Virtual Vacation!</title>
</head>
<body>

<form name="form1" method="post" action="upload_image.php" enctype="multipart/form-
data">

        <table border="0" cellpadding="5">
            <tr>
              <td>Image Name or Caption<br>
              <em>Example: Wish you were here!</em></td>
              <td><input name="image_caption" type="text" id="item_caption"
size="55" maxlength="255"></td>
            </tr>
            <tr>
              <td>Your Name</td>
              <td><input name="image_username" type="text" id="image_username"
size="15" maxlength="255"></td>
            </tr>
              <td>Upload Image:</td>
              <td><input name="image_filename" type="file"
id="image_filename"></td>
            </tr>
         </table>
        <br \>
        <em>Acceptable image formats include: JPG/JPEG</em>

        <p>Select your destination:</p>
        <table border="0" cellpadding="5">
           <tr>
              <td><img src="images/mountains.jpg"></td>
              <td><input type="radio" value="mountains" name="destination"></td>
           </tr>
           <tr>
              <td><img src="images/beach.jpg"></td>
              <td><input type="radio" value="beach" name="destination"></td>
           </tr>
           <tr>
              <td><img src="images/golfcourse.jpg"></td>
              <td><input type="radio" value="golfcourse" name="destination"></td>
           </tr>
        </table>

        <p align='center'><input type="submit" name="Submit" value="Submit">
         
        <input type="reset" name="Submit2" value="Clear Form">
        </p>
</form>
</body>
</html>
```

Then we have a page that processes the photos and merges them together, called
upload_image.php.

```php
<?php

//make variables available
$image_caption = $_POST['image_caption'];
$image_username = $_POST['image_username'];
$image_tempname = $_FILES['image_filename']['name'];
$today = date("Y-m-d");
$destination=$_POST['destination'];

//upload image and check for image type
$ImageDir="c:/Program Files/Apache Group/Apache2/test/images/";

$ImageName= $ImageDir . $image_tempname;


    if (move_uploaded_file($_FILES['image_filename']['tmp_name'], $ImageName))
    {

        //get info about the image being uploaded
        list($width, $height, $type, $attr) = getimagesize($ImageName);


        if ($type<>2) {
            echo "Sorry, but the file you uploaded was not a JPG file.<br>";
            echo "Please hit your browser's 'back' button and try again.";
        }
        else {

            //image is acceptable; ok to proceed

            $dstfilename = $ImageDir . $destination . ".jpg";

            $image = imagecreatefromjpeg($ImageName);
            list($width2, $height2, $type2, $attr2) = getimagesize($dstfilename);

            $image2 = imagecreatefromjpeg($dstfilename);
            imagecopymerge($image2, $image, 0,0,0, 0, $width, $height, 100);
        }

    header("Content-type:image/jpeg");
    imagejpeg($image2);
    }

?>
```

2. Have a page on your site with funny photographs or cartoons and allow your users to write
    the caption for them. Place the text in a speech bubble that is appropriately sized based on the
    length of the caption they submit.

A.   First, you need to have the page that gathers the input from the user (let's call this `input.php`):

```
<html>
<head>
<title>Write your own caption!</title>
</head>
<body>

<img src="images/cartoon.jpg">

<form name="form1" method="post" action="caption.php">
<p>Pick a caption for the above picture<br>
<em>Example: You talkin' to me?</em>
<br \><input name="image_caption" type="text" id="image_caption" size="25"
        maxlength="25">
<input type="submit" name="Submit" value="Send my Caption">
</p>
</form>
</body>
</html>
```

Then you need to put the text in the bubble. For our purposes here, we are using a simple ellipse shape that will stretch based on how long the text is. To do this, you would use the following code:

```
<?php

//make variables available
$image_caption = $_POST['image_caption'];
$image_username = $_POST['image_username'];

//get length of string
$length=strlen($image_caption);

//our cartoon without the caption
$image_filename="images/cartoon.jpg";

$image = imagecreatefromjpeg($image_filename);

//draw an ellipse based on string length
 //make our ellipse white
 $white = imagecolorallocate($image, 255, 255, 255);

//the center point for the bubble on our cartoon is at coordinates 134,14
 //alter your x/y coordinates as needed
 $el_x = 134;
 $el_y = 14;
 //for the width of the ellipse, assume each character is 10 pixels, plus 10
   pixels on either side for a cushion.
 $ell_width=($length*10)+20;
 $ellipse = imagefilledellipse($image, $el_x,$el_y, $ell_width, 25, $white);

//get starting point for text
$x = $el_x-((($length*10)/2)-10);
$y = $el_y+5;
```

```
//put the text in the bubble
imagettftext($image, 12, 0, $x, $y, 0, "arial.ttf", $image_caption);

header("Content-type:image/jpeg");
imagejpeg($image);
?>
```

You might want to note that you could have also used `imagettfbbox` to perform a similar task. We didn't cover this in Chapter 7, so you might want to refer to the manual at www.php.net for more information on this function.

3. Create a page for kids where they can choose different heads, bodies, and tails from animals, and put them together to make a new creation and a new image. Or create a virtual paper doll site where kids can place different outfits on a model, then save the images they create.

A. Although there are many ways to do this, we are going to have four separate pages, one for picking the head, one for picking the midsection, one for picking the behind/tail, and one for putting them all together and outputting our final result. We could easily create these images by taking stock photos of animals, resizing them so they are the same size, and then cutting them into three sections using Photoshop or another image manipulation software (or heck, we can even do this using PHP, right?). Assuming we have our sections all ready to go, our first page, `animal1.htm`, would look something like this:

```
<html>
<head>
<title>Create your very own animal!</title>
</head>
<body>

First, you must pick a head for your new animal.

<form name="form1" method="post" action="animal2.php">

        <table border="0" cellpadding="5">
            <tr>
              <td><img src="images/cowhead.jpg"></td>
              <td><input name="head" type="radio" value="cowhead"></td>
            </tr>
            <tr>
              <td><img src="images/pighead.jpg"></td>
              <td><input name="head" type="radio" value="pighead"></td>
            </tr>
            <tr>
              <td><img src="images/giraffehead.jpg"></td>
              <td><input name="head" type="radio" value="giraffehead"></td>
            </tr>
            <tr>
                <td><img src="images/elephanthead.jpg"></td>
                <td><input name="head" type="radio" value="elephanthead"></td>
            </tr>
          </table>

        <p align='center'><input type="submit" name="Submit" value="Pick a Body-
>"></p>
```

```
</form>
</body>
</html>
```

Our next file, animal2.php looks like this:

```php
<?php
$head=$_POST['head'];
?>
<html>
<head>
<title>Create your very own animal!</title>
</head>
<body>
Second, you must pick a body for your new animal.

<form name="form1" method="post" action="animal3.php">

        <table border="0" cellpadding="5">
            <tr>
              <td><img src="images/cowbody.jpg"></td>
              <td><input name="body" type="radio" value="cowbody"></td>
            </tr>
            <tr>
              <td><img src="images/pigbody.jpg"></td>
              <td><input name="body" type="radio" value="pigbody"></td>
            </tr>
            <tr>
              <td><img src="images/giraffebody.jpg"></td>
          <td><input name="body" type="radio" value="giraffebody"></td>
            </tr>
            <tr>
               <td><img src="images/elephantbody.jpg"></td>
               <td><input name="body" type="radio" value="elephantbody"></td>
            </tr>
            <input type="hidden" name="head" value="<?php echo $head?>"
        </table>

        <p align='center'><input type="submit" name="Submit" value="Pick a Tail-
>"></p>
</form>
</body>
</html>
```

And our next file, animal3.php looks like this:

```php
<?php
$head=$_POST['head'];
$body=$_POST['body'];
?>
<html>
<head>
<title>Create your very own animal!</title>
```

```
</head>
<body>

Third, you must pick a tail for your new animal.

<form name="form1" method="post" action="animalcreate.php">

        <table border="0" cellpadding="5">
            <tr>
              <td><img src="images/cowtail.jpg"></td>
              <td><input name="tail" type="radio" value="cowtail"></td>
            </tr>
            <tr>
              <td><img src="images/pigtail.jpg"></td>
              <td><input name="tail" type="radio" value="pigtail"></td>
            </tr>
            <tr>
              <td><img src="images/giraffetail.jpg"></td>
              <td><input name="tail" type="radio" value="giraffetail"></td>
            </tr>
            <tr>
               <td><img src="images/elephanttail.jpg"></td>
               <td><input name="tail" type="radio" value="elephanttail"></td>
            </tr>
            <input type="hidden" name="head" value="<?php echo $head?>"
            <input type="hidden" name="body" value="<?php echo $body?>"
        </table>

<p align='center'><input type="submit" name="Submit" value="Make your Animal!-
>"></p>
</form>
</body>
</html>
```

And finally, the file that combines the three images, our `animalcreate.php` file:

```
<?php
$head=$_POST['head'];
$body=$_POST['body'];
$tail=$_POST['tail'];

$imagedir="images/";

$head_file=$imagedir . $head . ".jpg";
$body_file=$imagedir . $body . ".jpg";
$tail_file=$imagedir . $tail . ".jpg";

$head_image = imagecreatefromjpeg("$head_file");
$body_image = imagecreatefromjpeg("$body_file");
$tail_image = imagecreatefromjpeg("$tail_file");

//each of our images is 100 pixels wide x 200 pixels high.
//also, our images were chopped horizontally
$new_animal = imagecreatetruecolor(300,200);
```

```
//merge blank image with the head
imagecopymerge($new_animal, $head_image, 0, 0, 0, 0, 100, 200, 100);

//now merge in the body
imagecopymerge($new_animal, $body_image, 100,0, 0, 0, 100, 200, 100);

//and finally the tail
imagecopymerge($new_animal, $tail_image, 200, 0, 0, 0, 100, 200, 100);

//output the final result:
header("Content-type:image/jpeg");
imagejpeg($new_animal);

?>
```

Chapter 8

1. Add validation to make the lead actor and director selections required.

A. In commit.php, add or change the lines highlighted below:

```
$movie_name = trim($_POST['movie_name']);
if (empty($movie_name)) {
  $error .= "Please+enter+a+movie+name%21%0D%0A";
}
if (empty($_POST['movie_type'])) {
  $error .= "Please+select+a+movie+type%21%0D%0A";
}
if (empty($_POST['movie_year'])) {
  $error .= "Please+select+a+movie+year%21%0D%0A";
}
$movie_leadactor = trim($_POST['movie_leadactor']);
if (empty($movie_leadactor)) {
  $error .= "Please+enter+a+movie+lead+actor%21%0D%0A";
}
$movie_director = trim($_POST['movie_director']);
if (empty($movie_director)) {
  $error .= "Please+enter+a+movie+director%21%0D%0A";
}
if (empty($error) ){
  $sql = "UPDATE movie SET " .
     "movie_name = '" . $_POST['movie_name'] . "'," .
     "movie_year = '" . $_POST['movie_year'] . "'," .
     "movie_release = '$movie_release'," .
     "movie_type = '" . $_POST['movie_type'] . "'," .
     "movie_leadactor = '" . $movie_leadactor . "'," .
     "movie_director = '" . $movie_director . "'," .
     "movie_rating = '$movie_rating'" .
     "WHERE movie_id = '" . $_GET['id'] . "'";
} else {
  header("location:movie.php?action=edit&error=" .
       $error . "&id=" . $_GET['id']);
}
```

```
            break;
        }
        break;
    case "add":
        switch ($_GET['type']) {
            case "people":
                $sql = "INSERT INTO people (people_fullname) " .
                        "VALUES ('" . $_POST['people_fullname'] . "')";
                break;
            case "movie":
                $movie_rating = trim($_POST['movie_rating']);
                if (!is_numeric($movie_rating)) {
                    $error .= "Please+enter+a+numeric+rating+%21%0D%0A";
                } else {
                    if ($movie_rating < 0 || $movie_rating > 10) {
                        $error .= "Please+enter+a+rating+" .
                                  "between+0+and+10%21%0D%0A";
                    }
                }
                $movie_release = trim($_POST['movie_release']);
                if (!ereg("([0-9]{2})-([0-9]{2})-([0-9]{4})",
                          $movie_release,
                          $reldatepart) || empty($movie_release)) {
                    $error .= "Please+enter+a+date+" .
                              "with+the+dd-mm-yyyy+format%21%0D%0A";
                } else {
                    $movie_release = @mktime(0, 0, 0, $reldatepart['2'],
                                             $reldatepart['1'],
                                             $reldatepart['3']);
                    if ($movie_release == '-1') {
                        $error .= "Please+enter+a+real+date+" .
                                  "with+the+dd-mm-yyyy+format%21%0D%0A";
                    }
                }
                $movie_name = trim($row['movie_name']);
                if (empty($movie_name)) {
                    $error .= "Please+enter+a+movie+name%21%0D%0A";
                }
                if (empty($_POST['movie_type'])) {
                    $error .= "Please+select+a+movie+type%21%0D%0A";
                }
                if (empty($_POST['movie_year'])) {
                    $error .= "Please+select+a+movie+year%21%0D%0A";
                }
                $movie_leadactor = trim($_POST['movie_leadactor']);
                if (empty($movie_leadactor)) {
                    $error .= "Please+enter+a+movie+lead+actor%21%0D%0A";
                }
                $movie_director = trim($_POST['movie_director']);
                if (empty($movie_director)) {
                    $error .= "Please+enter+a+movie+director%21%0D%0A";
                }
```

```
            if (empty($error)) {
              $sql = "INSERT INTO movie (movie_name,movie_year," .
                     "movie_release,movie_type,movie_leadactor," .
                     "movie_director,movie_rating) " .
                     "VALUES ('" . $_POST['movie_name'] . "'," .
                     "'" . $_POST['movie_year'] . "'," .
                     "'$movie_release'," .
                     "'" . $_POST['movie_type'] . "'," .
                     "'" . $movie_leadactor . "'," .
                     "'" . $movie_director . "'," .
                     "'$movie_rating')";
            } else {
              header("location:movie.php?action=add&error=" . $error);
            }
            break;
```

Chapter 9

In Chapter 9 you were shown three short snippets of code and asked to spot the errors and figure out how to fix them. Then you were asked to create a little error-catching script to catch the errors.

1.

```
<?
$query = "select * from table_name where name = '" . $_POST['name'] . "';"
$result = mysql_query($result) or die(mysql_error());
?>
```

A. Parse error from lack of semicolon at the end of the statement; the semicolon there is for the SQL statement.

2.

```
<?
if ($_POST['first_name'] = "Jethro")
{
echo "Your name is " . $_POST['first_name'];
}
?>
```

A. You always need to check equality with double equals (==), not single equals (=). Single equals is for setting a variable equal to a value.

3.

```
<?
$full_name = $_POST['mrmiss'] ". " $_POST['first_name'] " " $_POST['last_name'];
?>
```

A. This is missing concatenation operators between the variables and the strings.

Chapter 10

1. Add a "costume description" field to the character record, and provide a way to modify the costume description.

A. The three main tasks you need to accomplish in this exercise are to modify the database to hold the costume descriptions, modify the character edit page to provide a character description field, and modify the transaction page to process the extra field.

Start by adding a field to the `char_main` table in your database, something similar to the following:

```
costume varchar(250) NOT NULL
```

Then, modify `char_edit.php`, adding or modifying the lines highlighted below, starting first with the database queries at the top:

```
if ($char != '0') {
    $sql = "SELECT c.alias, c.real_name AS name, c.costume, c.align, " .
           "l.lair_addr AS address, z.city, z.state, z.id AS zip " .
           "FROM char_main c, char_lair l, char_zipcode z " .
           "WHERE z.id = l.zip_id " .
           "AND c.lair_id = l.id " .
           "AND c.id = $char";
    $result = mysql_query($sql)
      or die(mysql_error());
    $ch = mysql_fetch_array($result);
```

And then, further down the page in the HTML form:

```
<tr>
    <td>Real Name:</td>
    <td><input type="text" name="name" size="41"
        value="<?php if (isset($ch)) { echo $ch['name']; } ?>">
    </td>
</tr>
<tr>
    <td>Costume Description</td>
    <td><input type="text" name="name" size="41"
        value="<?php if (isset($ch)) { echo $ch['costume']; } ?>">
    </td>
</tr>
<tr>
    <td>Powers:<br><font size="2" color="#990000">
      (Ctrl-click to<br>select multiple<br>powers)</font>
    </td>
```

Finally, in `char_transact.php`, we change the following, starting with the "Create Character" case:

```
switch ($action) {
  case "Create Character":
    $sql = "INSERT IGNORE INTO char_zipcode (id, city, state) " .
           "VALUES ('$zip', '$city', '$state')";
    $result = mysql_query($sql)
```

```
      or die(mysql_error());

$sql = "INSERT INTO char_lair (id, zip_id, lair_addr) " .
       "VALUES (NULL, '$zip', '$address')";
$result = mysql_query($sql)
  or die(mysql_error());
if ($result) {
  $lairid = mysql_insert_id($conn);
}

$sql = "INSERT INTO char_main (id,lair_id,alias,real_name,costume,align) " .
       "VALUES (NULL, '$lairid', '$alias', '$name', '$costume', '$align')";
$result = mysql_query($sql)
  or die(mysql_error());
if ($result) {
  $charid = mysql_insert_id($conn);
}
```

And later in the "Update Character" case:

```
case "Update Character":
  $sql = "INSERT IGNORE INTO char_zipcode (id, city, state) " .
         "VALUES ('$zip', '$city', '$state')";
  $result = mysql_query($sql)
    or die(mysql_error());

  $sql = "UPDATE char_lair l, char_main m " .
         "SET l.zip_id='$zip', l.lair_addr='$address', " .
         "costume='$costume', " .
         "alias='$alias', real_name='$name', align='$align' " .
         "WHERE m.id = $cid AND m.lair_id = l.id";
  $result = mysql_query($sql)
    or die(mysql_error());
```

2. Modify the character listing to display the characters' locations alongside their powers.

A. This time, you only need to modify the `charlist.php` file. You're going to change the initial queries to return additional fields, and add those fields to the table display, as highlighted:

```
<?php
$sql = "SELECT c.id, c.alias, c.real_name AS name, c.align, z.city " .
       "FROM char_main c
        JOIN char_lair l ON c.lair_id = l.id
        JOIN char_zipcode z ON l.zip_id = z.id
        ORDER BY c.". $order[$ord];

$result = mysql_query($sql)
  or die(mysql_error());
if (mysql_num_rows($result) > 0) {
  $table = "<table border=\"0\" cellpadding=\"5\">";
  $table .= "<tr bgcolor=\"#FFCCCC\"><th>";
  $table .= "<a href=\"" . $_SERVER['PHP_SELF'] . "?o=1\">Alias</a>";
  $table .= "</th><th><a href=\"" . $_SERVER['PHP_SELF'] . "?o=2\">";
  $table .= "Name</a></th><th><a href=\"" . $_SERVER['PHP_SELF'];
  $table .= "?o=3\">Alignment</a></th><th>Powers</th>";
```

```
$table .= "<th>Location</th><th>Enemies</th></tr>";

// build each table row
$bg = '';
while ($row = mysql_fetch_array($result)) {
  $bg = ($bg=='F2F2FF'?'E2E2F2':'F2F2FF');
  $pow = ($powers[$row['id']]==''?'none':$powers[$row['id']]);
  if (!isset($enemies) || ($enemies[$row['id']]=='')) {
    $ene = 'none';
  } else {
    $ene = $enemies[$row['id']];
  }
  $table .= "<tr bgcolor=\"#" . $bg . "\">" .
            "<td><a href=\"charedit.php?c=" . $row['id'] . "\">" .
            $row['alias']. "</a></td><td>" .
            $row['name'] . "</td><td align=\"center\">" .
            $row['align'] . "</td><td>" . $pow . "</td>" .
            "<td>" . $row['city'] . "</td>" .
            "<td align=\"center\">" . $ene . "</td></tr>";
}
```

Chapter 11

1. Create code to send a message to an e-mail account, and blind carbon-copy (Bcc) yourself or another account.

A. This one is surprisingly short. All you really need is something similar to the following:

```
$to = 'youremail@yourdomain.com';
$bcc = 'anotheremail@yourdomain.com;'
$from = 'youremail@yourdomain.com';
$subject = 'Testing email';
$message = 'This is testing Bcc fields.';
$headers .= "BCC: " . $bcc . "\r\n";
$mailsent = mail($to, $subject, $message, $headers);
```

2. Create a simple Web form that e-mails comments or suggestions to an account of your choosing.

A. For this exercise you can create two files, one that provides a form for user entry of the required fields, and another to send the actual e-mail. The Web form should include something similar to the following:

```
<form action="mailit.php" method="post">
<p>Please provide you comments or suggestions
   to help make our site better!</p>
<textarea name="comments" cols="40" rows="10"></textarea>
</form>
```

And the processing page should be similar to this code:

```
$to = 'youremail@yourdomain.com';
$subject = 'Website comments';
$message = 'The following comments were entered: '.$_POST['comments'];
$mailsent = mail($to, $subject, $message);
```

Chapter 12

1. Create a "hidden" area that is only displayed to users that are logged in with your system.

A. You might be expecting to see a simplified PHP login/session example here, but we're going to go a different route. Instead, we're going to revisit the simple, yet effective, .htaccess solution.

Create a directory of your choosing, and create a .htaccess file in it:

```
AuthType Basic
AuthUserFile /usr/local/apache2/htdocs/demoauth #or your windows path
AuthName "Example restricted area"
<LIMIT GET POST>
require valid-user
</LIMIT>
```

Then, issue the proper htpasswd command for your system. Here's an example UNIX/Linux command:

```
/usr/local/apache2/bin/htpasswd -c /usr/local/apache/htdocs2/userauth john
```

Enter a password as needed.

2. Use cookies to retain some information for 30 minutes, dependent on logged users.

A. Here's one example of how it might be done:

```
session_start();
if ($_SESSION['user_logged']) {
  setcookie('testcookie', 'cows say moo', time() + 60 * 30);
  // * sets cookie for 30 minutes *
}
```

3. Create a system where certain users only have certain options dependent on their user level.

A. This exercise is actually a common component of many Web sites that use access levels to control what the user sees. For example, here's a sample navigation menu that presents the "Create News" link to users with access level 1 or higher, and the "Site Administration" link to users with access level 2 or higher:

```
<ul>
  <li><a href="index.php">Home</a></li>
  <li><a href="news.php">News</a></li>
  <li><a href="contact.php">Contact Us</a></li>
<?php if ($_SESSION['access_level'] > 0) { ?>
  <li><a href="createnews.php">Create News</a></li>
<?php } ?>
<?php if ($_SESSION['access_level'] > 1) { ?>
  <li><a href="admin.php">Site Administration</a></li>
<?php } ?>
</ul>
```

Chapter 13

1. **Delete when appropriate.** When reviewing an article, the delete button always shows up, regardless of what happens in the transaction page. Alter the code so the Delete button only shows up when the article is pending.

A. This one is as simple as wrapping the delete button markup with an `if` statement:

```
echo "<input type=\"submit\" class=\"submit\" " .
    "name=\"action\" value=\"Edit\"> ";
if (($row['access_lvl'] > 1) or ($_SESSION['access_lvl'] > 1)) {
  echo "<input type=\"submit\" class=\"submit\" " .
      "name=\"action\" value=\"$buttonType\"> ";
}
if (!$row['is_published']) {
echo "<input type=\"submit\" class=\"submit\" " .
    "name=\"action\" value=\"Delete\"> ";
}
?>

<input type="hidden" name="article"
  value="<?php echo $_GET['article'] ?> ">
```

2. Find out about the author. Authors of articles might want the readers to know a little more about them. Add the ability to enter extra fields in a user's profile, and provide a link on the article full-view page to the author's information.

A. We've covered adding a new field to a form and the corresponding database table before, so that should be familiar by now. Once the user form and database tables are modified to allow the extra information, you need to create a link in the `outputStory()` function, which is contained in `outputfunctions.php`:

```
if ($article) {
    $sql = "SELECT ar.*, usr.name, usr.user_id " .
            "FROM cms_articles ar " .
            "LEFT OUTER JOIN cms_users usr " .
            "ON ar.author_id = usr.user_id " .
            "WHERE ar.article_id = " . $article;
    $result = mysql_query($sql,$conn);

    if ($row = mysql_fetch_array($result)) {
      echo "<h3>" . htmlspecialchars($row['title']) . "</h3>\n";
      echo "<h5><div class=\"byline\">By: " .
          "<a href=\"authorinfo.php?id=" . $row['user_id'] . "\">" .
          htmlspecialchars($row['name']) . "</a>" .
          "</div>";
      echo "<div class=\"pubdate\">";
```

The link we added would pull up a page listing the author's profile. Such a profile page is really a simple matter of a `SELECT` query, and echoing the results to the screen.

3. Notify the author. Authors might want to be automatically notified when their stories have been approved. Add an e-mail notification upon approval, and give users the ability to toggle their notification on and off.

A. For this exercise, you'll need to make some modifications to the `transact-article.php` page, similar to the following highlighted lines:

```
case 'Publish':
  if ($_POST['article']) {
```

```
                    // Get author email
                    $sql = "SELECT u.email
                            FROM cms_users u
                            JOIN cms_articles a ON u.user_id = a.author_id
                            WHERE a.article_id = " . $_POST['article'];
                    $result = mysql_query($sql, $conn);
                    $row = mysql_fetch_array($result);
                    $authoremail = $row['email'];

                    $sql = "UPDATE cms_articles " .
                            "SET is_published=1, date_published='" .
                            date("Y-m-d H:i:s",time()) . "' " .
                            "WHERE article_id=" . $_POST['article'];
                    mysql_query($sql, $conn)
                      or die('Could not publish article; ' . mysql_error());

                    // Email author
                    mail($authoremail,'Article approved',
                        'Your article has been approved!');
                }
                redirect('pending.php');
                break;
```

Chapter 14

1. **Hide your users' addresses.** Modify the send message functionality to send the e-mails to your
    users using the "Bcc:" e-mail field, instead of the usual "To:" field.

A. Inside the "Send Message" case in `admin_transact.php`, modify the following highlighted
    lines:

```
            while ($row = mysql_fetch_array($result))
            {
              if (is_numeric($_POST['ml_id'])) {
                $ft = "You are receiving this message as a member of the ";
                $ft .= $listname . "\n mailing list. If you have received ";
                $ft .= "this e-mail in error, or would like to\n remove your ";
                $ft .= "name from this mailing list, please visit the ";
                $ft .= "following URL:\n";
                $ft .= "http://" . $_SERVER['HTTP_HOST'] .
                        dirname($_SERVER['PHP_SELF']) . "/remove.php?u=" .
                        $row['user_id'] . "&ml=" . $_POST['ml_id'];
              } else {
                $ft = "You are receiving this e-mail because you subscribed ";
                $ft .= "to one or more\n mailing lists. Visit the following ";
                $ft .= "URL to change your subscriptions:\n";
                $ft .= "http://" . $_SERVER['HTTP_HOST'] .
                        dirname($_SERVER['PHP_SELF']) . "/user.php?u=" .
                        $row['user_id'];
              }
              $bcc = "BCC: " . $row['email'] . "\r\n";

              $msg = stripslashes($_POST['msg']) . "\n\n";
```

```
        $msg .= "--------------\n";
        $msg .= $ft;

    mail(ADMIN_EMAIL,stripslashes($_POST['subject']),$msg,
        $headers . $bcc)
      or die('Could not send e-mail.');
  }
}
break;
```

2. **Reduce sending.** Modify the send message functionality to send e-mails to your users in groups of 10. That is, every e-mail that is sent should be sent to 10 users at a time (when possible), instead of 1 e-mail per user.

A. One possible solution requires editing the "Send Message" case in `admin_transact.php`, as highlighted:

```
$headers = "From: " . ADMIN_EMAIL . "\r\n";

$maillimit = 10;
$mailcount = 0;
$to = '';

while ($row = mysql_fetch_array($result))
{
  $mailcount++;
  if (is_numeric($_POST['ml_id'])) {
    $ft = "You are receiving this message as a member of the ";
    $ft .= $listname . "\n mailing list. If you have received ";
    $ft .= "this e-mail in error, or would like to\n remove your ";
    $ft .= "name from this mailing list, please visit the ";
    $ft .= "following URL:\n";
    $ft .= "http://" . $_SERVER['HTTP_HOST'] .
        dirname($_SERVER['PHP_SELF']) . "/remove.php?u=" .
        $row['user_id'] . "&ml=" . $_POST['ml_id'];
  } else {
    $ft = "You are receiving this e-mail because you subscribed ";
    $ft .= "to one or more\n mailing lists. Visit the following ";
    $ft .= "URL to change your subscriptions:\n";
    $ft .= "http://" . $_SERVER['HTTP_HOST'] .
        dirname($_SERVER['PHP_SELF']) . "/user.php?u=" .
        $row['user_id'];
  }

  $msg = stripslashes($_POST['msg']) . "\n\n";
  $msg .= "--------------\n";
  $msg .= $ft;

  if ($mailcount == $maillimit) {
    mail($to,stripslashes($_POST['subject']),$msg,$headers)
      or die('Could not send e-mail.');
    $mailcount = 0;
    $to = '';
  } else {
    $to .= $row['email'] . ", ";
  }
```

```
        }
      }
      break;
```

3. **Let the administrator know.** Add functionality to send an e-mail to an administrator when new users confirm their subscription to the mailing list.

A. This one is pretty simple. Add code to `user_transact.php`, similar to the following:

```
$subject = 'Mailing List Subscription Confirmed';
$body = "Hello " . $firstname . ",\n" .
        "Thank you for subscribing to the " .
        $listname . " mailing list. Welcome!\n\n" .
        "If you did not subscribe, please accept our " .
        "apologies.\n" .
        "You can remove this subscription immediately by " .
        "visiting the following URL:\n" . $url;

mail($email,$subject,$body,$headers);
```

```
mail("adminemail@yoursite.com",
    "Mailing list new subscription",
    "The following user just subscribed to the " . $listname .
    " mailing list: " .
    $_POST['firstname'] . " " . $_POST['lastname']);
```

```
$redirect = "thanks.php?u=" . $_GET['u'] . "&ml=" .
            $_GET['ml'] . "&t=s";
} else {
  $redirect = 'user.php';
}
break;
```

4. **Clean up any leftovers.** Add functionality to the administration page to allow an admin to purge the database of any subscriptions that haven't yet been confirmed.

A. The first step in this exercise is to add a link on the admin page to a new page you'll create, for example:

```
<a href="purge.php">Purge unconfirmed users</a>
```

Then, create the processing page (`purge.php`):

```
<?php
require('config.php');

$conn = mysql_connect(SQL_HOST, SQL_USER, SQL_PASS)
  or die('Could not connect to MySQL database. ' . mysql_error());

mysql_select_db(SQL_DB, $conn);

$sql = "DELETE FROM ml_subscriptions WHERE pending = 1";
mysql_query($sql, $conn);

echo "Records successfully purged.";
?>
```

Chapter 15

1. **Allow for tax.** Many states require that you charge sales tax on the orders shipped to the state where you have a physical presence, and some states require sales tax on all online orders. Set your code to check for customers in your own state and add the appropriate sales tax to those orders only.

A. Because you allowed for a sales tax field already in the main order table, this requires a simple `if` statement in the next to last step of the order, where everything is processed. You will also change your "total" to "subtotal." Locate the following lines of code in `checkout2.php`, and make your changes as highlighted below.

```
...
while ($row = mysql_fetch_array($results)) {
            extract ($row);
            $prod = "SELECT * FROM products WHERE
                products_prodnum = '$carttemp_prodnum'";
            $prod2 = mysql_query($prod);
            $prod3 = mysql_fetch_array($prod2);
            extract ($prod3);
            echo "<td>";
            echo $carttemp_quan;
            echo "</td>";
            echo "<td>";
            echo "<a href = 'getprod.php?prodid=" .
                $products_prodnum ."'>";
            echo "THUMBNAIL<br>IMAGE</td></a>";
            echo "<td>";
            echo "<a href = 'getprod.php?prodid=" .
                $products_prodnum ."'>";
            echo $products_name;
            echo "</td></a>";
            echo "<td align='right'>";
            echo $products_price;
            echo "</td>";
            echo "<td align='right'>";
        //get extended price
            $extprice = number_format($products_price * $carttemp_quan, 2);
            echo $extprice;
            echo "</td>";
            echo "<td>";
            echo "<a href='cart.php'>Make Changes to Cart</a>";
            echo "</td>";
            echo "</tr>";
        //add extended price to total
            //CHANGE
            $subtotal = $extprice + $subtotal;
            }

//add in tax if applicable, change to fit your state and tax rate
$taxstate = "CA";

if ($_POST['shipstate']==$taxstate) $taxrate = 0.07;
else $taxrate = 0;
```

```
$tax = $subtotal*$taxrate;
$subtotal=$subtotal+$tax;

?>


<tr>
 <td colspan='4' align='right'>If shipping to CA, there is a 7% sales tax.</td>
<td align='right'><?php echo number_format($tax, 2) ?></td>
</tr>


<tr>
<td colspan='4' align='right'>Your total before shipping is:</td>
<td align='right'> <?php echo number_format($subtotal, 2) ?></td>
<td></td>
<td></td>
</tr>
</table>
<input type="hidden" name="subtotal" value="<?php echo $subtotal?>">
<input type="hidden" name="tax" value="<?php echo $tax?>">

  <p>
    <input type="submit" name="Submit" value="Send Order --&gt;">
  </p>
  </form>
 </BODY>
 </HTML>
```

Then, you also need to change your checkout3.php as highlighted below:

```
<?php
session_start();
//connect to the database - either include a connection variable file or
//type the following lines:
$connect = mysql_connect("localhost", "root", "mysqlpass") or
      die ("Hey loser, check your server connection.");
mysql_select_db ("ecommerce");

//Let's make the variables easy to access in our queries
$firstname = $_POST['firstname'];
$lastname = $_POST['lastname'];
$firstname = $_POST['firstname'];
$add1 = $_POST['add1'];
$add2 = $_POST['add2'];
$city = $_POST['city'];
$state = $_POST['state'];
$zip = $_POST['zip'];
$phone = $_POST['phone'];
$fax = $_POST['fax'];
$email = $_POST['email'];
$shipfirst = $_POST['shipfirst'];
$shiplast = $_POST['shiplast'];
$shipadd1 = $_POST['shipadd1'];
$shipadd2 = $_POST['shipadd2'];
$shipcity = $_POST['shipcity'];
```

```php
$shipstate = $_POST['shipstate'];
$shipzip = $_POST['shipzip'];
$shipstate = $_POST['shipstate'];
$shipphone = $_POST['shipphone'];
$shipemail = $_POST['shipemail'];

//new
$tax = $_POST['tax'];
$subtotal = $_POST['subtotal'];

$sessid = session_id();
$today = date("Y-m-d");

//1) Assign Customer Number to new Customer, or find existing customer number
    $query = "SELECT * FROM customers WHERE
        (customers_firstname = '$firstname' AND
        customers_lastname = '$lastname' AND
        customers_add1 = '$add1' AND
        customers_add2 = '$add2' AND
        customers_city = '$city')";
    $results = mysql_query($query)
        or (mysql_error());
    $rows = mysql_num_rows($results);

    if ($rows < 1) {
        //assign new custnum
        $query2 = "INSERT INTO customers (
        customers_firstname, customers_lastname, customers_add1,
        customers_add2, customers_city, customers_state, customers_zip,
        customers_phone, customers_fax, customers_email)
         VALUES (
        '$firstname',
        '$lastname',
        '$add1',
        '$add2',
        '$city',
        '$state',
        '$zip',
        '$phone',
        '$fax',
        '$email')";
        $insert = mysql_query($query2)
            or (mysql_error());
        $custid = mysql_insert_id();
    }
    //If custid exists, we want to make it equal to custnum
    //Otherwise we will use the existing custnum
    if($custid) $customers_custnum = $custid;

//2) Insert Info into ordermain
    //determine shipping costs based on order total (25% of total)

    //CHANGE
    $shipping = $subtotal * 0.25;
    $total = $subtotal + $shipping;
```

```
        $query3 = "INSERT INTO ordermain (
                    ordermain_orderdate, ordermain_custnum,
                    ordermain_subtotal,ordermain_shipping,
                    ordermain_shipfirst, ordermain_shiplast,
                    ordermain_shipadd1, ordermain_shipadd2,
                    ordermain_shipcity, ordermain_shipstate,
                    ordermain_shipzip, ordermain_shipphone,
                    ordermain_shipemail,
                    ordermain_tax, ordermain_total
                    )
            VALUES (
            '$today',
            '$customers_custnum',

            //change
            '$subtotal',

            '$shipping'
            '$shipfirst',
            '$shiplast',
            '$shipadd1',
            '$shipadd2',
            '$shipcity',
            '$shipstate',
            '$shipzip',
            '$shipphone',
            '$shipemail',
            '$tax',
            '$total'

            )";
    $insert2 = mysql_query($query3)
        or (mysql_error());
    $orderid = mysql_insert_id();

//3) Insert Info into orderdet
    //find the correct cart information being temporarily stored
    $query = "SELECT * from carttemp WHERE carttemp_sess='$sessid'";
    $results = mysql_query($query)
        or (mysql_error());

    //put the data into the database one row at a time
    while ($row = mysql_fetch_array($results)) {
            extract ($row);
            $query4 = "INSERT INTO orderdet (
                    orderdet_ordernum, orderdet_qty, orderdet_prodnum)
                VALUES (
                '$orderid',
                '$carttemp_quan',
                '$carttemp_prodnum')";
            $insert4 = mysql_query($query4)
                or (mysql_error());
    }
```

```
//4)delete from temporary table
    $query="DELETE FROM carttemp WHERE carttemp_sess='$sessid'";
    $delete = mysql_query($query);


//5)email confirmations to us and to the customer
/* recipients */
$to = "<" . $email .">";

/* subject */
$subject = "Order Confirmation";

/* message */
    /* top of message */
    $message = "
      <html>
      <head>
      <title>Order Confirmation</title>
      </head>
      <body>
    Here is a recap of your order:<br \><br \>
    Order date: ";
 $message .= $today;
 $message .= "
    <br \>
     Order Number: ";
 $message .= $orderid;
 $message .= "
    <table width='50%' border='0'>
     <tr>
       <td>
        <p>Bill to:<br \>";
 $message .= $firstname;
 $message .= " ";
 $message .= $lastname;
 $message .= "<br \>";
 $message .= $add1;
 $message .= "<br \>";
if ($add2) $message .= $add2 . "<br \>";
 $message .= $city . ", " . $state . "  " . $zip;
 $message .= "</p></td>
    <td>
      <p>Ship to:<br \>";
 $message .= $shipfirst . " " . $shiplast;
 $message .= "<br \>";
 $message .= $shipadd1 . "<br \>";
if ($shipadd2) $message .= $shipadd2 . "<br \>";
 $message .= $shipcity . ", " . $shipstate . "  " . $shipzip;
 $message .= "</p>
      </td>
     </tr>
    </table>
    <hr noshade width='250px' align='left'>
  <table cellpadding='5'>
```

```
       <tr>";

//grab the contents of the order and insert them
//into the message field

    $query = "SELECT * from orderdet WHERE orderdet_ordernum = '$orderid'";
    $results = mysql_query($query)
        or die (mysql_query());
        while ($row = mysql_fetch_array($results)) {
            extract ($row);
            $prod = "SELECT * FROM products
                    WHERE products_prodnum = '$orderdet_prodnum'";
            $prod2 = mysql_query($prod);
            $prod3 = mysql_fetch_array($prod2);
            extract ($prod3);
            $message .= "<td>";
            $message .= $orderdet_qty;
            $message .= "</td>";
            $message .="<td>";
            $message .= $products_name;
            $message .= "</td>";
            $message .= "<td align='right'>";
            $message .= $products_price;
            $message .= "</td>";
            $message .= "<td align='right'>";
        //get extended price
            $extprice = number_format($products_price * $orderdet_qty, 2);
            $message .= $extprice;
            $message .= "</td>";
            $message .= "</tr>";
            }
```

```
//NEW
$message .="<tr><td colspan='4' align='right'>If shipping to CA, there is a 7%
sales tax.</td><td align='right'><?php echo number_format($tax, 2) ?></td></tr>";
```

```
$message .= "<tr>
    <td colspan='3' align='right'>
        Your total before shipping is:
    </td>
    <td align='right'>";
```

```
//CHANGE
$message .= number_format($subtotal, 2);
```

```
$message .= "
    </td>
    </tr>
    <tr>
    <td colspan='3' align='right'>
        Shipping Costs:
    </td>
```

```
            <td align='right'>";
  $message .= number_format($shipping, 2);
  $message .= "
      </td>
    </tr>
    <tr>
      <td colspan='3' align='right'>
        Your final total is:
      </td>
      <td align='right'> ";

  //CHANGE
  $message .= number_format($total, 2);

  $message .= "
      </td>
    </tr>
  </table>
</body>
</html>";

/* headers */
$headers = "MIME-Version: 1.0\r\n";
$headers .= "Content-type: text/html; charset=iso-8859-1\r\n";
$headers .= "From: <storeemail@email.com>\r\n";
$headers .= "Cc: <storeemail@email.com>\r\n";
$headers .= "X-Mailer: PHP / ".phpversion()."\r\n";

/* mail it */
//mail ($to, $subject, $message, $headers);


//6)show them their order & give them an order number

echo "Step 1 - Please Enter Billing and Shipping Information<br \>";
echo "Step 2 - Please Verify Accuracy and Make Any Necessary Changes<br \>";
echo "<strong>Step 3 - Order Confirmation and Receipt</strong><br \><br \>";

echo $message;

?>
```

2.   **Allow for inventory control.** Your shopping cart script can keep track of how many items you have in stock and display that to your customers. You can also show an "out of stock" message to your customers, letting them know that a particular item is temporarily out of stock but still available for purchase if they like.

A.   First, you need to alter your products table structure to include a field for "on-hand" quantity. You can easily do this by adding the following field through phpMyAdmin:

```
products_inventory INT(4) NOT NULL
```

Then, you can keep track of how many you have in stock by altering this field as necessary. Please note, our script does not allow for purchasing or receiving more items in, it will only decrease the quantity based on a completed sale. To show the in-stock quantity on the products detail page, you could make the following changes to the getprod.php file:

```php
<?php
session_start();
//connect to the database - either include a connection variable file
//or type the following lines:
$connect = mysql_connect("localhost", "bp5am", "bp5ampass")
  or die("Hey loser, check your server connection.");
//make our database active
mysql_select_db("ecommerce");

//get our variable passed through the URL
$prodid = $_REQUEST['prodid'];

//get information on the specific product we want
$query = "SELECT * FROM products WHERE products_prodnum='$prodid'";
$results = mysql_query($query)
  or die(mysql_error());
$row = mysql_fetch_array($results);
extract($row);

?>
<html>
<head>
<title><?php echo $products_name; ?></title>
</head>
<body>
<div align="center">
<table cellpadding="5" width="80%">
  <tr>
    <td>PRODUCT IMAGE</td>
    <td><strong><?php echo $products_name; ?></strong><br>
      <?php echo $products_proddesc; ?><br \>
      <?php
          if ($products_inventory <=0) {
            echo "<br><font color="red"><em>This product is currently
              out of stock, but is still available for purchase.</em></font>";
          }
          else {
              echo "<br>In-stock:" . $products_inventory;
          }
      <br>Product Number: <?php echo $products_prodnum; ?>
      <br>Price: $<?php echo $products_price; ?><br>
      <form method="POST" action="modcart.php?action=add">
        Quantity: <input type="text" name="qty" size="2"><br>
        <input type="hidden" name="products_prodnum"
          value="<?php echo $products_prodnum ?>">
        <input type="submit" name="Submit" value="Add to cart">
      </form>

      <form method="POST" action="cart.php">
        <input type="submit" name="Submit" value="View cart">
      </form>
    </td>
```

```
    </tr>
  </table>
  <hr width="200">
  <p><a href="cbashop.php">Go back to the main page</a></p>
  </div>
  </body>
  </html>
```

Then, to keep an accurate count of how many items you have in-stock, you want to delete any sold items from your current on-hand inventory. You need to make the following change to the final step in your checkout process (you wouldn't want to delete items that haven't been confirmed as being "sold"). Edit your checkout3.php as follows:

```
//3) Insert Info into orderdet
//find the correct cart information being temporarily stored
$query = "SELECT * FROM carttemp WHERE carttemp_sess='$sessid'";
$results = mysql_query($query)
  or (mysql_error());

//put the data into the database one row at a time
while ($row = mysql_fetch_array($results)) {
  extract($row);
  $query4 = "INSERT INTO orderdet (
            orderdet_ordernum, orderdet_qty, orderdet_prodnum)
            VALUES (
            '$orderid',
            '$carttemp_quan',
            '$carttemp_prodnum')";
  $insert4 = mysql_query($query4)
    or (mysql_error());

  //update the on-hand inventory for each product in cart
  $newinv = $products_inventory - $carttemp_quan;
  $query4a = "UPDATE products SET $products_inventory='$newinv'
            WHERE $products_prodnum = '$carttemp_prodnum'";
  $update4a = mysql_query($query4a);

}
```

3. **Show your customers your most popular items.** Which of your items are purchased the most? If an item is in the top 5 on your bestseller list, show a "bestseller" icon in the description of that item.

A. Again, there are several ways to do this, but probably the simplest way is to add another field to your products table that will keep a master count of the total quantity sold. You would alter your table (again, the easiest way is to use phpMyAdmin) and add the following field:

```
products_total_sold INT(4) NOT NULL
```

You want to check for a bestselling item when you show your product details, so you alter getprod.php as follows:

```
<?php
session_start();
//connect to the database - either include a connection variable file
```

```php
//or type the following lines:
$connect = mysql_connect("localhost", "bp5am", "bp5ampass")
  or die("Hey loser, check your server connection.");
//make our database active
mysql_select_db("ecommerce");

//get our variable passed through the URL
$prodid = $_REQUEST['prodid'];

//get information on the specific product we want
$query = "SELECT * FROM products WHERE products_prodnum='$prodid'";
$results = mysql_query($query)
  or die(mysql_error());
$row = mysql_fetch_array($results);
extract($row);

//function to determine bestseller list
function bestseller() {
global $prodid;
global $bestseller;
$querybest = "SELECT products_prodnum FROM products
        ORDER BY products_total_sold DESC LIMIT 5";
        $resultsbest = mysql_query($querybest);
        while ($rowsbest = mysql_fetch_array($resultsbest)) {
        extract ($rowsbest);
          if ($products_prodnum == $prodid) $bestseller = 'y';
        }
}

?>
<html>
<head>
<title><?php echo $products_name; ?></title>
</head>
<body>
<div align="center">
<table cellpadding="5" width="80%">
  <tr>
    <td>PRODUCT IMAGE</td>
    <td><strong><?php echo $products_name; ?></strong><br>

      <?php
       //check for bestseller list
        bestseller();
        if ($bestseller == 'y') echo "<img src='best.jpg'>";


      ?>
      <?php echo $products_proddesc; ?><br \>
      <?php
          if ($products_inventory <=0) {
            echo "<br><font color="red"><em>This product is currently
              out of stock, but is still available for purchase.</em></font>";
          }
          else {
```

```
                      echo "<br>In-stock:" . $products_inventory;
                }
        <br>Product Number: <?php echo $products_prodnum; ?>
        <br>Price: $<?php echo $products_price; ?><br>
        <form method="POST" action="modcart.php?action=add">
          Quantity: <input type="text" name="qty" size="2"><br>
          <input type="hidden" name="products_prodnum"
            value="<?php echo $products_prodnum ?>">
          <input type="submit" name="Submit" value="Add to cart">
        </form>

        <form method="POST" action="cart.php">
          <input type="submit" name="Submit" value="View cart">
        </form>
    </td>
  </tr>
</table>
<hr width="200">
<p><a href="cbashop.php">Go back to the main page</a></p>
</div>
</body>
</html>
```

Then just as you did with the inventory count, you would alter your `checkout3.php` file to update the total number sold with the customers current order information, as follows:

```
//3) Insert Info into orderdet
//find the correct cart information being temporarily stored
$query = "SELECT * FROM carttemp WHERE carttemp_sess='$sessid'";
$results = mysql_query($query)
  or (mysql_error());

//put the data into the database one row at a time
while ($row = mysql_fetch_array($results)) {
  extract($row);
  $query4 = "INSERT INTO orderdet (
              orderdet_ordernum, orderdet_qty, orderdet_prodnum)
              VALUES (
              '$orderid',
              '$carttemp_quan',
              '$carttemp_prodnum')";
  $insert4 = mysql_query($query4)
    or (mysql_error());

  //update the on-hand inventory and the total sold for each product in cart
  $newinv = $products_inventory - $carttemp_quan;
  $newtotal = $products_total_sold + $carttemp_quan;
  $query4a = "UPDATE products SET
              $products_inventory='$newinv',
              $products_total_sold = '$newtotal'
              WHERE $products_prodnum = '$carttemp_prodnum'";
  $update4a = mysql_query($query4a);

}
```

Chapter 16

1. Add code to `admin.php` to prevent unauthorized users from loading the page. Redirect them back to `index.php`.

A. This block of code should go at the top of `admin.php`:

```php
<?php
include "http.php";
session_start();
if ($_SESSION['access_lvl'] < 3) redirect('index.php');
?>
```

2. Create a regular expression that recognizes an e-mail address in a post and turns it into a link.

A. This is not the only answer but it gets the job done:

```
/[\w\-]+(\.[\w\-]+)*@[\w\-]+(\.[\w\-]+)+/
```

3. Add a bit of code to the pagination function to allow the user to go to the first page or last page. For example, if there are 14 pages, and the user is on page 8, and the range is 7, it should look something like this:

```
<PREV [1] .. [5] [6] [7] 8 [9] [10] [11] .. [14] NEXT >
```

A. Replace the appropriate lines of code with the following code snippets:

```php
    if ($lrange > 1) {
        $pagelinks .= "<a class='pagenumlink' href='" . $currpage .
"&page=1'>[1]</a>..";
    } else {
        $pagelinks .= "  ";
    }

    if ($rrange < $numofpages) {
        $pagelinks .= "..<a class='pagenumlink' href='" . $currpage . "&page=".
$numofpages ."'>" . $numofpages . "</a>";
    } else {
        $pagelinks .= "  ";
    }
```

PHP Quick Reference

This appendix lists some quick reference notes for your use. Consider the information in this appendix to be your "cheat sheet." These topics are covered in depth in Chapter 2.

PHP Syntax

The basic PHP syntax is as follows:

```php
<?php
// enter lines of code, make sure they end with a semicolon;
?>
```

Displaying to Browser

To display text in a browser, use the following syntax:

```php
<?php
echo "Enter text here";      //echo text
echo $variable;              //echo values
echo "<br>";                 //echo HTML text
?>
```

Assigning a Value to a Variable

To set a value to a variable, use the following syntax:

```php
<?php
$varname = value;        //for numeric
$varname = "value";        //for text
?>
```

Passing Variables

You can pass variables among pages in your Web site in three ways: through a URL, through sessions, and through a form.

Through a URL

To pass a variable through a URL, use the following HTML code:

```
<a href="http://www.localhost.com/index.php?varname=value">
```

Through Sessions

To pass a variable through a session, use the following PHP code:

```
<?php      //this must be the first line of the script, before HTML code
session_start();      //starts the session
$_SESSION['varname'] = value;      //sets values for the entire session
$_SESSION['varname2'] = value;
?>

<?php //this must be the first few lines of every
      //page accessing session variables
session_start();
?>
```

Through a Form

A form must reference the PHP script that will parse the variables:

```
<?php
$value = $_POST['varname'];      //this is how you will access the
                                 //values from the form
?>
```

if Statements

To use if statements, type the following syntax:

```
<?php if (this is true) //execute this command ?>
```

or

```
<?php
if (this is true) {
  //execute command 1;
  //execute command 2;
  //execute command 3;
}
?>
```

else Statements

To use `else` statements, type the following syntax:

```php
<?php
if (this is true) //execute this command;
else //execute this command
?>
```

or

```php
else {
  //execute command 1;
  //execute command 2;
  //execute command 3;
}
?>
```

Nested if Statements

You can use nested `if` statements by using the following syntax:

```php
<?php
if (this is true) {       //remember to use == for equals
  if (this is true) //execute this command;
  if (this is true) //execute this command;
  else //execute this command;
}
?>
```

Including a File

To include a file, use the following syntax:

```php
<?php include "header.php"; ?>
```

Using Functions

You can create and call functions using the following syntax:

```php
<?php
function funcname()      //defines the function
{
  //line of php code;
  //line of php code;
  //line of php code;
}
funcname();      //calls the function to execute
?>
```

Arrays

You can set the values for an array in one of two ways:

```php
<?php
$name = array("firstname"=>"Albert", "lastname"=>"Einstein", "age"="124");

echo $name["firstname"];
?>
```

or

```php
<?php
$name["firstname"] = "Albert";
$name["lastname"] = "Einstein";
$name["age"] = 124;
?>
```

If no keys are required, you can set the values for an array like this:

```php
<?php
$flavor[] = "blue raspberry";
$flavor[] = "root beer";
$flavor[] = "pineapple";
?>
```

for

You can execute a block of code a specified number of times with the following `for` statement:

```php
<?php
for ($n = 0; $n <= 10; $n=$n+1) {
  //these lines will execute while the value 'n' is
  //less than or equal to 10
  echo $n;
  echo "<br>";
}
```

foreach

You can apply the same block of code to each value in a specified array with the `foreach` statement:

```php
foreach ($arrayvalue as $currentvalue) {
  //these lines will execute as long as there is a value in $arrayvalue
  echo $currentvalue;
  echo "<br>\n";
}
```

PHP5 Functions

This appendix lists some of the functions that will be applicable if you are using the Apache/PHP/MySQL components. PHP has numerous other functions available to you, and you can find a complete listing in the manual at the source Web site, www.php.net. We have not included any function that may be in the experimental stage or that isn't fully documented on the PHP site at the time of writing.

Note that some of the functions listed here have optional parameters that can be used to further specify the function (noted in brackets in our listing). In the interest of simplicity, some of those optional parameters have not been explained here, so you are encouraged to visit the source Web site for more information.

Functions that were added in PHP5 are indicated in bold print.

> *Note to Windows users: Some PHP functions are designed to work on non-Windows platforms only. If you encounter otherwise unexplained errors in your code, you might try checking the source Web site to ensure that your function is Windows-compatible.*

Apache/PHP Functions

PHP uses these functions with the Apache server.

PHP Function	Description
apache_child_terminate()	Stops the Apache server from running after the PHP script has been executed.
apache_get_modules()	Returns an array of loaded Apache Modules.
apache_get_version()	Returns the version of Apache that is currently running.
apache_getenv()	Returns an Apache subprocess_env variable.

Table continued on following page

PHP Function	Description
apache_lookup_uri(filename)	Returns information about the URI in filename as a class.
apache_note(note_name [, note_value])	Returns or sets values in the Apache notes tables as strings.
apache_request_headers()	Returns all HTTP headers as arrays.
apache_response_headers()	Returns all Apache response headers as arrays.
apache_setenv(variable, value[, bool])	Sets an Apache subprocess environment variable.
ascii2ebcdic(string)	Converts ASCII code to EBCDIC, opposite of ebcdic2ascii().
ebcdic2ascii(string)	Converts EBCDIC to ASCII code, opposite of ascii2ebcdic().
getallheaders()	Returns all HTTP request headers as arrays.
virtual(filename)	Performs an Apache subrequest, returns an integer.

Array Functions

You can perform these functions on arrays of information.

Function	Description
array([...])	Depending on the parameters, this creates an array of values.
array_change_key_case(array[, case])	Converts the keys in the named array to either all uppercase or all lowercase.
array_chunk(array, size[, keep_keys])	Splits the array into chunks based on the named parameters.
array_combine(keys, values)	Combines two arrays with equal number of keys and values. Uses one array for keys and the other for values.
array_count_values(array)	Counts the number of times each value appears, and returns results in array format.
array_diff_assoc(arrays)	Finds the values from the first array that do not appear in subsequent arrays, but unlike array_diff(), this takes key values into account.
array_diff(arrays)	Opposite of array_intersect(), finds the values from the first array that do not appear in subsequent arrays, and returns results in array format.

Function	Description
array_diff_uassoc(arrays)	Similar to array_diff_assoc(), but allows a final check through a custom function.
array_fill(array, number, value)	Fills an array with named value, a named number of times.
array_filter(array[, criteria])	Returns only array values that fit the named criteria.
array_flip(array)	Flips the array values and keys and returns results in array format.
array_intersect_assoc(arrays)	Finds the values from the first array that do not appear in subsequent arrays, but unlike array_intersect(), this takes key values into account.
array_intersect(arrays)	Opposite of array_diff(), finds the values from the first array that appear in subsequent arrays, and returns results in array format.
array_intersect_uassoc(arrays)	Similar to array_intersect_assoc(), but allows a final index check.
array_key_exists(array, search)	Verifies whether or not a key exists for an array.
array_keys(array[, search_value])	Will find either all the keys in the named array, or those keys containing the search value specified, and returns results in an array format.
array_map(criteria, array)	Applies a criterion to every element of the array and returns the new array of elements that fit the applied criterion.
array_merge(arrays)	Merges named arrays together and returns results in an array format. If two arrays have the same string keys, the later array will overwrite an earlier key, and if two arrays have the same numeric keys, the array will be appended instead of overwritten.
array_merge_recursive(arrays)	Similar to array_merge(), but the values of the arrays are appended.
array_multisort(array[, mixed])	Sorts either a complex multidimensional array or several arrays at one time.
array_pad(array, pad_size, pad_value)	Copies the existing array and pads the named size and value, returns value in array format.
array_pop(array)	Similar to array_shift(), except this deletes the last value of an array and returns what was deleted.

Table continued on following page

Function	Description
array_push(*array*, *variables*)	Similar to array_unshift(), except this adds the named values to the end of the array and returns the updated number of values in the array.
array_rand(*array* [,*number*])	Chooses a random value from the named array and if *number* is specified, chooses *number* of random values from the named array. The random value that was chosen is returned (or if more than one value is chosen, results are returned in array format).
array_reduce(*array*, *function*)	Reduces the array to a single function based on the named parameters.
array_reverse(*array*)	Reverses the order of the values in the array, and results are returned in array format.
array_search(*exp*, *array*)	Searches the array for the named expression and returns the key if it exists.
array_shift(*array*)	Similar to array_pop(), except this deletes the first value of an array and returns what was deleted. Opposite of array_unshift().
array_slice(*array*, *offset*[, *length*])	Based on the named offset, this will create a subarray from the original array. New array that is returned will also be length (if named).
array_splice(*array*, *offset*[, *length*, *new_values*])	Based on the named offset, this will remove a section of the named array (and replace it with new values if they are named).
array_sum(*array*)	Calculates the sum of the values in the named array.
array_udiff_assoc(*arrays*)	Returns an array with all the values that are not present in any of the other arrays; allows an index check and user-defined callback function.
array_udiff(*arrays*)	Returns the difference in arrays using a user-defined callback function.
array_udiff_uassoc(*arrays*)	Returns the difference in arrays; allows an index check and compares data and indexes with a user-defined callback function.
array_uintersect_assoc(*arrays*)	Returns the intersection of arrays through a user-defined callback function; allows an index check.
array_uintersect(*arrays*)	Returns the intersection of arrays through a user-defined callback function.
array_uintersect_uassoc(*arrays*)	Returns the intersection of arrays; allows an index check and compares data and indexes with a user-defined callback function.

Function	Description
array_unique(*array*)	Deletes any duplicate values in array, and returns new array.
array_unshift(*array*, *variables*)	Similar to array_push(), except this adds the named values to the beginning of an array and returns the number of updated values in the array. Opposite of array_shift().
array_values(*array*)	Returns an array with the values in the named array.
array_walk(*array*, *function*[,*parameter*])	Applies the named function (based on named parameters) to every value in the array.
array_walk_recursive(*array*, *function*[,*parameter*])	Applies the named function recursively (based on named parameters) to every value in the array.
arsort(*array*)	Sorts the array in descending order (while maintaining the key/value relationship).
asort(*array*)	Sorts the array in ascending order (while maintaining the key/value relationship).
compact(*variables*)	Merges the variables named into one array, returns results in array format.
count(*array*)	Equal to sizeof(), this counts the number of values in the named array and returns the results in an integer format.
current(*array*)	Returns the current values in the named array.
each(*array*)	Creates an array with the key and value of the current element of the named array, and returns results in array format.
end(*array*)	Sets the last value as the current value.
extract(*array*[, *type*, *prefix*])	Takes the named array and imports values into the symbol table. The *type* option directs the server what to do if there is a conflict, and *prefix* adds a prefix to variable names.
in_array(*value*, *array*)	Lets you know whether or not a specified value exists in the array.
key(*array*)	Returns the key for the current value in the array.
krsort(*array*)	Sorts the keys in the array in reverse order and maintains the key/value relationship.
ksort(*array*)	Sorts the keys in the array and maintains the key/value relationship.
list(*variables*)	Lists the named variables.

Table continued on following page

Function	Description
natsort(*array*)	Uses "natural ordering" to sort alphanumeric strings (case-sensitive).
natcasesort(*array*)	Uses "natural ordering" to sort alphanumeric strings (case-insensitive).
next(*array*)	The opposite of prev(), returns the value of the "next" element from the current element and returns false if the current element is the last element in the array.
pos(*array*)	Returns the value of the current element. (This function is the same as current(*array*).
prev(*array*)	The opposite of next(), returns the value of the element "before" the current element, and returns false if the current element is the first element in the array.
range(*low*, *high*)	Creates a new array of integers between the named parameters, and returns results in an array format.
reset(*array*)	Sets the current element as the first element in the array, and returns its value.
rsort(*array*)	The opposite of sort(), this sorts the array in descending order.
shuffle(*array*)	Shuffles the array in random order.
sizeof(*array*)	Equal to count(), returns the number of values in the array.
sort(*array*)	The opposite of rsort(), this sorts the array in ascending order.
uasort(*array*, *function*)	Using the named function, this sorts the array accordingly and maintains the key/value relationship.
uksort(*array*, *function*)	Using the named function, this sorts the array by key.
usort(*array*, *function*)	Using the named function, this sorts the array by value.

Date/Time/Calendar Functions

The following are helpful functions built into PHP that you can use to work with dates, times, and calendar settings. Please note that if you have installed PHP on a Linux system, you will need to compile PHP with --enable-calendar.

Function	Description
cal_days_in_month(*calendar*, *month*, *year*)	Returns the number of days in the named month.
cal_from_jd(*julian_day*, *calendar*)	Converts a Julian Day Count into a date of a specified calendar.
cal_info([*calendar*])	Returns information about the named calendar.
cal_to_jd(*calendar*, *month*, *day*, *year*)	Converts a specified calendar date into a Julian Day Count.
checkdate(*month*, *day*, *year*)	Validates the named date and returns true or false.
date(*format* [, *timestamp*])	Returns the date (and time if named) of the local server based on the named format. See the next table for common formatting guidelines.
easter_date([*year*])	Gives the UNIX timestamp for midnight on Easter of the current year, or the named year if present.
easter_days([*year*])	Calculates the number of days between March 21 and Easter of the current year, or named year if present.
frenchtojd(*french*)	Converts from French Republican calendar to Julian Day Count.
getdate(*timestamp*)	Creates an array with the named date/timestamps.
gettimeofday()	Creates an array with the current time.
gmdate(*format*[,*timestamp*])	Formats a GMT date and time based on named parameters. See the next table for common formatting guidelines.
gmmktime([*hour*, *minute*, *second*, *month*, *day*, *year*, *is_dst*])	Gives the UNIX timestamp for GMT time/day based on the named parameters, or the current time/day if not named.
gmstrftime(*format*, *timestamp*)	Formats a GMT/CUT date/time based on geography. See the next table for common formatting guidelines.
gregoriantojd(*gregorian*)	Converts from Gregorian calendar to Julian Day Count.
idate(*string*[, *int*])	Formats a date/time as an integer.
jddayofweek(*julianday*, *mode*)	Gives day of week of Julian Day Count, based on format named in mode.
jdmonthname(*julianday*, *mode*)	Gives month of Julian Day Count, based on format named in mode.
jdtofrench(*julianday*)	Converts from Julian Day Count to French Republican calendar.
jdtogregorian(*julianday*)	Converts from Julian Day Count to Gregorian calendar.

Table continued on following page

Function	Description
jdtojewish(*julianday*)	Converts from Julian Day Count to Jewish calendar.
jdtojulian(*julianday*)	Converts from Julian Day Count to Julian Calendar Date.
jdtounix(*julianday*)	Converts from Julian Day Count to UNIX timestamp.
jewishtojd(*jewish*)	Converts from Jewish calendar to Julian Day Count.
juliantojd(*julian*)	Converts from Julian calendar to Julian Day Count.
localtime([*timestamp*, is_associative])	Finds and returns local time in array format.
microtime()	Calculates and returns seconds and microseconds since 00:00:00 January 1, 1970.
mktime([*hour*, *minute*, *second*, *month*, *day*, *year*])	Gives the UNIX timestamp for time/day based on named parameters, or current time/day if not named.
strftime(*format* [,*timestamp*])	Based on format and current location, this will format the local time and date. See the next table for common formatting guidelines.
strtotime(*time*[, *now*])	Converts a time/date format in common English into a UNIX timestamp.
time()	Gives current UNIX timestamp.
unixtojd(*timestamp*)	Converts from UNIX timestamp to Julian Day Count.

Dates can be formatted with the following formatting codes (in conjunction with date()):

Format Character	Description	What Is Returned
a	Lowercase ante meridian and post meridian.	am, pm
A	Uppercase ante meridian and post meridian.	AM, PM
B	Swatch Internet time.	000 through 999
c	**ISO8601 date.**	**2000-01-12T15:19:21+00:00**
d	Day of the month in 2 digits with leading zeros.	01 to 31
D	Day of the week in text, abbreviated to three letters.	Mon through Sun
F	Month name in text format, unabbreviated.	January through December
g	Hour in 12-hour format, without leading zeros.	1 through 12

Format Character	Description	What Is Returned
G	Hour in 24-hour format, without leading zeros.	0 through 23
h	Hour in 12-hour format, with leading zeros.	01 through 12
H	Hour in 24-hour format, with leading zeros.	00 through 23
i	Minutes with leading zeros.	00 to 59
I (capital "i")	Indicates if date is in daylight savings time.	1 if DST, 0 otherwise
j	Day of the month without leading zeros.	1 to 31
l (lowercase 'L')	Day of the week in text, unabbreviated.	Sunday through Saturday
L	Indicates if the current year is a leap year.	1 if it is a leap year, 0 otherwise
m	Month in numeric format, with leading zeros.	01 through 12
M	Month in text format, abbreviated to three letters.	Jan through Dec
n	Month in numeric format without leading zeros.	1 through 12
O	Difference to Greenwich time (GMT) in hours.	-0500
r	RFC 822 formatted date.	Mon, 25 Aug 2003 18:01:01 +0200
s	Seconds, with leading zeros.	00 through 59
S	English ordinal suffix for the day of the month, 2 characters.	st, nd, rd, or th
t	Number of days in the month.	28 through 31
T	Time zone setting of the server.	EST, MDT, and so on
U	Seconds since the Unix Epoch (January 1 1970 00:00:00 GMT).	
w	Day of the week in numeric format.	0 (for Sunday) through 6 (for Saturday)
W	ISO-8601 week number of year, weeks starting on Monday.	1–52
Y	Year in numeric format in 4 digits.	2000, 2001, and so on
y	Year in numeric format in 2 digits.	00, 01, 02, and so on
z	Day of the year in numeric format.	0 through 366

Table continued on following page

Format Character	Description	What Is Returned
Z	Time zone offset in seconds. The offset for time zones west of UTC is always negative, and for those east of UTC is always positive.	-43200 through 43200

Class/Object/Function Handling Functions

The functions in the table that follows are used when referencing and working with classes, objects, and custom functions in your PHP code.

Function	Description
call_user_func(*function_name*[, *parameters*])	Calls the named user-defined function.
call_user_func_array(*function_name*[, *parameters*])	Calls the named user-defined function based on the array of parameters.
class_exists(*class_name*)	Verifies whether or not the class has been defined.
create_function (*arguments*, *code*)	Creates a function based on the parameters and returns a unique name for the function.
func_get_arg(*argument_num*)	Returns an item from the argument list.
func_get_args()	Gets complete argument list.
func_num_args()	Returns the number of arguments in the argument list.
function_exists(*function_name*)	Verifies whether or not a function has been defined.
get_class(*object_name*)	Returns the name of the specified object's class.
get_class_methods(*class_name*)	Returns the methods for specified class, in an array format.
get_class_vars(*class_name*)	Returns the properties for the specified class, in an array format.
get_declared_classes()	Returns all the classes that have been defined, in an array format.
get_declared_interfaces()	Returns the names of the declared interfaces.
get_defined_functions()	Returns all the functions that have been defined, in an array format.
get_object_vars(*object_name*)	Returns the properties for the specified object, in an array format.

Function	Description
get_parent_class(*object_name*)	Returns the name of the specified object's parent class.
is_a(*object_name*, *class_name*)	Verifies whether an object is part of the named class or if the class is one of the object's parents.
is_subclass_of(*object_name*, *superclass*)	Verifies whether and object is a part of a subclass of the named superclass.
method_exists(*object_name*, *method_name*)	Verifies whether a method has been defined.
register_shutdown_function(*function*)	Sets up the named function to be executed when script has been processed.
register_tick_function(*function*)	Registers a function for execution upon every tick.
unregister_tick_function(*function*)	Unregisters a function previously registered using register_tick_function().

Directory and File Functions

These functions can modify your directory settings and allow you to work with files through your PHP script.

Function	Description
basename(*path*)	Returns the filename listed in the named path.
chdir(*directory*)	Makes the named directory the current one.
chgrp(*filename*, *group*)	Assigns the named file to the named group.
chroot(*directory*)	Makes the named directory the root directory.
chmod(*filename*, *mode*)	Changes the mode of the named file.
chown(*filename*, *owner*)	Changes the owner of the named file.
clearstatcache()	Clears the file stat cache.
closedir(*directory*)	Closes the named directory.
copy(*source*, *destination*)	Copies the named source file to the named destination.
dir(*directory*)	Returns an object with the value of the named directory.
dirname(*path*)	Returns the directory listed in the named path.

Table continued on following page

Function	Description
disk_free_space(*directory*)	Returns the amount of free space in the named directory.
disk_total_space(*directory*)	Returns the amount of space in the named directory.
diskfreespace(*directory*)	Equal to disk_free_space(), returns the amount of free space in the named directory.
getcwd()	Returns the name of the current directory.
fclose(*file_pointer*)	Closes the named file.
feof(*file_pointer*)	Verifies whether or not the end of file has been reached for the named file.
fflush(*file_pointer*)	Flushes the output to a file.
fgetc(*file_pointer*)	Returns the next character listed in the named file.
fgetcsv(*file_pointer*, *length*[, *delimiter*])	Returns the next line in the named file.
fgets(*file_pointer*, *length*)	Returns a line of up to (length–1) in the named file.
fegtss(*file_pointer*, *length*[, *allowable_tags*])	Returns a line of up to (length–1) in the named file, while removing all tags except those specified.
file(*filename*[, *usepath*])	Returns an entire file in an array format, with each line representing a new value in the array.
file_get_contents(*filename*)	Reads the entire file contents into a string.
file_exists(*filename*)	Verifies whether the named file exists.
fileatime(*filename*)	Returns the last time the named file was accessed.
filectime(*filename*)	Returns the last time the named file was changed (in UNIX timestamp format).
filegroup(*filename*)	Returns the owner of the named file's group.
fileinode(*filename*)	Returns the named file's inode number.
filemtime(*filename*)	Returns the last time the named file was modified.
fileowner(*filename*)	Returns the owner of the named file.
fileperms(*filename*)	Returns the permissions associated with the named file.

Function	Description
filesize(*filename*)	Returns the size of the named file.
filetype(*filename*)	Returns the type of the named file.
flock(*file_pointer*, *operation*[, *wouldblock*])	Locks or unlocks the named file.
fnmatch(*pattern*, *exp*)	Searches for a filename that matches the named parameters.
fopen(*filename*, *mode*[, *usepath*])	Opens the named file.
fpassthru(*file_pointer*)	Returns all remaining data in the named file.
fputs(*file_pointer*, *string*[, *length*])	Equal to fwrite(), writes the named string to the named file.
fread(*file_pointer*, *length*)	Reads the named file up to the named length.
fscanf(*handle*, *format*[, *var1*, *var2*...])	Parses input based on the named format from the named file.
fseek(*file_pointer*, *offset*[, *start*])	Moves the file pointer in the named file by named offset spaces from start.
fstat(*file_pointer*)	Returns information about named file.
ftell(*file_pointer*)	Returns the position of the file pointer in the named file.
ftruncate(*file_pointer*, *size*)	Truncates the named file to the named size.
fwrite(*file_pointer*, *string*[, *length*])	Equal to fputs(), writes the named string to the named file.
glob(*string*)	Finds path names that match the named string.
is_dir(*filename*)	Verifies whether the named file is a directory.
is_executable(*filename*)	Verifies whether the named file is an executable.
is_file(*filename*)	Verifies whether the named file is a file.
is_link(*filename*)	Verifies whether the named file is a link.
is_readable(*filename*)	Verifies whether the named file is readable.
is_writeable(*filename*)	Verifies whether the named file is writeable.
is_uploaded_file(*filename*)	Verifies whether the named file has been uploaded using HTTP POST.
link(*target*, *link*)	Creates a new link.
linkinfo(*path*)	Returns all information about the named link.

Table continued on following page

Function	Description
lstat(*filename*)	Returns information about named file.
mkdir(*pathname*, *mode*)	Creates a directory based on specified path name and mode.
move_uploaded_file(*filename*, *destination*)	Moves the named file to a different directory.
opendir(*path*)	Opens the named directory.
parse_ini_file(*filename*)	Parses the named configuration file.
pathinfo(*path*)	Returns information about the named path.
pclose(*file_pointer*)	Closes the named file pointer to a pipe.
popen(*command*, *mode*)	Opens a pipe with the named command.
readdir(*directory*)	Reads the named directory and returns the next entry.
readfile(*filename*[, *usepath*])	Reads the named file.
readlink(*path*)	Reads the named link and returns the target.
realpath(*path*)	Returns the absolute path.
rename(*name*, *newname*)	Renames the named file.
rewind(*file_pointer*)	Moves the pointer to the beginning of the file stream.
rewinddir(*directory*)	Moves the pointer to the beginning of the directory and resets the directory stream.
rmdir(*directory*)	Removes the named directory.
scandir(*directory*[, *sort_order*])	Lists the files and directories in the named path.
set_file_buffer(*file_pointer*, *buffer*)	Sets the file buffer for named file.
stat(*filename*)	Returns information about the named file.
symlink(*target*, *link*)	Creates a symbolic link.
tempnam(*directory*, *prefix*)	Creates a temporary file in the named directory.
tmpfile()	Creates a temporary file.
touch(*filename*[, *time*])	Sets the time the named file is modified.
umask(*mask*)	Modifies the current umask.
unlink(*filename*)	Deletes the named file.

Error Handling and Logging Functions

These functions can help you view and use errors to debug programs or alert you to potential problems in your scripts.

Function	Description
debug_backtrace()	Generates a backtrace and returns the information in an array format.
debug_print_backtrace()	Displays a generated backtrace.
error_log(*message*, *message_type*[, *dest*, *extra_headers*])	Adds an error message to the server's log, and anywhere else depending on the message type as defined in the given parameter. Message type 0 sends a message to PHP's system logger, type 1 sends an e-mail to the address specified in the *dest* parameter, type 2 sends a remote debugging message to the IP address or hostname specified in the *dest* parameter, and type 3 appends the error message to the file specified in the *dest* parameter.
error_reporting([level])	Determines which PHP errors will be displayed.
restore_error_handler()	Restores error handler functions.
restore_exception_handler(*function*)	Restores an exception handler function.
set_error_handler(error_handler)	Sets an error handler function.
set_exception_handler(*function*)	Sets a user-defined exception handler function.
trigger_error(*error_message*[, *error_type*])	Same as user_error(), displays a user-level error message.
user_error(*error_message*[, *error_type*])	Same as trigger_error(), displays a user-level error message.

HTTP Functions

These functions work with the HTTP protocol.

Function	Description
header(*string*)	Outputs the named HTTP header.
headers_list()	Returns an array containing the headers that will be sent.
headers_sent()	Verifies whether HTTP headers have been sent.

Table continued on following page

Function	Description
setcookie(*name*, [*value*, *expiration*, *path*, *domain*, *secure*])	Sends a cookie to the user based on the named parameters.
setrawcookie(*name*, [*value*, *expiration*, *path*, *domain*, *secure*])	Sends a cookie to the user without url encoding it first.

Image Functions

The following PHP functions enable you to manipulate and create images directly from your PHP code. Please note that you may need to have the GD library, which enables you to create dynamic images, installed to enable some of these functions. You can download GD from www.boutell.com/gd/.

Function	Description
exif_imagetype(*filename*)	Returns the type of named image file.
exif_read_data(*filename*)	Reads the EXIF headers in a JPEG or TIFF image, useful for reading digital images.
exif_thumbnail(*filename*[, *width*, *height*, *type*])	Reads the embedded thumbnail image of a JPEG or TIFF image.
gd_info()	Returns information about the currently installed GD library.
getimagesize(*filename*, [*image_info*])	Returns the size of the named file.
image_type_to_mime_type(*type*)	Gets the MIME-type for the named image type.
image2wbmp(*image*[, *filename*])	Outputs the image directly to a browser.
imagealphablending(*image*, *blendmode*)	Sets the blending mode for the named image.
imageantialias(*image*, *on_off*)	Toggles antialiasing on and off for the named image.
imagearc(*name*, *cx*, *cy*, *width*, *height*, *start*, *end*, *col*)	Draws a partial ellipse based on named parameters.
imagechar(*name*, *font*, *x*, *y*, *c*, *col*)	Draws a character horizontally based on named parameters.
imagecharup(*name*, *font*, *x*, *y*, *c*, *col*)	Draws a character vertically based on named parameters.
imagecolorallocate(*name*, *red*, *green*, *blue*)	Allocates a color for the named image and returns an identifier.
imagecolorallocatealpha(*name*, *red*, *green*, *blue*, *transparent*)	Similar to imagecolorallocate(), except allows the color to display at a certain level of transparency.

Function	Description
imagecolorat(*name*, *x*, *y*)	Indicates the color index of the pixel at the named coordinates.
imagecolorclosest(*name*, *red*, *green*, *blue*)	Returns the closest color in the palette of the named image.
imagecolorclosestalpha(*name*, *red*, *green*, *blue*, *alpha*)	Similar to imagecolorclosest(), except takes into account the alpha (transparency) level.
imagecolorclosesthwb(*name*, *red*, *green*, *blue*)	Similar to imagecolorclosest(), except also looks at hue, whiteness, and blackness.
imagecolordeallocate(*name*, *red*, *green*, *blue*)	Opposite of imagecolorallocate(), deallocates the color for the named image.
imagecolorexact(*name*, *red*, *green*, *blue*)	Returns the exact color in the palette of the named image.
imagecolorexactalpha(*name*, *red*, *green*, *blue*, *alpha*)	Similar to imagecolorexact(), except takes into account the alpha level.
imagecolorresolve(*name*, *red*, *green*, *blue*)	Returns either the index of the exact color or the closest color available in the palette of the named image.
imagecolorresolvealpha(*name*, *red*, *green*, *blue*, *alpha*)	Similar to imagecolorresolve(), except takes into account the alpha level.
imagecolorset(*name*, *index*, *red*, *green*, *blue*)	Sets the color for the palette of the named file.
imagecolorsforindex(*name*, *index*)	Returns value for red, blue, and green for the specified index.
imagecolorstotal(*name*)	Returns the number of available colors in the palette of the named image.
imagecolortransparent(*name*[, *color*])	Sets the named color as transparent in the named image.
imagecopy(*dest_name*, *source_name*, *dest_x*, *dest_y*, *source_x*, *source_y*, *source_width*, *source_height*)	Copies an image based on named parameters.
imagecopymerge(*dest_name*, *source_name*, *dest_x*, *dest_y*, *source_x*, *source_y*, *source_width*, *source_height*, *pct*)	Similar to imagecopy(), but copies an image based on named parameters including percent (when set to 100, acts identically to imagecopy()).
imagecopymergegray(*dest_name*, *source_name*, *dest_x*, *dest_y*, *source_x*, *source_y*, *source_width*, *source_height*, *pct*)	Similar to imagecopymerge(), except copies image in grayscale.

Table continued on following page

Function	Description
imagecopyresampled(*dest_name*, *source_name*, *dest_x*, *dest_y*, *source_x*, *source_y*, *dest_width*, *dest_height*, *source_width*, *source_height*)	Copies and resizes a resampled image based on the named parameters.
imagecopyresized(*dest_name*, *source_name*, *dest_x*, *dest_y*, *source_x*, *source_y*, *dest_width*, *dest_height*, *source_width*, *source_height*)	Copies and resizes an image based on named parameters.
imagecreate(*width*, *height*)	Creates a new image based on named width and height.
imagecreatefromgd2(*name*)	Creates a new image from a GD file or URL.
imagecreatefromgd2part(*name*, *x*, *y*, *width*, *height*)	Creates a new image from a part of a GD file or URL.
imagecreatefromgd(*name*)	Creates a new image from a GD file or URL.
imagecreatefromgif(*name*)	Creates a new image from the named GIF file.
imagecreatefromjpeg(*name*)	Creates a new image from the named JPEG or JPG file.
imagecreatefrompng(*name*)	Creates a new image from the named PNG file.
imagecreatefromstring(*name*)	Creates a new image from an image stream in the named string.
imagecreatefromwbmp(*name*)	Creates a new image from named file or URL.
imagecreatefromxbm(*name*)	Creates a new image from named file or URL.
imagecreatefromxpm(*name*)	Creates a new image from named file or URL.
imagecreatetruecolor(*x_size*, *y_size*)	Returns an image identifier based on a black image according to the named parameters.
imagedestroy(*name*)	Deletes the named image.
imageellipse(*name*, *cx*, *cy*, *width*, *height*, *color*)	Draws an ellipse based on the named parameters.
imagefill(*name*, *x*, *y*, *color*)	Fills the entire image with one color based on the named parameters.
imagefilledarc(*name*, *cx*, *cy*, *width*, *height*, *start*, *end*, *color*, *style*)	Draws a filled partial ellipse based on the named parameters.
imagefilledellipse(*name*, *cx*, *cy*, *width*, *height*, *color*)	Draws a filled ellipse based on the named parameters.

Function	Description
imagefilledpolygon(*name*, *points*, *num_of_points*, *color*)	Draws a filled polygon based on the named parameters.
imagefilledrectangle(*name*, *x1*, *y1*, *x2*, *y2*, *color*)	Draws a filled rectangle based on the named parameters.
imagefilltoborder(*name*, *x*, *y*, *border_color*, *color*)	Fills the entire image with a color and outlines it with a border color, based on named parameters.
imagefontheight(*font*)	Returns the height of the named font in pixels.
imagefontwidth(*font*)	Returns the width of the named font in pixels.
imagegammacorrect(*name*, *inputgamma*, *outputgamma*)	Corrects the gamma levels in a GD image.
imagegd2(*name*[, *filename*, *chunk_size*, *type*])	Outputs the named GD file to the browser based on the named parameters.
imagegd(*name*[, *filename*])	Sends the named GD file to the browser.
imagegif(*name*[, *filename*])	Sends the named GIF image to another file or to a browser as the named image.
imageinterlace(*name*[, *interlace*])	Toggles whether interlacing is on or off for the named image.
imageistruecolor(*name*)	Returns whether or not an image is truecolor.
imagejpeg (*name*[, *filename*, *quality*])	Sends the named JPEG image to another file or to a browser as the named image.
imageline(*name*, *x1*, *y1*, *x2*, *y2*, *color*)	Draws a solid line based on the named parameters.
imageloadfont(*filename*)	Loads the named font.
imagepallettecopy(*destination*, *source*)	Copies the named color palette.
imagepng(*name*[, *filename*])	Sends the named PNG image to another file or to a browser as the named image.
imagepolygon(*name*, *points*, *num_of_points*, *color*)	Draws an empty polygon based on the named parameters.
imagepsbbox(*text*, *font*, *size*, *space*, *width*, *angle*)	Returns the coordinates for a text box using a PostScript font, based on named parameters.
imagepscopyfont(*font_index*)	Makes a copy of an already loaded PostScript font.
imagepsencodefont(*encoding_file*)	Loads the named encoding vector for a PostScript font.

Table continued on following page

Function	Description
imagepsextendfont(*font_index*, *extend*)	Extends a PostScript font.
imagepsfreefont(*font_index*)	Frees the named PostScript font from memory.
imagepsloadfont(*filename*)	Loads the named PostScript font file.
imagepsslantfont(*font_index*, *slant*)	Slants the named PostScript font.
imagepstext(*name*, *text*, *font*, *size*, *foreground_color*, *background_color*, *x*, *y*[, *space*, *tightness*, *angle*, *antialias*])	Writes a text string using the named PostScript font and based on the named parameters.
imagerectangle(*name*, *x1*, *y1*, *x2*, *y2*, *color*)	Draws an empty rectangle based on the named parameters.
imagerotate(*name*, *angle*, *color*)	Rotates an image based on the named parameters.
imagesavealpha(*name*, *flag*)	Sets the flag to save with the image's alpha information.
imagesetbrush(*name*, *brush*)	Sets the brush for line drawing.
imagesetpixel(*name*, *x*, *y*, *color*)	Draws a pixel based on the named parameters.
imagesetstyle(*name*, *style*)	Sets the style for line drawing.
imagesetthickness(*name*, *thickness*)	Sets the thickness for line drawing.
imagesettile(*name*, *tile*)	Sets the tile image for fill functions.
imagestring(*name*, *font*, *x*, *y*, *string*, *color*)	Draws a horizontal string based on the named parameters.
imagestringup(*name*, *font*, *x*, *y*, *string*, *color*)	Draws a vertical string based on the named parameters.
imagesx(*name*)	Determines the width of the named image.
imagesy(*name*)	Determines the height of the named image.
imagetruecolortopallette(*name*, *dither*, *colors*)	Converts a true color image to a color palette based on the named parameters.
imagettfbbox(*size*, *angle*, *font_filename*, *text*)	Draws a text box using the named TrueType font and based on the named parameters.
imagettftext(*name*, *size*, *angle*, *x*, *y*, *color*, *font_filename*, *text*)	Writes a text string using the named TrueType font.
imagetypes()	Displays the image types supported by the PHP version currently being used.
iptcembed(*data*, *filename*)	Embeds International Press Telecommunications Council (IPTC) data into a JPEG file.

Function	Description
iptcparse(*iptcblock*)	Parses an IPTC block into tags.
jpeg2wbmp(*jpegfilename*, *wbmpfilename*, *height*, *width*, *threshold*)	Converts a JPEG file into a WBMP file.
png2wbmp(*pngfilename*, *wbmpfilename*, *height*, *width*, *threshold*)	Converts a PNG file into a WBMP file.
read_exif_data(*filename*)	Displays any EXIF headers from a JPEG file.

Mail Functions

Use these functions to send mail directly from your PHP script.

Function	Description
ezmlm_hash(*addr*)	Displays the hash value used by EZMLM scripts.
mail(*to*, *subject*, *message*[, *headers*])	Sends mail based on the named parameters.

Mathematical Functions

These functions allow you to perform mathematical calculations on your data while still in the PHP code.

Function	Description
abs(*number*)	Calculates the absolute value of a number.
acos(*argument*)	Calculates the arc cosine in radians.
asin(*argument*)	Calculates the arc sine in radians.
atan(*argument*)	Calculates the arc tangent in radians.
atan2(*x*, *y*)	Calculates the arc tangent of x and y.
base_convert(*number*, *startbase*, *endbase*)	Converts a number based on the named parameters.
bindec(*binary_string*)	Converts a binary string to a decimal, the opposite of decbin().
ceil(*number*)	Rounds fractions to next highest integer.
cos(*argument*)	Calculates the cosine in radians.
decbin(*number*)	Converts a decimal to a binary string, the opposite of bindec().

Table continued on following page

Function	Description
dechex(*number*)	Converts a decimal to hexadecimal, the opposite of hexdec().
decoct(*number*)	Converts a decimal to octal, the opposite of octdec().
deg2rad(*number*)	Converts degrees to radian, opposite of rad2deg().
exp(*argument*)	Calculates e to the named power.
floor(*number*)	Rounds fractions down to the next lowest integer.
fmod(*num1*, *num2*)	Returns the floating point remainder of the division of the two numbers.
getrandmax()	Calculates the maximum random value from the rand() function.
hexdec(*hex_string*)	Converts hexadecimal to decimal, opposite of dechex().
is_finite(*number*)	Returns whether or not the number is a finite number.
is_infinite(*number*)	Returns whether or not the number is an infinite number.
is_nan(*number*)	Returns whether or not the number is truly a number.
lcg_value()	Calculates a pseudo-random number between 0 and 1.
log(*argument*)	Calculates the natural log.
log10(*argument*)	Calculates the base 10 log.
max(*num1*, *num2*, ...)	Calculates the maximum of listed values.
min(*num1*, *num2*, ...)	Calculates the minimum of listed values.
mt_getrandmax()	Calculates the maximum random value from the mt_rand() function.
mt_rand([*min*, *max*])	Generates a Mersenne Twister random value.
mt_srand(*seed*)	Seeds the Mersenne Twister random number generator.
number_format(*number*[, *dec_places*, *dec_point*, *thousands*])	Formats the number based on the named parameters.
octdec(*octal_string*)	Converts octal to decimal, the opposite of decoct().
pi()	Returns pi to the number of digits set in the php.ini file.
pow(*number*, *exp*)	Calculates named number to the power of named exponent.
rad2deg(*number*)	Converts radians to decimal, the opposite of deg2rad().
rand([*min*, *max*])	Generates a random integer based on named parameters if applicable.
round(*number*, [*precision*])	Rounds the named number to the nearest integer.

Function	Description
sin(*argument*)	Calculates the sine in radians.
sqrt(*argument*)	Calculates the square root.
srand(*seed*)	Seeds the random number generator.
tan(*argument*)	Calculates the tangent in radians.

MySQL Functions

The following table lists the PHP functions that can be used with your MySQL server for added functionality in your PHP script.

Function	Description
mysql_affected_rows([*link_id*])	Returns the number of rows of records affected by the previous command.
mysql_client_encoding()	Returns the character set used by the current connection.
mysql_close([*link_id*])	Closes the active connection.
mysql_connect([*hostname*[:*port*] [:/*path/to/socket*], *username*, *password*])	Opens the connection to the server based on the named parameters. Similar to mysql_pconnect().
mysql_data_seek(*result_id*, *row_number*)	Moves to the named row of the results.
mysql_db_name(*result*, *row* [,*field*])	Gets data for result.
mysql_db_query(*database*, *query*[, *link_id*])	Executes the named query on the named database and returns results.
mysql_errno([*link_id*])	Displays the error number for the previous query.
mysql_error([*link_id*])	Displays the error message for the previous query.
mysql_escape_string(*string*)	Escapes the named string for use in a query.
mysql_fetch_array(*result* [, *type*])	Obtains the row of data based on the result from a previous query, returns result in an array format.
mysql_fetch_assoc(*result*)	Returns an associative array based on the query previously sent to the server.
mysql_fetch_field(*result*[, *field_offset*])	Returns the field based on the result from a previous query.

Table continued on following page

Function	Description
mysql_fetch_lengths(*result*)	Returns the length of each field in the result from a previous query.
mysql_fetch_object(*result*[, *type*])	Obtains data based on the result from a previous query, returns result in an object format.
mysql_fetch_row(*result*)	Obtains the row of data based on the result from a previous query, returns result in an enumerated array.
mysql_field_flags(*result*, *field*)	Displays the field flag of the named field.
mysql_field_len(*result*, *field*)	Displays the field length of the named field.
mysql_field_name(*result*, *field*)	Displays the name of the named field.
mysql_field_seek(*result*, *field_offset*)	Moves to the named field of the results.
mysql_field_table(*result*, *field*)	Displays the table of the named field.
mysql_field_type(*result*, *field*)	Displays the type of the named field.
mysql_free_result(*result*)	Frees any memory still used by the result from a previous query.
mysql_get_client_info()	Returns the MySQL client information.
mysql_get_host_info([*link_id*])	Returns information about the server host.
mysql_get_proto_info([*link_id*])	Returns the protocol information.
mysql_get_server_info([*link_id*])	Returns information about the server.
mysql_info([*link_id*])	Gets information about the previous query.
mysql_insert_id([*link_id*])	Returns the ID value of the most recently inserted auto_increment field.
mysql_list_dbs([*link_id*])	Lists the databases on the MySQL server.
mysql_list_fields(*database*, *table*[, *link_id*])	Lists the fields in the named database and table.
mysql_list_processes([*link_id*])	Lists the processes.
mysql_list_tables(*database*)	Lists the tables in the named database.
mysql_num_fields(*result*)	Shows the number of fields in the result from a previous query.
mysql_num_rows(*result*)	Shows the number of rows in the result from a previous query.
mysql_pconnect([*hostname*[:*port*] [:*/path/to/socket*], *username*, *password*])	Opens a persistent connection to the server based on the named parameters. Similar to mysql_connect().

Function	Description
mysql_ping([*link_id*])	Pings the server connection to verify the connection is working properly.
mysql_query(*query*[, *link_id*])	Executes the named query.
mysql_real_escape_string(*string*[, *link_id*])	Escapes a string to be used in the query, and takes into account the charset of the connection.
mysql_result(*result*, *row*[, *field*])	Obtains the data located in the named field/row of the results.
mysql_select_db(*database*[, *link_id*])	Selects the named database and makes it current.
mysql_stat([*link_id*])	Gets the current system status.
mysql_thread_id([*link_id*])	Returns current connection thread ID.
mysql_tablename(*result*, *index*)	Returns the table from which the result was obtained.
mysql_unbuffered_query(*query*[, *link_id*])	Queries the MySQL server without fetching and buffering the results.

Network Functions

The functions in the table that follows can be used to communicate with your network directly from PHP.

Function	Description
checkdnsrr(*host*[, *type*])	Equal to dns_check_record(), searches for DNS records based on the named parameters.
closelog()	Closes the connection to the system log, the opposite of openlog().
define_syslog_variables()	Initializes syslog constants.
dns_check_record(*host*[, *type*])	Equal to checkdnsrr(), searches for DNS records based on named parameters.
dns_get_mx(*host*, *mxhosts*[, *weight*])	Equal to getmxrr(), returns MX records based on the named host.
dns_get_record(*host*[, *type*)	Gets DNS records associated with the hostname.
fsockopen([*hostname*, *port*, *errno*, *errstr*, *timeout*])	Opens a socket connection based on the named parameters.
gethostbyaddr(*ip*)	Returns the hostname based on the named IP address.

Table continued on following page

Function	Description
gethostbyname(*host*)	Returns the IP address based on the named host.
gethostbyname1(*host*)	Returns multiple IP addresses based on the named host.
getmxrr(*host*, *mxhosts*[, *weight*])	Equal to dns_get_mx(), returns MX records based on the named host.
getprotobyname(*name*)	Returns protocol number based on named protocol.
getprotobynumber(*number*)	Returns protocol name based on named protocol number.
getservbyname(*service*, *protocol*)	Returns a port number based on named parameters.
getservbyport(*port*, *protocol*)	Returns the service based on named parameters.
ip2long(*ip*)	Converts a string with an IP address into a proper address.
long2ip(*proper_address*)	Converts a proper address into an IP address with dotted format.
openlog(*ident*, *option*, *facility*)	Opens a connection to the system log, the opposite of closelog().
pfsockopen([*hostname*, *port*, *errno*, *errstr*, *timeout*])	Opens a persistent socket connection based on the named parameters.
syslog(*priority*, *message*)	Writes the named message to the system log.

Output Buffer Functions

The functions in the table that follows enable you to control the output buffer from PHP.

Function	Description
flush()	Flushes the output buffer.
ob_clean()	Destroys the contents of the output buffer.
ob_end_flush()	Sends the output buffer contents and disables output buffering.
ob_end_clean()	Deletes the output buffer contents and disables output buffering.
ob_flush()	Sends the output buffer.
ob_get_clean()	Gets the contents of the output buffer and deletes the output buffer.
ob_get_contents()	Gets the contents of the output buffer.

Function	Description
ob_get_length()	Gets the length of the output buffer.
ob_get_level()	Gets the nesting level of the output buffer.
ob_gzhandler()	Callback function to gzip the output buffer.
ob_implicit_flush()	Toggles implicit flushing on and off.
ob_list_handlers()	Returns all output handlers being used.
ob_start()	Enables output buffering.
output_add_rewrite_var(name, value)	Adds values to URLs.
output_reset_rewrite_vars()	Resets any values added to URLs from the output_add_rewrite_var() function.

PHP Configuration Information

With these functions, you can easily determine what your PHP is communicating to the server based on its setup, and alter configuration options from your PHP script.

Function	Description
assert(assertion)	Verifies whether an assertion is false.
assert_options(what, [value])	Returns the assert flags.
extension_loaded(name)	Verifies whether or not an extension library has been loaded.
get_cfg_var(var)	Returns the named configuration variable value.
get_current_user()	Returns the owner of the PHP script.
get_defined_constants()	Returns an array with all the defined constants and their values.
get_extension_funcs(module_name)	Returns the functions in the named module.
get_include_path()	Returns the current include_path configuration option.
get_included_files()	Returns an array containing the filenames of those included or required in the script.
get_loaded_extensions()	Returns the compiled and loaded modules.
get_magic_quotes_gpc()	Returns the setting of magic_quotes_gpc.
get_magic_quotes_runtime()	Returns the setting of magic_quotes_runtime.
get_required_files()	Returns an array containing the filenames of those included or required in the script.

Table continued on following page

Function	Description
getenv(*var*)	Returns the value of the named environment variable.
getlastmod()	Returns when the page was last modified.
getmygid()	Returns the group ID for the current script.
getmyinode()	Returns the inode of the script.
getmypid()	Returns the process ID for PHP.
getmyuid()	Returns the user ID for the owner of the PHP script.
getopt()	Returns an array of options/argument pairs from the command-line argument list.
getrusage([*who*])	Returns resource usage.
ini_alter(*varname*, *newvalue*)	Updates the php.ini file based on the named parameters.
ini_get_all([*extension*])	Returns configuration options.
ini_get(*varname*)	Returns the named value from the php.ini file.
ini_restore(*varname*)	Restores the previous value in the php.ini file.
ini_set(*varname*, *newvalue*)	Sets the named value in the php.ini file.
memory_get_usage()	Returns the amount of memory allocated to PHP.
php_ini_scanned_files()	Returns a list of parsed ini files from an additional directory.
php_logo_guid()	Returns the PHP logo GUID.
php_sapi_name()	Returns the interface between the Web server and PHP.
php_uname()	Returns information about the operating system running PHP.
phpcredits(*flag*)	Displays the credits for PHP.
phpinfo()	Displays information about the current environment and configuration of PHP.
phpversion()	Displays the currently running PHP version.
putenv(*setting*)	Sets the value of an environment variable.
restore_include_path()	Restores the include_path configuration option.

Function	Description
set_include_path(*path*)	Sets the include_path configuration option.
set_magic_quotes_runtime(*newsetting*)	Turns the magic quotes feature on or off.
set_time_limit(*seconds*)	Sets the maximum amount of time a PHP script can run.
version_compare(*string1*, *string2*)	Compares two PHP version numbers.
zend_logo_guid()	Returns the Zend logo GUID.
zend_version()	Returns the current Zend engine.

Program Execution Functions

The functions in the table that follows allow PHP code to execute commands directly from the script.

Function	Description
escapeshellarg(*arg*)	Escapes a string to be used as a shell argument.
escapreshelllcmd(*cmd*)	Escapes shell metacharacters in the named command.
exec(*command*[, *array*, *return_var*])	Executes the named command and returns the last line of results.
passthru(*command*[, return_var])	Executes the named command and returns the raw output.
proc_close(*process*)	Closes processes opened by the proc_open() function.
proc_get_status(*process*)	Gets information about a process opened by the proc_open() function.
proc_nice(*number*)	Changes the priority of the current process according to the supplied number.
proc_open(string *cmd*, array *descriptorspec*, array &*pipes* [, string *cwd* [, array *env* [, array *other_options*)]]])	Executes the given command according to the given parameters.
proc_terminate(*process*)	Terminates a process opened by the proc_open() function.
shell_exec(*command*)	Executes a command through the shell.
system(*command*[, *return_var*])	Executes the named command and returns all the output.

Spelling Functions

You can have PHP perform spell checks for you, as long as you supply a reference it can use.

Function	Description
pspell_add_to_personal(*link*, *word*)	Adds the named word to a personal dictionary.
pspell_add_to_session(*link*, *word*)	Adds the named word to a session's wordlist.
pspell_check(*link*, *word*)	Using the named link as a reference, it will check the spelling of the named word.
pspell_clear_session()	Deletes a current session's wordlist.
pspell_config_create(*language*[, *spelling*, *jargon*, *encoding*])	Configures options to open a dictionary.
pspell_config_ignore(*link*, *n*)	Configures spell check so that words under *n* characters long will be ignored.
pspell_config_mode(*link*, *mode*)	Changes the number of suggestions offered.
pspell_config_personal(*link*, *file*)	Sets the file that will contain a personal wordlist.
pspell_config_repl(*link*, *file*)	Sets the file that contains replacement pairs.
pspell_config_runtogether(*link*, *flag*)	Determines if run-together words are valid.
pspell_config_save_repl(*link*, *flag*)	Determines if replacement pairs should be saved with the personal wordlist.
pspell_new_config()	Loads a new dictionary based on the supplied config.
pspell_new_personal()	Loads a new personal wordlist based on the supplied config.
pspell_new(*language*[, *spelling*, *jargon*, *encoding*, *mode*])	Loads a new dictionary with a personal wordlist.
pspell_save_wordlist(*link*)	Saves the personal wordlist to the named link.
pspell_store_replacement(*link*, *misspelled*, *correct*)	Stores a replacement pair for a word.
pspell_suggest(*link*, *word*)	Suggests a list of alternatives for the named word.

Session Functions

The functions in the table that follows are useful when utilizing sessions in your PHP scripts.

Function	Description
session_cache_expire([*new_cache_expire*])	Returns the cache expiration, or sets a new one (in minutes).
session_cache_limiter([*cache_limiter*])	Returns the cache limiter, or sets a new one.
session_commit()	Equal to session_write_close(), this ends the current session and stores all session variables.
session_decode(*string*)	Decodes the named session data.
session_destroy()	Destroys session data.
session_encode()	Encodes session data as a string.
session_get_cookie_params()	Gets information about session cookie configuration.
session_id([*id*])	Returns the session ID, or sets a new one.
session_is_registered(*varname*)	Verifies whether the named variable has been registered in current session.
session_module_name([*module_name*])	Returns the session module, or sets a new one.
session_name([*name*])	Returns the session name, or sets a new one.
session_regenerate_id()	Generates a new session ID for the current session and maintains session variables and their contents.
session_register(*name*[,*var1*, *var2*...])	Registers variables with the current session.
session_save_path([*path*])	Returns the path where session data is saved, or sets a new one.
session_set_cookie_params(*expiration*[, *path*, *domain*])	Configures the session cookie based on the named parameters.
session_set_save_handler(*open*, *close*, *read*, *write*, *destroy*, *gc*)	Sets user-level session storage based on named parameters.
session_start()	Starts a new session.
session_unregister(*name*)	Unregisters session variables.
session_unset()	Releases all session variables.
session_write_close()	Ends the current session and stores all session variables.

String Functions

There are times when you need PHP to manipulate strings for you, and luckily many functions help you do just that.

Function	Description
addcslashes(*string*, *charlist*)	Adds slashes before named characters in the named string.
addslashes(*string*)	Adds slashes to quoted characters in the named strings for database queries.
bin2hex(*string*)	Converts binary data into ASCII hexadecimal format.
chop(*string*)	Equal to rtrim(), deletes trailing spaces from the named string.
chr(*ascii*)	Returns the character based on the named ASCII code.
chunk_split(*string*[, *length*, *div*])	Divides the named string by inserting the character named by *div* every *length* characters.
convert_cyr_string(*string*, *from*, *to*)	Converts the named string from one Cyrillic character set to another.
convert_uudecode(*string*)	Converts a string encoded with the convert_uuencode() function.
convert_uuencode(string)	Encodes a string using the uuencode algorithm.
count_chars(*string*[, *mode*])	Counts the number of characters in the named string.
crc32(*string*)	Calculates the crc32 of 32-bit lengths of string.
crypt(*string*[, *char*])	Using named 2-character parameter, this will DES-encrypt the named string.
echo(*string*)	Displays the named string.
ereg(*exp*, *string*[, *array*])	Searches the named string for the named expression and stores the results in the named array.
ereg_replace(*exp1*, *exp2*, *string*)	Searches and replaces *exp1* with exp2 in the named string.
eregi(*exp*, *string*[, *array*])	Searches the named string for the named expression (case-insensitive) and stores the results in the named array.
eregi_replace(*exp1*, *exp2*, *string*)	Searches and replaces *exp1* with *exp2* (case-insensitive) in the named string.

Function	Description
explode(*separator*, *string*[, *limit*])	Divides the named string using the named separator and returns results in array format, the opposite of implode().
fprintf(*res handle*, *format*)	Sends a formatted string to a stream.
get_html_translation_table(*table*[, *quote_styles*])	Returns the named translation table.
hebrev(*text*[, *max_chars_per_line*])	Converts Hebrew text to visual text.
hebrevc(*text*[, *max_chars_per_line*])	Converts Hebrew text to visual text with newlines.
html_entity_decode(*string*[, *quote style*])	The opposite of htmlentities(), converts HTML entities into their applicable characters.
htmlentities(*string*[, *quote_style*])	Converts characters from the named string into HTML entities.
htmlspecialchars(*string*[, *quote_style*])	Converts special characters from the named string into HTML entities.
implode(*delimiter*, *array_name*)	The opposite of explode(), this combines bits of the named array together using the named delimiter tag, equal to join().
join(*delimiter*, *array_name*)	Equal to implode(), this combines bits of the named array together using the named delimiter tag.
levenshtein(*str1*, *str2*)	Calculates the Levenshtein distance between the two named strings.
localeconv()	Returns an array with local monetary and numeric formatting information.
ltrim(*string*)	Deletes spaces from the beginning of the named string.
md5_file(*filename*)	Calculates the MD5 hash of the named file.
md5(*string*)	Calculates the MD5 hash of the named string.
metaphone(*string*)	Calculates the metaphone key of the named string.
money_format(*format*, *number*)	Formats the number as a currency.
nl_langinfo(*item number*)	Returns specific information about the local language and numeric/monetary formatting.
nl2br(*string*)	Inserts the HTML code for before all line breaks in the named string.

Table continued on following page

Function	Description
number_format(*number*, *decimals*)	Formats the number based on the named parameters.
ord(*string*)	Returns the ASCII code of the first character in the named string.
parse_str(*string*[, *array*])	Parses the string and stores the results in the named array.
print(*string*)	Displays the string and returns a value of 1.
printf(*format*[, *arg1*, *arg2*, ...])	Displays a formatted string based on the named parameters.
quoted_printable_decode(*string*)	Converts a quoted-printable string to an 8-bit string.
quotemeta(*string*)	Escapes metacharacters in the named string.
rtrim(*string*)	Deletes trailing spaces from the end of the named string.
setlocale(*category*, *locale*)	Sets the locale information for functions in the named category.
sha1_file(*filename*[, *output*])	Calculates the sha1 hash for a file.
sha1(*string*[, *output*])	Calculates the sha1 hash for a string.
similar_text(*string1*, *string2*[, *percent*])	Determines the similarity between two named strings.
soundex(*string*)	Determines the soundex key of the named string.
split(*exp*, *string*[, *limit*])	Splits the named string using the named expression.
spliti(*exp*, *string*[, *limit*)	Splits the named string using the named expression (case-insensitive).
sprintf(*format*[, *arg1*, *arg2*...])	Displays the formatted string based on the named parameters.
sql_regcase(*string*)	Searches the named string (case-insensitive) and returns a regular expression.
sscanf(*string*, *format*[, *var1*, *var2*...])	Parses input from the named string based on the named parameters.
str_ireplace(*oldexp*, *newexp*, *string*)	Similar to str_replace(), except it is case-insensitive.
str_pad(*string*, *length*[, *pad_string*, *pad_type*])	Pads the named string to the named length with another string.
str_repeat(*string*, *number*)	Repeats a named string a named number of times.

Function	Description
str_replace(*oldexp*, *newexp*, *string*, [*count*])	Replaces one expression with another in the named string, and optionally returns the number of changes made.
str_rot13(*string*)	Performs the ROT13 encoding on the named string.
str_shuffle(*string*)	Randomly shuffles the string.
str_split(*string*[, *length*])	Converts a string into an array based on the optional length parameter.
str_word_count(*string*[, *format*])	Counts the number of words in the string.
strcasecmp(*string1*, *string2*)	Compares two named strings, case-insensitive.
strchr(*string*, *exp*)	Locates the named expression in the named string, equal to strstr().
strcmp(*string1*, *string2*)	Similar to strcasecmp(), except comparison is case-sensitive.
strcoll(*string1*, *string2*)	Compares the two strings based on locale.
strcspn(*string1*, *string2*)	Returns the number of characters at the beginning of *string1* that do not match *string2*, opposite of strspn().
strip_tags(*string*)	Removes HTML and PHP tags from the named string.
stripcslashes(*string*)	Removes C slashes from the named string.
stripos(*str1*, *str2*)	Finds the position of the first occurrence of *str2* in *str1*; case-insensitive.
stripslashes(*string*)	Removes escaped slashes from the named string.
stristr(*string*, *exp*)	Finds all occurrences of the named expression in the named string (case-insensitive).
strlen(*string*)	Returns the length of the named string.
strnatcasecmp(*string1*, *string2*)	Compares two named strings using "natural order" (case-insensitive).
strnatcmp(*string1*, *string2*)	Compares two named strings using "natural order."
strncasecmp(*string1*, *string2*, n)	Compares the first *n* characters of the two named strings (case-insensitive).
strncmp(*string1*, *string2*, n)	Compares the first *n* characters of the two named strings.

Table continued on following page

Function	Description
strpbrk(*string1*, *char_list*)	Searches *string1* for any of the characters in the named character list.
strpos(*string*, *exp*)	Returns the numerical position of the first occurrence of the named expression in the named string.
strrchr(*string*, *exp*)	Locates the last occurrence of the named expression in the named string.
strrev(*string*)	Reverses the named string.
strripos(*string*, *exp*)	Returns the numerical position of the last occurrence of the named expression in the named string (case-insensitive).
strrpos(*string*, *exp*)	Returns the numerical position of the last occurrence of the named expression in the named string.
strspn(*string1*, *string2*)	Returns the number of characters at the beginning of *string1* that match *string2*, the opposite of strcspn().
strstr(*string*, *exp*)	Finds all occurrences of a named expression in a named string (case-sensitive).
strtok(*string1*, *string2*)	Tokenizes named string based on named parameter, *string2*.
strtolower(*string*)	Converts the named string to lowercase characters.
strtoupper(*string*)	Converts the named string to uppercase characters.
strtr(*string*, *exp1*, *exp2*)	Translates characters based on the named parameters.
substr(*string*, *start*[, *num_char*])	Returns the named number of characters from the named start position in the named string.
substr_compare(*string1*, *string2*, *offset*[, *length*, [,*case*]])	Compares two strings from a given offset with the option of case-insensitivity.
substr_count(*string*, *exp*)	Returns the number of occurrences of the named expression in the named string.
substr_replace(*string*, *replacement*, *start*[, *num_char*])	Replaces text within the named string based on the named parameters.
trim(*string*)	Deletes extra space at the beginning and end of the named string.

Function	Description
ucfirst(*string*)	Converts the first character to uppercase.
ucwords(*string*)	Converts the first character of each word to uppercase.
vfprintf(*stream*, *format*, *arguments*)	Sends the formatted string to a stream.
vprintf(*format*, *arguments*)	Displays a formatted string.
vsprintf(*format*, *arguments*)	Returns a formatted string as an array.
wordwrap(*string*[, *width*, *break*, *cut*])	Wrap the string based on the named parameters, using the named *break* character.

URL Functions

The functions in the table that follows allow you to handle URLs within your PHP code.

Function	Description
base64_decode(*string*)	Decodes an encoded string, the opposite of base64_encode().
base64_encode(*string*)	Encodes a string, the opposite of base64_decode().
get_headers(*url*)	Gets the headers sent by the server.
get_meta_tags(*filename/url*)	Extracts and returns all meta tag information in a given file or URL.
http_build_query(*formdata*[, *prefix*])	Creates a URL-encoded query string based on data contained in an array.
parse_url(*url*)	Parses the URL into components.
rawurldecode(*string*)	Decodes a URL-encoded string, the opposite of rawurlencode().
rawurlencode(*string*)	URL-encodes a string, the opposite of rawurldecode().
urldecode(*string*)	Decodes an encoded string, the opposite of urlencode().
urlencode(*string*)	Encodes a string, the opposite of urldecode().

Variable Functions

Variables are a common tool used in PHP, and there are numerous functions to increase your ability to manipulate them.

Function	Description
`doubleval(var)`	Doubles the value of the variable.
`empty(var)`	Verifies whether the variable exists and has a non-zero value.
`floatval(var)`	Returns the float value of a variable.
`get_defined_vars()`	Returns all the defined variables in a script.
`get_resource_type(handle)`	Returns the resource type.
`gettype(var)`	Shows the field type of the variable.
`import_request_variable(types[, prefix])`	Imports GET/POST/Cookie variables into the global scope.
`intval(var[, base])`	Returns the integer value of the variable, using the named base.
`is_array(var)`	Verifies whether the variable is an array.
`is_bool(var)`	Verifies whether the variable is Boolean.
`is_callable(var)`	Verifies whether the variable can be called as a function.
`is_double(var)`	Verifies whether the variable is a double.
`is_float(var)`	Verifies whether the variable is a float.
`is_int(var)`	Equal to `is_integer()` and `is_long()`, verifies whether the variable is an integer.
`is_integer(var)`	Equal to `is_int()` and `is_long()`, verifies whether the variable is an integer.
`is_long(var)`	Equal to `is_int()` and `is_integer()`, verifies whether the variable is an integer.
`is_null(var)`	Verifies whether the variable is null.
`is_numeric(var)`	Verifies whether the variable is a number or numeric string.
`is_object(var)`	Verifies whether the variable is an object.
`is_real(var)`	Verifies whether the variable is a real number.
`is_resource(var)`	Verifies whether the variable is a resource.
`is_scalar(var)`	Verifies whether the variable is a scalar.
`is_string(var)`	Verifies whether the variable is a string.
`isset(var)`	Verifies whether the variable has been assigned a value.

Function	Description
print_r(*exp*[, *return*])	Displays readable information about a variable.
serialize(*value*)	Generates a storable version of variable.
settype(*var*, *type*)	Sets the named variable to the named type.
strval(*var*)	Returns the string value of the named variable.
unserialize(*string*)	Generates a PHP value from a stored version.
unset(*var*)	Deletes the named variable.
var_dump(*exp*)	Displays information about the named expression.
var_export(*exp*)	Outputs a string representation of the variable.

Miscellaneous Functions

The table that follows lists useful functions that don't exactly fit anywhere else.

Function	Description
connection_aborted()	Verifies whether or not the client connection has been aborted.
connection_status()	Verifies the client connection status.
connection_timeout()	Verifies whether or not the script has timed out.
constant(*name*)	Returns the value of the named constant.
define(*name*, *value*[, *case_insensitive*])	Defines a constant based on the named parameters.
defined(*name*)	Verifies whether or not a named constant exists.
die(*message*)	Displays the message and ends execution of the script.
eval(*string*)	Evaluates the named string as PHP code.
exit()	Ends execution of the script.
get_browser([*user_agent*])	Returns information about the user's browser.
highlight_file(*filename*)	Displays a highlighted version of the named file.
highlight_string(*str*)	Displays a highlighted version of the named string.
ignore_user_abort([*setting*])	Allows a script to continue executing if the user aborts a connection.
pack(format[, *arg1*, *arg2*...])	Packs the named arguments into a binary string.
php_check_syntax(*filename*)	Checks the syntax of the named file.

Table continued on following page

Function	Description
php_strip_whitespace(*filename*)	Returns the source code of the named file with comments and extra lines removed.
show_source(*filename*)	Displays a highlighted version of source code of named file.
sleep(*seconds*)	Pauses execution of the script for a named number of seconds.
time_nanosleep(*seconds*, *nanoseconds*)	Pauses execution of the script for a named number of seconds and nanoseconds.
uniqid(*prefix*[, *lcg*])	Assigns a unique ID based on the current time and named prefix.
unpack(*format*, *data*)	The opposite of pack(), this unpacks binary data into an array.
usleep(*microseconds*)	Pauses execution of the script for the named number of microseconds.

MySQL Data Types

See the table that follows for the potential data or field types in MySQL.

MySQL Field Type	Description
bigint(length)	Numeric field that stores integers from -9223372036854775808 to 9223372036854775807. (Adding the unsigned parameter allows storage of 0 to 18446744073709551615.) The parameter length limits the number of characters to be displayed. Please refer to the manual at http://www.mysql.com before performing mathematical calculations involving the bigint type.
bit	Equal to tinyint(1) field. A value of zero represents false; a non-zero value represents true.
blob	Equal to a text field, except it is case-sensitive when sorting and comparing. Stores up to 65535 characters.
bool	Equal to tinyint(1) field. A value of zero represents false; a non-zero value represents true.
boolean	Equal to tinyint(1) field. A value of zero represents false; a non-zero value represents true.

Table continued on following page

MySQL Field Type	Description
char(length)	Any characters can be in this field, but the field will have a fixed length. The length parameter can be between 0 and 255. If the length parameter is not defined, the default value is 1. Adding the BINARY attribute will make comparisons and sorting results case-sensitive.
date	Stores a date as yyyy-mm-dd. Allows values from 1000-01-01 to 9999-12-31.
datetime	Stores date and time as yyyy-mm-dd hh:mm:ss. Allows values from 1000-01-01 00:00:00 to 9999-12-31 23:59:59.
dec(length,dec)	Equal to decimal field.
decimal(length,dec)	Numeric field that can store decimals. The length parameter limits the number of digits that will be displayed, and the dec parameter limits the number of decimal places that can be stored. The length parameter does not count decimal points and "-" for negative values. A price field that would store prices up to 999.99, for example, would be defined as decimal(5,2). If the length parameter is not specified, the default is 10. Adding the unsigned attribute allows only non-negative values.
double(length,dec)	A medium-sized floating point number that stores values from -1.7976931348623157E+308 to -2.2250738585072014E-308, 0, and 2.2250738585072014E-308 to 1.7976931348623157E+308. The length parameter determines how many digits will be displayed; the dec parameter determines how many decimal places are displayed. (Adding the unsigned parameter allows only positive numbers to be stored.) Using double without parameters specified represents a double-precision floating point number.
double precision(length, dec)	Equal to double.
enum("option1", "option2", ...)	Allows only certain values to be stored in this field, such as true and false, or a list of states. 65,535 different options can be allowed.
fixed(length,dec)	Equal to decimal field.

MySQL Field Type	Description
float(length,dec)	A small floating point number that stores values from -3.402823466E+38 to -1.175494351E-38, 0, and 1.175494351E-38 to 3.402823466E+38. The length parameter determines how many digits will be displayed; the dec parameter determines how many decimal places are displayed. (Adding the unsigned parameter allows only positive numbers to be stored.)
float(precision)	Equal to float(length,dec) except the length and dec parameters are undefined. To be used with a true floating point number. (Adding the unsigned parameter allows only positive numbers to be stored.) The precision parameter can be from 0 to 24 for single-precision floating point numbers, and from 25-35 for double-precision floating point numbers.
int(length)	Numeric field that stores integers from -2147483648 to +2147483647, but can be limited with the length parameter. length limits the number of digits that can be shown, not the value. Mathematical functions can be performed on data in this field. Signifying the unsigned parameter permits positive integers (and zero) up to 4294967295.
integer(length)	Equal to int.
longblob	Equal to longtext except it is case-sensitive when sorting and comparing.
longtext	Allows storage of up to 4294967295 characters.
mediumblob	Equal to mediumtext field except it is case-sensitive when sorting and comparing.
mediumint(length)	Numeric field that stores integers from -8388608 to 8388607. (Adding the unsigned parameter allows storage of 0 to 16777215.) length limits the number of digits to be displayed.
mediumtext	Allows storage of up to 16777215 characters.
numeric(length,dec)	Equal to decimal field.
real(length,dec)	Equal to double field.
set("option1", "option2", ...)	Similar to enum field, but with set there can be none or more than one of the available options. Set allows up to 64 options.

Table continued on following page

MySQL Field Type	Description
smallint(length)	Numeric field that stores integers from -32768 to 32767. (Adding the unsigned parameter allows storage of 0 to 65535.) The length parameter limits the number of characters to be displayed.
text	Any character can be in this field, and the maximum size of the data is 64K (65535 characters).
time	Stores time as hh:mm:ss.
timestamp	Stores date and time as yyyy-mm-dd hh:mm:ss. Useful for automatically capturing current date and time.
tinyblob	Equal to tinytext field, except it is case-sensitive when sorting and comparing.
tinyint(length)	Numeric field that stores integers from -128 to 127. (Adding the unsigned parameter allows storage of 0 to 255.) The length parameter limits the number of characters to be shown.
tinytext	Allows storage of up to 255 characters.
varchar(length)	Any character can be in this field, and the data can vary from 0 to 255 characters. Maximum length of field is denoted with the length parameter. Adding the BINARY attribute causes comparisons and sorting results to be case-sensitive.
year(length)	Stores a year in 4-character format (by default). In this format, values from 1901 to 2155, and 0000 are acceptable. It is possible to specify a 2-year format by signifying so with the length parameter. In this format, the values from 70 to 69 are acceptable (1970-2069).

MySQL Quick Reference

This appendix lists some quick reference notes for your use. These topics are covered in more depth in Chapter 3 and on the MySQL Web site at www.mysql.com.

Database Manipulation Commands

Use the following commands to create and make changes to your database and tables.

Command	What It Does
CREATE *databasename*	Creates the database.
CREATE *tablename* (*field1*, *field2*, *field3*, and so on PRIMARY KEY(*field*))	Creates a new table.
ALTER TABLE *tablename* WHERE *condition*	Modifies a table in the database.
RENAME TABLE *oldtablename* TO newtablename	Renames a table in the database.
INSERT INTO *tablename* (*field1*, *field2*, . . .) VALUES ("*value1*", "*value2*" . . .)	Inserts information into the table.
UPDATE *tablename* SET *field1=value1*, *field2=value2* . . . WHERE *condition*	Changes information already stored in the table.
DELETE FROM *tablename* WHERE *condition*	Deletes a record from the specified table.
DROP *tablename*	Deletes the table.
DROP *database*	Deletes the database.
LOAD DATA INFILE "*filename*" INTO TABLE *tablename*	Loads a large quantity of data into the database.

Connecting to the Database

Before you can connect to the database, you need four things:

- ❏ Database name
- ❏ Host Server name
- ❏ Username
- ❏ Password

Connect to the database using the following command (in PHP):

```
$connection = mysql_connect("servername", "username", "password");
```

You then need to select the appropriate database by using the following command (in PHP):

```php
<?php
$database = mysql_select_db("databasename", $connection)
     or die("couldn't find the database");
?>
```

Accessing the Database

MySQL commands are inserted within your PHP code to access the database in this way:

```php
<?php
$query = mysql_query("UPDATE field1 FROM tablename WHERE condition1")
    or die("Couldn't find the table");
$result = mysql_fetch_array($query);
?>     //your information has now been updated
```

Retrieving Data from the Database

You can access the data stored in your tables with the following statement (you can use * to retrieve all fields):

```
SELECT field1, field2 FROM tablename
```

Condition Clauses

Use the following conditions in conjunction with this statement:

```
SELECT * FROM tablename WHERE
```

Conditions (use % for wildcard):

```
field = value
field > value
field < value
field >= value
```

```
field <= value
field != value (field is not equal to value)
field <> value (field is not equal to value)
field BETWEEN value1 AND value2
field NOT BETWEEN value1 AND value2
field LIKE value
field NOT LIKE value
field IS NULL
field IS NOT NULL
field IN (value1, value2, value3, etc)
field NOT IN (value1, value2, value3, etc)
```

Selecting from Multiple Tables

You can retrieve information from two or more tables at once by using the following statements:

```
SELECT table1.field, table2.field FROM table1, table2 WHERE
    table1.field = table2.field;
```

or

```
SELECT table1field, table2field FROM table1 LEFT JOIN table2 ON
    table1.table1field=table2.table2field;
```

Sorting the Results

You can sort the results of the SELECT query by using the following clause at the end of the statement (and the optional ascending or descending qualifier):

```
SELECT * FROM tablename WHERE field1=value1 ORDER BY field2 ASC|DESC
```

Limiting the Results

If you would like to limit the results returned from your query, you can modify your SELECT statement like this:

```
SELECT * FROM tablename WHERE field1=value1
ORDER BY field2 ASC
LIMIT offset, number_of_rows_to_be_returned
```

Comparison of Text Editors

Many software programs are available that you can use to enter all your code. Some have better options than others, so we've put together a chart to help you compare apples with apples. The following chart lists some of the more popular editors alphabetically and compares common text editor features, such as syntax highlighting.

Many of these editors provide similar features, so your decision really depends on your budget, your needs, and how comfortable you are with each user interface.

You can read more about features not listed here, because many of these editors provide other unique benefits. We encourage you to visit the following Web sites to download these programs and get more information:

- ❑ AnyEdit: www.anyedit.org
- ❑ Dreamweaver MX 2004: www.macromedia.com
- ❑ EditPlus: www.editplus.com
- ❑ HTML-Kit: www.chami.com/html-kit/
- ❑ jEdit: www.jedit.org
- ❑ Notepad: www.microsoft.com
- ❑ PhpED: www.nusphere.com
- ❑ PHPEdit: www.phpedit.net
- ❑ TextPad: www.textpad.com
- ❑ UltraEdit-32: www.ultraedit.com
- ❑ WordPad: www.microsoft.com

Editor	Highlighted Syntax	Spell Checker	Built-in FTP Access	Block Mode Editing	Line Numbers	Word Wrap
AnyEdit	✓			✓	✓	✓
Dreamweaver MX 2004	✓	✓	✓	✓	✓	✓
EditPlus	✓	✓	✓		✓	✓
HTML-Kit	✓	✓	✓		✓	✓
jEdit	✓		✓	✓	✓	✓
Notepad						✓
PhpED	✓	✓	✓	✓	✓	✓
PHPEdit	✓			✓	✓	✓
TextPad		✓		✓	✓	✓
UltraEdit-32	✓	✓	✓	✓	✓	✓
WordPad						✓

PHP Code Auto-Completion	WYSIWYG Web Design Editor	Database Connectivity	Content Preview	Multiple Undo/ Redo	Search and Replace	Price
✓				✓	✓	Free
✓	✓	✓	✓	✓	✓	$399
			✓	✓	✓	$30
✓	✓		✓		✓	$55
✓					✓	Free
					✓	Free
✓		✓	✓	✓	✓	$299
✓					✓	$90
				✓	✓	$29
✓			✓	✓	✓	$35
					✓	Free

Choosing a Third-Party Host

Many people like to run their own servers out of their homes or offices, and that is a feasible solution for hosting, if you have the time. But hosting your own Web site can lead to more problems than it's worth. You need to think about backup power, keeping the security holes patched, regular maintenance, regular upgrades, and many other issues. And keep in mind that not only do you need to have a Web server running, but you also need to have something to take care of your domain name servers (DNS servers).

With third-party hosting solutions, you have trained IT professionals who make sure your Web server stays up and running 24 hours a day. It's their job to make sure your site is secure and always available for viewing.

Hosting Options

Should you decide to have a third party host your site, you have many options to choose from when making your hosting choice. Here are a few criteria to look at when you select a host:

- ❑ **Supported languages:** PHP, JAVA, CGI, ASP
- ❑ **Supported databases:** MySQL, PostgreSQL, MSSQL
- ❑ **Server control:** Super User (root) access
- ❑ **Server access:** Such as FTP, telnet, SSH
- ❑ **Configuration ability:** Web server settings/configurations, cron jobs, htaccess
- ❑ **Administration GUIs:** E-mail, database, user setup
- ❑ **Bandwidth usage:** Web site, e-mail, streaming media, database connections
- ❑ **Price:** Based on features, contract time, and other criteria

Keep in mind that you aren't likely to have every combination and possibility with every host, so it's important that you know enough about hosts to make a well-thought-out decision before jumping into a long contract. To that end, let's get into a little more detail about each of those topics.

Supported Languages

First of all, we will talk about the supported languages. Obviously, because you bought this book, we're assuming you are looking into using PHP, but there are other languages you may need to use. There may be a time when another language, such as Java, is better suited for a job than PHP. For example, if you want live streaming audio or video on your site, you are likely to use a Java applet of some sort because PHP needs a request from the server to process information. PHP can do it with different calls to the server, but because it is more of a client request from the browser, a client-side language works much better for this task.

There may also be times when you need to use another programming language to accomplish something a client already has set up at a different host or server. If so, it is nice to at least have the option of using, say, a Perl script, rather than spending the time and money to redevelop the application in PHP.

Supported Databases

Again, because this book is geared toward MySQL, you will probably need a host that supports MySQL. However, you can use many other databases with PHP.

Here are just some of the databases that PHP can work with:

- ❑ MySQL
- ❑ PostgreSQL
- ❑ MS SQL Server
- ❑ MS Access
- ❑ Sybase

Depending on your situation, you may want to choose a host that has more than one of these databases set up by default. Some larger companies, for example, are using MS SQL as their database, usually because they are using ASP (Active Server Pages from Microsoft) for their programming. Should you need to convert any site to PHP, you will be glad to know that PHP can connect and work nicely with MS SQL as well. Also, keep in mind that you don't have to continue using the other databases; you can always port the data over to MySQL using PHP to ease the troubles of manual conversion.

Server Control and Access

Many hosts won't give a Web developer full access or control over their hosted domain. We tend to shy away from those hosts because you are more likely to run into problems with them when you want to do some custom configuration to the server.

Look into the type of access your host provides. Obviously, your host will give you FTP access so you can upload your files to the Web server. Some hosts, however, will give you FTP access, but nothing else. The problem is that you are likely to run into a situation in which you want to configure your server. For this you will need either telnet or SSH access to use the command line.

In fact, the ability to configure is often necessary when performing tasks that usually aren't allowed by hosts by default. For example, consider htaccess. With htaccess, you can deny and allow access to certain files and directories based on the users you allow in the `htpasswd` file. (See Chapter 12 for more information on htaccess.)

Along with htaccess, most hosts allow you to use cron jobs, but are not likely to set them up for you. Therefore, you need to telnet into the server and edit the crontab file to enable you to run scheduled tasks. There are countless configuration settings that you might want to change if your host allows you to configure them. Keep that in mind when choosing your hosting solution.

Administration GUIs

Certain hosts offer Administration GUIs or User Control Panels as a feature of their packages. A lot of people don't really care for GUIs, but when you don't have a choice, either because you don't have sufficient access to the server or you don't fully understand how to get things done through telnet, a point-and-click solution is a wonderful tool.

The interface can be as simple as one that allows you to view information about the server, or it can be as complex as one that allows you to install applications and programming languages with the click of a button. Also, keep in mind that many control panels have utilities that allow clients to administer their own e-mail users themselves. With such a feature, rather than having to call you or the hosting company to set up an e-mail account, the client can simply log on to the control panel and set up and delete users as the need arises.

Bandwidth and Site Usage

Bandwidth and site usage factor into the overall price of hosting. Hosting companies usually give out only so much bandwidth usage per site per month. If you go over that amount, there is usually a hefty charge.

Consider the following issues when looking into bandwidth:

- ❑ Web site traffic
- ❑ E-mail usage
- ❑ Database connections
- ❑ Streaming media

If you have heavy activity in any or all of these areas, before you know it, you might get billed for bandwidth overusage. You need to consider how many people will visit your site on average. In addition, some hosts count e-mail usage in the end-of-the-month calculation used to tally your bill. Some hosts will even go so far as to monitor your FTP access and count that toward the total bandwidth used.

Database connections don't really relate to bandwidth usage, but hosts often limit the amount of database connections you can make as another way to control the number of people allowed to visit the site at one time.

Finally, streaming media is very heavy on bandwidth; should you plan to use it as a form of conveying information to the end users of your site, your hosting bill could rise dramatically.

Pricing

You need to consider all the areas discussed so far when figuring out how much your host is worth to you. Rather than total price, look at the price per feature. You won't often get all the features you want for your site, but as long as you get most of them and you choose the host that has the lowest price per feature, you will probably make a wise hosting choice.

When using price to make your choice, ask yourself how much a particular feature is worth to you. Remember that some hosting companies require that you sign up for a full year and they won't offer a refund of any sort if you receive poor service or decide the service isn't worth the money you are paying. You want to find a host that will allow you to choose either monthly, quarterly, or yearly hosting options. That way you don't have to wait a full year to leave if you're dissatisfied. Just keep in mind that when you choose a shorter option, such as monthly or quarterly, the host will often charge a little more than if you pay up front, or they may charge service setup fees that might be waived if you pay up front.

Making the Choice

When making your hosting decision, it's very important to consider the criteria outlined in this appendix. You really don't want to get stuck in a situation in which you are unhappy with the service you are receiving or, worse yet, your paying client is disappointed with services you recommended.

The following is a list of 10 hosting options that we feel are the best bang for your buck. You may want to consider them when making your decision:

- ❏ www.olm.net
- ❏ www.lunarpages.com
- ❏ www.jumpline.com
- ❏ www.startlogic.com
- ❏ www.ipowerweb.com
- ❏ www.midphase.com
- ❏ www.infinology.com
- ❏ www.powweb.com
- ❏ www.interland.com
- ❏ www.websitesource.com

An Introduction to PEAR

PHP is a terrific scripting language. It is relatively easy to learn, especially if you already know other programming languages such as JavaScript, C++, or Perl. In no time at all, you can get some excellent pages up and running on your server, accessing databases, authenticating users, and providing dynamic, up-to-date content for your visitors.

So, you just spent six months creating your company's Web site. It's nearly perfect — users are being served up-to-the-minute content, and you have set up a complex Content Management System that enables almost anyone in the company to create new content. It's efficient, it's pretty, and you feel pretty darned good about it.

As you sit here thumbing through the appendixes, wondering if there are any more useful nuggets of information, in walks your boss, the IT Manager. She tells you once again what a fine job you did, congrats on the promotion — you know, the usual. As she gets up to leave, she stops in the doorway and casually mentions something that is going to completely overload your work schedule:

"Oh, by the way, HR is switching to an Oracle-based database accounting package. It's pretty slick. And we decided that since we'll be using Oracle anyway, all of our databases will be switched to Oracle. That won't be a problem, will it?"

Of course, the problem here stems from the way PHP accesses databases. The wonderful thing about PHP is that it supports a very wide variety of databases. The bad thing is that it has database-specific commands for each one.

Every developer has had this happen, so you are not alone. It might not be too difficult to change your code, but it will probably be time consuming, especially if you have hundreds of pages to update.

For example, here's how you would run a database query with various databases:

- ❑ **MySQL:** `mysql_query("SELECT * FROM table")`
- ❑ **Microsoft SQL:** `mssql_query("SELECT * FROM table")`
- ❑ **FrontBase:** `fbsql_query("SELECT * FROM table")`

❑   **Sybase:** `sybase_query("SELECT * FROM table")`

❑   **PostgreSQL:** `pgsql_query("SELECT * FROM table")`

Those may seem fairly simple to change, but this is just scratching the surface. Oracle doesn't even have a `_query()` function. You have to use `ora_parse()` on the SQL statement, and then run `ora_exec()`. You must also consider that there may be some specific functions you are using in MySQL that have no equivalent in Oracle. Perhaps you are even using very specific SQL statements in MySQL that are not supported in Oracle or are executed in a different way.

Now you can see how you might have your work cut out for you. Go ahead and give your IT Manager a resounding thump on the head for not foreseeing this change six months ago. (It's okay; just tell her we told you to do it.)

Wouldn't it be cool if there were a way to write your code more abstractly, so that when you run a function such as `get_query_results()`, it would be smart enough to know what type of database you are connecting to and perform all of the necessary steps to retrieve the data? Enter PEAR.

What Is PEAR?

PEAR stands for PHP Extension and Application Repository. It is an extensive online collection of free PHP modules and classes for many different functions. Modules exist for XML parsing, database processing, user authentication, and more. In most cases, these modules make life easier for the developer by hiding the details of more complex functions and by providing a friendly programming interface and function set for accessing low-level functions. This is called *abstraction*, and the interface module is referred to as the *abstraction layer*.

This appendix does not provide you with installation instructions or step-by-step instructions on how to use any specific modules. Rather, our intention is to tell you about some of the more popular PEAR modules and explain what some of their benefits and pitfalls may be. We will include simple examples for clarification of some points, but they are not intended to be used as-is.

> *If you would like more information about PEAR and the modules available, visit* `http://pear.php.net`.

Requirements

PEAR is designed to be used with PHP versions 4.0.4 or newer, although certain extensions may have stricter PHP version requirements. It is bundled with PHP, and the newest versions of PHP install PEAR by default. There is a very good chance that PEAR is already installed on your server, and you can begin using it right away.

For detailed installation instructions, visit `http://pear.php.net`.

The Packages

Many, many modules are available for PEAR. They are referred to as *packages*, and you can find them at `http://pear.php.net/packages.php`. Packages are written by PHP developers using specific coding standards. Each package is developed by a team or individual and must contain specific information such as documentation and a list of dependencies (both to and from other packages).

The packages are defined as *nodes* on a *tree*. For example, the XML_Parser node is grouped with other XML packages. This grouping is for organizational purposes only — dependencies have nothing to do with the locations of nodes on a tree. The Mail package, for example, depends on the Net_SMTP package, even though they are not connected nodes.

PEAR package developers are required to follow a strict set of coding standards called, logically enough, the PEAR Coding Standards. One of the great things about PEAR (and open source development in general) is that anyone can develop a package and have it inserted into the package tree. ("PEAR tree" — isn't that clever? We're just waiting for the first person to create a Partridge package.)

The big package discussed in this appendix is the database package PEAR DB. Although there are many excellent packages, this one is probably the most widely used. Many love it, and many hate it. It definitely has its benefits, but it has a few downsides, too. We'll touch on those shortly.

We'll also take a look at a few other package nodes, including Authentication, Mail, Payment, XML, and HTML.

PEAR DB

Before you delve into PEAR, you must be aware that most PEAR packages use objects and classes. If you are not familiar with PHP's implementation of Object Oriented Programming, you may want to read the Classes and Objects section of the PHP manual (www.php.net/oop5). PEAR DB is designed to work with PHP version 4.2.0 or greater.

To use PEAR DB (also written as PEAR::DB), you must include the file db.php in your page. This is your "window" to the PEAR DB classes, and it is the only file you need to include. It will implement a class called DB_common, which is contained in the DB/common.php file.

In common.php, you find the code that is common across different databases and some basic utility functions. If necessary, some of the classes will be overwritten, depending on the specific database driver file you load.

This brings us to the third file: driver. This file is loaded dynamically, depending on which database you specify as the one you will use. If you are using MySQL, for example, DB/mysql.php is loaded. It implements a class called DB_mysql that extends DB_common, and contains classes and functions specific to the needs of MySQL databases.

What does all this mean? Basically, it's mostly transparent to you as far as database access goes. You include db.php in your page and specify the database you are accessing (along with user, password, host, and database, as usual), and PEAR DB does the rest.

Suppose you have a database with the following two tables. You may remember these tables from Chapter 10. Let's use these tables in an example to see how PEAR DB compares to standard database functions. All of the examples will use these two tables.

id	league_id	alias	real_name
1	2	Average Man	Bill Smith
2	2	The Flea	Tom Jacobs
3	1	Albino Dude	George White
4	3	Amazing Woman	Mary Jones

id	league
1	Amazing People
2	Dynamic Dudes
3	Stupendous Seven
4	Justice Network

The first example uses MySQL-specific commands to retrieve all of the records and display them on the screen. For simplicity's sake, we will include the database constants in the same code. Just remember that the best coding practice is to put them into a separate `config.php` file and include them.

```php
<?php
$host = 'localhost';
$uname = 'bp5am';
$passwd = 'bp5ampass';
$db_name = 'comicsite';

$conn = mysql_connect($host, $uname, $passwd)
  or die('Could not connect to MySQL database. ' . mysql_error());

mysql_select_db($db_name, $conn);

$sql = "SELECT * FROM superhero s, league l WHERE l.id = s.league_id";
$result = mysql_query($sql)
  or die(mysql_error());

while ($row = mysql_fetch_array($result)) {
  echo $row['alias'] . " (" . $row['real_name'] . ") is a member of ";
  echo "the " . $row['league'] . " League.<br>";
}
?>
```

Here is what the code looks like if you use PEAR DB:

```php
<?php
$host = 'localhost';
$uname = 'bp5am';
$passwd = 'bp5ampass';
$db_name = 'comicsite';
```

```
$db_type = 'mysql';

require_once('DB.php');
$dsn = "$db_type://$uname:$passwd@$host/$db_name";
$conn = DB::connect($dsn);
if (DB::isError($conn)) {
  die ("Unable to connect: " . $conn->getMessage() . "\n");
}

$sql = "SELECT * FROM superhero s, league l WHERE l.id = s.league_id";
$result = $conn->query($sql);
if (DB::isError($result)) {
  die ("Query ($sql) failed: " . $result->getMessage() . "\n");
}

while ($row = $result->fetchRow(DB_FETCHMODE_ASSOC)) {
  echo $row['alias'] . " (" . $row['real_name'] . ") is a member of ";
  echo "the " . $row['league'] . " League.<br>";
}
?>
```

If you load either page in your browser, you will see the following on the screen:

```
Average Man (Bill Smith) is a member of the Dynamic Dudes League.
The Flea (Tom Jacobs) is a member of the Dynamic Dudes League.
Albino Dude (George White) is a member of the Amazing People League.
Amazing Woman (Mary Jones) is a member of the Stupendous Seven League.
```

The PEAR DB method takes more lines, and the syntax is a little different (which can be especially difficult if you are not familiar with objects). So why should you bother to use PEAR DB?

Remember that PEAR DB acts as an abstraction layer to help you interface with your database. If you look closely at the PEAR DB code, you'll notice that none of the functions refer to the type of database you are accessing. In fact, they are quite generic. In contrast, the first code snippet uses mysql_ functions throughout the code. That's not a problem, as long as you always use MySQL.

Remember your IT Manager's passing comment? Your company has just decided to switch from MySQL to Oracle. Which one of these small code segments would you prefer to modify? Okay, perhaps even the MySQL code would take only a couple of minutes, but try to imagine this on a grand scale. Also remember that Oracle commands are different — you must pass the SQL statement to the server and commit it. MySQL doesn't work that way.

Now you should see the benefits of using PEAR DB's abstraction layer. In fact, by keeping the $db_type variable (or an SQL_DB_TYPE) constant in an included file, all you should have to do to make your *entire* Web site work with the new database is change the $db_type variable from mysql to oci8 — theoretically, of course. This assumes that every SQL statement you used is compatible with both MySQL and Oracle (which is doubtful) and that every PEAR DB function you used for MySQL is compatible with Oracle (also doubtful). But at least you will have a lot less work to do.

There are definite benefits to using PEAR DB. For example:

❑ It enables you to easily change your code to work with any database backend supported by PEAR.

❑ It provides built-in error checking and error handling.

❑ It creates defaults for common methods (such as fetchRow()).

❑ It offers extended functionality — PEAR DB offers database functions that PHP does not provide natively. For example, a method (DB::isManip) tells you whether or not a SQL statement manipulates data or simply retrieves it. PHP has no equivalent function.

There are caveats to using PEAR DB as well:

❑ You must use SQL compatible with other databases or change your SQL statements when you change DB servers. You would have to do that without PEAR DB, of course, but you should know that PEAR DB does not solve this problem.

❑ PEAR DB is not as efficient as native PHP code, because you are running things in an abstraction layer, and there may be some very complicated things going on "under the hood."

❑ Not all database-specific functions are available through PEAR DB. For example, MySQL's function mysql_fetch_object has no PEAR DB equivalent. Workarounds exist for some functions (such as casting the results of a fetchRow to an object); of course, that defeats the purpose of having an abstraction layer.

So, should you install PEAR and use PEAR DB? Perhaps you should. You need to weigh the benefits against potential problems and determine if it's right for you. In the meantime, if you are working on a big PHP project, make sure you are absolutely sure what database you will be accessing. You can avoid a lot of headaches in the future (your IT Manager will thank you for that).

Other PEAR Packages

Pear::DB may be the most popular package available, but it is not the only package available. Let's take a look at a few of the other packages available in PEAR, including HTML, Authentication, Payment, and Mail.

For more information on PEAR DB and other PEAR packages, visit http://pear.php.net.

HTML

The HTML node contains quite a few packages, designed to make some HTML functions easier. A good example of this is HTML_BBCodeParser. This neat piece of code takes UBB style tags ([b], [img], and so on) and converts them to HTML (<b>, <img>, and so on). If you have ever been to a forum online (such as www.phpbuilder.com/board), you have seen these tags in action. This package allows you to create your own custom BBCode, and it claims to generate valid XHTML 1.0 code.

Other HTML packages include:

❑ HTML_Menu, which enables the easy creation and maintenance of an HTML menu navigation system.

❏ HTML_QuickForm, which provides methods for creating, validating, and processing HTML forms.

❏ Pager for HTML pagination (1–10, 11–20, and so on).

Authentication

The Authentication packages attempt to make it a little easier to add user authentication to your site. Auth offers the capability to use several different methods of storing and retrieving login data, such as databases supported by PEAR, SMTP mail servers, and SAMBA, to name just a few. Auth_PrefManager offers a method of storing and retrieving user preference data, to be used any way you see fit.

Payment

How cool would it be to be able to link your site up to several different online payment and credit card processing companies? Now you can. These packages provide a means to connect to these systems:

❏ CyberCash online payment API.

❏ CyberMut, which allows you to use the CyberMut Payment system of the Credit Mutuel (French bank).

❏ Payment_Clieop creates a `clieop3` file for sending to a Dutch bank. We can't tell you how many times we have needed this!

❏ Payment_DTA creates German data transaction files.

❏ SPPLUS allows you to use the SPPLUS payment system with the Caisse d'Epargne (French bank).

❏ TCLink connects with credit card processing through the Trust Commerce gateway.

Very international, wouldn't you say?

Mail

The PEAR::Mail package provides functions for sending mail with PHP. It supports the PHP `mail()` function, SMTP, and sendmail. It also provides e-mail address validation conforming to RFC 822 standards.

Other Mail packages include mailparse, which provides functions for parsing a mail message; Mail_Mime, which handles the creation and manipulation of mime e-mails; and Mail_Queue, which puts large groups of e-mails in a queue to be sent later (great for very large mailing lists).

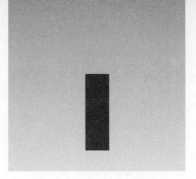

AMP Installation

This appendix guides you through installation of Apache, MySQL, and PHP for both Windows and Linux operating systems.

Installing with Windows

By following our step-by-step guide, you will successfully have all three components installed on your Windows system. This guide includes instructions for Windows NT, Windows 2000, Windows XP, and Windows Server 2003.

Install Apache

Apache will act as the server for your PHP/MySQL Web site. Installation is easy, as you will see.

This installation is for Windows NT, Windows 2000, Windows XP, and Windows Server 2003. You can find complete installation instructions for other versions of Windows at www.apache.org. Note that you must have TCP/IP running on your machine in order for your installation to be operational.

The following are the basic steps for installation:

1. Go to www.apache.org, and click the HTTP Server link.

   Although the Apache Software Foundation provides many different software packages, this is the only one we are concerned with at this time.

2. Click "Download from a Mirror" to choose an FTP site for downloading.

3. Click the Win 32 Binary (MSI Installer) link to download.

   If you experience problems downloading this file, you can try a different mirror site; click the drop-down box near the top of the screen to locate one.

4. Click the MSI file to initiate the installation wizard for the Apache software.

After accepting the installation agreement, you will see a screen that is equivalent to a `readme` `.txt` file — it gives basic information about the Apache software and where to go to find more information. We highly recommend that you read this file.

5. Click Next. You will see the Server Information screen.

6. Enter the following information:

    ❑   Domain name: For example, `domainname.com`

    ❑   Server name: For example, `server.domainname.com`

    ❑   Net administrator's e-mail address

    ❑   Who Are We Installing Apache For?

7. Because you are using Windows, you should install with the recommended option, "All Users."

8. Click Next to select a setup type.

    Typical installation is recommended for beginners and will suffice for most needs. Advanced users may feel more comfortable choosing Custom setup.

9. Click Next.

    The Destination Folder screen appears.

10. If you do not want your Apache files saved in the default path, click Change and select an alternate path; then click Next.

    The Ready to Install the Program screen appears.

11. Click Install to finish installation.

For configuration options and customization, please refer to Chapter 1 of this book.

Install PHP

This installation is for the PHP module on Windows 98, ME, and Windows 2000/XP/NT/2003. For all other Windows versions, please refer to the source Web site, `www.php.net`. Although there is an automatic PHP installer available at `www.php.net`, we strongly recommend that you use the manual installation. At time of publication, this installer is not complete, secure, or intended for use on live servers.

The following are the steps for installing PHP:

1. Go to the PHP Web site at `www.php.net`.

2. Scroll down to the Windows Binary section. If you are running your PHP on an Apache server, as we do in this book, click the PHP Zip Package link to be able to run PHP on Apache Server.

3. Click any FTP site to begin the download.

4. Unzip your file using any standard unzip program and save it to the directory of your choice.

    We recommend creating a directory named `c:\php` and unzipping it to this directory.

5. Before you can run PHP, you will need to rename `php.ini-dist` to `php.ini`. Make sure to save your new `php.ini` file to your `c:\windows` (or `c:\winnt`) directory so Apache can find it.

By default, the PHP installation provides two copies of your common configuration file: `php.ini-dist` and `php.ini-recommended`. The `php.ini-dist` file is meant to be used for development purposes, whereas `php.ini-recommended` should be used when your site goes live, because it has additional security measures in place that the `php.ini-dist` does not have. Depending on your reason for using PHP, you would choose the `php.ini` file that best suits your needs. For the purposes of this book, we are going to be using the `php.ini-dist` file simply because it is easier to work with and will present you with fewer obstacles. Once you are more familiar with PHP in general, we encourage you to switch to the `php.ini-recommended` file as your default. Therefore, you need to rename the configuration file as indicated in this step in order for your PHP installation to be complete.

6. Copy `php5ts.dll` into the `c:\windows\system32` or the `c:\winnt\system32` directory so that Apache can find it.

This file can be found in the `c:\php` directory, not the `c:\php\dlls` directory.

You now need to configure your PHP to run with Apache and MySQL. Please refer to Chapter 1 for more information on this step.

Install MySQL

MySQL is the database that holds all the data to be accessed by your Web site. This MySQL installation guide is for Windows 95, 98, 2000, NT, XP, and Server 2003. For all other versions of Windows, please refer to the source Web site at www.mysql.com.

Proceed with the following steps to install MySQL:

1. Go to the source Web site, www.mysql.com, and click "Developer Zone" then "downloads" on the navigation bar near the top of the page.

2. Scroll down to the latest stable version of MySQL, and click that link. It will be under the heading "MySQL database server & standard clients."

3. Scroll down to the Windows section of the downloadable files, and click Pick a Mirror.

4. Find a mirror and click to download (you can choose either HTTP or FTP to download).

5. Unzip the file to a temporary directory of your choice.

6. Click `setup.exe` to run the installation program. You will see the first of the Installation Wizard screens.

7. Click Next to display the informational screen.

We highly recommend that you read this screen before you continue.

8. Click Next, which brings you to the Choose Destination Location screen.

9. If the default directory is acceptable, simply click Next; otherwise, click Browse and select a different destination.

10. Click Next.

11. The next screen allows you to customize your installation; typical installation is sufficient for most users.

12. Click the setup type you prefer, and click Next to begin the installation.

After installing the appropriate files, the final screen will simply indicate the installation is complete. Click Finish to end the wizard.

You now need to configure your MySQL installation to fit your needs. See Chapter 1 for more information.

Installing with Linux

This section covers the installation of the three components of the AMP module using a Linux system.

In this instance, we will cover an installation from the source for all three AMP components. Other methods are available, such as RPM, deb, and ebuild. We've chosen to cover source installations instead because this method offers the most flexibility and works on nearly all UNIX-like systems.

Install MySQL

The following are the steps to install MySQL for a Linux system:

1. Go to the MySQL Web site (www.mysql.com) and download the latest stable version of the MySQL database server.

The link for this file is most likely located at the bottom under the heading Source Downloads.

2. Grab the tarball, named something along the lines of mysql-4.0.x.tar.gz.

3. Open a console window and change the directory (cd) to the folder where you downloaded the tarball.

4. If there isn't a user on the system dedicated to running the mysql daemon (typically mysql), you'll need to create one. To do this, in the console, enter the following commands:

```
> groupadd mysql
> useradd -g mysql mysql
```

5. Extract the tarball, and change to the directory it creates:

```
> tar -xzf mysql-VERSION.tar.gz
> cd mysql-VERSION
```

VERSION is the (sub)version of the mysql source tarball you downloaded, '0.20'.

6. Next, configure the source this way:

```
> ./configure --prefix=/usr/local/mysql
```

Using the --prefix switch tells the installer where to put the mysql libraries and binaries after they're built.

7. Compile the source:

```
> make
```

8. Install the libraries and binaries:

```
> make install
```

Note that you will need to be logged in as superuser (root) to perform this step and the following steps in the MySQL installation.

9. If this is the first time MySQL has been installed on your machine (in other words, not an upgrade), run this script to install the initial database/tables:

```
> scripts/mysql_install_db
```

10. Fix permissions on installed files, and copy over the default configuration file:

```
> chown -R root /usr/local/mysql
> chown -R mysql /usr/local/mysql/var
> chgrp -R mysql /usr/local/mysql
> cp support-files/my-medium.cnf /etc/my.cnf
```

Any changes you wish to make to customize MySQL should be made in this file.

11. Start the MySQL daemon:

```
> /usr/local/mysql/bin/mysqld_safe --user=mysql &
```

You'll probably want to add the previous command to whatever facilities are available to automatically start the daemon at boot. This varies by OS, so you'll need to find out what works on your system. Here is one easy way to add this that works with most systems (but may not be the best way):

```
> echo '/usr/local/mysql/bin/mysqld_safe --user=mysql &' >> /etc/rc.local
```

Install Apache

Follow these steps to install Apache:

1. Go to the Apache Web site (http://httpd.apache.org) and download the latest stable version of the Apache 2 Web server.

2. Grab the tarball, named something along the lines of httpd-2.0.x.tar.gz.

3. Open a console window, and change the directory (cd) to the folder where you downloaded the tarball.

4. Next, extract the tarball, and change to the directory it creates:

```
> tar -xzf httpd-2.0.52.tar.gz
> cd httpd-2.0.52
```

5. Configure the source:

```
> ./configure \
  --prefix=/usr/local/apache2 \
  --enable-so \
  --enable-mods-shared=max \
  --enable-modules=most
```

Using the --prefix switch tells the installer where to put the Apache server after it's built. For a complete list of configuration options, run ./configure -help.

6. Compile the source:

```
> make
```

7. Install the server:

> `make install`

Note that you will need to be logged in as superuser (root) to perform this step and the following steps in the Apache installation.

8. Start the Apache daemon:

> `/usr/local/apache2/bin/apachectl start`

9. Add the command to start Apache to whatever boot scripts you like, so the server starts every time you reboot. For example:

> `echo '/usr/local/apache2/bin/apachectl start`

Install PHP

Follow these steps to install PHP:

1. Go to the PHP Web site (`www.php.net`) and download the latest stable version of PHP.

2. Grab the tarball, named something along the lines of `php-5.0.x.tar.gz`.

3. Open a console window, and change the directory (`cd`) to the folder where you downloaded the tarball.

4. Next, extract the tarball, and change to the directory it creates:

> `tar -xzf php-5.0.2.tar.gz`
> `cd php-5.0.2`

5. Configure the source:

> `./configure \`
> `--with-apxs2=/usr/local/apache2/bin/apxs \`
> `--with-mysql=/usr/local/mysql`

Make sure you point to the correct locations for the Apache 2 apxs binary and the base of the MySQL installation directory. There are numerous configuration options for PHP, and we would almost need a chapter just to describe them all. For a complete list of configuration options, run `./configure -help`.

6. Compile the source:

> `make`

7. Install PHP:

> `make install`

You will need to be logged in as superuser (root) to perform this step.

At this point, you should configure your `php.ini` file as you like, verify that the necessary directives have been placed in Apache's `httpd.conf` file, and restart Apache. Refer to Chapter 1 for details on this.

Index